The Smell Culture Reader

SENSORY FORMATIONS

Series Editor: David Howes
ISSN: 1741–4725

- What is the world like to cultures that privilege touch or smell over sight or hearing?
- Do men's and women's sensory experiences differ?
- What lies beyond the aesthetic gaze?
- Who says money has no smell?
- How has the proliferation of "taste cultures" resulted in new forms of social discrimination?
- How is the sixth sense to be defined?
- What is the future of the senses in cyberspace?

From the Ancient Greeks to medieval mystics and eighteenth century empiricists, Karl Marx to Marshall McLuhan, the senses have been the subject of dramatic proclamations. Senses are sources of pleasure and pain, knowledge and power. Sites of intense personal experience, they are also fields of extensive cultural elaboration. Yet, surprisingly, it is only recently that scholars in the humanities and social sciences have turned their full attention to sensory experience and expression as a subject for enquiry.

This path-breaking series aims to show how the "sensual revolution" has supplanted both the linguistic and the pictorial turns in the human sciences to generate a new field—*sensual culture*, where all manner of disciplines converge. Its objective is to enhance our understanding of the role of the senses in history, culture and aesthetics, by redressing an imbalance: the hegemony of vision and privileging of discourse in contemporary theory and cultural studies must be overthrown in order to reveal the role all senses play in mediating cultural experience. The extraordinary richness and diversity of the social and material worlds, as constituted through touch, taste, smell, hearing, sight and, provocatively, the sixth sense, are addressed in the volumes of this series as follows:*

The Auditory Culture Reader (eds Michael Bull and Les Back) articulates a strategy of "deep listening"—a powerful new methodology for making sense of the social.

The Smell Culture Reader (ed. Jim Drobnick) foregrounds the most marginalized, and potentially subversive, sense of modernity, in addition to sampling how diverse cultures scent the universe.

The Book of Touch (ed. Constance Classen) maps the tactile contours of culture, exploring the powerful and often inarticulate world of touch, the most basic of our senses.

The Taste Culture Reader (ed. Carolyn Korsmeyer) serves up a savoury stew of cultural analysis, blending together the multiple senses of the term "taste."

Empire of the Senses: The Sensual Culture Reader (ed. David Howes) documents the sensual revolution in the humanities and social sciences, and reclaims sensation as a domain for cultural inquiry.

Cultures of Vision: The Alternative Visual Culture Reader (eds Elizabeth Edwards and Kaushik Bhaumik) explores and interrogates the multiplicity of scopic regimes within and without the Western tradition.

The Sixth Sense Reader (ed. David Howes) asks: What lies beyond the bounds of sense? Is the sixth sense ESP, electromagnetic sensitivity, intuition, revelation, gut instinct or simply unfathomable?

*Full publication details are available from the publishers, Berg, 1st Floor, Angel Court, 81 St Clements Street, Oxford OX4 1AW, UK; or consult http://www.bergpublishers.com

For Jennifer

Contents

Acknowledgments

One of the pleasures of editing an interdisciplinary book like *The Smell Culture Reader* is the opportunity to step outside one's established academic field and connect with a broader, diverse network. I am thankful for the enthusiasm and cooperation of all the authors invited to contribute to this book. It is interesting to note how smell inherently demands an interdisciplinary approach not only in the realms of theory and methodology but also in regards to the mutable identities of the writers themselves. Many of the researchers working with and on scent unreservedly adopt a varied relationship to their subject of analysis—for instance, perfumers who write history, scientists who collect perfume, anthropologists who practice aromatherapy, artists and scientists who collaborate with one another—a situation which demonstrates the protean vitality of scent and its dynamic influence on those attempting to understand its complexities.

I consider it a privilege to be a part of Berg's innovative *Sensory Formations* series. Managing Director Kathryn Earle's unwavering encouragement and Assistant Editor Hannah Shakespeare's adept guidance deserve to be lauded. Series editor David Howes, who invited me to edit this volume, made prodigious efforts to support the book in every way possible. Production Manager Ken Bruce ably steered the anthology through its successive stages and Felicity Marsh's careful copy editing improved the text in myriad ways. An anonymous Berg reviewer offered a number of helpful suggestions, to which I am grateful. Many of the contributors and copyright holders graciously agreed to waive or lessen their fees, which made a volume of this scope possible.

A grant from the Social Sciences and the Humanities Research Council of Canada, in the context of the Concordia Sensoria Research Team project "The Sense Lives of Things," sponsored invaluable research. I'd like to thank Concordia University's Office of the President; the Dean of the Arts and Sciences; Director of the MFA Programme Andrew Dutkewych, and CUPFA for subsidizing copyright permissions, translations, cover design and text editing. Translators Timothy Barnard and Kathryn Hunter conducted their tasks with superb conscientiousness. Lyle Robinson was indispensable for his work on early drafts of the texts. For the cover, I'd like to thank Anya Gallaccio for her immensely fragrant installation *Red on Green*, which I hope pervades the reading of this book, the Lehmann Maupin Gallery for granting permission, and the team at Associés Libres for their talented design work. Bob Strand kindly compiled the index.

The writing of the introductions was aided by the kindness of Carol Zemel and Yvonne Singer in securing a quiet place to think and write. Assistance from REF was much appreciated for creating the time to administer to the many details in the production of this anthology.

And to my intellectual compatriot and sparkling partner in art and life, Jennifer Fisher, I give the greatest thanks.

Jim Drobnick

Introduction
Olfactocentrism

Jim Drobnick

If everything were smoke, all perception would be by smell.

Heraclitus (qtd in Davenport 1990)

The act of smelling something, anything, is remarkably like the act of thinking itself.

Lewis Thomas, *Late Night Thoughts on Listening to Mahler's Ninth Symphony*

The sense of smell is mired in paradox. Considered earthy and animalistic, scents have nevertheless served as a long-standing component in spiritual practices. Enigmatically lacking a well-defined or extensive vocabulary, odors are unmatched in catalyzing the evocation of distant memories and places. Intensely visceral and emotional, fragrances are, however, the subject of an increasing degree of rationalization by the multi-billion-dollar perfume and flavor industry. Dismissed as vestigial and obsolete in an era dominated by information technologies, the sense of smell is now considered one of the means by which visual media's alienating effects can be mitigated. Often delimited as a mere "biological" sense, scents are, on the contrary, subtly involved in just about every aspect of culture, from the construction of personal identity and the defining of social status to the confirming of group affiliation and the transmission of tradition. There is a tendency to regard smells purely on the level of phenomenological immediacy, yet the manners and reasons people engage with the sense of smell are influenced by numerous cultural factors relating to the constructs a society creates integrating the environment, the bodies of its citizens and its symbolic worldview. In short, no act of perception is a pure or unmediated event; each society inflects and cultivates sensory practices according to its needs and interests. Societal influences, however, are not all-determining; individuals may challenge as much as conform to a reigning sensory regime. By examining a disparate array of Western and non-Western cultures, *The Smell Culture Reader* seeks to foreground some of the diversity of historical and contemporary practices of scent and form a context for continuing research and analysis.

Why should scent be the subject of an anthology, and why now? For a variety of reasons, the sense of smell is poised to break free from many of its assumed delimitations. The mystery of how smell works, for instance, has defied scientific understanding for centuries. However, with the award of the 2004 Nobel Prize in Physiology or Medicine to neuroscientists Richard Axel and Linda B. Buck, the basic code by which scents are perceived and cognitively processed seems to be on the verge of being cracked (Nobelprize. org 2004). Another delimitation concerns that of smell's inconsequentiality. In a study done in the early 1990s, smell was deemed the least valuable sense and the first one people would sacrifice if forced to choose among the senses (Synnott 1993: 183–4). However, given the recent effulgence in olfactory products and practices—oxygen bars, aromatic cookbooks, scented consumer items, custom-made perfumes, aromatherapy, designer room sprays, herbal spa treatments and toiletries, sensuous gardening, odor-enhanced entertainments and theme parks—it seems that smell is now the first and most popular sense people wish to *indulge*. Not only are individuals apparently unthreatened by smell's negative reputation, scents are being actively sought out to revivify overly sanitized environments and provide richer, more complex, sensory experiences (see Rose and Earle 1996; LaSalle and Britton 2003; Pink 2004: 67–9; Drobnick 2005). Even the concerns about air pollution, secondhand smoke, and scent bans, which seem to perpetuate olfactory stigmatization, evidence a heightened awareness about the physiological and psychological power of smells that in the end can promote a more responsible and conscious appreciation of olfactory effects.

Another transitional point resides in the realm of technology. Smell is often predicted to be a sense that will eventually disappear in the progress of human evolution, eclipsed in the apotheosis of pure mentality (Bradshaw 1982). With the advent of digital technologies and cyberworlds, complete disembodiment is theorized to be such a foregone conclusion that it is confidently claimed that "the senses have no future" (Moravec 1997). But as developments since the mid-1990s have shown, it is precisely in the field of technology that olfaction is gaining widespread applicability. Environmental fragrancing, odor biometrics, electronic noses, artificial fragrances and flavors, militarized smells, olfactory marketing—these are only some of the innovations demonstrating that smell is now in the process of becoming *instrumentalized*, that is, it is attaining scientifically verified, commercially commodified and legally patented utilizations (see Davies, Kooijmanb and

Warda 2003; Pearce et al. 2003; Field 2004; Korotkaya n.d.). Propelled by advances in chemical analysis and synthesis, sophisticated odor dispersion technologies and psychophysical research into olfactory effects, the near future promises to contain an ever-increasing use of rationalized scents in industry, the public sphere and everyday life. The discourse on these odoriferous implementations (some might call them manipulations) is for the most part generated within the parameters set by the developers themselves or subject to hyperbole in the popular press (see *Your Bionic Future* 1999), so there exists an urgent need for a broader understanding of the cultural context of smell in order to be able to critique and perhaps direct the uses of these new olfactory technologies, an understanding to which *The Smell Culture Reader* hopefully contributes.

My use of the term olfactocentrism for the title of this introduction is a sly response to the by now commonplace critique of vision implicit in the term ocularcentrism, a critique that ironically often results in the further inscription of visuality's predominance. Even though no sense operates in complete autonomy from the others, there is a certain strategic value in isolating the sense of smell. Many of the texts in this anthology include the other senses along with smell, yet smell is given priority so as to be able to ascertain its individuality and difference. By asking readers to adopt Heraclitus's smoky meditation quoted at the beginning of this introduction, the goal is to invite immersion into an evanescent olfactocentric realm and to consider how not only perception would change, but also thought. The connections between perception, thinking and smell, carried out in various ways throughout this anthology, is also summed up elegantly by Lewis Thomas's epigraph and his related comment that smell "may not seem a profound enough problem to dominate all of the life sciences, but it contains, piece by piece, all the mysteries" (1984: 41).

Unlike the voluminous discourse on the senses of vision and hearing, texts focusing on the sense of smell appeared relatively intermittently prior to the 1980s (see e.g. Bienfang 1946; Bedichek 1960; Moncrieff 1966; Largey and Watson 1972 [included in this volume]; Winter 1976). A watershed moment for smell, though, occurred in the early to mid-1980s when a series of publications came out that served as the inspiration for a broad range of subsequent scent-related writings and research (see Tuzin in this volume). The first, Alain Corbin's tour de force *The Foul and the Fragrant* (1986), originally published in French in 1982, not only focused on scent and the phenomenology of everyday life but drew out the profound influence of odors upon major social, political and cultural events during France's modernization in the eighteenth and nineteenth centuries. Secondly, German novelist Patrick Süskind, influenced by Corbin, created an international bestseller with *Perfume: The Story of a Murderer* (1986). Although the main character is a psychopath who reiterates the stereotype of the degenerate olfactophiliac, the evocativeness of the novel's world—completely suffused and oriented around odors—stirred literary and critical analyses within and beyond its own context (see Rindisbacher 1992; de Rijke, Ostermark-Johansen and Thomas 2000; Carlisle 2004; Hertel 2005; and Gray, in this volume). At the same time, an upsurge in psychophysical, biochemical and neurological studies attended to all aspects of olfaction, from clinical studies of smell disorders and the founding of aromachology to advances in perfumery and a campaign for fragrance education (see Engen 1982, Gibbons 1986; Gilbert and Wysocki 1987; Green 1988). These publication events, encompassing the domains of history, literature and science, can be said to have crystallized an agenda of sorts on smell, one that sought out the recovery, expression and explanation of smell on its own terms.

While Corbin's book served as a touchstone for a number of social sciences, there nevertheless were separate disciplinary precedents from which researchers also drew: for anthropologists, it was Marshall McLuhan and Claude Levi-Strauss (Classen 1997); for historians, Eric Hobsbawm and Lucien Febvre (Godfrey 2002; Smith 2003); for sociologists, Georg Simmel and Erving Goffman (Largey and Watson 1972). Since the mid-1980s, research on smell has been accompanied by a broader interest in the "lower senses" as a group and articulated under various but related disciplinary terminologies, such as "sensorial anthropology" (Howes 1991), "sensuous geography" (Porteous 1990; Rodaway 1994), "sensory history" (Classen 2001; Hoffer 2003), and culminating, perhaps, in Paul Stoller's overarching phrase "sensuous scholarship" (1997). Notable single-sense cultural histories of smell include Le Guérer's Scent (1992), Classen, Howes and Synnott's Aroma (1994), and several French anthologies, Odeurs du monde (Rey-Hulman and Boccara 1998), Géographie des odeurs (Dulau and Pitte 1998) and Sentir (Cobbi and Dulau 2004). The general public also has been well served by books explicating various aspects of smell, from Gonzalez-Crussi's The Five Senses (1989) and Ackerman's A Natural History of the Senses (1990) to Watson's Jacobson's Organ (1999), Glaser's The Nose (2002) and Burr's The Emperor of Scent (2002), not to mention lavishly illustrated books on perfume and a slew of publications on sexuality and scent, aromatherapy, and other aspects of a fragrant lifestyle.

Given the conundrum of smell and the challenge it has presented to scientists, a number of publications have come out since the late 1980s that bring together biology, neurology, chemistry, psychology, ethnology and cognitive science. Publications such as the two edited by van Toller and Dodd, Perfumery (1988) and Fragrance (1992), Engen's Odor Sensation and Memory (1991), Mueller and Lamparsky's Perfumes (1991), Serby and Chobor Science of Olfaction (1992), Ohloff's Scent and Fragrances (1993), Schab and Crowder's Memory for Odors (1995) and Rouby et al.'s Olfaction, Taste and Cognition (2002) variously examine the relationship of smell to hedonics, semiochemical communication, psychophysiology, evolutionary biology and consumer marketing, among other angles.

In considering the aforementioned publications, an underlying sense of smell's dialectical nature runs throughout, irrespective of disciplinary boundaries. An ambivalence between objective and subjective factors accompanies any odorous experience, yielding an intimate interplay between the physical level of materiality and physiology on the one hand, and the symbolic level of culture and ideology on the other. Perception, as researchers have pointed out, is inevitably influenced by the socialization of the senses and the contexts in which olfactory practices are engaged (see Classen, Howes and Synnott 1994), and this unconventional co-presence of phenomenology and culture contributes to smell's elusiveness and imponderability. Alfred Gell elegantly identifies this contradictory status of smell as one of "semiological ambiguity"—in which odors uniquely engage the characteristics of both a stimulus and a sign or symbol. Smells form a "restricted language," he argues, that partakes equally of matter and meaning, referring to the world as much as it alters the perceiver (see Gell in Part VII of this volume; Krogstad 1989). Such a shifting, unstable confluence between material and social realms, between sensation and perception, yields a remarkable diversity of olfactory phenomenon, as this anthology amply demonstrates: prominent odors that are ignored while subtle ones are fixated on (Cohen); imaginary smells projected onto others (Largey and Watson, Manalansan, Tuzin); smells variously interpreted as nostalgic or traumatic (Hinton et al., Hirsch); fragrant experiences transformed into metaphors, and vice versa (Rindisbacher, Shulman); olfactory evocations in texts (Gatten, Gray, Looby, Mavor, Stamelman, Turin); visual embodiments of smells (el-Khoury); ambient scents with psychophysical effects (Damian and Damian, Herz); spiritual olfactory phenomena (Classen, Guggenheim and Guggenheim, Steele); space- and identity-transforming fragrances (Aubaile-Sallenave, Graham, Porteous, Roubin), odors that can be variously abject, narcissistic or obsessive (Aftel, Corbin, Fisher and Drobnick), to mention only some of the more prominent themes which inform the following chapters.

The Smell Culture Reader is organized into seven sections. However, just as smells defy containment and refuse to respect borders, many of the themes and practices concerning scents cross over these, and indeed any, categorical divisions. Part I, Odorphobia, addresses the "fear" of smells in urban, moral and legal domains. With the eclipse of the zymotic theory of disease, which presumed that smells in themselves caused illness, the threat evoked by odors transmuted into social rhetorics justifying racism, exclusionary politics and the stigmatization of others, even torture. Part II, Toposmia, examines smell's spatial roles. Whether a location's ambiance serves as a distinctive sensory marker or is strategically added for ritualistic or manipulative purposes, odors define and subtly alter the functioning of places. Part III, *Flaireurs*, approaches the issue of scent and identity, especially in regard to individual differences in olfactory abilities, the subjectivity of memory and the personal affectivity of smells. Part IV, Perfume, examines its topic from the positions of novelist, perfumer, biophysicist, archeologist and cultural critic to foreground perfume's artistry, obsessiveness, healing potential and effectiveness as a literary device. Perfume is also relevant to Part V, Scentsuality, in which, along with body odors and pheromones, issues around scent and sexuality, eroticism, hygiene and fetishism circulate. Part VI, Volatile Art, brings forward examples of scents in entertainment, digital media, contemporary art and aristocratic pastimes, all of which point to the nascent formation of an olfactory aesthetics and counterpolitics. The last section, Part VII, Sublime Essences, investigates some fragrant aspects in the spiritual practices of ritual, divination, veneration, asceticism and meditation. Given the diversity of approaches represented among these essays, the definition of the word "culture" included in the title of this anthology could never be anything but polyvalent. Rather than attempting to forge a definition that might encompass the truly variegated examples listed below of artistic, folkloric, indigenous, popular and everyday cultures, I propose instead that readers consider how the attention to scents can rethink the idea of what constitutes culture, as well as the implications for reflexive and immersive research methodologies (see, for example, Classen 1997; Rasmussen 1999; Howes 2003).

The artwork featured on the cover, a view of Anya Gallaccio's installation *Red on Green* (1992), which featured 10,000 fragrant English tea roses, in many ways brings together the two strands of thinking about smells that run throughout this volume—the literal and the symbolic. The immense volume and unmistakable redolence of the flowers, especially when experienced in a typically sanitized exhibition space, creates for the beholder an emphatic encounter with the substance of the world, a strategy that could be considered a "realist" sensibility within olfactory artistic practice (Drobnick 1998). The fragrance of rose petals, in its subtle way, encourages a vibrant, confrontational experience of materiality beyond the purview of instrumental logic, commodity evaluation or technological mediation, not to mention the visualist imperative that Classen (1993) notes is endemic to the flower breeding industry. Yet the installation also works symbolically, although not in the expected sentimental manner that is most commonly associated with the rose, a sentimentality that nevertheless becomes overwhelmed by the artist's decision to leave the flowers to decompose over the course of several weeks. If refreshing floral scents are susceptible to romanticization, Gallaccio also recognizes that decay is an inevitable consequence of organic matter. The deteriorating roomful of roses—whereby an appealing scent gradually gives way to malodorous rot—exposes and confronts what Zygmunt Bauman (1993) terms modernity's "hidden truth" of mortality, and works to overcome the developed world's generalized ignorance of and alienation from biological processes (Press and Minta 2000). A dialog is configured between natural and cultural domains, and urbanized inhabitants are given the opportunity to reconnect with the environment's inherent but often obscured "cycle of smells" (see Cohen in Part II).

In sniffing through olfactory texts, it is striking to note the neologisms that arise. Invented no doubt to compensate for the paucity of vocabulary concerning smell, they are also an indicator of the innovativeness required to articulate olfactory matters. Interdisciplinarity is also a prominent feature of practically any attempt to understand scent as a cultural or physical experience. While *The Smell Culture Reader* brings to the fore work in the cultural sphere, threads of scientific research and discourse certainly weave throughout the chapters that follow. Despite their origins in vastly different domains of culture, art and science, researchers nonetheless parallel and mutually support one another in the task of understanding the complexities of olfaction. Even if the question of smell's neurological functioning is answered in the near future, and smell's scientific "mystery" resolved, there will still remain many untheorized odoriferous phenomena. As Montaigne (1958: 135) discerned many years ago, scents operate "to better fit us for contemplation"; this anthology is certainly the product of that contemplation as well a catalyst, perhaps, for further investigation into the role of smell in culture and history.

Bibliography

Ackerman, D. (1990), *A Natural History of the Senses*, New York: Random House.

Bauman, Z. (1993), "The Sweet Scent of Decomposition," in C. Rojek and B.S. Turner (eds), *Forget Baudrillard?*, London & New York: Routledge, pp. 22–46.

Bedichek, R. (1960), *The Sense of Smell*, Garden City, NY: Doubleday.

Bienfang, R. (1946), *The Subtle Sense*, Norman, OK: University of Oklahoma Press.

Bradshaw, J. (1982), "The Shape of Media Things to Come," in G. Gumpert and R. Cathcart (eds), *Inter/Media*, New York & Oxford: Oxford University Press, pp. 636–41.

Burr, C. (2002), *The Emperor of Scent*, New York: Random House.

Carlisle, J. (2004), *Common Scents*, Oxford: Oxford University Press.

Classen, C. (1993), "The Odor of the Rose," in *Worlds of Sense*, New York: Routledge, pp. 15–36.

—— (1997), "Foundations for an Anthropology of the Senses," *International Social Science Journal*, 153: 401–12.

—— (2001), "The Senses," in P.N. Stearns (ed.), *Encyclopedia of European Social History*, vol. 4, New York: Charles Scribner's Sons.

—— Howes, D. and Synnott, A. (1994), *Aroma*, New York: Routledge.

Cobbi, J. and Dulau, R. (eds) (2004), *Sentir*, Eurasie 13, Paris: L'Harmattan.

Damian, P. and Damian, K. (1995), *Aromatherapy*, Rochester, VT: Healing Arts Press.

Davenport, G. (trans.) (1990), *Herakleitos and Diogenes*, San Francisco: Grey Fox Press.

Davies, B.J., Kooijmanb, D. and Warda, P. (2003), "The Sweet Smell of Success," *Journal of Marketing Management*, 19(5–6): 611–27.

de Rijke, V., Ostermark-Johansen, L. and Thomas, H. (eds) (2000), *Nose Book*, London: Middlesex University Press

Drobnick, J. (1998), "Reveries, Assaults and Evaporating Presences," *Parachute*, 89: 10–19.

—— ([2002] 2005), "Volatile Architectures," in D. Howes (ed.) *Empire of the Senses*, Oxford: Berg.

Dulau, R. and Pitte, J.-R. (eds) (1998), *Géographie des odeurs*, Paris: L'Harmattan.

Engen, T. (1982), *Perception of Odors*, New York: Academic Press.

—— (1991), *Odor Sensation and Memory*, New York: Praeger.

Field, T.G. (2004), "Copyright Protection for Perfumes," http://www.piercelaw.edu/tfield/perfume.pdf.

Gibbons, B. (1986), "The Intimate Sense of Smell," *National Geographic*, 170(3): 324–61.

Gilbert, A.N. and Wysocki, C.J. (1987), "The Smell Survey Results," *National Geographic*, 172(4): 514–25.

Glaser, G. (2002), *The Nose*, New York: Washington Square Press.

Godfrey, S. (2002), "Alain Corbin," *French Historical Studies*, 25(2): 381–98.

Gonzalez-Crussi, F. (1989), *The Five Senses*, New York: Harcourt Brace Jovanovich.

Green, A. (1988), "Fragrance Education and the Psychology of Smell," in S. van Toller and G.H. Dodd (eds), *Perfumery*, London: Chapman & Hall, pp. 227–33.

Hertel, R. (2005), *Making Sense*, Amsterdam: Rodopi.

Hoffer, P.C. (2003), *Sensory Worlds in Early America*, Baltimore: Johns Hopkins University Press.

Howes, D. (ed.) (1991), *The Varieties of Sensory Experience,* Boulder, CO: Westview.

—— (2003), *Sensual Relations*, Ann Arbor: University of Michigan Press.

Korotkaya, Z. (n.d.), "Biometric Person Authentification: Odor," http://www.it.lut.fi/kurssit/03–04/010970000/seminars/Korotkaya.pdf.

Krogstad, A. (1989), "The Treasure House of Smell," *Folk*, 31: 87–103.

Largey, G.P. and Watson, D.R. (1972), "The Sociology of Odors," *American Journal of Sociology*, 77(6): 1021–34.

LaSalle, D. and Britton, T.A. (2003), *Priceless*, Boston: Harvard Business School Press.

Le Guérer, A. (1992), *Scent*, New York: Turtle Bay Books.

Moncrieff, R.W. (1966), *Odour Preferences*, New York: John Wiley.

Montaigne, M. (1958), *Essays*, trans. J.M. Cohen, Harmondsworth: Penguin.

Moravec, H. (1997), "The Senses Have No Future," http://www.frc.ri.cmu.edu/~hpm/project.archive/general.articles/1997/970128.nosense.html.

Mueller, P.M. and Lamparsky, D. (eds) (1991), *Perfumes*, London: Elsevier.

Nobelprize.org (2004), "The 2004 Nobel Prize in Physiology or Medicine," http://nobelprize.org/medicine/laureates/2004/press.html.

Ohloff, G. (1993), *Scent and Fragrances*, New York: Springer-Verlag.

Pearce, T.C., Schiffman, S.S., Nagle, H.T. and Gardner (eds) (2003), *Handbook of Machine Olfaction*, Berlin: Wiley-VCH.

Pink, S. (2004), *Home Truths*, Oxford: Berg.

Porteous, J.D. (1990), *Landscapes of the Mind*, Toronto: University of Toronto Press.

Press, D. and Minta, S.C. (2000), "The Smell of Nature," *Ethics, Place and Environment*, 3(2): 173–86.

Rasmussen, S. (1999), "Making Better 'Scents' in Anthropology," *Anthropological Quarterly*, 72(2): 55–73.

Rey-Hulman, D. and Boccara, M. (eds) (1998), *Odeurs du monde*, Paris: Inalco.

Rindisbacher, H. (1992), *The Smell of Books*, Ann Arbor: University of Michigan Press.

Rodaway, P. (1994), *Sensuous Geographies*, London: Routledge.

Rose, J. and Earle, S. (eds) (1996), *The World of Aromatherapy*, Berkeley: Frog Ltd.

Rouby, C., Schaal, B., Flolley, A., Dubois, D. and Gervais, R. (eds) (2002), *Olfaction, Taste and Cognition*, Cambridge: Cambridge University Press.

Schab, F.R. and Crowder, R.G. (eds) (1995), *Memory for Odors*, Mahwah, NJ: Lawrence Erlbaum Associates.

Serby, M.J. and Chobor, K. L. (eds) (1992), *Science of Olfaction*, New York: Springer-Verlag.

Smith, M.M. (2003), "Making Sense of History," *Journal of Social History*, 37(1): 165–86.

Stoller, P. (1997), *Sensuous Scholarship*, Philadelphia: University of Pennsylvania Press.

Synnott, A. (1993), *The Body Social*, New York & London: Routledge.

Tellenbach, H. (1968), *Geschmack und Atmosphäre*, Salzburg: Otto Müller-Verlag.

Thomas, L. (1984), "On Smell," in *Late Night Thoughts on Listening to Mahler's Ninth Symphony*, New York: Bantam, pp. 40–4.

van Toller, S. and Dodd, G.H. (eds) (1988), *Perfumery*, London: Chapman & Hall.

—— (eds) (1992), *Fragrance*, London: Elsevier.

Watson, L. (2001), *Jacobson's Organ*, New York: Penguin.

Winter, R. (1976), *The Smell Book*, Philadelphia & New York: J.B. Lippincott.

Your Bionic Future (1999), "Your New Senses," *Scientific American*, 10(3): 38–55.

Part I

Odorphobia

Preface

Celebration of Mistrust
On the first day of classes, the professor brought out an enormous flask.
"It's full of perfume," he told Miguel Brun and the rest of the students. *"I want to measure how perceptive each one of you is. Raise your hand as soon as you perceive the scent."*

And he removed the stopper. Moments later two hands were in the air. Soon five, ten, thirty—all hands were raised.
"May I open the window, professor?" a young woman asked, dizzy from the overpowering fragrance. Several voices echoed her request. The air, thick with the aroma of perfume, had quickly become unbearable for everyone.

Then the professor had the students examine the flask, one by one. It was full of water.

Eduardo Galeano, The Book of Embraces

The polarized response to smells—the like/dislike reaction that occurs almost instantaneously when encountering an odor—is one of olfaction's most distinctive characteristics. Eduardo Galeano's parable, above, illustrates the rapid trajectory that a smell can take in transforming from a faint, presumably pleasant experience into something disagreeable and suffocating. The fact that the "perfume" in question is really water only underscores the power of suggestion in regard to olfactory perceptions, and illustrates how easily an intolerance for even a nonexistent scent can be incited. "Celebration of Mistrust" uses odor to portray the dangers of an unquestioned belief in authority and how gullible conformity yields a passionate but mistaken collective opinion; yet the illusion and subsequent stigmatization of smell, especially when facilitated by and reinforced through group cohesion, is not an unusual occurrence as the chapters in this section attest.

"Odorphobia" may be a rather clinical sounding term by which to group the texts of this section, and it should be emphasized that the olfactory phenomena being discussed here have nothing to do with the neurological disorders characterized by a distorted or deranged sense of smell, for example, dysosmia, parosmia or cacosmia. My use of odorphobia relates to cultural, and in many cases ideological, intolerance toward smells, specifically as it is directed at places or people. As the following chapters demonstrate, odorphobia is often linked to state or majority agendas in which alterity is defined as a physical characteristic. Odors are the means by which the boundary between self and other is demarcated, as well as the supposed basis of prejudicial extensions of such demarcation; in other words, olfaction is the means to corporealize dislike and a prominent excuse for expressions of racism, sexism, classism and xenophobia (see Classen, Howes and Synnott 1994; Miller 1997; Carlisle 2004). The fear of odors, whether they can be actually smelled or not, naturalizes cultural disapproval, where immoral behavior is believed to produce a foul smell and, conversely, being odorous is tantamount to being odious (see van Beek 1992; Bubandt 1998; Telle 2002). Commensurate with these claims of foulness are inflamed anxieties over "contamination," which often justifies practices of segregation and colonialism (Stallybrass and White 1986; Cohen and Johnson 2005). The exception to the ideological use of odorphobia in this section is the concluding chapter, which concerns the deliberate use of smells as a tactic of oppression and terror.

The first chapter in this section addresses odorphobia and its relation to notions of place during that watershed moment in the modern Western history when sanitization campaigns became social policy and were instituted via the redesign of buildings, public spaces and entire cityscapes. Rodolphe el-Khoury's "Polish and Deodorize" revisits the thinking and hygienic practices of late eighteenth-century France. A number of anxieties about the purity of the atmosphere arose during this time—concerning putrefaction, telluric emanations, mephitic and morbific vapors—which led to a previously unmatched antipathy towards smells and an array of vigilant deodorization projects. Protecting citizens from subterranean miasmas by paving streets and sidewalks, sealing in residential odors by covering walls with plaster, moving noxious industries to the outskirts of the city, reorganizing and widening streets for better ventilation—these techniques sought to cleanse and purify the urban environment. Odorlessness became manifest by a visual logic articulated by white paint, shiny surfaces and panoramic vistas that continues to this day in architecture and city planning. Despite the prominence of these visible signs, the victory over stench was not entirely adequate until the introduction of city-wide sewer systems that took another hundred years (in Paris anyway), yet the influential architectural program begun at this time was more than enough to usher in what el-Khoury calls the reign of "olfactory silence."

Odorphobia directed at individuals and groups constitutes the second primary thematic of this section (Part II, Toposmia, will continue the discussion on smell and issues of place). The sociological dimension is foregrounded in the pioneering text by Gale Largey and Rod Watson who draw upon a diverse range of interpersonal and intercultural examples to propose that one fundamental role olfaction plays in society is as an indicator of moral status and value. On an individual level, pleasant smells are said to emanate from those who are virtuous and elevated on the social scale, while unpleasant smells cling to those who are corrupt and low-ranking. On a group level, similar dualistic judgments prevail. Groups considered "other" are generally considered malodorous, and good smells (or no odor at all) are believed to characterize the critic's own social group (see further, Classen 1993; Smith 2006). Avoidance behaviors, prejudicial comments and stereotypical characterizations are then rationalized by the supposed presence of a repugnant odor, which, in the end, turns out to be projected upon the other rather than actually perceived. Malodors thus function rhetorically and arbitrarily, for they can be attributed to any designated population segment, and in fact operate as a technique for in-group identification. Even within the in-group, however, odorphobia can be present in internalized form. Largey and Watson discuss the use of perfume as a method of impression management, and here the potential for self-scrutinized stigmatization continually threatens. Bad breath and body odor, especially when exaggerated by advertising ploys and a plethora of consumer products, constantly remind individuals to be on guard about the taboo of bodily emanations and keep odorphobia habitually engaged.

The next two chapters address particular instances of olfactory-based intolerance in the urban North American context. "Immigrant Lives and the Politics of Olfaction in the Global City," by Martin Manalansan, considers the circulation of odorphobic discourses in New York City generated by residents resistant to the influx of immigrants and changing neighborhood demographics. Smells, especially the aromas of culturally-specific cuisines, materialize as markers of difference, and offend mainstream sensibilities by virtue of being uncontainable, unfamiliar and representative of the supposed refusal of new citizens to assimilate and conform to majoritarian standards of odorlessness. Food odors become the ostensible and purportedly self-evident rationale through which a sensory politics, such as the euphemistically titled "Quality of Life" campaign, is enacted, but which has at its roots the goal of maintaining economic and racial stratification. Manalansan's primary research in the field and his interviews with Asian Americans also unveil the ambivalence created by these odorphobic discourses within immigrant communities. Already struggling with the upheavals involved in relocating to a new culture and environment, the smells of cooking create what the author calls a "quotidian dilemma": the aromas celebrate the sensorial knowledge of one's heritage and preserve cultural continuity, yet they also mark one's residence and body as distinctly "other" and thus vulnerable to being targeted. Finding ways to accomplish the former without invoking the consequences of the latter becomes a challenge requiring ingenuity and constant self-monitoring.

Alan Hyde's case study, "Offensive Bodies," centers on a US court decision to exclude a homeless man from a New Jersey public library's premises because of his odor. Hyde references the history of hygienic standards in the US, showing how the normative understanding of "clean" is a shifting and contingent one, rather than a convention that could be considered universal. What the emphasis on cleanliness over time does reflect, though, is the consistent policy of economic and social elites to subject the poor and other minorities to processes of purification—a policy with moral as much as physical implications. A tension, similar to the one Manalansan described, exists between two conflicting interpretations about the odor of the other: that either the smells pertaining to the body are conditional, in the sense that individuals possess the ability and, indeed, obligation to remove them; or that smells inherently adhere to the body, making them ineradicable, thus "justifying" the removal of persons themselves. Both positions, however, depend on the assumption that those in power are odorless or at least possess pleasing or non-offensive odors. Using Julia Kristeva's notion of the abject, whereby what is considered polluting is expelled in order to confirm the definition of one's own identity, Hyde argues that the expulsion of odorous others is the practice by which a political hegemony maintains its own self-assured status.

The moral implications for smell are even more pronounced among the Ilahita Arapesh of the East Sepik province of Papua New Guinea. Donald Tuzin's chapter, "Base Notes," discusses how smell is considered by the Ilahita to be the distillation of an object's (or person's) innermost being, and is a significant means by which communication, specifically of the moral kind, takes place. Smells project beyond an individual's body; at the same time, individuals permanently accumulate the smells of others and the environment. This is compounded by the fact that not all smells can be avoided. One must inhale, so often there is no choice but to ingest odors wafting in a person's immediate vicinity—whether they be good, bad or neutral. As the author remarks, the issue of morality usually entails some aspect of voluntary choice, yet given the necessity of breathing, one's moral condition for the Ilahita is not necessarily within voluntary control. Smells are thus a shared substance with mutually influential properties, necessitating mindfulness on the part of villagers to be careful of contagion from the ambiances encountered in everyday life. Alternately, odors can ensure useful and beneficent connections, such as between farmers and their crops or among marriage partners.

This section concludes with accounts of odorphobia generated specifically and intentionally by a state military apparatus. Olfactory-triggered panic attacks, the topic of investigation by Devon E. Hinton, Vuth Pich, Dara Chhean and Mark H. Pollack, differ from the above moral and ideological instances of odorphobia by being deliberate acts of intimidation and torture. Many of the Cambodian refugees who lived through the tyranny of the

Pol Pot regime and the terror it unleashed upon the country's population have been found by the authors to be afflicted with odor-induced panic attacks that are combined with horrifying flashbacks, debilitating physical symptoms and olfactory hypervigilance. The suffering is similar to the symptoms of post-traumatic stress disorder, but is compounded by traditional smell-sensitive Cambodian beliefs, especially those about the poisonous danger of smells and the anxiety stimulating potential of "wind attacks" to cause nausea and stroke. Even when the survivors are separated by distance and time from the original events, everyday smells such as cigarette smoke, car exhaust, garbage, perfume and burning food can invoke the traumas once experienced and lead to severe psychological and bodily effects. As much as olfaction was employed as a torture device, became intrinsically associated with the terrors of the Khmer Rouge and continues to incite torment in survivors decades later, the authors also point out smell's therapeutic value in retraining patients' odoriferous cognitions to alleviate fear and anguish.

Jim Drobnick

Bibliography

Bubandt, N. (1998), "The Odour of Things," *Ethnos*, 63(1): 48–80.

Carlisle, J. (2004), "Smelling Others," in *Common Scents*, Oxford: Oxford University Press, pp. 23–49.

Classen, C. (1993), "The Odor of the Other," in *Worlds of Sense*, New York: Routledge, pp. 79–105.

—— Howes, D., and Synnott, A. (1994), "Odor and Power," in *Aroma*, New York: Routledge, pp. 161–79.

Cohen, W.A. and Johnson, R. (eds) (2005), *Filth*, Minneapolis: University of Minnesota Press.

Galeano, E. (1991), *The Book of Embraces*, trans. C. Belfrage with M. Schafer, New York: Norton.

Miller, W.I. (1997), "Orwell's Sense of Smell," in *The Anatomy of Disgust*, Cambridge, MA: Harvard University Press, pp. 235–54.

Smith, M.H. (2006), *How Race is Made*, Chapel Hill: University of North Carolina Press.

Stallybrass, P. and White, A. (1986), *The Politics and Poetics of Transgression*, Ithaca: Cornell University Press.

Telle, K.G. (2002), "The Smell of Death," *Social Analysis*, 46(3): 75–104.

van Beek, W.E.A. (1992), "The Dirty Smith," *Africa*, 61(1): 38–58.

1

Polish and Deodorize
Paving the City in Late Eighteenth-Century France

Rodolphe el-Khoury

In Visible Environments

The unhealthy has the amorphous and the unnameable as its limits.

Jacques Guillerme

Two strikingly dissimilar images of *les halles* in the eighteenth century: a "realist" depiction of the existing marketplace and a rendering of its projected improvement in conformity with the latest principles of *embellissement*. The contrast encapsulates the urbanist impulse of the late eighteenth century, a systematic sanitization of urban space undertaken primarily through aesthetic—visual—means. Evidently, this contrast is not limited to visual discrepancies since the depiction of the two realities *implies* difference in more than one sensory register. These differences though are translated and conveyed in visual clues. While the bristling *melanges* of the existing market can bring to mind the "olfactory vertigo" evoked in Patrick Süskind's (1986) prose, the precisely delineated masses, the shiny surfaces and sharp edges of the projected square have a distinctly odorless look.

It is precisely in this capacity for the image to colonize and absorb nonvisual categories of experience that the urbanism of the eighteenth century reconciles the formal preoccupations of the past with the functional imperatives of rapidly growing cities. A long-standing tradition of town planning thereby confronts and adapts to the new agents in the production of space in which historians have identified a new paradigm of urban theory and practice. Urban historians have indeed spoken of a Copernican revolution in the Enlightenment's conception of the city. Beauty, once the governing principle of urbanism, is claimed to have been overthrown by health, hygiene and physiology—a constellation of operative concepts introduced by the scientific discourse. As a demonstration of this historical break, the aesthetic and fictional images of the baroque city are contrasted to the "functional" and "real" urbanism of the eighteenth century; the preoccupation with monumental vistas and axial composition is accordingly distinguished from the new concern for the optimal flow of air and merchandise in smooth and unobstructed street corridors.

Here is a characteristic rehearsal of the argument, quoted from a canonical work on eighteenth-century Paris:

> The old conception of the polis, inherited from the Renaissance and depicted in the paintings of Piero della Francesca, insisted first and foremost on cities' formal beauty; their monuments and their girdle of ramparts made them a priori pleasing to the eye and exhilarating to the spirit. The new design, however, which dates from the eighteenth century, somewhat neglects these aesthetic vaticinations and takes its inspiration from medicine. (Ladurie 1980–85: 203)

In the positivist/functionalist scenario, the interventions that led to the transformation of eighteenth-century Paris into the "capital of the nineteenth century" were guided by factors that eluded the disciplinary range of architecture. The term *embellissement,* which continued to describe the large-scale effort in street alignment, would seem to have survived by the force of habit. As an inertial vestige of a previous paradigm, it could not adequately describe a new mode of spatial production that was driven primarily by invisible forces. Recent studies have nevertheless demonstrated how these forces are defined and exercised in articulate spatial configurations that strive on visibility and are mediated by aesthetic criteria. Michel Foucault's analysis of the visual structure of the disciplinary apparatus is perhaps the most familiar (Foucault 1977, 1980; Mashek 1993; Evans 1971, 1982); its assimilation into architectural history has brought issues of power and aesthetics into previously unsuspected proximities.

Attention has, moreover, been given to the "superficial" aspects of the environment. Features that scholars have traditionally been trained to ignore in their quest for fundamental causes behind trivial symptoms are now recognized in their structural role. Mark Wigley's speculation on the function of white paint in modern architecture exemplifies this quasi-Nietzschean sensitivity to the depths of the surface: "modern architecture," he argues, "is never more than a surface effect" (Wigley 1995: 240).

Surface Effects

> The cleanliness of our [linen] clothing and the quantities in which we own it are worth more than all the baths in the world.
>
> Claude Perrault, *La Querelle des anciens et des modernes*

In his history of hygiene, Georges Vigarello underscores the primacy of the visual field in the construction of the concept of cleanliness; "only the visible counts" (Vigarello 1985: 94). Since the Middle Ages and until the modern practice of hygiene, cleanliness pertained mainly to the exposed areas or the body. Etiquette and civility manuals, which codified the behavior of the nobility in the medieval courts, insisted on the cleanliness of the face and the hands, making no further prescription for other parts of the body.

However systematic, the norms of cleanliness were moral rather than functional: cleanliness, or *propreté*, had more to do with "propriety" than with health. The instructions on the toilette of the hands were thus stated and adopted as a fixed code for the practice of "decency":

> Honorable child, wash your hands
> when you rise and when you dine
> and again at supper, all the time
>
> (Glixelli, "Les Contenances de table," fourteenth century,
> qtd. in Vigarello 1985: 54)

This partial and social cleanliness is visual and immediately discernible. Much like a vestimentary accessory, it has particular cultural and social associations that are indicative of certain distinctions. The clues are strictly visual because the visual sign "is without a doubt the most intuitive indication here, the one which convinces most 'naturally,' the one which can be subjected to the most effortlessly formulated norms. Through it, the signs of cleanliness are expressed and explained succinctly. The precepts seem 'limpid.' One need only look" (Vigarello 1985: 241).

White linen played the prominent role in the exercise and display of cleanliness. Its cleansing virtues had been promoted since the Middle Ages but only in the sixteenth century did it acquire a public function, as the white shirt began to emerge at the margins of the gown, spilling into the space of appearance at the collar and the sleeves, to eventually develop an elaborate rhetoric of display during the classical age. The overflowing shirt cascaded and folded over the dress, steadily claiming more exposure, transposing, metonymically, the hidden skin to the surface of the garment. The linen that had touched the skin intimately became an objectification of the private body and its whiteness an ostensible signifier of *cleanliness*.

Considering the visual and primarily accessory character of cleanliness, it is not surprising to find little concern for olfactory experience in the premodern practice of *propreté*. The odor of the body that nowadays would be considered the most evident index of cleanliness played a minor role in the theater of *propreté*. More important was the use of perfume, which was believed to have therapeutic effects as a counterodor, but also functioned as a mask in the olfactory display of cleanliness. The importance accorded to powders and fragrant sachets in the panoply of grooming accessories further testifies to the "visuality" of smell: they were the material support but also the visible traces of the evanescent perfume. Along with the oversized collar and cascading sleeves, immaculate whites, and abundant lace, they participated in the logic of the spectacle by constructing reality as an effect of the surface.

At the end of the eighteenth century, the emerging discourse on hygiene began to undermine the scenic code of cleanliness with Newtonian notions of dynamic influences and invisible forces. The proper functioning of internal organs—the new definition of health—eventually displaced the primacy of external appearance and was thereafter associated with physical vigor and dynamic stimulations of the body. Cold water was prescribed for tighter and firmer fibers and cleaner skin for the vital respiration of the pores—an evolution in health practices that Vigarello associates with the bourgeois economy of "vigors" that had just displaced the aristocratic strategies of appearance. But this shift to the internal functioning of the organ also entailed new strategies of representation that persisted with the effort to "visualize" the unseen, attempts to recover the hidden and the imperceptible in superficial and tangible traces (Stafford 1993). The visual practice of hygiene did not decline, as Vigarello would have it in his historical scenario; it was re-adapted to new registers of experience and levels of abstraction. The semiotics of the tanned skin testify to the recent realignments in the visualization of health.

This process was perhaps most effective in the visualization of smell; emphatically reasserted in the mid-eighteenth-century preoccupation with miasmic threats, olfactory vigilance ultimately served to reorganize the environment according to the dialectic of transparency and opacity that shaped the *aesthetic* of cleanliness. Permeable and transparent urban fabrics remedied the much maligned stagnation of the air while hard and impregnable surfaces satisfied the demand for prophylactic revetments.

Prophylactic Revetments

O superb city! what disgusting horrors are hidden within your walls! But let us not ask the reader's gaze to linger any longer on the shocking outcomes of a populous city.

Louis Sébastien Mercier, *Tableau de Paris*

The visual logic of cleanliness is evidenced in the treatment of the architectural surface, in floor pavements and wall coverings that exhibit a vestimentary "visuality" in the exercise of their professed sanitary function. The eighteenth century was very keen on the sanitary "coating" of the surface, especially when the miasmic threat reached its peak in the 1770s. Stone, plaster and even paint were among the most valued instruments of deodorization. Barely containing some of the noxious effluvia behind their scaling film, they brought temporary relief to the nose; their "superficial" effect on the eye nevertheless proved to be far more lasting.

Paving figured prominently in the projects of *embellissement*. Only the resonance of a multiplicity of circumstantial factors, of different agents promoting the value and utility of the paving project, could account for the urgency of its formulation and subsequent implementation. The practical advantages of paving are evident, however: it facilitated the rapidly increasing traffic of carriages, protected pedestrians from the dust and mud of the street, and could be washed easily by running water. The trend favored large granite flagstone rather than the conventional cobble as the material of choice. The paving stone was valued mostly for its sealing capacity: paving was held to constitute a hermetic surface that would contain the deadly "telluric emanation" below ground and thus safeguard the air of the city from miasmic contamination.

The anxiety caused by the telluric emanation has an enduring history in the French cultural imaginary. So engrained was the belief in the subterranean threats that the Abbé Dubos considered it a principal determining factor in his cultural geography. In his chapter titled "That the difference that fills the air of different countries can only be attributed to the nature of the emanations that issue forth from the earth and that are different in differing regions," he details how the vapors released from the fermenting substrata of the earth can have a drastic influence on the character of a given culture. Favorable conditions consist of an extended period of diminished telluric emanations while adverse climates are a consequence of increased subterranean activities. Genius is not possible in a land that is permeable to the gaseous influences of the telluric depth. Within the same land, different generations are furthermore conditioned by more or less favorable rates of earthly exhalations. The threatening vapors are held to emanate from a lower stratum that is composed of "minerals and clayey earth whose sap nourishes the exterior soil" (Dubos 1770: 318). "Prudent Nature" has taken the precaution to cover this dangerously fertile layer with a prophylactic crust of rubble, stone and sand. The trouble arises when the seal is broken by human intervention (building and agriculture) or natural catastrophes (earthquakes and volcanic eruptions):

> One lays open several locations of this rich and teeming envelope and exposes them to the instant action of air and sun, whereupon such unobstructed

contact triggers the release of molecules in too great a quantity ... Thus the
air of the region is corrupted. (Dubos 1770: 318–19)

One cannot help take notice of the sexual overtones in Dubos's language,
an indication that such irrational anxieties might have an origin in the
depths of a collective unconscious (see Bachelard 1949). But psychoanalysis
is not necessary here to diagnose the hysterical mistrust for the feminine
subterranean and its "morbific vapors"—old anxieties that were intensified in
the eighteenth century due to the mining industry and its recent excursions
into previously unknown subterranean depths. Scientific and medical reports
were indeed filled with references to the miner's battle with noxious vapors
of all kinds. Repeatedly mentioned among the perils of the quarries: a deadly
gas "exhaled by marble, tufa and certain stones, and which obviously attacks
the nostrils and the brain" (qtd in Corbin 1986: 23).

Not only did the mysterious earth concoct the much dreaded "emanations,"
its porous depths were also suspected of retaining the excremental waste
incessantly infiltrating the soil through cracks in the cesspools, only to
resurface eventually with more concentrated venom:

> The cesspools, often poor structures, allow the foul matter to seep into
> neighboring wells. This has not kept bakers, whose custom it is to use well
> water, from abstaining from doing so, and the most basic of staples is perforce
> impregnated by noxious and malevolent elements. (Mercier [1782] 1994:
> 116)

In the Parisian imaginary, the subterranean soil amounted to a gigantic
reservoir where the remains and waste of past generations precipitated into
a horrific brew. Under the street thus lay the excremental past of the city,
ready to burst forth again at any opportunity: a fissure in the ground, the
digging of a well, an excavation for a building's foundation.

More so than mining, archaeology cultivated the anxiety of terrestrial
depths. The excavation of layers of accumulated debris from past civilizations
made a tangible display of the excremental history of the earth. While
whole cities were excavated under the ashes at Pompeii and Herculaneum,
fantasies about a subterranean Paris were cultivated at the same pace; images
of a Swiss cheese-like underground, labyrinthine catacombs and galleries
bristling with hideous miasma and threatening to cave in at any moment
from under the overcrowded mass of the decaying city. Along with the terror
of depths bursting onto the surface, thus flourished a more apocalyptic
fantasy, that of the surface collapsing into an abysmal earth. This scenario
betrays a quasi-ecological hostility to the artifice of architecture, as evidenced
in Louis Sébastien Mercier's alarm at the incessant displacement of lapidary
mass from natural and stable sources below to contrived and precarious
accumulations above:

All that can be seen on the surface has essentially been pulled from the ground that serves as the city's foundation. Therein lies the reason for the terrifying chasms that open up beneath houses in many city neighborhoods. Houses nest on the abyss, and a not too considerable tremor will reclaim these stones for the very places from which they were so laboriously lifted. (Mercier [1782] 1994: 36)

The widespread preoccupation with paving is a manifestation of such anxieties. This is particularly evident in the adamant promotion of flagstone that was imported from England, at great cost, to systematically replace cobblestone. Also telling are the extreme instances where quasi-irrational arguments, such as recommendations for the paving of entire villages, including interiors, were urgently discussed at the academies. They consistently focused on the increasing permeability of the ground surface supposedly aggravated by the sedimentation of waste below as well as its accumulation on the streets and dumping sites above: intensifying osmotic pressures disrupting the natural crust that had previously protected the air from the mephitic emanations of the earth.

Yet the deodorizing properties of the paving stones are negligible next to their visual effectiveness in transforming the urban environment. In fact, little was achieved by way of paving in the fight against the foul Parisian smells. Urban odors seem to have lingered and intensified well into the nineteenth century. The worst ever were supposedly reported in the summer of 1880. Chlorine-based chemical compounds and an extensive sewage system were far more efficient in the deodorizing process than the stone surface that was meant to hermetically seal the miasmic vapors within their terrestrial reservoir.

The pavement could only fail in this impossible task but its virtues were never doubted, mainly because it was very effective in providing solutions to many other practical problems (see Mercier [1782] 1994: 1202). The sidewalk, an innovation imported from England, was one of its most celebrated applications. The first to be executed was in 1782 on the Rue du Théâtre François, and it was met with much enthusiasm by the bourgeoisie, for whom issues of pedestrian comfort had become evermore urgent. The revolted bourgeois, struggling to avoid the degrading filth of the street was an emblematic cliche, often invoked in protests against the inefficiency of government:

Little could amuse the passing foreigner more than the sight of a Parisian bounding and leaping across muddied streams in a three-cornered wig, white stockings and a coat festooned with garlands, speeding on tiptoe down sorry streets while roof gutters empty their gullets on taffeta parasols ... Mud in mounds and slime-glazed pavements and grease-laden axles and pitfall after pitfall to sidestep! He hurtles on nonetheless. At every street corner he stops and motions a crud-cleanser. (Mercier [1782] 1994: 110)

The *décrotteur* in question is the object of one of the *Tableau de Paris*'s most memorable characterizations (Mercier [1782] 1994: 1255–9). A polyvalent invention of the eighteenth century, his primary function was to assist the bourgeois with brushes and waxes, in the desperate attempt to maintain a proper appearance:

> A handy crud-cleanser awaits you at even street corner, an imperious brush darting from his dexterous hand. Only his tidying and grooming could make you fit to enter the houses of gentlemen and take your place amongst the ladies. A threadbare coat, coarse linens, cheap materials—all these can be overlooked, but no one, not even a poet, can come to the door ridden with crud. (Mercier [1782] 1994: 1255)

Other roles reserved to the *décrotteur* included stunt acts at the theater, in which they incarnated gods and monsters, suspended with cables from the machinery of spectacle. Furthermore, since they were readily available in great number, whole crowds of them were invited to visit new theaters on the boulevard so as to test their structural soundness before their official inauguration. In the exercise of all these different functions they consistently served as accessories of spectacle: they maintained the linen's whiteness, which was de rigueur in public appearance, and insured the proper functioning of the theatrical apparatus. In this context, Mercier's reference to the decorator and the painter, the other experts of stenography and representation, is all the more pertinent: "No apprenticeship for decorators … they take tip the brush and proclaim like the famous painter: and I, I also decrud" (Mercier [1782] 1994: 1256–7). "Why couldn't we have sidewalks like in London" is Mercier's reaction to the sight of the filthy street and the busy *décrotteur*. But his remark is little inspired by issues of health and safety; even less critical is the ease and efficiency of pedestrian circulation that a paved surface would most evidently favor. Rather, the capacity to shield from spattering mud is the sidewalk's most appreciated virtue. The sidewalk thus reproduces the role of the *décrotteur*: it serves to maintain the whiteness that is required of linen, to achieve an image of *propreté* according to the code of appearance.

Paving was no less visually minded in its other applications. This is particularly evident when its logic is extended to the treatment of the vertical surface, a site that has traditionally been more favored by aesthetic considerations. Paving's prophylactic potential also implicated the wall because telluric emanations were believed to permeate entire structures, infiltrating their most elevated section through the capillary action of the walls. This suspicion conceives of the wall, the vertical extrusion of the buried foundations, as an artificial extension of the earth. The notion is particularly plausible in the cases of stone and brick architecture, instances where the geological origin of the building material facilitates the conflation of the natural and the artificial. The paving imperatives thus extended to the walls: they had to be sealed at the surface. Otherwise, the mephitic sap that their porous sections incessantly drew through the foundation would be released into the atmosphere. In light of such threats, a crack in wall revetment would have caused much alarm; it was not merely a symptom of structural fatigue but also a breach in the seal that kept the telluric influence hermetically locked behind the surface.

Much like the soil that held the excremental history of the city, walls were known to absorb and retain the noxious vapors of the surrounding air. The persistence of this miasmic impregnation was noted by many "observers" who recognized a lingering odor emanating from surrounding walls years after its actual source had been removed from the space. The revetment was thus needed to shield the permeable wall from external influences as much as to contain the ascending ramifications of the miasmic earth. Mathieu Géraud argued that the thick wall tapestries of medieval interiors were better suited to this double task than modern wall papers and fabrics, which he considered far too flimsy and dangerously permeable (Géraud 1786: 34). Others promoted the virtues of wall tiles; the glazed kind were preferred, no doubt because their shiny surface is a visual demonstration of impregnability (see Howard 1994). Visual categories can accordingly account for the success of varnish in the armored protection against miasmic infiltration. Varnishes were recommended and applied to all kinds of surfaces, including clothing. Their effectiveness was convincingly displaced in their reflective properties: the shiny and slippery aspect they gave to the surface sufficed to guarantee its salubrity. This is largely because reflective surfaces are characteristic of hard and therefore impervious materials; by association, a soft but shiny taffeta can evoke the impregnability of glass, metal or polished stone. Still more effective is the visual allusion to a mineral realm, to inert substances that are not subject to the inevitable processes of organic putrefaction.

The reflective surface is one of the most "obvious" sites of overlap between the olfactory and the visual—instances where odors and images are confounded in the convergence of their semantic fields. Varnishes and glazed tiles could here translate an olfactory condition into a visual experience: to be shiny is to be odorless. This transposition has yet to lose its potency in the rhetoric of hygiene; the myriad of household products still devoted to the maintenance of the shiny/odorless surface testify to the longevity of miasmic mythology in the collective imaginary.

Equally lasting and far more critical in its architectural implications is the white wall. Plaster and whitewash had been available as wall finishes for quite a while but the medical reports of the late eighteenth century boosted their popularity to unprecedented highs. The potency of plaster as an antimephitic agent was demonstrated in the sulfurous gases it released while it was still fresh on the wall. The belief was that miasma could be effectively neutralized with counterodors such as aromatics because their characteristic volatility is supposedly antithetical to the earthbound density of organic miasma. Aromatic scents and sulfurous gases not only served to mask unpleasant odors but were accordingly held to constitute active antidotes to their mephitic counterparts. Hence the importance of perfumes, fumigations and incense burning in the fight against disease.

The antiseptic emanations of fresh plaster, however, were so potent that they constituted a health hazard in themselves for a few months after the coating of a wall. Newly plastered interiors were thus left vacant until the sulfurous gases dissipated. Mercier described an urban tradition known as *essuyer les plutres* ["wiping down the plasters"], whereby new structures were momentarily left at the disposal of the *filles publiques* until they could be safely occupied by the bourgeois (Mercier [1782] 1994: 923).

The sulfurous "counterodor" could indeed neutralize the mephitic exhalations of a decaying wall but the effect was only momentary and actually due to the sterilizing contact with the active chemical agents in the whitewash. If the white wall gradually gained a universal appeal, it is primarily because of its visual properties or, more precisely, by virtue of its capacity to translate the olfactory condition of odorlessness into an image. The rhetorical power of the white surface in demonstrating and insuring cleanliness can hardly be overestimated. White paint became a staple of modern architecture and its persistent efficacy in the space of the museum testifies to the complexity of its genealogy (Wigley 1996): not only did it once represent olfactory silence, it has also come to visualize the absence of visual stimuli.

Note

All translations from the French are by Nadia Benabid and the author unless otherwise noted.

Bibliography

Bachelard, G. ([1949] 1963), *La Terre et les rêveries de la volonté*, Paris: Librairie Jose Corte.

Corbin, A. (1986), *The Foul and the Fragrant*, Cambridge, MA: Harvard University Press.

Dubos, J.-B. (1770), *Réflexions critiques sur la poesie et sur peinture*, 2 vols., 7th ed., Paris: n.p.

Evans, R. (1971), "Bentham's Panopticon," *Architectural Association Quarterly*, April–June: 21–37.

—— (1982), *The Fabrication of Virtue*, Cambridge: Cambridge University Press.

Foucault, M. (1977), *Discipline and Punish,* trans. A. Sheridan, New York: Pantheon.

—— (1980), "The Eye of Power," in *Power/Knowledge*, trans. C. Gordon (ed.), New York: Pantheon.

Géraud, M. (1786), *Essai sur la suppression des fausses d"esance…*, Amsterdam: n.p.

Howard, J. (1994), *L'État des prisons, des hôpitaux et des maisons de forces en Europe au XVIIIe siècle*, Paris: Éditions de l'Atelier.

Ladurie, E.L.R. (ed.) (1980–85), *La Ville classique*, Paris: Seuil.

Mashek, J. (1993), "Bentham's Panopticon," in *Building—Art*, Cambridge: Cambridge University Press.

Mercier, L.S. ([1770] 1971), *L'An deux mille quatre cent quarante*, Bordeaux: Éditions Ducrox.

—— ([1782] 1994), *Tableau de Paris,* 4 vols., Paris: Mercure de France.

Roche, D. (1981), *Le Peuple de Paris*, Paris: Aubier Montaigne.

Stafford, B.M. (1993), *Body Criticism*, Cambridge MA: MIT Press.

Süskind, P. (1986), *Perfume,* trans. J.E. Woods, New York: Knopf.

Vigarello, G. (1985), *Le Propre et le sale*, Paris: Seuil.

Wigley, M. (1995), "White Out," in *Architecture: In Fashion,* Z. Efrat et al. (eds), New York: Princeton Architectural Press.

—— (1996), *White Walls, Designer Dresses*, Cambridge MA: MIT Press.

2

The Sociology of Odors

Gale Largey and Rod Watson

Universally, human animals are simultaneously emitting and perceiving odors. Ethologists, psychoanalysts, and biologists have seriously studied the phenomenon. Yet, with the exception of Georg Simmel (1908: 646–60), sociologists have either ignored odors or regarded them as an insignificant dimension of human interaction—a curious fact for the sociology of knowledge.

The sociological approach to odors might ask: What effects do differences in culture and life style have upon the perception and generation of odors? What social meanings are attributed to such perceived and generated odors? What social functions do such meanings fulfill? More specifically: Why are African Americans and lower-class persons often stereotyped as being "foul smelling"? To what extent are alleged malodors used as grounds for avoiding interaction? What is the social significance of the fart taboo? What are the dynamics of odor manipulation? Why, for instance, do people perfume? And does the use of incense during religious services have a sociological relevance? In this essay, we will attempt to examine these questions and point out that odors, though long neglected by sociologists, do indeed have a significant bearing upon human interaction.

Odors and Moral Status

Much of the moral symbolism relevant to interaction is expressed in terms of olfactory imagery. An untrustworthy person may be described as a "stinker," a "stinkoe," or a "stinkpot." In contrast, a holy or ritually pure person may be metaphorically described as emitting the "odor of sanctity" (see Wright 1967: 23–4). At the same time, groups may be termed "smelly and slovenly" or, on the other hand, "clean and orderly." In any case, particular odors, whether real or alleged, are sometimes used as indicants of the moral purity of particular individuals and groups within the social order, the consequences of which are indeed real.

For example, E. T. Hall (1969: 119) has observed that when intermediaries arrange an Arab marriage they often take great care to smell the woman, and will reject her if she "does not smell nice." In the same vein, Havelock Ellis (1928, IV: 64) cites a variety of situations where priests claim they are able to perceive whether a woman is a virgin by her odor. And, likewise, Pearl Buck (1946: 159) describes the association of odors with purity in Asian cultures. In *Pavilion of Women* she portrays the Chinese reaction to Westerners: they are "rank from the bone because of the coarseness of their flesh, the profuseness of their sweat, and the thickness of their woolly hair." And later she depicts Madame Wu assessing the character of one of her girls, Rulan:

> "Open your mouth" ... from it came a sweet, fresh breath ... she noted that all of the girl's skirts and inner garments were scented. She lifted the girl's hands and smelled the palms. They were scented, and her hair was scented, and from the body came a delicate scent. "You will do well, my child" Madame Wu said kindly. (Buck 1946: 262)

Historians inform us that during the Middle Ages perfumers were suspected of "moral laxity," and it is pointed out that "although it hardly mattered to them they were held ineligible for service as kings" (Baron 1957, III: 248). Also, it was commonly believed that "sorcerers and heretics could be detected by their foul and fetid odor" (see Summers 1956: 44); and it was widely held that deeply religious persons could generally ascertain the specific virtues and vices of those they met by the odor that was emanated. A particular vice at the time was being a Jew, and Jews were noted for emitting an unusually foul odor which was believed to miraculously disappear upon conversion and baptism into the Christian faith (Golding 1938: 59; Klineberg 1935: 130). Apart from illustrating the moral relevance of odors, the belief is interesting in that it drew much of its meaning from an additional belief that at Passover Jews would themselves sacrifice criminally obtained Christian children (in parody of the Passion of Jesus) and consume the blood in order to rid themselves of their fetid odor—an act intrinsic to only a fiendish faith, that is, an immoral group (see Hecker 1859: 38, 70–4).

Anthropologists have also afforded some fascinating examples of the association of odors with "purity" in the moral order. For instance, Reynolds (1963: 126) reports the activities of a diviner within the Nguni tribe: "Where he seeks out cannibals and necrographers he does so with his nose for they have the smell of flesh on their fingers ... the diviners frequently sniff vigorously when in the company of other people." Similarly, the nose-kissing practices of the Inuit and many other so-called primitive groups is usually associated with the mutual expression and assessment of character.

In modern societies there are many comparable examples. For instance, many males of the labor class associate the odor of cologne on a male with effeminacy—"he smells pretty." Consequently, it would be rare to find a steelworker who dabbed himself with cologne before going off to work. By the same token, a white-collar worker may be heard expressing a repugnance toward those who emit a "stinky sweat" or those who "smell like a farmer"—dirty and unclean. And his before-work ritual is more likely to include odorizing himself with cologne.

There are also echoes of the Middle Ages: "she smells like a whore," the implication being that a heavily perfumed woman is likely to be promiscuous. At the same time, advertisers are continuing to create a social consciousness that "bad breath," "ugly perspiration" or the "feminine odor" are signs of a contaminating character, a woman who rudely affronts others.

The linkage between one's olfactory identity and one's moral state is referred to in the so-called scientific, as well as the fictional, accounts of human life. For example, the British social psychologist Ronald Goldman (1969: 95), in writing of a youth club, strikingly describes a "problem member": "In personal terms... Tim was always smelly and dirty, and many teachers reported the obnoxious nature of the smell that came from him during school hours. Very few people who dealt with him could dissent from the judgment that he was sly, vicious and totally unreliable." In this case, Tim, the individual, stank physically and therefore morally.

Likewise, many alleged odors of groups are related with stereotyped notions about their moral laxity. For example, Pakistanis in Britain are described by a London dockworker in the following way: "They seem passive and weak. They smell, don't they?" (*Time,* May 20, 1970: 38). Similarly, an American white may be heard to speak of the "stench of niggers," suggesting that it arises necessarily from their failure to bathe and to follow "decent human standards," and because they "live like pigs" (see Faulkner 1948; Dollard 1957; Brink and Harris 1969: 138–40).

Finally, there is the "fart taboo," that is, the rule of etiquette which restricts flatus. It is so widely agreed upon that formal etiquette books do not even discuss it, and certainly anyone who "lets go a fart" in public is usually considered somewhat crass and undisciplined.

Curiously, social scientists have not touched upon the taboo, but its significance in human interaction is often vividly portrayed in novels. For example, in The Catcher in the Rye, J.D. Salinger describes a situation: "All of a sudden this guy sitting in front of me, Edgar Marsalla, laid this terrific fart. It was a very crude thing to do in chapel and all" (Salinger 1951: 48). Again, in The Sotweed Factor, John Barth describes the indignation that such a fart may evoke: "But this was a hard matter, inasmuch as for everie cheerie wave of the hand I signalled them, some souldier of Gentleman in my companie must needs let goe a fart, which the Salvages did take as an affront, and threwe more arrows" (Barth 1967: 371). One might also note that the stigmatization of an individual for so "letting go" often involves an attempt by the "crass one" to convince others that it was someone else.

In short, odors, whether real or alleged, are often used as a basis for conferring a moral identity upon an individual or a group. And certainly such moral imputations bear upon the processes of human interaction. Let us next consider olfactory boundaries and the patterns of avoidance and attraction as they are generated through olfactory definitions of individuals, groups and settings.

Odor-avoidance and Odor-attraction

A skunk is a symbol of avoidance, whereas a rose is a symbol of attraction. Upon encountering a skunk most persons carefully maintain distance and warn others nearby of potential contamination. On the other hand, if one smells a rose one is attracted toward it, and invites others to smell it and admire its aroma.

Avoiding the Skunk

From the sociological standpoint, the "skunk" we avoid may be an individual, a group, or even a setting, that is, a physical environment. If we encounter an individual "skunk" (e.g. a person with "bad breath"), it is commonly accepted that we may step back from the person so as to prevent further violation of our sense of smell. Usually, we mentally label such a person, and we may extend our discreditation by informing others that the person has a "problem." Strangely enough, these persons are seldom directly confronted about their "problem" because of the embarrassment it would cause the dishonored self to embarrass the dishonoring one. Nonetheless, it is quite clear that if sensorial involvement were disrupted repeatedly, then social involvement would become sharply jeopardized—particularly in modern societies in which, there appears to be a growing consciousness of odors.

The "skunky group" has more sociologically interesting aspects. As indicated previously, stereotypes and the dynamics of prejudice often derive from alleged, as well as real, odors given off by particular groups. Indeed, odors are often referred to as the insurmountable barrier to close interracial and/or interclass interaction, and they are repeatedly referred to in order to account for avoidance patterns and segregated ecological niches. In Poland, for instance, anti-Semitism is often expressed in terms of the odor of garlic. The novelist Prus presents a graphic example of this association in his work *Lalka* ("The Puppet"):

> The new assistant set to work immediately, and half an hour later Mr. Lisiecki murmured to Mr. Klein: "What the hell is it that smells of garlic?" And a quarter of an hour later, he added: "To think that the Jewish rabble

are pushing toward the Cracow suburb! Can't the damned nasty Jews stick
to Nalewki or St. George street?" Schlangbaum kept quiet but his red eyes
trembled! (Prus 1969: 68)

Like the hostile stereotypes of the Jews, racial prejudices, too, seek credence by reference to the malodor of the minority group. In fact, both
Dollard (1957: 381) and Klineberg (1935: 29) have pointed out that alleged
malodor is a crucial component in the white racist's conception of African
Americans—so much so, Dollard suggests, that a hypersensitivity to or
fastidiousness about body odors may become evident.

Class prejudices are equally supported by imputations that those of the
lower class are "foul smelling" and must be avoided if one is sensitive to such
odors. As Simmel observed:

[N]o sight of the proletarian's misery, much less the most realistic account
of it, will overwhelm us so sensuously and directly … that we can smell the
atmosphere of somebody is the most intimate perception of him … and it is
obvious that with the increasing sensitiveness toward impression of smelling
in general, there may occur a selection and a taking of distance, which forms,
to a certain degree, one of the sentient bases for the sociological [sic] reserve
of the modern individual. (Simmel 1908: 658)

It might also be added to Simmel's statement that given (a) the extremely
subjective nature of olfactory perception, (b) the simultaneous process
of social interpretation of these perceptions, and (c) socially generated
and maintained stereotypes influencing (a) and (b), the allegation of the
malodor of a group member can be imputed a priori rather than "accurately"
perceived, and the interpretation of the meaning of the odor may not reflect
the condition or the customs of either individuals or their group. Hence,
social distance may be maintained by conventionally imputed, rather than
"actually perceived," impressions of malodor. An example of this is contained
in a pamphlet that urged white parents to keep their children away from
youth camps allegedly dedicated to miscegenation: "How would you like it
if an exquisitely-formed white child was no longer white? … Its sensitive
mind no longer sensitive but apelike? Its beautiful body no longer beautiful
but black and evil-smelling?" (National Renaissance Bulletin 1963).

Finally, there are the urban–rural stereotypes. In Western societies urbanites
may be heard identifying farmers with manure or "earthy–dirty" work,
while the farmer may label the urbanite as "artificial-smelling," perfumed,
or factory-smelling.

A poignant description of similar urban–rural antagonisms in Chinese
society is offered by Pearl Buck:

Wang Lung and his wife and children were like foreigners in this southern
city … where Wang Lung's fields spread out in leisurely harvest twice a year

of wheat and rice and a bit of corn and beans and garlic, here in the small cultivations about the city men urged their land with stinking fertilizing of human wastes ...

In Wang Lung's country a man, if he had a roll of good wheat bread and a sprig of garlic in it, had a good meal and needed no more. But here the people dabbed with pork balls and bamboo sprouts and chestnuts stewed with chicken and goose giblets and this and that of vegetables, and when an honest man came by smelling of yesterday's garlic, they lifted their noses and cried out, "Now here is a reeking, pig-tailed northerner." The smell of the garlic would make the very shopkeepers in the cloth shops raise the price of blue cotton cloth as they might raise the price for a foreigner. (Buck 1931: 110–11)

As with individuals and groups, we are also prone to identify certain settings or physical environments in terms of real, as well as alleged, odors; and, we thereby seek to avoid them. Consider, for example, the avoidance feelings and patterns generated by the odor of a dental surgery, an unkempt greasy-smelling restaurant, or a smoke-filled tavern. Note the tendency to associate mental hospitals and wards for the elderly with the odor of urine (see Henry 1966: 406–8). Likewise, it may be observed that land use and development may be impaired in communities where the odors of a cannery, glue factory, brewery, tannery or paper mill dominate the setting. Too often in their concern with the political and economic institutions of a community, social scientists overlook its sensorial aspects—whether they be visual, auditory or olfactory.

Smelling Like a Rose

While "skunks" are to be avoided, "roses" suggest intimacy; and the individual who emits attractive odors relates effectively on at least one sensorial level. This fact is evidenced by the importance placed on odorizing and deodorizing rituals, as well as such practices as sending flowers or scented letters to one's lover.

Smelling, however, is not restricted to individual "roses." We also like bouquets. In other words, there are grounds for hypothesizing that group intimacy or alignments are at least partially established or recognized through olfactory stimuli. As pointed out by Herbert Spencer (1896, II: 15–16), the practices of nose-kissing and sniffing among the Inuit, Samoans and Philippine Islanders are not simply salutary gestures. More important, they are means of group identification and cohesion. And, quite possibly, those very odors that serve as indicants for avoidances by out-groups simultaneously generate a we-feeling in the in-group. In this regard, one may hypothesize that the odor of garlic, which constitutes a component of the anti-Pakistani complex among the British, may nonetheless contribute to an in-group identification among the Pakistanis themselves.

Finally, there is the "rose garden" that is, the odor setting that attracts and facilitates interaction. While we tend to have avoidance feelings toward urine-smelling asylums, we are drawn to pine-scented parks; while we are disgusted by canneries, we are enticed by bakeries; while we find cesspools and polluted streams repugnant, we delight at beaches permeated by the smell of salt and sand. In short, an odor is often a crucial component in the definition of, and orientation to, an environment and is instrumental in generating appropriate activity. While odor settings may be taken for granted in an unreflective manner, they are nonetheless cues to particular modes of involvement within the setting.

Impression Management Through Odors

Since odors do indeed bear social meaning, it is not surprising that various practices have developed by which olfactory identity and odor settings may be manipulated. Cross-culturally and historically one may observe efforts by actors to insure that they "give off" a creditable odor. Likewise, there are numerous examples of efforts to create a desirable odor setting. To establish and maintain a socially accepted olfactory identity, actors engage in two basic practices: deodorizing and odorizing. The first practice usually entails the removal of socially discreditable odors through such activities as washing, gargling and cleansing of teeth. There is usually a particular concern about the removal of perspiration. Odorizing, on the other hand, involves presentation of self with accreditable odors through the "art" of perfuming. The existent rationales for deodorizing include "health" and "cleanliness" while those for odorizing include "being fresh and pleasing to others." Through the use of deodorants and odorants an actor may anticipate his or her identifying label to be that of a "good, clean, and decent person" rather than a "stinker" or a "stinkpot." Through these practices an actor attempts to avoid moral stigmatization and present an olfactory identity that will be in accord with social expectations, in turn, gaining moral accreditation: one who smells good is good.

One's olfactory identity is particularly associated with racial, class and sexual identification; and, as noted earlier, perfuming is closely related to the presentation and manipulation of those identifications. It has already been observed that racial minority groups are often stigmatized in terms of odors, and, as Dollard (1957: 380) pointed out, the allegation that a minority group is "foul-smelling is an extremely serviceable way of fixing on him an undesirable lower-caste mark and by inference justifying superiority behavior." Likewise, Myrdal (1944, I: 107) noted that "the belief in a peculiar "hircine odor" of Negroes, like similar beliefs concerning other races, touches a personal sphere and is used to justify denial of social intercourse and the use of public conveniences which would imply close contact, such as restaurants, theaters and public conveyances."

Dollard (1957: 381) found that in order to cope with their stigmatization African Americans engage in a widespread use of perfume: "Perfume is an effort to avoid the odor-stigma of being ill-smelling which Negroes know to be one of the beliefs of white people about them." Unfortunately it might well be that the perfuming is seldom effective in the avoidance of the stigma. Instead, it may reinforce the white racist's belief that African Americans stink: if they didn't stink, they wouldn't have to cover themselves with perfume.

Like racial identity, class identity is often imputed in terms of odors. On the basis of reactions to forty-three different odors, Brill (1932: 40) reported that respondents "disliked most" the odor of perspiration; and he concluded that "this was not only because of its very sour smell, but, because it was associated with people of the lower class." Likewise, novelists and literary critics have noted that the odor of perspiration denotes lower class or status.

In a perceptive observation about Western society in the early twentieth century, Somerset Maugham asserted: "The matutinal tub divides the classes more effectively than birth, wealth or education ... the cesspool is more necessary to democracy than parliamentary institutions. The invention of sanitary conveniences has destroyed the sense of equality in men. It is responsible for class hatred much more than the monopoly of capital" (Maugham 1930: 140). In addition, Maugham thought it was significant that "writers who have risen from the ranks of labor are apt to make the morning tub a symbol of class prejudice" (see Brill 1932: 41–2).

The observation of Maugham may have been grossly exaggerated; none-theless, deodorizing–odorizing practices to avoid being "foul-smelling" and thus being associated with the lower class remain widespread. And, as with racial minority groups, it appears that the lower class often utilizes a great deal of perfume to avoid stigmatization—so much so that the lower class is sometimes described as being "scent smothered" or "daubed in cheap perfume," "cheap" being a term used to imply lower class.

At the same time, the middle and upper classes attempt to support their status position by the appropriate use of "expensive perfumes," perfumes that symbolize high status. These perfumes are known through their advertise-ments in middle- and upper-class magazines: *Fête*, "a really distinguished, sophisticated, classic perfume"; *Amalie*, "expensive"; and *Joy*, "the costliest perfume in the world." Often, too, these advertisements are associated with an aristocratic tradition, suggesting for instance, that Cleopatra or Queen Elizabeth used the perfume, and thereby appealing to a potential consumer's concern with class identity or status.

In short, one may observe that actors manipulate their olfactory identity to establish and/or to maintain their class identity. Often, too, they attempt to follow class rules set forth by etiquette books regarding the amount and type of perfume worn by those of the "proper class."

Historically, perfuming has also been associated with the enhancement of one's sexual attractiveness; and the belief that perfumes are erotic stimulants persists in most societies. For example, Beach (1965: 183–4) has described a Southwest Pacific society where there is an aphrodisiac based upon the similarity of vaginal odor to that of fish: "Men use a red ground cherry attached to the leader of a trolling line to attract fish. After having caught a fish in this way the ground cherry is believed to have the power to attract women in the same way as it attracted fish. Their vaginas, like elusive fish, will be attracted to the possessor of the ground cherry." Beach continues: "Other odors are also thought to be seductive. Most potent of these is a very musky aromatic leaf worn only by men when they dance and another is the somewhat astringent odor of coconut oil mixed with turmeric. Women rub this mixture in their hair."

In modern Western societies, the perfuming practices are quite similar. Perfumes themselves are widely used by both men and women, and odorants are usually added to toothpastes, shaving lotions, hand lotions and soaps, as well as hair oils (see Aikman 1951). Moreover, if advertising appeals indicate the legitimating motives for their use, then odorants are worn very often to enhance sexual identification. Consider the following advertisements of men's colognes: *Old Spice,* "Starts the kind of fire a man can't put out"; *Kent of London,* "It can't talk but women get the message"; *Pub,* "Uncorks the lusty life"; *By George,* "She won't? *By George,* she will!"; *007,* "*007* gives any man license to kill ... women." These types of advertisements are very often featured with nude or "sexually suggestive" women. They appeal to male desires to manipulate their olfactory identity so that it is sexually attractive.

Though less direct in approach, many advertisements for women's perfumes express a similar message: *Emeraude,* "Want him to be more of a man? Try being more of a woman"; *Tabu,* "The forbidden fragrance"; *Intimate,* "What makes a shy girl intimate?"; *Chanel No. 5,* "The spell of Chanel"; *L'Air du Temps,* "To summon a man, push this button"; *Maja,* "*Maja* is Woman. Genteel, earthy, provocative, poignant. The very mystique of a women"; *Ambush,* "Wait for him in *Ambush.*"

The extent to which a motive offered in an advertisement serves as a legitimating rationale for the use of a particular perfume needs further study; nonetheless, it can be hypothesized that a relationship does indeed exist. It is suggested that often the manipulation of an olfactory identity is related to a sexual identity.

Social actors realize, too, that the context within which they act sometimes influences behavioral patterns. They know that an odor often defines a setting. Thus, like olfactory identity, odor settings are subjected to manipulation. As previously mentioned, the odor of whole communities is sometimes described as "stinky"; and the label may be detrimental to the image and development of the community. It is therefore understandable that efforts have been made to control or alter the odor of communities.

In 1969, Washington DC adopted an air pollution code which outlawed odors injurious to the public welfare, the definition of welfare including reasonable enjoyment of life and property. To enforce the case the city acquired a scentometer, a scientific device for calibrating "stink" (reported in *Time*, October 19, 1970: 12). Other communities have adopted similar procedures, particularly to force industries and sewage treatment plants to deodorize. Each time the essential argument was: "Getting rid of the odor will stimulate a growth of the community through a more pleasant and healthy environment."

While communities are often concerned with deodorizing a setting to create a more aesthetic environment, other efforts have been made to odorize settings. For example, odorants were applied extensively in the Roman Colosseum during gladiatorial games, the intent being to create a communal or we-group feeling (McKenzie 1930: 56). Likewise, the Chicago White Sox baseball organization has attempted to spray the scent of hot buttered popcorn in its stadium because that "makes people feel good"; and at the 1964–65 New York World's Fair, the India exhibition was presented with the manufactured scent of curry and cows (Hamilton 1966: 84).

The use of incense is another example of the management of an odor setting. Religious groups have traditionally used incense to create an "odor of sanctity," an atmosphere of "sacredness" among the followers. It is burned so that the group may share a common experience. As followers introject "particles of the odor" within themselves, they are believed to more nearly achieve unity with others. Boulogne (1953: 95) has noted that the use of incense "provides for the senses a symbolic representation of the invisible action (communion) that is taking place" (see also Frazer 1951, I: 379–84). In the Durkheimian sense, the use of incense generates a truly social phenomenon.

The deodorizing and/or odorizing of other settings such as theaters, supermarkets, homes and rooms might also be considered. Again, each setting has a socially expected or desirable odor. Thus we find widespread use of aerosols, for example, the seasonal application of pine and spruce scents in homes to convey "the spirit of Christmas." As Hark (1952: 152) describes Christmas eve: "Throughout the room, intangible but definite, the faint perfume of spruce and moss and beeswax hovered like a benediction."

Finally, odors are sometimes used to control, rather than please, a group within a setting. The use of tear gas to disperse a crowd is one such example— though at the same time it creates a common or shared experience by which a we-feeling may be generated within a group, thus only reinforcing the crowd's further unity: "Did you get gassed by the cops?"

Conclusion

While much of this paper has of necessity been truncated and impressionistic we feel that it nevertheless points to a need for the study of a much-neglected field of sociological analysis. Simmel (1908) and Berger and Luckmann (1967:

203) are just about the only sociologists who even mention the possibility of a sociology of the senses, or "sociology of the body" (e.g. considerations of the alienation from one's "bodily self" social projection of the "bodily self," etc.). The sociology of odors and olfaction should, ideally, develop as one part of a more general sociological concern with the senses.

Bibliography

Aikman, L. (1951), "Perfume, the Business of Illusion," *National Geographic*, 99 (April): 531–50.

Baron, S.W. (1957), *A Social and Religious History of the Jews*, 3 vols, New York: Columbia University Press.

Barth, J. (1967), *The Sotweed Factor*, New York: Doubleday.

Beach, F. (ed.) (1965), *Sex and Behavior*, New York: Wiley.

Berger, P., and Luckmann, T. (1967), *The Social Construction of Reality*, London: Allen Lane.

Boulogne, C.D. (1953), *My Friends the Senses*, New York: Kenedy.

Brill, A.A. (1932), "The Sense of Smell in the Neuroses and Psychoses," *Psychoanalytic Quarterly* 1 (Spring): 7–42.

Brink, W., and Harris, L. (1969), *The Negro Revolution in America*, New York: Simon & Schuster.

Buck, P. (1931), *The Good Earth*, New York: Grosset & Dunlap.

—— (1946), *Pavilion of Women*, New York: John Day.

Dollard, J. (1957), *Caste and Class in a Southern Town*, New York: Doubleday.

Ellis, H. (1928), *Studies in the Psychology of Sex*, 4 vols, Philadelphia: Davis.

Faulkner, W. (1948), *Intruder in the Dust*, New York: Modem Library.

Frazer, J.G. ([1917] 1951), *The Golden Bough*, 12 vols, New York: Macmillan.

Golding, L. (1938), *The Jewish Problem*, London: Penguin.

Goldman, R. (1969), *Angry Adolescents*, London: Routledge & Kegan Paul.

Hall, E. T. (1969), *The Hidden Dimension*, New York: Doubleday.

Hamilton, A. (1966), "What Science Is Learning about Smell," *Science Digest*, 55 (November): 81–5.

Hark, A. (1952), *Blue Hills and Shoefly Pie*, Philadelphia: Lippincott.

Hecker, J.F.D. (1859), *The Epidemics of the Middle Ages*, trans. B.G. Babington, London: Trubner.

Henry, J. (1966), *Culture Against Man*, London: Tavistock.

Klineberg, O. (1935), *Race Differences*, New York: Harper.

McKenzie, D. (1930), *Aromatics and the Soul:*, New York: Hoeber.

—— (1966), "Burn Up Those Life Station Odors," *American City*, 81 (November): 80–2.

Maugham, S. (1930), *On a Chinese Screen*, New York: Doran.

Myrdal, G. (1944), *An American Dilemma*, 2 vols, New York: Harper & Row.

National Renaissance Bulletin (1963), *Youth Movements*, New York: National Renaissance Party.

Prus, B. (1969), *Lalka*, Warsaw: Governmental Publishing House.

Reynolds, B. (1963), *Magic, Divination and Witchcraft among the Barotse of Northern Rhodesia*, Berkeley: University of California Press.

Salinger, J.D. (1951), *The Catcher in the Rye*, New York: Harper & Row.

Simmel, G. (1908), *Sociologie*, Leipzig: Duncker & Humblot.

Spencer, H. (1896), *The Principles of Sociology*, 2 vols, New York: Appleton.

Summers, M. (1956), *The History of Witchcraft and Demonology*, New York: University Books.

Wright, L. (1967), *Clean and Decent*, Toronto: University of Toronto Press.

3

Immigrant Lives and the Politics of Olfaction in the Global City

Martin F. Manalansan IV

The Smelly Immigrant

The immigrant is a paradigmatic figure of modern alterity. Discourses around epidemics, natural disasters, crime and other catastrophes or social ills are constructed around the body of the immigrant as vector. Moreover, the immigrant body is culturally constructed to be the natural carrier and source of undesirable sensory experiences and is popularly perceived to be the site of polluting and negative olfactory signs.

Scholars have often pointed out how aromas and smells have been important constituent elements in the cultural construction of difference and inequality. Classen (1992) echoes a long line of scholars when she suggests that smell is a pivotal index of moral, racial, ethnic, class and cultural difference and marginality. In the modern West, the olfactory process has historically been denigrated in relation to vision. At the same time, other researchers have argued that modern Western discourses have established aromatic phenomena to be "non-Western," pre-civilized and primitive. For example, Le Guérer (1990) goes further to accuse Westerners of becoming "olfactory invalids" because the sense of smell has become compartmentalized in daily life and relegated to highly specialized commodified spaces such as aromatherapy clinics or perfume stores. At the same time, McPhee (1992) characterizes US culture as a deodorized one. According to Howes (1991: 128, 131), the emergent interest in the sense of smell is in part due to the "universal association between olfaction and transition" and that smell is the "liminal sense par excellence." As a social marker that evokes change and liminality, smell therefore provides a strategic mode of communicating identities, bodies and temporalities that are betwixt and between.

The "smelly immigrant" trope may be seen as always and already an ignorant stereotype unworthy of any serious study. However, as I demonstrate in this chapter, the trope does not conjure the easy and linear narrative of assimilation where the immigrant figure is symbolically and materially fumigated—divested of the repellent olfactory, moral and political underpinnings and eventually transformed into an odorless yet modern entity. Instead, I would argue for a strategic use of the "smelly immigrant" trope as a way to understand corporeal politics and sensory meanings within the frame of global capitalist restructuring. To pose the project in terms of a question—if sensory experiences are ways of knowing the world, what can we learn through a politicized and historically situated conception of the olfactory process?

I pursue this inquiry through a study of Asian American communities in New York City. I conducted field work from January to early August, 2001 in the Asian neighborhoods in Queens, New York. Asian Americans have historically been directly associated with food and indirectly with specific aromas (see Tchen 1999; Lee 1999). Filipinos, Koreans and Vietnamese have been branded as dogeaters. The Chinese have been accused of cooking and eating cats, rats and every animal imaginable. Indians are charged with being guilty of creating a fiery, spicy cuisine that defies human capacities. At the same time, economic realities have also rendered the stereotypical conjunctions of Asian Americans and food. Asians, particularly the Chinese, have been associated with the food service industries as waiters, busboys and cooks. Chinese food is the ubiquitous and the "most ethnic" of American fast food. Yet, while studies of the alimentary constructions of Asian Americans mark their abjection in American immigration history and culture, these works are characterized by their dependence on the hegemonic visual and gustatory apparatuses. One crucial exception is Aihwa Ong's (2000: 89–90) study that demonstrates how Cambodian refugees are ushered into American life through a guidebook and training sessions that admonish them to bathe, use deodorants and, in general, avoid unpleasant odors in cooking and maintaining their homes. Despite this notable work, it is telling that smell, which occupies the lowest rung in the Western hierarchy of the senses, has never been usefully deployed in these kinds of analyses. Nowhere is this gap more telling and ironic than in Asian Americans who inhabit the sensory spaces of New York City.

New York City and the "Restructuring" of the Senses

The global city of New York is more than a serendipitous choice for study. Cinematic and literary renditions of the city characterize it as a sensory overload. This urban locale is the site for the ironic juxtaposition of sensory stimuli, and an arena for contesting, creating and imposing regimes of olfactory meanings and corporeal practices. Smells abound in New York City streets, subways and other public spaces, but despite this reality, the city is almost always visually represented by the mythical image of an odorless Manhattan skyline. This skyline and its odorless quality are constitutive elements of its modernity and its centrality as a global center of finance and technology. Odorlessness, which is the basis for the utopic myth of the modern city and the visual dimension of the skyline, masks a more complex arrangement or logic of things (see e.g. Illich 2000; Corbin 1986; Pinard 1991).

Immigrants from the Third World and communities of color from impoverished rural and urban centers in the USA have migrated to this city to provide the services of the secondary labor market and make possible the awe-inspiring silhouette of a global center. The city has therefore been popularly perceived as constituted by a duality. The dual-city model proposes that the global city's gleaming modernity is made possible through a hierarchical stratification. The city's modern financial superstructure is propped up and made possible by a substratum of service-oriented industries staffed mostly by immigrants, women and people of color.

This economic and racial stratification can be mapped and grafted into a vernacular topography of the city. People in the outer boroughs of Queens, Bronx, Staten Island and Brooklyn, or "the bridge and tunnel crowd," as they are disparagingly called by Manhattanites, are stereotypically portrayed as lacking international cosmopolitanism and their districts deficient in the gleaming rational modernity evoked by the Manhattan skyline. This "lack" of the outer boroughs and their denizens is often couched in denigrating terms and the sites are depicted as being enclaves of smelly immigrants, home to working-class culture of pre-modern or archaic tradition. These outer boroughs form a temporal and cultural counterpoint to the island across the East River. Seen as other worlds and anachronous spaces, one informant jokingly stated that his Manhattan friends often have to take their passports along when they cross over to the outer boroughs. Queens in particular is constructed as the home of people fresh off the immigration boat and a haven for INS (Immigration and Naturalization Service) raids. But what is sorely lacking in these largely untenable dualisms is a critical understanding of the relationship between Manhattan and its others. This relationship can be firmly and critically delineated with the politics of smell and the struggles of Asian immigrants in the borough of Queens.

This popular image is also manifested in the political and cultural machinery that attempted to maintain the post-Fordist dream of separate worlds between the financial elite and the teeming service workers. This machinery is best exemplified by a series of laws and ordinances as well as police directives called the "Quality of Life" campaign, which was first hatched under the administration of Rudolph Giuliani who was mayor of the city from 1994 to 2001. At face value, this corpus of directives, laws and ordinances can be seen as harmless and admirable attempts to rid the city of crime and unwanted noise, panhandling, lewd conduct, urinating in public, dirt and garbage, but on closer inspection, they are part of a Manichean attempt to foist disciplinary regimes to control the foreign, the queer, the poor and visible minorities (McArdle and Erzen 2001). The transformation of Times Square in the late nineties is the crystallization of this campaign. The writer Samuel Delaney (1999) chronicles the "cleaning-up" and gentrification of this district that not only removed the adult business establishments but also displaced numerous inhabitants of color from the streets and buildings.

The idea of a dual city has been criticized by numerous urban theorists. Saskia Sassen (1994, 1996) suggests that the emergence of New York City as a global city is part of its subsequent deindustrialization and eventual growth as a financial and cultural center. As such, New York operates as a consolidating force in the global arena not because of its putative social duality but due to its effective operation as a unified specialized center of world finance. Mollenkopf and Castells (1991) criticized and nuanced this idea of a fragmented and divided city by rightly countering that the city's cleavages no more signal a separation than a symbiotic yet oppressive unequal relationship where structures do not diverge but rather interpenetrate each other. In other words, New York City as a global urban space is made possible by the cosmopolitan financial elite and their political and cultural machinery, which attempts to localize immigrants and racialized others. It is against this tableau that the corporeal narratives of Asian American immigrants and the cultural politics of olfaction are set and read.

Smell, particularly in the America and New York City of the early twenty-first century, is a *code* for class, racial and ethnic differences and antagonisms. I submit that the sense of smell is the basis for recognition and misrecognition and that it provides an opportunity to affiliate, to belong as well as to disidentify and to ostracize. Most importantly, olfaction provides the means in which to narrate the permeability of the two worlds of financial and cosmopolitan modernity and immigrant alterity. By doing so, the narrative can contribute to a critical understanding of New York's urban modernity. While smell is widely considered to be the antithesis of modernity, I demonstrate that modernity itself, with its hegemonic seemingly monumental force, is fragmented and contradictory. This fragmentation allows for vernacular renderings of modernity that run counter to its monolithic construction.

Domesticating Odors: Bodies, Households and Aromatic Intimacy

The whole house smelt of fried onion, the goodly smell which gets stale so soon and fills the very bricks of these mining villages with such a reek that you can tell them from far away in the country by the strong scent of poor man's cookery.

Emile Zola, *Germinal*

Asians smell of food. It is funny, but we Asians really smell of what we eat. We walk around and our kitchens stay with us. You know, Koreans smell of garlic, Indians smell of curry, Filipinos smell of vinegar ... and so on. Caucasians—a lot of them just smell bad.

Jun, Chinese American informant, 24 years old

Government reports about immigrant enclaves in the early twentieth century described the visual and olfactory abjection of immigrant neighborhoods (Claghorn 1901). Immigrant homes were deemed to be no more than unsanitary niches of social derelicts and outcasts that reeked of their moral deprivation. However, aromas, particularly those of food and bodies in contemporary immigrant homes in Queens, suggest more complex reactions, images and constructions than the old reports. These reactions and images involve struggles around memory, identity construction and creating a sense of belonging.

Recent studies have focused on the aromatic and other sensory travails of diasporic groups. David Sutton (2001) emphasized the mnemonic dimensions of sensory experiences around food among the Greek inhabitants of Kalymnos Island. He suggested that these sensory experiences "move" with people in migration and other travels. Most importantly, Sutton argued that these sensory experiences become part of a struggle against the displacement and fragmentation of migrant experiences. Lisa Law's ([2001] 2004) study of Filipina domestics in Hong Kong focused on their attempt to mitigate diasporic displacements through cooking, which then creates "smellscapes" or fluid domestic spaces that go beyond physical geography.

In Asian immigrant homes, such sensory experiences evoke memories and, at the same time, constitute many quotidian dilemmas and struggles around immigrant embodiment. Numerous informants in my research marveled at and celebrated the smell of their native food. This celebration revolved around the idea of social reproduction and cultural continuity. As one Indian man said, "This is the food of my childhood. I want my children to experience the taste and smell of the food so they will know their roots."

However, not all of the informants considered native food smells in terms of nostalgia and cultural socialization and perpetuation. Many had an ambivalent attitude towards these aromas. For Gloria, a Filipina immigrant with a husband and two children, specific food smells were not only nostalgic fuses that triggered memories but they also provoked anxiety. Food smells, according to Gloria and several other informants, did not just waft into the air and disappear. These odors adhered to clothes, to walls and to bodies. Part of Gloria's anxiety about such situations was due to the fact that the smell marked or indexed her household and her family member's bodies as "immigrant." Gloria said: "One time, my office supervisor made a surprise visit to my house. I just cooked *binagoongan* [a pork dish made with fermented shrimp paste]. The whole house reeked of the shrimp paste. It was so embarrassing."

She reasoned that, at work, she had maintained the respect of her colleagues through a skillful accumulation of cultural capital, such as having a fashionable taste in clothes, speaking seemingly unaccented English and the like. The unexpected visit virtually marked her as an FOB—an ignorant new immigrant "fresh off the boat." The same concerns related to her tenacity regarding the smell of her children's clothes and bodies. Gloria's mother visited her the previous year, and one weekday morning decided to feed the family fried *tuyo* (small sardine-like dried fish—very salty and odoriferous). Gloria's apartment was so small that even with the doors closed, the smell just virtually attacked their clothes and, she said, the kids had to go to school reeking of fish. Gloria longed for the day when she could have two kitchens, as do many middle- to upper-class homes in the Philippines: a clean one for all to see, and another "dirty" one, usually located outside, where the maid can cook the family meals. She was very sensitive to what her neighbors, mostly other Asian immigrants, might think of her home. Despite the fact that several of her next-door neighbors actually do cook foods with pungent aromas, Gloria always worried about the possibility of complaints and gossip about this issue.

Sometimes, the problem was not only about the size of the kitchen or apartment. Interracial couples I interviewed also talked about compromising their food preferences because of smell. Kara, a Korean woman married to a Caucasian man, had tried to create a heavily boarded-up pantry to contain the smell of kimchi and other Korean food items, but she was never really successful. She had resigned herself to eating Korean food only when her husband was away on business, in Korean restaurants, or at friends' and family's houses. Gloria, on the other hand, marveled at the fact that the big Filipino grocery in Woodside now carried cooked food items—particularly fried fish and pork intestines. Now, she can just buy the food without having to encounter the smell. In these two situations, food odors become the medium through which identities are amplified or marked. At the same time these odors also signal how the seemingly seamless intimate spaces of the home are actually marked by porousness, tensions and conflicts. These tensions and conflicts of disciplining odors are rendered in strongly gendered and racialized terms.

The burden of trying to contain these smells is left to the women, who were seen as the bearers of tradition (Ray 1998). The men I interviewed were concerned only when the smells crossed over to their public and occupational personas. One of them said: "I want people to smell Calvin Klein and not my wife's curries." Although some of them expressed not caring whether other people perceived anything peculiar with their body odors. Alfred, a Filipino clerk who works in Manhattan, said: "If I don't notice anything coming out of me, then I really don't give a damn about what people smell."

I interviewed two Asian realtors who were in the business of selling homes in Queens. Mrs Ng, a Chinese American realtor, told me that she advised Asian homeowners to paint drab walls, fix the faucets and showers, and, most importantly, to clean their houses thoroughly. By cleaning she really meant to deodorize the entire house:

> There is nothing that will annoy a potential home buyer but to be met at the door with the smell of years of fried food and spicy cooking. The buyer will assume that the smell is permanent and cannot be scrubbed out. You know, there is some truth to that since I have been in houses that have been scrubbed until the walls and floors have been virtually stripped bare.

She further admitted that while some buyers may not be alarmed or dismayed with the smell of pets, many react more violently with the heavy aroma of food lingering in the hallways.

A Korean American realtor, Mr Kim, advised the homeowner to cook something American such as pot roast or, even better, apple pie. While most homeowners selling their homes will balk at this suggestion, Kim had an easier trick of having several apples and a stick or two of cinnamon inside a low oven. He argued that while many of the homebuyers are Asians themselves, they were upset when confronted with what they believed to be permanent olfactory "damage."

The domestic struggles around food aromas in Asian American homes suggest the inflection of gender, class, race and ethnicity with sensory meanings. At first glance, the experiences of families parallel, in part, the experiences of the other ethnic and racial minorities in different settings at the moment of their assimilation into middle-class status (see e.g. Kaplan 1991; Gay 1984; Elias [1939] 1982). However, this should not be taken as a facile transhistorical and transcultural bridging of divergent processes of emerging bourgeois cultures. Rather, to contextualize this project within twenty-first century New York City, the struggles of containment and domestication of food aromas around Asian immigrant homes are part of competing economic and political interest of global capital in perpetuating racial and class subordination (Sassen 1996).

The concerns behind containing smells can also be about not getting oneself into trouble with the police. Some informants were aware of how animosities between neighbors can easily escalate into accusations of public disturbance and how the police can get involved. Garbage, noise and other intolerable behavior have been criminalized to such an extent that many of the Asian American immigrants I interviewed were wary of making any kind of public display of their difference. In many cases, some feared that police intervention might unearth a person's illegal immigration status.

Odors, in these situations, acquire contradictory meanings. Informants' yearnings to become "middle class," "modern," "respectable" and "American" should be read against the more complicated counter-struggles and yearnings to be "safe," "rooted," "traditional" and "nationalistic." Their bodies are no mere vessels for aromas and odors but the arena for negotiating these identities. At the same time, these domestic quotidian settings should be set against the events of border crossing between these intimate spaces to more public ones. These border crossings involve smell "out of place" and run counter to the increasing privatization of a post-Fordist New York City under Rudolph Giuliani.

Odors on the Run: Aboard the Number 7 Train

> Imagine having to take the 7 Train to the ballpark [Shea Stadium] looking like you're riding through Beirut, next to some kid with purple hair, next to some queer with AIDS right next to some dude who just got out of jail for the fourth time right next to some twenty-year old girl with four kids. It's depressing... The biggest thing I don't like about New York are the foreigners. I'm not a very big fan of foreigners. You can walk an entire block of Times Square and not hear anybody speaking English.
>
> John Rocker (qtd. in Pearlman 1999)

What happens when food smells, which are stereotypically considered to be part of the private realm of social life—the home, crosses the border into the public sphere? In my interviews, people talked about encountering people on the train and how their bodies, specifically the food odors emanating from specific bodies, acted as a sign of their marginality.

The Number 7 train the New York City subway has been popularly dubbed "the Oriental Express." It runs from Times Square and ends up in the Flushing neighborhood in Queens. Included in the train's path are numerous Queens neighborhoods that are deemed to have their own peculiar odors. Jackson Heights, Elmhurst and Flushing are considered to be neighborhoods with strong peculiar smells and not surprisingly, they have the biggest number of Asian American residents: Filipino, Korean, South Asian and other Asian business establishments like restaurants, as well as residences, line the streets of these neighborhoods or districts.

Odors do not just characterize or mark particular neighborhoods, these food odors mean something symbolically and politically for different people. For the first-time rider of any New York City subway train, the force of visual and olfactory elements is immediately apparent. This "assault on the senses" is apparent in the controversial statements by the baseball athlete John Rocker about the experience of riding the Number 7 train. His fear and dismay over the varied forms of alterity that one can encounter in this subway ride—differences in sexuality, class, language, cultural expression and ethnicity—is one typical reaction of outsiders (especially privileged ones).

The subway ride is a moment where bodies are kept in more confining spaces and where aromas are amplified. The subway ride pushes urban bodies in closer proximity than in many daily rituals. It therefore creates an anomalous "intimate" moment in a visibly public, anonymous space. The reactions and sensory experiences become part of struggles to demarcate spheres of separation, of maintaining both physical and social distance.

The struggles around maintaining boundaries, preventing instances of pollution and containing "private" aromas, are not just part of public quotidian life. These struggles were also elevated to the level of urban politics during the Rudolph Giuliani era in New York. Neighborhood and borough politics around property values, hygiene and "quality of life" implicated struggles around odors and aromas. This was forcefully demonstrated in the case of community politics in Flushing, New York—the endpoint of the Number 7 train in Queens and a place dubbed "the new Chinatown" because of the massive settlement of Chinese, Taiwanese and Korean residents and merchants.

In the mid-1990s, Julia Harrison, an elderly, long-time resident, was voted into council office on the strength of her platform to bring back the "old glories" of Flushing. She argued that these new, mostly Asian, immigrants tarnished and transformed the "old" Flushing with their new businesses—mostly restaurants with "strange" food, smells and signs in foreign languages. According to Harrison, unlike the "authentic" European immigrants at the turn of the twentieth century who were escaping death from the pogroms, these mostly Asian immigrants were only there for economic profit. Harrison, buoyed by an older, Jewish voting minority (as opposed to a largely immigrant, non-voting Asian majority), further constructed the alterity of the new settlers by characterizing them as "speaking languages the old-timers don't understand and selling foods they have never tasted" (Dugger 1996: 38). *New York Times* reporter Celia Dugger reported on this vitriolic politician by trailing Harrison as she went around her jurisdiction: "Mrs Harrison drives to the Waldbaum's in College Point to do her grocery shopping. On a recent walk in downtown Flushing, she paused at a greengrocer's and sniffed a bunch of Chinese broccoli covered with delicate yellow buds. 'I think it's dandelion,' she said. She examined a star fruit and asked, 'What is this? Papaya?'" (Dugger 1996: 1).

On other side of the cultural and political spectrum, critic Calvin Trillin (2003) celebrates the varied exotic spaces of food in Queens. He manages to sanitize a ride aboard the Number 7 train as one filled with a kind of touristic awe and enthusiasm of the "foodie." The train becomes a physical and symbolic vehicle that provides him access to the culinary delights and sensory knowledge of immigrant neighborhoods. Here lies the kind of privileged positionality that consumes the culinary cultures of these neighborhoods as part of an accumulation of cultural capital. Foodies such as Trillin are in search of "authentic" culinary experiences, including being able to experience what may be abhorrent to the visual, olfactory and gustatory sensibilities of the *hoi polloi*. Therefore, the olfactory experience here becomes part of the touristic cosmopolitanism exuded by the "cultured" foodie.

These opposing poles of attitudes and positions are not significant influences in Asian American immigrants' daily lives. The Number 7 train is a vehicle for their economic and social survival that enables them to literally and figuratively override the issues around odor containment. This situation amplifies the ways in which odors intrude upon and complicate the easy divide between public and private, and between the dual realms of the global city.

Al, a 27-year-old Chinese worker, told me that the Number 7 train and his home are not sharply demarcated olfactory spaces as they are for other people. At the same time, the food and the aromas either at home or in the streets and subways are so much a part of his daily routines that they are barely noticeable or perceptible. Therefore, immigrant residents lay claim to these streets, subways and other public spaces in a different and less possessive way than would privileged white subjects such as Harrison and Trillin.

This situation brings to mind the idea of the flâneur, the figure of urban modernity who is classically constructed as a white, upper-class male able to traverse the various sections of a modern city with a knowing eye and, I suspect, a discriminating nose. If one were to posit a *flâneur* of color, preferably one who is an Asian immigrant woman, we are faced with complicated figure who then would stake a claim not for an all-encompassing, masculine, privileged form of modernity, but one that is filled with gaps and conflicting allegiances between tradition and modernity. In other words, if one were to examine the ways in which odors in general and food aromas in particular are politicized, policed and disciplined in New York City, the immigrant subject's claim on the city's modernity will be constituted in partial and ambivalent ways. In Asian immigrant informants' attitudes and ideas around odors I found a contradictory yet flexible form of negotiation involved in the relationship between identity, olfaction and modernity that is not characterized by overt resistance or complete submission.

Some Brief Aromatic Reflections on Power and Knowledge

In light of my analysis of the "smelly immigrant," olfaction is a political and cultural process that should be seen in terms of the visceral or the emotional which includes shame, fear, disgust and shock. This process not only affects immigrant life in the urban context, but also the anthropological enterprise itself, for both fieldwork and everyday life are always enmeshed in some kind of power struggle. I argue that anthropologists should be made aware of the vitality and integral value of the "visceral"—primarily the olfactory in the anthropological engagement with the operations of power.

I would advocate the centering of the emotional content in order to denaturalize the bifurcated anthropological understanding of the senses that is at once universal (as fieldworker's tools) and also culturally specific (as part of subjectivity). I encourage the act of self-questioning to uncover the motives underlying sensorial predispositions in ethnographic fieldwork. Consider the following excerpt from my own field journal:

> It was another one of those cramped two-bedroom apartments in the borough of Queens, New York City. If you were watching a film, it will not be marked by anything out of the ordinary, maybe a trinket or two, a bottle of soy sauce, but nothing to really mark it as an Asian household unless you are able to smell the surroundings. The Park family, who immigrated to the US, in the early 1980s from Korea, keeps their household clean and sparkling. I suspect they cleaned up when I told them I was going to visit them and conduct an interview about their culinary practices and beliefs. As I walked through the kitchen I noticed, at least according to my storehouse of recognizable aromas, vestiges of spicy cooking. Was it kimchi—the only spicy Korean food that I know? Was I looking for a specific smell—one that would have indicated or hinted something about the people who lived in this space? (Manalansan 2001)

In what ways were my own presuppositions about odors influencing my own actions, feelings and reactions in that domestic space? Was I—the anthropologist—authority figure, causing specific anxieties and emotions among the members of the Park family? In other words, the new anthropology of the visceral should make explicit the emotions and power entanglements that proliferate in everyday life, including shame, pride and disgust. These emotions, I suggest, form part of the embodied (sometimes read as "gut") reactions in the lives and sensory experiences of immigrants who create paradoxical and incomplete negotiations, refusals, resistances and capitulations between competing ideas and experiences of modernity and tradition, the public and the private, self and the other and between the odorless and the malodorous.

Acknowledgments

Research for this chapter was funded by grants from the Asian American Studies Program, the Center for Democracy in a Multiracial Society, and the Campus Research Board at the University of Illinois, Urbana-Champaign. Versions of this chapter were presented at the Sociocultural Anthropology Workshop of the University of Illinois, the Feast and Famine Colloquium at New York University and at the annual meetings of the American Studies Association and American Anthropological Association. I would like to thank the many colleagues and friends who made this project possible, especially Nancy Abelmann, Amy Bentley, Edward Bruner, Matti Bunzl, Brenda Farnell, Dara Goldman, Shanshan Lan, Anita Mannur and Nicole Tami.

Bibliography

Claghorn, K.H. (1901), "The Foreign Immigrant in New York City," *Reports of the Industrial Commission*, vol. XV, Washington, DC: US Government Printing Office, pp. 465–92.

Classen, C. (1992), "The Odor of the Other," *Ethos*, 20(2): 133–66.

Corbin, A. (1986), *The Foul and the Fragrant*, Cambridge, MA: Harvard University Press.

Delaney, S. (1999), *Times Square Red, Times Square Blue*, New York: New York University Press.

Dugger, C. (1996), "Queens Old Times Uneasy as Asian Influence Grows," *New York Times*, 31 March.

Elias, N. ([1939] 1982), *The Civilizing Progress*, Oxford: Basil Blackwell.

Gay, P. (1984), *Bourgeois Experience*, vol. 1, *Education of the Senses*, Oxford: Oxford University Press.

Howes, D. (1991), "Olfaction and Transition," in D. Howes (ed.), *The Varieties of Sensory Experience*, Toronto: University of Toronto Press, pp. 128–47.

Illich, I. (2000), "The Dirt of Cities, the Aura of Cities, the Smell of the Dead, and Utopia of an Odorless City," in M. Miles, T. Hall and I. Borden (eds), *The City Cultures Reader*, London: Routledge.

Kaplan, M.A. (1991), *Making of the Jewish Middle Class*, Oxford: Oxford University Press.

Law, L. ([2001] 2004), "Home Cooking," in D. Howes (ed.), *Empire of the Senses*, Oxford: Berg, pp. 224–41.

Lee, R.G. (1999), *Orientals*, Philadelphia: Temple University Press.

Le Guérer, A. (1990), "Le Declin de L'olfactif," *Anthropologie et Société*, 14(2): 25–45.

Manalansan, M.F. IV (2001), unpublished journal, 21 March.

McArdle, A. and Erzen, T. (eds) (2001), *Zero Tolerance*, New York: New York University Press.

McPhee, M. (1992), "Deodorized Culture," *Arizona Anthropologist*, 8: 89–102.

Mollenkopf, J.H. and Castells, M. (eds) (1991), *Dual City*, New York: Russell Sage.

Ong, A. (2000), "Making the Biopolitical Subject," in M.F. Manalansan IV (ed.), *Cultural Compass*, Philadelphia: Temple University Press, pp. 85–112.

Pinard, S. (1991), "Taste of India," in D. Howes (ed.), *The Varieties of Sensory Experience*, Toronto: University of Toronto Press, pp. 221–30.

Ray, K. (1998), "Meals, Migration, Modernity," *Amerasia*, 24(1): 105–127.

Pearlman, J. (1999), "At Full Blast," <http://sportillustrated.cnn.com/feature/news/1999/12/22/rocker/>.

Sassen, S. (1994), *Cities in a World Economy*, Thousand Oaks, CA: Pine Froge Press.

—— (1996), "Identity in the Global City," in P. Yaeger (ed.), *Geography of Identity*, Ann Arbor: University of Michigan Press, pp. 131–51.

Sutton, D. (2001), *Remembrance of Repasts*, Oxford & New York: Berg.

Tchen, J.K.W. (1999), *New York Before Chinatown*, Baltimore: Johns Hopkins University.

Trillin, C. (2003), *Feeding a Yen*, New York: Random House.

Zola, E. (1933), *Germinal*, New York: E.P. Dutton.

4

Offensive Bodies

Alan Hyde

He whose odor is unpleasant shall be punished and ostracized.

Egyptian pyramid inscription (Le Guérer 1992: 30)

Law facilitates the construction and abjection of hated Others whenever it permits classification and exclusion around issues of sameness or propriety. Abjection is not just about hatred of immigrants or particular races. It is part of the psychological process of the formation of the self and is particularly associated with the purification of the body and maintenance of body boundaries. Social concern with hygiene is inseparable from division of the population into high and low, and control of the lower orders. Such abjection is well illustrated by a recent case upholding the power of a public library to exclude a homeless patron who smelled bad.

Richard Kreimer is a homeless man who lives in various outdoor public spaces in Morristown, New Jersey, and at one time spent a great deal of time in the public library. The library expelled him more than once because his offensive odor "prevented the Library patrons from using certain areas of the Library and prohibited Library employees from performing their jobs." The library also asserted that Kreimer, in addition to smelling bad, stared at and followed patrons and talked loudly to himself and others. Inasmuch as Kreimer's attack on library rules was "facial," the courts made no factual findings on the library's allegations (*Kreimer* 1992: 1242). Lawyers close to the case have told me that, in their opinion, Kreimer's alleged odor was the fundamental reason for his exclusion from the Library.

The court held that Richard Kreimer had a right under the First Amendment to receive information, and that the public library was a "limited public forum," "intentionally opened ... to the public *for expressive activity,* namely 'the communication of the written word'" (*Kreimer* 1992: 1250–5, 1259, emphasis in original). The library's rule provided that "patrons whose bodily hygiene is offensive so as to constitute a nuisance to other persons shall be required to leave the building." The court noted that this rule "would require the expulsion of a patron who might otherwise be peacefully engaged in permissible First Amendment activities within the purposes for which the Library was opened" (*Kreimer* 1992: 1264).

Nevertheless, held the Court, the library's rule was "narrowly tailored" (as Mr. Kreimer surely was not) "to serve a significant government interest." That interest is ensuring, in the library's words, that "all patrons [may] use its facilities to the maximum extent possible during its regularly scheduled hours." Since, according to the library, "Kreimer's odor was often so offensive that it prevented the Library patrons from using certain areas of the Library and prohibited Library employees from performing their jobs" (*Kreimer* 1992: 1247), a regulation excluding Kreimer would protect library attendance by everyone else.

The main reason the court permitted the library to exclude Kreimer was then that his odors allegedly prevented others from using the library. (The rule also "promotes the Library's interest in maintaining its facilities in a sanitary and attractive condition.") If this should be true, it may say more about library patrons than it does about Kreimer. We do not have a history of American odors to match Alain Corbin's (1986) or Georges Vigarello's (1988) of France. Moreover, we do not know with much precision how Kreimer smelled, as a legal matter, because no findings of fact were made and, as a discursive matter, because our language of odors is nowhere near as precise as our language for sight and sound. Odors cannot be named in any European language; the closest we can come is to say something smells like something else (Classen, Howes, and Synott 1994: 3). Indeed, it has been suggested that the physical location of the sense of smell, in the most primitive, reptilian part of the brain, makes it inaccessible to the language centers of the brain that develop much later (Rivlin and Gravelle 1984: 88–9).

However, if Kreimer's were simply the odors normally attendant on one who does not bathe—they may well have been worse—it is likely that there have been patrons with similar odors ever since there have been public libraries. Offense at the unbathed other is a comparatively late development in American social history; it is intimately linked with social stratification.

Bathing was in fact widely believed until the 1850s to constitute a hazard to health. Vigarello summarizes the legal bans on bathing in plague-infested areas of sixteenth- and seventeenth-century Western Europe:

> The skin was seen as porous, and countless openings seemed to threaten, since the surfaces were weak and the frontiers uncertain. Behind the simple refusal of proximity lay a very specific image of the body: heat and water created openings, the plague had only to slip through... Baths and steam-baths were dangerous because they opened up the body to the atmosphere. (Vigarello 1988: 9)

It thus followed that dirty bodies would be healthier than clean ones (Corbin 1986: 31; Vigarello 1988: 7–17).

These attitudes disappeared very slowly. Throughout nineteenth-century America, baths were an occasional indulgence for the upper classes. They were not part of anyone's daily life; they were not accessible to the lower classes; and they were still associated with health hazards. Law played a role, in constructing this normative unbathed body, that was even more direct than *Kreimer*'s contemporary construction of the normatively bathed body. Law in Boston as late as 1845 prohibited bathing during the winter except on medical advice, and Philadelphia nearly adopted a similar ban the decade before (Eberlein 1978: 340). Law did not need to construct the denial of access of the poor to bathing, beyond law's general regime of private property and conceptualizing of bathing as a private privilege.

The rise of bathing in nineteenth-century America has been documented by Richard L. Bushman and Claudia L. Bushman, and attributed to a combination of a general "civilizing process"; changing medical thought as to the skin and perspiration, now emphasizing the unhealthy quality of perspiration and the need to remove it from the body; and, though of lesser importance, religious tracts and preaching on cleanliness. These intellectual influences were largely in place at the turn of the nineteenth century but took over half a century to alter much behavior: "[P]robably not until 1850 did regular personal washing become routine in large numbers of middle-class households." Baths in which the entire body was immersed were even rarer. "The proposal to install a bathroom in the White House in 1851 raised a furor over the unnecessary expense. By 1860 there were 3,910 baths reported in Boston in a population of 177,840; probably most were portable tubs and not plumbed. Albany, New York, reported just 19." As late as 1906, only one dwelling in five in Pittsburgh had a bathtub (Bushman and Bushman 1988: 1213, 1225–6, 1231).

Interestingly, the medical learning on respiration through the skin and the necessity of cleaned, open pores was linked, at least in France, to thermodynamics and the analogy of the body to a steam engine, running on combustion (Vigarello 1988: 170–2). So the machine body became a cleaned body just when the machine analogy changed from clockwork to steam engines. The discovery of microbes by the end of the century gave further impetus to the growing popularity of cleanliness, although as late as 1900 families that never bathed can be identified (Corbin 1986: 217–18; Vigarello 1988: 175).

The history of cleanliness alerts us to another aspect of *Kreimer*: the mobilization of norms of cleanliness and good odor in a larger policing project of ethnic and economic elites against poor and minority populations (Corbin 1986: 142–75). The discovery of offensive odor is always necessarily at least in part a Kristevan abjection script in which purity is maintained through the expulsion of the polluting member.

The body may indeed be common to us all, but an almost universal aspect of human behavior is the insistence that one's own social group is inodorate while others smell. This attitude is not confined to the uneducated. It finds its way into classics of modern social analysis, such as Georg Simmel's *Soziologie*, which includes the following jarring paragraph in its self-consciously scientific approach to modern society:

> The exclusion of the Negro from high society in North America appears to be due to his body odor, and the complex and deep mutual aversion to Jews and Germans has been attributed to the same cause. (Simmel 1908: 657, trans. by the author)

George Orwell thought he had penetrated "the real secret of class distinctions in the West ... summed up in four frightful words ... *The lower classes smell*" (Orwell 1958: 159). Today we are more inclined to say of Simmel and Orwell what anthropologists say generally: "Rather than a cause of ethnic antipathy, ... olfactory aversions are generally an expression of it" (Classen, Howes, and Synnott 1994: 165). Since smell can be perceived at a distance, it has been speculated that smell may be particularly salient in the observation of people with whom one is not intimate, does not converse or embrace (Classen 1993: 79–105).

Every step in the history of public health measures for the encouragement of personal hygiene, the spread of bathing and eradication of filth, is always and necessarily a form of political hegemony. Distinct odors are attributed to hated ethnic groups, foreigners, the poor, homosexuals (Corbin 1986: 142–51; Stallybrass and White 1986: 125–48). Richard Bushman and Claudia Bushman (1988: 1227–31) document the frequency with which popular literature of the nineteenth century use cleanliness to divide people into two worlds, a high world of refinement and a detested lower world. In the optimistic version of this myth, the freed slave, the immigrant could well ascend into the higher world, should he or she simply be induced to bathe regularly; Simmel's is the pessimistic account in which odor, like race itself, inheres in the body, not in our construction of it.

Kreimer's case represents a post-nineteenth century, individualized version of the myth, in which Kreimer's odors are in some sense peculiar to him as an individual. Sensitivity to each individual's odor and a belief that everyone might become inoffensive graphically represent an individuation of the person; in earlier periods bodily odors, if noticed at all, could only represent the forces of nature or a less differentiated mass of people. An insistence on individuals' controlling their own odors helps reiterate and embody the abstract, liberal political program of self-government.

To describe the library's conduct as Kristevan abjection is not to say that it should stop forthwith. We cannot live without abjection. This detour into Kristevan abjection then does not demonstrate that the *Kreimer* case was wrongly decided. No doubt if so many people thought that Richard Kreimer smelled bad, he did, and if this sensitivity to odor is historically contingent, then so be it—what other sort of sense of odor could we have except that of our own era? If there is to be such a category as people whose odors are so offensive as to prevent others from working, I can think of no alternative source for the definition than the good sense of library staff. Given language's weak range of descriptions of odors, objective rules do not seem feasible. I wasn't in the library with Kreimer, and perhaps removing him really was like the expulsion of waste that lets us live.

Perhaps. Yet I do not think a court that was self-conscious about this complex of abjection problems, in which bodies are figured as polluting, from drugs and immigration to racial segregation, could have written an opinion as unself-conscious as the opinion in *Kreimer,* with its narrow tailoring and weighing of interests.

The benefit of this discussion of abjection might be a greater judicial self-consciousness about what it is doing in a case like *Kreimer.* I would like law to develop a pause here, a sudden stopping of the hand at the recognition that law has constructed and abjected an Other, the kind of recognition that comes when the prototype is firm in our minds and we recognize it everywhere. Perhaps we are too quick to identify our security with firm boundaries and internal purification and fail to see how the security we prize comes only from the way we enter into communication with people around us, particularly people who might as easily be constructed as Other and abjected.

For an alternative treatment of the odorous body, consider John Donne's 1622 Lenten sermon on the text "Jesus Wept," as described by Elaine Scarry:

> [Donne] imagines that Jesus could have looked at the four-day rotting corpse of Lazarus and said, "There is no such matter, he doth not stink," but says instead, He is rotting, there is a stench, but yet he is my friend ("but though he do, my friend shall not lack my help."). This, finally, is Donne's most characteristic reflex, to bring forward the human hand at moments of both desire and repulsion; to say, but yet he is my friend. (Scarry 1988: 97)

Bibliography

Bushman, R.L. and Bushman, C.L. (1988), "The Early History of Cleanliness in America," *Journal of American History*, 74: 1213–38.

Corbin, A. (1986), *The Foul and the Fragrant*, Cambridge: Harvard University Press.

Classen, C. (1993), *Worlds of Sense*, London: Routledge.

Classen, C., Howes, D., and Synnott, A. (1994), *Aroma*, London: Routledge.

Eberlein, H.D. (1978), "When Society First Took a Bath," in *Sickness and Health in America*, J.W. Leavitt and R.L. Numbers (eds), Madison: University of Wisconsin Press.

Kreimer v. Bureau of Police for the Town of Morristown (1992), 958 F.2d, 3d Cir.

Le Guérer, A. (1992), *Scent*, New York: Turtle Bay Books.

Orwell, G. (1958 [1937]), *The Road to Wigan Pier*, New York: Harcourt Brace.

Rivlin, R. and Gravelle, K. (1984), *Deciphering the Senses*, New York: Simon and Schuster.

Scarry, E. (1988), "Donne: 'But Yet the Body Is His Booke,'" in *Literature and the Body*, E. Scarry (ed.), Baltimore: Johns Hopkins University Press.

Simmel, G. (1908), *Soziologie*, Leipzig: Duncker und Humblot.

Stallybrass, P. and White, A. (1986), *The Politics and Poetics of Transgression*, Ithaca: Cornell University Press.

Vigarello, G. (1988), *Concepts of Cleanliness*, Cambridge UK: Cambridge University Press.

5

Base Notes
Odor, Breath and Moral Contagion in Ilahita

Donald Tuzin

Is it not curious that anthropology, a discipline chartered to explore humanity's cultural and biological wholeness, has had relatively little to say about the senses? There have been some notable contributions, of course: the researches of Edward T. Hall (e.g. 1966) come immediately to mind, as do the excellent work on sensory topics by Alfred Gell (1980 and in this volume) and Uri Almagor (1990). John Blacking's edited volume (1977) on the anthropology of the body must be mentioned, and there have been several pieces dealing with various sound stimuli in relation to reported religious experience (e.g. Needham 1964; Freeman 1968; Rouget 1980; Tuzin 1984). For the most part, however, ever since the Abbé de Condillac's famous treatise of 1754 (Condillac 1930), sensory phenomena have been left to philosophy and psychology. This is a shame, for culture has much to do with how we see, hear, smell, taste and touch the world (Ackerman 1990; Howes 1991; Classen 1993).

Conversely, because the sensory hardware is commonly judged to be standard for our species, it follows that many of the sensory idioms that recur widely (if not universally) in world cultures represent an elaboration that is, so to speak, invited by precultural peculiarities of the modalities themselves (Tuzin 1984). Thus, Gell's observation that smell-signs are semiologically ambiguous, in that they are not fully detached from "the world of objects to which they refer" (Gell 1977: 26), may have application even beyond the Proustian domains of taste and olfaction. At the very least, the further development of an anthropological perspective on sensory phenomena should help to illuminate (non-reductively, one would hope) both the perceptual bases of culture and the cultural bases of perception.

That, then, is the larger program. In this chapter, I wish to speak only of smell and its close companions. Smell—a sense that, with the simultaneous release of Patrick Süskind's relentlessly olfactory novel *Perfume* (1986), Alain Corbin's fascinating history (1986) of smell in the French imagination and the unprecedented smell survey conducted in the September 1986 issue of *National Geographic Magazine*, suddenly became airborne as an object of popular and scholarly interest. Subsequent works have broadened awareness of culture and olfaction and entered it more firmly on the anthropological agenda (e.g. Classen, Howes and Synnott 1994).

And yet, in all this flurry of interest in the different faces of smell, the distinctively *moral* implications of this sense have not been explored at length. The association of smell with memory and emotion is well known; its role in identifying self and other is also well described. Evolutionary and comparative biology have examined smell in an even broader explanatory framework. These features make smell singularly available to the development of the moral aesthetic of good and bad, right and wrong, kin and non-kin, the familiar and the alien, the safe and the dangerous. George Orwell grasped the morality of olfaction when he bluntly stated, "The real secret of class distinction in the West can be summed up in four frightful words ... *the lower classes smell*" (qtd. in Watson 2001: 136). Olfaction has been called "the sense of sympathy"—but also "the witch's sense" (Watson 2001: 143, 147). Saints in the Middle Ages exuded the "odor of sanctity" (Le Guérer 1992: 122), but certain persons and ideas were and are repelled as "stinking."

This pervasive dualism in the moral inflection of olfaction may derive from the sense's most primitive features. While Sigmund Freud and others make much of the fact that human olfaction is much less acute than that of other mammals ("repressed"), and that dogs and rabbits have hundreds of *times* more receptors than we do, two other facts are worth noting. First, although less hairy than other primate species, humans have many more apocrine glands, making them the smelliest of all primates (Stoddart 1990); one must wonder what all of that perfume is for, if not to affect behavior in some way. Secondly, while humans may have fewer receptors and therefore less olfactory input, they also have a much larger neocortex with which to process that input. "And that opens the door to an unexpected conclusion," writes Watson (2001: 212), "far from being poor smellers, we may in some ways be the most evolved of all species in this respect." If humans have taken olfaction to the level of high art, with thousands of perfumes, not to mention the many other exudations of industrialized society, it is because of what our higher cortical capacities have done with material that is quite simple and primitive, signaling only what the organism needs to know to survive; and at that level, the issue reduces to some version of the simple binomialism—good or bad. Borrowing a term from the perfume makers, these are the "base notes" of moral reckoning. These arouse the feeling-states that validate moral responses; they are the fixatives that grace the moral mixture with "warmth, texture and lasting qualities." They do not overpower the higher notes, but enhance them and act as a "true accompaniment" (Stoddart 1990: 158).

Among the Ilahita Arapesh of the East Sepik Province, Papua New Guinea, the moral salience of smell is highly cognized and culturally embedded. But if smell in Ilahita holds its own in importance with its sister senses, the hypothetical injunction "Smell no evil" presents a dilemma not found with the others, namely, that evil smells cannot always be avoided or, indeed, detected. If morality is generally about choice, then olfaction is a paradoxical moral sense, in that daily life is full of odors we do not choose to inhale, but we do so all the same. One does what one can, and hopes for the best. As will be seen, the people of Ilahita are aware of this problem, and have used it to further their cultural purposes.

At a deep cultural and emotional level, the Ilahita judge smell to be the distillation of physical and, more importantly, moral essences—of goodness and badness, of purity and pollution. Though in Ilahita all living or once-living things have essences, only some have a detectable odor; it is this feature that renders them morally identifiable and problematic. Just as Western science classifies olfaction as a chemical or "contact" sense, the Arapesh understand that smell is the *communicable* aspect of its source, which is the innermost core of the object emitting it. In humans and other animals this core is located in the *okom*, or heart, while in inanimate things such as aromatic leaves, piles of ordure and stinking dead bodies, it is diffused throughout the object's substance. One cannot be wholly indifferent to a smell, as one can to visual and aural objects, because during sensory contact the perceiver directly ingests the volatile essence into his or her own *okom*, where it remains permanently. Because, then, the goodness or badness of a thing is transmitted in its smell, the vapors of everyday life are a constant source of moral contagion. And, in the nature of moral classification, things are either "good" or "bad." Informants are able, under the duress of questioning, to rate one smell as better or worse than another, but in the end there are really only good and bad smells, just as there are only good and bad moral qualities.

Arapesh ideas concerning smell also apply to gustatory ingestion, which in these terms is the swallowing of smell. Of the food we eat, part goes to renewing blood and bodily tissue, part is excreted, and the morally imbued part—the essence—lodges in the *okom*. As the Germans say, *Man ist was Man ißt*: we are what we eat. Ordinarily, one is able to control what one eats—the nose helps to guide us in this matter—but the contagion requires only a small, perhaps undetectable amount slipped into one's food. This happens, for example, during initiation into the several grades of the men's cult, when novices are surreptitiously fed fecal material and other noxious substances, the essences of which find their way to the *okom* and thereafter insure that any violation of ritual food taboos will cause bodily harm, possibly death, to the person who has been initiated—the perfect, embodied, unsleeping censor of one's moral acts.

Another technique, using the same purported mechanism, is available to women who desire that their husbands stop beating or tyrannizing them. The woman tucks a piece of coconut meat in her armpit for a time long enough for it to acquire her smell, then she pricks her finger and allows some drops of blood to fall on it. The treated coconut is fed to her husband in his yam soup, thus changing him from bad to good in his behavior toward her. These examples illustrate my major theme, which is that among the Arapesh one's moral condition is accessible to—may be coerced, tricked or beguiled by—olfactory sensations of either personal or impersonal origin. By the same token, one may affect a moral situation by manipulating its olfactory components.

My first inkling that the people with whom I lived had (what by Western standards must be) an exaggerated olfactory aesthetic, occurred early during fieldwork. My pet cat had chosen to give birth in my book box, and as soon as was practicable I removed her and her brood to another location and closed the box against her return. The dame seemed desperate to get back into the box, but I was unyielding. A few days later, following my nose, I discovered that a newborn kitten had been overlooked and was now decomposing between Mead and Malinowski. When I casually asked my paid assistant—a man of the village—to dispose of the remains, he evinced such horror at the prospect, with such grimacing, spitting, gagging and moaning, that to insist would have been out of the question. I was amazed. Agreed, the smell was not pleasant; but it was only a *little* kitten, with not much flesh to begin with, and the stench seemed hardly sufficient to incapacitate my assistant. The incident did alert me, though, to the possibility that the ideas and experiences surrounding olfaction in Ilahita are elaborated to a remarkable extent. This suspicion was later confirmed.

Two examples might convey the aroma of smell in Arapesh behavior and ideology.

1.   I had obtained the use of a truck with which to drive myself and a few villagers to the port town of Wewak, which was one hundred bumpy, swervy miles from Ilahita. The man who was to ride with me in the cab arrived with a small, roasted yam that had been partially split lengthwise. It was the reddish-skinned, spectacularly aromatic variety known locally as *nematap*. When I made some comment about his sensibly bringing a snack with him for the long journey, he replied that the yam was not to eat, but to smell. He explained that he was prone to motion sickness, and that when he felt the nausea rising he had only to breathe deeply the fragrance of the yam, and the discomfort would go away. And, indeed, frequently during the drive he successfully used the yam as an inhalator. Several times over the following months, I observed individuals using

yams in this way, not only to counteract nausea, but as a tonic when they were feeling dispirited or out of sorts. In the latter situation, smelling their favorite food—the food that in many ways means most to them, and is a direct link to their ancestors (see Tuzin 1972)—has a cheering effect; in the case of nausea, the good smell of the yam, felt on the tongue and penetrating to the *okom*, drives away the badness that is the source of discomfort. Whatever biochemical mechanisms may have been involved in this effect, it was plain to me that the psychocultural significance of yams for these people is an important factor in counteracting negative states that, like nausea, have a strong psychological component.

2. When I once asked a group of senior men to decide among themselves what smell was the worst imaginable, they took little time in agreeing that it is the Breath of a Ghost. (I capitalize this to convey the sense of awe that accompanied their response.) They described the Breath of a Ghost as reminiscent of the fumes of a rotting body—only much worse: a distillation of evil essences, the smell exceeds normal putrescence in the same way that the ghost itself exceeds the dead body. Elsewhere I have described how Arapesh traditional mourning practices involved placing the corpse in a shallow, leaf-covered grave in the ground-house floor, so that during the period of decomposition family members may express piety by sleeping with and inhaling the odors of decay (Tuzin 1975). This implies that the essence of the deceased is literally incorporated into the *okom* of the bereaved. Here it is that a physically unpleasant smell is morally positive, and yet a certain ambivalence is suggested by the idea that the smell of corruption, when carried on the breath of a ghost, becomes horrific both in itself and in what it signifies.

More specifically, the smell of death *is* the power of life released from its corporeal containment in the *okom*. In life this power, viewed as a kind of elixir—one man characterized it as a cross between blood and bone—enables a man to perform competently in war, pig hunting, yam growing and tree felling; in curing and in romancing; and, interestingly, in grave digging. Women do not possess this power. It is acquired by males through the succession of initiations into the men's cult (the Tambaran) that begins immediately after weaning and continues in five stages up to the gates of great old age. In particular, one develops this power by studiously observing the food taboos that attend each grade of the cult. Witness the case of the old woman La'wai, who, it is said, lost her nose many years ago because her husband spoke angrily to her shortly after he had eaten the dangerous, initiatory foods of the Tambaran. So powerful was his *okom*, that the breath exploding from it caused the poor woman's nose to rot away. Similarly, the man Supalo made the mistake of working too close alongside Watasiwi, a magician and master artist whose *okom* was reputedly one of the most powerful in the village. Watasiwi's breath accidentally swept across Supalo's face. Later that day, Supalo's eyesight began to fail, and by the next morning he was blind. It was only Watasiwi's ministrations—using his breath, but this time in a controlled, deliberate fashion—that restored him.

As part of the same logic, the explanation given for the general incompetence of certain other men is that they were undisciplined in their youth, were negligent about the ritual taboos, and, therefore, had never developed their masculinity. They are now abject, luckless, hen-pecked sorts who on the rare occasions they do attempt to assert themselves only succeed in being ridiculous. If a man of this type buries a body, the earth will not contain its smell. This is because the grave-digger's powers are not strong enough to create a new confinement for the smells that, at death, begin to seep, later to flood, from the *okom*. As one person commented, "Burying a body is something like planting a yam. It is more than just a matter of knowing what to do. You must have 'good power' (*atamb bimbaomb*), or else the effort must fail."

It is important to note that grave making of the six-feet-under variety is a recent custom in Ilahita, imposed in the late 1950s as a health and sanitation measure by the Australian colonial administration. From having regarded decomposition odors as something to be piously endured—or, at any rate, as a necessary though unsettling contact between the living and the newly dead—the Ilahita were told that these smells must be avoided by interring the corpse in a deep hole in a public cemetery, some distance away from the nearest occupied hamlet. Removed from the privacy of the family, potentially available to strangers seeking to imbibe and manipulate them, the smells of death lost their psychologically redeeming features and became, at best, merely unpleasant, and, at worst, a source of ghostly peril and negative moral contagion to the community. In objective sensory terms—if there is such a thing—the smells may not have changed; but their moral polarity was reversed, and that made them both frightening and odious.

For reasons of their own, therefore, given that colonial law required them to abandon their disposal customs, the villagers took to heart the patrol officer's admonition and thereafter sought to master rather than submit to the smell of death. Because this implied, also, mastery of the powers released at death, grave making joined that category of tasks (war, gardening, hunting etc.) requiring the strength of essential masculinity.

For good or ill, then, the contagion of death is transmitted through smell. So are other sorts of contagion. Casanova, it is famously said, once confided to a friend the secret of his conquests: at a point during the evening of the campaign, perhaps while dancing, he would contrive to wipe the brow of his intended with a handkerchief that he had carried tucked in his armpit. The subliminal effect of his smell was to make the woman helpless before his advances. Whether the story is apocryphal or not, the Ilahitans whom I told about it had no trouble in believing that the famous lover's trick would be effective. To know a person's smell is to recognize and like him or her, but more than that it is to experience the intimacy of shared substance. Love philters operate on this principle, and they are sometimes so effective that I hesitate to call them "magical" in the usual sense of the word. Thus, perfumes extracted from a wide variety of aromatic leaves, and more recently talcs, colognes and scented body oils purchased from trade stores, are considered by men to be *de rigueur* in the amorous quest. Women, they explain, like the perfume and will pant for it, taking into their *okom* the commingled scent of the man himself, and thereby opening themselves to his advances. Their attraction to him is precisely that of a moth to a flame, for the people say that what irresistibly attracts the insect is the "smell" of the light. Other techniques involved the woman being surreptitiously fed a trace of the man's smell. Similarly, but overtly, during the ritual cleansing following a couple's honeymoon seclusion, the bride eats some of the blood which the groom lets from his penis (Tuzin 1980: 21). This is to insure love and fidelity on her part, and it also imbues her with the smell that the husband's ancestral yams recognize and tolerate as their own. Without this credential the yams—who identify humans by their smell—would be alarmed by her strangeness in the garden and their spirits might abandon the couple. So, too, would they reject their own master, if he entered the garden with the scent of a strange woman on his penis.

The point is that smell is the medium of moral recognition, of shared substance, of mutual trust and identity, and, perhaps, of love. Olfactory intercourse unites and in a moral sense defines the filial and conjugal circle and by attenuation comes to embrace the entire community of which individuals feel themselves to be a part. That is why a drifter, a man who constantly shifts residences, is described by the transitive expression, *Nahia pengen* ("He who smells"), meaning that he is searching for a smell and not finding it. It is one of the saddest things that can be said of anyone, for it means that the person has no home.

Just as the ingestion of a smell establishes a spiritual bond between sender and receiver, so one might try to mitigate olfactory contamination by spitting. Missionaries and other Europeans tend to regard the more or less constant spitting that goes on as merely a filthy habit, but in view of the ideas attached to olfaction in this culture, and of the many smells that infect everyday life—some perceived, others not—simple prudence and regard for one's health and personal autonomy are reason enough for frequent spitting. Apart from this kind of absent-minded expectoration, there are times when spitting is deliberate. It can be a serious insult, a sign of distaste and moral–aesthetic revulsion, when used in the presence of an enemy and with the appropriate snort and grimace. In cult ceremonies, ritual spitting is performed by initiators on the threshold of the spirit house as a magical way of intensifying the ordeal that the novices will momentarily undergo upon entering the house; fathers combat this effect and mitigate the ordeal by spitting, themselves, on the threshold. And, again, spitting a fine spray of saliva on the patient is the shaman's way of empowering his magic. Finally, it is thought that a person who spits immediately upon awakening will be able to remember the dream(s) he or she has just had; as a rather nice analogue of Freudian repression, it is understood that if you swallow at the moment of wakefulness, you swallow your dreams, sending them beyond recall into the innermost part of your being.

In summary, spitting and exhaling can serve either to prevent unwelcome smells from penetrating to the *okom*, or to project one's personal powers outside the body for some practical purpose. Saliva and breath can go in either direction. In this respect they are unusual body products, unless one wishes to count nasal mucus—which, as far as I could discover, has no cultural significance whatever for the Arapesh—or, intriguingly, feces, *insofar as they may sometimes be eaten*. In a sense, what happens in the mouth and nose expresses immediate experience; and it is the person's choice whether to affirm or submit to (by swallowing), or reject (by expelling), the implications of the moment. This may be why olfaction and the allied sensation of taste are so closely tied to moral reckoning, both as verbal idioms and as modalities through which substantiated moral values may be variously recognized, assimilated, and rejected—to wit, *bodily experienced*. Moral systems, by their nature, posit only two choices: anything more requires the notion of system transcendence. Thus, we say that a moralist "sees things only in black and white," implying that a more sophisticated (transcendent) perspective would acknowledge "shades of gray." The Arapesh, on the other hand, understand that morality is not something to be known from afar; not something to be "visualized" in any hues at all; not something to be escaped or transcended without the penalty of solitude. For them, morality dwells within the body. It is experienced intimately, and it smells either good or bad.

In conclusion, olfaction in Ilahita is the vehicle and vocabulary of moral reckoning. One's moral character is formed by smells taken into the body, while the unavoidable constancy of inspiration means that one is always vulnerable to unwelcome changes in that character and in the existential contours of life itself. These features, derived in substantial measure by the inherent properties of this sensory modality, in turn provide much material for further cultural elaborations in the domains of power, gender, dominance, identity, piety and personal autonomy. Indeed, the shared component of *smell* is precisely the way in which these various domains become moralized. No wonder, then, that the people of Ilahita treat smell with such seriousness, and cannot abide the stinking carcass of a kitten.

Acknowledgments

Fieldwork was conducted in Ilahita village during twenty-one months in the period 1969–72 and eleven months during 1985–6. The author is grateful to the Australian National University, the Wenner-Gren Foundation for

Anthropological Research, and the National Science Foundation for their generous support.

Bibliography

Ackerman, D. (1990), *A Natural History of the Senses*, New York: Random House.
Almagor, U. (1990), "Odors and Private Language," *Human Studies*, 13: 253–74.
Blacking, J. (ed.) (1977), *The Anthropology of the Body*, ASA Monograph 15, London: Tavistock.
Classen, C. (1993), *Worlds of Sense*, London: Routledge.
—— Howes, D., and Synnott, A. (1994), *Aroma*, London: Routledge.
Condillac, E.B. de ([1754] 1930), *Treatise on the Sensations*, Los Angeles: University of Southern California.
Corbin, A. (1986), *The Foul and the Fragrant*, Cambridge, MA: Harvard University Press.
Freeman, D. (1968), "Thunder, Blood, and the Nicknaming of God's Creatures," *Psychoanalytic Quarterly*, 37: 353–99.
Gell, A. (1977), "Magic, Perfume, Dream..." in I. Lewis (ed.), *Symbols and Sentiments*, London, New York and San Francisco: Academic Press.
—— (1980), "The Gods at Play," *Man*, 15(2): 219–48.
Hall, E.T. (1966), *The Hidden Dimension*, London: The Bodley Head.
Howes, D. (ed.) (1991), *The Varieties of Sensory Experience*, Toronto: Toronto University Press.
Le Guérer, A. (1992), *Scent*, New York: Turtle Bay Books.
Needham, R. (1964), "Blood, Thunder, and the Mockery of Animals," *Sociologus*, 14: 136–49.
Rouget, G. (1980), *La Musique et la Transe*, Paris: Gallimard.
Stoddart, D.M. (1990), *The Scented Ape*, Cambridge: Cambridge University Press.
Süskind, P. (1986), *Perfume*, trans. John E. Woods, New York: Alfred A. Knopf.
Tuzin, D. (1972), "Yam Symbolism in the Sepik," *Southwestern Journal of Anthropology*, 28(3): 230–54.
—— (1975), "The Breath of a Ghost," *Ethos*, 3(3): 555–78.
—— (1980), *The Voice of the Tambaran*, Berkeley: University of California Press.
—— (1984), "Miraculous Voices," *Current Anthropology*, 25(5): 579–89, 593–6.
Watson, L. (2001), *Jacobson's Organ*, New York: Penguin.

6

Olfactory-Triggered Panic Attacks Among Khmer Refugees

Devon E. Hinton, Vuth Pich,
Dara Chhean and Mark H. Pollack

The human ritual of renewal meant relearning old habits from her "former" or pre-Auschwitz life: how to use a toothbrush, toilet paper, handkerchief, knife and fork; how to smile, first with the lips, then with the lips and eyes; how to recapture forgotten odors and tastes, like the smell of rain.

Implicit in the procedure of renewal, however, annealed to it with the epoxy of disruptive memory, is the "counter-time" of Auschwitz, where the rain stank of diarrhea and beat down on the camp, the victims, "the soot of the crematoriums and the odor of burning flesh."

Lawrence Langer, *Holocaust Memories*

In this quotation, Langer highlights the salience of olfaction in the Holocaust traumatic ontology, and its centrality in attempted recovery. Traumatic events are encoded into memory by auditory, olfactory and visual cues. The sensory modality of olfaction—whose afferent tracts connect directly to the limbic system—seems to play a pre-eminent role in emotion and alerting to threat (Ledoux 1996). Though sights and sounds are commonly assessed triggers of flashbacks, odor cues in individuals diagnosed with post-traumatic stress disorder (PTSD) and panic disorder have been minimally investigated by psychiatrists and psychologists.

We conducted a survey to determine the prevalence of olfactory-triggered panic attacks among Cambodian refugees attending a psychiatric clinic, and to delineate the phenomenology of olfactory panic attacks. The survey revealed that Cambodians frequently have a panic reaction to the following odors: (1) car exhaust fumes, (2) cigarette smoke, (3) trash odors, (4) cooking smells (i.e. gas-stove fumes or the odor of burning food) and (5) certain other scents (e.g. perfume, nail polish, fresh paint, bleach or new clothes). In that study, we discovered that many Cambodian refugees had trauma memories triggered by these odors, and that the Cambodian refugees often fear dying during the odor-triggered panic attacks, that is, they have catastrophic cognitions during the olfactory-triggered panic episodes. Also, the patients had severe panic symptoms during the olfactory-triggered panic attacks.

Below, we will first present some vignettes of Cambodian refugees at our psychiatric clinic who have olfactory-triggered panic attacks, then discuss some of the mechanisms by which olfactory panic is generated, and conclude by discussing treatments for Cambodian refugees with odor-triggered panic attacks.

Cases

Ry

Three years prior to the present interview, Ry began psychiatric treatment. The then forty-six-year-old patient had panic attacks triggered by car exhaust, cigarette smoke and trash odors. In the car exhaust-triggered panic attacks, the patient experienced flashbacks of an event that took place during the Vietnamese invasion of Cambodia: a mortar shell exploded next to her, killing several friends. Panic attacks triggered by cigarette smoke or trash odors were not accompanied by flashbacks. The patient was diagnosed with PTSD and panic disorder and treated with medication (clonazepam and sertraline) and therapy.

In the four weeks prior to the interview, she had experienced two panic attacks, both triggered by cigarette smoke. On the day of her most recent clinical visit, when Ry walked into the vestibule at the entrance to the clinic, she encountered someone smoking a cigarette. As she passed the smoker, Ry suddenly experienced a constellation of symptoms: strong nausea, dizziness (*loengii loengoe*), shortness of breath, palpitations, diaphoresis, the urge to urinate and defecate, and the feeling of imminent syncope. The "wind attack" caused her to fear dying of a heart attack, stroke or some other medical event, and her reaction to the odor confirmed her self-diagnosis of "weakness" and "weak heart." Even after Ry moved into a smoke-free area, her symptoms persisted for another ten minutes. She did not report having flashbacks during this cigarette-induced panic attack.

Ry related the story of her exposure to severe bombing. While Vietnamese were fighting the Khmer Rouge at a site next to her natal village, she and some fellow villagers sought refuge in a nearby banana-tree grove. A mortar shell exploded very close by and the acrid smell of sulfur infused her nostrils with a burning sensation. There was also the odor of burnt vegetation and flesh along with a strong scent of blood. As she looked around, Ry saw that one person had been severed at the trunk, another's legs had been torn from the body, and blood was splattered everywhere. A few days later, a mortar shell exploded even closer to Ry, resulting in shrapnel injury and loss of consciousness. She explained that the smell of car exhaust is identical to the sulfurous odor of fumes from an exploded bomb. Ry also described how, during the Pol Pot period, she often encountered foul-smelling decaying corpses.

Sokha

Upon first presenting to the clinic, Sokha, who was then forty-five years of age, was diagnosed with PTSD and panic disorder. Initially, his main complaint consisted of severe startle: loud noises would cause him to have palpitations for thirty minutes. Sokha worried that his startle sensitivity indicated a weakness of heart and that he could die during a tachycardic episode. After we explained that startle-induced palpitations were normal in such situations and verified (through consultation with his physician) the healthiness of his heart, Sokha's startle-induced palpitations decreased to just one minute in duration and caused him only minimal distress. During the olfactory survey, our team learned of another phenomenon of great concern to Sokha. Upon encountering the smell of fresh paint or new clothes, he had a panic attack (in his words, a "wind attack") along with a Pol Pot flashback of decaying corpses. And if the car ahead of him on the road emitted much exhaust—particularly in the case of diesel trucks—he would develop dizziness, palpitations, shortness of breath, nausea, sweating and fear but without flashbacks.

During the Pol Pot period, Sokha lived in an area of Cambodia where many people were killed. Every day, new people arrived for execution; the bodies were piled on wood, then torched. The scent of burning flesh was omnipresent and overwhelming, and Sokha wondered whether this would soon be his fate. During his escape journey to Thailand following the Vietnamese invasion of Cambodia, Sokha saw multiple bodies in a state of putrefaction along the roadside. The corpses emitted an overwhelming stench. Flies swarmed around—and alit upon—the corpses, creating a constant buzzing. Many of the bodies were swollen to twice the original size, the skin cracking, a fluid exuding from the fissures and, in certain sections, invaded by undulating masses of maggots. Even after passing well beyond the corpses, Sokha could smell the odor for days, as if the stench had stuck to his body. As he described the image, Sokha looked suddenly ill, saying that just recalling the image made him feel dizzy and nauseated and made his hands grow cold and his head ache. He extended his hands outward for the first author to verify. They were icy cold. Sokha also explained that he had been exposed to the sulfurous smoke of bombs and gunfire.

When Sokha learned that it was common among Khmer refugees to have a strong physiological response to traumatic event reminders such as smells, that this reactivity was an expected and benign aspect of trauma-related disorder, he no longer ascribed his odor-provoked symptoms to "inner wind," "weakness" or a "weak heart." As a further therapeutic intervention, we suggested that Sokha keep a Vicks™ sniffer in his pocket, utilizing it upon exposure to objectionable odors. While sniffing the Vicks™ tube, Sokha conjured the image of a garden scene, imagining that he smelled the fragrance of sweet flowers. During the visualization, he practiced muscle relaxation, especially of the shoulders, along with a head rotation, imagining his neck and spine to be the stem of a lotus and his head to be like a bloom dancing playfully in the wind. Sokha was also taught that he could take a half-pill of a benzodiazapine should the sniffer fail to relieve his anxiety. After these interventions, Sokha no longer experienced olfactory-triggered panic attacks and only occasionally felt a mild sense of distress upon encountering a formerly problematic odor.

Chan

Three times a week during the month prior to the interview, fifty-nine-year-old Chan experienced severe episodes of dizziness upon standing. He would immediately sit down, fearing "wind overload." A panic attack would ensue that lasted about an hour. During about a third of the orthostatically induced panic attacks, Chan had a flashback of either his brother's execution or of stacks of body parts. Whenever Chan was exposed to cigarette smoke, he suffered a panic attack (cold extremities, dizziness, nausea, shortness of breath and fear) lasting thirty minutes—which he described as a "wind attack"—in conjunction with a flashback of his brother's execution. Such a cigarette-triggered panic attack had occurred once in the four weeks prior to interview. To relieve the symptoms of the olfactory-triggered panic attack, Chan immediately began to "coin" himself (dragging a coin across the skin) in order to remove excessive inner wind (see Hinton, Um and Ba 2001a, b); Chan considered cold extremities, dizziness and other symptoms to result from the blockage of vessels in the limbs and an inner accumulation of wind.

In the Khmer Rouge period, just before the Vietnamese invasion of his village, Chan and his two brothers were farming rice about an hour's walk from the village. Suddenly, six Khmer Rouge showed up at the rice field and proceeded to arrest Chan and his brothers. The soldiers had learned that Chan's two brothers had served as soldiers prior to the Khmer Rouge invasion. (The Khmer Rouge routinely hunted down and executed all former soldiers.) While Chan had always worked exclusively as a rice farmer, he nevertheless was arrested as well. He was charged with two crimes: being related to a soldier and not revealing his brothers' identities to the authorities. Three Khmer Rouge soldiers escorted Chan's brothers to a distance of about fifty yards while another three Khmer Rouge remained behind to guard Chan. One of the guards lit a cigarette and, while exhaling smoke directly into Chan's face, told him that they intended to kill and eviscerate his two brothers and consume their livers. Chan's heart pounded against his rib cage, his chest tightened, and his face flushed with blood, while his head was sent into a whirling spiral of fear and rage and cigarette fumes. He watched as his brothers' hands were bound behind their backs and a Khmer Rouge fired a rifle into each brother's chest in turn. One and then the other brother collapsed backwards, and the odor of sulfurous gunshot fumes filled the air. The soldiers then escorted Chan to his dead brothers and forced him to watch as they eviscerated the bodies with a long knife and placed the livers on a banana leaf. The stench of blood and sulfur was overpowering. Chan was overcome with panic, nausea, dizziness and leg weakness and feared he would collapse. The soldiers then let him go, saying that this would be his fate if he committed any errors.

Upon arriving back at his village, Chan found the Khmer Rouge commanding the villagers to assemble before the leader's house in order to view the butchered corpses of twelve people who had tried to escape the village. There was one pile of limbs, severed at the knee and elbow; in an adjacent mound were the heads; and beside that lay the eviscerated trunks, the abdomens splayed open with flaps of skin draping down, the livers having been extricated for consumption by the Khmer Rouge. Weak-kneed, dizzy, and nauseated, Chan stared at the horrifying image of his own likely fate. When the Vietnamese invaded his village a few hours later, he seized the moment to escape, and managed to reach the Thai border.

The Generation of Olfactory Panic Attacks among Cambodian Refugees

The generation of olfactory panic involves the complex interaction of various factors. Below we will discuss three major aspects of the multiplex model as applied to olfactory panic in the Cambodian population: (1) trauma associations to odors; (2) catastrophic conditions regarding odors and odor reactivity; and (3) metaphoric resonances of odors.

Trauma Associations to Odors

A patient may react to certain cues linked to past traumas without actually having ideational recall of the traumatic events (Clark 1999). In other words, a patient may have experienced a trauma (e.g. exposure to bombing), which in turn leads to a certain cue triggering a panic attack (e.g. the sulfur of car exhaust), yet the patient does not recall the event itself during exposure to the cue and the ensuing attack. For Khmer refugees, conditioning plays an extremely important role in the generation of olfactory panic attacks. For example, above, we demonstrated that car exhaust fumes and cigarette odors trigger flashbacks of battle scenes. Below are six kinds of traumas strongly encoded by an odor.

Sulfurous Smoke of Bombs and Bullets To patients, car exhaust smells just like the sulfur (*rumseew*) of exploding bombs and fired guns. Nearly every Cambodian refugee was exposed to bombing—often multiple times; many barely escaped alive. Gun battles and execution by shooting were also common. Before the Khmer Rouge period Americans dropped large bombs in parts of the country that were controlled by the Khmer Rouge. As the Khmer Rouge took over the country in 1975, fierce gun battles ensued; and during the Pol Pot regime, execution by gunshot frequently occurred. At the time of the Vietnamese invasion, in 1979, the vast majority of Cambodians were forcibly moved to new areas by retreating Khmer Rouge. Many attempted to escape by crossing over to the Vietnamese-controlled areas or by traversing the Thai border. Cambodians had existed at near-starvation levels since the time of the Khmer Rouge takeover, and as vast numbers of people were forced to re-locate, food became even scarcer. Most fleeing Cambodians were caught, often more than once, in the crossfire between the Khmer Rouge and Vietnamese forces. As patients who had been soldiers before the Khmer Rouge period explicated, being situated between fighting troops is much more traumatic than fighting on one or the other side: it is noisier, the smell of sulfur and smoke is much stronger, and there is a sense of passive helplessness. Often the person would be trapped in the zone between fighting troops for a day or more; if there were no place to take cover, one would have to run through the crossfire to reach a safe zone. During the battle, all the senses were assaulted: one smelled the sulfurous smoke of exploding projectiles and the fumes of burning houses, vegetation and animal and human flesh; one saw shrapnel wounds, the severing of limbs, evisceration and spilled blood; and one heard the deafening clamor of mortal shells, grenades, machine guns and rifles. The original exposure to bombing prompted a pairing of multiple odors (fresh blood, singed hair, burned flesh, burning vegetation and the sulfur of bombs) with (1) a certain situation (the sight of decapitated bodies, intestines protruding from shrapnel-injured abdomens and skulls with the brain spilling out), (2) specific somatic states (e.g. hunger, palpitations) and (3) fears (being killed by bombs and shooting).

Cigarette Smoke During the Khmer Rouge period, cigarette smoking was an extremely common habit. For one, it helped to keep away insects such as mosquitoes. The Khmer Rouge constantly smoked, having greater access to tobacco, especially pungent high-quality varieties. Hence, tobacco smoke—

and the image of the cigarette itself—became a marker of starvation and trauma (Foa and Kozak 1998). Furthermore, if a perpetrator smoked, then the victim often developed an aversion to cigarette smoke. Such linkages continue to occur; the first author has had several female patients who developed reactivity to cigarette smoke in the United States after spousal abuse by husbands who smoked.

Burning Flesh In Cambodia, the dead are cremated; the body is placed on wood and then ignited. Patients reveal that cremation produces a very strong odor of burning flesh and hair. Sometimes it is described as sulfurous, at other times it is compared to the odor of perfume or burning food. (Just before cremation, large amounts of perfume are applied to the deceased's body by the surviving relatives, causing some patients to associate perfume with cremation and death.) The odor of burning flesh was encountered during bombings, and burning was also sometimes used as a means of execution and torture. More rarely, large numbers of those who had been executed were burned (see the case of Sokha), though usually the bodies were left to slowly putrefy.

Decaying Corpses It is estimated that 1.5 million Cambodians out of a population of 8 million died during the four-year Pol Pot period due to starvation, overwork, illness, malnutrition or execution (Kiernan 1996). Often these bodies were purposefully left unburied in shallow holes, a warning to those that might transgress against the regime. Khmer Rouge frequently dumped the bodies of their victims into the water-filled rice fields to serve as "fertilizer," and many patients encountered such decomposing corpses while tilling the paddy. During the Pol Pot period, almost every Khmer came across dead bodies—usually on multiple occasions—often bloated and maggot-infested and exuding an overpowering stench. The antithesis to the adjustment to death that burial rites allow for the living (Uwanyiligira 1997): such was the effect of viewing the omnipresent corpses that slowly decomposed in a sickening and macabre image of progressive decay—and viewing the corpses conjured memories of relatives who had been killed and left to the same fate, not receiving proper burial. The corpses also embodied the probable soon-to-be state of the living.

Torture-associated Smells Torture often involved exposure to strong odors. In many cases, patients who were being tortured were confined to small cells, and, like those held there before them, were forced to defecate and urinate within the confines of the prison cell.

House Burning In Cambodia, many patients experienced deliberate or inadvertent burning of their homes or those of their neighbors. Even in America, since patients tend to live in poorer housing districts, it is not uncommon for them to have either experienced or observed residential fires.

Catastrophic Cognitions Regarding Odors and Odor Reactivity

Odors as Head Turners and Dizziness Inducers When in a state of weakness, Cambodians consider the stimuli-scape to be dizziness inducing. Khmer react to smells as would an American to a sudden sound; they demonstrate "smell startle"; there is an orienting response, a turning of the head to find the source of an odor. But it is the forced turning of the head that is most disliked; it causes dizziness. If there are several bad odors, then multiple orienting responses—multiple rotations of the head—occur, and dizziness results. The disturbing effects of a bad odor are compounded by a continual "smell startle," that is, a forced turning of the head in search of the odor's source.

Idioms Configuring Odors as Poisonous Khmer idioms configure odors as dangerous substances that provoke a physical reaction. Various idioms enshrine the idea of a bad odor having the power to invade and poison the body, to provoke "inner wind" (i.e. panic attacks), and to send the brain to spinning. *Chuol* (literally, "penetrating odor") means that the vapor enters the nasal cavities and invades the body and may well cause choking and other bodily symptoms (*Dictionnaire Cambodgien* 1967). *Choengioem chuol* (*choengioem* "burning smell," *chuol* "penetrating odor") describes the pungent and disturbing smell of a burning body (e.g. the sulfurous-like smell of ignited hair). Upon exposure to some unpleasant smell—for example, car exhaust—patients frequently speak of "odor poisoning" (*thwoe aoy pul*). *Lâp* means "to turn or spin, to be overwhelmed and anxious, or to be crazy" (*Dictionnaire Cambodgien* 1967); when a Cambodian claims to be anxious to the point of being *lâp*, the meaning is frequently not only metaphorical: *lâp* denotes the actual spinning of brain matter in the cranium. Cambodians often speak of a strongly pungent smell as causing them to be *lâp*; the patient will aver that the odor was *choengioem lâp* (*choengioem* "burning smell," *lâp* "making-my-brain-spin"; this might be best translated as "making-my-brain-spin burning smell").

"Inner Wind": Smell Sensitivity and "Wind Attacks" Having somewhat increased inner wind (literally, "to be on the verge of a wind attack" *châng kaoet khyâl*) predisposes one to reacting to an odor, and encountering an odor is thought to provoke a "wind attack" (*kaoet khyâl*); that is, the panic symptoms triggered by the odor are interpreted as being produced by "inner wind" (*khyâl*). Cambodians explain most somatic anxiety symptoms by a pathomechanics of wind (see Hinton, Um and Ba 2001a, b): dizziness indicates excessive wind in the head; sore joints, that wind does not travel normally in the limbs and may cause stroke; and nausea, that wind is hitting upward in the body and may ascend to cause dangerous havoc in the body. And any time that bodily symptoms are noticed upon encountering an odor, the symptoms

will be considered evidence of an incipient "wind attack" (*kaoet khyâl*), thereby giving rise to concerns about possible dire events resulting from a pathophysiology of inner wind.

Weak Heart and Smell Sensitivity Khmers believe that "bodily weakness" (*khsaoy kamlang*), especially "heart weakness" (*khsaoy beh doung*), creates smell sensitivity. Being "weak" or having "heart weakness" predisposes one to reacting to odors and, in turn, reacting to an odor "weakens" the body. The body is considered to have a certain reservoir of energy that once exhausted leads to death; a person having a "weak heart" is thought to be at significant risk of dying as a result of heart failure during periods of palpitations. "Heart weakness" is a key aspect of the Khmer traumatic ontology (Hinton, Um and Ba 2002); a sufferer of "weak heart" displays cardiac over-reactivity in response to any stimulus, for example, to a loud noise or an odor. When psychologically distressed, a Khmer may well make the self-diagnosis of "weak heart" and consequently worriedly assess sensitivity to smells. Smell sensitivity in turn confirms the self-diagnosis of "weak heart" and generates fear of death as a result of heart arrest during odor exposure.

Syndrome-generated Olfactory Fear Cambodian illness syndromes—e.g. ideas about "on the verge of a wind attack," "wind attacks," "weakness," and "weak heart" (i.e. the "wind syndrome," "weakness syndrome," and "weak heart syndrome")—result in hypervigilance to olfactory stimuli for those who consider themselves to be suffering from those conditions. In American populations, such syndromes as the "chronic fatigue syndrome," "multiple chemical sensitivity" or the "Gulf War syndrome," likewise lead to olfactory hypervigilance. In the same way, one can speak of *syndrome-generated orthostasis fears* (i.e. fears of dizziness upon standing) in the American syndrome of "chronic fatigue" (Schondorf and Freeman 1999), the Japanese syndrome of "orthostatic dysregulation" (Nozawa et al. 1996), and the Khmer syndrome of "weak heart." Illness syndromes produce anticipatory anxiety about reacting in a particular way to specific situations; bring about significant self-focused attention (in search of the predicted bodily symptoms) as well as anxiety upon being in the feared situation (e.g. encountering the odor or standing); and lead to catastrophic cognitions upon recognizing any bodily symptom indicative of the feared syndrome when in the feared situation (e.g. when encountering the odor or standing).

Metaphoric Resonances to Odors

In a given language, olfactory terms used to label unpleasant smells may serve simply as a classification of unpleasant smells. Or, in other cases, the olfactory terms may be used metaphorically to describe emotional state and person or situation evaluation. For Khmer speakers, bad odors metaphorically elicit ideas of rude speech, poor reputation, evil action, worthlessness and a state of exasperation. For a Khmer, a bad odor may activate multiple metaphoric resonances; a foul odor conjures self-worth, financial, existential and interpersonal issues. Upon being exposed to a disagreeable odor, the related metaphoric meaning networks are activated, bringing to mind present life circumstances that have been encoded in memory—cognized—as being a kind of stench. In addition, as soon as the odor activates a sensation (e.g. nausea, shortness of breath or dizziness), each of these sensations may activate metaphoric resonances. The metaphoric resonances to those sensations (and trauma associations and catastrophic cognitions connected to the odor and those sensations), may contribute to the production of panic.

Therapeutic Approaches to the Treatment of Cambodian Patients with Olfactory Panic Attacks

The multifactorial origins of smell reactivity predisposition should be explored and addressed. The therapeutic approach to the patient with olfactory-triggered panic attack follows from the processes outlined in the multiplex model of panic attack generation (see Hinton et al. in press).

Trauma Associations

Exploring trauma associations to odors acts as a form of exposure that promotes successful emotional processing—modification of trauma networks (Foa and Kozak 1986; Pennebaker 1993; van der Kolk and van der Hart 1991). The patient begins to transform the visual, auditory, kinesthetic and affective aspects of the trauma-event schemas—previously experienced in a fragmentary manner—into linguistic structures that form part of a coherent narrative (Brewin 2001). The act of verbalization changes the nature of representation, that is, transforms a "reliving experience" into a verbal narrative, thereby decreasing the flashback intensity.

   To help the patient successfully cope with the constant undesired recall of traumatic events triggered by olfaction, the patient may be taught to use mindfulness, that is, a multi-sensorial awareness of being-in-the-present-moment, as in attending to the particular color of the sky; the specific shape of a cloud in the sky; the speed by which a cloud drifts along; how the wind causes a leaf to dance in a certain manner; the feeling of wind on the skin; the proprioceptive sense of a particular bodily posture and movement; the inhalation and exhalation of breath in and out of the body at the mouth and nose, accompanied by a rise and fall of the chest; and ambient sounds. Mindfulness may be framed as a form of merit making for the deceased. The person is reminded of the culturally sanctioned duty to make merit for the deceased; survival guilt and a sense of life purpose is thereby promoted.

The patient might be instructed in the utility of carrying a sniffer or "wind oil" upon encountering an odor that triggers trauma memories. The visualization of a soothing scene and muscle relaxation are paired with the aromatic scent of the sniffer. Muscle relaxation and visualization promote recovery in trauma victims (Foa and Rothbaum 1998).

Catastrophic Cognitions

As suggested above, patients may be afraid that flashbacks and reactivity to trauma reminders indicate incipient insanity or bodily demise (Falsetti and Resnick 1997). These fears must be addressed. The patient is taught that panic attack symptoms, as in dizziness and palpitations, may be elicited by reminders of past trauma; they do not indicate "a weak heart" or other physical disorder. The patient should be queried about catastrophic cognitions regarding smell sensitivity (e.g. weak heart or "wind fears"). An alternative model of symptom production is offered; the Western scientific model of the symptoms as being generated by the physiology of the autonomic nervous system (e.g. cold hands as due to non-dangerous vasoconstriction) should be explained.

Metaphoric Resonances

Metaphoric resonances of the sensations induced by the odor should be discussed. For example, an odor may resonate with feelings of being in a state of "the face being enveloped by a poisonous smell" (*krâpul muk*)—metaphorically meaning, surrounded by problems—owing to problems such as an acting-out child.

Dysphoric Associations to Symptoms Induced by the Odor

Patients often have dysphoric associations to the symptoms induced by the odor, as in to dizziness or nausea or shortness of breath. These dysphoric associations—for example, trauma associations, catastrophic cognitions and metaphoric associations—need to be delineated.

Re-association and the Making of a Euphoric Odor Cosmology

In treating olfactory panic, the sufferer should be taught an active—rather than a passive—stance to the olfactory-scape. One chooses, to a significant extent, the odors one encounters and the associations to those odors. The patient should be encouraged to create positive associations to the problematic odor. For example, the smell of gasoline could be used to conjure the pleasure of travel, past joyful car ventures or visiting a particular loved landscape (Classen, Howes and Synnott 1994: 2, 79). In addition, the patient should try to surround her- or himself with pleasurable scents by placing flowers in the home or using perfumes; in this way, olfactory sensations become a gateway to joy and positive memory rather than pain. The patient is encouraged to carry a sniffer and to associate this odor with relaxation and empowering imagery. The slow sipping of fragrant jasmine tea should become a daily meditation. One guides the patient in creating a pleasurable olfactory cosmology. A cosmology at the level of a society is simply a field of potential ways of being. Each person dwells in her or his own cosmology, an enacted and lived-in field of being. One moves through—and dwells in—certain sensori-scapes; smells of the sensori-scape acquire specific "dynamic interpretants" (as defined by Charles Peirce; see Hinton and Hinton 2002). The sensori-scape forms an idio-cosmology, an idio-sensori-cosmology; the odors, acted upon by poesis (Kirmayer 2002, 2003), give rise to an idio-odor-cosmology. A ritual that involves odor only succeeds to the extent that the daily encountered odors now take on new dynamic interpretants that inspire and invigorate.

Summary of Therapeutic Approaches

The following nine core techniques—based on the multiplex model of panic attack generation—can be applied in treating olfactory panic: (1) identifying the trauma associations to the odor; (2) teaching a protocol to be utilized at times of flashback (e.g. an attitude of mindfulness and loving kindness); (3) addressing the catastrophic cognitions concerning odor reactivity; (4) exploring the metaphoric associations to odor reactivity; (5) attempting to create a positive re-association (i.e. new positive dynamic interpretants) to the offensive odor; (6) teaching relaxation; (7) suggesting the use of a sniffer and other essences to gain control of olfactory experience; (8) maximizing the positive associations of the olfactory substance carried by the person – be this a sniffer or other fragrant substance—thereby creating positive associations and visualizations to accompanying the olfaction of the substance; (9) promoting, more generally, positive olfactory experiences (e.g. the mindful drinking of fragrant jasmine tea); and (10) providing the patient with a medication to utilize at times of olfactory panic, as in a benzodiazapine or meclizine.

Olfactory-triggered panic attacks represent an important aspect of trauma-caused disorder in the Khmer refugee population. Future studies should investigate this phenomenon in other groups. Olfactory-triggered panic attacks need to be investigated in a systematic manner in trauma victims and those persons suffering PTSD and panic disorder. Surveys and ethnographic studies of smell sensitivity in trauma victims—and syndromes marked by olfactory sensitivity such as "chemical sensitivity"—represent an important area of future research and clinical intervention. By considering both multifactorial origins of initial odor reactivity and the escalating spiral of panic, a more adequate model of olfactory panic generation emerges.

Note

The authors' facility, Southeast Asian Clinic at Arbour Counseling Services, is located in Lowell, MA.

Bibliography

Brewin, C. (2001), "A Cognitive Neuroscience Account of Posttraumatic Stress Disorder and Its Treatment," *Behaviour Research and Therapy*, 39: 373–93.

Clark, D.M. (1999), "Anxiety Disorders," *Behaviour Research and Therapy*, 37: S5–S27.

Classen, C., Howes, D., and Synnott, A. (1994), *Aroma*, London: Routledge.

Dictionnaire Cambodgien (1967), Pnom Penh: Edition de l'Institut Bouddhique.

Falsetti, S.A. and Resnick, H. (1997), "Frequency and Severity of Panic Attack Symptoms in a Treatment Seeking Sample of Trauma Victims," *Journal of Traumatic Stress*, 10: 683–9.

Foa, E. and Kozak, M. (1986), "Emotional Processing of Fear," *Psychological Bulletin*, 99: 20–35.

Foa, E. and Rothbaum, B. (1998), *Treating the Trauma of Rape*, New York: Guilford Press.

Hinton, D.E., Chhean, D., Pich, V., Safren, S.A., Hofmann, S.G. and Pollack, M.H. (in press), "A Randomized Controlled Trial of CBT for Cambodian Refugees with Treatment-resistant PTSD and Panic Attacks," *Journal of Traumatic Stress*.

Hinton D. and Hinton S. (2002), "Panic Disorder, Somatization and the New Cross-cultural Psychiatry," *Culture, Medicine and Psychiatry*, 26: 155–78.

Hinton, D., Hinton, S., Um, K., Chea, A. and Sak, S. (2002), "The Khmer 'Weak Heart' Syndrome," *Transcultural Psychiatry*, 39: 323–44.

Hinton, D., Um, K. and Ba, P. (2001a), "*Kyol Goeu* ('Wind Overload') Part I," *Transcultural Psychiatry*, 38: 403–32.

—— (2001b), "*Kyol Goeu* ('Wind Overload') Part II," *Transcultural Psychiatry*, 38: 433–60.

Kiernan, B. (1996), *The Pol Pot Regime*, New Haven, CT: Yale University Press.

Kirmayer, L. (2002), "The Refugee's Predicament," *Evolutionary Psychiatry*, 67: 724–42.

—— (2003), "On the Cultural Mediation of Pain," in S. Coakley and K. Shelemay, (eds), *Pain and Its Transformations*, Cambridge: Harvard University Press.

Langer, L. (1991), *Holocaust Memories*, New Haven, CT: Yale University Press.

Ledoux, J. (1996), *The Emotional Brain*, New York: Touchstone.

Nozawa, I., Imamura, S., Hisamatsu, K. and Murakami, Y. (1996), "The Relationship Between Orthostatic Dysregulation and the Orthostatic Test in Dizzy Patients," *European Archives of Otorhinolaryngoly*, 253: 268–72.

Pennebaker, J. (1993), "Putting Stress into Words," *Behaviour Research and Therapy*, 6: 539–48.

Schondorf, R. and Freeman, R. (1999), "The Importance of Orthostatic Intolerance in the Chronic Fatigue Syndrome," *American Journal of Medical Science*, 817: 117–23.

Uwanyiligira, E. (1997), "La Souffrance psychologique des survivants des massacres au Rwanda," *Nouvelle Revue d'Ethnopsychiatre*, 34: 87–104.

van der Kolk, B. and van der Hart, O. (1991), "The Intrusive Past," *American Imago*, 48: 425–54.

Part II

Toposmia

Preface

What a delight to move from one realm of odor to the next, through the narrow streets of an old town! The scent sphere of a candy store makes one think of the innocence and curiosity of childhood; the dense smell of a shoe-maker's workshop makes one imagine horses and saddles, harness straps and the excitement of riding; the fragrance of a bread shop projects images of health, sustenance and physical strength; whereas the perfume of a pastry shop makes one think of bourgeois felicity. Fishing towns are especially memorable because of the fusion of the smells of the sea and of the town; the powerful smell of seaweed makes one sense the depth and weight of the sea, and it turns any prosaic town into the image of the lost Atlantis.

Juhani Pallasmaa, *The Eyes of the Skin*

Many theorists of spatial experience gesture toward the necessity of under-standing places via all of the senses, noting that something like synesthesia or "simultaneous perception" is required (e.g. Hiss 1990; Abram 1996). Yet these theorists neglect to follow through and explore the ramifications of such statements, only to reiterate, ultimately, a methodology centered on visualist and discursive modes. A few examples of smells in certain locations—such as at a farm, bakery or paper mill—may demonstrate the point but leave the more challenging questions of what exactly these sensory experiences mean and how they factor into individuals' cultural and emotional lives unasked and unanswered. What is required is a field of inquiry that could be named *toposmia* ("place" + "smell"), which investigates the spatial location of odors and their relation to particular notions of place (see Drobnick 2002). Explorations of the dynamics of toposmia necessarily integrate a number of disciplines, namely geography, cultural history, sociology and urban studies, as well as aesthetics.

A first step in the toposmic understanding of place is to define how olfac-tion alters traditional visualist conceptions of the landscape, design and architecture (see Tuan 1995; Malnar and Vodvarka 2004). The sensuous geo-graphy demonstrated in J. Douglas Porteous's pioneering essay, "Smellscape," argues that, unlike the information present in vision, olfactory experiences are inherently discontinuous, fragmentary and episodic, that is, time-based. The more subjective and indeterminate qualities of intensity, complexity and affect replace considerations of perspective, scale or distance. Besides exceeding ocularcentric approaches, Porteous outlines several social factors that condition the appreciation and analysis of smellscapes. The sanitization imperative in contemporary culture that seek the removal of all environmental odors—in operation since the era explored by el-Khoury in Part I—contributes to a desensitization of experience, creating what Porteous calls "blandscapes," areas so empty of stimuli that they lead to an alienating sense of placelessness. This is compounded by ever-increasing "smogification," whereby the diversity and subtlety of smellscapes, mostly in urban centers, are overwhelmed by the odors of metal, oil and exhaust fumes. Porteous shows how, despite the trend towards homogenization and increase in pollution, aromatic places remain a significant influence in memory, personal history and sensory cultivation (see also Rodaway 1994; Dann and Jacobsen 2003).

Perhaps because of the diminution of smellscapes an interest in them becomes ever more enhanced. To discover the olfactory in the midst of the aseptic becomes both a challenge and a thrill. "Vagueness Gridlocked," by Eleanor Margolies, discusses the contradictory relationship between mapping and smells, as the rational, authoritative mandate of the map confronts the elusive, evanescent nature of odors. Margolies models her navigation through olfactory New York on previous mapping projects in the eighteenth and nineteenth centuries. The maps of Jean-Noel Hallé, Arthur Young and Charles Booth, in France and England, sought to locate and identify fetid smells, earthly miasmas and stenches produced by humans. Their agenda? To vividly describe what they sniffed in order to spur civic action on the issues of hygienic ventilation, the supervision of natural resources and, covertly, the moral "improvement" of disenfranchised populations. By contrast, Margolies's search for scents within the city's grid is not based on the motive to find and eradicate, but to recover and savor, a task that contains something of an activist element: firstly for the enjoyment of smells that persist despite the best efforts of technological and governmental deodorizing schemes, and secondly as a recognition and valuation of the nonconformist, entrepreneurial lifestyles and the culturally varied communities referenced by those smells (see also University of Minnesota Design Institute 2003).

If the contemporary Western metropolis is an unlikely, though surprisingly fragrant, site for toposmic analysis, places in rural locales where pre-modern agricultural practices are still in operation would seem to offer the full experience of what Erik Cohen (and Uri Almagor) term the "cycle of smells." In this formulation, smells bear meaning not intrinsically, based on their material origin, but contextually, via their position in the continuing ecological cycle of birth, maturation, ripeness, putrefaction and waste.

Items associated with fertility accrue a favorable scent, while those of death are repellent. What is cyclical about these smells, however, is that what was once fertile eventually decays, and what decays eventually serves as fertilizer; hence smells deemed agreeable turn disagreeable and then agreeable once more—thus "completing" the ecological cycle. What causes the cycle to "break," as found in Cohen's title and discussed in his chapter, is the modernist propensity to compartmentalize the elements of the cycle into separate domains, so that the interaction between the pleasing and repulsive stages of smells becomes unnaturally separated and fixed. Examining the squatter settlements in Bangkok in which the transition from rural to urban is incomplete and still in progress, Cohen finds a unique situation of "olfactory dualism," where environmental stenches fade into the background of consciousness, but personal and relatively mild body odors are attended to with hypersensitive vigilance.

Toposmic studies include places where smells organically adhere or exude, yet there are many sites which gain their olfactory dimension through intentional and applied actions. Festival and ritualistic spaces, as investigated in Lucienne A. Roubin's chapter, are often demarcated and consecrated by the introduction of specific, culturally-charged aromas. Such scents performatively configure the boundaries of a temporally defined ritual arena, serve as an aromatic emblem or signal of the event's occurrence, as well as suffuse the air with an unmistakable ambiance intended to please or confront (see also Roubin 1990). Whether it is thirteenth-century *talemeliers* (bakers) employing rosemary as a symbol of acceptance into the professional ranks of the guild, or a bereaved Nepalese family conducting funeral rites and using basil to create a way station for the departed soul to communicate before heading off into the afterlife, or tradesmen in Tarascon who circulate a series of offensive malodors during an annual city-wide procession to keep disasters at bay, scent is an active, facilitating agent in transforming spaces from the ordinary to the ceremonial.

As much as smells can be said to abide in certain locations, they also resist containment and easily transgress boundaries. Hans J. Rindisbacher's "The Stench of Power" is a harrowing analysis of the degrading conditions and unthinkable abuses at Nazi concentration camps. Bringing together accounts by both survivors and perpetrators, Rindisbacher examines the heightened olfactory significance registered in their writings—as the means to debase internees forced to live in filthy, hellish conditions, as the ineradicable evidence that betrayed the truth of the camps' genocidal activities, and as an aesthetic means by which to represent and condemn the criminal inhumanity of the holocaust. This example of toposmia strikingly, painfully, perversely inverts everyday conventions of olfactory associations. Perfume manifests as an instrument of torture; the unidentifiable "sweetish" odor enveloping the camp misleads inmates about the true nature of their fate; the stench of death provides prisoners with the cover for an escape, allowing a few individuals to live; the overpowering odors of the camps mark their horror in the memory of survivors, liberators and, ultimately, to readers after the fact. Here power is enacted upon, evidenced and denounced via olfaction.

In an era of stealthy aroma diffusion technologies, sick building syndrome and scent-free zones, the atmosphere can no longer be taken for granted and has instead become a publicly contested entity. The last chapter in this section, "Environmental Fragrancing," written by aromatherapists Peter Damian and Kate Damian, questions the ethics and efficacy of the recent trend towards ventilating workplaces, institutions, retail outlets and other communal spaces with synthesized scents. Ostensibly promoted to beautify the surroundings and reinvigorate tired employees, the authors argue that the practice of artificially disseminating scents engenders a number of problematics concerning the use of involuntary olfaction for marketing strategies and for subconscious behavior modification. In this case, toposmia is the furthest away from the naturalist conceptualization of smellscape as an anchor for being-in-the-world: odors can be as simulated and as mediated an encounter as any other perceptual feature of the built environment, with the added caveat that the manner in which scents induce physical and psychological effects is little understood—thus little protected against. Perfume bans have been one response to the unconsenting inhalation of manufactured scents, but these measures tend to indiscriminately brand all smells as dangerous and outlaw them for every individual, and so again the specter of odorphobia re-enters the discourse on olfaction.

Jim Drobnick

Bibliography

Abram, D. (1996), *The Spell of the Sensuous*, New York: Vintage.
Dann, G.M.S. and Jacobsen, J.K.S. (2003), "Tourism Smellscapes," *Tourism Geographies*, 5(1): 3–25.
Drobnick, J. (2002), "Toposmia: Art, Scent and Interrogations of Spatiality," *Angelaki*, 7(1): 31–46.
Hiss, T. (1990), *The Experience of Place*, New York: Vintage.
Malnar, J.M and Vodvarka, F. (2004), *Sensory Design*, Minneapolis: University of Minnesota Press.
Pallasmaa, J. (1996), *The Eyes of the Skin*, London: Academy.
Rodaway, P. (1994), *Sensuous Geographies*, London: Routledge.
Roubin, L. (1990), *Le Monde des Odeurs*, Paris: Méridiens Klincksieck.
Tuan, Y. (1995), *Passing Strange and Wonderful*, New York: Kodansha.
University of Minnesota Design Institute (2003), *Twin Cities Odorama*, http://www.design.umn.edu.

7
Smellscape

J. Douglas Porteous

Smell is immensely meaningful to humans. Combined with gustatory sensations, it is responsible for flavor in foods. It is an efficient warning device against contamination. There may be an olfactory component in sexual attraction, and a human pheromone has been isolated. This importance in the matter of food, disease and sex suggests a basic species-survival function for smell. However, Westerners seem keen to eliminate their personal smells, replacing their erased bodily secretions with perfumes derived from, or created as surrogates for, the bodily secretions of other mammals.

Further, smell is an important sense in that it is primarily a very basic, emotional, arousing sense, unlike vision and sound, which tend to involve cognition. Certain smells are, therefore, deeply meaningful to individuals. The smell of a certain institutional soap may carry a person back to the purgatory of boarding-school. A particular floral fragrance reminds one of a lost love. A gust of odor from a spice emporium may waft one back, in memory, to Calcutta. And above all, as we shall see, smells can be memory releasers for the reconstruction of one's childhood.

Environmental aestheticians have called for a more thorough investigation of the environmental aspects of the non-visual senses (Porteous 1982). This chapter will, therefore, pioneer the exploration of the landscape of smell, beginning with an overview of recent findings in psychology. Using the triad person–time–space as an organizing framework, I will investigate smell as a function of person, of place, and of time.

Psychological Bases

Olfactory research in psychology has progressed remarkably since William James (1893: 69) asserted that nothing was known of the chemical senses.

Some of the more important findings, largely based on Engen (1982), are presented here.

The concept of adaptation is vital. The perceived intensity of a smell declines rapidly after one has been exposed to it for some time. Not that the smell disappears, but the perceiver becomes habituated to it, as, in Aesop's fable, the tanner gradually learned to ignore the stench of tanning hides. In everyday terms, one's house has a characteristic smell readily perceived by visitors but apparent to the occupant only after having been away from home for some time. This habituation effect is crucial to humanistic studies, for it will be apparent in later discussions that almost all literary descriptions of smells (with the important exception of childhood memories, which are distanced in time rather than space) are the work of non-residents. Thus, in the humanistic study of smellscapes, as elsewhere, the insider/outsider antinomy (Relph 1976) is a crucial one.

A second important feature relates to the psychology of hedonics. Of the estimated 400,000 existing odorous compounds, Hamanzu (1969) estimates that only twenty per cent are regarded as pleasant by humans. Further, there appears to be a strong tendency to judge unfamiliar smells as unpleasant; this finding relates to the concept of habituation. A matrix with pleasant/unpleasant and familiar/unfamiliar dimensions would yield an overwhelmingly high incidence of odors in the polarized familiar/pleasant and unfamiliar/unpleasant cells. This dichotomy relates to the alerting, warning, function of smell, and provides some support for the importance of the insider (familiar)/outsider (unfamiliar) antinomy in smell perception.

Vast individual and group differences in the sensory response to smell are a third major finding (Gilbert and Wysocki 1987). Although all persons are likely to judge an unfamiliar smell as unpleasant, the same smell may be familiar and pleasant to one individual but unfamiliar and unpleasant to another person. This experience is a common one for outsiders, such as tourists, inner-city visitors to farms and urban newcomers to country living. Industrial occupation is also an important factor. Besides the distinctive odor of coastal fish-packing, the Western Canadian smellscape contains both "sweet" and "sour" regions, product, respectively, of timber processing and natural-gas drilling. The rotten-egg smell of gas can drift for scores of miles, and occasionally envelops the cities of Calgary and Edmonton. Although such smellscapes may be offensive to city dwellers, modern Canadian folklore includes the pulp-mill worker who tells the offended middle-class environmentalist that the sulphite odor of his plant "smells of money," a variation of the old Yorkshire saying, "Where there's muck there's brass."

Further, odor tolerances and preferences appear to be age-related. Children are much more tolerant of basic body smells, such as of sweat and feces, than are adults. Few smell preferences are innate (Engen 1979); most are learned, which shows the importance of cultural adaption and insideness. There is, in fact, little evidence that universally pleasant or unpleasant smells exist, unless the almost universal adult dislike of the feces odor can be so considered. However, generalized preferences, at least among Westerners, appear to favor natural scents, from flowers, fruits and vegetables (Moncrieff 1966). Recent world smell surveys (Gilbert and Wysocki 1987; Radford 1989) suggest banana as the most, and natural gas as the least, preferred smells on the global scale. Inexplicable regional differences, however, are apparent. Generalized dislikes tend to include many chemical and synthetic smells, especially those emitted by chemical factories, food-processing plants, refineries, garbage dumps and most of all, engines, especially diesel engines. Given such generalized preferences, it is unfortunate that the majority of mankind in industrial societies is confined to urban areas dominated by machinekind.

Finally, psychological research indicates that olfaction seems to stimulate emotional or motivational arousal (Engen 1982: 129), whereas visual experience is much more likely to involve thought and cognition. Vision clearly distances us from the object. We frame "views" in pictures and camera lenses; the likelihood of an intellectual response is considerable. By contrast, smells environ. They penetrate the body and permeate the immediate environment, and thus one's response is much more likely to involve strong affect.

Smellscape

The concept of smellscape suggests that, like visual impressions, smells may be spatially ordered or place-related. It is clear, however, that any conceptualization of smellscape must recognize that the perceived smellscape will be non-continuous, fragmentary in space and episodic in time, and limited by the height of our noses from the ground, where smells tend to linger. Only rarely will we find examples of smell isopleths, as in Spencer's *The Salt Line* (1984) where a character remarks: "There's a place along the road where you can smell the Gulf ... You could draw the line of that salt smell on the map."

Smellscape, moreover, cannot be considered apart from the other senses. Many smells provide little information about the location of their source in space. Yet it is common experience that smells are not randomly distributed, but are located with reference to source, air currents and direction and distance from source. In combination with vision and tactility, smell and the other apparently "non-spatial" senses provide considerable enrichment of our sense of space and the character of place. We are all familiar with the fact that places may be characterized individually, or even typed, by smell, from the smell of India, of Mexico, of London from a generation ago during a "pea-souper," of Los Angeles today during a smog alert, to hospitals and the smoking section at the rear of a passenger airplane.

A major problem in studying the non-visual sensory landscape is the general lack of an appropriate vocabulary. Anglo-Saxonically, I incline to "smellscape" and "smell" rather than "odorscape" and "odor." Synonyms for smell are rarely positive (fragrance), often neutral (odor, scent) and frequently negative (stink, stench, reek, pong, hum), while particularly bad smells may be adjectivalized as "noisome," an apparently auditory term. The metaphoric load carried by smell is ambivalent. We may be in bad odor, and thus unlikely to achieve the odor of sanctity. I smell a rat and sniff it out, savoring the sweet smell of success. Further, individual smells are often difficult to describe or name, even though instantly recognizable. This verbalization difficulty is known as the "tip-of-the-nose" problem (Lawless and Engen 1977).

A basic spatial vocabulary can be derived from soundscape studies. Soundscapes consist of sound events, some of which are soundmarks (compare landmarks). Similarly, smellscapes will involve *smell events* and *smellmarks*. "Eyewitness" is replaced by "earwitness" and *nosewitness*. Visual evidence becomes hearsay and *nosesay*. The heightening of visual perception becomes ear-cleaning and *nose-training*.

Surveys and mapping of smellscape may perhaps be performed via *smellwalks* (compare soundwalks, and the Lynchean "walk around the block"). Environmental assessment of smells can be undertaken by questionnaire and interview surveys of the general population, or by teams of highly sensitized, nose-trained experts. A World Smellscape Project might match the former World Soundscape Project, but would find great difficulty with recording. Historical research, in particular, must rely on nosewitness (compare oral history), but it is likely that insiders may not be the best witnesses because of habituation. Recent soundscape work, for example, has cast doubt on the World Soundscape Project's use of elderly residents of a locality as expert earwitnesses (Porteous and Mastin 1985). The value of the elderly as respondents is also reduced by the general decline in sensitivity, discrimination and recognition of sounds, smells and tastes with advancing age.

One alternative is to explore the depiction of smell, both spatially and temporally, in literature. The use of odor in literature emphasizes that, while one may stand outside a visual landscape and judge it artistically, as one does a painting, one is *immersed* in smellscape; it is immediately evocative, emotional and meaningful. Literature, largely British and twentieth-century, provides ample data for the discussion of smells of persons and landscapes in space and through time.

The Smell of Persons

Personal smells vary according to race, ethnicity, culture, age, sex and class. North Americans attempt to banish personal smells and secretions, and prefer floral perfumes, whereas, in the East, "perfumes are heavy, intriguing, sleepy and mildly intoxicating" (Moncrieff 1966: 297). Early-twentieth-century

British writers were astounded by the use of patchouli in the Balkans; until recently, Continentals were far less averse to male perfumery than were the abstemious British (Lowenstein 1966). The milky smell of babies is often liked, whereas the smell of old people or the sick is avoided. An odor of sanctity pervades the corpse of a saint. No war novel is complete without reference to the sweet stench of bloated human remains.

The Viet Cong were reputedly able to scent American troops by their cheesy odor, product of a high consumption of milk derivatives. Similarly, the Japanese once knew Europeans as *bata-kusai* ("stinks of butter"). Europeans and Americans make reciprocal claims. It may no longer be appropriate to mention the highly differentiated smells of the basic human racial groups. In a less anxious age, however, Graham Greene recalls the smell of his Liberian carriers during a trek through the bush:

> [I]t wasn't an unpleasant smell, sweet or sour, it was bitter, and reminded me of a breakfast food I had as a child ... something vigorous and body-building which I disliked. The bitter taint was mixed with the rich plummy smell of the kola nuts ... with an occasional flower scent one couldn't trace in the thick untidy greenery. All the smells were drawn out, as the heat increased. (Greene 1971: 78)

It is significant that Greene records these smells on the first day of the trek; thereafter his record of smells is non-existent.

The northern races have their own peculiar odors. Maclean (1964: 54) records inter-war Russian peasants as "gnarled beings whose drab, ragged, sweat-soaked clothes exhaled a sour odor of corruption." Numerous child-hood reminiscences of English rural life record the strong, wild, acrid smell of Gypsies, a compound of body, food and woodsmoke. Irish laborers were also singled out. Kitchen (1963: 44) came across a group of Irish farm workers boiling potatoes: "The potatoes smelled good, but the Irishmen didn't." Less judgmental was Alison Uttley, who was proffered "a penny with the Irishmen's smell all over it, which she kept in a little box, safe with its penetrating odor, to remind her of them when they were far away" (Uttley 1931: 201).

These may be class smells, for the social classes were, until a generation or two ago, readily distinguished by smell. Laboring peoples' work was dirty and promoted sweating, yet their sanitary arrangements prevented complete cleanliness. Conversely, the well-off sweated less and could wash more. Little wonder, then, that the working classes were long noted for their offensive smell, from Shakespeare's crowds in their sweaty nightcaps to Huxley's (1977: 55) painfully sensitive Denis: "how unpleasant the crowd smelt! He lit a cigarette. The smell of cows was preferable." George Orwell's forays into the foreign fields of Burma, Spain and working-class northern England resulted in writings rich in smells. Sensitive to the prevailing inter-war notion among the elite that the working classes stank, he nevertheless painfully recorded their odoriferous peculiarities, to the intense discomfiture of bourgeois communists.

Within the mass of "great unwashed," of course, some individuals smell much more rankly than others. The limits of tolerance are met in Roberts's *Ragged Schooling* (1976: 40) in the persons of the homeless outcast Ignatius and the "two girls who lived behind the fish frier's you could smell ... at a distance of six feet." As a schoolboy, H.E. Bates (1969: 42) was especially indignant at being made to "sit next to a boy who stinks." This smell event remained strong in his memory: "the peculiar acrid stench of the unwashed lingers in my nostrils." I can confirm the importance of similar episodes, my rural childhood being well-stocked with poor children, Irishmen and Gypsies, whose smells, however, seemed much less important than their interesting selves.

Smell in Space and Place

People are identified with place, and thus become components of a general smellscape. Some smellscapes are large; world geographical regions can be defined *inter alia* by intersubjective odor impressions. Almost invariably, for the reasons already noted, odorous descriptions are the work of outsiders.

No account of India, from Kipling to the recent popular novels of M.M. Kaye and the accounts of Geoffrey Moorhouse and the Naipauls, fails to invoke the peculiar smell of that subcontinent a mixture of dung, sweat, heat, dust, rotting vegetation and spices. The intimate relationship between smell and the exotic, between smell and primeval urges, is exemplified by Kipling's joyous celebration of India's "heat and smells and oils and spices and puffs of temple incense and sweat and darkness and dirt and lust and cruelty" (Fitzgerald 1983).

Africa is equally well-served. Native African writers, such as Ngugi wa Thiong'o, rarely supply significant smell descriptions, unless referring to the impact of the city upon a rural African. White visitors, however, associate certain smells with the continent, as when Greene, smelling the smoke drifting over the sea from Freetown, Sierra Leone, exclaims that "it will always be to me the smell of Africa" (Atkins 1966: 67).

White Africans, however, are aware of greater detail than a simple capsule odor. Entering a "native slum," the white is overcome by visual, auditory and odorific sensations, especially the stench of "urine and dung and rotting meat" (Ruark 1964: 97). Indian bazaars in Nairobi, in particular, are redolent of the Orient: "The howling, reeking bazaars, where every smell known to the East was mingled in one magnificent ripe stink of rotting fruit and dust and dung and curry powder and wet plaster and no plumbing and ancient filthy habits" (Ruark 1964: 97). It is notable that the same author never conjures up the smell of white Africa, and rarely goes beyond sound and visual impressions when dealing with blacks, except when black African meets white and scents a contrast:

> Today he had a great deal of thinking to do, and he did not want to do it permeated by the white smell—the smell of the white man, the white man's food and drink and clothing, the greasy stink of the white man's petrol fumes and belching diesel exhausts. He wanted to do his thinking surrounded by the smells with which he had grown up, the comfortable smells of wood smoke and the acrid reek of goats and the old greasy odor of the hut in which the food was cooked and children born and goats kept at night for safety. (Ruark 1964: 149)

The smell of the internal-combustion engine has become normal in the cities of the Third World, as in the North. For Malcolm Lowry, Mexico City of the 1930s was chiefly noise and smell, and the smell was a compound of old and new, organic and inorganic, "the familiar smell ... of gasoline, excrement and oranges" (1972: 115).

The occupation of the Falkland Islands by Argentine troops in 1982 heightened the contrast between Latin American and British cultures. Returning to windy Stanley after the restoration of British control, Ian Strange noted that the soundscape had radically changed because of the introduction of many more telephone lines. But smellscape changes were more important:

> To me the most striking feature was the smell of the town, a smell of a distinct nature I had noted on weekend evenings during a stay on the outskirts of Buenos Aires: a smell of wood smoke mixed with barbecued meat and seasoned sunflower-seed oil. Although not unpleasant, the wood smoke was alien to this little town, and it brought home yet another feature that demonstrated yet again how different the two cultures are at an individual level. (Strange 1983: 32)

The Third World, then, has its distinctive smell regions. One may distinguish Cuernavaca from Cairo, from Calcutta, from Canton by the nose alone. The urban-industrial world, however, is not immune to regionalization by olfaction. Here the great divide is East and West, First and Second worlds, Capitalist and Communist. Anthony Burgess has characterized the smell "of the essential Russia (an Edwardian smell, really, to match the furniture): tobacco, spirits, port-type wine, fried butter, leather, metal polish" (Burgess 1963: 159) but few visitors to Russia have analyzed so clearly the inescapable indigenous odor of that country as the Scot Fitzroy Maclean, who becomes aware of it, as did Greene in Liberia or Sierra Leone, immediately upon entering the country:

[I]t was then I first noticed the smell, the smell which, for the next two and a half years, was to form an inescapable background to my life. It was not quite like anything that I had ever smelt before, a composite aroma compounded of various ingredient odors inextricably mingled one with another. There was always, so travellers in Imperial Russia tell me, an old Russian smell made up from the scent of black bread and sheepskin and vodka and unwashed humanity. Now to these were added the modern smells of petrol and disinfectant and the clinging, cloying odor of Soviet soap. The resulting, slightly musty flavor pervades the whole country, penetrating every nook and cranny, from the Kremlin to the remotest hovel in Siberia. Since leaving Russia, I have smelt it once or twice again, for Russians in sufficiently large numbers seem to carry it with them abroad, and each time with that special power of evocation which smells possess, it has brought back with startling vividness the memories of those years. (Maclean 1964: 11)

Maclean fails to mention boiled cabbage in this passage. Yet it is notable that many Western writers, wishing to evoke everyday life in totalitarian regimes, resort to the boiled-cabbage smell. Boiled cabbage lingers pungently in the corridors and canteens of Orwell's *1984* (1954). It persists in numerous prison novels. It surfaces in schools, and is used as a reliable indicator of the hopeless, monotonous self-imprisonment of lonely people in boarding-houses; Huxley, for example, laments the despair associated with institutional *"crambe repetita"* (1978: 10).

Continents, countries, regions, neighborhoods (especially "ethnic" ones) and houses have their particular smellscapes. I can recall, for example, the exotic smells of India; the wild-herb scents of rural Greece; the peculiar odor of Humberside mud; the smells of horse, sea and grass on Easter Island; Italian pasta and aniseed in Boston's North End; Arab and Chinese food in its South End; the cedar kindling and dried alder in my woodshed.

The urban–rural distinction is clearly identifiable through the nostrils. In urban areas, as already noted, individual smell events are as figure to a ground of omnipresent vehicle vapors, dimly perceived because of habituation. Individual cities, even urban types, may be distinguished by smell. Pulp-mill towns, colliery towns, leather-working towns, chemical towns, smelting towns, each has its particular type of smell. The small town of Tadcaster, North Yorkshire, home of three breweries, can be distinguished afar by the rich, thick smell of brewing. Nearby Knottingley has an equally rich, biting scent of creosote and tar. A local saying on the Monterey Peninsula once characterized three major towns as Carmel-by-the-sea, Pacific-Grove-by-God (originally a religious retreat), and Monterey-by-the-smell. But change is constant: on returning to Cannery Row in the early 1960s John Steinbeck was met by the scent of tourists rather than by the sickening stench of fish (Hartman 1986).

In heavy industrial centers bad smells were associated with pollution. Until well after the Second World War, every small English town had its gasworks, where coal was gasified for the supply of the town. It was a sweet, sickly and ultimately poisonous smell. Roberts tells of the "noxious vapors" that bourgeois environmentalists claimed had killed a Salford wood early this century. Less concerned with trees than human health, he retorts: "These same 'noxious vapors' we ourselves breathed in concentrated form: our own streets stood immediately under the gasworks in the path of the prevailing winds. Sometimes the air stank abominably for days on end. But very few questioned the right of industry to ruin our health and environment in pursuit of profit. The poor were expendable" (Roberts 1976: 133). Not only expendable, but also invisible and unsmellable. It is not by accident that the West Ends of English cities were located upwind of the East Ends, where lived "the great unwashed."

Judging by accounts such as Roberts's, most urban smells were evaluated negatively. Some individuals, such as Roberts's father, "used to damn the odors endemic to [the] neighborhood" (Roberts 1976: 39), but, in general, the working classes had to adapt to noxious fumes while the well-off moved to suburbs or countryside.

In contrast, accounts of country life, even among the poor, are far more positive with regard to smellscape. Analysis of Beckwith's (1973) autobiography suggests that, while most urban smells are negatively rated, almost all rural smells are regarded as positive. The cottages of the poor were, of course, the scene of bad odors resulting from inadequate sanitation. Cottage life was idealized by the Victorian middle classes, armed with sketchbooks; *Punch,* however, had a different view, at once satirizing middle-class visual perceptions and pointing out the grim reality of another sensory modality:

> The cottage homes of England
> Alas! How strong they smell.
> There's fever in the cesspool,
> And sewage in the well.

> (Woodforde 1969: 5)

Moreover, smelly cottages could soon be left behind for the more positive smellscapes of farm and field. At the farm was "the sweet smell of the cows and the ringing of the milk against the zinc pail" (Ashby 1961: 168). In the fields, "the faint weedy smell ... from the river" and, again, "the sweet animal smell of cows" (Huxley 1978: 118). In farmhouses, "the kitchen had the warm, half-buttery, half-milky smell in which was also mingled the odor of cows and cow manure. There was also about the entire house an ancient and church-like smell, strong with woodsmoke and dampness." On the coast, "the smell of the sea, of seaweed drying in the sun, of plaice being fried for breakfast, of horse-dung and the whiff of vinegar from whelk-stalls." But, on the road, "a pile of soddened dung always steamed on the air, the ammoniac sting of it powerful enough to kill even the aroma of baking" (Bates 1969: 166, 72, 70).

Early-twentieth-century rural smellscapes, then, were redolent with the odors of animals, notably horses and cows. That vegetation was also important in the smellscape will be seen below in "Smellscape in Time." Late-twentieth-century rural places, now well-supplied with pre-packaged food, with high rates of automobile usage, and with factory farming, have lost their distinctive odoriferous character. Indeed, the massing of animals in production-line industrialized agriculture has become a major source of rural smell pollution.

Whether urban or rural, smells identify places in the lived-world, as is especially apparent in H.E. Bates's *Vanished World*. Bates was repelled by the local boot factory, with its "stench of leather and gaslight," and hardly more pleased by long waits in the barber's, where "the smell of shag, after two or three hours, had the power to move mountains." Much more preferable was the bakery: "There was always a great heavenly warmth about it, together with the even heavenlier fragrance of new-baked bread." Indeed, in a few pages Bates provided us with a complete smellscape, not of a house and garden, as Proust did, but of the significant components of a small agrarian town (Bates 1969: 36, 37, 70).

Finally, early-twentieth-century travel was associated with smells one is unlikely to perceive today. The town child was delighted with the sensuous quality of a horse-brake: "the gleaming brass and neatsfoot oil of the harness, the odors of horse-flesh and horse droppings, the summer dust, the harsh crunch of metal wheel rims on the rough stones of the road" (Bates 1969: 32). In contrast, a rural farm laborer is pleased with the new bus service in the 1930s, but still has much regret for the sensuous quality of former travel modes: "In one thing would the carrier's cart beat the modern bus, and that was in the variety of smells. There was tarpaulin over all. Then came leather, then apples and cow-cake, with occasionally a calf or a crate of chickens" (Kitchen 1963: 92). Speed and convenience have clearly been paid for in terms of odoriferous pleasure. Bates's (1969: 85) reaction is clear when he speaks of the advent of the "horseless carriage stinking of oil and petrol."

Smellscape in Time

There appears to be no general history of environmental smells. Social historians of Britain give but passing mention to ambient odors. Yet it is clear that any future historian of the smellscape would have to include: the medieval ripeness of houses, persons and foods; the characteristic smells of "occupational" streets in pre-modern towns, from Bristol's Milk Street to York's Shambles, where one would have encountered the raw reek of butchery and blood; the changes in country scents that came with the planting of many miles of thorn hedges during Enclosure; the animal odors of cities before the development of long-distance milk transport and mechanical intra-urban conveyances and the like.

The development of empire was clearly responsible for the diffusion of exotic smells into traditional smellscapes. I think of the "British" smells of the Indian subcontinent: railways; the English flowers of Indian hill-stations; the characteristic smells of drains, Christian churches and hollyhocks in Rangoon. The process was a two-way one; Victorian gardeners radically altered English smellscapes by importing and acclimatizing hundreds of alien species of flowering plants. In the present century, the growing homogenization of the world smellscape, under the pressure of American-style "sanitization" in housing, clothing and food packaging and display, is a process worthy of study.

Perhaps the most striking change, still possibly accessible to oral historians, is the fairly recent adaptation of huge urban populations to a basic "keynote" smell compounded by metal and oil products. On the more positive side, late-twentieth-century pollution legislation has considerably reduced our opportunity to experience the formerly characteristic odor of British cities, compounded of coal fires, industrial processes and smog.

In this chapter, however, I am chiefly concerned with smells that may be personally experienced on a cyclical basis, smells that recur daily, weekly, seasonally or annually. Smells vary both from day to day and throughout the day. Frosty or dewy mornings are especially conducive to smell generation. At daybreak and at dusk, smells are especially apparent. Weather conditions are important, for rainstorms may stir up "a rich smell of elder flower, hemlock and dogroses" (Kitchen 1963: 24). The landscape smells clean after rain.

The first half of the twentieth century was noted for its weekly smell events. Domestic economy required wash day and baking day. Wash day occurred on Mondays, and children were fascinated by its smells of heat and moisture, to be followed by "the hot smell of iron on calico." Baking day was even more odorous, when "the house smelt rich and sweet of cakes and buttermilk scones and hot jams" and "men and boys came in to enjoy the orgy of heat and scent and promise" (Ashby 1961: 109, 209, 215).

Smells are also indicative and evocative of seasonal change. English villages sixty years ago abounded in seasonal odors. In early summer, at hay-making time, "always the air in June seems to have been clotted with the intoxication of mown grass, or May blossom, of moon-daisies dying along the paling swathes ... the air full of the scent of it, mixed with the fragrance of honeysuckle and meadowsweet and an occasionally pungent pong as the horse broke wind" (Bates 1969: 53, 86). Few rural accounts fail to mention the smellfulness of haymaking, when "all the air is full of scent and hazy mists" (Kitchen 1963: 152). By late summer, "down in the hollows, hovering in the crisp night air, drifted a most appetizing smell of herrings being fried for a late meal ... the warm night was sometimes fragrant with the scent of cut grass; and about this season too, the pungent odor of shallots lying out in the garden to ripen off came in soft whiffs across the hedges" (Bourne 1912: 11). This is a blend of both season-specific and idiosyncratic smells, whereas, for fall, there is only one indicator smell: "raking and burning weeds, the slow blue smoke and pungent smell of which is perhaps the most autumnal of autumnal things" (Horn 1976: 71).

Even in winter, when the sense of smell may be deadened by cold, Kitchen appreciates the healthy "heady smell" of farm manure and "the sweet smell of tobacco on a frosty morning" (1963: 222). Indoors, throughout the winter, store-rooms "smelled of apples, ripe and sweating and laid out ... for keeping" (Bates 1969: 96). And, in spring, one returned to "the smell of new-turned earth, the free life and the fresh air" (Kitchen 1963: 129).

The seasons of rural Portugal are equally explicitly identified by non-visual cues. "The mountain changes its scents and sounds throughout the year" (Jenkins 1979). In spring, the strong smell of eucalyptus fails to mask the wild rosemary or the strong apricot smell of chanterelles. The early summer scent of wild lavender on upper slopes and orange and lemon at lower elevations gives way to a general smell of heated earth in late summer, followed by the "most delicious smell of all ... the sweet freshness of the first autumn rains" (Jenkins 1979: 21).

Annual and occasional events are also recognizable by their associated smells. One recalls the musty smell of church, the deep smell of graveyard earth at a funeral, and the grave release of the rich-smelling "ham tea" that followed. Or the crisp smell of new clothes at Whitsuntide, the rich animal smell of a new pair of shoes actually soled with leather, or the "Flower Show ... the most scented day of all the summer" (Ashby 1961: 202). Irish country fairs are reported perhaps most realistically: "The pleasant smell of fresh dung, the warm smell of animals, and old clothes and tobacco smoke" (O'Brien 1963: 129).

The loss of formerly familiar smells is also a measure of the passage of time, of modernization and change. Many paleotechnic smells will rarely be smelled again. Few of us bake our own bread now. I well remember the sudden advent of soft, wrapped, sliced, steam-baked bread during my childhood in the 1940s. Factory bread merely exemplifies the growing modern tendency towards homogenization and placelessness (Relph 1976). As early as the turn of the century, there was considerable concern that civilization's tendency to eliminate odors would have deleterious effect on human sexuality and aesthetic life in general (Engen 1982). Aldous Huxley, always avant-garde, expressed this in novelistic terms. An English couple enter an Italian store, "filled with a violent smell of goat's milk cheese, pickled tunny, tomato preserve and highly flavored sausage." The lady chokes, reaching for her Parma violets. The shopkeeper retorts:

"*I forestieri sono troppo delcati.*" "He's quite right," said Mr. Cardon. "We are. In the end, I believe, we shall come to sacrifice everything, to comfort and cleanliness. Personally, I always have the greatest suspicion of your perfectly hygienic and well-padded Utopias. As for this particular stink," he sniffed the air, positively with relish, "I don't really know what you have to object to it. It's wholesome, it's natural, it's tremendously historical. The shops of the Etruscan grocers, you may be sure, smelt just as this does." (Huxley 1978: 190)

Relph's fear of placelessness is expressed mainly in visual terms. He may be sure that the world-wide homogeneity of faceless glass buildings will be matched by continuous Muzak and wholesale deodorization. The American motel bathroom, "sanitized for your protection," is the antiseptic symbol of sensuous death. Because all environmental smells cannot be pleasant, we will have none at all.

Smell and Memory

In environmental aesthetics, the intuitive discoveries of humanists or writers are often confirmed, perhaps centuries later, by experiment (Porteous 1982). Nowhere is this truer than in what is now described, by psychologists, as "the Proustian hypothesis of odor memory" (Engen 1982: 98). The adult Proust is irresistibly reminded of the beloved Combray of his childhood by the taste and smell of *petites madeleines*. He generalizes this effect as:

> But when from a long-distant past nothing subsists, after the people are dead, after the things are broken and scattered, still, alone, more faithful, but with more vitality, more unsubstantial, more persistent, more fragile, the smell and taste of things remain poised a long time, like souls, ready to remind us, waiting and hoping for their moment, amid the ruins of all the rest; and bear unfaltering, in the tiny and almost impalpable drop of their essence, the vast structure of recollection. (Proust 1970: 36)

Recent psychological experiments (Engen and Ross 1973; Engen 1977) have confirmed that, while we may distinguish between smells with only twenty per cent accuracy, we are able to remember these smells with almost the same degree of accuracy up to a year later. In contrast, visual recognition shows an almost 100 per cent accuracy within minutes of the original test, but this accuracy rapidly falls off with time. According to Engen (1982: 107–8), "our data clearly support the observations of so many writers, as well as individual experiences [that] time seems to play no role in odor memory." It is suggested that olfactory receptors are plugged directly into the brain's limbic system, the seat of emotion, and that this direct connection between smell and emotion had strategic evolutionary value for our ancestors.

So significant was Proust's suggestion that many subsequent writers have used his smell-generated flashback technique. As early as 1925, Huxley uses the smell of an Italian bay-leaf to take a character back through years of time to the bay rum of a London hairdresser (1978: 46). T.S. Eliot (1974: 23, 28) explicitly links smell with reminiscence in his world-weary urban evocations of "female smells in shuttered rooms," "smells of steaks in passageways," "And cigarettes in corridors/And cocktail smells in bars." Less obviously mannered is Maclean's (1964: 523) meeting with Soviet forces in Yugoslavia: "in a flash I was back in the Soviet Union: the taste ... the stuffiness ... the cold ... and, above all, the smell: that indefinable composite aroma of petrol, sheepskin and vodka, black bread and cabbage soup [there it is!], Soviet scent and unwashed human bodies." Perhaps the most compelling odoriferous description in Greene is his vivid memory of the contrasting smellscapes on either side of the green baize door that divided an alien institutional school from a beloved home (his father was a headmaster): "There would be a slight smell of iodine from matron's room, of damp towels from the changing rooms, of ink everywhere. Shut the door behind you again, and the world smelled differently: books and fruit and eau-de-Cologne" (Greene 1947: 13).

It is less likely that Flora Thompson, an English village postmistress, had read Proust, although she may have encountered similar notions in Kipling or Victor Hugo. Nevertheless, one of her characters "had smelled a beanfield in bloom. The scent had so vividly brought back to her the bean rows by the beehives in her father's garden that she had felt an irresistible longing to see her old home. She no longer had anyone belonging to her living in Restharrow and had not herself been there for twenty-four years, but the impulse was so strong it had to be obeyed" (1948: 10). The "beanflower's boon" was a common feature of memories of Victorian rural summers. More apposite, perhaps, in an era of war and tourist travel, are the musings of James A. Michener (1974: 413): "But in human beings it is the sense of smell ... least regarded of the senses ... which is most powerful in evoking memories; so that now if I smell burnt chicory I am in Fiji, if I smell clean ocean fish, I'm in the Tahiti market. Or a whiff of burnt sulphur can pitch me back into the sugar factories of Queensland."

Most of the early-twentieth-century reminiscences noted earlier are products of this sharp, emotion-laden memory we have for smell. Smell seems especially important in childhood, and adults tend to associate childhood and the childhood home with certain smells. Charles Kingsley, confessing to an insatiable *Heimweh,* frequently mentions olfactory sensations: "the very smell is a fragrance from the fairy gardens of childhood" (Chitty 1974). Jung (1965) tells us that one of his first memories is that of being aware of the "characteristic smell of milk ... It was the moment when, so to speak, I became conscious of smelling. This memory ... goes very far back." And on his first visit to Tunis, archetypically, he felt that the landscape smelled of blood, of perennial soakings from Carthage to the French occupation.

Applications

Whereas zoning regulations have only recently come to grips with the notion of visual pollution, both the legal concept of "nuisance" and general urban zoning laws have long recognized smell as a problem. Noxious land uses, such as chemical factories, glue plants and slaughterhouses, must be adequately segregated from residential and commercial areas. Celebrated cases of nuisance include the foul smell of the Thames in London's Houses of Parliament and the olfactory aggression of a pulp mill on the sister institution in Ottawa. On the positive side, tactile museums for the blind have been matched by the construction of odoriferous gardens for the visually handicapped. Properly designed, such a garden can provide rich olfactory sensations, give directional information and confirm the passage of the seasons. Commercially, odor is an important tool in marketing. The flavor/fragrance industry is involved in most commercial products and ancient treatments such as aromatherapy are being revived in an age of holistic medicine.

Environmental odor, however, has generally been considered only as a negative problem. Just as soundscape is dominated by noise research, so the investigation of smellscapes is almost wholly devoted to odor pollution. A considerable amount of applied research in Scandinavia has dealt with olfactory evaluations of indoor-air quality (Berglund and Lindvall 1979). Traffic smells have aroused considerable interest. Since the late 1960s, a series of international clean air congresses have dealt with problems of theory, measurement and application. The trend appears to be away from mechanical "artificial noses" towards the use of public evaluation and olfactometry. Indeed, Engen (1982: 137) considers that "the human nose may in fact be a better indicator than physical or chemical analysis of pollutant concentrations, especially when the data are obtained by investigators trained in psychophysics." Such an investigator is the aptly named James Rotton, whose work in both laboratory and real world suggests that malodorous pollution may impair task performance and help trigger aggressive behavior, family violence and psychiatric emergencies (see e.g. Rotton 1983).

About half of all complaints about air pollution involve smells. In Sweden complaints about odors range from twenty-seven per cent of rural interviewees to up to seventy-eight per cent in urban areas. Smell-control technology includes odor dilution through heightening emission stacks and the use of scrubbers or combustion. Masking by the introduction of pleasant smells may be effective. Although still largely an urban issue, smell problems are increasing in rural areas. With the introduction of factory farming the noxious smell of animal manure has become a major rural problem. In Britain, officers of the Institute of Environmental Health investigated 3,600 reported nuisances in 1981, fifty per cent more than in 1975. Of these complaints, fifty-nine per cent concerned pigs, twenty-seven per cent poultry, and fourteen percent cattle units. In terms of operations, twenty-seven percent of the incidents involved animal housing, twenty-nine per cent the storage of manure, and forty-four per cent the spreading of manures (Whitlock 1982).

At the household level, smell-masking devices and air fresheners are being replaced by electrostatic air cleaners. Salubrious smells can be programmed into the air-conditioning systems of buildings. This, together with Muzak and "white noise," is yet another step in the regression of urban–industrial civilizations towards total asepsis. On the positive side, it is clear that there is some public interest in the preservation or resynthesis of historic ambiences. To take only two recent examples, the Viking Museum in York tries to re-create the smells (fish, leather, earth) of tenth-century Jorvik, while the smell of the Glasgow underground (subway) system was so addictive that "people in the city have come up with ideas for recreating the smell ... the search to synthesize the whiff of the past goes on. And the idea of preservation takes on a whole new dimension" (qtd. in Goodey and Menzies 1977: 2).

Further, recent research has shown that respondents can readily be trained to improve their skills in the identification and differentiation of smells (Engen 1982). The gap between perfumers, wine-tasters and the general public could, it seems, be narrowed by environmental education (nose training). The French Institute of Taste has already begun to organize taste and smell consciousness-raising classes in schools (Boddaert 1989). Preliminary results suggest that the students enjoy greatly improved sensorial relationships with food, readily become more discriminating than most adults, broaden their sensibilities generally, and even become less resistant to reading Proust!

This is one of the most hopeful results from the psychological research on smell. For to retain a rich, placeful world, individuals must come to appreciate the sensuous complexity of their environments. Smells are an important, though neglected, part of our perceived sensescape. Life in future blandscapes will be severely impoverished if negative smells are annihilated and little effort made to promote pleasant environmental odors. The smellscape is an emotive environment, not an intellectual one, and as such, should be cherished. Asked what they missed during their record-making 211 days in space in 1982, Soviet cosmonauts replied: "the smell of flowers, the city noises, city smells" (Berezovoy 1983).

Bibliography

Ashby, M.K. (1961), *Joseph Ashby of Tysoe 1859–1919*, Cambridge: Cambridge University Press.

Atkins, J. (1966), *Graham Greene*, London: Calder & Boyars.

Bates, H.E. (1969), *The Vanished World*, London: Michael Joseph.

Beckwith, L. (1973), *About My Father's Business*, London: Arrow.

Berezovoy, A. (1983), "Salyut Seedlings Comfort Spacemen," *The Guardian*, 7 January.

Berglund, B. and Lindvall, T. (1979), *Olfactory Evaluation of Indoor Air Quality*, Copenhagen: Danish Building Research Institute.

Boddaert, A. (1989), "French Refine Their Tastebuds in Class," *The Guardian*, 5 March.

Bourne, G. (1912), *Change in the Village*, London: Duckworth.

Burgess, A. (1963), *Honey for the Bears*, London: Heinemann.

Chitty, S. (1974), *The Beast and the Monk*, London: Hodder & Stoughton.

Eliot, T.S. (1974), *Collected Poems 1909–1962*, London: Faber.

Engen, T. (1977), "Taste and Smell," in J.E. Birren and K.W. Schaie (eds), *Handbook of the Psychology of Aging*, New York: Van Nostrand.

—— (1979), "The Origin of Preferences in Taste and Smell," in J.H.A. Kroeze (ed.), *Preference, Behaviour and Chemoreception*, London: Information Retrieval.

—— (1982), *The Perception of Odor*, Reading MA: Addison-Wesley.

—— and Ross, B.M. (1973), "Long-term Memory of Odors with and without Verbal Descriptions," *Journal of Experimental Psychology*, 100: 221–7.

Fitzgerald, V. (1983), "Remembering the Raj," *The Guardian*, 4 September.

Gilbert, A. and Wysocki, C. (1987), "The Smell Survey," *National Geographic*, 172: 514–25.

Goodey, B. and Menzies, W. (1977), *Sensing the Environment*, London: Town and Country Planning Association.

Greene, G. (1947), *The Lawless Roads*, Harmondsworth: Penguin.

—— (1971), *A Sort of Life*, New York: Simon & Schuster.

Hamanzu, T. (1969), "Odor Perception Measurement by the Use of an Odorless Room," *Sangyo Kogai*, 5: 718–23.

Hartman, R. (1986), personal communication.

Horn, P. (1976) *Labouring Life in the Victorian Countryside*, Dublin: Gill & Macmillan.

Huxley, A. (1977), *Chrome Yellow*, Harmondsworth: Penguin.

—— (1978), *Those Barren Leaves*, Harmondsworth: Penguin.

James, W. (1893), *Psychology*, New York: Holt.

Jenkins, R. (1979), *The Road to Alto*, London: Pluto Press.

Jung, C.G. (1965), *Memories, Dreams and Reflections*, New York: Vintage.

Kitchen, F. (1963), *Brother to the Ox*, London: Aldine.

Lawless, H.T. and Engen, T. (1977), "Associations to Odours," *Journal of Experimental Psychology*, 3: 52–9.

Lowenstein, O. (1966), *The Senses*, Harmondsworth: Penguin.

Lowry, M. (1972), *Dark as the Grave Wherein My Friend Is Laid*, Harmondsworth: Penguin.

Maclean, F. (1964), *Eastern Approaches*, New York: Time.

Michener, J. (1974), *Return to Paradise*, New York: Fawcett Crest.

Moncrieff, R.W. (1966), *Odor Preferences*, New York: Wiley.

O"Brien, E. (1963), *The Country Girls*, Harmondsworth: Penguin.

Orwell, G. (1954), *1984*, Harmondsworth: Penguin.

Porteous, J.D. (1982), "Approaches to Environmental Aesthetics," *Journal of Environmental Psychology*, 2: 53–66.

—— and Mastin, J. (1985), "Soundscape," *Journal of Architectural and Planning Research*, 2: 169–86.

Proust, M. (1970), *Swann's Way*, New York: Vintage.

Radford, T. (1989), "Banana Wins by a Nose," *The Guardian*, 8 January.

Relph, E. (1976), *Place and Placelessness*, London: Pion.

Roberts, R. (1976), *A Ragged Schooling*, Manchester: Manchester University Press.

Rotton, J. (1983), "Affective and Cognitive Consequences of Malodorous Pollution," *Basic and Applied Psychology*, 4: 171–91.

Ruark, R. (1964), *Uhuru*, London: Corgi.

Spencer, E. (1984), *The Salt Line*, New York: Doubleday.

Strange, I. (1983), "Falkland Islands: Passing of a Lifestyle," *Geographical Magazine*, 55: 30–5.

Thompson, F. (1948), *Still Glides the Stream*, London: Oxford University Press.

Uttley, A. (1931), *The Country Child*, London: Faber.

Whitlock, R. (1982), "Restoring the Sense of Smell," *The Guardian*, 14 March.

Woodforde, J. (1969), *The Truth About Cottages*, London: Routledge & Kegan Paul.

8
Vagueness Gridlocked
A Map of the Smells of New York

Eleanor Margolies

Key to an Invisible Map

Buoys: Moveable Navigation Markers (Trestle Tables, Wheeled Stands, Portable Racks)

It is possible to navigate by smell. Were you to walk through the city blindfold, you'd know Chinatown by the smell of distinctive vegetables, fish and herbal medicines, or the Financial District by the harsh perfumes and colognes. These odors are not fixed to a site like a shop or a factory, but recur predictably, marking certain districts.

#1 Caramelized sugar: *Peanuts $1/Almonds $2/Cashews $2*. All down the lower half of Broadway, caramelized nuts are prepared, stirred with sugar in heated copper basins. The stoves are kept going even when trade is slow, wafting an olfactory advertisement under pedestrians' noses, a message delivered directly to the sweet-tooth's hypothalamus. This part of Broadway, like Oxford Street, smells of hot sugar; the stands are often on corners, so that you can orientate yourself towards Broadway as you walk down a cross-street.

#5 Incense: *Satya Sai Baba Nag Champa Agarbatti Bangalore (Insist For This Label: To Avoid Imitation Buy From Reputed Dealers Only)*. Higher up Broadway, from Houston and around Union Square, as well as in the East Village, there are sellers of incense, the smoke from one stand blending into the neighbor's. Many also offer religious literature. One man proclaims: *Faggots Will Burn, Lesbians Will Burn*.

#4 Pretzels (Museum Mile): Also candyfloss in bags hanging from a broomstick (the ultimate portable display unit), knishes, fried onions, hotdogs and burgers. Without a permit, traders have to be ready to pack up and move instantly; in any case, at the end of the day, the stands are wheeled away to lock-ups on side-streets or in the suburbs.

Historical Features

Smells can also be navigation points in time, persisting over years, connecting the past and present of an individual or a group of people.

#11 Fish being smoked (Lexington Ave).

#13 Warm laundry: From launderettes with glass fronts (Rivington Street) but also from vents in the broad sidewalks of the Upper East Side, where the big hotels are. Hidden deep below, someone is doing the laundry.

#3 Christmas trees: Heaped at intervals along the streets of SoHo, next to bags of fabric scraps on Mercer Street, and on Park Avenue. Seven six-foot trees outside the Robert F. Kennedy school. The density of households living above the street is revealed, and the streets are never so green as when these trees, still fragrant, are thrown out at the end of the holidays.

#16 Old books (Mercer Street; Astor Place): Musty, discarded books that might eventually take on the smell of a different place, a new reader.

#10 Earth (The New York Earth Room, 141 Wooster Street): The first floor is twenty-two inches deep in earth. The odor of soil is called *geosmia*.

#8 Kossar's Bialystok Bialys: Walk down to Water Street, towards the rich smell of this bakery set among tall apartment blocks. Behind the counter, floury men in white aprons are rolling pieces of dough and setting them to prove on wooden trays. This smell is a node in time: a landmark for A., who grew up in this neighborhood; for me, a smell characteristic of previous visits—a walking breakfast in a brown paper bag. A node in an individual's history, and in the history of the city. Bialys—soft flattened rolls with a dab of sweet, almost burnt, caramelized onion in the center—are named after Bialystok, a city in the east of modern Poland. New York still enjoys the smells of Eastern Europe. (Other evidence: pretzel stands, just like the glass-fronted *obwarzanki* trolleys in Krakow, pickles for sale in huge open barrels outside a store on the Bowery.) And everywhere the smell of vegetables, baked goods and hair-oils that are unfamiliar to me evoke other places, distant homes that are at home here. The persistence of smell is the olfactory equivalent of the "persistence of vision" which creates the illusion of movement from still pictures; smell animates the frozen architecture of the city without our conscious awareness.

Human Smells

Smell is itinerant—carried by people moving through the grid of streets in unpredictable patterns.

#7   Subway: The distinct smells of underground systems in different cities: Glasgow's damp and warm; Paris smells of hot rubber. People are crowded together. A woman is reading a book called *Molecules and Emotions*. A man outside the subway says: "It's gonna rain. I got a cold, but I can smell it."

#14 Stale urine: A man on a subway train in 1996: "Excuse me ladies and gentlemen, I'm grateful for your attention, I've got AIDS and TB…"

#17 Cheesy rotting cloth: On Fifth Avenue a man holds a notice: *Resumes Typed One Hour*. His job is to stand still.

    You can stride through the streets, listening to music and averting your eyes but smells register before you can pinch your nostrils closed. You are forced to acknowledge the presence of other people, of smells you're supposed to like but don't (*Opium, Obsession, Dune*) and smells no one is supposed to like. Perhaps your nausea comes from living in an artificially deodorized environment? If revulsion is a natural reaction what about common humanity? Bad smells feed atavistic fears: talk of drug-resistant TB spores reactivates the old fear of invisible miasmas. In 1996 I was afraid of the coughs of homeless travelers on the subway, more afraid than a healthy, well-fed young person with access to free health-care need have been.

Global Smells

#12 Fragrance Cassette Herbal Pine (Cafe, West Broadway): *Employees Must Wash Their Hands*. An automatic dispenser sprays every visitor to the toilets with fragrance. Now I'll smell like someone who smelt so bad they had to be disinfected.

#6   Perfume store (Mercer Street):
Creative scents: *note coco, note fleur d'oranger, note clementine, note rose, note fraise*
Heavenly scents: *note pomme, note miel*
Warm scents: *note vanille*
Sensuous scents: *note pacifique, note marine, note violette, note romarin*
Colorful scents: *note passion, note fraise, note framboise, note caramel*
Unique scents: *note pacifique, note ciel, note cascade*

    While personal smell is ruthlessly eliminated, a "unique" or "creative" scent identity can be purchased for $2. Smell is branded and trademarked just like words and images.

#15 Detergent: Kellie said: "You smell so good, you smell like Tide."

#2   **PVC** (Canal Street Plastics Warehouse): The delicious smell of vinyl. When I went from America to England on a plane the first time, I had a transparent blue case for my book and coloring pencils and it smelled heavenly, like the soft heads of dolls. The smell of mold, of rot, signals danger, but we cannot directly sense phthlates, dioxins, radioactivity. We may even be trained from infancy to prefer materials that contain these hidden dangers.

Mapping Smells

Each image that came from America I would sniff, so to speak, with the voluptuousness with which one welcomes the first whiffs of the inaugural fragrances of a sensational meal of which one is about to partake. "I want to go to America, I want to go to America."

Salvador Dali, 1935 (qtd in Koolhaas 1994: 261)

Smells are notoriously difficult to capture or record, each odor being a complex mixture of hundreds of volatile chemicals. Moreover, there seems to be a contradiction between "smelling" and "mapping": maps are made of permanent features, while smell is evanescent, temporary and transitory. A practical map allows users to relate its markings to the landscape they see, but a smell-map records odors that may exist only at the moment of its making; modern maps take an imaginary aerial view, but a smell-map has a human viewpoint, and is made on the ground, walking.

Nonetheless, there have been important attempts to map smells, to record the occurrence of distinct odors in space. A series of smell-maps were made by Jean-Noel Hallé, the first holder of the chair of public hygiene established in Paris in 1794. Early one morning in 1790, for example, Hallé and his friend Boncerf walked about five kilometers along the right bank of the Seine, returning on the opposite bank, keeping a meticulous record of all the odors they encountered. In the same period an English agriculturist and traveler, Arthur Young, was drawing a map of the smells of France: "those at Rouen, Bordeaux, Pamiers, and above all Clermont, choked him" (Corbin 1996: 27). Charles Booth's *Descriptive Map of Poverty* (first published in 1889–91 with *Life and Labour of the People in London*) depends mainly on visual evidence and the views of informants, although references to chemical works, gas works, costers' barrows and meat markets give an impression of the olfactory landscape, and there are occasional descriptions of the air-quality: near the railway, a "large amount of open ground ... compensates for smaller gardens and ... the air is fresh and pure," while in Watergate Street, a "faint fetid smell prevails, overpowered in places by disgusting stench. Rough women, one with head bandaged; others with black eyes; one old harridan sitting on doorstep with dirty clay pipe; shoeless children. Costers, street-sellers, gut-cleaners" (Steele 1997: 145, 151).

Booth's maps had an immediate purpose for, as Rosemary O'Day and David Englander put it, "Social inquiry, for Booth, was not an academic pursuit but a guide to social action" (Steele 1997: 5). Other records of perception may seem less purposeful. However, like prehistoric star maps in stones, or weather notes buried in diaries of previous centuries, what seems to be merely idiosyncratic observation may later become significant. Like the records of changing skies, the perception of the smell world depends on changes in the sensuous texture, and so is unavoidably subjective. It would have been of little help for this map had I used a portable gas spectrometer to provide the chemical analysis of each odor, or even invented sophisticated collecting bottles that would allow you to smell exactly what I smelled. For the cultural meaning of smells is made in interaction with their location and with the previous experience of the one who smells. Gershom Scholem's comment on Walter Benjamin's early interests is suggestive: he "occupied himself with ideas about perception as a reading in the configurations of the surface, which is the way prehistoric man perceived the world around him, particularly the sky" (Scholem 1982: 61). Perception is a "reading": the reading of scientific instruments requires experience and sensitivity to the changes that temperature and pressure can make, as well as the range of human error; in a more literary sense, any reading of the configurations of a surface (a window display, a line of verse) both draws on the experience of the reader and changes the reader. To pay attention transforms the environment—the activity of "collecting" produces a shadow map, a trace of what cannot yet be recorded.

The Vagueness of Smell

The apparent incompatibility between the rational mastery represented in a map and the evanescent, subjective nature of "smelling" is embodied in the encounter between the street-plan of Manhattan and the city's odors. It has been staged many times as a battle between the New World and the Old, between legibility and vagueness, between the visual and the invisible. But smell does not battle or argue back—it evades and persists, insinuating itself into the grid.

Odors—both good and bad—are associated with clouds and smoke, with the intangible and the vague. The word "perfume" comes from the "fumes" of smoke which were originally its medium: concentrated oils or resins were burnt on charcoal, or formed into cakes of incense. Censers are swung in many religious ceremonies; in nineteenth-century Arabia, incense was used to perfume visitors' clothes (Classen, Howes and Synnott 1994: 128–9). Perfume also "goes up in smoke" symbolically: it is an appropriate offering for gods, and it is a luxury because it is always "wasted." Alain Corbin, the great historian of smell, encapsulates the eighteenth-century bourgeois objection to perfume:

What disappeared or became volatile symbolized waste. The ephemeral could not be accumulated. The loss was irremediable. One could dream about recovering and reutilizing waste or about recycling excrement; evaporation was beyond hope. For the bourgeois there was something intolerable in this disappearance of the treasured products of his labor. Perfume, linked with softness, disorder and a taste for pleasure, was the antithesis of work. (Corbin 1996: 69)

If the volatility of precious smells was seen as wasteful, the volatility of bad smells posed a far greater danger. Anxiety about airborne disease is now, as always, an unstable mixture of current scientific opinion and dark imaginings. Newspapers mix reports that one-third of the world's population carries the TB bacterium with features suggesting that obesity might be caused by a "fat virus," caught like a cold on public transport. The vagueness of smells' boundaries is one of their most troubling aspects: a sniff of something bad might remain a trace, or might suddenly overwhelm you. Alain Corbin describes the aim of eighteenth-century pneumatic chemistry as the elimination of "the vagueness of the putrid" in Jacques Guillerme's memorable phrase (qtd in Corbin 1996: 16).

Smells pose a pungent challenge to philosophies of autonomous action—although, according to Auden in "Prologue: the Birth of Architecture":

Some thirty inches from my nose
The frontier of my person goes
And all the untilled air between
Is private pagus or demesne

(Auden 1996: 14)

– smells do not remain attached to their source, nor respect boundaries. US legislation for smoke-free public buildings, workplaces and restaurants appears to be a peculiarly isolated recognition that some actions are not self-contained—an insight that is not applied to other forms of pollution either locally or globally.

Though smell is "vague" in terms of its lack of boundaries and the difficulty in establishing its precise contents, smells can also be "unmistakable" markers of a specific substance or individual. Lyall Watson cheerily lists the smells characteristic of some illnesses:

Typhoid fever smells of freshly baked brown bread. Tuberculosis carries the sour scent of stale beer. Encounters with yellow fever are reminiscent of visits to a butcher's shop. The breath of some diabetic patients has the sharp odor of acetone. (Watson 1999: 114)

The links between disease and odor, now given far less emphasis than other forms of diagnosis, were once a vital aspect of the doctor's training. Hallé, the medical smell-recorder of the eighteenth century, describes the smells encountered in hospital:

> There is a stench that is similar to the one exuded by clothes, and there is a moldy smell that is less noticeable but nevertheless more unpleasant because of the general revulsion it arouses. A third, which might be called the odor of decomposition, may be described as a mixture of the acidic, the sickly and the fetid; it provokes nausea rather than offending the nose. This mixture accompanies decomposition and is the most repellent among all the odors to be encountered in a hospital ... Each infectious material has its distinctive exhalation. Doctors know the special smell of a septic wound, of a cancerous agent, and the pestilential odor that is spread by caries. (Corbin 1996: 3–4)

Although smells appear "vague," they are in fact highly specific, just as each cloud is unique, although vague in form. They appear vague at the limit of our abilities to perceive them—the trained nose of a perfumer or scientific analysis reveal a complexity we cannot "naturally" perceive, but which affects us nonetheless. There are, for example, hundreds of varieties of rose, and the scent of each will vary depending on the conditions in which they are grown, the season, the time of day and even the distance from the rose, because the chemicals that make up the scent vary in proportion and in volatility. So "the smell of roses" that an individual remembers from childhood is specific not generic. The words for smells are evocative for this reason: to speak of smell is to employ poetic openness—"the scent of your mother's hair" is descriptively "vague" but recalls something particular for each individual. However, the scent given to modern manufactured products is universal and unchanging. Under test conditions, most people prefer simulated to natural smells—they are heightened but simplified. As simpler, universal odors replace a variety of complex odors, the diffuseness of "shared" experience narrows.

The Rational Grid

> Architecture = the imposition on the world of structure it never asked for and that existed previously only as clouds of conjectures in the minds of their creators.
>
> Rem Koolhaas, *Delirious New York* (1994: 246)

For Koolhaas, Manhattan was "the product of an unformulated theory *Manhattanism*, whose program—to exist in a world totally fabricated by man, i.e. to live *inside* fantasy—was so ambitious that to be realized, it could never be openly stated" (1994: 10). The structure of this fantasy was the grid, "clouds of conjecture" made solid. Rosalind Krauss describes the grid in modern art as an ambivalent structure, which seems to draw attention to the materiality of paint and canvas, while its artists speak of "Spirit" or "Universal" qualities: "The grid's mythic power is that it makes us able to think that we are dealing with materialism (or sometimes science, or logic) while at the same time it provides us with a release into belief (or illusion, or fiction)" (Krauss 1985: 12).

Everyone knows the image of the Manhattan grid as an expression of dynamic modernism. The abstraction takes a bird's-eye view, rather than a street-level view, using numbers rather than names, blocks rather than landmarks. It gives the stranger the same rights as the long-term resident: once you have a mental image of the island, with its "up" and "down" giving the direction of numbering streets, you can emerge from a subway station in a new district and work out which way to go without having to ask anyone. A rational plan reduces the need for interaction on the street. (In the 1980s this became a principle—tourists were warned not to get out maps as this would invite mugging, but to keep walking as if they knew where they were going—perpetuating the estrangement between residents and visitors.) London, in contrast, has to be learned—its medieval street plan, its alleys, hidden squares and streets at odd angles continue to surprise the resident.

Skyscrapers and Stenches

In the spiraling Guggenheim Museum, a text on the wall near Mondrian's *Still Life with Ginger Pot* (1912) describes the grid as the "supreme structure of spiritual balance and rationality." The painting seems, retrospectively, to anticipate his grid paintings. But what happened to the smell of ginger?

The Manhattan Grid was laid out by Simeon deWitt, Gouverneur Morris and John Rutherford (1811) with twelve avenues running north–south and 155 streets running east–west. The plan of the new city was to leave no room for odors that drift, curl and spiral. New York was to be a "counter-Paris, an anti-London," rejecting those cities' narrow streets, dog-legs and dead-ends, where smells could gather, and air stagnate. This "Futurist city" was to be the bracing spa, "the Baden Baden of that dying stench called Europe" (Benjamin de Casseres qtd by Koolhaas 1994). Cities—European cities—had long been associated with stinks. A writer of 1779 claimed that "Paris may be smelt five miles before you arrive at it." Dickens specialized in London's murky horrors. *Bleak House* opens with a description of the insidious, ubiquitous fog, and its account of the "nauseous air" of the district of Tom-All-Alone's is pivotal to the novel. "Tom" is the name given to the collective emanations of the corrupt individuals who live along this "stagnant channel of mud." Our heroine catches a disfiguring fever from the crossing-sweeper, and so loses the good looks which have visibly connected her to her noble mother, showing that miasmas cross social boundaries and level all ranks of society through infection.

The organization of Manhattan's streets was designed to make the city a self-ventilating system, with the street blocks acting as the shafts and blades channeling stale air out to sea. The architects of the grid compared New York's situation to that of cramped European towns:

> It may, to many, be a matter of surprise, that so few vacant spaces have been left, and those so small, for the benefit of fresh air, and consequent observation of health. Certainly, if the city of New York were destined to stand on the side of a small stream such as the Seine or Thames, a great number of ample spaces might be needful; but those large arms of the sea which embrace Manhattan island, render its situation, in regard to health and pleasure, as well as to convenience and commerce, peculiarly felicitous. (Koolhaas 1994: 20)

The success of this image of the city grid as a hygienic structure can be seen in its immediate exportation to Europe, where many hospital architects made explicit reference to New York in the grid arrangements of wards and skyscraper sanatoria.

Skyscrapers may have thrived in New York thanks to the island's rocky substrate, but they also conformed to one of the principles of the aerist theories, which so influenced Enlightenment architecture: upper stories were believed to be more healthful than cellars and ground-floor rooms. With the help of the elevator (from 1870), residents were liberated from earthy emanations, rejoicing in a "metropolitan paradox" that the "greater the distance from the earth, the closer the communication with what remains of nature (i.e. light and air)." However, as Koolhaas points out, this makes the elevator "the ultimate self-fulfilling prophecy: the further it goes up, the more undesirable the circumstances it leaves behind" (Koolhaas 1994: 82).

Ventilation and surveillance were both promoted by the combination of grid and tower. Alain Corbin argues that the "inextricable link between these hygienic imperatives [proximity to a reserve of pure air and control of the flow of air], between the panoptic aim and the wish to improve moral standards" had been revealed by Jules Michelet, who wrote of the dwellings of the great under the *ancien régime*: "Ventilation, cleanliness, supervision, three equally impossible things—these infinite labyrinths of corridors, passages, secret staircases, little inner courtyards, finally the roofs, and the flat balustrade roofs provided a thousand hazards" (Corbin 1996: 165). Eighteenth-century reformers "nursed the plan of evacuating both sewage and vagrants, the stenches of rubbish and social infection all at the same time" (Corbin 1996: 93). Later, Foucault's accounts of the hospital as a *"machine a guérir"* described the link between hygienic and moral imperatives, a connection that continues to be made, sometimes for the crudest propaganda purposes, as in the Dover newspaper that described "asylum-seekers" as "human sewage."

Mayor "Squeegee" Giuliani has "helped to transform New York City from a scary and anarchic war zone into one of the nation's safest cities. Homicides have plunged by two-thirds, the overall crime rate is at its lowest level in decades" (Grunwald 2001). The success of his "clean-up" campaigns depends on the successful application of an analogy between crime's progress and the epidemiology of infectious diseases; according to Malcolm Gladwell, the idea "that social problems behave like infectious agents" has "begun to attract serious attention in the social sciences." In the subway, graffiti and fare dodging were seen as "broken windows" that "invited" further disorder and serious crime; by addressing smaller offences, the crime level was kept below the epidemic's "tipping point." In the city, "a team of officers go around and break up the groups of young people who congregate on street corners, drinking, getting high and playing dice—and so remove what was once a frequent source of confrontations" (Gladwell 1996).

The targets of the clean-up have been diverse, including "cab drivers, Legal Aid lawyers, bike messengers, hot-dog vendors, street artists, community gardeners" (Grunwald 2001) as well as jay-walkers, people who dodge over subway turnstiles and the homeless. These figures share some qualities: they are not established in permanent locations, but move across the city, living on their knowledge of side streets and abandoned buildings—they are dangerously "vague." Like the whiff of a bad smell that might become a dangerous stench, they need to be directed and rectified. Epidemic theory actually complicates policy-making, because it shows that change is not linear, and that results are not directly proportional to investment. However, the analogy between crime and disease often seems to shape Giuliani's approach to problems in a much simpler way. The homeless are less visible, but their number is no fewer.

What model of city life is promoted by these policies? Is discouraging unofficial gardens and aimless wandering the cost of safety? Can unhealthy and unpleasant smells be reduced without indiscriminate deodorization? In Krzysztof Wodiczko's work on the *Homeless Vehicle Project*, he accepted that given the violent and dehumanizing conditions of the hostels, many homeless people have made a rational choice to live on the streets. Wodiczko worked with homeless individuals to design mobile shelters adapted to the facts of their life—the cold and wet, the need to move with all your possessions at short notice, the collection of recyclable rubbish. A secondary aspect of the vehicles was their visibility. While the sight or sound of other people can be habitually ignored, smell makes the presence of others felt, and its particular power to do so makes it especially reviled. Wodiczko's vehicles make a dramatic statement of presence in a more acceptable medium than smell. Working with people to design their own vehicles, Wodiczko allowed them to define their visual presence. The manipulation of smell messages remains a privilege of those who have access to medicine, bathrooms, a change of clothes and a choice of food.

The Persistence of Smell

"How close are we all to the ground? How much contact do we have with the social terrain when pacing or enjoying that creative freedom? To what degree is our creative life-machine under the control of our ethical consciousness?" asks Wodiczko (1999: xv). Smell, for all its affinity with the clouds, emanates from things and people that lie close to the ground. Merleau-Ponty's rejection of the philosophy of pure vision may recall the contrast between "mapping" and "smelling" with which I began:

> For a philosophy that is installed in pure vision, in the aerial view of the pan-orama, there can be no encounter with another: for the look dominates; it can dominate only things, and if it falls upon men it transforms them into puppets which move only by springs. (Merleau-Ponty 1968: 77–8)

Even in the city of the grid and the skyscraper, designed to be self-ventilating and supposed to have eliminated the vague, smell persists. There should be no time in New York for reverie, nothing to slow the efficient movement of people, and yet odors rise from cracks and vents, from basement kitchens and laundries, and drift round corners from street markers and bakeries. Moving across the ruled lines of the grid, you breathe: air spirals up the nose, over the folds of the brain and down into the fractal folds of the lungs.

Bibliography

Auden, W.H. (1996), *About the House*, New York: Random House.
Classen, C., Howes, D. and Synnott, A. (1994), *Aroma*, London: Routledge.
Corbin, A. (1996), *The Foul and the Fragrant*, London: Macmillan.
Gladwell, M. (1996), "The Tipping Point," http://www.gladwell.com.
Grunwald, M. (2001), "Cruel to be Kind," *The New Republic*, 15 January.
Koolhaas, R. (1994), *Delirious New York*, Rotterdam: 010 Publishers.
Krauss, R.E. (1985), "Grids," in *The Originality of the Avant-Garde and Other Modernist Myths*, Cambridge MA: MIT Press.
Merleau-Ponty, M. (1968), *The Visible and the Invisible*, Evanston IL: Northwestern University Press.
Scholem, G. (1982), *Walter Benjamin*, London: Faber & Faber.
Steele, J. (ed.) (1997), *The Streets of London*, London: Deptford Forum Publishing.
Taylor, J. (1991), *Hospital and Asylum Architecture in England 1840–1914*, London: Mansell.
Watson, L. (1999), *Jacobson's Organ*, Harmondsworth: Penguin.
Wodiczko, K. (1999), *Critical Vehicles*, Cambridge MA: MIT Press.

9

The Broken Cycle
Smell in a Bangkok Lane

Erik Cohen

In our programmatic paper on the sociology of smell, Uri Almagor and I broach the idea of "the cycle of smell" as a heuristic device through which the structure of the totality of smells in a simple society could be understood.[1] We argue that smells associated with fertility and birth, at the beginning of the cycle, are generally considered pleasant, smells associated with maturation and ripeness, are also well-liked, though they tend to become unpleasant as they intensify into smells of over-ripeness; smells of putrefaction, decay and death, and the associated smells of refuse, garbage and excrement, particularly of human excrement, are considered repellent. However, as substances bearing such smells are used to produce new life, e.g. as fertilizers, they tend to become more pleasant again. Hence, we further argue, the experience of smell ought to be understood emically, in terms of its meaning within the cultural context, and cannot be fully grasped etically, i.e. merely from the olfactory characteristics of the smelling substance. As the meaning of the smell varies according to its location in the olfactory cycle, so does its appreciation. Hence, the smells of animal dung or urine may be appreciated when used, e.g. as symbols of fertility or birth (Almagor 1987); elsewhere, when these same substances are perceived merely as animal excrements, their smell will be experienced as repellent. This argument extends, in fact, the conception that human attitudes to, and actions in, the environment are mediated by culturally determined "environmental orientations" (Cohen 1976), into the area of the anthropology of smell.

In tribal and rural society, particularly prior to the introduction of modern Western agricultural techniques and materials, the cycle of smell is closely associated with the ecological cycle of life. Insofar as the latter is closed, the former will tend to become closed: the odious smell of refuse, through ecological recycling, will become the pleasant smell of the life-giving fertilizer. In contemporary Western urban society, however, the cycle of smells is absent. Instead of an ideally ever self-renewing cycle, a separation takes place between more or less permanent and static "domains of smell," which are closely related to the social organization of space and interpersonal relations within it. Permanently bad and even repugnant smells are legitimate in strictly limited, non-residential, industrial or commercial zones, out of bounds to the general public. Public spaces such as residential quarters, parks, shopping and entertainment areas are supposed to be olfactorily neutral—and smells of any kind in such areas are considered offensive and often banned by municipal sanitary by-laws. Smells are legitimate again in the private space of the home: the regions of personal interaction are made to smell positively, e.g. by flowers or artificial odorizers, while bad smells, e.g. in the toilet, are overcome by powerful deodorizers. Only in the sphere of intimate interaction, such as sexual intercourse, does penetration into the "olfactory bubble" (Hall 1968) of another person's body odors become fully legitimate; under these circumstances, body odor may be perceived as pleasant. However, if a person's "olfactory bubble" extends beyond the immediate environment of his or her body, it may become offensive to others in interpersonal (but not intimate) interactions. Modern civility dictates olfactory neutrality.

The "domains of smell" of the modern Western city are thus ideally arranged along a range, with legitimate bad smells of industrial non-public space on the one extreme, and good smells of personal and eventually intimate space on the other; in between is the olfactory neutral zone of public space. This ideal arrangement is spatially expressed in the modern city in the separation, often by zoning laws, between industrial and residential areas; and in the modern habitation, in the separation between areas of merely personal interaction—e.g. the guest-room or "salon"—and those of intimate contact—e.g. the bedroom.

However, such an ideal arrangement is usually not achieved even in the modern Western city: even here often emerges a "no-man's land" of semi-public space, which is neither under municipal control nor under that of private households. Such semi-public spaces often become depositories of refuse and urinals, whose smells are perceived as offensive, and thus as interfering with the olfactory well-being of the inhabitants of residential areas: the best known example is probably the stench of urine in the entrance halls and staircases of high-rises and slum houses.

I argue in this chapter that between the (ideally) closed cycle of smell of traditional agriculture and the (ideally) statically arranged "domains of smell" of the modern Western city, there is a third typical case—that of the "broken cycle" of smell, found in the slums and squatter settlements of rural-to-urban migrants of Third World cities. Here the natural process of transformation of refuse and garbage has collapsed under the impact of the transition from rural to urban land uses and growing population densities; the "domains of smell," however, have not yet stabilized, due to the perseverance of rural customs of garbage disposal, insufficient or faulty municipal sanitary services and the absence or ineffective enforcement of zoning and other municipal regulations. I shall describe such a situation as it developed in the slum areas of a *soi* (lane) in Bangkok, in which I lived for extensive periods of time between 1981 and 1984, conducting an urban anthropological study.

Smell is of considerable importance in Thai culture. I am, however, unaware of any systematic examination, in the extensive anthropological literature on Thailand, of the classification, meaning or appreciation of smells in Thai society. My own experience in the *soi* indicates that Thais are keenly but selectively sensitive to smells: they are highly sensitive to body odors, but almost oblivious to the stench of disintegrating refuse in the deteriorating environment of the slums in the *soi*. This "olfactory dualism" drew my attention to the place of smell in Thai culture, and forms another basic problem which this chapter seeks to explore.

Smell in Soi Sunlight: The Tolerance for Environmental Stench

A *soi* is a lane or a "small street branching off a main road [*thanon*]" (Allison 1978: 223). In contrast to the roads, the *soi*s are generally narrow, and often deficient in terms of infrastructure, sewerage and sanitation. Dead-end *soi*s are frequently quiet residential neighborhoods; through-*soi*s, which serve as links between roads, however, are often heterogeneous in terms of land uses and population, noisy and congested. The *soi* under investigation, here to be called Soi Sunlight, is a through-*soi*, about 1.5 km long, connecting two of the busiest traffic arteries of the city. Since the ecology of the *soi* has been described at length elsewhere (Cohen 1985), only some basic information relevant to present purposes is given here.

Up to the end of the Second World War, the area of Soi Sunlight was in purely agricultural land-use; it consisted of rice-fields and orchards, which have by now virtually disappeared. In the course of the rapid postwar growth of Bangkok, the rice fields were gradually turned into residential areas occupied by in-migrants from rural regions. These came at first from the provinces surrounding Bangkok, and later on from more remote regions, particularly the depressed North-East (Isan) of the country. Soi Sunlight sprang up along a secondary *klong* (irrigation canal). The wooden shacks constructed on the rice fields adjoining it gradually turned into slums. As the area came to be occupied by the semi-rural neighborhoods of the in-migrants, the Chinese also moved into it, constructing shop houses along Soi Sunlight itself, and on several of the many sub-*soi*s which branch out of it. More recently modern residential houses were added, mostly in the quieter hinterland of the *soi*.

These various kinds of construction penetrated into land originally occupied by the slums. In recent years, especially, substantial parts of the slum area were cleared, to make place for more intensive urban development. Two slums nevertheless still survive in Soi Sunlight, a small one close to Sukhumvit Road, the central artery of this part of the city, and an extensive one closer to the Klong Toei area, which adjoins the port of Bangkok. Altogether, several thousand inhabitants still live in these two slums.

The rice fields on which the slums have been constructed lied low; and since the land has normally not been filled in before the construction of the wooden shacks began much of the area is still swampy: in many places stilted or elevated houses stick out of the water. Narrow, elevated wooden or concrete footpaths run through the slum area and provide an often precarious approach to the shacks from the main *soi*. During the rainy season, the whole slum area is frequently flooded, and even the narrow paths are often half a yard under water. Soi Sunlight itself, though asphalted and several feet higher than the slum area, is badly drained and hence also frequently flooded during the rainy season.

The stagnant swampy water under the shacks and the floodwater on the main *soi* are the principal sources of pollution and stench in the area of the *soi*. The floodwater floats up the refuse which has accumulated at the bottom of the swampy plots and along the narrow paths and deposits it, moist, on the surface. Until recently, the floodwater would also mix with the overflowing sewerage in the middle of the *soi*, in an area adjoining a little market, in front of the bigger of the two slums. Here a black, putrid mass, emitting an acrid stench of human excrement covered the side-street of the market for days on end, while several feet away, in the market area, stall-owners displayed their wares—mainly staple food-stuffs and vegetables—undeterred by the stench.

But even if there are no floods, the stagnant swampy water under the shacks, suffused by accumulated garbage and other refuse, emits a permanent, stifling smell. In the shack in which I lived in 1981, the smell would enter my room on the ground floor through the cracks in the wooden planks, particularly during the evening hours, and provoke a light nausea lasting to the next morning. The stench was occasionally commented upon by the inhabitants, but no actions were taken to eliminate it, e.g. by cleaning out the refuse which accumulated around the habitations. In sharp contrast to even light body odors, the stench did apparently not significantly disturb them.

That the accumulated refuse does not constitute a serious environmental concern to most of the inhabitants of the slums can also be inferred from their treatment of garbage. Like in other slum areas of Bangkok (*The Nation* 1972) garbage removal by municipal garbage trucks is hampered by the ecology of the slums: the trucks cannot enter the narrow paths leading into the interior. The inhabitants are therefore forced, if they desire garbage to be removed, to carry it in big baskets to the main *soi*, where it usually accumulates for a few days, until it is removed by the municipality. Only part of the inhabitants, predominantly those living in the vicinity of the main *soi*, go into the trouble of depositing their garbage on the *soi*. Many, and particularly those living further inside, prefer to throw it onto empty lots within the slum area, in which huge piles of untreated garbage have accumulated over the years. But some people do not go even that far—rather, they simply depose their garbage into the stagnant water under or around their shacks (cf. *The Nation* 1972) or throw it in front of their yards, where it accumulates along the foot-paths. I assume that this custom has been transferred to the urban environment from the rural areas from which most inhabitants hail. In the villages, garbage is frequently simply thrown away to rot in the vicinity of the household compound, often to be later burned or otherwise used as fertilizer. In the urban slum, the garbage cannot be put to agricultural use. Moreover, a significant part of the garbage is of industrial rather than vegetable origin, and hence does not simply rot and disintegrate. In poorer slums, e.g. in Klong Toei, part of the garbage is recycled, as inhabitants try to make a living from the retrieval of such discarded materials as plastic bags. In the somewhat better off slums on Soi Sunlight, however, no such recycling takes place; the garbage is simply left to accumulate, or sink into the swampy waters, only to be floated to the surface during the floods affecting the area.

The pollution of the environment surrounding the habitations is greatest in the smaller of the two slums, in the area along the main *soi*. Here is located a rooming house area of densely built shacks, inhabited by a highly mobile population of singles, mostly single girls, working in tourism-oriented prostitution in the various establishments of a nearby major touristic entertainment area (Cohen 1982, 1985, 1995). The heaped-up refuse along the foot-paths is here in places several feet deep. Big fat rats live beneath the broken wooden planks of the foot-paths, and at night invade the rooms, devouring whatever food has not been safely stored away. During the floods, the refuse creates a messy, stinking mixture with the dirty water, in which float plastic bags, waste paper, tubes, sanitary napkins and an occasional bloated dead rat. The inhabitants waddle through that mess to reach their rooms. The girls, who usually live for just a few months at a time in one place, are altogether oblivious to the filth and stench surrounding them, virtually reaching their doorsteps; in fact, they themselves substantially contribute to it by disposing their garbage around their rooms. Their disregard stands in stark contrast to the extreme care which they devote to their personal cleanliness, to be discussed below.

While the slum areas of the *soi* are thus under a virtually perennial cover of garbage, the main *soi* is marked by a different, but to an outsider not less annoying ambiance. Being a through-*soi*, Soi Sunlight suffers from a heavy load of traffic, particularly during rush hours, when its exits are frequently jammed. The flow of vehicles of various descriptions, and particularly the ubiquitous motorcycles and *tuk-tuk*s (motorcycle-taxis) emit almost continuously a loud noise, which makes communication on the sidewalks and in the many small open restaurants and eating places along the *soi* virtually impossible. The vehicles, and particularly the motorcycles, also disseminate large amounts of smoke into the *soi*. The smoke mingles with the dust and the oppressive, humid heat to create a smog, which lies heavily on the street, entering the lungs of passersby, shop and stall keepers and customers of stores and restaurants. However, the strong smell of oily vehicles, of the smog and of the refuse accumulated on the sidewalks, is to all appearances not particularly offensive to the inhabitants of the *soi*. The little open restaurants and eating stalls are often packed, particularly in the late afternoon and evening hours, when the traffic is heaviest. The noise, smog and smell seem not to disturb the relish with which the locals enjoy their food and drinks.

But not only adults eat and drink in the dirt and smell of the *soi*. Small children belonging to households adjoining the main *soi* are left undisturbed to play, often naked, on the dusty and dirty sidewalks in front of the slums among the piles of stinking, accumulated garbage waiting for disposal.

Environmental degradation and stench are not limited to the slum areas; they are also found in other parts of the *soi* and particularly in the rooming houses adjoining them which also serve a transient population. I lived for a while in one such three-storey house; in the front yard, facing the entrance, an open pile of garbage accumulated for weeks between removals, spreading its stench throughout the area. Several food peddlers sold their products in the yard. In one corner, beneath the staircase, a keeper of a food stall prepared the various hot Thai dishes on open charcoal ovens every morning. Smoke mingled with the acrid smell of burned chili peppers, spread into the staircase and thence into the rooms of the upper floors. Though obviously disturbing the neighbors, nobody objected or asked the stall owner to remove her cooking area elsewhere; rather, most of the residents bought their meals at her stall. This example furnishes further proof that smells which are not of human origin are not perceived as personally offensive in Soi Sunlight; the inhabitants bear with them, as they bear with smells emanating from the environment.

Smell in Soi Sunlight: The Sensitivity to Body Odor

Set against the obliviousness of the inhabitants to the dirt and stench prevalent in their environment, stands their keen sensitivity to odors emanating from the human body.

Personal cleanliness and neatness (*riab roi*) are generally held in high regard in Thai society. In the villages, most people bathe at least once a day, towards the evening, after returning home from work. Even in the slums in the *soi*, people normally bathe at least once and during the hot season often several times a day. Similar attention is paid to the cleanliness of the clothing: many people change clothing every day, some even several times a day, after every outing. Women in particular tend to sniff their clothes, and if they emit even a slight odor, they are discarded and laundered.

While most people in the *soi*, including the slum areas, pay attention to their personal cleanliness and neat appearance, this is particularly the case with the single Thai girls working in tourist-oriented prostitution in the nearby touristic entertainment area. Every evening close to the opening hours of the various establishments, a stream of freshly washed, cleanly dressed, often heavily made-up Thai girls can be observed coming out of shabby shacks of the slum and from other habitations in the *soi*, catching a taxi or *tuk-tuk* on their way to work. Their impeccable appearance stands in sharp contrast to the squalor prevailing in their surroundings. However, while their evening "occupational" attire highlights this contrast, it is important to note that even during the diurnal hours, when they are at leisure at home, they are very much preoccupied with matters of toilet and personal cleanliness. Much of their spare time is spent in bathing, washing of hair and clothes and otherwise taking care of their body and appearance. Their rooms in the slum, though often only sparsely furnished, are generally kept meticulously clean, even if that cleanliness is achieved by the simple expedient of throwing all garbage onto a heap in the yard or onto the narrow path just outside the front yard.

Among the various aspects of personal toilet, particular attention is paid to body odor. Much care is taken to prevent any part of the body from smelling. Like most Thai women, the girls carefully extricate the hair under their armpits, and apply deodorants to them. Perfume, called in Thai literally "smelling water" (*nam hom*), is frequently but discreetly used. Unlike in some other cultures, however, perfume is not used as a substitute for personal cleanliness, but applied only after the body has been carefully washed and deodorized. I was informed that the girls facetiously change the word for "perfume" from *nam hom* to *nam men* (stench water) when someone applies it in order to cover up the odor of his or her unwashed body.

The careful attention to cleanliness and smell which the girls pay to their own appearance is also extended to their customers. In contrast to brothel girls, girls working in tourist-oriented prostitution out of bars and coffee-shops, are able to exercise considerable freedom in the choice of their customers. Body odor is a cardinal criterion of choice: most girls are less repulsed by a man who is old, ugly or obese, than by one who exudes bad body odor. Such men are much despised. Indeed, the term *men* (stench) may be used as a metonym for a general antipathy or dislike for a customer. Some ethnic groups are denigrated by the girls in terms of olfactory stereotypes: thus, many girls refuse to take on Arab customers, though Arabs usually reward the girls more generously than do the *farang* (white European) customers. The almost unanimous explanation given for that refusal is "*Arab men*" (Arabs stink) (cf Hall 1966: 149–50). While for some girls this expression of rejection may be based on actual sense impressions gained from entering the olfactory bubble of Arabs, it appears that for many it is merely a shorthand for their diffuse antipathy for Arab customers, which may be based on such characteristics as their manner with women or their sexual preferences and conduct. It is significant, however, that this antipathy and rejection are expressed in an olfactory idiom.

Discussion

The principal finding emerging from this case study is that the inhabitants of the slum in the *soi*, and in particular the girls engaging in tourist-oriented prostitution, are marked by a pronounced "olfactory dualism": an obliviousness to the non-human smell emanating from the public and, particularly, semi-public spaces; and a keen sensitivity to human body odors, emitted into private or intimate space. Indeed, the stench penetrating a room from the outside, which to a foreigner may appear nauseating, seems to be a much less significant nuisance for the Thai inhabitants of the slum, and hence less a matter of attention and concern, than even a slight odor emanating from the human body. I shall now attempt to interpret this finding in terms of the interplay of some ecological and cultural factors.

Most people in the slums hail from the countryside, even though many of them left their home villages many years ago. Many of the girls, however, moved only recently to the city, mostly from the impoverished Isan region, and some of them still engage in circular migration, going home for the season of extensive agricultural work, and returning to the city during the dead agricultural season.

It appears that the stench in the environment of the slum originates, to a large extent, from the breakup of the typical ecological cycle, and following that, of the "cycle of smell," found in rural areas. In the slum, the refuse is not circulated; neither is it removed by the municipality, owing to faulty sewerage and obstacles to garbage removal from the inner areas of the slum. Refuse accumulates around the slum habitations, as inhabitants keep to the rural habits of discarding garbage into the swampy water on which their shacks are built, and onto yards, empty lots or foot-paths. I suggest that the inhabitants are not concerned with the stench of their surroundings because the smells in the slums resemble those found in the rural areas from which the inhabitants came—although, in the urban environment, the smells are static and do not constitute a "cycle of smell." Due to a kind of "cultural lag" the stench of disintegrating garbage has apparently not yet acquired a negative cultural connotation for the slum dwellers.

To this should be added the fact that the source of the stench is found in the public and semi-public spaces, even though it may penetrate from there into private spaces. Many authors have noted the absence of a civic spirit in Thailand—a low regard and consideration for public matters, which also expresses itself in a marked disregard for the cleanliness and tidiness of public areas; this disregard stands in sharp contrast to the pronounced concern for such matters in the private sphere. The temporariness of a large proportion of the inhabitants of the slums in Soi Sunlight causes an even more limited concern for communal and public matters that can be found in other, more sedentary slums in Bangkok. People do not want to bother with public matters, and confine themselves to the privacy of their homes, in the case of the single, highly mobile girls, to the narrow circle of friends and neighbors living in the same yard. It is significant that in the crowded frontal area of the smaller slum, inhabited mostly by singles, tall fences of corrugated iron have been constructed around the shacks, thus isolating the inhabitants from the wider environment; such fences are not ordinarily found in other slums in Bangkok.

There are two implications to this attitude: first, the inhabitants do not mind the deterioration of their environment, to which they themselves contribute significantly by disposing their garbage in it. Secondly, and more important for our purposes, the impersonal smells emerging from this environment have no negative cultural meaning, and are therefore not offensive to the inhabitants. It could be assumed that if the latter had a high regard for the community, they would not only be concerned with the cleanliness of its environment, but they would also find littering a culturally significant fact—a lack of regard for the community—and hence be aware of and offended by the stench of garbage.

The marked sensitivity of these same people to body odor, in contrast, is closely related to the personalistic character of Thai social structure (Kemp 1984), and the related concern with the preservation of "face" (Mulder 1979: 656) in interpersonal relations. This concern gives rise to an etiquette of appearance and conduct which emphasizes consideration for the other person (*kreng chai*) (Mulder 1979: 64), cleanliness and neatness (*riab roi*). Body odor is repulsive not merely owing to its physical qualities, but because it is a culturally significant, personal smell, which infringes upon the norm of consideration for others, or, in Goffman's (1963: 196–7) felicitous phrase, upon the "situational properties" prescribed in Thai culture. It is important to note that those offended by body odor are not an impersonal public (which can be offended with impunity) but rather concrete other individuals with whom one is in direct, personal contact. Hence, the same person may freely dispose his garbage in the public or semi-public space and thus befoul the environment, or even fill a whole rooming house with acrid smoke; this will not be perceived as a personal offence to others. But he, or particularly she, will have to take much care not to disseminate body odor in interpersonal contact—this will be offensive and cause a loss of face. A smelly person is ridiculed and rejected. For the girls engaged in tourist-oriented prostitution, finally, the prevention of body odor and the use of perfumes became part of the grooming prescribed by their particular occupational subculture; the criteria of selection of their customers, however, among which olfaction plays a major role, continue to be derived from the traditional Thai cultural norms by which the conduct of others, even foreigners, is judged.

The case study thus furnishes additional proof of the argument that human attitudes and reactions to smell are not a direct consequence of the olfactory impressions of the senses, but result from a further elaboration and interpretation of these impressions; these in turn depend on the cultural significance attributed to the smells. In the olfactory sphere, like in all other spheres of human experience, the impressions coming from nature are culturally filtered—and such filtering, in turn, determines human reactions. Since, however, these reactions act back upon nature, they may have important ecological consequences (cf. Rappaport 1971: 246–7, Cohen 1976: 59–60). Thus, malodorous garbage, the stench of which is inoffensive to the Thai slum dwellers, is permitted to accumulate in the environment, even as individuals take considerable care to avoid much weaker body odors, which are culturally offensive. These differential reactions lead, in turn, to a growing deterioration of the environment, accompanied by a contrary tendency towards meticulous personal cleanliness.

Note

1. The citation of this text, unfortunately, could not be located.—ED.

Bibliography

Allison, G.H. (1978), *Jumbo English–Thai Dictionary*, 3rd ed., Bangkok: Odeon Store.
Almagor, U. (1987), "The Cycle and Stagnation of Smells," *Res*, 13: 106–21.
Cohen, E. (1976), "Environmental Orientations," *Current Anthropology*, 17(1): 49–70.
—— (1982), "Thai Girls and *Farang* Men," *Annals of Tourist Research*, 9(3): 403–28.
—— (1985), "A *Soi* in Bangkok," *Journal of Siam Society*, 73(1/2): 1–22.
—— (1995), "Open-ended Prostitution as a Skilful Game of Luck," in M. Hitchcock, V.T. King and M.J.G. Parnwell (eds), *Tourism in South-East Asia*, London & New York: Routledge.
Goffman, E. (1963), *Behavior in Public Places*, New York: Free Press.
Hall, E.T. (1966), *The Hidden Dimension*, Garden City NY: Doubleday.
—— (1968), "Proxemics," *Current Anthropology*, 9: 38–108.
Kemp, J.H. (1984), "The Manipulation of Personal Relations," in H. ten Brummelhuis and J.H. Kemp (eds), *Strategies and Structures in Thai Society*, Amsterdam: Universiteit van Amsterdam, pp. 55–69.
Mulder, N. (1979), *Everyday Life in Thailand*, Bangkok: Editions Duang Kamol.
The Nation, (1972), "The Slum People," 12 March: 11.
Rappaport, A. (1971), "Nature, Culture and Ecological Anthropology," in H.L. Shapiro (ed.), *Man, Culture and Society*, London: Oxford University Press.

10

Fragrant Signals and Festive Spaces in Eurasia

Lucienne A. Roubin

The multitude of scents enveloping humanity surrounds social groups with a heterogeneous and seasonal procession of a widely varying spectrum of smells. This influx of smells delivers a number of messages during daily work or festive activities in the form of a collectively understood ensemble.

This system, created out of olfactory data, designates, classifies and prioritizes objects, animals and humans in the space occupied by the group; simultaneously, it situates them in the temporal course of the seasons. Indeed, by integrating the processions of odors into a network of correlative significations, humans make odor the carrier of a latent message which incites them to action. In other words, in all parts of the world, chains of odors are inherent to a given space, and these odors describe that space by operating within it on a passing or permanent basis.

However, privileged spaces and objects with a maximum concentration of scent can be found in the heart of the human environment. Among these are the places chosen by the group for its festivities. Moreover, whatever the kind of festivity involved—a family celebration of the stage in an individual's life cycle, city or village dwellers' celebrations around a patron saint, or a ceremony to mark admission to a trade or profession—it is set off from the flow of quotidian life. The scenario that keeps the collective memory alive—which is, moreover, always open to innovation—forms its own customs (Frigout 1965), cut off from daily contingencies and completely devoted to accomplishing certain functions which are the reason for its existence.

Moreover, in the case of annual rural festivals, which renew the tacit solidarity among the people of a region under the protection of the patron saint, the order found in the festive space seems to radically invert the day-to-day order. It is a time of "outdoing existence" (*surenchéssiment d'existence*), to use Arlette Frigout's expression (Bastide 1970), and sometimes even of excess, but never to the point of rendering the festivities chaotic.

The Role of the Fragrant as a Messenger of Festive Time

Between examining the numerous links between spectrums of smells and festive spaces, odor's constant role as a messenger of the festive event should be emphasized. All around the world, preparations for festive days inevitably bring with them a series of activities to clean the areas in which the festivities will take place—public buildings, family homes, neighborhood streets and squares. This cleaning campaign creates a regal concentration of scents around it, situating the festive space in the realm of the pleasant. Certainly since antiquity, and probably since neolithic times, human settlements have maintained around their inhabited spaces a register of odors which they believe to be beneficial to their survival, especially in these moments of preparing for upcoming festivities. In sum, as the celebrations approach, processions of fragrances announce the event and prepare the people, in the depths of their existence, by creating an uplifting ambience.

Celebrations also reveal another constant: they configure the festive space itself. This space takes shape in a precise location, one known to all participants, whose borders are often marked by a system of bright signs made of scented bouquets, garlands of greenery or flowers, and multi-colored paper streamers. In this way, the festivity organizes spatial zones which are clearly delineated within the spaces of inhabitation, creating small islands which stand apart from the celebrations. For example, in the discussion below, families grieving a recent loss isolate themselves from the festive area.

Within this known perimeter, fragrant boundary markers are often used to mark out the way to the focal point of the celebrations. Thus fragrant plants are strewn about the ground, a practice found throughout the Middle Ages in Europe, transmitted to Latin America, particularly Guatemala, and still practiced today in the Mediterranean region.

Père Saravelli-Retali's (1910) study of Sartène reveals that at the turn of the twentieth century this custom was still practiced in Corsica for marriages. Small bouquets of flowers, propped up with stones, were placed on the path to the home of the bridegroom. The wedding guests gathered them up and, to the great delight of the children, replaced them with a few small coins.

Today, in Greek churches, laurel and myrtle are strewn in the central aisle on festive days, while on Maundy Thursday on Hydra Island fresh sage is strewn about the holy place (Adam 1971).

With respect to the use of scent to demarcate ordinary and festive spaces, what is the role of fragrance in the very heart of the ceremonial space? What is its place in the metamorphosis of a given geographical space—a village square, a mountain slope, a room for gatherings in a home—from a simple place of things, as Halbwachs (1992) described it, to a revered space that transmits a coherent ensemble of collective images and is thereby made suitable for the celebrations about to take place there?

I will examine these fragrant actors at work in two examples, first in the initiation into a trade in France under the ancien régime, and then in funeral rites in Nepal.

Fragrant Influxes as the Organizer of Trade Practices in France under the Ancien Régime

Thanks to Étienne Boileau's thirteenth-century *Le Livre des Métiers* ("The Book of Trades"), it is known that the guild of *talemeliers*, who were to become known as bakers in the sixteenth century, was classified in the first group of trades in the food industry. It paid the king superintendence fees and, with every change of king, also had to pay a fee to confirm its privileges. After three years of apprenticeship, which were necessary to accede to the title of Companion, a sort of valet/foreman, a member of the guild had to pass another three years in his master's shop, often moreover becoming a part of the family through marriage to the master's daughter. At the end of this final stage, the title of Master, which was out of reach of many son-in-law Companions because of the cost of the banquets and masterpieces that had to be produced, conferred upon the recipient the highest category in the guild. It was bestowed by the guild's leader, the *Grand Panetier*.

For our purposes, it is instructive to examine the framework and modalities of the reception ceremony. The ceremony, a sort of rite of passage from the title of Companion to Master, took place three years after admission to the apprenticeship as Master. It was held in the home of the master *talemelier*, in a room reserved for this purpose. The ceremony was always held on the first Sunday following Epiphany. The new master baker, having paid all the necessary fees, had to bring a new pot of green clay or pottery containing a rosemary bush, complete with its roots. Candy, "sugar peas," oranges and other fruit in season were suspended from its branches (Hivonnait 1990: 168). With the help of other masters and jury members, the new master offered the pot to the *Grand Panetier* with the words "Master, I have completed my time." The *Grand Panetier* then asked the jury members and senior bakers accompanying him "If this is true, if the pot is in the prescribed shape, and if the request can be heard." If the answer was yes, the *Grand Panetier* received the master and admitted him to the guild.

Since antiquity and throughout Europe, rosemary, *Rosmarinus officinalis*, has been a particularly revered aromatic plant. The vast swaths of land that were given over to its cultivation, from England to Poland by way of

Provence, Alsace and Crete, confirm its status even today as a nuptial plant (Roubin 1990). In addition, rosemary was for a long time burned as a religious funerary offering as a substitute for expensive incense.

Rosemary's prestigious status helps explain the induction ceremony of the guild of *talemeliers*. The ceremony was organized around the introduction of the aromatic plant into the guild's hall; the plant had to be living, rooted in earth, and decked out for the celebration, its branches decorated with candies. Properly speaking, it was the influx of scent that put the candidate in a position to be accepted into the guild. The *Grand Panetier*'s question assumes all its symbolic meaning because of the pot of rosemary: being "in the prescribed shape," according to custom, guaranteed the candidate's professional abilities.

In this professional space, the reception hall was protected by the scent of the fragrant emblem and the ritual could proceed in the most favorable way possible. Here, the aromatic fragrance consecrated both the place chosen for initiation into the guild and the recognized professional capabilities of the new member.

Collective memory thus maintains a close connection between fragrance and certain places, with the former transmitting to the latter a quality and power that these in turn confer upon the events taking place in them.

Scented Space and Funeral Rites in Nepal

The Kuswar's celebrations to mark the end of mourning reveal an even deeper connection between festive space and a number of fragrant plants. Ultimately, this connection results in direct communication between the world of the living and the world of the dead and the great beyond. In Nepal, the Kuswar belong to the caste of boatmen and live along the waterways which irrigate the high Himalayan valleys. Corneille Jest has spent many years observing the group, and his work has made it possible to examine this particularly significant ceremony.

Along with the veneration of their ancestors, the Kuswars' beliefs concerning the realm of the dead are an essential element of their religious life:

> Their invisible universe is abundantly populated by *Pitr* (the souls of the dead), to both good and evil effect. Feared by their servants, the lower-ranking divinities known as *Botes*, as well as by various kinds of genies and spirits, [the *Pitr* are] capable of entering the human body. When people are possessed in this way, they acquire certain supernatural powers. (Jest 1994)

The ceremony examined here must be carried out within a year after death. The ritual, which centers on the return of the soul of the deceased, takes place over three days. Jest reports that "It is perfectly codified, and requires the participation of the entire community."

Two complementary sequences are contained within the ceremony, two sequences in which the fragrant takes on radically inverted forms. The first involves the mourning family calling the soul of the deceased and preparing for its welcome in the village before, finally, receiving it into the family home, where its own dwelling has been symbolically drawn. In this space, which is clearly designated by a certain fragrance, the deceased makes his or her wishes known through the voice of a woman in trance possessed by the deceased. The second sequence is that of the villagers' celebration of the *Pitr*. They offer it provisions and a symbolic horse, which are essential to its long journey back to the world of the dead, to which the ceremonial songs insistently invite it to return.

This celebration reveals, from beginning to end, the primordial role the collective consciousness assigns to fragrant plants. These plants, by virtue of their ability to dispense pleasantness, open up communication between the villagers and the world of the deceased and divinities. Several fragrant plants are successively called upon in the songs which structure the ceremony, but the decisive role is reserved for basil, known as *babari* by the Nepalese.

In Eurasia, basil, *Ocimum basilicum*, ranges from a mere culinary herb in the western Mediterranean region to a revered spice that is a means of social exchanges and used in funerary offerings throughout the Middle East (Roubin 1994). It is the Nepalese Kuswar, however, who give it its greatest meaningfulness.

It is already glorified on the first day of the ritual, when songs are sung about the return of the *Pitr* among the living:

> The *babari* flower has a nice scent.
> The *godaveri* flower has a nice scent.
> The *makamali* flower has a nice scent.
> The *diturchangi* flower has a nice scent.
> Come smell the nice scent.

After the family's guests, who have sometimes come from a distance of a day's walk, have entered the house in mourning, the deceased's home is solemnly drawn, in white paint, on the wall facing the door of the house. It is depicted by a large frame divided into sections by vertical and horizontal lines in which the *Pitr*'s belongings are also drawn. Once the drawing is finished, a small cord is hung in front of the frame, from which are hung new clothes for the soul of the deceased about to return. Also hung along this cord are large bunches of basil. During the three ritual days, the space of this individualized drawing on the wall will remain a sacred space. The second day of the ritual is taken up with the preparation of the elevated altar to the souls of the deceased's descendants. This altar is located within the limits of the village but at some distance from its houses. The *Bote*, that secondary divinity which is a servant to the deceased, must also come and take possession of a human body, a young man in his early twenties. Basil is omnipresent in this young man's clothing and accessories.

The young *Bote*, his legs and face smeared with clay, holds a saber with a small bell in his right hand and branches of basil in his left. A little later, the young man, in a trance, begins to dance, and then, accompanied by four young attendants, goes over to the altar built by the village elders. At dusk, the head of the deceased's family, escorted by drums, also goes to the altar. An offering to the deceased's soul is made to the four cardinal points. They then dance about the altar, and then the procession returns to the house while seven young men, their bodies smeared with clay and holding branches of basil in their hands, chant:

> We have in our hands
> branches of *babari*.
> The *babari* flower has a nice scent.
> The *makamali* flower has a nice scent.
> The *godaveri* flower has a nice scent.
> Come, *Pitr*, come!
> Come, *Pitr*, come!

As a rule, Jest explains, the soul of the deceased settles on the basil when the "song of the flowers" is sung without interruption on the way back to the home of the deceased. The basil then begins to tremble, and the person holding it is possessed by the soul of the deceased. The song of the fragrant flowers is once again intoned upon arrival at the *Pitr*'s house. Towards evening, it is sung again inside the house by all present. The members of the family then go out, as does the young *Bote*, carrying his saber and basil. Then a young woman, a branch of basil in her hand, enters into a trance, dances, and soon the soul of the deceased takes possession of her. Hurrying inside the house, she sits at the foot of the drawing on the wall, which is to say in front of the *Pitr*'s home, and begins to speak in a high-pitched voice while those present gather round to listen to her. The head of the family then interprets her words, just as, in ancient Greece, the Delphic priests interpreted Pythia's words at Apollo's oracle. Pythia, we might note, did not hold basil in her hands, but she did chew laurel, another fragrant plant. This account of the Kuswar ritual is an important ethnological contribution to the understanding of ancient rituals still being practiced today.

Thus, throughout the night, the deceased's soul makes its last wishes known. The young woman possessed by this soul anoints the foreheads of the family members with a special oil in order to cleanse them of the impurities of the mourning. The singers intone once again the "song of the flowers and nice scents" as the dawn of the third day of the ritual breaks and the second sequence takes its place.

An initial aspect of this second sequence, which is significant to the analysis here, must be noted: in this second sequence, the basil disappears completely from the ceremonial events. The songs no longer mention it, and the young *Bote*, embodying attendance on the soul, no longer holds basil in his hand but rather sesame flowers. Finally, the song, the signal for the *Pitr*'s departure on its voyage to the land of the dead, refers to the presence of basil on the first day of the ritual but ignores it when it takes leave of the deceased. This is how the *Pitr* returns. It has visited its family, made known its wishes, and must now depart. At the same time, the basil, which for three days has been the *Pitr*'s fragrant incarnation in the village space, disappears in turn. This space is thereby liberated of its visitor from the great beyond and is fully returned to the world of the living.

Through this ritual, the Kuswar of Nepal provide an exemplary illustration of the charge conferred upon the fragrant influx on the space they have prepared. This fragrance, by investing one or another of its different sectors, opens up for these sectors a brief communication with the great beyond, during which the alliance between the entire community and this invisible and fearsome other world is renewed.

Fragrance thus marks out the space of the festivities with a range of permanent or fleeting signals with precise functions. So far in our discussion, all of these fragrances have been pleasant, and it is here that the aesthetic preferences of the group concerned are clearly asserted.

Malodorous Complexes in the Ceremonial Space

An enlarged survey, on the other hand, one attentive to various categories of celebrations, reveals in some cases a series of malodorous complexes which submit the ceremonial space to a veritable hegemony of the disgusting, whose meaning it is our task to decipher.

The festivities carried out around the Tarasque in the Rhone valley in Provence are particularly clear in this respect. The most startling is the one in Tarascon, which takes place the Monday of Pentecost. It centers on the sacrificial procession of the Tarasque, bringing together every member of the trades (Benoit 1949: 242–3). The ceremony was fixed by King René himself who, in 1474, founded the order of *Tarascaïres*, or the Knights of the Taresque. Led by St Martha, patron saint of the city and draped in a blue coat, the Knights were charged with vanquishing the monster.

The procession tours the city, thereby surrounding the houses in a protective circle. This ritual is accompanied by whiffs of malodorous smells which, traditionally, the monster releases, and to which are added misdeeds of all kinds against the people in attendance: here, shepherds smear people with cade (juniper) oil, while further on sailors spray them with dirty water smelling of slime. The approach to the Taresque is particularly fearsome: flares and serpents issue from the mouth and eyes of the monster, while its long tail, a kind of rod carried by fifty men, sweeps passersby out of its path.

Michelet reports that when he attended the event in the nineteenth century, the celebration was not considered successful unless at least one spectator's arm was broken! This sort of outrage shines light on the festivity's primary function: the dragon associated with the Tarasque is part of a family of fantastic beings, identified as early as Greco-Roman antiquity, as having fetid breath. The Hydra of Lerna, Metz's Graoully and the Dragon of Niort, among others, strike down with their stinking breath anyone who comes near.

We know in addition the connection that exists everywhere between social disorder and foul smells. Since Mesopotamian times, this connection derives from the constant collusion between disgusting smells and demonic forces, while pleasant smells are always associated with benevolent divinities.

The procession of the Tarasque is consistent with this point of view. Through the ceremonial use of misdeeds connected to the mythical monster in the malodorous procession, a sort of gigantic abscess of fixation is established. Periodically provoked, it guarantees the inhabited space circumscribed by it an impunity that for ages the inhabitants have entrusted to the protection of their patron saint, St Martha, whose blue coat—Michel Pastoureau's (2001) magnificent work on color proves this—recalls the victory over the monster.

Unlike the pleasant influx, the malodorous, when spread over a given space, becomes a messenger of reprobation towards social disorder and natural catastrophe, and in all cases is a ringing protest against dangers which could be potentially disastrous to a community.

These few examples serve to demonstrate how widespread the practice is of using fragrance to circumscribe festive spaces. In these deployments, specifically chosen scents preside over social gatherings and inculcate a sense of joy and harmony with the environment.

Note

Translated from French by Timothy Barnard.

Bibliography

Adam, G. (1971), private communication.
Bastide, R. (1970), private communication.
Benoit, F. (1949), *La Provence et le Comtat Venaissin*, 3rd ed., Paris: Gallimard.

Frigout, A. (1965), "La Fête Populaire," in *Histoire du Spectacle*, Paris: Gallimard, pp. 265–92.

Halbwachs, M. (1992), *On Collective Memory*, Chicago: University of Chicago Press.

Hivonnait, P. (1990), *Histoire de la Corporation des Anciens Talemeliers à Paris du XIIième au XVIIIième siècle*, Paris: Librairie de la Société du Recueil Sirey, Larorse et Tenin.

Jest, C. (1994), "Le Tambour à Deux Voix, ou le Monde à l'Envers," *Eurasie* 5: 16–57.

Pastoureau, M. (2001), *Blue: The History of a Color*, Princeton: Princeton University Press.

Roubin, L.A. (1990), *Les Monde des Odeurs*, Paris: Méridiens/Klincksieck.

—— (1994), "Hiérophanies Odorantes," *Eurasie* 5: 59–73.

Saravelli-Retali, F. (1910), *Si Sartène m'Était Conté*, Sartène: n.p.

11

The Stench of Power

Hans J. Rindisbacher

Fascism, be it said in passing, will arise in Europe out of this obsession; loathing for what is unclean, hatred for what is impure.

Michel Serres, "Corruption—The Antichrist"

However wild the imagination runs, however sensorially distorted the fictionally created universe—or indeed reality itself—maybe, the original point of reference is always human sensory perception as we know it. Perception is, short of paraphysical and parapsychological phenomena, our only access to what we take to be the world. Regardless of the technological gadgets in use throughout the fantastic worlds of the imagination, they infallibly turn out to be extensions or distortions of the five senses by which we live in our everyday world. It is on this common phenomenological ground of sensory perception that we are able to approach and compare the categorically different texts in this chapter. It is the sense of smell that will validate an experience, fictional or real, as authentic and human. This is a grand claim for the humble sensory mode at the center of this inquiry. It will be modified as it takes shape in our move from one interpretation to the next. Important verification will come from the juxtaposition of two texts by Auschwitz survivors with those written by Nazis directly involved in the running of that camp.

Five Chimneys is the harrowing account of Olga Lengyel from Transylvania, married to a surgeon and in the medical profession herself, who follows her husband, together with her children and her parents, unsuspectingly to Auschwitz/Birkenau, to which he is deported in 1944. She is the sole survivor of the family. The family is carted away in a cattle car, crammed with ninety-six passengers, into the unknown. This "wooden gehenna" is almost surreal, and during the journey to the hell of the camp she tries "to forget reality,

137

the dead, the dying, the stench, and the horrors" (1947: 10). When the train stops, the odors of the dead bodies "in various stages of decomposition" are "so nauseating that thousands of flies had been attracted." The entrance into the camp is marked by a "cool wind that carried to us a peculiar, sweetish odor, much like that of burning flesh, although we did not identify it as that. This odor greeted us upon our arrival and stayed with us always" (1947: 14, 16). The emphatic end position of "always" helps to mark off the camp as the territory of the "sweetish odor," the stench of death. As the newly arrived are marched off to their dwellings, "the strange, sickening, sweetish odor which had greeted us upon our arrival, attacked us even more powerfully now," but the guide tells them that it "is a camp 'bakery'" (1947: 22). Smell is enveloping the camp. Just as there is no smoke without fire, there is no smell without a source. The naive search by the new arrivals for a source and explanation of the odor, and their tracing it to "the bakery" is particularly gripping because it is so tragically ironic. Olfactory conceptualization, always linking the phenomenon to a source, is fooled here because the atrocity of the truth is as yet beyond the grasp of the prisoners, whose encoding mechanism is civilian and human and does not, in any case, include burning human bodies as the source of the smell they notice.

In the life of the camp it is the contrast between the actual smell of things and normal social, civilian associations and encodings that creates permanent alienation: soup normally has a pleasant aroma; in the camp, however, its "odor was sickening"; it is an "evil-smelling liquid" (Lengyel 1947: 27, 29). As olfactory, gustatory and tactile perceptions are senses of proximity and do not allow for even limited distancing, they are the source of constant revulsion. Taste is much less commented on than smell or used to describe the atmosphere of the camp. The reason seems to lie in the two senses' respective importance for survival: in this world of starvation, to eat, regardless of the taste, becomes a more urgent necessity than to smell or to avoid smells.

Because of its relative unimportance in the struggle for survival and because of its strong evocative and associative powers and its memory-triggering function, smell retains a degree of freedom and can be used by the writer to stress the outrageousness of the prisoners' situation, the incredible discrepancy with "normal" civilized life. With (bad) smell is clearly associated the feeling of inferiority vis-a-vis the outside world in whatever limited form it is present. "The herd of dirty, evil-smelling women inspired a profound disgust in their companions and even in themselves" (Lengyel 1947: 45). When Primo Levi, the second principal author discussed here, and two fellow prisoners are allowed to work in the Buna laboratories and are confronted with the regular employees, Levi notices how badly he compares with them: "We are ridiculous and repugnant." But above all he notices how badly he and his companions smell: "We are accustomed to our smell, but the girls [at the lab] are not and never miss a chance of showing it" (Levi 1986: 142).

Two elements are mixed here: the contrast of the camp and civilization, and the awkwardness of meetings with the opposite sex. Whereas the impressions of the other senses fuse into the overall reality of the camp and create this world of its own beyond which an outside hardly seems to exist anymore and within which sensory experience has turned into pain, smell with its strong memory component continues to hint at a civilized life, an outside. The most striking example is Lengyel's account of one of the appearances of the feared Irma Griese, the "blond angel," an "exceptionally beautiful" SS woman. "Her beauty was so effective that even though her daily visits meant roll call and selections for the gas chambers, the internees were completely entranced, gazing at her and murmuring, 'How beautiful she is'" (1947: 147). It is in this "aesthetic torture," degrading the prisoners by hinting at the world outside, that smell plays an explicit role and in fact comes very close to being used actively as an "instrument of torture" and being perceived as such:

> Wherever she went she brought the scent of rare perfume. Her hair was sprayed with a complete range of tantalizing odors: sometimes she blended her own concoctions. Her immodest use of perfume was perhaps the supreme refinement of her cruelty. The internees who had fallen to a state of physical degradation, inhaled these fragrances joyfully. By contrast, when she left us and the stale, sickening odor of burnt human flesh, which covered the camp like a blanket, crept over us again, the atmosphere became even more unbearable. (Lengyel 1947: 147–8)

The "refinement" of perfume versus the "sickening odor of burnt human flesh," the luxury product of an advanced society versus the olfactory trace of its uttermost degradation: this is the span within which the aesthetically or hedonistically defined good and bad smells of normal life take on an ethical and moral dimension. And it is here that the silent truce of power with olfactory aesthetics is laid open to criticism.

Primo Levi's account in *Survival in Auschwitz* and the story of his liberation, followed by his tortuous journey home to Italy through parts of Russia, Rumania and Hungary in *The Reawakening*, are of a less immediate nature, focusing less on explicit cruelty and atrocities than on incidents of a more intimate and individual kind, both positive and negative, thereby creating a more subtle, almost laconic horror, but also leaving room for hope. His first experience after crossing through the gate with its ominous *"Arbeit macht frei"* ("Work will set you free") is of unbearable thirst and of the water he has to spit out because it is "tepid and sweetish, with the smell of a swamp" (1986: 22). The first chapter establishes the camp as a system of rigid rules, as a network of structures that are cut off from everything outside and that completely overturn values and perceptions generally held in the world, but soon become the new norm inside the camp. They do not connect with the outside, yet they allow for strange niches of vague anarchism, both of particular brutality and surprising humanity. Inside, this system is complicated by the confusion of languages, which is "a fundamental component of the manner of living here: one is surrounded by a perpetual Babel, in which everyone shouts orders and threats in languages never heard before, and woe betide whoever fails to grasp the meaning." When language breaks down, the body is in jeopardy. In this state of emptied-out normal meaning and forced understanding of new meanings one "learns quickly enough to wipe out the past and the future" (1986: 38, 36). Before the chemistry exam that will eventually permit him to work at the Buna factory, smell comes up as a social marker: "we will have to go in front of some blond Aryan doctor ... and he will certainly smell our odor, to which we are by now accustomed, but which persecuted us during the first days, the odor of turnips and cabbages, raw, cooked and digested" (1986: 102–3).

When language fails, and all the senses report pain and degradation, smell remains a clearly understood realm of social signification. Smell arises by necessity in an inhuman system, marking victims, separating them from the perpetrators. At the same time, however, and thanks to its function of triggering memory and because it is not essential for survival, smell can imaginatively break through the barriers of the system. It both rubs in the inferiority of the victims and recalls the last remains of imaginative or imagined freedom: "It was warmish outside, the sun drew a faint smell of paint and tar from the greasy earth, which made me think of a holiday beach of my infancy" (Levi 1986: 111). When Levi enters for the first time the well-equipped Buna chemical labs he exclaims:

> How clean and polished the floor is! ... The smell makes me start back as if from the blow of a whip: the weak aromatic smell of organic chemistry laboratories. For a moment the large semidark room at the university, my fourth year, the mild air of May in Italy comes back to me with brutal violence and immediately vanishes. (1986: 139)

Levi emphasizes cleanliness, an issue with which smell is closely associated. In particular he talks about the bathing and cleaning rituals that he undergoes as he passes through the hands of various authorities after the liberation, and he particularly remembers the American procedure: "The only efficient equipment [at the transit camp of St Valentin in Austria] was in the baths and the disinfection room, the West took possession of us by this form of purification and exorcism ... There were about twenty wooden cabins, with lukewarm showers and bath wraps, a luxury never seen again" (1986: 368). There are two earlier accounts of bathing, particularly memorable the one after the prisoners passed into Russian hands:

> Here too, as at every turn of our long itinerary, we were surprised to be greeted with a bath ... I am not questioning that a bath was opportune for us ... But in that bath, and at each of those three memorable christenings, it was easy to

perceive behind the concrete and literal aspect a great symbolic shadow, the unconscious desire of the new authorities, who absorbed us in turn within their own sphere, to strip us of the vestiges of our former life. (Levi 1986: 188)

Bathing and cleaning, the unquestionably necessary medical and hygienic procedure, constitutes a symbolic act. The eradication of the olfactory trace and the restoration of hygiene is a ritual for returning into civilization. One cannot help but think of the perversion of this ritual used by the Nazis at the prisoners' entry into the camps, the promise of a shower, disinfection and fresh clothes.

Smell, with its free play of meaning, becomes invested with the significance of civilization in the prisoners' self-perception. It marks most clearly the borderline of the camp and the world outside in terms of sensory perception. It denounces the abuse of power on the human body. Smell plays an essential role in an *aesthetics of resistance* (Weiss 1975). *Because* it is passive, it is always only reflecting existing power structures, denouncing them.

In support of the claims made for the extraordinary representational role of the olfactory sense in the survivors' accounts, we need to investigate the other side, the people directly involved in the operation of the death camps and the textual strategies employed by them in their dealing with the experience. *KL Auschwitz Seen by the SS* unites three firsthand accounts by Rudolf Höss, Johann Paul Kremer and Perry Broad (Bezwinska 1984). Kremer's is a candid, personally revealing narrative, revealing in its laconic tone, in what it does not say. It permits some immediate insight into a man who, with both a medical and a philosophical doctoral degree, belongs to the intellectual elite of the Third Reich. The diary includes numerous accounts of food and eating. These entries are placed side by side with comments such as: "Quarantine in camp on account of numerous contagious diseases (typhus, malaria, diarrhea)" (10 August 1942). For the following day we read: "Tropical climate with 28 centigrades in shade, dust and innumerable flies! Excellent food in the Home," followed by a detailed description of the meal: "This evening, for instance, we had sour duck livers for 0.40 mark, with stuffed tomatoes, tomato salad, etc. Water is infected. So we drink seltzer water which is served free." These few excerpts from Kremer's early days at Auschwitz suffice to give us an impression of his *modus operandi*. He is clearly aware of the unsanitary conditions around him, the din, dust, the flies, as he is aware of the health risks involved. While he takes appropriate measures for his own person, which is really the only focus of his interest, the prisoners inside the camp, for whom he technically has the medical responsibility, do not even enter his thoughts. Reading Kremer's entries against each other and his whole account against Lengyel's and Levi's reveals a serious disturbance of his perceptive capacities, showing his complete obtuseness toward a large part of the reality surrounding him.

It is this utter disregard for the suffering fellow human beings that is the most striking aspect of this account. The psychological defense mechanism of the Nazi personality takes the form of blocking out the victims' reality and in compensation focusing on one's own bodily and physical reality. Completely in line with, in fact an integral part of, the defense mechanism is the absence of olfactory impressions from Kremer's notes. Smells, with their strong memory component would threaten the psychological closeout mechanism. They would imply participation, involvement, being part of the same reality as the prisoners—and precisely this is to be avoided. It is the outrageous "banality of evil" that strikes one in this diary, the ruthless juxtaposition of comments on the weather, on food, on coat measurements, with gassings and shootings of hundreds of people at a time. It is a psychological and emotional depravity of stunning proportions.

For our purpose, the fact that there are no smells mentioned is significant, and we will return to this point. "Smell no evil, know no evil," seems to be Kremer's motto. Pery Broad's account of his involvement with Auschwitz is drastically different from Kremer's, first and foremost in its form and author–reader relationship. It is a longer and coherent text, written specifically for the British authorities by whom he was arrested after the liquidation of the camp. It is a factually accurate description of the general procedures and daily atrocities of the SS, and it often shows a stance of indignation, criticism and implicit distancing. To an unwary reader it might at first sight even appear as a camp inmate's story, for it takes a seemingly critical position vis-a-vis the SS. It does so, however, by completely omitting the role and the place of the "I"-narrator in the events described: he is simply not present as a person in his own narrative. His stance is that of the classical omniscient narrator who is removed, yet, of course, constantly within observable distance of the events he relates.

It is interesting to observe how this man, living at Auschwitz and taking part in the operations of the camp, employs smell in an open and truthful text that at the same time serves to create distance between its author and the events he relates. While Broad's narrative stance is misleading in its intended distancing effect, it is again at the perceptual level that it becomes clear beyond doubt on which side the narrator really stands. In contrast to Kremer, Broad does mention smells while leaving out all references to food, eating and taste. In the opening pages he describes the living conditions at Birkenau as "considerably worse than in Auschwitz where they were bad enough" and mentions the "sticky bog" and the "mire underfoot" everywhere in the camp and particularly bothersome in "wet and cold weather." In addition to that, "there was nearly no washing water," and "barbarous hygienic conditions, insufficient food rations and hard work, together with other torments" led to innumerable deaths among prisoners after only a short time in the camp (Bezwinska 1984: 141). Broad's tone of near-reproach, which he maintains over the next few pages, is put to the test when he uses smell as a descriptive device. He levels direct accusations against Aumeier, the camp manager, and Grabner, the head of the Political Section, where Broad works. The following scene takes place on the occasion of one of Aumeier's periodic actions of "dusting out" the prison cells in the basement of Block 11:

> The air in these underground corridors was so stifling that breathing seemed almost impossible. The weird atmosphere was enhanced by the suppressed whisperings behind the cell doors, the glaring light of the bulbs, the sharply contrasting [sic] consisted of the warder of the prison and some blockleaders and finally by the death's heads glittering upon the caps of the SS men. (Bezwinska 1984: 146)

This is a scene of truly Gothic proportions, and it is seen from close up. Although not grammatically marked, the narrator gives away his presence in the sensory detail, "the death's heads glittering" and by his breathing the stifling air. "A prison warder opened the first cell door ... A choking stench issued from the crowded, narrow cell" (1984: 146). That he is not inside the cell, but rather with the SS men in the corridor is indicated by the "issuing" of the stench. For the next moment, the narrator steps back a little when he notices that "some of those walking skeletons had spent months in the stinking cells, where animals would hardly be kept," but he closes in again for the description of the shooting that is now to take place and for which the helpless prisoners are led out into the yard between Block 10 and 11. "They felt, [sic] the cold, bloody muzzle of the gun against their necks, they heard the pulling of the trigger." Grabner, Broad adds with the intention of revealing the former's cruelty and brutal unconcern, "could enjoy a substantial breakfast" after a series of such executions (Bezwinska 1984: 149, 150).

Having previously shown the importance of the olfactory in the survivors' accounts, and knowing from other witnesses' testimonies that Broad's is a factual and faithful report of camp life, we may safely claim that he must have been present at the events he describes, and we can even determine with considerable certainty on the basis of this evidence which side he was on. Further clues in this olfactory criminal investigation help us solve the question. We find one when Broad describes in some detail the first crematorium, and then talks about problems with its exhaust system:

> The smoke did not always rise above the chimney in transparent, bluish clouds. It was sometimes pressed down to the ground by the wind. And then one could notice the unmistakable, penetrating stench of burnt hair and burnt flesh, a stench that spread over many kilometers. When the ovens, in which four of [sic] six bodies were burnt at the same time, were just heated, a dense, pitch-black smoke coiled upwards from the chimney then there was no doubt as to the purpose of that mound. (Bezwinska 1984: 159)

The spreading of the smoke or stench over a great distance into the world outside the camp makes the crematorium a focal point of his perspective. He anxiously follows on its escape the trace of the crime that ought to be kept secret. This is unmistakably the perpetrator's perspective. The underlying fear of the spreading of the stench—a fear the victims do not share, while they do notice the stench, as we have shown above—becomes more nagging in the following passage, describing the olfactory emissions after the mass graves of Russian prisoners begin to leak. "The sun shone hotly that summer [1942] upon Birkenau, the only partially decomposed bodies began to fester and a dark red mass poured out from gaps in the ground. The resulting stench was indescribable. Something had to be done about it and quickly" (Bezwinska 1984: 170–1). The concern about the stench becomes even more urgent when the corpses are exhumed and then burned, with Jewish prisoners doing that horrible work and the SS men supervising them receiving extra food and vodka rations in compensation for their unpleasant job. "One could, for long weeks, see dense, whitish smoke clouds rising toward the sky from several spots. Nobody was allowed to come near those places without a special pass, but the stench betrayed the truth about which people round Birkenau had begun to whisper" (Bezwinska 1984: 171). This is, in spite of the grammatically and lexically neutral construction ("one could see..."; "nobody was allowed ...") clearly the SS perspective, the viewpoint of those in the know about the origin of the stench and aware that it should be prevented from spreading. Broad never talks about the smell of everyday objects, of food, for instance; and smell never occurs as an associative stimulus of memory. This would have established him as an individual in his own narrative, a concrete person, which is precisely what he tries to avoid in his choice of narrative stance. It is nevertheless revealed in the perspective and the reference to the stench of the burning bodies. The point is further illustrated in the following scene: "One night the wind drove the unbearably stinking smoke low to the ground. No guard could bear to stay there. That fact was used by two prisoners who knew they had nothing to lose, if they did not gain something, by escaping, and so they made their get away from the spot under cover of the smoke." Although the prisoners escape "under cover of the smoke," which implies visual cover, it is the stench of the smoke that drove the guards away in the first place. The lurking fear associated with this incident has its roots in the threatening revelation of the secret of Auschwitz. "What would happen, if the fugitives, one a French and the other a Greek Jew, managed to get abroad or started to tell the German population about the happenings at Birkenau? It was unthinkable!" (Bezwinska 1984: 171, 172). Broad's concept of revelation seems somewhat naive in its immediacy. Rumors and proofs were already at that time spreading far beyond the neighborhood of Auschwitz, and they were traveling along channels other than smoke signals. As a symbol, however, the events described and Broad's attitude toward them are striking:

how the smoke escapes from the place of the crime; how it transforms itself into words in people's whispering; how it materializes in the two fugitives, confirming the rumors, giving substance to the smoke and stench; how the crime, in short, translates into text across the medium of stench. According to Broad, another such incident occurred, and again stench is at its origin. A "guard got sleepy due to the heat and the stunning smell of the smoke. Two prisoners ran away." They are recaptured, and Broad mentions specifically how much "the *SS-Schütze* Strutz [the failing guard] felt relieved" about it (Bezwinska 1984: 172).

The stench of Auschwitz is a Nazi obsession. It is the unmistakable symbol of their abuse of power, of a power that has degenerated into violence and is aimed directly at the annihilation of its subjects, who are reduced to victims. The obsession with the stench is, in a certain way, the last remnant of bad conscience that the Nazi death machine still reveals. Höss, the ultimate technocrat of that machine, its most diligent and creative administrator, is busily working toward eliminating that bad conscience by eliminating the stench. Höss is a monster of technology, but even he fears the stench escaping from the chimneys of Auschwitz.

Höss's autobiography, written while he was in Polish custody after serving as a witness at the Nuremberg trials, is the most detailed of the three accounts; it is also the most technical and administrative. Höss appears, although he is in charge of the whole operation, as the one most removed from its sordid everyday details. Like Kremer, he is a master at blocking out certain aspects of his surrounding reality. The factual, businesslike tone aiming at explaining technical and administrative details, discussing personnel problems, and giving approximate "production" figures breaks down only in a few places to give way to more human emotions and feelings, some personal worries and complaints. It is these passages that afford us some insight into the psychological and perceptual makeup of the man Höss.

On just one occasion the olfactory is involved, indicating his presence, despite his repulsion, at such a scene of horror. Smell expresses proximity and involvement, and it marks the inescapability of his task and his loyalty to it and to those carrying it out (the guards, I should add, not the Jewish prisoners specially detailed to do the most bestial work), as well as to those who gave the orders. The images he is able to chase away whereas about the memory of the stench we do not know. But it is interesting that in the following it is again vision, the sense of distance, and smell, the sense of proximity, that are combined in the descriptive makeup of the scene. In 1942, as larger and larger contingents of Jews were beginning to arrive at Auschwitz, it became evident that their dead bodies could no longer simply be burned in the open air:

> During bad weather or when a strong wind was blowing, the stench of burning flesh was carried for many miles and caused the whole neighborhood

> to talk about the burning of Jews, despite official counter-propaganda ...
> Moreover the air defense services protested against the fires which could be
> seen from great distances at night. Nevertheless, the burnings had to go on,
> even at night, unless further transports were to be refused. (Bezwinska 1984:
> 112)

Here we have it again, the Nazi concern with the fire that can be seen and
the stench that can be smelled and is stronger than the official propaganda.
Fire and death, the flame and the dead body, two of the most powerful and
archaic human symbols, signifiers of two of the deepest human fears as
well as fascinations, known and commented on for a long time. What has
received much less attention is the action of the former on the latter, the fire
on the corpse, which is not simply its clean and traceless destruction, but
the production of a stench, horrible and loathsome, settling in the olfactory
memory indelibly. The ashes are no cause for concern, neither in the real
world of things nor in the world of memory. They "fell through the grates
... and were taken in lorries to the Vistula, where they immediately drifted
away and dissolved" (Bezwinska 1984: 136), out of sight, out of mind. This
is not so for smell, however, and the odorless burning of the corpses remains
an eternal Utopia of the perpetrators of evil.

In Barbara Hyett's *In Evidence*, the narrated experience is not even of camp
prisoners but of soldiers present at the liberation of the camps, eyewitnesses
of the moment when the gates were opened. "In spite of what preparation
their soldiering might have provided, those who entered the camps could
not believe what they saw there" (Hyett 1986: xii), she says in the preface,
where she also briefly outlines her work, which consists of interviews
with veterans. Her attempt to put these statements into an adequate form
for publication results in turning them into poems. The passage is worth
quoting fully:

> Two years after the first interview, I began the poems about the liberation. At
> first, I tried to write as a child on the train to Dachau, but I could not speak
> for the victims. Then, I wrote as an observer, but these poems were faceless. So
> I listened to all the tapes again, and this time heard the music in the words. I
> selected details from the accounts, maintaining the language as it was spoken,
> changing very few words, and then only for the sake of clarity. I arranged the
> poems to create a narrative sequence, imagining a voice—a young soldier
> who is there, watching, not necessarily comprehending, letting the horror
> wash over him. (Hyett 1986: xii)

The perceptual comments by the liberators in their accounts show how
much smell marks the world of horror they encounter and to what degree
it infiltrates their own reality as an inescapable trace:

The ovens,
the stench,
I couldn't repeat
the stench. You
have to breathe.
You can wipe out
what you don't want
to see. Close your
eyes. You don't want
to hear, don't want
to taste. You can
block out all senses
except smell

(Hyett 1986: 8)

Even for the liberators smell is the experience that marks most dearly the borderline between the camp and the world outside. For one of the soldiers, the stench makes it altogether impossible to exercise other forms of perception:

And I went in
to take a picture
and the stench was so much
I couldn't.

(Hyett 1986: 83)

Smell, from whichever perspective, denounces the abuse of power on the human body. Its construction within an aesthetic frame means the organization of sensory perception not in terms of beauty but of the power structures that underlie the phenomenological and perceptual experience on which the artwork draws. Because the olfactory is a registering rather than a productive device; it does not itself shape symbolic, representational structures; but it infallibly reveals and highlights them.

Bibliography

Bezwinska, J. (ed.) (1984), *KL Auschwitz Seen by the SS*, New York: Howard Fertig.

Hyett, B.H. (1986), *In Evidence*, Pittsburgh: University of Pittsburgh Press.

Lengyel, O. (1947), *Five Chimneys*, Chicago: Ziff-Davies Publishing.

Levi, P. (1986), *Survival in Auschwitz* and *The Reawakening*, trans. S. Woolf, New York: Summit Books.

Serres, M. (1986), "Corruption—*The Antichrist*," trans. C. Bongie, *Stanford Italian Review*, 6(1/2): 31–52.

Weiss, P. (1975), *Ästhetik des Widerstands*, Frankfurt am Main: Suhrkamp.

12
Environmental Fragrancing

Peter Damian and Kate Damian

In Japan, "the era of perfume dynamics has arrived," according to Masakuni Kiuchi, an engineer for Shimizu, one of the three largest, if not the largest, of Japanese architectural, engineering and construction firms. Quickly responding to Japanese research showing enhanced efficiency and reduced stress among workers exposed to scents, Shimizu is one of an increasing number of construction firms that over the past few years have developed a computerized environmental fragrancing system to deliver such scents into the workplace, both their own and those of other businesses. Moreover, since the late 1980s, Shimizu has been designing new offices and hospitals to include Shimizu's "Aroma Generation System," whereby liquid fragrances compressed into mist are pumped into working or living quarters through air-conditioning ducts and vents. Scented environments are not entirely new in Japan, which has a long tradition of various social rituals using incense, but these days even the Tokyo Stock Exchange has taken to fragrancing its inside air each afternoon with peppermint essence to invigorate and refresh employees.

It seems that in Japan not only are new and old buildings being scented, but some peculiar consumer goods are also being manufactured, among them an alarm clock that uses a built-in fan to blow a "forest scent" shortly before awakening the sleeper, a futon dryer that also spreads a floral fragrance over the bedding, and scent-infused pantyhose, all of which are now available for export to Europe and the United States. Is Japan merely giving us a whiff of our own medicine, or is this a sniff of things to come? In Japan, Europe and America, some people hope the latter is so. Others have real doubts and reservations, even fears, about this "era of perfume dynamics" in an increasingly fragrant society. More specifically, many think that the very idea of environmental fragrancing stinks.

In early 1992, urged by the Citizen Commission on Human Rights (CCHR; an arm of the Church of Scientology), a Massachusetts state legislator introduced a bill to ban any use of perfumes to "covertly control the behavior of others." The CCHR-sponsored ban would specifically prohibit the secret or subliminal use of aromas, scents, perfumes or fragrances in businesses and public places. While citing the Japanese for already implementing such practices to increase worker productivity, the CCHR is also responding with alarm to current US research aimed at developing scents to be vented into the New York City subway system to "induce a chemical euphoria as a method of reducing aggression." Is this a case of paranoia, or is environmental fragrancing an impending social problem requiring preemptive social or political action? Historical precedent for the CCHR's legitimate concern and for government intervention already exists, dating back to ancient Greece and Rome. Of course, some concerns about the effects of fragrances are less legitimate than others.

Some years ago, upon suffering a migraine headache she claims was caused by contact with a magazine scent sample, a New York woman, rather than sensibly avoiding such contact in the future (even assuming that the magazine was solely or partly responsible for her headache), petitioned her state legislator, who subsequently introduced a bill requiring scent samples in magazines sold in New York state to be sealed. More recently, according to *The Wall Street Journal*, employees at a "scent-free" New Jersey insurance agency have been prohibited from wearing fragrant cosmetics, including hair spray. "People are fed up with fragrances; they're so pervasive and intrusive," insists a New Jersey environmental health group activist who distributes buttons proclaiming "Perfume Pollutes." In apparent agreement, a San Francisco theater chain has removed the air fresheners from all fourteen of its theater restrooms. Meanwhile, in Marin County, California, the "National Foundation of the Chemically Hypersensitive," trumpeting its protection of the innocent from the evils of cologne and after-shave lotion, has demanded that designated "fragrance-free zones" be required in all restaurants and state-owned buildings. Julia Kendall is one of the more extreme activists in the group; because personal perfumes make her ill, she wants them prohibited everywhere. Based upon her own peculiar aversion to scents (the mere approach of someone wearing perfume causes her jaw to tighten, leaves her gasping for breath and eventually gives her a severe headache), Kendall extrapolates that perfume is a public menace. The same sort of extended interpretation of personal experience characterizes the other members of her group. (Indeed, it is typical human behavior among various kinds of grievance groups.) Susan Molloy, who attends public meetings carrying an oxygen mask and tank, believes that scented personal products worn by others infringe upon her air space and that she is being unfairly driven from society by their presence. Terri White, executive director of the ironically named Center for Independent Living, and a backer of Molloy and her cause, desires that warning signs be posted on all buildings to deny entrance to anyone who wears perfume or whose clothing may be carrying the odor of smoke, dry cleaning or fragrances. She wants the "chemically hypersensitive" to be legally represented as another disability or handicapped group and given protection under federal law.

These events in New York, New Jersey, and California, reported to illustrate a point, also require commentary. The elevation of a person's "victim status," which is established by one's membership in a specially designated social grievance group, has become a highly competitive and often highly profitable exercise in our increasingly contentious and litigious society. A tiny minority with an unfortunate idiosyncrasy and an overactive imagination, the "chemically hypersensitive" have literally raised that exercise to an art form by their hysterical claims of dangerous "second-hand scents" and unreasonable demands for odor bans and "fragrance-free zones" (as if such things were truly possible). The "chemically hypersensitive" (who, no doubt, are emotionally hypersensitive, since odor allergy is one of the more plainly psychogenic or psychosomatic ills) are now counted among those odd few factional groups who, rather than seeking individual solutions for their personal problems, instead demand that the larger society adapt, hinder or inconvenience itself for their sake, regardless of the actual merits or consequences of their cause. It is instructive, however, that these phenomena and other idiosyncratic or otherwise incidental allergic reactions to scents and fragrances are neither attributable to aromatherapy nor the consequence of pure essential oils. Yet, while we recognize that synthetic scents or isolated, artificial ingredients are more likely to invite or provoke hypersensitivity or severe allergic response, such adverse reactions are hardly pandemic and form no basis for government restrictions upon personal odor or behavior. They certainly do not require the creation and advancement of yet another social cause, or public awareness campaign, or a new "victim class" of citizens. Nevertheless, what might happen if the same artificial, chemical scent ingredients were not randomly worn by individual people but instead were deliberately sprayed into public arenas is another matter altogether. Entirely new and truly public health risks would be created, some obvious and some not so obvious, which we will explore. But environmental fragrancing presents more than a social health problem; it creates an ethical predicament involving social and personal liberty that must be equally addressed.

The Objectives of Environmental Fragrancing

The ostensibly benign objectives of "ambient fragrancing," as it is some times called, are essentially these: (1) to increase or enhance aesthetics, (2) to optimize performance and creativity at large and (3) to improve air quality—that is, to relieve the multisymptomatic health problems of "sick building syndrome," so named because it is thought to be acquired by inhabiting tight, poorly ventilated homes and offices that inhibit the circulation of fresh air. The term now generally refers to health problems arising from occupying any stale, denatured or de-energized artificial or closed environment, especially those in which low-level toxic emissions (from rugs, paints etc.) and unfiltered proliferating microorganisms are vented, usually through air conditioning systems. In actuality, according to latest statistics provided by a National Institute for Occupational Safety and Health study of 529 buildings, inadequate ventilation is the primary cause (fifty-three percent) of poor indoor air quality. Inside or outside contaminants account for fifteen percent and ten percent, respectively. Microorganisms are responsible for only five percent of indoor air contamination; building materials cause only four percent. Unknown causes account for the remaining thirteen percent.

As a new element of interior design (which already incorporates lighting, sound, color and space), "sensory engineering"—as Sivon Reznikoff, professor at Arizona State University terms it—would design fragrancing to match or otherwise suit the needs of any architectural structure or interior environment. The expected results would include increased individual and social performance (memory, organization, mental acuity), job satisfaction, compliant cooperation, personal incentive, heightened vigilance and accuracy. Immediately, one wonders how such a grandiose plan would account for a wide spectrum of individual needs, tolerances and choices and about how it would require consensus of the targeted participants. Experimental scientific evidence or expert opinion about the "valuable results" of the plan might be initially convincing, but because human smell is a deeply subjective, personal and diverse phenomenon, hardly uniform in preference and response, the plan is bound to elicit objections from the "fragrance-free" crowd, arouse suspicions of behavior modification and mind control, and meet resistance from just plain folks who have their familiar habits and own aesthetic ideas about how a particular environment ought to smell—and also their own ideas about what's good for them. Odors do not become consciously perceptible until quite strong, but they are always subconsciously effective—and just as effective even when undetectable by the nose.

Scent Plans

A central problem with implementing any public plan or social strategy involving smell, whether intended to resolve health and aesthetic concerns or requirements, or designed to produce a particular performance result or behavioral response, is that everybody's sense of smell is different. Indeed, everyone is different in a variety of important ways. Because of that, proper scent selection, itself requiring wisely intelligent judgment, becomes more problematical. As Susan Knasko at Monell Chemical Senses Center observes, some people can smell only some of the ingredients in any given perfume, while others cannot smell any ingredients at all. Hence, the response to and effects of an odor, cognitively or subliminally, may be different. Knasko illustrates her point by saying that only half the population can smell androstenone, and among those who can, half perceive it as a subtly pleasant odor, while the rest say that it smells strongly disgusting. Maralyn Teare, marriage and family counselor and a clinical instructor of psychiatry at the University of Southern California in Los Angeles, cites her own experiential research and adds that all scents do not work on all people: "Scent is very person-specific; what may work for you may not work for someone else."

This uncertainty has not deterred environmental fragrancing in Japan where, beginning several years ago, Shimizu has devised at least twenty varieties of a "scent plan" to anticipate its clients' requests and better suit their business needs for greater efficiency or stress relief. For example, Shimizu says that a bank has specific needs requiring invigorating scents (e.g. lemon) in working areas to alert the staff, and calming scents (e.g. lavender) for bank customers. (If the novel idea that a bank can have "needs" is not curious enough, there also seems to be the implication that an alert bank staff needs some means to subdue its customers.) In partnership, Shimizu and Takasago, Japan's largest fragrance company, have implemented their scent plans for subliminal environmental fragrancing based upon the brain-wave research of Professor Shizuo Torii of the Toho University School of Medicine. Maybe the subliminal aspect of the scent plan is to tactically avert individual objections to the scents, but it has not escaped the attention of the Citizen Commission on Human Rights, which cites the Japanese in its campaign and support for legislation to prohibit the practice of subliminal fragrancing in Massachusetts.

In the earlier years of its joint venture development of Shimizu's Aroma Generation System and scent plan, Takasago conducted a series of experiments testing the efficiency of computer and word-processing operators. Takasago found, after thirteen operators were monitored eight hours a day for a month, that per-hour punching errors were reduced by nearly twenty-one per cent when lavender scent was released into the office air, reduced by thirty-three percent using jasmine, and reduced by fifty-four percent using lemon scent. By reducing errors, the scents had increased work efficiency and productivity; increasing improvement was shown by the use of a more stimulating scent. One wonders, given the disparate results of lavender and lemon, how the apparent trade-off between lowering work stress (with lavender) at a cost of thirty-three percent reduced efficiency and productivity (as compared with lemon) is to be considered. Other questions arise: Would the effect of this ambient fragrancing diminish by habituation after continual exposure over a longer period of months? Other than habituation, what are the long-term health effects of continuous exposure to artificial scents? The questionable

use of synthetic or denatured scents in environmental fragrancing is virtually
guaranteed by the fragrance industry's large investment and involvement in
the idea. (Takasago's "aromatherapy" fragrance creations for Japanese and
American cosmetic companies, such as Avon, said to be based on aromatherapy
principles, are not likely based entirely on essential oils.) Answering for the
well-being of the participating keypunch operators, Junichi Yagi, a senior vice
president of S. Technology, Shimizu's Massachusetts subsidiary, said that they
enjoyed the fragrances, adding, "They reported feeling better than they did
without it." Yagi also maintains that the fragrances were selected according
to the principles of aromatherapy. The distinction here is that utilizing the
principles of aromatherapy does not necessarily guarantee or require the use
of the products of aromatherapy—pure essential oils—unless, of course, one
believes, as do true aromatherapists, that the use of odorous substances other
than genuine essential oils somehow violates those principles.

At the Kajima Corporation, another large Japanese construction company
in Tokyo, another systemized "scent plan" adapted to the seasons, the
weather, and the time of day cyclically emits scents to influence employees
throughout each day. In the late 1980s, Kajima's scent plan was conceived
by Shiseido, Japan's largest cosmetics manufacturer, and originally installed
and tested in a then new three-building complex in Tokyo that holds a
thousand Kajima employees. At first, oddly blending the separate principles
of aromatherapy and democracy, Shiseido selected the fragrances to be used
according to the scent preferences of the Kajima employees. For example,
since jasmine was preferred more by women than by men, that fragrance
would be used in offices where women constitute the majority, said Shiseido
spokeswoman, Yukiko Fukuda.

The Kajima complex was centered on an atrium (plants and a waterfall)
that can be seen from any one of the six lounges or the single meeting room
nearby, into which a "forest scent" is pumped, thus enabling employees to
breathe and view the "great outdoors" while still indoors. Otherwise, via
the air conditioning unit, trees in the interior garden are made to emit a
refreshing citrus aroma in the morning, a calming floral scent as the work
day actually begins and a supposedly invigorating (?) scent of cypress during
lunch hour.

The Shiseido–Kajima partnership has sold dozens of environmental
fragrancing units in Japan at $8,000 each. That seems inexpensive by
comparison with Shimizu's customized systems, which cost about $20,000
per room, according to Junichi Yagi, whose Boston-based S. Technology
subsidiary is preparing systems for sale in this country. Whether Shimizu's
marketing strategy meets the same opposition elsewhere in the United
States that it has encountered in Massachusetts remains to be seen. In Japan,
meanwhile, people seem less concerned about being "led around by the
nose" than they are about national corporate success and smart business. It
is instructive to remember, however, that Japan is a small nation (slightly

smaller than California) with a homogeneous population (99.4 percent Japanese) that, despite a century of Western modernization, has a long history of social and behavioral conformity and traditional acceptance of "social aromatics" in public rituals.

Subliminal Shopping

"We've long controlled other parts of the retail environment, such as lighting, temperature and decor," says J'Amy Owens, Seattle office president of Retail Planning Associates. "Now, we're finally realizing the influence smells can have on buying habits. Used properly, they can be a very powerful tool." As an environmental psychologist at Monell Chemical Senses Center, Susan Knasko has observed how scents make shoppers linger. Placing potpourri in a jewelry store during the 1990 Christmas holiday season made shoppers stay in the store longer, but they did not necessarily buy more jewelry. Yet, Knasko says, "Manipulating the ambiance through scent could be as powerful as setting a mood with lights or music." That is exactly how Mark Peltier, founder of Aromasys in Richfield, Minnesota, views environmental fragrancing. "This is olfactory Muzak," beams Peltier. "This is very, very big," which is how Peltier hopes his sales of "mood-altering fragrance systems" (ranging from $100 desktop models to $10,000 centralized units) will grow. His first commercial system has already been installed in the Miami Marriott Hotel, and he has received requests from several companies and universities, most frequently asking him to induce alertness, relaxation and refreshment. Peltier reports that to "perk people up" he offers a blend of peppermint, lemon, eucalyptus, rosemary and pine; to calm them down, he uses lavender and clove with "floral notes and a whiff of woodland"; and to refresh, he blends "citrus notes with pine and eucalyptus." (Without critically commenting upon Mr. Peltier's selective judgment, we needn't conclude that his "aromatherapy" is based solely upon essential oils.)

In Britain, scientists at Warwick University are developing scents for a group called Marketing Aromatics, designed to influence staff and customers in work environments for everything from stress reduction to use of scented company stationery with a "corporate odor identity," all tailor-made for each business's needs. So-called "signature scents" are becoming prevalent on both sides of the Atlantic. Victoria's Secret, a lingerie chain store and mail-order house, has adopted a potpourri scent for its feminine identity. Knot Shops tie stores emit a fragrance blend of spice, leather and tobacco to convey masculinity. Dr Alan R. Hirsch, director at the Smell and Taste Treatment & Research Foundation in Chicago, has been hired by one of the "Big Three" US automobile manufacturers to develop a showroom scent that will increase car sales. Marketing Aromatics is doing the same while also secretly testing its mood-altering ideas in more than a hundred British stores, including department stores and travel agencies. Is this sly subliminal manipulation or simply clever marketing salesmanship? As observed, retailers already extensively employ music for shoppers; but is it the same thing when retailers and vendors insert subliminal odors into their products and stores to induce customers to buy? Is subliminal fragrancing more or less devious than using hidden, subliminal video or audio messages to urge buying and discourage shoplifting? Is it deception when a creditor laces payment bills with a faintly musky, chemical pheromone intended to intimidate customers into paying their bills more promptly? This has been tried in Australia by a mail-order cosmetics company whose scented final-notice bills sent to delinquent debtors were paid seventeen percent more readily and rapidly than were bills sent on untreated paper. Meanwhile, in Las Vegas, Nevada, scents are being used to increase slot-machine and other gambling revenues by relaxing players and thus encouraging them to take more chances.

A Brave New World

Dr Charles Wysocki is an olfactory research scientist at Monell who notes the unique immediacy of smell's access to the limbic system and brain: "Smell is our most intimate, individualistic sense," he says. "It is primitive, uneducated and therefore vulnerable." He warns that human emotions, with which smell is associated, can be readily exploited through the use of odors, scents, fragrances and aromas. Dr Trygg Engen of Brown University cautions that aromatic mood control could backfire: "Studies have shown that unidentified odors make people anxious. Other studies have shown that if a person feels he is being controlled, even by perfume, he is likely to find the aroma disagreeable."

Dr Susan Schiffman of Duke University also has expressed reservations about environmental fragrancing. After more than twenty years of using fragrances such as chocolate and apricot to help alleviate depression and anxiety and to reduce aggression in her patients, she says she is disinclined to mass-market her findings: "The most powerful and effective aromatic suggestions remain highly personal and idiosyncratic." Yet, contradictorily, Schiffman's research is leading exploration of environmental fragrancing to reduce aggression in New York City subways. "We have to find ways to reduce aggression," says Schiffman. "We're looking at whether we can pump certain odors into a subway to make people less violent" and also into prisons "to reduce stress," which many, like the Church of Scientology and its Citizen Commission on Human Rights, interpret to mean the experimental mind control of a literally captive audience. Like so many others whose research is financially supported by the fragrance industry via its Fragrance Research Fund, Dr Schiffman envisions many potential uses for fragrances, saying that scientific evidence gathered in sponsored studies by the FRF (for which Dr Schiffman has served as scientific director) indicates a vast range of clinical, developmental, sociological and physiological applications. Long before, in 1985, Henry Walter enthusiastically agreed, speaking as the chairman of the board of International Flavors & Fragrances in New York, the world's largest producer and supplier of scents. The IFF has made a multimillion-dollar commitment to research, investing huge sums of money in grants to universities, research centers and individuals since the Fragrance Research Fund began in 1982. "We're putting our money where our nose is," remarked Walter, who likened the burgeoning market of fragrance products for "aromatherapy" to, in his own words, "the beginning of antibiotics." "We envision a zillion different possibilities," added Walter, including pumping stimulating aromas into schools to wake people up. But in this brave new world of odors envisioned by and divided between the synthetic fragrance industry and the conventional medical establishment, there is little or no room for traditional, holistic aromatherapy or real essential oils.

Artificial Inhalation

Dr Alan Hirsch has already concluded that our frame of reference for aromas is gradually drifting away from nature and toward manufactured compounds. Numerous clinical and observational studies can be recounted that indicate how the human nose is being deceived by manufactured odors, which, coupled with our modern urbanized detachment from nature, is causing confused and distorted identity associations between odors, tastes and their sources. Dr James A. Steinke, director of flavor development and application at Fries & Fries, a Cincinnati laboratory that compounds flavors for the food industry, notes: "People raised on strawberry Kool-Aid will prefer the Kool-Aid-type berry flavor over a completely natural berry. Actually, if you squished fresh berries and blindfolded these tasters, they would say it wasn't fruit."

That for a rapidly increasing number of human beings, an artificial "fruit flavor" represents what they now believe is the "real" scent and flavor of fruit, and that real fruit no longer smells "real," tells us something important about what Monell's Dr Wysocki calls the "primitive, uneducated and therefore vulnerable" nature of smell and about how the human nose and tongue, inundated with bogus odors and phony flavors, can be falsely satisfied by artificial stimuli that while "pushing the right buttons" and saturating the senses offer no therapeutic or nutritional benefits whatever. Artificial substances do this not by mere equal substitution for the real thing but by false exaggeration, which provides us more of the hedonic stimulus and response we like, even while providing us less of everything else we really need or expect. Often, only because they smell and taste like those things that are good for us, we are duped into eating, drinking and smelling things that are not good for us.

As if ersatz scents masquerading as the real thing weren't enough of a problem, the cross-proliferation of scented products, "natural" or otherwise, further complicates our ability to correctly identify odors. "It's getting confusing," says Susan Knasko of Monell. "Everything is scented. Many people learn scents out of context and it's starting to affect my research." For some people, lemon scent means lemonade; for others it's furniture polish, and so on. Knasko reports that in research studies when subjects eighteen to forty-five years old smell pine scent, they often think it's a cleaning product or otherwise misidentify the odor as lemon because lemon and pine are so commonly mixed in cleaning and household products. The age range of her subjects is telling, since other studies reveal that younger generations are gradually being conditioned and acclimated to synthetic chemical odors which are rapidly replacing natural scents, fragrances and aromas in our work and home, indoor and outdoor environments, food and beverages, toys, clothing and other products. While contemplating the countless substances and materials of modern industrialism and technology that have been introduced to our olfaction during the latter half of the twentieth century, one begins to realize how present and future generations will be increasingly influenced emotionally, hedonically and nostalgically by fabricated fragrances rather than by natural odors. What this portends is unknown, but the implications and consequences could be tremendous. Perfumers and flavorists are well aware of this olfactory shift observed by Dr Hirsch and others. Having 10,000 mostly synthetic aromatic substances available to fashion fragrances, and 5,000 mostly artificial ingredients to fabricate flavors for packaged foods, the fragrance and food industries are quite busy furthering that trend.

On the Wrong Scent

In producing their psycho-physiological effects, essential oils traverse the blood–brain barrier not only by virtue of their lipid solubility when utilized transdermally or by ingestion but also by triggering nerve impulses olfactorally when they are inhaled. This is not exclusive entry; other substances can do likewise. But since all odors are not created equal, the question is, what message, what information, does each offer or carry to the brain? Varied scientific processes of manipulating or tampering with naturally occurring matter or substances (whether genetically, chemically, molecularly or atomically) can produce mutations, denatured or unnatural substances that are synthesized, isolated chemical constituents or artificial replications. Always there is the risk of imbalancing or somehow distorting the effects or character of the original that is being processed or imitated, consequently creating something that is less healthful, therapeutically effective, or valuable yet more psycho-physiologically active or potent in a narrow, limited and disturbing way. This is often what likewise creates abnormalities of human response to such unnatural substances, ranging from simple allergies to toxicity or addiction. Considering what we've learned about olfaction, is it possible to become chemically and psychologically addicted to false scents? That is, can we learn to prefer or rely upon them more than we do natural aromas and fragrances? Judging by the human experience with numerous modern synthetic drugs variably classified as hypnotics, sedatives, tranquilizers, narcotics, stimulants, depressants and hallucinogens, we ought to conclude that the answer is yes. First, to be effective, an inhaled "aroma drug" need only find the right receptor by imitating a natural substance. A potent enough synthetic odor would then operate in much the same way as oral, injected and nasal drugs already do, by exaggerating hedonic response, intensifying the psycho-physiological stimuli and effects, and creating an increased desire for and eventual dependence upon the synthetic odor.

It is instructive that the Citizen Commission on Human Rights's opposition to the notion of pumping "behavioral fragrances" into our prisons, schools and subways is a continuance of the Church of Scientology's war against psychiatry or, more specifically, against what Scientology views as the psychiatric profession's misuse of mind-altering, psychoactive drugs that reduce people into zombies. It may first be recognized in this dispute that synthetic scents and artificial fragrances are another generation of imposters, which, if handled as drugs are and have been handled, could harm individuals and threaten society in much the same way. Do we need or want another generation of synthetic drugs—this time "behavioral fragrances" or "olfaction drugs"—that treat symptoms rather than people and will likely generate more personal and social problems than they resolve? It is incumbent on phytoaromatherapists to encourage the use and supply of natural botanicals and aromatics, to counter the disturbing modern trend toward synthetic scents and artificial substances, and to educate all concerned about the increasingly important need for authentic fragrances that have true therapeutic and aesthetic value.

Aromatherapy Questions and Answers

In all capacities, essential oils, herbs and other plant remedies provide a safe, sane and healthful alternative to the synthetic products of the chemistry lab. Essential oils are foremost among those medicines created out of the earth which a wise man ought not abhor. Certainly, if one generally disapproves of synthetic drugs or artificial foods, one cannot condone the synthetic odor chemicals preferred by manufacturers only for the sake of reduced costs and higher profits and made for the commercial exploitation of emotional hedonic responses, or to produce behavioral modification with short-sighted goals and superficial or deleterious results. A purpose of authentic aromatherapy is to maintain or restore healthy, natural olfactory and psychological responses and to promote genuine, enduring self-improvement through the use of essential oils. Whole, pure essential oils, like whole foods, are better received by the human organism; they are more psycho-physiologically nourishing, carrying complete, intelligent information and messages to the human being.

Their effects are not superficially stimulating but are safely therapeutic and capable of engendering real and profound changes. The subtle subjectivity of individualized smell and the complexity of essential oils may be too inconvenient or complicated for the consideration or objectives of medical establishment and fragrance industry practices, but they remain as necessarily vital to aromatherapy as they are personally important to the individual human being. Socialized environmental fragrancing is not aromatherapy. Mass aromatherapy of any kind, by practice or production, contradicts holistic individualized treatment and personal self-improvement—the purpose of aromatherapy's "individualized prescription" as declared by Marguerite Maury.

Modern man is in olfactory recession partly because of the evolution of other, more advanced senses but also because we are saturated and desensitized by the odorous stimuli of a more complex world and existence. Since we are already besieged by countless odors, scents, fragrances, perfumes and aromas, there is reason to be more selective or more prohibitive with deliberate environmental fragrancing by still more synthetic aromatic substances. (We cannot predict that real essential oils or otherwise natural scents will be used in environmental fragrancing; yet, for ethical and philosophic reasons we ought not to endorse such use.) What are the potentially adverse health effects of widespread environmental fragrancing? Despite the increased likelihood of sensitization, synthetic fragrances will probably be favored for their lower manufacturing costs, and because of the reproducibility and predictability of human response to the narrow spectrum of components in synthetic scents. Yet, synthetic odors are apt to exacerbate concerns over the dangers of "second-hand scents" and heighten the debate over natural versus artificial substances. Scents are everywhere—but what of increased scented packaging? Already the "chemically hyper-sensitive," or people with allergies, have successfully protested "scratch 'n' sniff" advertising and perfumed magazines. Responding to one of environmental fragrancing's proposed objectives, one might ask how "sensory engineering" hopes to actually improve air quality by generating more synthetic, artificial odors, regardless of how aromatically pleasing they may be. We ought to expect that artificial scents bring artificial results that are transient and superficial. Always, the issue of environmental fragrancing carries both health and ethical implications, the latter a clash between indiscriminate collectivism versus individual needs, preferences, choice and liberty.

Using natural scents to attain therapeutic psycho-physiological effects in medical offices, hospitals, nursing homes, spas or wherever else they might be expected or personally desirable (as at home, where one retains individual controls) is quite different from having government authorities pump fragrances into subways in the hope of deterring urban crime. (Religious liturgical incense rituals are not a sure argument for public environmental fragrancing, because people in church presumably share a single, common mental and spiritual imperative and expectation and are willingly bound by a single, unifying spiritual purpose arrived at voluntarily.) As for business offices, it will no doubt be argued that environmental fragrancing is both an employee benefit as well as an employer's advantage. But in any case, or more specifically in public subways, schools or even prisons, environmental fragrancing is nonetheless mass medication akin to the fluoridation of water. Modern medical practitioners and civic authorities have, for their own reasons, chosen to ignore the existing and mounting scientific evidence that fluoride ingestion from city water is hazardous and injurious, owing not only to fluoride dosage alone but also to fluoride's interaction with other chemicals also present in the treated water. What is the interaction of synthetic scents with other odorous (and odorless) chemicals already present and interacting in the air, which synthetic fragrances may mask but do not eliminate, detoxify or disarm? Always vulnerable to the law of unintended consequences, good intentions are not enough. Otherwise, we'd pump antibiotics into the air and water during respiratory or other epidemics.

These are some of the topics for debate generated by the matter of environmental fragrancing, especially in a pluralistic society such as that in the United States. Voluntary, informed individual consent, which may allow much smaller group consensus, is the best answer. Of course, natural scent ingredients, preferably essential oils, should always be selected, whether by collective consensus or individual choice. Ideally, the desired goals must be articulated and the results demonstrated to the satisfaction of those involved. More likely, no matter how well intentioned, environmental fragrancing will meet resistance, much of it justified, as it expands too far, too fast.

In addressing the behavioral modification aspects of environmental fragrancing, it is instructive that the effects of those social olfaction experiments recounted earlier were neither unanimous, total, nor scientifically reliable, because so many other factors and stimuli were unaccounted for. As if other sensory mixing or intrusion into our smell appreciation were not complicated enough, human response to scents, fragrances, odors and aromas has many peculiar psychological variables—learned association or experience, associated or cognitive expectation—as well as other sensory, environmental reinforcements. The psycho-physiological effects of odors are difficult to trace or differentiate because individual differences profoundly affect any therapeutic result, even as shown by olfactory research involving simple synthetic scents—all of which complicates any strictly biological explanation for the effect of smell, or scent, upon human behavior. Correspondingly, the power of mind over matter may obviate or allay some fears of a sinister "scent slavery" like that practiced by the predator ants upon their victims, just as the exercise of individual free will mitigates the supposed irresistibility of suggestion.

Part III

Flaireurs

Preface

Sniffing at every risk-filled corner for a rhyme.

Charles Baudelaire, "Le Soleil" (Buck-Morss 1989)

One effect of the sanitization drive beginning in the eighteenth century was the appearance of hyperattentive smellers, individuals who either sniffed for stenches to eliminate or cultivated ultra-refined olfactory experiences. Widespread odor intolerance, then, set off a rebound effect of sorts and created the context for the emergence of aromacentric personalities. If smell lost much of its former importance as an epistemological method, a utilitarian tool or as a disease-causing threat, its symbolic and affective aspects compensated by gaining increased prominence. There is an under-theorized figure in this olfactory history of modernity, namely that of the *flaireur*, or "smeller," for whom smell is a pre-eminent aspect of being in the world (see Drobnick 2002). The most extreme *flaireurs* exist on the periphery of social and ethical respectability: snobbish olfactory-oriented dandies, wealthy scent-collecting "heros of the nose," or notorious "sniffers" who swooped down on female customers in nineteenth-century department stores to smell their perfumed napes (see Stamelman in Part V; Camporesi 1994: 122–8; Corbin 1986: 208–9). Yet *flairerie* can be an everyday, commonplace practice as suggested by Margolies' olfactory tour of New York City (in Part II), tourists pursuing aromatically attractive locales (Dann and Jacobsen 2002), public curiosity about the putrid "corpse flower" *Titan arum*, which often draws large crowds eager to inhale its rotting-meat aroma (Cannon 1999), or books for children such as the scratch 'n' sniff series *Smelly Old History* (e.g. Dobson 1997).

There is a certain equivalency between the *flaireur* and the better documented *flâneur* (see Tester 1994). Both are conditioned by similar origins within the processes of modernity—urbanization, shifting class structures and so on—although the *flaireur* arises somewhat earlier. Baudelaire, an arch exponent and definer of *flânerie*, could be said to be himself a *flaireur*,

163

as hinted at by the line from his poem "Le Soleil" quoted above, as well as by his famous self-assessment as one existing in that indeterminate state between vaporization and condensation. For the *flaireur*, "smelling well" connotes not only the acts of relishing fragrances and presenting oneself in a pleasingly scented manner, but, more significantly, serves as an olfactory model upon which one's core identity is constructed (see Drobnick 2003). All of the chapters in this section address aspects of *flairerie*, whether it be via the link between selfhood and smell, olfactory super-sensitivity, scent nostalgia or the individualistic formation of odor preferences.

Alain Corbin's chapter, "The New Calculus of Olfactory Pleasure," from his influential book *The Foul and the Fragrant*, describes a momentous shift that accompanied the deodorization campaigns in eighteenth-century France. Along with the ventilation of cities and the eradication of stenches, there arose a parallel phenomenon in the realm of personal hygiene and in the fashion preferences for perfume. The suspicions attached to water and bodily cleansing lifted with the promotion of vitalist theories of health. Similarly, the aristocratic elite adopted and popularized new rituals of the toilette, and set a more urbane standard for self-presentation. Most important was the waning of animal-derived scents, especially musk, and the associated use of overpowering olfactory façades in favor of subtle, floral scents and the acceptance of individuals' natural aromatic atmospheres. Personal satisfaction, pleasure, identity and even self-expression, now became channeled through the medium of fragrance. Corbin articulates this sensualist ethos as "narcissistic," but it must be kept in mind that this engagement with one's own odors and the enjoyment of scent coincided with the upsurge in autobiographies and confessional writings, the rising concern with memories, sentiment and inner feelings and the growth of romanticism's notion of the soulful unity with the world (Corbin 2004). Such a shift in the appreciation both of odors and of one's olfactory aura presaged the modern formation of one's personality as a unique and notable existence.

The next two chapters explore the capabilities of individuals with extraordinary olfactory sensitivities, *flaireurs* par excellence—Helen Keller and Stephen D., a neurology patient examined by Dr Oliver Sacks. Keller's elegant prose argues for the nobility of the sense of smell and extols its virtue as a "potent wizard" with the power to attune individuals to the environment, gather subtle knowledge, invoke rapturous emotional responses and dramatically store the memories of events and places. She also comments frankly about the existence of distinctive and captivating "person-scents." Shorn of the embarrassment and anxiety typically attached to the discussion of body odors, her compelling remarks reveal the information about other's vocations and residences that it is possible to glean from their smell, as well as the vitality and inner essence of their being. Stephen D.'s temporary hyperosmia, an intensification of the sense of smell, bestowed upon him the remarkable ability to perceive scents emanating from almost any object.

He could recognize every street, corner and store by his nose alone, and, like Keller, each person he encountered exhibited a particular and evocative "smell-face." Despite the vividness of such a sensory awareness, Sacks hints at the potential for social opprobrium that it occasioned—that is, Stephen D. had to be careful not to indulge in his olfactory curiosity with others present lest he be judged inappropriate and peculiar. Sacks' chapter also records the experience of a patient with the opposite condition, anosmia, or the complete loss of smell. Taken for granted by most persons, the contribution smell makes to the savoring of everyday experience only becomes noticeable, lamentably, upon its absence.

For *flaireurs*, the most telling indicator perhaps of their personal and intimate relation to smell is the type of odor that evokes nostalgic feelings. Most of these smells are drawn from childhood experiences and the specificities of one's home locale. In the previous section, Porteous explained the significance of odors in childhood because of their newness and one's heightened awareness towards the sensations of the world during the process of growing up. The evocative power of smell can also be traced to its operation as a symbolic reference. That is, smells bypass language and directly connect the material world to one's inner state (Sperber 1975: 115–9). What makes scent impractical for predictable, systematic communication makes it ideal for represencing emotional experience. The excerpt by Alan R. Hirsch featured here, from "Nostalgia, the Odors of Childhood and Society," considers this memorative olfactory phenomenology on a collective scale by charting the types of odors particular to a succession of age groups over the course of the twentieth century. The decade by decade progression of the types of odors that spark nostalgic feelings provides telling evidence not only of personality type and lifestyle, but also of the shifting nature of the olfactory milieu due to changes in residential patterns, the increasing presence of technology (and pollution) in everyday life and the prominent availability of synthetically scented consumer products since the 1960s.

Besides the context of nostalgia, personal associations are also paramount in differentiating between smells suitable to appreciate and those deemed repugnant. Rachel S. Herz examines whether there are any grounds to the generalized belief in innate reactions to smells and whether an individual's like or dislike of an odor can be influenced by learning or experience. Briefly surveying the physiology of smell and current theories of olfactory reception, she draws upon studies with pregnant mothers and newborns to show that even at early developmental stages odor preferences are acculturated and keyed into conditional aspects of the family's environment (see also Schaal 1997). Comparing international studies of scent preferences, she finds that therapeutic uses of scent likewise depend upon contextual factors regarding emotion, language, psychology and cultural background. In terms of human evolution, a flexible rather than predetermined relationship to odors may have held a number of advantages, allowing the sense of smell to adapt to changing circumstances and permit social knowledge to play a role in perception.

Jim Drobnick

Bibliography

Buck-Morss, S. (1989), *The Dialectics of Seeing*, Cambridge, MA: MIT Press.

Camporesi, P. (1994), *Exotic Brew*, trans. C. Woodall, Cambridge: Polity Press.

Cannon, W. (1999), "Something Rotten in Seattle," *American Scientist*, November-December, http://www.americanscientist.org/template/AssetDetail/assetid/15819.

Corbin, A. (1986), *The Foul and the Fragrant*, Cambridge, MA: Harvard University Press.

—— (2004), "Charting the Cultural History of the Senses," in D. Howes (ed.), *Empire of the Senses*, Oxford: Berg, pp. 128–39.

Dann, G.M.S. and Jacobsen, J.K.S. (2002), "Leading the Tourist by the Nose," in G.M.S. Dann (ed.), *The Tourist as a Metaphor of the Social World*, New York: CABI Publishing.

Dobson, M. (1997), *Tudor Odours*, Oxford: Oxford University Press.

Drobnick, J. (2002), "Toposmia," *Angelaki*, 7(1): 31–46.

—— (2003), "Trafficking in Air," *Performance Research*, 8(3): 29–43.

Schaal, B. (ed.) (1997), *L'odorat chez l"enfant*, Paris: Presses Universitaires de France.

Sperber, D. (1975), *Rethinking Symbolism*, trans. A.L. Morton, Cambridge: Cambridge University Press.

Tester, K. (ed.) (1994), *The Flâneur*, London & New York: Routledge.

13

The New Calculus of Olfactory Pleasure

Alain Corbin

Pleasure and Rose Water

Among the elite, changes in tastes and in fashion sanctioned the experts' discrediting of heavy scents. The smells of private space became less strong and were enriched and varied by more delicate and subtle fragrances. The new behavior patterns reflected the fascination with airy space. The balsamic effluvia of springtime meadows became an obsession. The interiors of Tiepolo's paintings corresponded to the inarticulate expression of a new sensitivity to smell. Lowering the thresholds of perception not only created intolerance of excremental odors; it also emphasized the social function of personal toilette as an aspect of good manners, which were being codified in an increasingly strict and precise manner. Intrusive perfumes as well as indiscreet body odors had to be avoided lest they cause discomfort.

Ernst Platner, the authority most commonly referred to in the late eighteenth century, listed the theoretical dangers of bodily un-cleanliness. Dirt obstructed the pores; it held back the excremental humors, favored the fermentation and putrefaction of substances; worse, it facilitated the "pumping back of the rubbish" that loaded the skin (qtd. in Baumes 1789: 189). This foul-smelling pellicule, too often regarded as a protective coating against miasmas, impeded the aeriform exchanges necessary for organic equilibrium. It was therefore important to increase the frequency of ablutions. Platner, like Jacquin, recommended that faces, hands and feet be washed often, and even the whole body "from time to time" (qtd. in Baumes 1789: 191).

In this way a very cautious, somewhat uncertain bodily hygiene was encouraged, its spread limited by a multitude of restraints. Vitalists and iatromechanists appealed for prudence. The loss of vitality that Bordeu stressed was not the only danger from water. Rash use of baths relaxed the fibers, weakened the organism, led to indolence. Like Boyle and Lancisi not long before, Hallé (1785) emphasized the septic effect of soap, particularly in time of plague. But moralists were afraid of the pleasure, the sensual glances, and the autoerotic temptation of baths. Privacy was provided as a proof against seduction in the dressing rooms of the period; nakedness was risky.

In any case, such practices were bound to be confined to a small elite. Inadequate control of running water prevented private bodily hygiene from becoming widespread. For most people, the use of water remained collective. Bathing, which did in fact become more widespread at the end of the century, at least in Paris, was more a therapeutic practice than anything else. Furthermore, Moheau (1778: 110) noted, ablution was useful for the common laborer only when he was not working; for the rest of the time the movement of his sweat was enough to clear his pores.

Nevertheless a popular pedagogy of private hygiene was sketched out; norms were formulated within limited circles—the same circles that gave rise to the keenest anxiety; schools and, even more, prisoners' cells, hospitals, barracks and Cook's ship became the laboratories for little-known experiments.

Among the elite, the new use of perfumes coincided with the new ritual of the toilette: the individual must not betray poor hygiene by wearing a scented mask. Quite the contrary, the individual atmosphere revealing the uniqueness of the "I" must be allowed to break through. Only some vegetable odors, chosen with discernment to express a certain olfactory harmony, could enhance allurement of the individual person. The woman developed a wish to breathe and control her fragrances at the same time that she began using the looking glass. The psychological and social function of delicate scents justified the new fashions. "It is necessary to do something to make us pleasing to ourselves," wrote the perfumer Déjean concerning the use of vegetable perfumes. "That makes us lively in gatherings and in that way we please others; that is what makes society. If by some misfortune we are displeasing to ourselves, whom will we please?" (1764: 147). This comment confirms a development of the greatest importance, which Roger Chartier has already stressed with regard to school manuals: the movement away from a code of good manners primarily intended to avoid causing embarrassment to other people, toward a body of hygienic precepts that also aimed at narcissistic satisfaction (Chartier, Julia and Compère 1976: 144). Woman wanted to be breathed; she thereby affirmed her wish for self-expression. By this discreet allusion to the body's élan, by this search for an image, she created an aura of dream and desire. One might say that the shift from a "mosaic" to a "syntactic" model, which was to underlie the emergence of high perfumery at the end of the nineteenth century, had been prepared for much earlier.

The new fashion, all subtlety and delicacy, translated the major historical shift discerned by Robert Mauzi: the movement from provoked sensation to received sensation, from artifice to nature (1960: 427). What unleashed sensual agitation was the vagueness of the soliciting message. "Perfumes are used," wrote Déjean, "to satisfy the sensuality of the sense of smell ... not with those strong and violent odors, but with those sweet odors which can be neither distinguished nor defined" (1764: 457).

The application of these principles led to the rejection of animal perfumes. Ambergris, civet and musk went out of fashion, "since our nerves have become more delicate," according to the 1765 *Encyclopédie*. Musk-scented gloves were no longer tolerated; their odor was too violent. There is a vast amount of evidence on this subject. Musk had become old-fashioned, declared Nicolas Le Cat (1767: 256). Déjean alluded to the disrepute into which this perfume had fallen as if it were self-evident, and was content to plead the cause of ambergris (1764: 91). Nevertheless there is some evidence of more conservative attitudes. Whereas animal perfumes were the subject of abuse, a belated craze developed for "extracts of royal ambergris." The resistance, contested but indisputable, is explained by the interplay of taboo and desire, a subject that demands special attention.

Havelock Ellis rightly analyzed this discrediting of musk as a major fact in sexological history. In his opinion, up to the end of the eighteenth century women did not use perfume to mask their odor but to emphasize it (1905: 91, 99). Musk had the same function as corsets that accentuated the contours of the body. According to Hagen (1901), master of sexual osphresiology, women until then had sought out the strongest, most animal perfumes for that purpose.

From this viewpoint, the decline in these perfumes at the end of the eighteenth century only registered the decline in the "primitive attractiveness" of sexual odors (Ellis 1905: 99). Havelock Ellis took up Bordeu's timid analyses. Western man and woman would henceforth endeavor with increasing skill to disguise body odors that had become burdensome; it was a way of denying the sexual role of the sense of smell, or at least of shifting the field of olfactory stimulation and allusion; thereafter it fell to the delicate exhalations of perspiration, and not to the powerful odors of secretions, to presage the intimate liaison. Never before had there been so great a revolution in the history of sexual invitation; except, Freud wrote twenty-two years later, when man stood upright and thus for the first time reduced the role played by olfaction in unleashing desire (Freud 1975: 99–100).

There is nothing to oppose the idea that sensualism contributed to the victory of that prohibition on animal perfumes. The excremental odor of the emunctories situated near the genitals—as is the case with the musk deer's abdomen—would explain the sense of shame and, in the final analysis, the feelings of modesty that the genitals aroused. Hartley was convinced of this connection: "The mental displeasure that accompanies shame, the idea of indecency, etc. come to a considerable degree from the disagreeable odors of fecal substances of animal bodies" (Hartley 1755: 332). Thus the English philosopher justified an idea dear to the fathers of the Church; his theory led implicitly to a condemnation of the use of musk, ambergris and civet.

We have already considered, in all its strange complexity, the theoretical justification for the decline of animal perfumes. It was accompanied by an enormous vogue for "odoriferous spirits," "essential oils" and "scented waters" extracted from spring flowers. What was new was their great variety (Déjean 1764: 8ff). At the court of Louis XV, etiquette prescribed the use of a different perfume every day. The great success of rose water was shared by violet, thyme and, above all, lavender and rosemary water. "Lavender water," noted Malouin, "is the most generally pleasing of all the odors" (1750: 275). The 1760s saw the launching of "eaux de la maréchale" and "eaux de la duchesse," whose fashionable image reinforced sensitivity. A few years later vegetable odors "from the islands" contributed an exotic note to the range of floral essences. Men as well as women obeyed the new injunctions; Casanova made fun of the young Baron Barois, whose chamber smelled sweetly of the odor of the pomade and scented waters he applied (1977: 255).

Delicate "odors" became part of the ritual of bodily hygiene. Of course, several doctors, Platner foremost among them, advised the use of pure water and avoidance of perfumed mixtures. They were barely heeded. "L'eau d'ange" was much in vogue in the seventeenth century, but according to Déjean its use had lapsed by 1764. It was followed by waters with fruit scents, soap and paste with floral perfumes, odoriferous balls to rub on the body in the bath. Master perfumers prepared scented pellets and powders to scent the hands—a subject that aroused lively interest. The custom developed of washing out the mouth with rose water, perfuming the breath with iris paste.

Courtly literature was quick to record the discrediting of musk. Notions of hygiene and ablutions are central to Restif de La Bretonne's eroticism. Rose water had a surprising monopoly; it was ceaselessly refreshing Conquette-Ingenue's feet and private parts (L'Anti-Justine). The bidet became the accessory of pleasure. Casanova's story has the same monotony as far as the use of scents is concerned: washing the woman's body in rose water assumed the form of a ritual (1977: 448). Perfume played hardly any role except in setting the scene for pleasure; it had moved away from the desired body. It would even disappear from the erotic scenario of the marquis de Sade's novels.

The persistent emphasis on the skin's absorptive power justified the caution regarding the use of strong scents. This caution, however, was counterbalanced by the use of perfumed powder, which, more than other cosmetics, revealed the personality of the person using it. It "varies," Déjean noted, "according to each person's taste and is composed of distinctive perfumes" (1764: 423). Powder "à la maréchale" retained its prestige for nearly a century; it consisted of a skillful mixture of iris, cloves, lavender, rose, orange and marjoram, perfected by the maréchale d'Aumont. Apart from this mixture, the ones most commonly used were iris powder, cypress powder and, above all, carnation powder. Carnation powder came to the fore in the reign of Louis XV; its success signified the triumph of vegetable scents.

A predilection for flowers quite logically accompanied this craze. Fashionable Parisian ladies grew cloves and basil in pots. Large vases of flowers decorated ladies' toilette tables. Ladies of fashion draped themselves with honeysuckle and wildflowers: buttercups, hyacinths, jonquils, lilies of the valley, convolvulus and ranunculus. A veritable cult surrounded violets. Marie Antoinette consolidated and extended a set of behavior patterns that had appeared well before she imposed her own image on the court.

Strong odor, now old-fashioned, became the prerogative of aged coquettes and peasants. Animal scent belonged to the masses. "The gentleman of fashion no longer exhales ambergris," noted Louis-Sébastien Mercier (1782–88, 2: 158). Casanova nearly fainted when an old nymphomaniac duchess made her appearance, smelling of musk from twenty steps away. He himself used only myrrh and storax to concoct the magician's sulfurous apparatus. The captivating Celestine nevertheless rejected Casanova by mocking scented waters and revealing her peasant origins through the avowal that she used goat's fat (Casanova 1977: 295, 185, 139).

"Apart from philosophers ... everyone smelled nice," Alexandre Dumas wrote in 1868 of the elite at the end of the ancien régime. Edmond de Goncourt and Huysmans helped to establish the myth that the eighteenth century was flower and perfume mad. There is an element of truth behind this myth, which the contributors to the *Encyclopédie* recognized. The practice of using perfume to embellish the environment and the objects in it acted as a counterweight to the disappearance of musk and civet. Perfumers offered "concoctions to wear on one's person," "perfumes for pleasure," with no therapeutic purpose (*Le Parfumeur royal* 1761: 83). "Odors are carried only in bottles," Déjean (1764: 4) specified, "for fear of annoying those who do not like them." Cotton wool soaked in perfumes was concealed in miniature perfume-pans or in tiny tassels sewn onto an item of dress. Gentlemen of fashion vied in the art of analyzing the concoctions. Possession of a royal perfume was a sign of membership in the aristocracy of refinement. Casanova took good care of his bottle from the suite of Louis XV. Sade dispatched persistent pleas to his correspondents to send him rich "odors" when he was imprisoned in the Bastille.

The perfumed handkerchief, a favorite component of feminine wiles, remained fashionable into the nineteenth century. Both perfumers and coquettes made up "pads to wear on the person" and filled them with lightly musked violet powder. "English" sachets in Florentine silk or taffetas—because linen corrupted the odors—were fabricated at home. Containing a small layer of perfumed cotton wool or a pinch of fragrant powders, they were attached by ribbons to negligees or were placed in cupboards, chests of drawers and the drawers of bedside tables.

It was also the custom to perfume toilet accessories. Delicately scented Provence gloves replaced musked gloves. Perfumed fans spread and moderated scents from breasts and bouquets. The harmony established by the odor of the perfumed glove was a sign of the subtlety of the composition of the scents. "English" or "Montpellier" styles of dress cut in odoriferous fabrics were less common. The wearing of negligees that had been kept in delicately perfumed containers confirmed the change in fashions of sexual solicitation.

Everything worn, even medals and rosaries, could caress the sense of smell. Forbidden to smoke in the presence of ladies, men used snuff smelling of jasmine, tuberose or orange blossom. Cooks busily perfumed their dishes.

The atmosphere of private space was tinged with delicate odors: perfumed boxes, baskets of scent and, above all, skillfully prepared potpourris, some of which kept their odor for ten or twelve years, perfumed the apartments of the rich. Their concoction, like the concoction of pomades, powders and scented waters, fostered a domestic art of preserving odors that competed with the master perfumers."

This moderate advance in bodily hygiene made the dressing room one of the sanctuaries of seduction. There, as in the adjoining boudoir, the smell of the environment, combined with the effect of hangings and mirrors, lent itself to the transactions of intimate exchange. Parny, following Rousseau, dwelled reverently on this favored place for sexual invitation, epitomized by Pompadour (1861, 3: 78–9). On the other hand, the extreme example supplied by the duc de Richelieu, who had odors skillfully wafted about in his apartments to set the stage for seduction, does not seem to have caught on.

The Perfume of Narcissus

Providing an accessible locale that would allow both the chosen sensation to be welcomed and the pleasures and feelings it aroused to be experienced was the first injunction of the sensualist ethic. Rousseau made this art of sensations, based on the choice and arrangement of objects, the first technique of happiness. It was a difficult calculation, involving constant care to avoid obtrusive sensations that created distractions or even aroused repulsion. Enjoyment of the true pleasures of the sense of smell therefore presupposed a flight far from mud and dung, far from the putrefaction of living bodies, far from the confined places of the town as well as from the cramped lands of the valley. Even in the countryside, flight was necessary; the village had become a cesspool, declared Girardin (1777: 59). "I see a hundred crowded thatches," deplored Obermann, "an abominable cluster where roads, stables and kitchen gardens, damp walls, floors and roofs, even clothes and furniture, all seem to be part of the same slime. Where all the women bawl, all the children weep, and all the men sweat" (Senancour 1844, 1: 71).

Thus was the repugnance to "social emanations," still vague but intensely felt, displayed (Senancour 1844, 1: 71). Ramond de Carbonnières (1789: 346), who did so much to spread the fashion for mountains, thought that the "commerce in emanations" took place only on the horizontal plane; it was limited to the social activities of the people of the plain or valley. The elite should be able to escape it by taking to the heights, leaving the stenches of congestion to the confined masses.

The rich man had to enjoy pure air. The wide casements of his dwelling, the unrestricted space that surrounded him were not enough. Tronchin advised him to take walks for fresh air and warned him against the stagnation of repose. Diderot and Sophie Volland left Paris every summer, one for Chevrette or the Grand Val, the other for Isle. Saint-Preux was surprised that vaporish people were not sent to the mountains. In 1778 Thouvenel endeavored to promote aerotherapy, still in its early stages and made fashionable by the philosophers. Jurine advocated "aerial baths" (1789: 95). The "air cure," still a vague idea, became a medical prescription before public health experts in the next century improved its practice and expertly adapted it to age, sex and temperament (Dagognet 1959: 76, 85).

Remedial properties were attributed to gardens and mountains, the antitheses of putrid places. Géraud pleaded for more public parks so that the city dweller could go and release his miasmas under their protective shade (1786: 95). But mountains remained the supreme reference point. Remaining at an altitude might, of course, prove hazardous, Saussure warned his readers (1779–96, 1: 518). The air breathed in the "confines of the ether is dry and devoid of emanations from the inhabited earth" (Senancour 1844, 1: 54). It was distressing to the reckless tourist. The "degeneration" of the Swiss mountain dwellers, the ugliness of their wives, the cretinism of the inhabitants of the Maurienne all were reasons for prudence (Senancour 1844, 2: 174). But these lonely places at least permitted the access that was vital to the pleasure of sensation. It was the silence of the mountain pastures that provided the context allowing Obermann to enjoy the sound of the fountain.

The garden's seclusion also permitted the creation of the "romantic situation," which Girardin defined as follows: "without being wild or unkempt [it] ... must be tranquil and solitary so that nothing distracts the soul and it can give itself up entirely to the sweetness of a deep emotion" (1777: 128). Here, the sense of smell was invested with powerful affects— despite its devaluation by those who regarded it as the sense of animality.

"The pleasures of the senses must have a basis, or at least a pretext, in nature so that they do not injure reason," decreed Watelet (1764: 34). This requirement for "landscapes or selected nature" led to the obsolescence of the skillful combination of perfumes in flower beds in favor of a very limited range of scents. The odor of newmown hay was henceforth the supreme balsamic reference point. Louis-Sébastien Mercier, Ramond de Carbonnières and Senancour, here following Loaisel de Tréogate, praised its refreshing subtlety. "Around four o'clock I was awakened by daybreak and the odor of hay that had been cut in all its freshness by moonlight," Obermann disclosed (1844, 1: 23). Thus the perfume known as "Newmown Hay" made its name. Henceforth most references to smells in the literature devoted to the pleasures of nature were divided among jonquils, violets and jasmine. Roses, so highly valued by perfumers, seemed old-fashioned. Strawberries tended to epitomize the pleasant odor of fruit.

Making the garden the source of olfactory pleasures initially seems paradoxical. A garden was, of course, primarily, a picture. Its composition was based on "the mechanism of sight" (Lefaivre and Tzonis 1977: 74). Architects were clearly guided by the desire to indulge sight and hearing above the other senses. The English garden provided the opportunity to consecrate and enact a hierarchy of the senses in a manner that resembled a religious litany. Girardin (1777: 123) extolled the superiority of sight with its more immediate, keener, subtler impressions. Hirschfeld summarized the position decisively in 1779: Of all the senses "the sense of smell, which receives the sweet exhalations of plants and vegetables, seems to be the last, unless it is joined with the coarser sense of touch, to experience the refreshing action of the air"; consequently the artist, "though without neglecting the sense of smell entirely," had to "work for the eye and the ear, particularly for the eye. Therefore, the gardener will mainly endeavor to expose the visible beauties of rural nature" (1779–85, 1: 185, 186). Although these developments diminished the role of flowers, the latter continued to be used primarily to gratify the eye; their first function was to carpet the hillside, to dot the meadow, not to delight the sense of smell. The increased number of theatrical scenes set in "picturesque gardens" confirmed the primacy of the visual. Only the ear, reassuring witness of the purifying movement of wind and, even more, of water, could compete temporarily with the eye in the scale of sensual enjoyment. Neither Thomas Whately (1771), whose influence was considerable, nor Jean-Marie Morel (1776) alluded to olfactory pleasure.

Nevertheless, the sense of smell did form part of the sensual palette available to the artist who wanted to vary the production of sensations and feelings. Perfume could help to perfect a strategy of emotional satisfaction. Thenceforth it would be irrelevant to try to analyze too exclusively what originated from each sense; to do so would amount to rejecting the quest for "corresponding perceptions," which, according to Hirschfeld, were essential if gardens were to be places that sated the senses. "A grove embellished by fresh foliage and smiling prospects is even more delightful when at the same time we hear the song of the nightingale, the murmur of a waterfall, and when we breathe the sweet odor of violets" (Hirschfeld 1779–85, 1: 185).

Analysis of the discourse on landscapes, parks and gardens makes it appear that references to the sense of smell involve only a limited number of places, attitudes and feelings. The sense of smell was solicited primarily to accommodate the wish for repose. The approaches to the house and to the bedroom, the arbors sheltering the bower or resting place, the bed of moss that invited a halt in the depths of the valley and, in a more general way, "serene regions" called for plants with odoriferous flowers or foliage in the vicinity (Girardin 1777: 52). No one has defined this subtle imperative— already expressed by Horace Walpole (1785)—better than Hirschfeld. The model here was not so much Julie's garden as the bower that sheltered the love of the first couple in Eden's "wilderness of sweets" in *Paradise Lost*.

The sense of smell was solicited wherever running water bestowed its freshness and encouraged sensory associations. Girardin recommended decorating banks of streams with odoriferous plants. In the heart of the oak wood, near the source, "simple aromatics, wholesome herbs, and the resin from odoriferous pines perfume the air with a balsamic odor that expands the lungs" and invited reverie (Girardin 1777: 48). Hirschfeld advised strewing flowers near bridges where strollers liked to sit down (1779–85, 1: 51).

It was also possible to deploy heady perfumes when work and the need for fertilization justified them. Locating a flowery close next to the apiary was a practical measure: "Thyme, lavender, marjoram, willow, limes, poplar grow in profusion there and scent the air one breathes over a wide area. Here the luxury of flowers and perfumes is allowed" (Watelet 1764: 34).

The optimistic identification of the natural with the vital and the wholesome was a way of acknowledging both the attraction exercised by the perfume of growing plants and the odoriferous sensuality of the open air. The penetrating odor of some country flowers could intoxicate; it was an inducement to sexual pleasures, as was suggested by the resemblance between the facial expressions of a woman when smelling a flower and when making love. According to some experts, this ambiguous marriage between the woman and the flower she smelled could end in orgasm. The perfumed arbor, the bower it sheltered, places of solitude, repose and dreams were easily transformed into privileged theaters of vertiginous abandon. The perfume of nature merged with the incense of voluptuousness. The young countess's seduction by the guilty Dolbreuse, like the excitement of the open-air wedding night, owed a great deal to the alliance of natural perfumes (Tréogate 1783: 80, 174). Orange blossom, jasmine and honeysuckle perfumed the loves of Sydney and Félicia (Nerciat [1776] 1979). The subtle hedonism of plant life surpassed even the skillfully perfumed backcloths constructed for pleasure by the libertine.

The bulky literature devoted to the "English" garden should not eclipse the continued existence of the flower garden, a perfumed enclosure round the house. Both Girardin and Hirschfeld persistently emphasized the bourgeois fashion for this "pleasure garden." Women and, even more, young girls found in it something to stir their sensibilities. They went there to compose their vapors by breathing "sweet, delicate, pleasing and refreshing perfumes, suited to revive their spirits" (Hirschfeld 1779–85, 5: 66).

The essential function of olfaction in all these favored places was clearly to encourage narcissism. Far from the *theatrum mundi*, informed by the staleness of worldly intercourse, tempted by hermitages, grottoes in picturesque gardens, or mountain rocks, the reader of Rousseau's *Rêveries*, Werther's confidences, or Young's *Nights* dreamed of intensely experiencing the existence of the "I." Because it contributed to awareness of the flight of the self, the sense of smell was henceforth the favored sense for the perception of time. The landscape artist had to observe the clock of the smells of nature; there were morning, midday or evening gardens, and he had to choose among them. If he intended to give particular importance to perfumes, he chose evening scents, because it was undisputed that the exhalation of plants emphasized with particular intensity the flight of day. According to Ramond de Carbonnières, this was what made the odor of the Pyrenean fringed red carnation so moving (1789: 165). Olfaction thus played a large role in the endlessly savored theme of the seasons.

What was really new was the power of odors to stir the affective memory; the search for the "memorative sign" (as Rousseau put it) (see Starobinski 1971: 196), the violent confrontation of the past and present engendered by recognition of an odor, could produce an encounter that, far from abolishing temporality, made the "I" feel its own history and disclose it to itself. Just as the growing fashion for subtle perfume gave the remembered image of the Other a poetic resonance, so literary descriptions of smells concentrated on their power to engender reminiscence itself. Two examples will suffice among the thousands available.

"There is something indefinable in perfumes that powerfully awakens memory of the past. Nothing so much recalls beloved places, regretted situations, the passing of those minutes that left as deep imprints on the heart as they left few in the memory. The odor of a violet restores to the soul the pleasures of many springs. I do not know what sweeter moments in my life the flowering lime tree saw, but I feel keenly that it disturbs long tranquil fibers, that it rouses from deep slumber memories linked with beautiful days; I found a veil between my heart and my mind that it would perhaps be sweet—perhaps sad—for me to lift." So wrote Ramond de Carbonnières (1789: 88). Obermann told his correspondent that the odor of mown hay at Chessel made him remember the "lovely barn where we used to jump when I was a child" (Senancour 1844, 2: 58).

Yves Castan (1980), following Lucien Febvre and Robert Mandrou, has shown that hearing was for a long time accepted as the sense of social communication, as opposed to sight, source of intellectual knowledge. The increased role of sight was manifested in legal procedure; in the courts, hearsay was gradually subordinated to eyewitness testimony. But from the mid-eighteenth century on, a new aesthetic movement tended to make olfaction the sense that generated the great movements of the soul.

"Odor," noted Saint-Lambert, "gives us the most intimate sensations, a more immediate pleasure, more independent of the mind, than the sense of sight; we get profound enjoyment from an agreeable odor at the first moment of its impression; the pleasure of sight belongs more to reflections, to the desires aroused by the objects perceived, to the hopes they give birth to" (qtd. in Mauzi 1960: 320).

The sense of smell, by virtue of the very transience of its impression (sad tribute to the power of odor to penetrate consciousness), aroused the sensitive soul, which was then unable to flee from the sensations it had inspired. A strange correspondence was established between the transience of indescribable odor and the revelation of that vague desire, without hope of satisfaction, that was the basis of narcissism. "Jonquil! violet! tuberose! You last but moments!" regretted Obermann, fascinated yet disappointed by the precariousness of the feelings they suggested (Senancour 1844, 2: 268). Of all the senses, smell was best able to produce the experience of the existence of an "I" conceived as the "contraction of the whole self around one single point" (Mauzi 1960: 114). The means of access that it offered to the inner void differed from the approach offered by listening to the rhythms of water. Given his importance in defining new notions of the self, Rousseau's flagrant anosmia, at least in his writing, has probably led later historians to minimize the importance of the role of the sense of smell in the period.

It was already apparent that the sense of smell reveals more idiosyncrasies than does any other sense. "Everyone has his unknown nervous disposition," noted the author of the article "Odorat" in the *Encylopédie*, concerning the close connection between the respiration of odors and the discharge or retention of vapors. The intolerance to musk henceforth evinced by the elite reflected the intensification of individual sensibilities. Disorders, which we are tempted to see as allergic, were analyzed in terms of idiosyncrasy for nearly a century. According to the most prominent osphresiologists, notably Hippolyte Cloquet, behavior in relation to smells gave vent to the individual's most secret inclinations and imposed them on the whole organism.

The inner experience resulting from the transient effect produced by the odor of the ephemeral flower should be compared with the reaction to excremental odors. We have seen how obsessive perceptions of the progress of putrefaction in living bodies proved at that time. "We live in infection, carrying an intolerable odor inside ourselves always," exclaimed Caraccioli (qtd. in Mauzi 1960: 195). The place for defecation became specific and individualized. The privatization of waste tended to make it the place for an inner monologue. The only English type water closets installed at Versailles were reserved for the king and Marie Antoinette. Thus they were among the first individuals in France to experience a new privacy. Their example favored that individuation of social practices which encouraged narcissism. Tombs soon became individual and lost their stench. There was already a tendency to discharge hospital patients who could not be cured because they themselves were putrefying. In 1813 Fodéré recommended the exclusion of the scrofulous, "constantly confined in an atmosphere impregnated with the putrid emanations from their bodies" (1813, 6: 526).

The sense of smell, again more than the other senses, permitted the individual to experience the harmony of the organization of the universe. Natural odor, by its very transience, introduced into feeling something of that universal harmony which rendered death incomprehensible and allowed hope of a better world. The "shock of the transient" became a "sudden call" (Senancour 1844, 2: 269, 268). Robert Mauzi's analysis throws considerable light on the depth of the change: "Unity between nature and man gives the illusion of a unity within man. Sensation reestablishes the thread that was broken between heart and mind. A simple perfume grows into a sudden awareness of self. This has the effect of associating the 'I' with nature, until then foreign to it" (Mauzi 1960: 317).

Experience of this coexistence encouraged a new sensuality that was no longer instinctive voracity but, so Watelet defined it, the art of the "most perfect relationships among external objects, the senses, and the state of the soul" (qtd. in Mauzi 1960: 319). No one expressed better than Senancour that vertiginous power of the sense of smell available to individuals endowed with refined sensitivity. Spring flowers issued to the chosen soul sudden calls to "the most inward life." "A jonquil was blooming. This is the strongest expression of desire: it was the first perfume of the year. I felt all the happiness set aside for man" (Senancour 1844, 1: 113). "Most people could not conceive the relationships between the odor that a plant exhales and the way to happiness in the world. Ought they to regard the sense of these relationships as an error of imagination because of this? Are these two perceptions, which to many minds seem so foreign one to each other, foreign to the spirit who can follow the chain that joins them?" (Senancour 1844, 1: 244–5).

It is impossible to overemphasize the importance of the flower of the field, with its shy, natural, capricious perfume, a free gift, an infinitesimal ripple that taught the true value of the first stirring of the heart. Revealing unfathomable desires, it was the model on which the image of the young girl was structured.

At the end of the eighteenth century gardens and mountains became places for a multiple quest. The traveler came not only to seek repose or sensual pleasure in their perfumed solitude. Flight from the putrid crowd allowed for the possibility of reminiscence, awakened narcissism, admitted a presentiment of universal harmony, favored the outpourings of the solitary lover. But it was the odor of the jonquil, more than the sight of the landscape composed by the garden artist or the contemplation of rocky vastness, that led to this new sensuality. Later, the functions attributed to springtime scents would progressively devolve on perfumes during the era of the aesthetics of smell.

But for the time being, the focus was on the deodorization of bodies and the environment in order to produce the sensory calm deemed indispensable to the voluptuous disturbances of the "I." Medical instructions for checking putrid fevers and stemming miasmas, the metaphysical anxiety engendered by the advance of putrefaction to the very depths of being, the rise of narcissism and the desire for physical access to scents that it aroused, the wish to be perpetually on the alert to receive natural odors revealing the existence of the "I" and the harmony of the world, the fear aroused by social emanations that were still confused and undifferentiated—all these factors combined to promote the deodorization tactics put into effect from the mid-eighteenth century on. These facts explain the lowering of the threshold of tolerance for stench, the emergence of a fashion for delicate perfumes, and the limited advance in bodily hygiene. Moreover, beyond its formal articulation in medical discourse, this revolution in perception spread, polymorphously, throughout the whole of society.

Bibliography

Baumes, J.-B. (1789), *Mémoire*, n.p.: n.p.

Casanova, G.J. (1977), *Mémoires, 1744–1756*, Paris: n.p.

Castan, Y. (1980), communication to a colloquium on the history of prisons, held at l'Ecole des Hautes Etudes en Sciences Sociales, 19 December.

Chartier, R., Julia, D. and Compère, M.-M. (1976), *L'Education en France du XVIe siècle*, Paris: n.p.

Dagognet, F. (1959), "La Cure d'air," *Thalès*, 10: 75–98.

Déjean, M. (Antoine de Hornot) (1764), *Traité des odeurs*, n.p.: n.p.

Dumas, A. (1868), "Les Parfums," in *Le (Petit) Moniteur Universel du Soir*, 16 October.

Ellis, H. (1905), *Sexual Selection in Man*, vol. 4 of *Studies in the Psychology of Sex*, Philadelphia: F.A. Davis.

Fodéré, F.-E. (1813), *Traité de médecine légale et d'hygiène publique oui de police de santé*, n.p.: n.p.

Freud, S. (1975), "Civilization and Its Discontents," in *The Standard Edition of the Complete Psychological Works of Sigmund Freud*, J. Strachey (ed.), vol. 21, London: Hogarth Press.

Géraud, M. (1786), *Essai sur la suppression des fosses d'aisances et de toute espèce de voirie*, Amsterdam: n.p.

Girardin, R.-L. (1777), *De la composition des paysages*, n.p.: n.p.

Hagen, I.B. (1901), *Die Sexuelle Osphrésiologie*, Leipzig: n.p.

Hallé, J.-N. (1785), *Recherches sur la nature et les effets du méphitisme des fosses d'aisances*, Paris: n.p.

Hartley, D. (1755), *Explication physique des sens, des idées et des mouvements tant volontaires qu'involontaires*, vol. 1, Paris: n.p.

Hirschfeld, C.C.L. (1779–85), *Théorie de l'art des jardins*, 5 vols., Leipzig: n.p.

Jurine, L. (1789), *Histoire et Mémoires de la Société Royal de Médecine*, 10, n.p.: n.p.

Le Cat, N. (1767), *Traité des sensations et des passions en general et des sens en particulier*, n.p: n.p.

Lefaivre, L. and Tzonis, A. (1977), "La Géométrie du sentiment et la paysage thérapeutique," *XVIIIe Siècle*, 9.

Malouin, P.-J. (1750), *Chimie médicinale*, n.p.: n.p.

Mauzi, R. (1960), *L'Idée du bonheur au XVIIIe Siècle*, Paris: n.p.

Mercier, L.-S. (1782–88), *Tableau de Paris*, 12 vols., Paris: n.p.

Moheau (A. Auget, baron of Montyon) (1778), *Recherches et considérations sur la population de la France*, n.p.: n.p.

Morel, J.-M. (1776), *Théorie des jardins*, n.p.: n.p.

Nerciat, A. de ([1776] 1979), *Félicia ou mes fredaines*, Paris: n.p.

Le Parfumeur royal (1761), n.p.: n.p.

Parny, E.-D. D. de (1861), "Le Cabinet de toilette," in *Oeuvres de Parny*, 3 vols., n.p.: n.p.

Ramond, L.-F. (1789), *Observations faites dans les Pyrénées pour servir de suite à des observations sur les Alpes*, n.p.: n.p.

Saussure, H.B. de (1779–96), *Voyages dans les Alpes*, 4 vols., Neuchatel: n.p.

Senancour, E. (1844), *Obermann*, 2 vols., n.p.: n.p.

Starobinski, J. (1971), *La Transparence et l'obstacle*, Paris: n.p.

Tréogate, L. de (1783), *Dolbreuse*, n.p.: n.p.

Walpole, H. (1785), *Essay on Modern Gardening*, London: n.p.

Watelet, C.-H. (1764), *Essai sur les jardins*, n.p.: n.p.

Whately, T. (1771) *Observations on Modern Gardening*, London: n.p.

14
Sense and Sensibility

Helen Keller

Smell is a Fallen Angel

For some inexplicable reason the sense of smell does not hold the high position it deserves among its sisters. There is something of the fallen angel about it. When it woos us with woodland scents and beguiles us with the fragrance of lovely gardens, it is admitted frankly to our discourse. But when it gives us warning of something noxious in our vicinity, it is treated as if the demon had got the upper hand of the angel, and is relegated to outer darkness, punished for its faithful service.

In my experience smell is most important, and I find that there is high authority for the nobility of the sense which we have neglected and disparaged. It is recorded that the Lord commanded that incense be burnt before Him continually with a sweet savor. I doubt if there is any sensation arising from sight more delightful than the odors which filter through sun-warmed, wind-tossed branches, or the tide of scents which swells, subsides, rises again wave on wave, filling the wide world with invisible sweetness. A whiff of the universe makes us dream of worlds we have never seen, recalls in a flash entire epochs of our dearest experience. I never smell daisies without living over again the ecstatic mornings that my teacher and I spent wandering in the fields, while I learned new words and the names of things. Smell is a potent wizard that transports us across a thousand miles and all the years we have lived. The odor of fruits wafts me to my Southern home, to my childish frolics in the peach orchard. Other odors, instantaneous and fleeting, cause my heart to dilate joyously or contract with remembered grief. Even as I think of smells, my nose is full of scents that start awake memories of summers gone and ripening grain fields far away.

The faintest whiff from a meadow where the new-mown hay lies in the hot sun displaces the here and the now. I am back again in the old red barn.

My little friends and I are playing in the haymow. The sense of smell has told me of a coming storm hours before there was any sign of it visible. I notice first a throb of expectancy, a slight quiver, a concentration in my nostrils. As the storm draws nearer, my nostrils dilate the better to receive the flood of earth-odors which seem to multiply and extend, until I feel the splash of rain against my cheek. I know by smell the kind of house we enter. I have recognized an old-fashioned country house because it has several layers of odors, left by a succession of families, of plants, perfumes and draperies.

In the evening quiet there are fewer vibrations than in the daytime, and then I rely more largely upon smell. The sulphuric scent of a match tells me that the lamps are being lighted. Later, I note the wavering trail of odor that flits about and disappears. It is the curfew signal; the lights are out for the night.

The Elusive Person-odor

From exhalations I learn much about people. I often know the work they are engaged in. The odors of wood, iron, paint and drugs cling to the garments of those that work in them. Thus I can distinguish the carpenter from the ironworker, the artist from the mason or the chemist. When a person passes quickly from one place to another I get a scent impression of where he has been—the kitchen, the garden or the sick-room. I gain pleasurable ideas of freshness and good taste from the odors of soap, toilet water, clean garments, woolen and silk stuffs and gloves.

I have not, indeed, the all-knowing scent of the hound or the wild animal. None but the halt and the blind need fear my skill in pursuit; for there are other things besides water, stale trails, confusing cross tracks to put me at fault. Nevertheless, human odors are as varied and capable of recognition as hands and faces. The dear odors of those I love are so definite, so unmistakable, that nothing can quite obliterate them. If many years should elapse before I saw an intimate friend again, I think I should recognize his odor instantly in the heart of Africa, as promptly as would my brother that barks.

Once, long ago, in a crowded railway station, a lady kissed me as she hurried by. I had not touched even her dress. But she left a scent with her kiss which gave me a glimpse of her. The years are many since she kissed me. Yet her odor is fresh in my memory.

It is difficult to put into words the thing itself, the elusive person-odor. There seems to be no adequate vocabulary of smells, and I must fall back on approximate phrase and metaphor.

Some people have a vague, unsubstantial odor that floats about, mocking every effort to identify it. It is the will-o'-the-wisp of my olfactive experience. Sometimes I meet one who lacks a distinctive person-scent, and I seldom find such a one lively or entertaining. On the other hand, one who has a pungent odor often possesses great vitality, energy and vigor of mind.

Masculine exhalations are as a rule stronger, more vivid, more widely differentiated than those of women. In the odor of young men there is something elemental, as of fire, storm and salt sea. It pulsates with buoyancy and desire. It suggests all things strong and beautiful and joyous, and gives me a sense of physical happiness. I wonder if others observe that all infants have the same scent—pure, simple, undecipherable as their dormant personality. It is not until the age of six or seven that they begin to have perceptible individual odors. These develop and mature along with their mental and bodily powers.

15

The Dog Beneath
the Skin

Oliver Sacks

Stephen D., aged 22, medical student, on highs (cocaine, PCP, chiefly amphetamines).

Vivid dream one night, dreamt he was a dog, in a world unimaginably rich and significant in smells. Waking, he found himself in just a world. "I had dreamt I was a dog—it was an olfactory dream—and now I awoke to an infinitely redolent world—a world in which all other sensations, enhanced as they were, paled before smell." And with all this there went a sort of trembling, eager emotion, and a strange nostalgia, as of a lost world, half-forgotten, half-recalled.

"I went into a scent shop," he continued. "I had never had much of a nose for smells before, but now I distinguished each one instantly—and I found each one unique, evocative, a whole world." He found he could distinguish all his friends—and patients—by smell: "I went into the clinic, I sniffed like a dog, and in that sniff recognized, before seeing them, the twenty patients who were there. Each had his own olfactory physiognomy, a smell-face, far more vivid and evocative, more redolent, than any sight face." He could smell their emotions—fear, contentment, sexuality—like a dog. He could recognize every street, every shop, by smell—he could find his way around New York, infallibly, by smell.

He experienced a certain impulse to sniff and touch everything ("It wasn't really real until I felt it and smelt it") but suppressed this, when with others, lest he seem inappropriate. Sexual smells were exciting and increased—but no more so, he felt, than food smells and other smells. Smell pleasure was intense—smell displeasure, too—but it seemed to him less a world of mere pleasure and displeasure than a whole aesthetic, a whole judgment, a whole new significance, which surrounded him. "It was a world overwhelmingly concrete, of particulars," he said, "a world overwhelming in immediacy, in immediate significance." Somewhat intellectual before, and inclined to reflection and abstraction, he now found thought, abstraction and categorization somewhat difficult and unreal, in view of the compelling immediacy of each experience.

Rather suddenly, after three weeks, this strange transformation ceased—his sense of smell returned to normal; he found himself back, with a sense of mingled loss and relief, in his old world of pallor, sensory faintness, non-concreteness and abstraction. "I'm glad to be back," he said, "but it's a tremendous loss, too. I see now what we give up in being civilized and human. We need the other—the 'primitive'—as well."

Sixteen years have passed—and student days, amphetamine days, are long over. There has never been any recurrence of anything remotely similar. He has no regrets—but he is occasionally nostalgic: "That smell-world, that world of redolence," he exclaims. "So vivid, so real! It was like a visit to another world, a world of pure perception, rich, alive, self-sufficient, and full. If only I could go back sometimes and be a dog again!"

I have recently encountered a sort of corollary of this case—a gifted man who sustained a head injury, severely damaging his olfactory tracts and, in consequence, entirely losing his sense of smell.

He has been startled and distressed at the effects of this: "Sense of smell?" he says. "I never gave it a thought. You don't normally give it a thought. But when I lost it—it was like being struck blind. Life lost a good deal of its savor—one doesn't realize how much 'savor' *is* smell. You *smell* people, you *smell* books, you *smell* the city, you *smell* the spring—maybe not consciously, but as a rich unconscious background to everything else. My whole world was suddenly radically poorer..."

There was an acute sense of loss, and an acute sense of yearning, a veritable osmalgia: a desire to remember the smell-world to which he had paid no conscious attention, but which, he now felt, had formed the very ground base of life. And then, some months later, to his astonishment and joy, his favorite morning coffee, which had become "insipid," started to regain its savor. Tentatively he tried his pipe, not touched for months, and here too caught a hint of the rich aroma he loved.

Greatly excited—the neurologists had held out no hope of recovery—he returned to his doctor. But after testing him minutely using a "double-blind" technique, his doctor said: "No, I'm sorry, there's not a trace of recovery. You still have a total anosmia. Curious though that you should now 'smell' your pipe and coffee..."

What seems to be happening—and it is important that it was only the olfactory tracts, not the cortex, which were damaged—is the development of a greatly enhanced olfactory imagery, almost, one might say, a controlled hallucinosis, so that in drinking his coffee, or lighting his pipe—situations normally and previously fraught with associations of smell—he is now able to evoke or re-evoke these, unconsciously, and with such intensity as to think, at first, that they are "real."

This power—part conscious, part unconscious—has intensified and spread. Now, for example, he snuffs and "smells" the spring. At least he calls up a smell-memory, or smell-picture, so intense that he can almost deceive himself, and deceive others, into believing that he truly smells it.

16

Nostalgia, the Odors of Childhood and Society

Alan R. Hirsch

As children grow up, moving into new environments and new relationships, they must, even in the best of circumstances, relinquish something pleasant in the life that is left behind. As the old milieu recedes, the screen of memory emphasizes the pleasant aspects and filters out the unpleasant ones. More than any other sensations, odors are particularly effective in inducing a vivid recall of an entire scene or episode from the past. A special odor may revive a clear image of the past and, more important, the enhanced emotional state associated with that image.

Healthy individuals can smell 10,000 odors, but no two people will respond to a particular odor in exactly the same way. Who they are, where they live, whether they have smelled the odor before and under what circumstances all enter into the reaction. Among people from the Eastern United States, the scent of flowers prompts nostalgic feelings; among those from the South, the scent of fresh air; among those from the Midwest, the smells of farm animals and among those from the West Coast, the smells of meat cooking or barbecuing often prompt such feelings. The most common odor known to stimulate an olfactory-evoked recall in people, regardless of their geographic origin, is the odor of baked goods.

In September 1991, we interviewed nearly 1,000 shoppers (511 females and 478 males), selected at random at Water Tower Place on Michigan Avenue in Chicago. While most of them had grown up in the city or suburbs, forty-five states and thirty-nine countries were represented. Their responses showed that eighty-five percent were susceptible to certain odors that triggered nostalgic feelings. This was true both for those who reported that they had happy childhoods and for those who said their childhoods were unhappy.

Equal numbers of men and women, about one person out of twelve, reported having had an unhappy childhood. We had anticipated that an unhappy childhood might preclude nostalgic feelings, but, surprisingly, this was not the case. Yet there was one remarkable difference between the groups who reported happy childhoods compared to those with unhappy childhoods. People with unhappy childhoods were twice as likely to have an olfactory-evoked recall precipitated by an odor that most of us consider foul, such as body odor, dog waste, mothballs, sewer gas and bus fumes.

We interviewed people who were born before 1930 in less urbanized and industrialized times who mentioned such natural odors as pine, hay, horses, sea air and meadows as reminiscent of childhood. But those born after 1930 were more apt to mention food and artificial odors such as plastic, scented markers, airplane fuel, Vaporub® and Play-Doh® as reminiscent of their childhood.

Responses to the same odors can also change over time. When we questioned the shoppers who had happy childhoods, those born before 1960 liked the smell of newly cut grass, but those born between 1960 and 1979 disliked the smell, associating it with the "unpleasant necessity" of having to mow the lawn. This is a striking illustration of how history, lifestyle and changing technology affect perceptions.

What this shift may presage, we can only speculate. But the implications for our changing values may not be encouraging. If nostalgia for the odors of the natural world experienced in childhood is an important impetus behind our concern to preserve the environment, that concern may fare poorly in another generation when the children of today become adults who can only experience olfactory-evoked recall in response to manufactured chemical odors. In that event, society will certainly feel less urgency to preserve a natural environment that has lost its power to appeal to special nostalgic yearnings.

Odors Often Evoke Feelings of Nostalgia

People born in the 1920s:
  flowers, grass, roses, pine, soap, manure

People born in the 1930s:
  flowers, hay, sea air, pine, baby powder, burning leaves

People born in the 1940s:
  baby powder, mother's perfume, hay, cut grass, flowers, sea air, roses, tweed

People born in the 1950s:
  baby powder, mother's perfume, dad's cologne, crayons, pine, Play-Doh®

People born in the 1960s:

baby powder, mother's perfume, chlorine, window cleaner, dad's cologne, detergent, paste, Play-Doh®, disinfectant, refineries/factories, motor oil, exhaust

People born in the 1970s:

baby powder, mother's perfume, mothballs, plastic, hair spray, suntan oil, chlorine, felt-tip pens

17

I Know What I Like

Understanding Odor Preferences

Rachel S. Herz

Do you like the smell of skunk? I do, and I bet a few of you are nodding your heads in agreement. But most are no doubt wondering what sort of strange people find the smell of skunk pleasant. Your response to my question is the subject of fundamental inquiry into the perception (and psychology) of olfaction, the science of smell.

Why do we like some odors and not others? Are we born hardwired to like or dislike certain smells, or do we acquire these preferences? I argue that our odor preferences are not innate and rather that we have *learned* through experience to like or dislike all the scents in our repertoire. I like the smell of skunk because the first time I smelled it, on a lovely summer's day, my mother said: "Isn't that smell nice?" Ever since then, it has indeed smelled nice to me.

Most olfactory scientists agree that olfactory responses are learned, but not all are convinced. You, too, may initially disagree, but my goal is to present you with evidence that our responses to odors are learned; our specific personal history with specific odors gives them meaning, making them pleasant or unpleasant to us.

How We Perceive a Smell

Odors are volatile molecules; they float in the air. When we breathe, air enters the nostrils and is swept upward into the nasal passages, where odor molecules settle on a mucous membrane called the olfactory epithelia. The olfactory epithelia contains olfactory sensory neurons, small nerve cells covered with cilia that protrude into the mucus that coats the nasal epithelium. These cilia, which are actually the dendrites of olfactory neurons, have odorant receptors on their tips. Research by Linda Buck and Richard Axel (1991) showed that mice have about 1,000 different types of odor receptors, with specific genes regulating each different receptor. In humans, however, the number of types of functioning receptors appears to be between 300 and 400. Nevertheless, we have about 20 million olfactory receptors covering the epithelia of our right and left nostrils. Although this is more receptors than we have for any other sense except vision, contrast our measly 20 million olfactory receptors with those of a bloodhound, which has about 200 million, and you can see why we are considered relatively poor smellers.

The journey of an odor from the nose into the brain is an extremely short path. From the nose, the axons of the olfactory neurons connect directly to the brain by passing through tiny, sievelike holes of a bony structure called the cribiform plate. The axons from each nostril then bundle together to form the olfactory nerve, which transmits electrical impulses to the olfactory bulbs. Unlike the wiring in other senses, olfaction is "ipsilateral," which means that the right olfactory bulb receives information from the right nostril and the left olfactory bulb receives information from the left nostril. There is no crossover from right to left, as in the case of the visual system.

From the olfactory bulbs, sensory information is routed to the primary olfactory cortex, part of a brain area called the piriform cortex that is connected to the limbic system, where brain structures responsible for emotion are found. The chief limbic structures that communicate with the olfactory system are the amygdala and the hippocampus. Only two synapses separate the olfactory bulb from the amygdala, which is critical for the expression and experience of emotion. Only three synapses are needed to connect to the hippocampus, which is necessary for associative learning and various forms of memory. The connections between the olfactory area and the amygdala and hippocampus are more direct than the connections between these brain areas and any other sense. This uniquely direct neuroanatomical link between olfaction and the parts of the brain related to emotion and learning-memory is the key to understanding why odor-evoked memories are distinguished from other types of memories by their emotional potency—and also why associations between odors and emotions are so readily formed.

From the limbic system, olfactory information makes its way to the orbitofrontal cortex, which also receives taste information and is the place where the brain interprets flavor. From the orbitofrontal cortex, olfactory information is then sent to structures in the neocortex for cognitive processing.

An important distinction must be made here between taste and flavor. Taste comprises only the five basic tongue sensations of salt, sour, sweet, bitter and (the latest addition) *umami*, or savory. Flavor, on the other hand, is a combination of these basic tastes, plus smell. You distinguish the flavor of a cold cup of coffee from a glass of red wine only by smell, not taste.

How the System Works

Olfaction did not attract much scientific attention until fairly recently. In the last decade, a spike in olfactory research has occurred, particularly at the molecular level. But despite more than ten years of intense study of the genetics, biochemistry and neurophysiology of olfaction (along with psychological research), we still do not know for sure how the molecular composition of an odorant is translated into the psychological perception of "aha, the smell of banana" or "aha, the smell of mildew."

The most widely accepted hypothesis today is what scientists call "shape theory." Odorant receptors have different shapes, and how well an odor molecule is detected is determined by how well it fits into the olfactory receptor. Note that there are many molecules that are too big or do not meet other criteria to fit into olfactory receptors, and therefore cannot smelled at all. Once a sufficient number of molecules have stimulated a receptor, the receptor fires an action potential (a nerve impulse). Recent biochemical and molecular work indicate that different odorants activate arrays of olfactory receptors in the olfactory epithelia producing specific firing patterns of neurons in the olfactory bulb. According to shape theory, the specific pattern of electrical activity in the olfactory bulb determines the scent we perceive. The smell of a banana elicits a different pattern of neural impulses from the smell of mildew.

Shape theory is not accepted by all. Some, such as Luca Turin, Chandler Burr's emperor in *The Emperor of Scent* (2002), propose a vibration theory. Here, the perception of scents is proposed to be due to the different vibrational frequencies of the molecules that comprise them—with vibrationally similar molecules producing perceptually similar scents. This has been shown to be true for some scent categories, such as citrus, but overall there is much more evidence in favor of shape theory.

A complete understanding of the translation from odor stimulus to perceived smell sensation will require combined efforts by scientists in molecular biology, neurophysiology and psychology. Through molecular biology and neurophysiology, we should be able to identify and determine the biochemical and structural mechanisms and pathways between the nasal epithelia and the olfactory bulb. Psychologists will have to explore whether you and I both experience the same sensation when we label what we smell as rose or skunk. Where does the sensory perception of a smell end and the emotional appreciation of that smell begin? Can we even separate the two? Undoubtedly, as we begin to answer questions in some of these areas, more answers—and more questions—will emerge in others.

Losing the Sense of Smell

The inability to smell, called anosmia, is not unusual. The rate in the US adult population is typically given as one in a hundred, but this is likely an underestimation. People commonly become anosmic through injury or illness. The easiest way is from a car accident or a sports injury, when a sharp blow to the head knocks the cribiform plate out of its normal alignment. As it moves, it shears off the olfactory axons that pass through it. In this case, because the axons have been cut off from their cell bodies, there is no way to regain the sense of smell. You can also lose your sense of smell through upper respiratory viral infections or by developing nasal polyps. In these cases, smell function sometimes can be regained, particularly from surgical intervention to reduce nasal obstructions.

Many people have specific anosmias—the inability to smell one type of compound only, where smell perception is otherwise normal. Most specific anosmias are to steroidal musk compounds and appear to be genetic in origin.

The specific anosmia that has been most extensively studied is to the musk compound androstenone. Half the population has a specific anosmia to androstenone. Interestingly, of the half who can smell it, about half of them describe the smell as sweet musky-floral and the other half describe it as an unpleasant urine-like odor. In this instance, perception of this compound appears to be hardwired in our bodies, which is potential evidence that olfactory responses are innate. But even here, experience can alter this biological determinism. People who formerly could not smell androstenone report being able to detect it after repeated exposure. Moreover, whether a particular person likes the smell of urine or dislikes florals is a psychological issue, different from how that person perceives a specific chemical. In other words, the separation is between denotation—detecting and classifying the scent as something—and connotation—liking or not liking it. Here I am primarily concerned with showing that the connotation of odors is acquired, although there is a complex overlap between how an odor is denoted and how it is connoted.

The Feel of a Smell

An important dimension of olfaction, which is often not appreciated, is that most smells have a feel to them. Menthol feels cool, ammonia is burning. We perceive this feel through the trigeminal nerve, which runs throughout the face and the nose. In addition to giving odors their pungent and temperature qualities, the trigeminal nerve is responsible for our tears when we cut onions and for our sneezes when we smell pepper. Almost all odors have a trigeminal component, varying from mild to intense. For example, geraniol (sweet rose) is mild, benzyl acetate (synthetic pear-like) is moderate, and acetone is strong. Intense trigeminal stimulation can be irritating, even painful. Odors that do not stimulate the trigeminal system are extremely rare, but include vanilla and hydrogen sulfide (rotten eggs).

In many cases, it is difficult to distinguish whether a sensation is arising from the olfactory or the trigeminal system, as in the case of smelling gasoline. The elicitation of a strong and irritating trigeminal response by an odor may explain why certain odors can be immediately disliked.

Learning Our Olfactory Likes and Dislikes

We learn the meaning (the connotation) of odors by association. We experience every smell in a context: semantic, social, emotional, physical. That context always has some emotional content, good or bad, albeit sometimes only weakly. The meaning and emotional feel of the context attach to the odor, which thereafter is interpreted according to this first experience—for example the comforting smell of fresh baked bread. Of all our senses, olfaction is especially predisposed to become associated with emotional meaning because of its neuroanatomical relationship with the amygdala–hippocampal complex, critically involved in forming and remembering emotional associations.

My argument is that the olfactory system is set up so that, through experience, meaning becomes attached to odor stimuli. This is in contrast to the proposition that we are hardwired to like or dislike various odor stimuli before ever smelling them. The two major sources of direct evidence in support of my argument come from research with infants and children and cross-cultural studies.

Where Odor Preferences Begin

We begin to learn the meaning of odors while still in the womb. Julie Mennella and her colleagues found that what a mother consumes during pregnancy or nursing can scent the chemical composition of her amniotic fluid or breast milk. Studies of in-utero exposure to volatile substances such as cigarette smoke, garlic and alcohol found that infants exposed to them showed preferences for these odors after birth, in contrast to infants who had not been exposed (Mennella and Beauchamp 1991). Further research has shown that when presented with toys scented with vanilla or alcohol, and identical unscented toys, infants who have at least one parent who consumes alcohol regularly preferred to mouth toys scented with alcohol than vanilla scented or unscented toys. These studies show how the arbitrary pairing of odor with experience leads to the formation of preferences.

By the same token, we have no physical predisposition to respond to odors like mother's milk; this must be learned, as well. Research with newborns showed that there is no initial preference for the smell of their mother's breast; the preference for breast odor builds as the infant feeds. In exactly the same manner, infants quickly learn to prefer perfume smells if those smells are paired with cuddling. We can conclude from this that our responses to both biologically meaningful and serendipitous odors are acquired by the same process; both types of odors acquire meaning through experience.

If they have had no prior exposure, infants and young children do not differentiate between odors that adults typically find either very unpleasant or pleasant. For example, studies by Trygg Engen (1988) showed that newborns gave the same response to asafetida (foul onion) and anise (licorice). Similarly four-year olds did not show different emotional reactions to butyric acid (rancid cheese) and amyl acetate (banana). The typical response to all these odors was avoidance. Other research with infants has even shown that sometimes they demonstrate responses opposite to those of adults, for example, liking the smell of synthetic sweat and feces. But by age eight, most children's responses to odors mimic those of the adults in their culture.

Only one study has suggested that children make adultlike responses to pleasant and unpleasant odors. Hilary Schmidt and Gary Beauchamp (1988) presented three-year-olds with various scents and then asked them to give the scent either to Big Bird (good) or Oscar the Grouch (bad). Children tended to give butyric acid (rancid cheese) to Oscar and methyl salicylate (wintergreen) to Big Bird, although their responses varied considerably. Some children gave the only other unpleasant odor tested, pyridine (spoiled milk), to Big Bird, even though all the adults in the sample rated it as unpleasant. It is worth noting, though, that by age three quite a bit of olfactory learning has already taken place.

Throughout our lifetime we acquire the emotional meaning of odors through experience, but first experiences are pivotal. This is why childhood, a time replete with first experiences, is such a training ground for odor learning. The first associations made to an odor are difficult to undo. A woman once told me that she could never get over disliking the smell of rose because the first time she smelled roses was at her mother's funeral when she was a child. I continue to like the smell of skunk, despite social disapproval.

In many instances, what we think an odor is influences our responses to it—sometimes even more than the impact of the odor itself. For example, in studies in my laboratory we have found that presenting exactly the same odor stimulus, but with two different labels—one good and one bad (for example, vomit versus Parmesan cheese)—can create an olfactory illusion. The stimulus in one case is perceived as very unpleasant and in the alternate case as very pleasant. Moreover, not only is the odor believed to be what it has been labeled when presented as such, but people do not believe that the stimulus is the same when it is labeled differently, showing how powerful suggestion and context are in odor perception (Herz and von Clef 2001). We are cued to whether we should like or dislike an odor by what its name connotes, even before we smell it. If the denotation of an odor stimulus is neutral, we may need more direct interactions with it for emotional impressions to form.

What about smelling things we have never smelled before, without any labels or obvious odor source, and saying: "I like that" or "I don't like that"? My explanation for the immediate emotional responses in these situations is that we are experiencing smells similar to others we have already encountered and consider pleasant or unpleasant (or, sometimes, when we say we do not like a novel smell, find too unfamiliar). Thus, although we may not have direct experience with the exact stimulus in question, it is similar enough to other odors for which we already have impressions that it becomes assimilated with them and appreciated accordingly.

I Say Candy, You Say Medicine

Culture also plays a key role in developing our odor preferences. Look at ethnic differences in food preferences, where one man's meat can literally be another man's poison. Evidence for culturally learned odor associations also emerges from a comparison of two independent studies that examined olfactory emotional responses. One was conducted in the United Kingdom (Moncrieff 1966), the other in the United States (Cain and Johnson 1978). Among the odors examined in both studies was methyl salicylate (wintergreen). In the United Kingdom study, this smell was given one of the lowest ratings for pleasantness, but in the United States study, wintergreen was given the highest rating of all odors tested. Why? The most likely explanation is cultural history. In the United Kingdom, the smell of wintergreen is associated with medicine and, particularly for the subjects in the 1966 study, with rub-on analgesics that were popular during World War II, a time that these subjects might not remember fondly. Conversely, in the United States, the smell of wintergreen is almost exclusively the smell of candies. A similar effect is anecdotally reported for the smell of sarsaparilla, which in the United Kingdom is a disliked medicinal odor and in the United States is the smell of a popular soft drink: root beer.

Most people find it easier to accept that there is no universally appealing odor than that there are no universally repelling odors. Yet there is compelling cross-cultural evidence for this notion. Recently the US military tried to create a stink bomb as a tool for crowd dispersion. Researchers tested a series of foul odors, including a toilet smell, in countries around the world, but failed to find any odor that was consistently evaluated as repelling.

There is one possible exception. Odors with strong trigeminal stimulation (for example, ammonia) are often immediately repelling. The irritation caused by trigeminal nerve activity when we are exposed to the odor produces an avoidance response. So it may well be that when an odor is automatically repelling, with no prior exposure to it, we are avoiding the unpleasant trigeminal aspect, not the olfactory aspect per se. One avenue of future research in the psychology of odor perception might be to develop a test to separate the trigeminal from the pure olfactory aspects of various odors and to examine how responses to the olfactory aspect change when it is evaluated in isolation.

Another as yet unstudied area is the extent to which there are genetically based individual differences in sensitivities that may predispose different people to like or dislike specific smells. Scientists have recently learned that individual differences in the variability of the distribution of genes relating to olfactory perception may account for why certain people have specific anosmias and why others have heightened or weakened odor perception. These differences in sensitivities may account, in part, for a predisposition to like or dislike specific scents. In this way of thinking, we could speculate that I like skunk because I cannot detect some of the more pungent volatiles in the skunk bouquet the way someone who is truly repelled by the odor can. There may be similar genetic differences among various ethnic groups as well, which would explain why a universally effective stink bomb has not been found.

The Advantages of Learning Odors

There is also an evolutionary argument for why we are not hardwired to like or dislike any odors. When organisms first evolved as single-cell creatures, their primary function was to take in or reject substances from the outside world. This approach or avoidance response is called chemotaxis. As organisms evolved to be multicellular, they needed a way to detect on their outside what was good or bad (for example, food or nonfood), and to communicate that information to the rest of the cells of the body. This is how the chemical senses (olfaction and taste) are thought to have evolved. From an evolutionary perspective, the function of odors is to impart information about what to approach and what to avoid—for example, prey and predator.

If an organism lives in a small, specifically defined ecological habitat, with particular local prey and predators, it will be adaptive for that organism to be hardwired with a system for detecting what food sources versus predators smell like. For example, the caterpillar of the monarch butterfly needs to know that only milkweed is food. These organisms are specialists. If, however, the organism could live in any ecological habitat and accept a wide variety of sources as food, it would not make evolutionary sense to have responses to acceptable versus nonacceptable smells wired in. These organisms are generalists.

Along with rats and cockroaches, we humans are the world's most successful generalists. We can live in any ecological habitat on the planet and survive by eating the available foods. If we had been hardwired to accept only fishy smells as food, we would never have survived in the savannah. For generalists, the function of olfaction is to learn how to respond appropriately to a particular smell source when it is encountered, and not to hold a predetermined set of responses to particular odors. Thus animals that are specialists should have innate olfactory responses to prey and predators, whereas animals that are generalists should not. Rather, generalists should be prepared to learn from experience what is good and what is bad.

Evidence for this can be found in a number of studies of animal behavior. Animals who are specialists display the ability to recognize predators without prior experience and to behave appropriately to them; this is true of a wide variety of vertebrate species, including birds, rodents and fish. Moreover, it has been demonstrated that the cue by which these predators are detected is most often olfaction. For example, both lab-born and wild-reared ground squirrels show a discriminative defensive response to their natural predators, rattlesnakes, as compared to gopher snakes. This discrimination is made on the basis of subtle olfactory cues that differentiate the two snakes. The squirrels show the same specificity in seeking food sources. Finding this specific behavior in both lab-reared and wild squirrels suggests that their olfactory responses are innate.

Paul Rozin (1976) has discussed the generalist–specialist issue in detail. He points out that specialists find the food they eat by using a hierarchy of "search images," first olfactory and then visual. Still, even in species with a narrow set of potential foods, there is evidence for some experiential influences on food selection: specifically, a general preference for familiar over unfamiliar foods. For example, young garter snakes develop a selective preference for fish or worms on the basis of prior exposure, but this effect of experience is reversible. Even specialist species are able to modulate innate olfactory responses based on experience.

For generalists and specialists alike, *neophobia*—a cautious response to novel foods and odors—is universal. This response is particularly adaptive for generalists because of the enormous array of possible food choices available and the greater risk of exposure to poisons. What has already been consumed is safe; what is unknown may or may not be safe. The behavior of young humans attests to this. Infants and young children generally react with dislike to novel smells and flavors, regardless of the emotional tone that adults use in offering them. It is only after these smells become familiar or attractive, as a result of appropriate modeling by the adults, that children make discriminative responses.

Pleasurable and Painful Smells

We can see further evidence that learning is the key mechanism by which generalists acquire odor responses if we look at aversions to tastes. Rats (and humans)—who will eat anything—can be made to avoid a flavor by being made sick after consumption. For example, presenting a rat with a sweet-tasting banana-smelling drink and then injecting the rat with lithium causes nausea and creates a conditioned avoidance of this smell in the future. Similarly, if you eat pepperoni pizza and then get severe stomach flu, you will find pepperoni pizza unpalatable for quite a while. Researchers have shown that the conditioned aversion is to the smell, not the taste, of the substance (Bartoshuk 1989). Although potentially socially disruptive, the long-term effects of learned taste aversion are clearly adaptive. If poison is ingested, it is best to learn to avoid it permanently, rather than having to repeat the mistake until it kills you. The key point is that for generalists, banana and pepperoni are not inherently meaningful smells in themselves; rather, their association to pleasure or pain is what makes us interpret them as good or bad.

There are important differences between emotional responses to taste and to smell. Research shows that the emotional response to sweet and bitter tastes is present at birth. Placing a drop of sugar on a newborn's tongue elicits a smile, while placing a drop of quinine on the tongue elicits the characteristic "yuck" face that expresses disgust. Responses to salt and sour tastes are also generally stereotypical, but some physical maturation after birth is required before they are elicited and the concentration of the substance also affects the emotional reaction. By contrast, emotional responses to odors must be learned.

All the essential constituents of foods—vitamins, minerals, proteins, carbohydrates and fats—are odorless. The smells of beef versus fish, for example, are the result of the volatiles in their fat. These volatile chemicals give fish and meat their distinctive odors, but there is nothing olfactory that announces that either one of these substances is nutritive; you must learn this through experience. By contrast, some aspects of foodstuffs do have tastes: the sweetness of sucrose, the saltiness of sodium, and the bitterness of many poisons. Sweet signals carbohydrates, which are good to eat, and bitter can signal poisons, which are bad, so it is adaptive for the taste system to have a built-in like/dislike response so that the substance can be swallowed or rejected when it first reaches the tongue. Similarly, the trigeminal avoidance response to certain odors may be adaptive because toxic gases are often highly trigeminally irritating.

So olfaction can direct our food choices, but only after we learn what the odors mean in relation to the foods in question. A poisonous mushroom may smell somewhat different from an edible one, but there is no a priori poison mushroom smell. We must learn these differences by experience—preferably in the form of wisdom communicated by other members of our species, not direct contact. It is evolutionarily advantageous for the olfactory system of generalists not to be hardwired to like or dislike any particular odors, but rather to be readily predisposed to learn and remember what is good and what is bad based on experiences with them.

Aromatherapy: The Power of Suggestion

If we, as generalists, must learn our responses to odors, what does this say about the possible benefits of aromatherapy? Aromatherapy is based on the belief that various natural odors have an intrinsic (essentially pharmacological) ability to influence mood, cognition and health. For example, inhalation of mint is said to have a stimulating effect and lavender a sedative effect on our mood and physical state. There is no evidence, however, that these effects are anything but learned associations. The claim that certain odors can have a relaxing effect and others a stimulating one may be true, but this is because of the acquired meaning of the odors, not any intrinsic potency.

Research reports on studies of the effects of odors on moods clearly point to the principle that odors people like induce a pleasant mood; odors they do not like induce an unpleasant mood. Participants in experiments where purportedly pleasant odors are tested will not show the expected mood effects if they dislike the odor being presented. Moreover, positive mood effects supposedly elicited by pleasant ambient odors can be induced without any odor present (Knasko 1992). The joys of aromatherapy are in the mind of the smeller, produced not by direct action of the odor but rather by associations the individual has learned to connect with the odor.

The context in which we typically encounter an odor helps support its aromatherapeutic effects, for example, in Western culture, lavender is commonly found in bath oils and soaps. Since people take baths to relax, lavender is easily construed as relaxing. In contrast, we have linked the term "refreshing" with mint, and mint is purportedly stimulating. But as our earlier wintergreen example illustrates, culture can be decisive in eliciting emotional responses to fragrances. Yes, odors may alter mood and relax or invigorate us, but this is due to the emotional associations we have previously made with them—not to any inherent or innate influences on us. If a Martian were given a vial of lavender to smell, my hunch is that she would not become relaxed.

What about using odors for psychological benefits in the workplace? In Japan, some work environments, particularly manufacturing plants, use ambient scenting to help reduce worker fatigue and boredom. This manipulation works, but only temporarily. Adding fragrance to a previously unscented room is the equivalent of changing the furniture or putting in new lights. The change increases attention and makes people more positively aware of their environment, but after a while, these effects diminish. This occurs very quickly with odors. You may have noticed that when you enter a house that has a peculiar smell, it takes about twenty minutes before you no longer smell it. This is because the olfactory system is geared to detect change (a novel odor); but once the novelty wears off, the receptors cease to respond, and you cease to smell it. This does not mean the smell has gone; it merely illustrates the effect of olfactory adaptation. This process can lead to overuse of cologne or perfume by a wearer who no longer can smell the scent from the bottle. Rest assured that others still can.

Pheromones

Any discussion of innate responses to odors invariably turns to pheromones. A pheromone is a chemical produced by one animal that elicits a specific behavior or physiological response in another animal of the same species. Pheromones are a form of chemical communication. Although most important for communication among social insects (ants, termites and bees), they convey important information for almost all species—above all, information about reproductive state.

Humans do demonstrate a pheromonal response, but in only one situation that has been verified experimentally; when women of childbearing age live together, over time they may fall into menstrual synchrony. This is known as the "McClintock effect," after Martha McClintock's (1971) discovery of this phenomenon while she was a college student. The McClintock effect is what is known as a primer pheromone effect: Over long-term exposure, chemicals transmitted by one individual induce a physiological change in another of the same species. Primer pheromones are distinguished from releaser pheromones, which trigger prompt responses such as mating or alarm. Although releaser pheromone effects have been shown in many animals, including higher primates, they have never been observed in humans. So, despite advertising claims to the contrary, the human aphrodisiac has not been found.

Note that pheromones are not odors. In fact, they need not be smelled at all. In non-human species, pheromones are not even perceived through the olfactory system but by an organ near the nose, above the roof of the mouth, called the vomeronasal organ (VNO). The VNO is a separate sensory system, independent of the olfactory system. It evolved to detect large molecules and nonvolatile molecules that could not be processed through the olfactory receptors. An intact VNO is critical to the reproductive physiology and behavior of reptiles, rodents and some primates.

A major problem with the hunt for human pheromones is that we do not have a functional VNO. Human embryos do have one, but it disappears shortly after birth. How can we perceive pheromones without a VNO? How does the McClintock effect work? One possibility to explore is whether the chemicals responsible for inducing menstrual synchrony are transmitted through skin contact. If so, one person's sweat could be absorbed through the skin of another, enabling chemicals from the first to enter the bloodstream of the second and alter the receiver's endocrine system to produce menstrual synchrony. Interesting, but this is purely my conjecture. At present, we do not know how or to what extent chemicals emitted by fellow humans may influence us, and whether olfaction is explicitly involved.

Thinking it Stinks

My argument that our responses to odors are learned, not innate, has several methodological and as yet unsolved experimental issues. The first problem is separating the trigeminal from the nontrigeminal aspects of odor perception. The second is determining whether genetic differences in response to certain volatiles may predispose certain people to experience the smell of skunk, for example, differently. Third is the ubiquitous problem in odor research of determining whether the label "rose," when used by you to describe a smell, denotes the same experience that I label "rose." A final problem is that all the possible odors in this world have not been scientifically tested or universally experienced. We cannot know, therefore, whether an universally repelling or appealing odor does exist.

I have presented an argument that human responses to odors are based on associative learning; they are not innate, not wired into us. We associate an odor with the circumstances under which it was first experienced. If the circumstance is good, then we like the odor; if it is bad, we dislike the odor. Evolution made us generalists, able to be exposed to an enormous potential array of prey and predators and learn through our experiences how to identify which is which. The relationship between specific odors and these myriad good and bad sources is, however, relatively random. This is why it makes better adaptive sense to learn the meaning of odors based on how we experience them rather than being ready-set.

If we have any innate response to odors, it is caution. Infants and young children show wariness when exposed to unfamiliar odors, regardless of whether the odors are classified as pleasant or unpleasant by the adults around them. This uneasiness in the face of uncertainty is adaptive. It is better to be cautious than reckless when approaching the unknown. Knowing what smells we like and dislike, and why you and I may not agree on how they smell, comes about because of our specific personal and cultural histories and experiences.

Nothing stinks, but thinking makes it so.

Bibliography

Bartoshuk, L.M. (1989), "The Functions of Taste and Olfaction," *Annals of the New York Academy of Sciences*, 575: 353–62.

Buck, L. and Axel, R. (1991), "A Novel Multigene Family May Encode Odorant Receptors," *Cell*, 65: 175–87.

Burr, C. (2002), *The Emperor of Scent*, New York: Random House.

Cain, W.S. and Johnson, F. Jr. (1978), "Lability of Odor Pleasantness," *Perception*, 7: 459–65.

Engen, T. (1988), "The Acquisition of Odor Hedonics," in S. Van Toller and G.H. Dodd (eds), *Perfumery*, New York: Chapman & Hall.

Herz, R.S. and von Clef, J. (2001), "The Influence of Verbal Labeling on the Perception of Odors: Evidence for Olfactory Illusions?," *Perception*, 30: 381–91.

Knasko, S. C. (1992), "Ambient Odor's Effect on Creativity, Mood and Perceived Health," *Chemical Senses*, 17: 27–35.

McClintock, M.K. (1971), "Menstrual Synchrony and Suppression," *Nature*, 229: 244–5.

Mennella, J.A. and Beauchamp, G.K. (1991), "The Transfer of Alcohol to Human Milk," *New England Journal of Medicine*, 325: 981–5.

Moncreiff, R.W. (1966), *Odour Preferences*, New York: Wiley.

Rozin, P. (1976), "The Selection of Food by Rats, Humans and Other Animals," in J.S. Rosenblatt, R.A. Hinde, E. Shaw and C. Beer (eds), *Advances in the Study of Behavior*, New York: Academic Press, pp. 21–76.

Schmidt, H.J. and Beauchamp, G.K. (1988), "Adult-like Odor Preferences and Aversions in Three-year-old Children," *Child Development*, 59: 1136–43.

Part IV
Perfume

Preface

> What is the deeper meaning of the simple yet magical expression "to smell nice"? That intangible aura emanating from the skin embraces a hint of linen, a flashing image, a caress of silk and a musical rustle, in other words a direct and powerful link with the unsaid, the unperceived, the unimagined, the impossible and the intangible.
>
> Dominique Rolin, *La Voyageuse* (qtd. in Barillé and Laroze 1995)

A particular variant of the *flaireur* discussed in the previous section is the perfume connoisseur. Such is the mystique enveloping perfume—with ancient roots in ritual, myth and medicine—that no matter how concerted an effort is made by puritanical and parsimonious critics to consign it to the realm of indulgent excess or unnecessary luxury it has blossomed over the course of the last century into a multi-billion dollar industry with hundreds of new scents introduced each year. Explanations of perfume's allure have centered upon a variety of reasons: its similarity to magical potions conferring power and insight (Maple 1973), its mythological associations with vital fluids such as sap and blood (Le Guérer 1992), its antecedents in alchemy and the search for the essence of transformation and immortality (Aftel 2001), its roots in apothecary potions and aromatic panaceas (Palmer 1993), its reputation as an addictive intoxicant (Barillé and Laroze 1995), its technical achievement as a blend of art and science (Newman 1998) or its debt to the sheer effectiveness of packaging and advertising to incite glamorous fantasies (Craik 1994: 167). (Part V will addresses perfume's aphrodisiacal qualities.) Regardless of the cause, perfume has maintained an irresistible aura over the centuries (see Genders 1972; Morris 1984). Smell's seeming defiance of concrete language and rational logic, and its ability to synesthetically encompass a diversity of experience, as expressed by Dominique Rolin above, makes perfume difficult to convincingly deconstruct and, conversely, facilitates the conscription of ever-new worshipful converts.

The section begins with two instances of perfume obsessions—one literary and the other professional. Marcel Proust's short story, "Another Memory," chronicles the experience of a depressed traveler vacationing at a beach resort who chances upon an unforgettable encounter with a "rare and delectable scent." The exaltation caused by the perfume incites the protagonist to embark on an obsessive quest to seek out its owner and procure a sample of the precious liquid, even if it turns out to be a few desperate drops. Though the pursuit of a fragrance contradictorily inspires lofty sentiments (love and spirituality) as well as its lowly opposites (jealousy and possessiveness), it embraces the mythic origins of perfume as the ambrosial food of the gods. Mandy Aftel's chapter, "Perfumed Obsession," similarly pivots on the intoxicating nature of perfume, especially one of the industry's most beloved components—jasmine. According to the author, upon inhaling the flower's complex scent, one's senses are seized, "worlds open," and a transformation occurs as if one had sipped an elixir. This rapture, however, is only possible thanks to the intense efforts on the part of the perfumer as Aftel discusses the technical workings of scent extraction and distillation, the difference between natural and synthetic fragrances, and the counter-intuitive fact that many euphoric smells are constituted of earthy and fecal aromachemicals. Like all obsessions, perhaps, the passion for perfume combines elements of both arousal and disgust—a motif that will continue in some of the texts in Part V, Scentsuality.

Except for redolent displays in department stores and the abundance of poetic, sometimes risqué, advertisements, the world of perfume is for many an esoteric one. The competitiveness of the industry is matched only by its professional code of secrecy, and into this discursive void arrive the opinionated, insightful and informed reflections of Luca Turin. The perfume reviews featured here critique and praise a range of recent and classical scents, from mass-marketed perfumes to couturier namesakes to artisanal creations. The author's insider status as both an olfactory scientist and a perfume collector, as well as an individual sporting a distinctively acute sense of smell, provides him with access to a wealth of knowledge about the history of perfumes, the art and craft of parfumerie and the processes of chemical synthesis and composition. Besides being a luxury consumer good or a fashionable means of adornment, perfume is a complex social entity that intimately blends science, culture and everyday life to create, in the author's words, "the most portable form of intelligence."

The two primary qualities of perfume mentioned so far in this section—intoxication and intelligence—are central to John J. Steele's examination of the psychoactive uses of perfume in South America. While the technology exercised in the manufacture of contemporary perfumes is readily appreciable, there is another sense in which perfume has been considered a technology in and of itself, a technology that has been practiced by healers and mystics since Paleolithic times. *Perfumeros* are only one of several types of shamanic individuals discussed by Steele who employ perfumes, along with aromatic brews, tobacco and other herbs, for magical rituals and to induce altered states of consciousness (see also Wilbert 1987). In cultures throughout the Amazonian rainforest, odoriferous substances are an essential element in generating a diverse range of transformational experiences: inculcating trances, exorcising evil influences, controlling the weather, curing illnesses, communicating with spirits and ancestors, and garnering what the author calls "ecstatic wisdom," among other pursuits. If the intoxication of perfume in the West at times appears to be merely recreational, here the transcendence of normative perception offered by fragrance accomplishes instrumental goals regarding health, protection, fertility and divine knowledge.

The intoxicating experience of perfume, however, does not necessarily translate into benevolence or altruism. That olfactory power is as corruptible as any other serves as the keystone for Patrick Süskind's novel *Perfume*, as well as for Richard T. Gray's critical analysis in "The Dialectic of 'Enscentment.'" The novel, set in eighteenth-century France and notable for its vivid portrayal of the era's reeking atmospheres, follows the life of perfume genius and psychopath Jean-Baptiste Grenouille as he searches for the creation of a scent that will grant him ultimate mastery over others. Perversely, this task requires him to murder virginal women so that their odor can be incorporated into his abominable tincture. While the Age of Enlightenment is most widely characterized as the epitome of the belief in rationality and the progress of systematized knowledge, for Gray Grenouille's actions transpose the Enlightenment's epistemic mechanisms onto the realm of the olfactory, and thus expose their underlying inhumanity. Despite scent seeming to be the antithesis of reason, Grenouille's macabre passion nevertheless engages with the same manipulative intentions and colonizing goals, eventually provoking his own gruesome immolation. The obsession for perfume here leads not to beauty or wisdom, as for the perfumers and *perfumeros* discussed above, but to alienation and self-destruction.

Jim Drobnick

Bibliography

Aftel, M. (2002), *Essence and Alchemy*, New York: North Point Press.
Barillé, E. and Laroze, C. (1995), *The Book of Perfume*, New York & Paris: Flammarion.
Craik, J. (1994), *The Face of Fashion*, New York and London: Routledge.
Genders, R. (1972), *A History of Scent*, London: Hamish Hamilton.
Le Guérer, A. (1992), *Scent*, New York: Turtle Bay Books.
Maple, E. (1973), *The Magic of Perfume*, New York: Samuel Weiser.
Morris, E.T. (1984), *Fragrance*, New York: Scribner's.
Newman, C. (1998), *Perfume*, Washington, DC: National Geographic Society.
Palmer, R. (1993), "In Bad Odor," in R. Porter and W.F. Bynum (eds), *Medicine and the Five Senses*, Cambridge: Cambridge University Press.
Wilbert, W. (1987), "The Pneumatic Theory of Female Warao Herbalists," *Social Sciences and Medicine*, 25(10): 1139–46.

18
Another Memory

Marcel Proust

Last year I spent some time in T., at the Grand Hôtel, which, standing at the far end of the beach, faces the sea. Because of the rancid fumes coming from the kitchens and from the waste water, the luxurious banality of the tapestries, which offered the sole variation on the grayish nudity of the walls and complemented this *exile* decoration, I was almost morbidly depressed; then one day, with a gust that threatened to become a tempest, I was walking along a corridor to my room, when I was stopped short by a rare and delectable scent. I found it impossible to analyze, but it was so richly and so complexly floral that someone must have denuded whole fields, Florentine fields, I assumed, merely to produce a few drops of that fragrance. The sensual bliss was so powerful that I lingered there for a very long time without moving on; beyond the crack of a barely open door, which as the only one through which the perfume could have wafted, I discovered a room that, despite my limited glimpse, hinted at the presence of the most exquisite personality. How could a guest, at the very heart of this nauseating hotel, have managed to sanctify such a pure chapel, perfect such a refined boudoir, erect an isolated tower of ivory and fragrance? The sound of footsteps, invisible from the hallway, and, moreover, an almost religious reverence prevented me from nudging the door any further. All at once, the furious wind tore open a poorly attached corridor window, and a salty blast swept through in broad and rapid waves, diluting, without drowning, the concentrated floral perfume. Never will I forget the fine persistence of the original scent adding its tonality to the aroma of that vast wind. The draft had closed the door, and so I went downstairs. But as my utterly annoying luck would have it: when I inquired about the inhabitants of room 47 (for those chosen beings had a number just like anyone else), all that the hotel director could provide were obvious pseudonyms. Only once did I hear a grave and trembling, solemn and gentle male voice calling "Violet," and a supernaturally enchanting female voice answering "Clarence." Despite those two British names, they normally seemed, according to the hotel domestics, to speak French—and without a foreign accent. Since they took their meals in a private room, I was unable to see them. One single time, in vanishing lines so spiritually expressive, so uniquely distinct that they remain for me one of the loftiest revelations of beauty, I saw a tall woman disappearing, her face averted, her shape elusive in a long brown and pink woolen coat. Several days later, while ascending a staircase that was quite remote from the mysterious corridor, I smelled a faint, delicious fragrance, definitely the same as the first time. I headed toward that corridor and, upon reaching that door, I was numbed by the violence of fragrances, which boomed like organs, growing measurably more intense by the minute. Through the wide-open door the unfurnished room looked virtually disemboweled. Some twenty small, broken phials lay on the parquet floor, which was soiled by wet stains. "They left this morning," said the domestic, who was wiping the floor, "and they smashed the flacons so that nobody could use their perfumes, since they couldn't fit them in their trunks, which were crammed with all the stuff they bought here. What a mess!" I pounced on a flacon that had a few final drops. Unbeknownst to the mysterious travelers, those drops still perfume my room.

In my humdrum life I was exalted one day by perfumes exhaled by a world that had been so bland. They were the troubling heralds of love. Suddenly love itself had come, with its roses and its flutes, sculpting, papering, closing, perfuming everything around it. Love had blended with the most immense breath of the thoughts themselves, the respiration that, without weakening love, had made it infinite. But what did I know about love itself? Did I, in any way, clarify its mystery, and did I know anything about it other than the fragrance of its sadness and the smell of its fragrances? Then, love went away, and the perfumes, from shattered flacons, were exhaled with a purer intensity. The scent of a weakened drop still impregnates my life.

19

Perfumed Obsession

Mandy Aftel

The truth is, I've always been obsessive. When I'm not interested in a subject—or a person, for that matter—nothing on earth can get me to pay attention to it. But when I'm drawn to something, I want to know all about it, and I want to get it from the source.

My passion for working with beautiful materials led me to my grand obsession, natural perfume. I fell into it the way I've fallen into most things in my life, roundabout. I was researching a novel I wanted to write, and I'd gotten the idea that the heroine should have a sensual and exotic occupation. Perfumer seemed ideal. I began by searching out turn-of-the-century perfume books, because I was only interested in perfume that was created from authentic materials—from the beginning, chemicals in test tubes held no fascination for me. The books were charming, beautiful and eccentric, and before long I had amassed a collection of more than one hundred of them. I felt the thrill of being the first one into the cave that harbored the relics of a lost civilization—the unsullied pottery and intact arrowheads. In the stories of perfume, you could see the world being discovered, people searching for spices and learning to extract the aromatic oils from the exotic plants they were finding in faraway places. In intricate woodcuts and engravings, old distilling apparatuses looked like a cross between lab equipment and witchcraft.

Soon I was buying essential oils and trying my hand at making natural perfumes. The materials were simply too inviting, too ... insistent. The names themselves seduced—*ambergris* and *costus, ylang ylang concrète. Choya loban, orange flower, boronia, civet, tonka bean, champaca.* Even those I recognized—*jasmine, sandalwood, frankincense, myrrh, bitter orange, vetiver*—conjured up ancient civilizations and exotic customs, long journeys and sensual torpor. The endless variations on each theme fanned my obsession. Once I discovered rose absolute, I had to try not only the Bulgarian version but the Russian,

Moroccan, Turkish, Indian and Egyptian as well. Every time I came upon a passage in one of my books that introduced a new essence to me, I had to track it down and start working with it. I loved the complicated histories of the materials, and their complex characters—at once delicate and harsh, putrid and fresh, floral and fecal—which made the perfumer's palette so intense. I literally had to get my hands on them.

Take *Jasminum grandiflorum*, which is arguably the most important perfume material. Its small, waxy white blossoms exhale a perfume so peculiar as to be incomparable. To walk past the flowering shrub in the evening is to be assaulted with the most glorious odor, finely floral but heavy in the air, turning an ordinary street corner into a boudoir. The essence derived from the flower intensifies the experience. Worlds open and the ocean parts when you inhale. It is a deeply floral, warm, rich and highly diffusive odor, with a peculiar honeylike sweetness and tealike, fecal undertone. Its almost cloying sweetness gives way to a drier note as it evolves, but jasmine has considerable tenacity—staying power—and it retains its warmth and depth all the way down to the dryout, the last note you smell before the scent evaporates entirely. Jasmine flower is one of the essential elements, and sometimes the main pillar, in the structure of the greatest perfumes. No perfume fails to be improved by jasmine's ability to impart smoothness and a radiant quality, which is why everyone in perfumery knows the adage, "No perfume without jasmine."

Enfleurage, the traditional process of rendering the jasmine flower into a perfume material, is as intricate and sensual as the material it yields. Jasmine does not render an oil per se—like many flowers, its blossoms are too delicate to survive steam extraction, the process through which most essential oils are produced. Instead, it is rendered as a more viscous absolute. Each flower is picked by hand, usually at dawn, when it exudes its most exquisite perfume. It takes a little over 2,000 pounds of flowers to produce a little less than two pounds of jasmine absolute. But jasmine flowers only contain an insignificant quantity of their perfume at a given moment. The flower produces it and exhales it in a continuous fashion, and its character continues to develop even after the blossoms have been detached from the plant, as the blossoms fade and deteriorate. Enfleurage captures more essential oil from the flower than it ever possessed in a given moment of life. A more apt metaphor for the obsessive's quest—for the essence of a thing that is somehow greater than the thing itself—would be hard to imagine.

Enfleurage makes use of the fact that the volatile perfume material flowers produce is soluble in fat. Glass plates, each supported in a wooden frame, are coated on both sides with fat—tallow and lard. Flower petals are laid on the plates, and the plates are piled on top of one another, so that as the petals release the volatile oils, they are caught in the layers of fat above and below. When all the perfume from the petals has been absorbed by the fat, they are replaced by a fresh supply, and the process is repeated until the fat is saturated with the perfume. This saturated fat is known as a pomade, and it is then dissolved in an alcohol-based solvent in order to obtain the essential oil.

Enfleurage, alas, is so time-consuming a process that it is no longer commercially viable. It has been replaced by a process of solvent extraction, which has been likened to dry cleaning. Flowers are placed on racks in a hermetically sealed container. A liquid solvent, usually hexane, is circulated over the flowers to dissolve the essential oils. This produces a solid, waxy paste called a concrète. The concrète is then repeatedly treated with pure alcohol (ethanol), which dissolves the wax and yields the intensely aromatic dark orange (upon aging, reddish-brown) semiviscous liquid known as an absolute.

The process has changed, but for the material itself there is no viable substitute. Jasmine is the only floral whose scent cannot be approximated by the artful blending of other odorous materials, natural or chemical. Synthetic jasmine, vapid and cloying, does not even come close. This uniqueness satisfies and stimulates one of the deep desires of the obsessive as well, to capture, to experience most fully, what is elusive, evanescent and irreplaceable.

For authentic things act on us in a way that facsimiles don't. Rich and warm, heavy and fruity, intensely floral, jasmine is almost narcotic in its ability to seize the senses and the imagination. Yet powerful as it is, jasmine refreshes rather than oppresses, possessing antidepressant as well as aphrodisiacal properties.

It is the intensely narcotic aura that strikes you most, though, inducing a sense of receptivity and surrender, almost of being ravished. This feeling of intoxication derives from the fecal undertone that is the source of the yin–yang appeal of some of the most coveted perfumes. The magic ingredient is indole, a major element in jasmine, as well as tuberose and orange flower, that is also found in human feces. This odor of indole, reminiscent of decay, lends jasmine the putrid–sweet, sultry–intoxicating nuance that makes jasmine essences the same delicate aphrodisiac today as they were in the past.

It is the indole, above all, that cannot successfully be synthesized. It can be approximated, but the loss of its delicate natural nuances extinguishes the synergistic effect they achieve. That is why attempts to replicate jasmine essences result in an unpleasantly dominant note of indole and demonstrate the limitations of the synthetics in general. It is not that naturally occurring indole smells different from the synthetic, or that its chemical structure is different; it is that nature, in the composition of its odor complexes, likes to include, in addition to the quantitatively predominant and identifiable components, minute amounts of materials that, by virtue of their intensity, play a decisive role in the character of the entire complex and its delicate "naturalness." These materials are hard to identify due to their trace levels.

As an isolated element, indole loses its magic, much as acting in a particular manner in an effort to be sexy often isn't. But as an element of a natural essence entwined with other essences in an intricate fragrance, indole plies the fine line between arousal and disgust, orchestrating a genuine eroticism. As in nature itself, complexity and context are the field conditions for awakening passion. The intensely earthy scents of the body that trigger libido are not, for example, erotic in themselves any more than the blatant, unmodulated come-on of a "sexy" synthetic blend is. Scent can be sexual without being erotic. In our sexuality, we are purely in the domain of nature; in our eroticism, we are specifically human.

While lust can be easily triggered, eroticism is subtle, complex and, above all, dependent on context. The fecal essence of our most pungent bodily odors draws us, even as it repels us. The precarious balance between arousal and disgust is sexual in its very nature, creating erotic tension and heightening arousal. It is manifested in the pervasive scatological references in folklore, superstition and literature, and in the universality of coprolagnia, sexual practices that link human excretion with eroticism. A truly aphrodisiac perfume is one that triggers our unconscious memory of our animal nature in all its erotic manifestations. It is an artful construction of scents *based on* the impolite smells of the human body. It points to a little-acknowledged truth about the relationship of scent to sexuality: sexy smells are subliminally reminiscent of the smell of sweat and of the hairy regions of the human body. The odor of our species at its most animal is at the heart of eros.

You see where obsession gets you. It doesn't stop there, though. In eros we descend into our hidden animal nature. But eros is also about the transcendence of the ordinary into the sublime. The true obsessive dives deep in order to touch the universal. Jasmine's aroma, irreducible and narcotic, transports you into the polymorphous intensity of the present, in all its inchoate sensuality. Obsession is at once specific and collective, earthly and otherworldly, cutting a wide and layered swath through my own life, and life itself. It reconciles seeming opposites, rather than reducing them to contradiction. And nothing brings together these seeming contradictions than a drop of jasmine.

20
Accords and Discords
Perfume Reviews

Luca Turin

Amarige (Givenchy)

Opinions differ: some rate *Amarige* as the most unfortunate perfume of the past decade, others find it fresh and pleasant, which suggests that it may sit on a genetic fault-line. The author of these lines finds it simply unbearable: built on a towering tuberose note buttressed by mighty synthetics, it exemplifies the escalation in power typical of the late 1980s. *Amarige* is an olfactory typhoon, it will put you off your food, ruin a concert, stifle a conversation, turn an elevator into a torture chamber, revive calls in Parliament for a ban on fragrances in public spaces and disrupt radio traffic. This being said, it is unforgettable.

Alabaster (Mary McFadden)

A very modern, rather mannered perfume with interesting creamy-green headnotes reminiscent of *marron glacé*. A solid, well-constructed heart follows, in the eighties tradition of *Ivoire* and *Madame Carven*. The early drydown has a very melodious feel, at once nutty and soapy, but later becomes slightly tiresome and chemical as the quality runs out.

Amour Amour (Patou)

One whiff of *Amour Amour* suffices as a reminder of how far perfume has moved on, not always for the better, since the 1920s. There is a dissonant, ephemeral, almost poignant freshness about *Amour Amour* that suggests a vanished world of maverick elegance and devil-may-care luxury, the world of Lartigue photographs and Poulenc compositions. Not a momentous fragrance by any means, but as moving as an old newsreel.

Aqua Allegoria (Guerlain)

The gradual decadence of natural perfumery in the last two decades has left only a handful of houses making high-quality natural raw materials in once-great Grasse. A reaction had to come: firms like Aveda, and many bogus "aromatherapy" outfits, have made a lot of money from a return to nature. Guerlain, from its eyrie on the Champs-Elysées, has watched these upstarts launch "simple," natural fragrances for years. Such had been the sway of chemistry, and for so long, that suddenly a simple lavender water smelled wonderful.

This nouvelle cuisine of fragrance, like its edible counterpart, stands or falls on the quality of raw materials. Great firms like Guerlain have access, exclusive in some instances, to wonders that remind us that God is still the greatest perfumer. They enter into masterpieces like *Mitsouko* and *Shalimar*, but popular taste now wanted them in more legible form. So far Guerlain, constrained by the canons of great perfumery, seemed reluctant to compose jingles when it could do whole symphonies.

Now, belatedly, comes a masterstroke. The five *Aqua Allegoria* (surely -ica, but Guerlain are clearly better perfumers than classical scholars) create what may be a new category of perfume. It is close to what the French touchingly used to call a *sent-bon* ("smells-good"), but stamped with greatness. These are unfussy, clear compositions with enough intelligence to be called fragrances, with all their structure explicit, and made with stuff that most other firms can only dream of. Something had to go, of course, to make this possible; in the event, duration was sacrificed. Five concise pieces, then, though more substantial than the competition. Get them all and smell "natural" history in the making.

Boucheron (Boucheron)

The first perfumery effort of this opulent jeweler turned out to be a masterstroke. Boucheron has a big-boned, majestic, impassive structure vaguely reminiscent of *l'Heure Bleue*, very slow in development and tenacious without aggressive tendencies. It is perhaps the most successful attempt to date at rendering an effect of natural complexity through dexterous deployment of aromachemicals. In a slightly humorless, virgin-goddess sort of way, this is one of the great fragrances of the last twenty years.

Câline (Jean Patou)

Jean Patou, one of the few firms still employing its own perfumer and by all accounts as obsessed with quality as Chanel and Guerlain, brought back some of its great classics some years ago. In all fairness, while the quality of the fragrances is consistently high, most of them show their age, being constructed as variations of top and middle notes on a very similar, nutty-ambery drydown in the "modular" thirties style. *Câline* is an exception, with *Y* (Saint Laurent) the only surviving member of the distinguished family of green chypres, including notably the lamented *Futur* (Piguet) and *Sous le Vent* (Guerlain). *Câline* exemplifies the dry, aquiline, almost bony beauty of the genre. Had she lived long enough, or for that matter had she lived at all, Proust's Oriane de Guermantes would have liked this one: for the day, to be worn with a black-and-white hound's-tooth *tailleur*, on serious errands such as an expedition to Berthillon to sample the sorbets. Impeccably elegant, stunning on a man in small doses.

Chanel No. 5 (Chanel)

It is good, at regular intervals, to refresh one's memory of what unalloyed luxury is about. Chanel's manic attention to detail and quality, combined with one of the great structural inventions of perfume history, deserves to stand under a glass jar next to the reference meter and kilogram at the Pavillon des Poids et Mesures. Rumor has it that *Chanel No. 5* does poorly in blind panel tests against contemporary fragrances, and it is easy to see why. Those who have been brought up on stunted, suburban fragrances must find it hard to accept the existence of such a regally beautiful thing. The top notes surprise every time: a radiant chorus of ylang and rose floating like gold leaf on the chalk-white background of aldehydes. Curiously this most modern of perfumes evokes an image of great antiquity, perhaps a Scythian jewel on a white dress. The drydown fades the way white flowers do, slowly becoming soft and flesh-colored. To get an idea of *No. 5*'s quality, smell it on a paper strip after twenty-four hours. Now try this with whatever else you're wearing now. See?

Chanel No. 19 (Chanel)

Chanel's combined mastery of raw materials and orchestration shines through once again. Tremendous leafy-peppery green start without a hint of harshness, like the earthy breath of a lush jungle after a storm. The genius of *No. 19* lies in maintaining this unripe greenness, like a tense unresolved musical chord to the very end, without succumbing to the temptation of sweet afterthoughts. The effect is one of rigorous intellectual elegance and restraint. An absolute masterpiece, great on men too.

Dark Vanilla (Coty)

The name suggests a beguilingly sinful, high calorie confection. Instead, the fragrance has all the charm and mystery of a neon-lit shopping mall, and smells of cheap chocolates with a fruit heart. A case of pastel-clad obesity.

Destiny Woman (Harley Davidson)

I have over the years been rather partial to some of the fragrances Harley-Davidson has produced, chiefly *Castor Oil* and *Nitromethane*. I suppose one must get used to the idea that a motorcycle manufacturer lends its name to things that come in bottles: After all, Hermès used to be a saddler... The demurely named *Destiny Woman* is an appropriately big-haired fragrance of the straight-exhaust school inaugurated by *Angel* (Thierry Mugler) some years back, but less headstrong than its model. This loud but cute creature is best worn at dragster races, preferably while lounging on the purple fiberglass nose of an Unlimited.

DK (Donna Karan)

Donna Karan's perfumes have been nothing if not courageous, and *DK* started the trend. This is in essence a feminine reinterpretation of the fascinatingly artificial *Azzaro Homme*. An unusual, slightly camphoraceous top note sets the scene for a smooth development of a creamy, velvety heart endowed with the weight and feel of suede. The last drydown is unexpectedly fresh and airy. All in all, a strange creature, unearthly but lovable.

Dolce e Gabbana (Dolce e Gabbana)

After an interesting fern-like green start, settles down to an intensely colored and very powerful fruity-musky chord. A sturdy, slightly coarse fragrance, the olfactory equivalent of maroon *dévoré* velvet.

Dune (Dior)

Dune's slow unveiling has the stately pace of classical perfumery, and culminates after an hour or so in the clangor of a strange, muffled atonal chord of vanilla/patchouli/indole, imbued with the desert-earth hues of a powder compact. *Dune* is more coherent and original than all the perfumes it has inspired (such as *Allure*) but remains curiously aloof. Distinctive without being pleasant, refined without being pretty, it radiates a rare and somewhat sullen elegance. Easier to admire than to like, but very good nevertheless.

Dzing! (L'Artisan Parfumeur)

When the history of perfume is written, the small firm of *L'Artisan Parfumeur* will get a whole chapter. In its early days, under the guidance of Jean-François Laporte, it came up with some of the great perfumery ideas of the past twenty years: the first to associate vanilla and the candy floss note of ethylmaltol in *Vanilia*, the first to use coffee in *L'Eau du Navigateur*, more recently the first to come up with a convincing fig-leaf fragrance, *Premier Figuier*. *Dzing!* is as original as any of these, and withal a fragrance of superlative oddness. For the first twenty minutes, it simply smells of cardboard. For those prosaic souls who would question a pressing need to smell of cardboard, a few words of explanation. One of the most surprising things about smell is the fact that complex combinations often give simple results, if simplicity is defined by our ability to name things unambiguously. Conversely, despite its workaday origins, cardboard is actually a rich, warm, woody smell with a spicy angle. Much in the way that a great painter like Giorgio Morandi can transfigure for our benefit the homeliest of objects, a great perfumer can reveal to us beauty where it is often most safely hidden: right under our noses. *Dzing!*

Eden (Cacharel)

A rare instance of finely tuned coherence between the celadon-colored pack-aging and the opalescent green smell. Love it or hate it, *Eden* is one of the most distinctive perfumes in recent years, with an extraordinary raspy-suave, peculiarly stagnant start, little or no evolution in time and tremendous tenacity. Owning it makes perfect sense, but wearing it is another matter. *Eden* is undoubtedly a brilliant, cerebral exercise in perfumery, but who wants to smell like wet cashmere?

Freedom for Her (Hilfiger)

Hilfiger finds it hard to shed a somewhat naïf "tracksuit at the mall" image, and this fragrance is no exception, complete with a waisted bottle for women, square one for men (should have been bulging the other way, really). The fragrance is far better than that, however, a magnolia and tea affair, solidly built, very clean, with an excellent fresh drydown and an overall feel of comfortable quality, not unlike a *Tommy Girl* seen through sunglasses. Nice on a man, I'll wager.

Herba Fresca (Guerlain)

Exercise: use mint as a core note in a fragrance without recalling toothpaste. Most perfumers would desist, but Guerlain gives it a try. First of all, use the weird mint (oba) that the Japanese sometimes use to wrap sushi, and which has an almost anisic feel. Secondly, marry it with the freshest, most deliciously soothing infusion of lime, verbena and tea, with a floral touch to offset the almost medicinal effect. Stir well, and serve in a lovely bottle decorated with Merovingian bees. Simple, really.

Hervé Léger (Hervé Léger)

The last two years have seen a revival of a class of synthetic raw materials known as lactones (cyclic esters, for readers who remember Chemistry 200) whose smells range from coconut to peach via warm milk. They formed the backbone of the great sixties feminine fragrances like *Femme* (Rochas) and *Dioressence* (Dior). Interestingly, high quality sandalwood essence also has a warm-milk feel to it, which is impossible to replicate with synthetic ingredients. *Hervé Léger* cleverly associates a strong milky note with a sandalwood and rounds the whole thing off with a fresh twist, to give a sweet, smooth, monochrome effect that is reminiscent of Léger's fashion style and, like it, will no doubt work to opulent effect on a tanned skin.

Je Reviens (Worth)

A strange, abstract, curiously artificial construction, part biker-girl, part blue-stocking. It used to be vastly weightier and better than the present rather dilute version. Nevertheless it still gives a faded but otherwise faithful impression of the extraordinary opal green glow of the original, the sort that emanates from a numinous uncut gem in a Rider Haggard epic. Its soapy-leathery drydown is wonderful and, though quiet, instantly identifiable from afar. Give it to someone you love, or wear it to attract someone of above-average intelligence. Great on a man.

Je T'Aime (Holzman and Stephanie)

Blessed with a superlatively gauche name, *Je T'Aime* is a pleasant green floral, notable for what seems to be an early use of the fig-leaf note of stemone, a fascinating oxime compound that has since become the rage in bucolic fragrances. Agreeable and well-constructed. Great in summer.

Jovan Musk (Jovan)

Notable for its once spectacularly gauche seventies packaging, *Jovan Musk* is, as its name indicates, a phalanx of synthetic musks of the sort that a competent perfumer could muster in fifteen minutes. Contrary to popular belief, musks do not in any way evoke the back end of a furry animal, but rather a creamy, sweet cleanliness. Some of the best ones have been outlawed for such worthy reasons as skin irritation or environmental concerns, and Jovan makes do with what's left. The result is rather nice, about as feminine as a steel wrench and altogether reminiscent of a Norman Rockwell barbershop. Suave, but uninspiring.

Jovan White Musk (Jovan)

"It says what it does, it does what it says" could be the slogan for this perfume. *Jovan White Musk*'s medley of synthetic musks is, not least, of scientific interest, because it illustrates the curious fact that these hefty eighteen-wheeler molecules are to olfaction what white noise is to hearing. After some time spent close to this deafening olfactory waterfall, one begins to smell fruity, aldehydic and animalic notes that are probably absent from the mix. Tremendously tenacious, because musks don't easily take flight, and solidly unpretentious. It is hard to imagine it worn by anyone much above voting age.

Jungle Elephant (Kenzo)

Perhaps the fairest way to describe *Jungle Elephant* is as an intelligent failure. A strikingly monochrome confection of velvety dried fruit notes that fades in time without evolving, it has a dark, rich timbre recalling a bass clarinet practicing scales. The novelty of it holds the attention for a moment. Unfortunately, the note itself is not original, and derives from a composition called Prunol which has been around since the 1950s. Prunol was once used to give a low contralto register to some great chypres like *Diorama* and *Jolie Madame*. Used all by itself, it feels unfinished and falls short of real perfumery. To this reviewer's nose, it recreates a curious impression familiar to those who have done their shopping in small French grocers' in summer: the proximity of floor polish and ripe peaches sometimes adds up to a wonderful accord, and *Jungle Elephant* reproduces it to perfection.

Lacoste for Women (Lacoste)

A curious drift has taken place, little by little, in women's fragrances over the last couple of years. The search for clean freshness in places other than marine, citrus and lily of the valley has turned up a series of very natural magnolia-like accords, which come in a range of pale colors ranging from cream to buff depending on whether they are at the floral or woody end of the spectrum. In combination with minty notes, which recently became plausible as a perfumery raw material, they give very abstract, long-lasting clean fragrances devoid both of the aggressiveness of marine notes and of floral color and sweetness. In the process, they have lost almost all "feminine" connotations, indeed have become proper unisex fragrances, that is to say things that simply smell great without any further designs. With *Lacoste for Women*, a restful, orderly fragrance as quiet and airy as a Japanese garden, the genre has arrived. Like a record one puts on very late at night in reflective moods, it is something one needs, an oasis of peace away from the bustle of modern fragrance chemistry.

Lavande Velours (Guerlain)

What could be more obvious, more hackneyed in principle than a lavender fragrance? Not any more! Guerlain's miraculous skill in dodging cliché starts with a startlingly intense, almost winelike lavender, adds a touch of honeyed hay to offset its airy blue feel and crowns the whole thing with a sentimental violet note, a knowing homage to Tiemann and Kruger's discovery of synthetic ionone, just over a century ago. Seldom has a perfume been so aptly named.

Le Feu d'Issey (Issey Miyake)

The surprise effect of *Feu d'Issey* is total: smelling it is like pressing the play button on a frantic videoclip of unconnected objects that fly past one's nose at warp speed: fresh baguette, lime peel, clean wet linen, shower soap, hot stone, salty skin, even a fleeting touch of vitamin B pills, and no doubt a few other UFOs that this reviewer has failed to catch the first few times. Whoever did this has that rarest of qualities in perfumery, a sense of humor. Bravo also to those who did not recoil in horror at something so original and agreed to bottle it and sell it. Let us hope this fragrance succeeds. Whether you wear it or not, it should be in your collection as a reminder that perfume is, among other things, the most portable form of intelligence.

OH! de Moschino (Moschino)

A precursor of *Contradiction*, with a ketonic nail-varnish remover top note reminiscent of a spray paint shop, on a woody-vanillic base of some distinction. Well put together, clean, a little dull, perhaps a bit bare. Would be great in a shampoo or a tanning lotion. Use it on holidays.

Organza (Givenchy)

Organza was the first major fragrance in recent years to dare the break with the wispy-low calorie trend of the early 1990s, and turned out to be a major commercial hit. An unashamedly vulgar orchestration of somewhat tuneless floral and vanillic notes, it serves as a humorous reminder that perfumery need not be phobic and cerebral to appeal to the modern audience. Unoriginal yet convincing, *Organza* is a perfect antidote to postmodern dirges.

Pamplelune (Guerlain)

This fragrance is a high-wire act with sulfurous notes, those demons of perfumery present in trace amounts in, for example, grapefruit and blackcurrant (*Pamplelune* is a conflation of *pamplemousse*, the French for "grapefruit," and Pampluna in Spain). To understand how sulfur notes work, try this at home: put some *Pamplelune* on the back of your hand, allow the alcohol to dry, then cut some garlic (another sulfuraceous) and smell both at once. See how close a wonderful fragrance like *Pamplelune* is to calamity? Only the very skilled can pull this off…

Parfum Sacré (Caron)

The venerable but struggling firm of Caron is one of France's national treasures, offering a confidential and uniquely chic line-up of perfumes comparable to Guerlain's in beauty and historical importance. One of the most widely available, *Parfum Sacré* is a full-throttle symphonic poem on a rose theme, brilliantly balancing the slightly soft effect of Turkish otto with a spicy-woody structure. Roses of this quality have a heady, wine-like feel. Let this be a reminder to the user: read Omar Khayyam, smell this on your loved one, sip claret from a gold goblet and remember that life is short.

Poême (Lancôme)

Allegedly derived from the delicate effluvia of a rare Himalayan flower, no doubt pared down by scores of hard-nosed chemists. *Poême* is notable for its thundering, sweet-peppery bubblegum top note, a sort of dessert version of *Amarige*. The drydown smells exactly like the reception area of a fragrance company, a lusty chorus of all the fiercest aromachemicals escaped from the lab down the hallway. A tinselly, tacky perfume, ideal for nine-year old beauty queens.

Poison (Dior)

Perfumers usually act like Professor Higgins when dealing with the untutored beauty of tuberose, smoothing the edges and filling in the gaps as in *Oscar de la Renta* or *Fracas*. *Poison* opts for the opposite strategy, and doubles the stakes by mixing it with a novel, prodigiously potent fruity note. That gave would-be imitators a lot of sleepless nights at the mass spectrometer trying to figure out what it was made of. This is a loud, invasive fragrance that may work wonders in private but remains totally unpresentable. The almost universal dislike it inspires today is exactly proportional to the love it initially elicited. A remarkable piece of perfumery nevertheless. Own it but don't wear it out of doors.

Rive Gauche (Yves Saint Laurent)

Rive Gauche is an object lesson in perfection. Firstly, it illustrates the mastery of time achieved by the greatest perfumers. Its large, sculptural, seamless form smoothly and gradually emerges from within the mist of the top notes and stands revealed in full glory only after several hours. All the while, the fragrance seemingly gets stronger and more distinct. Secondly, it shows that one can use a huge rose note without any of the sentimental sweetness that hampers most other attempts. In fact, the rose of *Rive Gauche* is so unusual in its smoky, almost rubbery character, and blends so well into its woody-powdery surroundings that it takes an effort to discern it even when warned. Thirdly, its kinship to the earlier and slightly softer *Calandre* shows that in perfumery, as in all the serious arts, imitation is legitimate when allied with genius. One of the great fragrances of all time. Excellent on a man as well.

Shalimar (Guerlain)

The fact that *Shalimar* has been a best seller since 1925 suggests that it must be a seriously good fragrance. Just how good, however, only emerges as one becomes familiar with it and compares it with its many followers and imitations. *Shalimar* is the reference oriental, a red-plush-and-gilt marvel of smooth vanilla, sweet amber, somber woods and saucy animalic notes. Guerlain invented the rules of the genre, and is therefore allowed to flout them. Unlike modern perfumes eager to make a good first impression, *Shalimar* is an intricate machine designed to project an olfactory effect remote in both time and space. It does not smell "good" in the strict sense for at least half an hour after being put on skin. It also often feels rather strange up close, while radiating a quietly melodious aura. But just as we patiently sit through an overture in anticipation of the aria at the end of the first act, we rightly expect *Shalimar* to come on song in an hour's time, and to be better appreciated from the stalls than the stage. How does Guerlain achieve this? A century of practice and two or three perfumer geniuses along the way certainly help, but there is another, more earthbound reason: Guerlain's raw materials are of a different order than the stuff that merely mortal firms can get their hands on. Their vanilla absolute is sensational, their civet tincture is unique, and no doubt they have the sort of know-how that makes great cuisine more than the sum of its parts. Whatever the secret is, let us hope that the sale of the Guerlain family silver to the giant international group LVMH won't dilapidate it in short order. Buy *Shalimar* now as an insurance in case things go wrong.

Sublime (Patou)

The French are uniquely good at modernizing their works of art while remaining within the remit of the Grand Manner, witness for example the glass pyramids in the courtyard of the Louvre. *Sublime* is a case in point, an architectonic work equilibrating a classically smooth and silken sweet-amber base with a soaring, streamlined, ozonic-blue accord of vetiver and ambergris notes. These two mighty wings are joined up by a quiet but warm floral-powdery structure. The balance point must have been devilishly difficult to find and happens to be exactly right. Familiarity with this splendid fragrance breeds respect. Should probably be sprayed on clothes rather than skin to prolong its graceful arc. Great on a man, if he dares.

Tocade (Rochas)

Perfumers spend a large fraction of their creative life assimilating novelty, fitting never-before-smelt raw materials into legible structures. Once in a while, though, a perfume comes along that uses nothing new and yet achieves a fresh, uncharted, entirely pristine effect. *Tocade* is exactly that, a contralto coming back on stage after a demanding concert to sing an encore of old-fashioned blues. In less expert hands, *Tocade*'s structure of rose, amber and vanilla would have been a sentimental cliché. Instead, the sassy greenness of the top notes sets a summery, joyful scene, and endows this smiling fragrance with the feel of suntanned, sweet-smelling skin dusted with salt from a swim in the sea. Happiness in a bottle.

Vanilla Musk (Coty)

The name of this fragrance is clearly meant to reach the heart via the engine rooms, as in "food and sex." Curiously, this combination of two hugely popular notes manages to be at once totally unappetizing and deeply unsexy. The vanilla note is nasty, more cheap chocolate than orchid seedpod, while the musky part is tenacious and rasping, and reeks of low-budget muscle ingredients. To be avoided.

White Linen (Estée Lauder)

A fine example of successful top-down design. Everything meshes together with this perfume, the splendid name, the spotless image, and of course the resplendent fragrance. Loosely based on the great but curiously confidential *Chanel 22*, it exploits the unblemished whiteness of aldehydes to the full. *White Linen* is the smell of a large white bath soap scaled up to symphonic proportions of power and radiance. If powder snow had a smell, this would be it. Not to be missed.

Ysatis (Givenchy)

At the time of its launch, *Ysatis'* demure, marmoreal coolness seemed almost too reticent, as if the fragrance were reluctant to join the ambient fun. With the benefit of hindsight, *Ysatis* now appears a perfectly judged construction, deceptively simple and shy, radiating the quiet but steady glow of a sheltered candle. Its lemony-floral accord is fresh but not watery, sensual but not heavy and polite without seeming tepid. *Ysatis* is perhaps the best introduction to perfumery for first-time users.

21

Perfumeros and the Sacred Use of Fragrance in Amazonian Shamanism

John J. Steele

The West is currently witnessing an olfactory renaissance in which there is a renewed interest in the psychoactive and transformational nature of botanical fragrances. Aromachology, the recently inaugurated scientific study of fragrance's behavioral impact (see Green 1988), has ancient roots in shamanic practices, a worldwide Paleolithic transformational technology which utilized controlled access to ecstatic wisdom for healing, weather control, divination of food sources and danger, and deep communication with plants, animals, ancestors and spirits. Shamans are masters of curing plants for body and soul. They combine intuition with heightened sensory abilities. Following recent advances in the field of the anthropology of the senses (see Howes 1987), instead of viewing a culture from the perspective of Western sensory biases, an attempt is made here to examine how Amazonian cultures perceive their own sensoria, the operating totality of blended senses which determines the way reality is understood.

Tobacco Shamanism

Tobacco is the most widespread magical plant used in South America. There are thirty-seven native species in the subcontinent which have evolved from the genus *Nicotiana* of the nightshade family. Johannes Wilbert (1987) has collected an impressive array of evidence which suggests that tobacco species may be the oldest cultivated plants in the Americas. The scent of tobacco permeates many aspects of South American Indian cultures. Shamans consider tobacco a medium with which to commune with the spirit world. Tobacco shamans become nicotine-intoxicated by hyperventilating smoke through their mouth and nose. Wilbert reports that "shamans require tobacco in all their activities. They blow tobacco smoke to cure patients, to protect their fellow men from evil spirits, to sanctify new maize and the first honey of the season, and to exorcise any possible evil from fresh game." Shamans "eat" smoke by forcing down large gulps of smoke from their pipes to induce dreams and trances in which they encounter the "Supernaturals." In a mutually beneficial symbiosis, tobacco feeds the spirits who in turn protect humans. Wilbert observes that South American Indians use tobacco to amplify vital human energy and fertility. Tobacco smoke is sometimes blown over women before marriage or giving birth. The smoke is also a way of making visible the pneumatic power of the shaman's breath. He further remarks that "belief in the life-giving force of tobacco becomes apparent in myth when women are created from clay over which tobacco smoke is blown and when shamans blow tobacco smoke to 'resurrect' the dead."

Carana

Wilbert (1987) comments that "Warao shamans perfume their cigars with pulverized or granulated *carana* resin." Tobacco cigars smoked with *carana* are blown over people and objects to purify them. He also mentioned that *carana* was used as a substitute for frankincense in the Catholic church (Wilbert 1991). The paramount gods of the Warao, with the exception of the cardinal god of the West, are nourished by tobacco smoke. "They appreciate it especially," states Wilbert (1987: 178), "when it has been perfumed with *carana* incense." To the Warao, the combination of tobacco smoke and *carana* is the most esteemed aroma. *Carana* belongs to the Burseraceae or myrrh family, which is also the source of balsamic resins used as perfume materials. Schultes (1990) relates that the Tanimuka Indians of southern Colombia burn the *carana* resin (*Protium hetaphyllum*) and blow the perfumed smoke into powdered coca, thus marrying fragrance with intoxicating substances.

Ayahuasca

Ayahuasca is a hallucinogenic brew made by boiling the bark of the Malpighiaceous forest vine, *Banisteriopsis caapi,* with the leaves of admixture plants, such as *Psychotria viridis,* which intensifies its visions in different ways (McKenna 1984). *Banisteriopsis caapi,* which grows throughout the Amazon basin, is called "the vine of the spirits." *Ayahuasca* is taken to telepathically divine the origins and cures of illness, to locate game or enemies and to learn the mysteries of life beyond normal perception. Taken ritually, it induces brilliantly colored fluid visions that reveal supernatural and mythological beings which sometimes re-enact creation myths of the tribe: the origins of plant, animal and tribal life (Reichel-Dolmatoff 1978). An ethnobotanist noted that in one tribe *ayahuasca* was given to women in childbirth, and in another tribe to introduce young children into the tribal way of seeing (McKenna 1991). Luis Eduardo Luna (1986) explained that "tobacco is the food of *ayahuasca*. It is blown over the vines before they are cut and over the bottle of *ayahuasca* before you take it." He added that the *icaro*, the magical healing song of the shaman, is derived from the Quichua Indian word *ikaray* which means "to blow smoke in order to heal." *Ayahuasca* is also called a "plant teacher" because it teaches the correct way to live. A shaman prepares himself for it by going on a restricted diet which is low in protein and high in carbohydrates (yucca, manioc, banana, rice and dried fish) for several weeks. No fat, sugar, salt, pork, chicken or industrially produced food is allowed. Foods must be avoided with contaminating smells. According to Luna, who has extensively studied the use of *ayahuasca* in Peruvian Mestizo populations near Iquitos and Pucallpa, the diet alters the body's semiochemistry and this, in turn, alters the shaman's body scent so that it becomes *olor a monte*, "the smell of the forest." With *olor a monte* a shaman can go into the forest and commune with the animals and spirits which will not sense him as an enemy, "as other" (Luna 1991). Thus as it changes your body scent, it changes your aura.

Janet Siskind described an aspect of the *ayahuasca* ritual of the Sharanahua Indians, a small tribe that lives in the eastern Amazonian region of Peru: "They take *ayahuasca* to seek the cause of illness and to learn or to know." She said that after taking the brew, "for twenty minutes men chant quietly or gaze toward the distant blank silhouette of the forest, lighting small pipes of Peruvian tobacco, picking a few stalks of an odorous plant (*Ocimum mircanthum*), whose smell will protect them from bad visions." The shamans guide the young men, "teasing them into chanting, blowing on their faces and stroking their foreheads if they appear too deep in frightening trance, holding the sweet-smelling plant under their noses to bring them out" (Siskind 1990).

Shamanic Aromachology

Ocimum mircanthum possesses a mysterious capacity to reorient the mind in a positive way and to avoid the fearful imagery of an *ayahuasca* trance. Biopsychologist Avery Gilbert (1991) suggests that the plant's anti-anxiety effect may be due to the its ability to "block the anxiety receptors, acting like a beta-blocker of the adrenergic nerves. Beta adrenergic blockers decrease blood pressure, heart rate and serve to limit the symptoms of anxiety. When you smell the plant it would effectively stop the autonomic cascade and calm you down." This hypothesis was supported by ethnopharmacologist Dennis McKenna (1991), who suggested that *"Ocimum mircanthum* might be a neuroleptic, a tranquilizing agent."

Schultes (1990) has stated that *Ocimum mircanthum* is used as a fragrance by forest cultures: "the twigs are inserted under wristbands or crushed and rubbed on the shoulders for perfuming the body. The Siona and Secoya Indian names both mean *"chica* perfume," suggesting that the plant may be employed to scent *chica* (a fermented drink usually made from Cassava)." In addition, McKenna (1991) mentioned that *Ocimum mircanthum* was a very commonly used admixture for *ayahuasca* and that "it is the indigenous Amazonian form of basil, commonly cultivated in everybody's herb garden." The pieces of this aromatic puzzle begin to fit together. Robert Tisserand (1983) remarks that "oil of basil is an excellent, indeed perhaps the best, aromatic nerve tonic. It clears the head, relieves intellectual fatigue and gives the mind strength and clarity. It is of great value in states of nervousness, anxiety and depression. It is uplifting."

To sum up, the behavioral aromatic dynamics of Amazonian basil on the *ayahuasca* trance are as follows: when the mind becomes hypnotically fixated on a frightening image in a closed loop of anxiety, it goes unconscious, suspending its capacity to reprogram itself or to change its frame of reference. The fragrance of basil synesthetically shifts the weight given to the visual imagery and by this means unlocks the anxiety loop by restoring the natural fluidity of the mind. These psychological dynamics illustrate the compelling cross-sensory effect of the sense of smell on the sense of vision.

A shaman, Manuel Cordova Rios, relates that when he had several Lamisto Indians of Chazuta in an *ayahuasca* ceremony in the Peruvian Amazon, the first thing he did in the deep forest clearing was to chant as he made a fire: "fragrant leaves, tranquil smoke, prepare our minds for visions to come." As he prepared the *ayahuasca*, "a billowing white cloud of pungent, fragrant smoke from the burning leaves floated up into the treetops, enveloping us at the same time in the spell of its aroma. A trance-like tranquility prevailed as we breathed in the fragrant smoke" (Lamb 1985). Perhaps the fragrant plant was *Ocimum micanthum*. In any case, it was used to perform a similar function of creating a serene aromatic atmosphere for a sacred visionary experience.

Perfumeros

A *perfumero* is a healer who uses the scents of fragrant plants and perfumes. Sometimes they take *ayahuasca* and sometimes not. They are extremely sensitive to the many naunces of body odors caused by diet, emotions and scent imbalances due to sorcery-induced illness. They anoint the forehead and arms of the patient, then they take off his clothes and anoint and bathe the whole body in scent. After the treatment perfume is applied several times to reinforce this change. They usually have many plant scents and perfumes to choose from (Luna 1991). For example, as a remedy for insanity or mental derangement, Cordova Rios, the shaman mentioned above, suggests the fresh bark of the Ashango tree, which is chopped up and put in cold water for several hours. After bathing in the water, he says, "let the patient smell the fragrant oil extracted from the wood, and rub this oil on his temples and neck. Very quickly the patients will return to normal and be cured" (Lamb 1985).

A *perfumero* attempts to heal not only physical illness, but also bad luck in love and work. For example, if someone has bad luck in business and few customers, this can be cured. "There is the possibility of affecting your smell, your pheromones, changing your chemistry in one way or another. You take baths of certain plants, like the onion-scented *sacha-ajos* (*Mansoa alliacea*), which makes you feel like a magnet, you attract the attention of the people and everybody wants to help you" (Luna 1985). With the skillful use of fragrance, *perfumeros* can transform the auric field, the energetic/emotional envelope that surrounds a person. These shamans understand the plasticity of this field and that it can be manipulated through fragrance and diet. In the magical tradition, fragrance can "magnetize or irradiate" a weakened aura.

In South America, some diseases are thought to be caused by spirits rather than by biological organisms. Someone's soul is stolen, entrapped or poisoned by an adversary spirit. The forest indians and Mestizo populations on the outskirts of cities are subject to sorcery battles and telepathic duels between the forces of good and evil magic. *Ayahuasca* is often used to determine the magical source of disease. It gives power to a shaman to counter the black magic of sorcerers.

Florecer

During a treatment, a *perfumero* may also take a small amount of perfume in his mouth and then, after inhaling some tobacco smoke, blows the mixture on the patient. "This is called *florecer*, the spitblowing–spraying of perfumed essences through pressed closed lips and that in turn relates to the pneumatic power of the shaman. The Indians believe the pneuma, the breath, is endowed with curing powers, so to blow tobacco or spray essences is an extension of this" (Giese 1989). *Florecer* means "to blossom, to do well, to advance, to make whole or to flourish." It means to give persons the vital force and awareness necessary to protect themselves. It means that the patient should blossom in every aspect of life. *Florecer* is more than anything the payment to the spirits through the perfume. If the correct scent is missing on an altar, everything in the healing ritual disintegrates. "Without perfume," notes Giese who has studied traditional healing in northern Peru, "you cannot do anything" (Giese 1989). In a typical healing ritual the assistants spray fragrance over the patients, the shamans and then the altar of sacred objects. This makes it easier for the spirits to manifest, especially the spirits of power plants like *ayahuasca*. *Cananga* water, another floral spray, is used later to defend against negative powers by the shamans. The spirits of the mountains are invoked by offering them incense (Giese 1989).

Another example of cross-sensory activation comes from Luna (1991) who reported that several years previously he had taken *ayahuasca* with a shaman in Iquitos. The shaman asked him if he was having any visions. When Luna said that he was not, the shaman took some perfume in his mouth, mixed it with tobacco smoke, and blew it directly on the top of his head. At that moment Luna reported that visions literally exploded in his brain.

Shamanism and Synesthesia

The Shipibo-Conibo Indians, who live on the eastern slopes of the Andes in lowland Peru, also use *ayahuasca* in their synesthetic healing rituals. Gebhart-Sayer (1987) observed that "together the shamans and spirits hear the curing songs and patterns and smell and sing them." These restorative body patterns operate on the auric field and can only be perceived and manipulated by the shaman. At the start of the healing treatment the shaman sees the body of the patient like an X-ray. A sick person's visual body pattern is like a mixed-up pile of garbage and its pathological aura has a vile stench which is the mark of the attacking spirit. The healing ritual involves both the restoration of a healthy visual body pattern and the neutralization of the pathogenic aura through life-enhancing fragrance. After the shaman has taken the *ayahuasca,* he replaces his rattle with a bunch of herbs with which "he beats a smelling rhythm. The air is now full of aromatic tobacco smoke and the good scent of herbs." Vibrant scents are essential shamanic tools because they attract beneficial spirits. The shaman knows that fragrance is a two-way channel which can also carry messages from the forest spirits (Gebhart-Sayer 1987).

David Howes (1987) has theorized that "there is an intrinsic connection between olfaction and transition, or category change. This association would appear to be universal for it finds expression in the context of diverse rites-of-passage all over the world." Olfactory synchronization, be it through incense, perfume, or the scent of cooking, accompanies life transitions in rites-of-passage from birth to death and in religious observances. In Amazonian cultures, there is ample evidence for this hypothesis. Fragrance facilitates transformations in religious, magical and healing rituals.

In shamanic cultures, fragrances and perfumes are accorded the status of life-giving substances which positively amplify the energetic/emotional envelope of the human aura. Fragrance is a reciprocal medium: the gods or spirits manifest through scent, are nourished by it, and messages are sent to them through fragrance. There is also a recognition of the alliance of fragrance and hallucinogens. Furthermore, it is a synesthetic culture in which smell is ranked highly. The synesthesia of the rituals dissolve the conditioned psychological boundaries which rigidify and compartmentalize the mind, and serve to make it more amenable to positive transformations.

The perception of fragrance creates a deep chemical sense of immediacy in the body which somatically integrates more distant optical and acoustical senses in the synesthetic experience. Because of its chemical (molecular) immediacy, fragrance gives a sense of the immediate present, of being in present time. Within the context of shamanic thought, present time is the optimum window in which to effect a change in consciousness. It implies a state of total attention and awareness.

Fragrance is an indispensible part of the enlightened sensorium. The West has been nose-blind too long. Shamanic cultures have much to teach about smell and fragrance. As more sensorial anthropology (and archaeology) is done in the future, knowledge of other cultures who have developed the sense of smell will contribute to the West's own olfactory awakening.

Bibliography

Gebhart-Sayer, A. (1987), *Die Spitze des Bewusstseins Untersuchungen zu Weltbild und Kunst der Shipibo-Conibo*, Munich: Klaus Renner Verlag.

Giese, C. (1989), *Curanderos Traditionelle Heiler in Nord-Peru*, Munich: Klaus Renner Verlag.

Gilbert, A. (1991) Paper presented at the 1st Aromacology Symposium, New York: Fragrance Foundation, 12 November.

Green, A. (1988), "Fragrance Education and the Psychology of Smell," in S. Van Toller and G.H. Dodd (eds), *Perfumery*, London: Chapman & Hall, pp. 227–32.

Howes, D. (1987), "Olfaction and Transition," *Canadian Review of Sociology and Anthropology*, 24: 398–416.

Lamb, F. (1985), *Rio Tigre and Beyond*, Berkeley: North Atlantic Books.

Luna, L.E. (1985), "Shamanism among the Mestizo Population of the Peruvian Amazon," paper presented at the Ayahuasca Conference, Esalen Institute, Big Sur, CA, August.

—— (1986), *Vegetalismo*, Stockholm: Almqvist & Wiskell.

—— (1991), personal communication with the author.

McKenna, D. (1984), "Monoamine Oxidase Inhibitors in South American Hallucinogenic Plants," *Journal of Ethnopharmacology*, 10: 195–223.

—— (1991), personal communication with the author.

Reichel-Dolmatoff, G. (1978), *Beyond the Milky Way*, Los Angeles: UCLA Latin American Center Publications.

Schultes, R.E. (1990), *The Healing Forest*, Portland: Dioscorides Press.

Siskind, J. (1990), "Shavarahua Songs of Transformation," *Shaman's Drum*, 20: 24.

Tisserand, R. (1983), *The Art of Aromatherapy*, Saffron Walden: C.W. Daniel.

Wilbert, J. (1987), *Tobacco and Shamanism in South America*, New Haven: Yale University Press.

—— (1991), personal communication with the author.

22

The Dialectic of "Enscentment"

Patrick Süskind's *Perfume* as Critical
History of Enlightenment Culture

Richard T. Gray

...eternalized scent is paradoxical.

Theodor W. Adorno, *Aesthetic Theory*

Patrick Süskind unquestionably established himself as the wunderkind of the German literary scene of the 1980s. Although he published only four slender volumes in the past ten years, two of these, the one-man drama *The Contrabass* and the novel *Perfume: The Story of a Murderer* (1987) (*Das Parfum: Die Geschichte eines Mörders*), held top spots in the German literary hit parade of the decade. But the novel's success has by no means been restricted to Germany: it has been translated into no fewer than twenty-five languages, and by the beginning of 1990 it had registered worldwide sales of over two million copies (Hage 1990: 101).

Initial critical responses to Süskind's novel, while on the whole positive, have only rarely reflected the enthusiasm of the reading public. One reason for this is that contemporary German literary critics often suspect commercially successful works of collaborating with the trivializing tendencies of the postmodern culture industry. Because such assessments operate within the discourse of what Andreas Huyssen has called the "great divide," presupposing an absolute dichotomy between popular culture and high art, between postmodernism and critical aesthetics (1986: viii–x), they fail to do justice to Süskind's novel, to which this dichotomy no longer applies. For

Perfume, especially in the historical dimension of its narrative, moves well beyond a mere clever retreading of the popularized detective story and the self-indulgent playfulness of postmodern pastiche; in fact, it strategically appropriates these techniques of popular and postmodern literature to relate in fictive-parabolic form a critical *histoire des mentalités* of Enlightenment culture. This project is informed by two distinct yet related traditions: on the one hand, the critique of enlightened instrumental reason developed by the early Frankfurt school theoreticians and formulated most succinctly by Max Horkheimer and Theodor Adorno in their *Dialectic of Enlightenment;* on the other hand, the tradition of French sociocultural historiography extending from the *Annales* historians through Michel Foucault to Alain Corbin. Süskind, who studied history in Munich and Aix-en-Provence during the period of student unrest in the late 1960s and early 1970s, most certainly came into close contact with these intellectual currents, which prominently informed the discourse of student revolt in both France and Germany. What these movements have in common, of course, is their critical inquiry into the systematization of knowledge and their sympathetic interest in the elements of thought and human conduct that Enlightenment culture sought to exclude from the discourse of the "rational." *Perfume* extends the critical counterhistorical practices embodied in such sociohistorical examinations into the domain of historical fiction, constructing a fictional narrative that exposes the epistemic mechanisms of Enlightenment culture by transposing those mechanisms into the alienating realm of the olfactory.

If, as Judith Ryan has claimed, the opening paragraph of *Perfume* presents a "consummate imitation of historical narrative" (1990: 399), this mimicry serves not merely to promote intellectual titillation and postmodern play but also to establish from the outset the sociohistorio-graphic thrust of the novel:

> In eighteenth-century France there lived a man who was one of the most gifted and abominable personages in an era that knew no lack of gifted and abominable personages. His story will be told here. His name was Jean-Baptiste Grenouille, and if his name—in contrast to the names of other gifted abominations, de Sade's, for instance, or Saint-Just's, Fouché's, Bonaparte's, etc.—has been forgotten today, it is certainly not because Grenouille fell short of those more famous blackguards when it came to arrogance, misanthropy, immorality or, more succinctly, to wickedness, but because his gifts and his sole ambition were restricted to a domain that leaves no traces in history: to the fleeting realm of scent. (Süskind 1987: 3)

Aside from locating the novel in the genre of historical fiction, this paragraph adumbrates the critical position the text takes vis-a-vis the historical narrative it relates. The passage indicates that during the historical period in question—the Age of Enlightenment, or what Foucault terms the "classical" age, with its reliance on the principle of mastery through visual representation (1973:

46–77)—genius is inextricably interwoven with misanthropy and wickedness, and history, including that of Süskind's protagonist, Grenouille, is the history of "gifted and abominable personages." The narrator acknowledges the marginality of the story he recounts but at the same time insists that Grenouille is representative of the Age of Enlightenment, even though the character's sensory forte lies outside the domain of sight. Grenouille's deeds are not intrinsically less noteworthy—that is, less gruesome—than those committed by "more famous blackguards" of eighteenth-century France, but since he accomplished these deeds in the realm of the olfactory, a sensory sphere whose impressions the Enlightenment attempted to suppress, they are not recorded in its history. In *Civilization and Its Discontents*, Freud explicitly associates the rise of civilization with the suppression of olfactory stimuli (1974: 229–30, 235–6); the coterminousness of this emergence and repression is expressed in *Perfume* by the paradox that the history the novel narrates at once exemplifies the Enlightenment's historical sensibility and is marginalized by that sensibility. This incongruity has its counterpart in the seemingly aporetic charge assigned to Süskind's narrator: the reconstruction of a history that has left no vestiges whatsoever in official history. Insofar as the novel is concerned with the recollection and documentation of what has been wiped off the slate of historical memory, it pursues a project of critical anamnesis. It is no coincidence, moreover, that this counterhistory relies specifically on the documentation of olfactory data, since it is a commonplace of modern osphresiology that of all the senses, olfaction is the one most intimately connected to the function of memory (Corbin 1986: 220; Tellenbach 1968: 103–4).

It is generally recognized that *Perfume* was inspired in part by Alain Corbin's study of the relation between odor and the French social imagination, *The Foul and the Fragrant*. Besides borrowing certain specific motifs from Corbin—for example, the stench of Paris in the eighteenth century and the especially attractive fragrance attributed at that time to redheads and virgins (Corbin 1986: 27–8, 38, 85)—Süskind replicates Corbin's historiographic strategy: both works attempt to tell the hidden but all-important history of olfaction in the Enlightenment. But the historical demeanor of *Perfume* draws more generally on procedures characteristic of the *Annales* historiographers, transposing into the sphere of historical fiction the search for "deep-down history" typical of that school (Braudel 1977: 85). Süskind and these writers have both a common purpose and a similar method. *Annales* historiography operates under the presupposition that "the vast world of the habitual, the routine" constitutes the "great absentee in history" (Braudel 1977: 16). Its aim is to bring to light the domain of the "unthought," to identify the paradigmatic constants that are masked by the epiphenomenal narratives of traditional historiography they underlie. It pursues this task by isolating marginal phenomena of sociocultural production and scrutinizing them for features representative of broad historical patterns. Süskind applies a similar methodology in *Perfume:* by projecting the career of Grenouille, the abominable olfactory genius with no scent of his own, onto the historical backdrop of the Enlightenment, Süskind can uncover certain "deep-historical" practices and epistemic routines inherent in the culture of the period. In other words, the anecdotal story of the scentless Grenouille and his hypersensitive nose acts as a fictional foil to throw the prejudices and obsessions of enlightened thought into critical relief. In this parable of the nose demon who destroys living creatures to capture and control their "spirits" or "absolute essences," Süskind dramatizes the consequences of enlightened reason's destructive dialectic.

If the French poststructuralist critique of Western "logocentrism" has found relatively little resonance in contemporary German critical circles, one reason is that the German intelligentsia was already familiar with the primary lines of this argument through the theories of the Frankfurt school. Indeed, decades before deconstructive philosophy introduced the term *logocentrism* into critical discourse, Horkheimer and Adorno coined the word *logozentrisch* (*logocentric*) in their *Dialectic of Enlightenment,* where it already displays the critical undertones specific to its current usage (1971: 61). For Horkheimer and Adorno Enlightenment logocentrism names an epistemological canon according to which knowledge must be disclosed and organized to be accepted as true or valid. The cornerstone of this knowledge regime is formal logic, the "great school of standardization," which provided Enlightenment thinkers with "the schema of the calculability of the world" (1971: 10). Within this system of knowledge the modern "subject," whose central characteristic is the drive to control, manipulate and dominate the totality of its natural environment, is born as the rationally organizing center of an objectified world. But, as Horkheimer and Adorno stress, human beings as enlightened subjects "pay for the increase in their power with alienation from that over which they exercise power. Enlightenment behaves toward things as a dictator behaves toward human beings: he knows them insofar as he can manipulate them." In this logically controlled universe, uniqueness disappears, and individuals are reduced to mere placeholders in an artificially inducible, infinitely iterable formal structure: "Being is viewed under the aspect of manufacture and administration. Everything—even the individual human being, not to mention animals—becomes a repeatable, replaceable process, a mere example for the conceptual models of the system." The solidification of Enlightenment thinking occurs as the formulation and formalization of a specific language that no longer expresses but "calculates, signifies, betrays, incites to murder" (Horkheimer and Adorno 1971: 225).

In his development from naive sniffer to master perfumer, Grenouille exemplifies the enlightened subject in the historical process of perfecting technological knowledge as a formulaic "language" of control. The self-destruction with which he pays the price for this rise to dictatorial power encapsulates that absolute self-alienation which Horkheimer and Adorno regard as the logical consequence of enlightened purposive rationality. Viewed in this context, *Perfume* appears as an inverted, indeed perverted, *bildungsroman*: the novel relates the progressive integration of its singular protagonist into his sociohistorical and epistemic environment, but it depicts this process negatively, showing Grenouille appropriating and applying reason to establish an egocentric reign of terror. The successive refinements he accomplishes "in the conventional language of perfumery" consolidate his knowledge of the world of scents, and he cunningly exploits his knowledge to gain power over his fellow human beings (Süskind 1987: 110). In his *Anthropology from a Pragmatic Point of View*, Kant registers the inescapability of smells and condemns olfaction as "opposed to freedom" and hence unworthy of cultivation (1977a: 452–3). Like the Enlightenment philosopher Kant, Grenouille too recognizes smells as unavoidable, but it is precisely for this reason that he considers olfactory sensations the most effective medium for influencing and manipulating sensate creatures. On the basis of this recognition, Grenouille formulates his olfactory program for tyranny:

> He [Grenouille] would be the omnipotent god of scent, just as he had been in his fantasies, but this time in the real world and over real people. And he knew that all this was within his power. For people could close their eyes to greatness, to horrors, to beauty, and their ears to melodies or deceiving words. But they could not escape scent. For scent was a brother of breath. Together with breath it entered human beings, who could not defend themselves against it, not if they wanted to live... He who ruled scent ruled the hearts of men. (Süskind 1987: 189)

With cold-blooded deliberation, Grenouille formulates a plan to rule humankind through the inevitable entrancement—Kant's "unfree" quality—resulting from particular olfactory sensations. Because scents enter into the very being of anyone who perceives them (Kant 1977a: 452), they represent an ideal means of colonizing the emotions of others by establishing control from within. Just as Horkheimer and Adorno sought to understand "why humanity, instead of entering into a truly human condition, sinks into a new kind of barbarism" (1971: 1), Süskind fictionally documents as a dialectic of "enscentment" the methodological, systematic and logical principles that account for the degeneration of the dream of technological "progress" into a nightmare of technocratic despotism.

Perfume can be divided into four sections, each containing a specific developmental station through which Grenouille must pass on his way to becoming an olfactory tyrant. In keeping with the *bildungsroman* model, each is organized as an educational encounter between the protagonist and one or more representatives of his sociohistorical environment. Moreover, the stations correspond to particular stages in the history of Western aesthetics;

Grenouille's progress in the art of perfumery parallels the progression from classical to modernist art, culminating in the commodity aesthetics of the culture industry. This imbrication of enlightened reason and aesthetic modernism constitutes the primary critical thrust of *Perfume*. As Huyssen has argued, "[P]ostmodernism's critical dimension lies precisely in its radical questioning of those presuppositions which linked modernism and the avant-garde to the mindset of modernization" (1986: 183), and it is this linkage that Süskind interrogates through the fictional history of the olfactory artist and terrorist Grenouille. The first segment of the novel (chs. 1–8) relates Grenouille's birth and early childhood. The second section (chs. 9–22) deals with Grenouille's apprenticeship to the perfumer Giuseppi Baldini and ends with Grenouille's attainment of journeyman's papers, his departure from Paris, and the catastrophe that befalls Baldini. The third section (chs. 23–34) portrays Grenouille's retreat from the world into the realm of his olfactory imaginings, his subsequent return to civilization, and his experiences as a guinea pig for the marquis de La Taillade-Espinasse. The fourth part (chs. 35–50) depicts Grenouille's perfection of his perfumery skills, his triumph over Antoine Richis in the competition for possession of Richis's daughter, and the olfactory metamorphosis of Grenouille's execution into a bacchanalian rite. This section concludes with a chapter that recounts Grenouille's return to his birthplace, the Cimetière des Innocents in Paris. Here he dons his artificial aura, the perfect perfume, and thereby "inspires" a mob with the same deadly passion that has motivated him throughout his life, causing the crowd to dismember and devour him. At the novel's conclusion Grenouille thus meets the same fate as his countless victims have, falling prey to his own will to mastery.

While the second, third and fourth sections of *Perfume* each depict Grenouille's socialization by juxtaposing him with a single primary antagonist (Baldini, Taillade-Espinasse and Richis, respectively), the first section disseminates the role of antagonist among a number of characters. This diffraction is consistent with the purpose of the novel's introductory segment, to provide an atmospheric description of the decades leading up to the French Revolution, which function as the sociohistorical backdrop for Grenouille's story. Indeed, one antagonist is this sociohistorical context itself. In the opening pages of the novel Süskind draws on Corbin's social history of odor in evoking the putrid smells of civilized Paris. The infernal stench pervading the metropolitan center of the European Enlightenment parallels the infernal lovelessness Süskind attributes to the city's populace. Without exception, the secondary characters of this opening section—from Grenouille's mother to Father Terrier, from the nannies Jeanne Bussie and Madame Gaillard to the tanner Grimal—perceive the child Grenouille either as an unwanted burden to be disposed of in the quickest and easiest manner possible or as a material "good" to be exploited for profit. The unadulterated heartlessness of this "civilized" society is concretized in the efforts of

Grenouille's mother to bury the product of the "revolting birth" shortly after bearing him (Süskind 1987: 5). The reifying attitude this society takes toward human beings is suggested by the demeanor of Grenouille's mother, who icily refers to the infant as a lump of "bloody meat" and as a "newborn thing" (Süskind 1987: 5–6). The state, which punishes Madame Grenouille for her reckless brutality, acts with a similar disregard for human life: "for reasons of economy" it transports as many as four foundling children to the state orphanage in a single bark basket, even though this method of transport is known to drive the mortality rate extraordinarily high. Grenouille is spared the horror of such a transport only because a "whole series of bureaucratic and administrative difficulties" cause him instead to be handed over to the cloister of Saint-Merri (Süskind 1987: 7).

As depicted by Süskind, the secular institutions of prerevolutionary France manifest a coldhearted bureaucratic reason that accepts a higher mortality rate as the price of greater efficiency, and the same coldheartedness characterizes the ecclesiastical institutions of that era. These are represented by Father Terrier, whom the narrator explicitly identifies as an enlightened thinker, a man who relies on his critical faculties and who does not shy away from "mak[ing] use of [his] reason" to combat "the superstitious notions of the simple folk" (Süskind 1987: 16). The references to reasoned critique and the struggle against superstition, as well as the allusion to Kant's famous definition of Enlightenment as the "making use of one's own reason" (1977b: 53), identify Father Terrier with the Enlightenment spirit. Consistent with this is Terrier's valorization of "sharp eyes" capable of perceiving "the light of God-given reason" over the "primitive organ of smell," which he, like Kant, identifies as "the basest of the senses" (Süskind 1987: 17). Although Terrier is prudent, God-fearing and reasonable, the uncanniness of the scentless infant Grenouille gets the better of him, and he too casts the child off, arranging to have him reared by Madame Gaillard.

Madame Gaillard proves to be the perfect nursemaid for Grenouille in one respect: having lost her sense of smell as the result of a childhood beating administered by her father, she is unaware of Grenouille's peculiar scentlessness. She lacks not only her sense of smell, however, but also human passion (Süskind 1987: 22). This absolute emotionlessness, the narrator suggests, is related to her "merciless sense of order and justice," a virtue central to Enlightenment culture (Süskind 1987: 23). As if these characteristics were not enough to throw into doubt Madame Gaillard's suitability as a nursemaid, the reader also learns that she is motivated to perform her duties neither by pity nor by charity but by the desire for profit: she lays aside half the payment she receives for the expenses of each child to save enough to provide herself with a "private" death. It is symptomatic of the bleakness of this world that Madame Gaillard's efforts are ultimately in vain. Her dream is swept away by the rampant inflation that accompanies the introduction of paper money, and she dies the same public death at the Hôtel-Dieu that befell her husband. The narrator's digression on Madame Gaillard's ignoble demise elucidates not only the general hopelessness of the sociohistorical conditions within which Grenouille's story takes place but also the futility of systematic calculation and long-term planning in a world governed by unforeseeable forces. Madame Gaillard's fate thus undermines the Enlightenment belief in the inherent ability of human beings to control their own lives through reasoned deliberation.

The three persons largely responsible for Grenouille's childhood development—his mother, Father Terrier and Madame Gaillard—represent the values Süskind associates with enlightened society in the mid-eighteenth century: egocentrism, calculating rationality, emotionlessness, orderliness, "justice." Given this context, it is small wonder that Grenouille decides with his first whiff of the rank effluvia of civilized society to privilege self-interested calculation over humanitarian feeling.

> The cry that followed his birth, the cry with which he had brought himself to people's attention and his mother to the gallows, was not an instinctive cry for sympathy and love. That cry, emitted upon careful consideration, one might almost say upon mature consideration, was the newborn's decision against love and nevertheless for life. Under the circumstances, the latter was possible only without the former, and had the child demanded both, it would doubtless have abruptly come to a grisly end. (Süskind 1987: 24)

The narrator's condemnation of enlightened society could scarcely be stated more explicitly: he depicts this world as one in which love and life are mutually exclusive. Throughout the novel love is dialectically intertwined with brutality and death. Grenouille's murders, committed to preserve and eternalize the attractive power of love, exemplify this dialectic, as does the novel's conclusion: the lustful mob that tears Grenouille apart is said to act out of love (Süskind 1987: 310). From the very moment of his birth, the gifted and abominable Grenouille embodies in exaggerated form the dark underside of "enlightened" society. Grenouille's first act, the calculated, egocentric cry with which he calls attention to himself, concretizes the pernicious dialectic of enlightened rationality: the cry both marks the possibility of Grenouille's self-preservation and leads directly to the death of another human being.

It is this darkly cynical vision of the inception of Enlightenment culture—a vision shared by Corbin, the early Foucault and the authors of *Dialectic of Enlightenment*—that lurks behind the often ironically humorous facade of *Perfume*. The chapters depicting Grenouille's birth and childhood establish the alienating, reifying interpersonal relations characteristic of enlightened society, and the chapters dealing with Grenouille's years of virtual enslavement to the tanner Grimal narrow this focus by concentrating on the socioeconomic conditions of emergent industrial society. Aware that Grenouille, if forced to work with the caustic, often poisonous fluids used in the tanning process, would have little chance of survival, Madame Gaillard experiences "not the slightest twinge of conscience" when she sells her eight-year-old charge to Grimal for fifteen francs (Süskind 1987: 33). In Grimal's shop Grenouille is forced to work for a meager keep and constantly subjected to his master's physical brutality. In this environment, in which human beings are an expendable natural resource, Grenouille comes to understand intimately the rule of tyranny, recognizing that his life "consisted only of whatever utility Grimal ascribed to it" (Süskind 1987: 36). A paradigm of Darwinian adaptability, Grenouille adjusts even to these abject conditions. His obsequiousness earns him the freedom to explore Paris in search of fresh scents for his olfactory vocabulary.

It is during one such interlude of relative independence that Grenouille first detects the scent that promises to provide an "aesthetic principle" to help him organize the chaos of his olfactory imagination (Süskind 1987: 43).

> He had the prescience of something extraordinary—this scent was the key for ordering all odors, one could understand nothing about odors if one did not understand this one scent, and his whole life would be bungled, if he, Grenouille, did not succeed in possessing it. He had to have it, not simply in order to possess it, but for his heart to be at peace. (Süskind 1987: 45)

Grenouille is driven not by lust for possession but by passion for systematic knowledge: his need to capture this supreme scent reflects an obsession with order, a compelling impulse to organize his olfactory sensations into an austere and inviolable system. Following the aromatic trail, Grenouille is led to a beautiful—that is, beautiful-smelling—redheaded girl who sits in a garden along the Seine cleaning yellow plums. As he inhales the scent of unadulterated beauty, he recognizes that without its elementary presence all his "edifices of odors" are doomed to remain meaningless (Süskind 1987: 49). In pursuit of this absolute meaning, the transcendental signifier without which his entire catalog of olfactory sensations remains without significance, Grenouille becomes a murderer: he kills the girl, the source of this fragrance, to revel in her aromatic beauty undisturbed. This murder triggers in Grenouille an epiphany of rebirth as he discovers his mission in life: acknowledging for the first time his own olfactory genius, he envisions himself as a revolutionary in the world of scents, potentially the greatest perfumer of all time (Süskind 1987: 51).

The night after his first murder, Grenouille formulates as his life project a rationalist systematization of the entire domain of scents. He arranges the uncountable scent fragments in his memory in a "systematic order," establishes a hierarchical "catalogue of odors ever more comprehensive and differentiated," and erects "the first carefully planned structures of odor" (Süskind 1987: 51). The vocabulary Grenouille uses to articulate his program betrays his reliance on the logic of enlightened codification, and he reflects the shadowy aspect of this epistemic formation in his incognizance of or indifference to the relation between his plan and the act of murder that makes it possible. If, as Horkheimer and Adorno maintain, enlightened rationality attains mastery over nature only at the price of increased alienation from it, Grenouille must kill the natural source of this ethereal essence he wishes to dominate. But Süskind also goes beyond Horkheimer and Adorno's analysis and approaches the ideas of Foucault and Corbin insofar as he implicates the domain of aesthetics in the pursuit of rational systematization: for Grenouille's desire is to capture the essence of beauty, to establish a pure and systematic aesthetic.

The second section of *Perfume*, which describes the symbiotic relationship between Grenouille and the perfumer Baldini, forms the historicocultural core of Süskind's text. The account focuses on a paradigm shift in the art of perfumery, a historical transformation parallel to the aesthetic revolution that gave birth to bourgeois modernism in the second half of the eighteenth century. Initially Baldini represents a premodernist aesthetic in which creation is predicated on adherence to a canon; this aesthetic conception is tied to a professional self-understanding informed by the regulative authority of the guild. Although aware that the perfumer's trade is undergoing revolutionary changes as it turns away from traditional artisanship toward daring innovation, Baldini upholds a conservative position. He expresses his convictions through attacks on his adversary, Pelissier, whose originality and productivity strike Baldini as distastefully "unpredictable" (Süskind 1987: 63). Baldini is suspicious not only of this "inflationist of scent," whose reckless creativity represents a threat to the ancient trade of perfumery, but also of the fashion consciousness and profit mongering his rival represents (Süskind 1987: 64). Pelissier is everything Baldini is not: whereas Pelissier manifests inspiration, originality, experimentation, aesthetic anarchy, mass production, fashion and a market orientation, Baldini reveres tradition, the age-old rules of his trade, the rigidity of the guild system, artisanship and perpetuation of the tried-and-true. The philosophy of subjective creativity and infinite production promulgated by the "modernist" Pelissier contrasts with the philosophy of rule-governed imitation and limited reproduction advocated by the classicist Baldini. Because Pelissier's attitudes correspond more closely to those disseminated by enlightened, protomodernist culture, Baldini the classicist is reduced to the status of a mere epigone, surviving only by copying the novelties Pelissier's genius concocts. Baldini's increasing marginalization is reflected in the deterioration of his business, and it is not surprising that he lashes out at Enlightenment thinking, which he considers responsible for his decline. Baldini identifies the debilitating crisis of legitimation that the Enlightenment's relentless questioning unleashes; to his way of thinking, this "century of decline and degeneration" is intimately connected to the ideas of such enlightened "scribblers" as Diderot, d'Alembert, Voltaire and Rousseau (Süskind 1987: 69). Baldini predicts with oracular authority: "But that was the temper of the times, and it would all come to a bad end" (Süskind 1987: 69). What he does not yet know, however, is that he himself will be converted to this new philosophy and that this conversion, true to his prophecy, will result in his annihilation.

Grenouille's arrival marks a radical turnaround in Baldini's fortunes. Much like Grimal, Baldini is motivated solely by the desire to exploit Grenouille's talents. With Grenouille's help, Baldini successfully outmaneuvers his rival, Pelissier. Justifying the acquisition of this apprentice by pointing to the theory of "division of labor and rational systematization," Baldini recognizes that he is fighting his enlightened adversary with his adversary's own weapons (Süskind 1987: 106). Baldini thus assumes the role of a Faust figure who sells his soul to the modernist progressivity symbolized by Grenouille's infinitely creative, Mephistophelian genius. With the help of this "sorcerer's apprentice" (Süskind 1987: 107), Baldini ultimately commits the very acts he found distasteful in Pelissier: he asserts his preeminence by flooding the market with an endless stream of novel perfumes, and his commercial success is so great that he must eventually open a small factory in which his fragrances are produced and bottled on an assembly line (Süskind 1987: 121–2). This new enterprise manifests not only a sellout of classicism for aesthetic modernism but also the shift from the individually crafted product of the guild system to the mass production of the industrial age. What Süskind illustrates in the career of Baldini is the birth of the culture industry out of the spirit of modernist aesthetics, the strategic harnessing of modernism's aesthetic principles as the motor driving the productivity and profit of industrial modernization.

Baldini's meteoric rise to wealth and power ends as abruptly as it begins: the night the perfumer releases Grenouille from apprenticeship, the bridge on which the shop is located collapses, and Baldini and all his wealth disappear into the Seine. While the narrative makes no causal connection between this "minor catastrophe" (Süskind 1987: 135) and Baldini's new loyalty to enlightened modernism—aside from obliquely implying that the sheer weight of his hoarded riches may have compounded the stress that caused the bridge to fall (Süskind 1987: 133)—Süskind develops an elaborate allegory that explicitly suggests this association. On the eve of Grenouille's arrival, Baldini stares into the river and imagines it washing millions of gold coins in his direction (Süskind 1987: 78); suddenly, however, this image of boundless wealth reverts to one of impending doom: "The view of a glistening golden city and river turned into a rigid, ashen gray silhouette" (Süskind 1987: 78). Baldini correctly interprets this vision as an omen and impulsively decides to sell his shop the next day. Instead, however, he is seduced by the profit to be gained by exploiting Grenouille's remarkable olfactory genius. With this betrayal of his prior values and acquiescence in the principles of the "degenerate" modern age, Baldini unwittingly sets the stage for the realization of his vision: his "golden" rise to unimaginable wealth is the harbinger of his "ashen" demise, with which it is inextricably coupled. Baldini's story thus lays bare the linkage between enlightened progress and human self-destruction, manifesting the inescapable "principle of fatal necessity," which Horkheimer and Adorno identify as the internal dynamic of instrumental reason (1971: 14).

Grenouille and Baldini are joined in a relationship of mutual benefit: as Baldini profits from the fruits of his apprentice's genius, Grenouille learns from his master techniques that will enable him to distill the olfactory essences of natural objects. From Baldini, Grenouille expects to acquire the two prerequisites for creating the perfect perfume: "the cloak of middle-class respectability" in the form of his journeyman's papers and knowledge of the perfumer's craft, of the way scents are produced, concentrated, preserved and thereby made available for "higher ends" (Süskind 1987: 111). Through his association with Baldini, Grenouille learns to liberate the "scented soul" of living objects from the "stupid stuff" of their material being (Süskind 1987: 114). Grenouille's obsession with the ethereal "essences" of things and his disregard for their empirical existence represent a caustic satire of the "essentialism" characteristic of Western metaphysics, which privileges soul and spirit to the detriment of the physical body. Indeed, Grenouille's artistry concretizes the alliance of essentialist metaphysics and technological intelligence that Horkheimer and Adorno consider the heart of enlightened rationality.

The third stage of Grenouille's *Bildung* begins with an interruption of his training as a perfumer: instead of traveling to Grasse to complete his technical education, Grenouille sets out on a Romanticist journey inward, taking refuge for the duration of the Seven Years' War in a mountain cave where he is insulated from the effluvia of civilization. This retreat is motivated not only by Grenouille's growing disgust with human society but also by his desire to indulge in the fantasies of his olfactory imagination. In this self-imposed isolation, Grenouille plays the part of the autonomous modern artist who retreats from the banalities of the empirical world to cultivate undisturbed the empire of his imagination. Grenouille articulates his newfound aesthetic sensibility even before leaving Baldini's shop, designating as his artistic purpose the free expression of his olfactory fantasies. Grenouille's project has obviously undergone a radical shift in emphasis: whereas his technological education in the art of perfumery is directed outward toward the appropriation of the "essences" of objects in the empirical world, his attention is now trained on the subjective domain of his internal being. No longer concerned with olfactory mimesis, the re-creation of objectively detectable scents, Grenouille becomes fascinated with subjective self-expression. The numerous allusions to Romantic literature in this portion of the text reflect Grenouille's passage through a decidedly Romanticist phase (Ryan 1990: 396). This stage of his development is characterized by the solidification and fortification of his "innermost empire," a process that culminates in a grandiose fantasy of self-apotheosis (Süskind 1987: 150). Grenouille pictures himself as the God of scents, as Grenouille the Great, the absolute ruler of the olfactory universe; and a quasi-biblical discourse echoing that of Nietzsche's Zarathustra demonstrates this self-deification. It is especially apparent in this section of the work that the literary allusions in the narrator's discourse do not simply stitch together a textual pastiche but in fact serve a strategic purpose: they reflect the state of Grenouille's soul and underwrite the historicizing thrust of the novel by situating the distinct stages of the protagonist's artistic development in specific epochs of the history of aesthetics.

Grenouille's Romantic–aesthetic retreat to the sanctuary of the imagination ends suddenly with an "inner catastrophe" (Süskind 1987: 163) precipitated by the realization that aside from all the smells he has cataloged in his olfactory memory, one scent has escaped him: his own odor. Capable of detecting the subtlest fragrance at great distance, Grenouille is paradoxically unable to perceive his own odor, that most intimate and omnipresent of all smells. In the fictional universe of *Perfume,* to lack odor is to lack essence, and the final product of Grenouille's phase of Romanticist self-obsession is the knowledge that he has no essence. This gives rise to an anxiety hitherto unknown to him, "the fear of not knowing anything much about himself" (Süskind 1987: 167). With this, Grenouille is catapulted from the magnificent, self-aggrandizing vision of himself as Grenouille the Great to the reality of his inability to attain genuine self-knowledge: he is doomed to remain ignorant of any stable and enduring "essence" that might be identifiable as his self.

The self-critical awareness that he is by definition a man without qualities impels Grenouille to return to the civilized world and resume his quest. But in the wake of his sudden insight, this pursuit assumes a new dimension: Grenouille's aim is no longer simply the acquisition of the technical knowledge that will enable him to create the perfect perfume; he now sets his sights on the development of an artificial "essence" that will compensate for his natural scentlessness. His next mentor, the eccentric marquis de La Taillade-Espinasse, performs the important function of awakening Grenouille to the significance of semblance in human relations. In the scientistic quacksalver Taillade-Espinasse, Süskind presents a caricature of the experimental scientist bred by Enlightenment culture. Subscribing to the theory that the earth emits a *fluidum letale* that deteriorates living organisms, Taillade-Espinasse believes he has discovered in Grenouille— whose physical condition degenerated markedly during his seven years in the cave—incontrovertible evidence to support his hypothesis. Like all Grenouille's previous mentors, the marquis is interested only in exploiting Grenouille. For him Grenouille is merely a scientific specimen to be put on display. Using Grenouille, he hopes to accomplish the "veritable divine act" of transforming a beast into a human being by dispelling the *fluidum letale* (Süskind 1987: 175). When his ventilation treatment effects no perceptible changes in Grenouille's condition, however, Taillade-Espinasse sets about altering the superficial details of Grenouille's appearance: he has Grenouille bathed, given a set of fashionable new clothes, shaved, coiffed, fitted with a shoe to compensate for his crippled foot, packed in makeup and—last but not least—doused with the marquis's personal perfume.

What Grenouille learns from his encounter with the marquis is the importance of semblance and dissemblance in human intersubjective relations. In an enlightened world in which the truth of the seen is indubitable, clothes indeed do make the man. What matters in this environment, Grenouille recognizes, is not what one in essence is but what one appears to be, since one is judged not according to one's visually imperceptible being but only according to the impression one makes on others. Thus Grenouille comes to understand the importance of acquiring "a practiced routine for lying," that is, of learning to use semblance to manipulate others' sensibilities (Süskind 1987: 195). This realization brings with it a final transformation in Grenouille's aesthetic program: abandoning the self-expressive, autonomous aesthetics of Romanticism, he embraces instead an aesthetics of reception that valorizes semblance in the name of rhetorical effect. In short, Grenouille learns that aesthetic illusion is the most powerful weapon in the arsenal of the demagogue.

In keeping with the peculiarities of his genius, Grenouille transfers this insight from the realm of the visual into that of the olfactory. This displacement, however, produces a significant shift in meaning; whereas visual deceit as dissemblance amounts merely to disguising essence behind an arbitrary mask, olfactory delusion as "disenscentment" involves adopting an entirely new "essence." It is at this point that Süskind's strategy of enciphering the visual prejudices of enlightened thought in an osphresiological allegory begins to pay high critical dividends; for, once displaced into the domain of smells, the dichotomy between semblance and essence that dominates enlightenment metaphysics collapses: in the moment of aesthetic reception artificial scent becomes "essence" in a double sense, both as fragrant mask and as intrinsic being. In his encounter with Taillade-Espinasse, Grenouille thus solves the crisis of self-identity that disrupted his Romantic fantasy world in the cave: he arrives at the crucial insight that "essence" is a function not of the real but of what Jean Baudrillard has termed the "hyperreal." "Essence," like the entire reality of enlightened, industrial civilization, is not merely something that can be reproduced; the real is a simulation, "*that which is always already reproduced*" (Baudrillard 1983: 146). Taillade-Espinasse is the quintessential representative of the world in which reality disappears behind the simulations of hyperreality. Thus, although he cannot help knowing that Grenouille has been superficially altered rather than fundamentally transformed through science, Taillade-Espinasse never questions that the transformation is essential to Grenouille's being and that it confirms the fluidal theory. Through Taillade-Espinasse, Süskind exposes the scientific "knowledge" codified by enlightened reason as a series of carefully fostered illusions. Moreover, from this experience Grenouille comes to understand that the power to manipulate other human beings is intimately bound up with the ability to control simulations and their effects. The lesson Grenouille learns from Taillade-Espinasse is an eminently political one: the secret of controlling the emotions of human beings through simulations calculated to evoke specific responses. To be sure, it is precisely Grenouille's own "essence-lessness" that defines his suitability to become a master dissimulator, since the absence of essence makes appropriation of any and all essences possible. Thus, the man without qualities becomes a man with all (artificially induced) qualities, a perfect chameleon, capable of adapting his constitution to the demands of the moment. Once he achieves insight into reality as simulation, Grenouille—now the modern man par excellence—has at his disposal all the theoretical knowledge required for the formulation of his plan for dominion over all humanity. Yet he still lacks two significant elements for the realization of his design: familiarity with the advanced techniques of enfleurage and a human source from which to distill the keystone scent for his system of olfactory terror. In Grasse, the setting of the fourth section of the novel, both these needs are fulfilled, the first through his apprenticeship in Madame Arnulfi's perfumery, the second by his discovery of Laure Richis and her inescapably seductive odor.

Grenouille encounters his most challenging adversary in Antoine Richis, the father of his prospective victim. Two factors in particular account for Richis's ability to compete with Grenouille in the game of human mastery: his adherence to the mechanisms of enlightened thought and his ability to empathize so greatly with the murderer Grenouille that he can divine the method underlying Grenouille's lethal madness. Richis can project himself into Grenouille's thoughts and determine his motive because Richis and Grenouille have fundamentally similar modes of cognition. Both are systematic, methodical thinkers able to map out a tactical plan and pursue it with guile and tenacity. By identifying Grenouille's mode of thinking with that of Richis, the paragon of calculative reason, Süskind underscores once again that his protagonist embodies the principles of the Enlightenment episteme. Richis's description of the murderer's method and motives reads like a general characterization of enlightened rationality:

> The murderer ... had a system. It was not just that all the murders had been carried out in the same efficient manner, but the very choice of victims betrayed intentions almost economical in their planning ... In any case, it seemed to him, as absurd as it sounded, that the murderer was not a destructive personality, but rather a careful collector. For if one imagined—and so Richis imagined—all the victims not as single individuals, but as parts of some higher principle and thought of each one's characteristics as merged in some idealistic fashion into a unifying whole, then the picture assembled out of such mosaic pieces would be the picture of absolute beauty, and the magic that radiated from it would no longer be of human, but of divine origin. (Süskind 1987: 246)

This efficiency, when combined with precise planning and systematic rigidity, underwrites not only the murders perpetrated by Grenouille but also Richis's plan to achieve economic and political power. Although Richis thinks in visual metaphors while Grenouille follows olfactory pursuits, the structure of their thought remains the same. As described by Horkheimer and Adorno, enlightened rationality is distinguished by a tendency toward abstraction that reduces real entities to mere idealities. Grenouille's murders, Richis realizes, are predicated on the ability to overlook the concrete singularity of the women he destroys. Grenouille views his victims instead as "parts of a higher principle," that is, as elements in an abstract, formal system. In the words of Horkheimer and Adorno, "abstraction, the tool of enlightenment, treats its objects as did fate ... : it liquidates them" (1971: 15). Grenouille's murders exemplify the perverse consequences of abstract idealism run amok.

The intellectual similarity between the enlightened thinker Richis and the murderer Grenouille is further exhibited by their essentially parallel undertakings. Grenouille, after all, is not the only calculating strategist for whom Laure forms the keystone in an idealistic edifice: indeed, "Laure was also the keystone in the edifice of his, of Richis's own plans" (Süskind 1987: 248). Richis's "fatherly" love for his daughter is invariably tied to her utility for his self-serving ambitions, since her blossoming beauty provides him with an efficient means to accomplish his plan for sociopolitical advancement. The marriage he has arranged for her with the son of a wealthy aristocrat will enable Richis "to found a dynasty and to put his own posterity on a track leading directly to the highest social and political influence" (Süskind 1987: 241). For both Richis and Grenouille, Laure is a token to be wagered in a game whose stakes are economic and sociopolitical power.

Richis, of course, comes out the loser in this contest—not because his rival has more cunning or better methods at his disposal but because Grenouille has cultivated to perfection the principles underlying enlightened rationality. At the same time, Grenouille profits from the osphresiological insight that visual appearances are fundamentally secondary to olfactory emanations, which are the first stimuli to leave impressions in the infant's brain (Dragstra 1984: 115, 173; Tellenbach 1968: 13). Grenouille's preeminent refinement of Richis's system consists precisely in transferring visual metaphors and prejudices into the realm of the olfactory. The strategic edge this displacement brings Grenouille is demonstrated by the relative effectiveness with which each man establishes his incognito. Richis and his entourage attempt to beguile potential pursuers as they flee Grasse by changing their clothes; in contrast, Grenouille, who knows the advantages of olfactory dissimulation, disguises himself with an "odor of inconspicuousness" (Süskind 1987: 259). Grenouille's reliance on olfactory rather than visual sensation constitutes the measure of his superiority over Richis: disregarding visual clues, he tracks down father and daughter by following his nose. Conversely, when Richis discovers Grenouille sleeping in the stall of an inn, Richis's suspicions are dispelled by the olfactory impression of insignificance and harmlessness emanating from Grenouille's artificial "aura." Because of his superior skills of dissimulation, Grenouille subsequently has no difficulty whatsoever in reducing Laure to yet another of his aromatic trophies.

The conflict between Richis and Grenouille, with which *Perfume* reaches its apogee, is prefigured in many respects by the competition between Pelissier and Baldini in the second section of the novel. Pelissier and Richis, both paradigmatic proponents of Enlightenment thought, are defeated by opponents who beat them at their own game. But neither Baldini nor Grenouille, the apparent victors, can enjoy the fruits of his victory for long. Baldini's violent end, as I have noted, is linked with his appropriation of the principles of Enlightenment and of a dialectic that proves lethal. Ultimately this dialectic affects Grenouille's destiny as well, and in this sense, the fall of Baldini anticipates the fate of the novel's protagonist. Grenouille is at the peak of his power when he dons the perfume created from the scents of Laure and the other murdered women, thereby transforming the ritual of his own execution into a bacchanalian rite at which he is worshiped as a god. In this moment Grenouille makes real the fantasy of Grenouille the Great that occupied his imagination during the years of his seclusion; but far from being able to relish this triumph, he is overtaken by a pervasive anxiety:

> Yes, he was Grenouille the Great! Now it had become manifest. It was he, just as in his narcissistic fantasies of old, but now in reality. And in that moment he experienced the greatest triumph of his life. And he was terrified. (Süskind 1987: 292)

In the moment when Grenouille's elation gives way to terror he recognizes that his success, like Baldini's, is dialectically coupled with self-destruction. Grenouille's conquest and the triumph of enlightened reason are both ultimately Pyrrhic victories. Like the sorcerer's apprentice in Goethe's poem "The Sorcerer's Apprentice," Grenouille is unable to control the powers that he unleashes. When he is dismembered and devoured in the name of the same abstract, idealizing "love" that motivated his destructive quest, the novel reaches its all too logical conclusion.

Through Grenouille, *Perfume* voices an allegorical critique of enlightened reason and the spirit of industrial modernization. Framing this critique within the history of post-Enlightenment aesthetics allows Süskind to implicate Western aesthetics in the self-destructive dialectic of Enlightenment. In his *Aesthetic Theory* Adorno notes, "Precisely by attempting to lend duration to the ephemeral—to life—seeking to rescue it from death, works of art kill it" (1973: 202). Adorno calls this reflex the "negativity" of the work of art: "Works of art are a priori negative because of their adherence to the law of objectification; they kill what they objectify by tearing it from the immediacy of its existence" (1973: 201). In this objectifying compulsion modern art participates in the abstracting, alienating mechanisms of the enlightened episteme. In *Perfume* Süskind points out the parallel between modernist aesthetic practices and the principles of instrumental rationality; indeed, he exposes the destructive impulse inherent in Enlightenment metaphysics by examining its operation in the domain of aesthetics.

Perfume follows the patterns of that sub-genre of the *bildungsroman* known as the *Kunstlerroman* (Hallet 1989: 285), narrating the gradual perfection of its protagonist's technical skills and aesthetic sensibility in the art of perfumery. However, the novel relates this artistic education as an evolution unto death, a betrayal of nature for an artificial simulation of nature that is accomplished under the pretext of preserving its absolute essence. In this sense, Süskind's novel stands in close relation to two of the best-known novels of postwar Germany, Thomas Mann's *Doctor Faustus* and Gunter Grass's *The Tin Drum*. Both Mann and Grass interweave the evolution of their artist-protagonists, Adrian Leverkuhn and Oskar Matzerath, with the rise of national socialism in Germany, and both novels, furthermore, make use of the technique of historical allegory to present their fictional exposition of the causes and consequences of nazism. Süskind's *Perfume* is indebted in both respects to these literary forerunners, but it is distinguished from them by its wider focus. Instead of limiting his perspective to Germany's fatal flirtation with fascism, Süskind portrays fascism's propagandistic dissemblances and its irrational cult of personality as a historical consequence of enlightened rationality. In this Süskind follows Horkheimer and Adorno, who likewise interpret fascism not as a narrowly German phenomenon but as the culmination of a larger historical–epistemological process. *Perfume* articulates this more encompassing critique of the modern(ist) world as a *histoire des mentalités* of Enlightenment culture, describing the destructive epistemological mechanisms of that culture through the fictional history of the olfactory genius–terrorist Jean-Baptiste Grenouille.

Note

Unless otherwise marked, all translations are by the author.

Bibliography

Adorno, T.W. (1973), *Ästhetische Theorie*, G. Adorno and R. Tiedemann (eds), Frankfurt: Suhrkamp.
Baudrillard, J. (1983), *Simulations*, trans. Paul Foss et al., New York: Semiotext(e).
Braudel, F. (1977), *Afterthoughts on Material Civilization and Capitalism*, trans. P.M. Ranum, Baltimore: Johns Hopkins University Press.

Corbin, A. (1986), *The Foul and the Fragrant*, Cambridge: Harvard University Press.

Dragstra, R. (1984), "Der witternde Prophet," in D. Kamper and C. Wulf (eds), *Das Schwinden der Sinne*, Frankfurt: Suhrkamp, pp. 159–78.

Foucault, M. (1973), *The Order of Things*, New York: Vintage-Random.

Freud, S. (1974), *Das Unbehagen in der Kultur*, vol. 9 in A. Mitscherlich et al. (eds), *Freud-Studienausgabe*, Frankfurt: Fischer.

Hage, V. (1990), *Schriftproben*, Reinbek: Rowohlt.

Hallet, W. (1989), "Das Genie als Mörder," *Literatur für Leser*: 275–88.

Horkheimer, M. and Adorno, T.W. ([1944] 1971), *Dialektik der Aukflärung*, Frankfurt: Fischer.

Huyssen, A. (1986), *After the Great Divide*, Bloomington: Indiana University Press.

Kant, I. (1977a), *Anthropologie in pragmatischer Hinsicht*, vol. 12 in W. Weischedel (ed.), *Immanuel Kant Werkausgabe*, Frankfurt: Suhrkamp.

—— (1977b), "Beantwortung der Frage," in *Schriften zur Anthropologie, Geschichtsphilosophie, Politik und Pädagogik I*, vol. 11 of W. Weischedel (ed.), *Immanuel Kant Werkausgabe*, Frankfurt: Suhrkamp.

Ryan, J. (1990), "The Problem of Pastische," *German Quarterly*, 63: 396–403.

Süskind, P. ([1985] 1987), *Perfume*, trans. J.E. Woods, New York: Pocket.

Tellenbach, H. (1968), *Geschmack und Atmosphäre*, Salzburg: Müller.

Part V

Scentsuality

Preface

What does a vagina smell like?
Earth. Wet garbage. God. Water. A brand-new morning. Depth. Sweet ginger.
Sweat. Depends. Musk. Me. No smell, I've been told. Pineapple. Chalice
essence. Paloma Picasso. Earthy meat and musk. Cinnamon and cloves. Roses.
Spicy musky jasmine forest, deep, deep forest. Damp moss. Yummy candy.
The South Pacific. Somewhere between fish and lilacs. Peaches. The woods.
Ripe fruit. Strawberry–kiwi tea. Fish. Heaven. Vinegar and water. Light, sweet
liquor. Cheese. Ocean. Sexy. A sponge. The beginning.

Eve Ensler, *The Vagina Monologues*

The continual fascination with the mythical allure of perfume, the self-consciousness paranoia about body odors and, recently, the subconscious enchantment of pheromones, attests to the significance of smell in sexuality, either as an irresistibly persuasive or repelling force. One hundred years ago, individuals expressing more than a passing interest in smell would have been diagnosed with "olfactophilia"—a term that I take the liberty to rehabilitate here. For Richard von Krafft-Ebing ([1886] 1965), a pronounced interest in odors, especially in regards to any kind of sexual behavior, was a sign of dementia, disease or moral degeneration. Havelock Ellis furthered the regulation of olfactory pleasure by concluding that olfaction only plays a role for neuraesthenics, "inverts" and "primitives." Should any of the presumedly Euro-American and bourgeois readers identify with one of the plethora of examples of scentsuality described in his research, Ellis reassured that "refined and educated" people did not fit the profile of the "olfactory type," even if they fell under the infatuation of odors from time to time (Ellis [1905] 1942: 111). While Krafft-Ebing and Ellis stigmatized olfactophilia through appeals to sexual, class and cultural deviancy, it was Sigmund Freud (1961) who raised the stakes to the ultimate level—the survival of the human species. Smell was too powerful a sense, because of its close link to animality and sexuality, and needed to be sacrificed as a precondition for civilization itself.

To foreground the sense of smell to any significant degree in erotic practice is thus to tempt the label of "perversion." Often, in the literature on the erotic, smell is considered to be just an aphrodisiacal prelude, essential to the stages of seduction or foreplay but never an end in itself. The seeming unorthodoxy of olfactophilia certainly qualifies it as an erotic behavior that would be categorized as a "peripheral" or "petty" sexuality (Foucault 1980: 48; Grosz and Probyn 1995: x–xi)—a form of libidinality outside the realm of procreative ideologies. However, given the predominance of the multi-billion dollar fragrance industry and the pervasiveness of its marketing, could it not be the case that it is a *majority* of the population, by virtue of perfume and cologne consumption alone, who are practicing (but unacknowledged) olfactophiliacs? By placing emphasis on the nose, aromatic locations across the body and the fragrant aura (natural or artificially enhanced) that inevitably accompanies individuals, consumers become scentualists and disturb reductivist conceptions of sexuality based on phallocentric terms. The radical implications of olfactophilia—despite its tacit acceptance in the commonplace purchase of perfumes and other scented products—resides in its problematizing of the genital economy of sexuality, and the pluralizing of eroticism to every available sniff (see Stoddart 1990; Kohl and Francoeur 1995; Drobnick 2000). Once considered subversive to the regulation of emotions and behavior supposedly necessary to societal organization, smell's ability to invoke what Marcuse called "unsublimated pleasure" (1962: 36) is now a well-accepted and eagerly pursued objective.

The first chapter in this section reprises the subject of perfume from Part IV, here focusing on it as the vaporous embodiment of sexuality and death. Richard H. Stamelman's "The Eros—and Thanatos—of Scents" examines the traces of perfume in the Bible, Shakespeare, Greek mythology and nineteenth- and twentieth-century writings to find a continuing thematic of smell's summoning of eroticism and loss. Given the enduring co-presence of erotic and thanatopic principles in fragrance-filled poetry and literature over the course of several millenia, it is no wonder that similar concepts also infuse the naming of contemporary perfumes and influence the slogans accompanying their marketing campaigns. Within the terse but evocative copy of perfume advertising, there lie lyrical capsulizations of ancient mythology, philosophical ideas and cultural narratives about love and expiration. The figure of the olfactophiliac appears again and again in various guises, especially as the object of passion succumbs and scent symbolizes all that which is intense but ultimately fleeting. As much as scent serves as a muse for poetic ruminations on sexuality and death, the author maintains that poetry itself is based on an evanescent logic of form confronting formlessness.

Eve Ensler's question, "What does a vagina smell like?," addressed to a wide range of women interviewed during the process of writing of *The Vagina Monologues*, dares to confront the always–already stigmatization that clings to body odors, sexual or otherwise. The variety of answers—from the comical to the earthy to the profound—hints at a complexity that goes a long way to undermining simplistic cultural discourses of olfactory and corporeal disapproval. Carol Mavor's discussion of *odor di femina* likewise seeks to debunk discourses that configure women as the negative or absent gender, especially in the scientifically discredited but nevertheless still theoretically influential field of psychoanalysis. She critiques the inadequacy of visualist psychoanalytic paradigms by drawing attention to female versions of fetishism (which typically include olfactory and tactile sensations), scouring through Freud's "fetid footnotes" to expose masculinist, Eurocentric views, and following the logic of Lacan's cryptic mentions of odor to unintended results. If the authority of vision positioned women as different and objectified, the equating of women with smell positioned them as inferior and abject. Yet, the volatility of odor and atavism of the sense of smell embody a certain type of radicality that permits women to undo both the primacy of the visual and overdetermination in the discursive field.

Odor di femina's male vaporous counterpart—*aura seminalis*—is a term equally endowed with mythical power and yet subject to approbation. Christopher Looby's chapter on "The Odor of Male Solitude" centers on the odors that diffuse out of nineteenth-century textual depictions of masculinity. The scent of men, especially semen, when recognized by other men, tends to perturb the unstable olfactory repression and homophobia of the era. Walt Whitman's autoerotic indulgence in bodily aromas, Herman Melville's allusions to homoeroticism through the gelatinous fragrance of whale flesh, and Francis Parkman's olfactory hallucination of and subsequent "averse desire" for the perfume of a Bostonian—these examples demonstrate the olfactophilic deviancies that were ever present in male cultural domains and liable to be unleashed unexpectedly. The most harrowing of Looby's source material is Homer Bostwick's virulent anti-masturbation tract, with its antagonism towards non-procreative bodily pleasures and its promotion of sadistic therapeutic techniques. As Looby remarks, Bostwick's olfactory-laden text vividly evokes that which he is expressly seeking to stigmatize, contradictorily creating difficulty in distinguishing whether it nullifies or incites an interest in self-pleasuring acts.

In the twentieth century, photography, advertising and television commercials become a predominant means of articulating sexual mores and projecting models of gender behavior (see DeLong and Bye 1990; Tannen 1994; Amy-Chinn 2001). Once resolutely heterosexual, perfume ads now embrace gay, lesbian, bisexual and androgynous preferences. Seducing the opposite sex, the overriding purpose expressed in postwar ads, yields instead to the shifting desires found in the postmodern, late-capitalist context of blurred and interchangeable gender identities. Mark Graham's "Queer Smells" analyzes a recent series of perfume ads that, even as they attempt to exemplify the heteronormative order of sexual relations, threatens its very foundation. Partly due to the inherent ephemerality and flux of smells, which resist notions of constancy and stability, and partly due to the introduction of unisex scents, which disregard gender dichotomy and its singular, reciprocal vector of attraction, these ads adopt a queer sensibility by configuring desire as performative. This is particularly the case, the author argues, with the promotion of pheromone-based scents, whether intended for hetero- or homosexual users. In effect, they bottle desire as an essentialized and autonomous entity, making it available to anyone, in any situation, independent of biology, gender and sexual orientation, and thus open to mobile desires and a multiplicity of persuasions.

Noritoshi Hirakawa straightforwardly addresses the paradoxical dimension of olfactophilia by foregrounding an unexpectedly intimate encounter with body odors in the participatory artwork *Garden of Nirvana* (1996). In this installation, featuring women's underwear hanging from the ceiling like musky chandeliers, visitors were invited to not only experience but to contribute (if female) their own worn intimate clothing. As Jennifer Fisher and Jim Drobnick indicate, the piece at once celebrates the effects of corporeality and caters to fetishists, as well as draws upon Buddhist ascetic practices where the mind is trained by confronting socially taboo and abject sensations. The funky *odor di femina* that Mavor discusses as a discursive phenomenon, and which has recently garnered attention as a consumer product (Levin 2004), here actually circulates in the gallery air and raises perplexing questions: Does the smell on display combat or substantiate gynophobia? Does it liberate individuals from oppressive dictates of hygiene or does it entrench these standards even more anxiously? Is women's vaginal odor reclaimed as an everyday, natural occurrence or does it represent a further degree of colonization by male desire? While the immediacy of the smell and the viscerality of the body are beyond doubt, *Garden of Nirvana* generates misogynist and emancipatory interpretations that uneasily coexist.

Jim Drobnick

Bibliography

Amy-Chinn, D. (2001), "Sex Offence: The Cultural Politics of Perfume," *Women*, 12(2): 164–75.

DeLong, M.R. and Bye, E.K. (1990), "Apparel for the Senses," *Journal of Popular Culture*, 24(3): 81–7.

Drobnick, J. (2000), "Inhaling Passions," *Sexuality and Culture*, 4(3): 37–56.

Ellis, H. ([1905] 1942), *Studies in the Psychology of Sex*, New York: Random House.

Ensler, E. (1998), *The Vagina Monologues*, New York: Villard.

Foucault, M. (1980), *The History of Sexuality*, vol. 1, trans. R. Hurley, New York: Random House.

Freud, S. (1961), *Civilization and Its Discontents*, trans. J. Strachey, New York: Norton.

Grosz, E. and Probyn, E. (eds) (1995), *Sexy Bodies*, London & New York: Routledge.

Kohl, J.V. and Francoeur, R.T. (1995), *The Scent of Eros*, New York: Continuum.

Krafft-Ebing, R. von ([1886] 1965), *Psychopathia Sexualis*, trans. F.S. Klaf, New York: Bell.

Levin, R.J. (2004), "Smells and Tastes—Their Putative Influence on Sexual Activity in Humans," *Sexual and Relationship Therapy*, 19(4): 451–62.

Marcuse, H. (1962), *Eros and Civilization*, New York: Vintage.

Stoddart, D.M. (1990), *The Scented Ape*, Cambridge: Cambridge University Press.

Tannen, M. (1994), "Sex in a Bottle," *New York Times Magazine* (9 October): 72–3.

23

The Eros—and Thanatos—of Scents

Richard H. Stamelman

The Eros of scent—its drive toward life and its impulse toward love—is many things. It is *Biblical*. The Shulamite and her lover in *The Song of Songs* celebrate their passion through olfactory metaphors that are as ecstatic as they are erotic: "My king lay down beside me / and my fragrance / wakened the night. / All night between my breasts / my love is a cluster of myrrh" (Bloch and Bloch 1995, 1: 12–13; 4: 6). The Eros of scent is *Shakespearean* as well. Cleopatra's barge enters Alexandria floating on the water like the intoxicating vision of a golden cloud of incense: "Purple the sails and so perfumed that / The winds were love-sick with them" (*Antony and Cleopatra*, II, ii, 198–9). And the Eros of scent is "Parisian," long before it was French. When Hera, Pallas Athena and Aphrodite suddenly appear before a confused Paris, tending sheep on a remote hillside outside of Troy, to demand that he select the fairest among them, Paris decides, under the pressure of their bribes, to award the golden apple not to Hera, who promises to make him lord of Europe and Asia, not to Athena, who promises to help him lead the Trojans to victory over the Greeks, but rather to Aphrodite, who has come to him under the name of Hedone, goddess of sensual pleasure. Smothered in spellbinding perfumes and "all proud of the power of desire," as Euripides reports (Detienne 1977: 62), Hedone succeeds in turning Paris's head with the vision of the hedonistic pleasure that the body and soul of Helen, the fairest woman in the world, will give him (Hamilton 1942: 179).

The Eros of scent is also *chemical*. For years scientists have known that ovulating female animals use pheromones (chemical signals with the power to modify biology and behavior when exchanged between individuals of the same species) to attract males. A sow in estrus will immediately place

herself in a spread-legged mating position when she smells the pheromone
contained in the saliva of a male boar (Stoddart 1990: 77). While the power
of odors (in the form of pheromones) to excite sexual attraction and provoke
mating in animals has been clearly proven, the same cannot be said, at least
for now, about humans. "Research into whether human body odors play
any part in human sexual behavior," D. Michael Stoddart remarks, "have
been largely inconclusive." Yet "the role of odors in the sexual physiology
of non-human primates and other mammals," he continues, "is sufficiently
clear for there to be a very strong possibility that they do indeed play some
role in our own species" (1990: 118–19).

In its represented forms as myth, poetry, song, legend, fable, narrative and,
of course, as advertisement and object of fetishistic desire and consumption,
perfume has been lauded, celebrated, extolled, mystified, hyperbolized and,
of course, eroticized. Such a celebration has often highlighted the paradox,
mystery and instability (if not the indeterminacy) inherent in the effect of
scent on the body and on the image of the woman who wears it. From the
conflict and then fusion of odors emanating from his mistress's body as
she undresses herself—which the English poet Robert Herrick (1591–1674)
describes as "This *Camphire, Storax, Spiknard, Galbanum*: / These *Musks*, these
Ambers, and those other smells," migrating from "silken bodies" to "passive
Aire" (1957: 156)—to Calvin Klein's slogan for his 1997 oriental perfume
Contradiction—"She is always and never the same"—the erotic figuration
of scent envelops the woman in ambivalence, complexity and mutability,
emphasizing her hybrid, unsettled, undefined and therefore capricious and
threatening reality. Yet perfume is notable for giving the female body—even
in its paradoxical state of being—a voice, a language, an expressive presence:
"Without perfume, the skin is silent" announces a series of advertisements
from the 1980s for the *Comité français de parfum* (Ghozland 1987: 86). But
such expression also does away with the body, transforming it into spirit
and therefore into absence, especially at those times when vision is forced
to yield to the superior perceptual powers of olfaction: "One must smell a
woman before having even seen her," the perfumer Marcel Rochas remarks,
and "what lingers of a woman at night," asks the perfumer Jean-Paul
Guerlain, "if not her perfume?" (Barillé and Laroze 1995: 86, 120). Encircled
by scent, the body is at once present (as emanation, effluvium, aroma, aura,
vapor) and absent (as spirit, trace, memory and *sillage*): "To wear a perfume,"
remarks the couturiere Sonia Rykiel, "is to expand, melt away, blend in. To
leave behind something strange that causes one to do a double-take: once
to see and once to ask what one has seen" (Barillé and Laroze 1995: 124).
In the many images she is given, the scented woman exists in a perpetual
state of ambiguity, of decorporealized corporeality: at once a body *and* a
soul, a presence *and* an absence. By means of the Eros of scent, woman
becomes a hybrid, a hyphenated being: visible–invisible, proximate–distant,
corporeal–spiritual, ephemeral–enduring, earthly–celestial, base–sublime,
primitive–civilized, expressive–mute, innocent–seductive.

Different images, stories and names have expressed over the centuries the erotic *imaginary* that scent possesses. A list of some of the names of perfumes from the early 1900s to the present evokes, with different degrees of subtle and not-so-subtle innuendo, the link between scent and love and scent and seduction, confirming, as the perfumer Robert Ricci has succinctly declared, that "a perfume is an act of love" (Barillé and Laroze 1995: 90). Each name constitutes the embryonic beginning of an amorous narrative, literally a *pre*-text, which fantasy (usually, but not necessarily, male) is called on to enhance and complete. From before the Second World War, Eros or the erotic is implied in perfume names like *Séduction* (Gellé Frères, c. 1913), *Fruit défendu* (Maison Rosine, 1914), *Premier Oui* (Arys, 1919), *Jouir* (Fioret, 1920), *Ouvrez-moi* (Lubin, 1920s), *My Sin* (Lanvin, 1925), *Moment suprême* (Patou, 1929), *Scandal* (Lanvin, 1932), *Shocking* (Schiaparelli, 1937), *Tabu* (Dana, 1931), *Ardente Nuit* (Corday, 1931), *Audace* (Rochas, 1936) and *Aphrodisia* (Fabergé, 1938). Since the 1950s, erotic and sexual realities are conjured in names no less suggestive or laconic than those of earlier decades, although such names are somewhat more evocative of the *paradis artificiels* that perfumes create: *Intimate* (Revlon, 1955), *L'Interdit* (Givenchy, 1957), *Opium* (Yves Saint Laurent, 1977), *J'ai osé* (Guy Laroche, 1977), *Poison* (Dior, 1985), *Boudoir* (Vivienne Westwood, 1998), *Ce soir on jamais* (Anick Goutal, 1999), *Organza Indécence* (Givenchy, 2000), *Volupté* (Oscar de la Renta, 1992), *Le Secret de Vénus* (Weil, 1996), *Rush* (Gucci, 1999).

In addition to these names, each a narrative node unto itself for an as yet unwritten story, certain perfumes carry appellations that already encapsulate imaginary scenarios that are both *prêt-à-porter* and *prêt-à-emporter*. When a perfume is called *Chamade* (Guerlain, 1969), it evokes surrender, or when it displays the word *Guet-Apens* (Guerlain, 1999) on its blue, lantern-shaped bottle, it provokes images of entrapment. Or when it is known as *Ophélie* (Cardin, 1995) or *Amazone* (Hermès, 1974) or *Shéhérazade* (Jean Desprez, 1983) or *Le Styx* (Coty, 1911) or *Venezia* (Laura Biagiotti, 1992), it appropriates the mythic and poetic resonance—the ideological and cultural *imaginary*—such literary, historical and geographical figures and realities possess in Western and Oriental societies. A scent with the name *Panthère* (Cartier, 1987) may call to mind the powerfully graceful, sleek and stealthy movements of a stalking cat, but it evokes as well strategies of entrapment, for the panther was the only animal, according to the Ancients, to emit a perfumed odor that attracted victims to its hiding place and to their deaths (Fellous 1987: 103).

Moreover, beyond the succinct, compact, poetically and erotically charged name of the perfume—an onomastics of sexuality where the two or three syllables of the word explode like a cry (*Fracas, Poison, Obsession, X-S, Fétiche, Balafre*) or caress like a whisper (*Sense, Caline, Pleasures, Chant d'arômes*) or soothe the spirit with a dream of bliss (*L'Idéal, Truth, Joy, Happy, Eden, Timeless, Eternity*) or promise the passionate and fatal intensity of mad love (*Turbulences, Farouche, Volcan d'Amour, Chaos, Vertige, Pour Troubler*)—exists another register of poetic and erotic evocativeness: namely, the gnomic, haiku-like slogan accompanying the perfume. The Eros of scent is intensified and concentrated—even before the fragrance has been smelled, since most consumers read an advertisement in a magazine or see one on television before they get to a store and open the bottle—by slogans expressive of very different messages. They may predict, somewhat pretentiously perhaps, a better life for humankind—"Un jour la tendresse s'étendra sur le monde" (*Anaïs, Anaïs*, Cacharel)—or declare the poetic power of silence and smell over that of language and visibility—"Parfois les mots ne disent pas tout" (*Poême*, Lancôme)—or give personal advice—"Toute femme mérite d'être première" (*First*, Carrier)—or offer a lesson in self-affirmation and confidence—"Vous seule savez ce qui est vraiment important" (*Knowing*, Estée Lauder)—or promise women a new sexuality, independence, autonomy and sense of empowerment—"Parfum pour une nouvelle femme" (*Jaïpur Saphir*, Boucheron), "L'audace a son numéro" (*Chanel No. 19*)—or offer lessons in erotic comportment—"Le secret de charme est de ne pas tout dévoiler" (*Mitsouko*, Guerlain)—or finally fantasize scenes of infinite bliss, joy, reverie, happiness and transgression—"A drop of perfume … an ocean of love" (*Hanae Mori*), "The best dreams happen when you are awake. Who needs night?" (*Dreams by Tabu*, Dana).

Some slogans present perfume as if it were a philosophy of life—"Le parfum qui fait s'interroger sur la valeur de la civilisation" (*Coriandre*, Jean Couturier)—or an existential teaching—"La vie est plus belle quand on l'écrit soi-même" (*Champs-Elysées*, Guerlain)—or an original interpretation of Freudian theory—"L'inconscient a son parfum" (*Fantasme*, Ted Lapidus)—or an acceptance of self so evident that only tautology can express it—"Je suis comme je suis" (*Cabotine*, Grès)—or finally as an irrefutable and anti-idealist truth of being—"The senses don't lie" (*Truth*, Calvin Klein). Moreover, perfume names can have a syntax of their own, coming together to form not only a sentence or a slogan, but a fable. Jacques Worth (grandson of Charles Frederick Worth, the father of couture) who with the perfumer Maurice Blanchet founded Parfums Worth in the 1920s, designed five perfumes over ten years, of which each name serves as a fragment in a short, romantic poem evocative of an insuppressible, bewitching love: *Dans la Nuit* (1924), *Vers le Jour* (1925), *Sans Adieu* (1929), *Je Reviens* (1932), *Vers Toi* (1934) ("In the night, just before dawn, because I can't bear to say goodbye, I'm coming back to you") (Edwards 1996: 81).

These encapsulated, *prêt-à-porter* narratives are also often linked to exotic, legendary names like *Mitsouko, Shalimar, Nahema* and *Samsara*, fragrances created by the house of Guerlain in 1919, 1925, 1979 and 1989, respectively. While *Mitsouko* (from a word meaning mystery), a chypre-based fragrance heavily scented with wood moss and peach and presenting a new idea of femininity, alludes to the impossible love between an English naval officer and Mitsouko, the wife of a Japanese admiral during the Russian–Japanese war, and while *Shalimar* evokes the beloved wife of a shah who once haunted the Indian gardens near the Taj Mahal, and *Nahema* (meaning "fille du feu") recalls the name of an oriental princess who, as Sheherazade tells the tale, possesses an enigmatic and passionate temperament, it is the name *Samsara*, from a Sanskrit word meaning the transmigration of beings and symbolic of spiritual renewal, eternal rebirth and the endlessly turning wheel of life, that is expressive more of an idea than of a story. For *Samsara* invokes a philosophical way of being in the world, the notion, according to Guerlain's publicity, of "an imaginary, sacred, mysterious place at the juncture of East and West, the symbol of harmony and of the absolute interaction [osmosis] between a woman and her perfume, a spiritual journey leading to serenity and inward contemplation." Dominated by the scents of sandalwood and jasmine, *Samsara* is associated with the experience of the absolute, of nirvana (a word with which it shares a final syllable), of perfection, as its slogan asserts; "A few drops of *Samsara*, a few drops of eternity." The red-glass bottle, modeled after the silhouette of a Khmer dancer found in the Musée Guimet in Paris, whose hands are clasped in a gesture of offering, invokes the fullness of being and the flowering of femininity. The stopper, in accord with the overarching *imaginary* of serenity, harmony, elegance, mysticism and exoticism that the constellation of name (with its weighty consonants followed by airy vowels), bottle and scent (an "oriental *ambré*") seek to establish, has been fashioned to represent the eye of the Buddha, symbol of the meditation, in this instance more olfactory than visual, that will lead to detachment and reawakening (Fellous 1987: 30, 73–4, 128–31, 150; "Les Secrets du parfum": 15, 24; Atlas and Monniot 1997: 282–3; "Le Livre de Samsara": 5, 17, 27). It is not clear, however, how the sensuality of the perfume—and *Samsara* is a perfume that leaves a remarkably heavy and long-lasting *sillage*—will lead to a transcending of the senses.

In all these names, but especially that of *Shalimar*, a myth, a philosophical idea or a narrative, hardly known to the general public at the time of the perfume's debut, become part of the very image and imaginary the fragrance attempts to embody and, of course, to offer for consumption. Not only is the myth or story used to sell the scent; it becomes the narrative armature upon which the advertising, the slogan, the bottle and the packaging are hung. Image and design depend on a story that needs to be taught to the consuming public at the same time the product, the perfume, is introduced. Publicity and pedagogy coincide. Eventually, as has happened most successfully with *Shalimar*, whose image, reputation and mythic status as a "classic" fragrance—one of the five great perfumes of the twentieth century—have made it popular among at least four generations of women, the scent and the myth, the perfume and the imaginary it incarnates, become one. As the product becomes a classic, the myth associated with it sinks its roots into the culture. "Say *Shalimar*" or "*S'Afficher Shalimar*" as an ad from the 1980s declares (Chevrel and Cornet 1993: 183), and there will come to mind not only the unique bottle with its bat-wing form or the singular blend of bergamot, jasmine, iris and especially vanilla, which give the perfume its distinctively warm, exotic, smoldering, sensual fragrance, but a full-fledged narrative hovering over bottle and perfume.

Shalimar makes reference in name and aroma to the gardens of Shalimar (a Sanskrit word meaning "the Abode or Hall of Love") located in Agra, India, and constructed in 1619 by the Mogul emperor Shah Jahangir. Eleven years later, Shah Jahan, having succeeded his father to the imperial throne, and in mourning at the death of the favorite of his wives, Mumtaz Mahal, begins the construction of the Taj Mahal as a funerary monument in her memory (Edwards 1996: 55–9). History and myth join in the imaginary that *Shalimar*, the perfume, puts forth. Here, eternal love and eternal death are commemorated, unending memory and permanent loss coexist. Even the bottle itself, with its upwardly arcing lines evocative of the surge of water in the many fountains of the Shalimar gardens and with its fan-shaped stopper of the deepest blue, "the color of sky at dusk when the sun disappears behind the horizon" ("Genèse de Shalimar": 7), has an "architecture" fusing events that reappear with those that disappear: the memory of a love reasserting itself and climbing heavenward like a *jet d'eau* and the mourning of a loss, which, in tandem with the dying sun, sinks again into oblivion. Like perfume, which is after all a liquid immediately changed into vapor, a body or a skin transformed into evanescent air, a presence coinciding with its own absence, a sign effaced and replaced by a trace, *Shalimar* embodies the myth and reality of presence and absence, the fiction and truth of possession and loss: it joins together the scent of Eros and the aroma of Thanatos.

The popularity of perfumes with enduring *sillages*, like *L'origan* (Coty, 1905)—its "fauvist sensibility" made it the first "violent" scent of the century (Barillé 1995: 82)—*Shalimar* (1925), *Opium* (1977) and *Samsara* (1989), has over the twentieth century waxed and waned. A cycle of heavy, captivating scents has, in reaction to the styles of the time, yielded to lighter, more discreet versions of established fragrances, as happened in the early 1990s, for example, with the launching of *Un Air de Samsara* (Guerlain) and *Tendre Poison* (Dior). But in the nineteenth century, single-floral scents—an *eau de lavande*, for example, was composed primarily of lavender—were the rule and not the exception, as is the case today with more richly complex, multifaceted combinations of natural and synthetic ingredients. During the Restoration and into the years of the July Monarchy, when manuals of *savoir-vivre* insisted on the importance of cleanliness and purity, only floral-scented waters or oils were tolerated. Strong animalic scents, like musk, ambergris and civet, were strictly banned, and if they were worn it was only by women of questionable morals. Moreover, single-flower scents were never applied directly to the body, but were used to perfume common, everyday objects like fans, gloves, handkerchiefs, lace or stored linen (Barillé and Laroze 1995: 6–7). Style dictated light, soft fragrances, as Mme Celnart, author of a small manual on perfume (1833), indicated in quite precise and assertive detail: "Strong odors like musk, ambergris, orange blossom, tuberose and other similar scents should be completely avoided" (Fellous 1987: 22). The ideal of beauty for most of the century celebrated a woman's naturalness.

Although the style in perfumes from the beginning of Louis XVI's reign to the appearance of Coty's compositions at the beginning of the twentieth century tended to favor sweet, floral scents, there were, nevertheless, in this long time span oscillations in olfactory taste and fashion; "every half-century," Alain Corbin observes, "musk and ambergris unleashed short counteroffensives" (1986: 195). In his *Le livre des parfums* (1870) the perfumer, Eugene Rimmel, chastised the society of his time for its "deep aversion to perfume," finding in this "antipathy for what had been created solely to please" a sign of "corrupt taste" (1870: 25–6). His was not a cry in the wilderness. Writers of the July Monarchy, the Second Empire and the Third Republic, including Balzac, Gautier, Baudelaire, Flaubert, Huysmans, Maupassant, Edmond de Goncourt, Zola, Cros and Mallarmé, most of whom were remarkably knowledgeable about contemporary styles of fashion, were united in their sensitivity to and fascination with perfume. This passion for perfume did not, of course, give pride of place to the sweet, innocent, floral scents preferred by the puritanical purveyors of olfactory morality. Only heavy, spellbinding, intoxicating, soulful, opiate scents like musk, ambergris, frankincense, benzoin and jasmine could produce the spiritual, otherworldly states of sublime sensuality favored by a poet like Baudelaire: "Reader, you know how a church can reek / from one grain of incense you inhale / with careful greed—remember the smell? / Or the stubborn musk of an old sachet?" ("Le Parfum"). These were perfumes that, like the other "flowers of evil" (ennui, beauty, Paris, wine, drugs, hair, death), possessed the power to transport the poet's spirit to idyllic, exotic lands of "pleasure, peace and opulence" ("L'Invitation au voyage"). These fragrant substances of transcendence, "rich, corrupt and masterful—/ possess the power of such infinite things / as incense, amber, benjamin and musk; / to praise the senses' raptures and the mind's," generated an oceanic feeling of oneness with the Absolute ("Correspondances") (Baudelaire 1982: 43, 58, 15).

Baudelaire and other writers of the second half of the nineteenth century would not have disagreed with Edmond de Goncourt's observation that "certain odors seem to have been composed to deepen the enchantment of amorous embraces" (Barillé and Laroze 1995: 68). Nor would they have felt uncomfortable with his ironic and misogynistic description in the novel *Chérie* (1883) of Marie Chérie Haudancourt's taste for perfumes, an obsession she shares with other upper-class Parisian women who impregnate their clothes, hair and skin with "the strongest and most *nauseating* odors that the perfume industry can distill from animal and vegetal matter" (1883: 223). Chérie lives continuously in a cloud of scent composed of an "elusive blend of spirits of tuberose, orange blossoms, jasmine, vetiver, opoponax, violet, tonka bean, ambergris, sandalwood, bergamot, neroli, rosemary, benzoin, verbena, patchouli" that give her a sensation of felicity, well-being, and from time to time "something resembling a nearly imperceptible spasm," which resembles the addictive hunger and the subsequent stupor of the opium-eater: "Chérie lifted herself up, deeply and passionately inhaling once again the scent, in a movement that pushed her chest—and tilted her head ever so slightly—backwards, her eyes closing with pleasure" (1883: 223–4). Like a knight searching for the Grail, Chérie ardently longs to have in her possession a grain of musk; in this desire she resembles the empress Josephine whose overuse of musk made her rooms at Malmaison nearly uninhabitable to Napoleon. When Chérie does purchase this tiny, precious substance, extracted from the sexual glands of a small deer found in the Himalayas of Tibet and China, she keeps it in a small gold-lacquered box with her jewelry. Chérie's "addiction" to perfumes finds its erotic apotheosis, however, in a scene of sensual bliss and vertiginous unconsciousness akin to orgasm, where body and soul, touched and penetrated by scent, undergo a distillation into vapor and air. Woman is literally transformed into perfume. Every morning upon waking, Chérie, though still half asleep, reaches for a vaporizer and sprays the scent of white heliotrope under the covers of her bed, where she then buries her head, taking care not to let any of the scent escape into the room. The infiltration of one's being by perfume, the filling of the soul with intoxicating odors, the vaporization of the self as the body loses all sense of its physical contours and limits characterize the Eros of scent. Flaubert felt it, as these lines from a letter written to Louise Colet the night of August 6–7, 1846 indicate: "I look at your slippers, handkerchief, your hair, portrait, I reread your letters, I smell their musky odor. If you only knew what I'm feeling right now! ... in the night, my heart expands and a rose of love pierces it. A thousand kisses, a thousand, everywhere, *everywhere*." And two nights later, caressing Louise's slippers, he writes: "I smell them, they give off the scent of verbena, and your odor expands my soul" (Flaubert 1973: 280, 284). Flaubert, like Baudelaire and like Chérie, is *un olfactif*. The body of the woman is sublimated into liquid and air, prepared to be absorbed, drunk, inhaled, interiorized by the bewitched male, a ritual of penetration and invasion that affects both women and men. "The use of perfumes, by man as well as woman," writes Shaykh Umar ibn Muhammed al-Nefzawi, the sixteenth-century writer of *The Perfumed Garden*, an erotic manual, "excites to copulation" (1964: 79), thus reiterating the belief in the sexuality of perfume acknowledged as far back as the ancient Egyptians. But under the Eros of scent lies the hidden, yet enveloping note of Thanatos. The loss of consciousness, the swooning, the invasion by material substances, now airborne, into the inner recesses of self and spirit, the effacement of physical and corporal boundaries, the suspension of time and space, the feeling of a vaporized and liquefied self flowing into a formless, abstract world—elements characteristic of the poetic and narrative representation of perfume—point as well to the symbiotic copresence of sexuality and death in the *mise-en-scène* of scent.

In the wake of Sade and Freud, Georges Bataille was sensitive to the fetid odor of mortality, decomposition and sexuality hidden within all representations of beauty; in this respect, he follows in the footsteps of Baudelaire, who had perceived in the rotting, worm-infested corpse of an animal lying in the road the image—albeit, a future incarnation—of his beloved ("Une Charogne"). Insofar as perfume compositions combine scents extracted from flowers, plants and trees with those removed from animals, in particular from glands or sacs near the animals' sexual organs—civet comes from the Ethiopian cat, musk from the Tibetan deer, castoreum from the abdomen of the beaver, and ambergris, with no anatomical sexual connection whatsoever, from the intestinal lining of the sperm whale—and insofar as these animalic scents (most of which today are synthesized compounds) serve as "fixatives" holding in place, within the architecture of a fragrance, the top and middle notes and giving to the base note its distinctive tenacity and permanence, it could be suggested that in perfume humanity and animality, spirituality and materiality, beauty and corruption coexist. Bataille would agree, although with his usual tendency toward hyperbole he would see in this conjunction of the sublime and the "base" the very nature of human eroticism: "In the union of bodies, human beauty reveals the opposition between humanity at its most pure and the repulsive animality of organs" (1957: 160). Love and whatever inspires love—be it beauty, art, poetry, even perfume—are sublimations beneath which lie pain, anguish, uncleanness, obscenity, depletion, bestiality, baseness and death: "At the opposite pole of spirituality lies an exuberant sexuality that signifies the tenacity of animal life in us" (1957: 160). Coincident with the spasms of orgasm are loss, loneliness, expenditure and the paroxysm of *la petite mort*: "The spasms of death and those of pleasure are alike" (1976a: 537); "The most tender kisses have the aftertaste of a rat" (1976b: 156). Wherever eroticism is evoked, wherever it is stimulated and provoked, even by the sensual, seductive air of an erogenic perfume, death follows, because "the movement of love, at its utmost, is the movement of death" (1957: 47). Without going too far, one might suggest that what Bataille says about the erotic reality of poetry—its tendency to blur limits, to confuse reality with dream, to blend spirit with matter and form with formlessness—could be applied equally to the sexual power of scent. The "fumes" of perfume (from the Latin *per-fumum*) create the same kind of vagueness, imprecision and mistiness as well as the same wedding of form to formlessness, of permanence to ephemerality, of life to death, as poetry does.

In his essay "The Language of Flowers," Bataille demystifies a predilection in Western culture for the representation of human endeavor as an ideal and sublime experience, one, unfortunately, that both silences the death rattle and masks the death's head. "If one says that flowers are beautiful," he writes, "it is because they seem to *conform to what must be*, in other words they represent, as flowers, the human ideal." Yet, flowers can be hideous and perverse in appearance, since "even the most beautiful flowers are spoiled in their centers by hairy sexual organs." The apparent elegance of a flower only masks its inner sordidness (*souillure*), covers over "the filth of its organs," and disguises the fragility of its corolla, so easily and indecently touched by rot and a "garish withering." Emerging from dirt, from "the stench of the manure pile," and giving, as it climbs vertically and heavenward in a "flight of angelic and lyrical purity," the illusion of having escaped the base matter of its origin, the flower becomes the symbol of a failure, of an Icarian fall. Ashes to ashes and dust to dust, it "relapses abruptly into its original squalor: the most ideal is rapidly reduced to a wisp of aerial manure." What is true of the upper reaches of the flower affects the nether regions as well: "While the visible parts are nobly elevated, the ignoble and sticky roots wallow in the ground, loving rottenness just as leaves love light" (Bataille 1985: 12–13). Therefore, Bataille concludes, love, purity, sacredness and the ideal smell like death, baseness, perversion and matter.

If the language of flowers is that of death and eroticism, then the language of scents "given the aura of sweetness, purity, romance and beauty enveloping them and the technical processes of sublimation, distillation and vaporization producing them—are they not called 'essences' and 'spirits' after all?" is a language of Eros and Thanatos. Many perfumes have carried and still carry the names of flowers or plants: *Fougère Royal* (Houbigant, 1882), *Véra Violetta* (Roger & Gallet, 1892), *Jasmin de Corse* (Coty, 1906), *Muguet* (Guerlain, 1908), *Narcisse noir* (Caron, 1911), *Héliotrope* (Coty, 1913), *La Violette Ambrée* (Coty, 1914), *Mimosa* (Caron, 1917), *Géranium d'Espagne* (1925), *La Fête des Roses* (Caron, 1936), *Gardénia Passion* (Annick Goutal, 1989), *Tubereuse Criminelle* (Serge Lutens, 1999). To apply Bataille's demystifying logic to these floral-based fragrances is to see perfume as not only a substance that establishes presence but as one that in the same act of creation initiates absence, disappearance, decomposition, dissipation, effacement and loss. We have already seen in the example of Goncourt's Chérie how the drug-like dominance of a perfume causes human drive, energy, movement, activity and lucidity to surrender to stupor, intoxication, passivity, immobility and befuddlement. If flowers are inherently eaten away by mortality, if the perfect homage to a rose is that performed by the Marquis de Sade, who tossed petals into a ditch filled with liquid manure (Bataille 1985: 14), then perfume must not hide the death it inaugurates, must not disguise its evanescent ephemerality behind such absolute names as *L'Idéal* (Houbigant, 1900), *Eternity* (Calvin Klein, 1988), *Eden* (Cacharel, 1994), *L'Infini* (Caron, 1970), *Sublime* (J. Patou, 1992), *Présence* (Houbigant, 1933), *Je Reviens* (Worth, 1932). Although many perfumes are named after love, like *Amour Amour* (Patou, 1928), it will be a long while before the word "absence," or "loss," or even "death" appears in one of them.

That death is an essential partner of love in creating the *imaginary* of perfume can be seen in a number of literary representations written over a century: from Huysmans's story of a *poète-parfumeur* in *A rebours* (1884) to Italo Calvino's postmodern tale "The Name, The Nose" (1972) and Patrick Süskind's quasi-allegorical novel *Perfume: The Story of a Murderer* (1986), the subtitle of which renders synonymous the Eros and Thanatos of scent. The only way to capture and eternalize the rare loveliness of an ephemeral scent is, according to Süskind's antihumanist vision, to make the art of perfumery coincident with murder and atrocity, to make scent pass through the alembic of death. Besieged by headaches, dizziness and hallucinations from an olfactory neurotic disorder occasioned by a mysterious and imaginary odor of frangipani that only he, among the inhabitants of his chateau, can smell, Des Esseintes, Huysman's dandy hermeneut of scents, labors feverishly to invent fragrances that, by means of a kind of "nasal homeopathy," will mask the offending natural odor with a sublime and complex blend of ingredients that only art, imagination and genius can create. Despite the new language and syntax of scents Des Esseintes invents—the harmonious refrains, the melodious aromatic stanzas, the sonorous scented phrasings, the recurring olfactory motifs, the balanced accords and notes, the "fragrant orchestration" that inspires him to blend styrax, jonquil, coal tar, linden and "new mown hay" with allspice, sandalwood, jasmine, hawthorn and verbena in the hope of giving musical, lyrical form to his poem of scent—the obsessive miasma of frangipani returns, invading the countryside around his castle and bringing him to the brink of unconsciousness and death.

Similarly, the three major characters of Italo Calvino's "The Name, the Nose," each in his own and very different way a hermeneut of scents, start out on a passionate search for a particular odor and the particular female who once embodied it, only to find her at the moment of her death. As the point of departure for the hunt and as the stimulus for the frenetic pursuit of the other, Eros once wedded to scent leads irremediably to death. The three stories—that of a nobleman in nineteenth-century Paris, that of a quadruped pre-human (on the threshold of erect posture) roaming the savannas during a prehistoric time, and that of a drummer with a rock band in the seventies in London—are told in intertwined narrative fragments that, like perfume vapors, coil around and lap over each other. The French nobleman makes a desperate appeal to his *parfumeur* to help him identify the scent of an unknown, masked woman he had encountered the previous night, but his olfactory memory grows more and more dim as he describes the perfume; words, Calvino suggests, are much too weak to meet the descriptive challenge posed by experiences of evanescence and loss like memory, scent and sensuality. The male hominid, part of a pack of pre-human animals, aggressively follows the scent of a female whose odor has attracted him but whom he cannot yet distinguish from the group. The rock drummer, after a night spent sleeping on the floor with his mates and a host of groupies, seeks out the scent of an anonymous woman to whom he had been drawn earlier in the night and with whom he had made love in total darkness.

In each of Calvino's three narratives, the female object of desire possesses neither face, nor identity, nor personality, and the male pursuer has been seduced by a scent, which, because of the poverty and nominative insufficiency of language and the erosion of olfactory sensitivity among humans over the course of evolution, can only be discovered at the moment it blends with the odor of death. The masked Frenchwoman is discovered lying in her coffin, the female hominid thrown in a heap of rotting, lacerated bodies, and the groupie asphyxiated by the smoke of a fire in the apartment. Perfume and death are synonymous, and language, faced with the Eros of scent and with loss, is powerless to offer any possession or knowledge of the real—be it that of a name, or a person, or a love. The Frenchman enters the masked woman's home and is immediately struck by "a heavy smell, as of rotting vegetation" circulating among the wreaths, garlands and funereal flowers surrounding the veiled and faceless corpse. And yet he recognizes "the base, the echo of that perfume that resembles no other, merged with the odor of death now as if they had always been inseparable" (1988: 81). The hominid as well senses in the stinking miasma of death the flower of life and love: "The odor I was following was lost down there, and it rises with the stink of the clawed cadavers, the breath of the jackals that tear them apart" (1988: 82). As for the drummer, his attempt to isolate the seductive, life-enhancing and therefore truly erotic, scent of the faceless woman (now reduced to a "thing") from the mass of confusing, undifferentiated, disgusting, yet clearly funerary odors—his description constitutes the story's concluding sentence—strikingly confirms Bataille's *mélange* of eroticism, death, horror, baseness and animality, all of which gravitate, according to Calvino, around the ineffable, word-denying experience of odor, which yields no knowledge other than that of indeterminacy, loss and mortality:

> On the floor the thing I see before I writhe in a lit of vomiting is the long, white, outstretched form, face hidden by the hair, and as I pull her out by her stiffened legs I smell her odor within the asphyxiating odor, her odor that I try to follow and distinguish in the ambulance, in the first-aid room, among the odors of disinfectant and slime that drips from the marble slabs in the morgue, and the air is impregnated with it, especially when outside the weather is damp. (1988: 83)

Where Calvino presents death as the ultimate defeat of knowledge, love, language, memory and sensorial experience, Süskind, in *Perfume*, reveals it as the ultimate preserver of life, as a counter to loss, as a fixative (like those stabilizing ingredients used in perfumery) that functions to reverse the erosions of time and gives permanence to all that is evanescent in life. Paradoxically, it is *through* the medium and agency of death that odors are preserved, for Jean-Baptiste Grenouille, Süskind's eighteenth-century master perfumer, is a gifted artist of exquisite sensitivity and an evil creature of intense misanthropy and horror, more animal than human, as the innumerable references to him as a blood-sucking tick (as well as a toad, spider, crab, mole, vermin) testify. He possesses an extraordinary, truly inhuman sense of smell. Yet, strangely, he himself has no odor. Thus he sets about to endow himself with a scent so distinctive that it would make him "the world's most fragrant human being" (1986: 256). In his pursuit of the perfect scent, the odor that will give him power over all of humankind and make him the greatest perfumer of all time, Grenouille consistently sacrifices humanity on the altar of Art. The pursuit of power through artistic genius and an estheticism inseparable from death turns the delicate perfumer into a brutal fascist. The end—in particular, the search for a sublime, enchanting, magical, hypnotizing scent—justifies the means, and Grenouille's means are manipulative, violent and murderous. As part of his self-imposed training, he kills animals and by means of a once widely used technique of perfume extraction called *enfleurage* causes their smells to be absorbed in fat. He does the same with twenty-four young virgins. But the two great murders that begin and conclude the novel involve young women whose fragrance is so magical and yet so precarious and ephemeral, especially as they advance into puberty and the odor of their bodies changes, that the scent must be seized at the very moment it explodes into ripeness, not unlike the picking of jasmine petals, which occurs only in certain seasons (July in Grasse) and at certain hours of the day (dawn) when the scent is at its peak.

Behind Grenouille's multiple killings and their coincidence with his perfume creations is a desire to invent a perfume of love for himself that would make him beloved of all humankind. Indeed, this does happen at the novel's conclusion in a final murder, this time self-inflicted (and collective), which in Bataillean fashion draws Eros, perfume and death together in a horrible and bestial apotheosis. Covering himself in the fragrance whose notes and accords have been constructed from the stolen odors of murdered virgins, Grenouille is set upon by a group of homeless thieves, whores, cutthroats, who cannibalistically want to possess a piece of this sublimely smelling creature. Grenouille's death, a form of suicide by perfume, embodies an Eros and a Thanatos synonymous with the rapture of love and with the divine seductiveness of scent. Love at its most extreme turns into death, as Bataille remarked and as the final, corrosively ironic sentences of Süskind's novel affirm. The exhausted crowd of "cannibals," their orgy of eating completed, smile at each other. "They were uncommonly proud. For the first time they had done something out of love" (1986: 310). And what they have done "out of love" is murder. Eros impelled by the need for possession turns into hysterical cannibalism, the bestial appropriation of the other. The crowd devours Grenouille with lust and in total unconsciousness. They ingest and consume his smell, his flesh, his body. They internalize his odor. But is this cannibalism any different from love in general, from an Eros that seeks to capture, possess and ingest the being of the beloved, or, for that matter, from olfaction, which longs to inhale, to absorb, to interiorize, to fill the lungs with the scent of the other? In the voluptuous desire to become one with the beloved, love and smell, Eros and perfume seek the death of the other. Under the powerful influence of the Eros and Thanatos of scent, we cannot help, even if it only be in our unconscious dreams and fantasies, to love the other to death.

That poetry and perfume are sister arts has been reiterated from *The Song of Songs* to the most recent advertisements for Lancôme's fragrance, *Poême*: "Sometimes words are not enough / to reveal your heart, to describe your love." Perfume is the silent poem ("Say it all without a word," advises another ad for *Poême*). It is the "poem one breathes," as Nicolas Mamounas, the "nose" for parfums Rochas, writes (Girard 1990: 171). It is the volatile poem of love expressed as a thin vapor, as an invisible spirit, as the almost nothingness of air. It articulates the ineffable; it gives voice to the vague, misty, evanescent spaces into which words cannot venture. One such space of inexpressibility is love and one is death. Although perfume and love may hide the reality of death, the mask of scent, even with its symphony of head, heart and base notes, is only paper thin and skin-deep. It disappears leaving in its wake the irreversible presence of loss as "voiced" again and again by a vestige, a fragment, or a trace. But the magical power of perfume, of love and of poetry is to fill the void, to replace the absence of things with an illusory, if not sometimes hallucinated, presence and to place the world under the spell of the imaginary. The perfumed woman is, Kristeva writes, "a lover so intimately and guiltily involved with carnage and death that she can perfume, disguise, and forget them, making you live among the vapors of caprice and impulse alone" (1988: 7). The Eros of scent charms death itself; it keeps Thanatos in thrall—but only for a moment. For death breaks the spell; the real dispatches the imaginary; and perfume and poetry confront again the loss at the heart of being: that death which is the most permanent, immobilizing and truly base of the three notes that compose the music of perfume: its odes of love and its threnodies of death.

Bibliography

Atlas, M. and Monniot, A. (1997), *Guerlain*, Toulouse: Milan.
Barillé, E. (1995), *Coty*, Paris: Assouline.
—— and Laroze, C. (1995), *Le livre du parfum*, Paris: Flammarion.
Bataille, G. (1957), *L'érotisme*, Collection 10/18, Paris: Editions de Minuit.
—— (1976a), *L'histoire de l'érotisme*, vol. 8 of *Oeuvres complètes*, Paris: Gallimard.
—— (1976b), *L'impossible*, vol. 3 of *Oeuvres complètes*, Paris: Gallimard.
—— (1985), "The Language of Flowers," in *Visions of Excess*, A. Stoekl (ed. and trans.), Minneapolis: University of Minnesota Press.

Baudelaire, C. (1982), *Les fleurs du mal*, trans. R. Howard, Boston: David R. Godine.

Bloch, A. and Bloch, C. (trans.) (1995), *The Song of Songs*, Berkley: University of California Press.

Calvino, I. ([1972] 1988), "The Name, the Nose," in *Under the Jaguar Sun*, trans. W. Weaver, San Diego: Harcourt Brace Jovanovich.

Chevrel, C. and Cornet, B. (1993), *Grain de Beauté*, Paris: Somog Editions d"Art/ Bibliothèque Forney.

Corbin, A. (1986), *The Foul and the Fragrant*, Cambridge: Harvard University Press.

Delbourg-Delphis, M. (1981), *Le sillage des élégantes*, Paris: J.C. Lattès.

Detienne, M. (1977), *The Gardens of Adonis*, trans. J. Lloyd, Atlantic Highlands, NJ: Humanities Press.

Edwards, M. (1996), *Perfume Legends*, Levallois: HM Editions.

Fellous, C. (1987), *Guerlain*, Paris: Denoel.

Flaubert, G. ([1862] 1970), *Salammbo*, Collection Folio, Paris: Gallimard.

—— (1973), *Correspondance*, vol. 1, J. Bruneau (ed.), Bibliothèque de la Pleïade, Paris: Gallimard.

"Genèse de Shalimar Fragments de papiers oubliés" (1995), Paris: Guerlain.

Ghozland, F. (1987), *Perfume Fantasies*, Toulouse: Milan.

Girard, S. (1990), *Le livre du parfum*, Paris: Messidor.

Goncourt, E. de (1883), *Chérie*, Paris: Ernest Flammarion et Eugène Fasquelle.

Hamilton, E. (1942), *Mythology*, New York: New American Library.

Herrick, R. (1957), "Upon Julia's Unlacing Her Self," in F.W. Moorman (ed.), *Hesperides*, Oxford: Oxford University Press.

Huysmans, J.-K. (1969), *Against the Grain*, New York: Dover.

Kristeva, J. (1988), "Préface," in G. Pillvuyt (ed.), *Histoire du parfum de l'Egypt au XIXe siècle*, Paris: Denoël.

"Le livre de Samsara" (n.d.), Paris: Guerlain.

"Les secrets du parfum par Guerlain," (n.d.), Paris: Guerlain.

Rimmel, E. (1870), *Le livre des parfums*, Paris: E. Dentu.

Stoddart, D.M. (1990), *The Scented Ape*, Cambridge: Cambridge University Press.

Süskind, P. (1986), *Perfume*, trans. J.E. Woods, New York: Washington Square Press.

Umar ibn Muhammed al-Nefzawi, S. ([1886] 1964), *The Perfumed Garden*, trans. R.F. Burton, New York: G.P. Putnam's Sons.

24
Odor di Femina
Though You May Not See Her, You Can Certainly Smell Her

Carol Mavor

A wild odor emanates from the "function of *seeingness (voyure)"*: so says Jacques Lacan (1978: 82). Taking a cue from Lacan's provocative claim, this chapter seeks to unearth Lacan's conceptualization of the gaze as an expanded constellation of the senses, in which sight loses its pride, its authority and its maleness. My goal is to excavate Lacan's notion of the gaze in order to loosen the gaze's hold on the site of seer/seen, subject/object and, especially, sight/smell: a smell rank with heterosexual presumption. For, to open Lacan's writing on the gaze is to open Pandora's box. While you cannot see Hope hiding under the lid, you can certainly smell her. Hope's wild odor, like Lacan's own slippery mirror writing, resists codification and celebrates the unmarked, which is not necessarily, as Peggy Phelan has pointed out, invisible (1993). I value Hope and Lacan. I value their unmarkedness: their odor. Not only their olfactory productions, but also their sounds rustling in the leaves of language. As my finger slowly opens Pandora's box, I am overcome with the strange *odor di femina*. I let the lid drop...

Seeing with Freud

Freud developed his important theories of sexuality and the unconscious around *visual representations*. For example, Freud (1899) *imaged* the unconscious as an invisible receptacle of filmic and still screen memories that selectively play themselves out as signs. Impressions are made even before the child's "psychical apparatus" is "completely receptive" and like "a photographic exposure ... can be developed after any interval of time and transformed into a picture" (Freud 1939). Similarly, in his "A Note Upon the 'Mystic Writing Pad,'" Freud (1924) images the unconscious as a waxen, magic writing tablet (a *Wunderblock)* that retains memories/pictures/marks from the past, even though they are not always readily accessible. The experiences/images are consciously forgotten (apparently wiped clean), as if the cover-sheet of the *Wunderblock* had been lifted.

Here it is not only the content of the inscriptions that takes weight, but also the *Wunderblock* as an object of visual attention, a surface to be looked at, where text (and images) become pictured and (almost) vanish ... white writing. Likewise, Freud's recasting of the Oedipal myth as the entry into adult sexual life falls on the problem of seeing. Or rather, on the problem of seeing nothing (the mother without a penis). This, in turn, calls for a stopping of the look retrospectively, by re-fixing the gaze on an object that was on or near the mother before the horrifying primal glance. The (fetishized) object then stands in for the missing penis. This action of seeing and not seeing simultaneously (which makes a so-called absence into a presence) stands at the center of the fetishizing gaze. "It is," as Emily Apter writes, "a 'not looking' sustained paradoxically through visual fixation on the substitute phallus" (1991: xiii).

The overriding sense and even documentation of fetishism as both male and visual is at the center of Freudian psychoanalytic theory. As Apter has pointed out, "despite [Freud's] admission ... that 'all women ... are clothing fetishists,'" Freud typically supplied a male agent to the perversion by associating it with male homosexuality and (as we shall see) *feminized* coprophilic pleasure (1991: 102).

Apter undoes the gendered-biased reading of fetishism, by discovering fetish objects of women spilling out of the drawers of not only turn-of-the-century French literature (Guy de Maupassant), but also in the cabinets of French psychiatry (Gaëtan Gatian de Clérembault) or the cupboards of feminist art (Mary Kelly). While sniffing out traces of female fetishism, Apter comes across special boxes and bureaux and albums and other private places enshrouded with veils and fabrics and fur—all belonging to women—whose sole purpose is to preserve the relics of departed loved ones. The stories of loss range from spoiled love to death to merely growing up. Inside these feminine spaces we find letters, pressed flowers, locks of hair, nail clippings, pieces of clothing. Apter points out that this "bric-a-brac-cluttered world" has been largely overlooked, even when it reaches a space of "manic collectomania" because it has been naturalized as part of feminine culture (1991: 100, 105). Apter reads the work of the contemporary American artist Mary Kelly (who collected and framed, among other things, her son's soiled nappy liners, fragments of his baby blanket and little cotton T-shirts) as "ironically aestheticizing the negative associations surrounding [a mother's] rituals of melancholia ... [by transforming] the maternal reliquary into a feminized poetics of mnemonic traces, constitutive in turn of a (now positively valorized) genre of sentimentality" (Apter 1991: 115).

Apter's examples of female fetishes are often visual, sometimes olfactory. Most, however, feel haptic, fixated as they so often are on the textures of hair, cloth, jewelry. Apter's story suggests that tactile stimulation has been used (especially in Clérembault's psychoanalytic work and Maupassant's fiction) to separate the girls from the boys; this is not unlike Freud's computation of smell with the feminine. It is as if women are to be seen ... not seeing.

Not surprisingly, Freud characterized his own teacher, Jean-Martin Charcot, the father of hysteria, as a "seer" (1893). This characterization is in keeping with Charcot's own disposition towards the visual. Charcot is famous for his appointment of a resident photographer to photograph the hysterics who inhabited the famed Salpêtrière clinic. For many of the women, Charcot's linking of hysteria with the photographs caused them to image themselves as one with the clinical pictures. Their identity became so determined by the camera that they performed according to the doctor's expectations. The best "performers" were rewarded with more photographs taken and became the "stars" of Salpêtrière (Didi-Huberman 1987: 67).

The reality of the photograph was used not only to index the hysteria of the patient, but also to give the patient a model of how to represent herself. (All the clinicians were male and most of the patients photographed appear to be women.) The women of Salpêtrière were encouraged to see themselves as pure image—as artwork carved out by a Frankensteinian Pygmalion, housed not in an artist's studio, but in an asylum. It is no wonder, then, that in 1862, when Jean-Martin Charcot became the head of the Salpêtrière clinic in Paris, he described it and its five thousand inmates as a "living museum of pathology" (Didi-Huberman 1987: 67). Charcot's "museum" as is suggested by both his own account and by Freud's, became a kind of art institute in which the power play between the male artist and his female model/muse was played out on both her body and her mind.

Probing still deeper into the walls of the female body imaged as a waxen Galatea (as a *tabula rasa,* a mystic writing pad), we find that the clinicians of Salpêtrière actually wrote on the bodies of their hysterics with needle-like instruments. They sowed their impressions (in needlepoint), words like "*Démence précoce*" or a mysterious date and signature, "*OCT 91 EC*" or the labeling of "*Satan,*" or the name of the clinic on these anything but patient bodies. These dermagraphed bodies became signed signs of the doctors' own creative visualizations. When the inscriptions became welts and scabs, the doctors read them as proof of the hysteria that they had already diagnosed long ago. As clinical artists, sorcerers of sorts, these doctors claimed that many of the lurid inscriptions appeared unassisted. Or, if they acknowledged assistance, they attributed the "unnatural" bubbling up to excessive sensitivity to the slightest touch: a hypersensitivity that was simply understood as a blossom of the patient's hysteria. The doctors took the vision to be demonstrative truth. The dermagraphed skin (which inevitably recalls the branding of black slaves in America, the tattooing of Holocaust victims in Germany, and many of the other horrors of body scarring that have marked the other in history) was read as a representation of the patient's hysteria—itself a representation of woman's diseased body. Dermagraphism is a focus on skin that determines those who are not male (hysterics), not sane, not same.

I have always been struck by the artistic treatment of the dermagraphic photographs. For instance, the surreal beauty in the picture-body that rose to completion on *"OCT 91"* complemented by the doctor's monogram "EC" (Èlie Chatelain). Each carefully inscribed letter, evenly spaced across her back as if her body were a fine piece of thick white cotton paper, as if the doctor were making art. The serifs on each letter "C" are incomprehensibly cruel—extra strokes of unfathomable callousness—tiny marks of horrific, carefully carried out artistry. Relentlessly tied to the conventions of fine art, the photograph's dramatic casting of lights and darks artistically emphasizes the curve of the patient's strong shoulders, the curvaceous form of an ornamental ear (a starlit moon with its own dark shadow), and the grand sweep of an embossed back. Cropped to perfection, the photograph invites the desire to caress. Like *"Démence précoce"* or *"Satan,"* it has the kind of beauty prescribed by nineteenth-century French art: a bather painted by Jean Auguste Dominique Ingres or a nude photographed by Eugène Durieu and posed by Eugène Delacroix.

Akin to Man Ray's woman as a violin (*Le Violin d'Ingres,* 1924), these picture-body hieroglyphics prefigure all the convulsive beauty and all the violence of surrealism. It is no wonder that the surrealist journal, *La Révolution Surréalist* (no. 11, 1928), celebrated the fiftieth anniversary of hysteria by reprinting "six large photographs drawn from the *Iconographie de la Salpêtrière* showing Charcot's star patient, Augustine, in various *"attitudes passionelles"* (Suleiman 1990: 106).

While all systems of representation may be composed of signs, the visual has been used most effectively to signify women's difference as her inferiority. Visual signs have authority: they do not easily disappear; they endure time; they take time to fade away. Moreover, they share the representational status of someone who speaks "the truth" for another who is apparently incapable of self-representation—like the lawyer who represents the accused, or the guardian who represents the child. Or like the dermagraphed women of Salpêtrière who were *sentenced* by their doctors: faceless, they *appear* incapable of speaking. In these photographs, the women are represented not as individuals (these pictures are not portraits), but as objects without sensate bodies. The materiality of their actual bodies has been replaced by the media of photography. They are all paper and chemicals.

The power of the doctor's gaze, masculinist, objectifying and monological, is preternaturally real in the Salpêtrière photographs. The pictures are a horrific exaggeration of the nudes painted, sculpted and photographed throughout the history of art. As Johannes Fabian has so powerfully argued in *Time and the Other*, visualism, in its most abstract and general form, is a monological discourse that denies a language of difference, and thereby paints over the possibility of the heterological, constructing difference as sameness and as lacking. That is why we are encouraged to understand, to "see" the other through a theory of knowledge which turns on "visualism" so much so "that the ability to 'visualize' a culture or society almost becomes synonymous for understanding it" (Fabian 1983: 106).

Undoing the Primacy of Visualism: Or, Smelling with Freud

Despite Freud's usual emphatic privileging of a masculine, homological, monological standard of sight, it appears that difference permeates his *Civilization and Its Discontents* in a most unexpected and non-visual way. This text is, in fact, riddled with *sexual difference discontent,* which is articulated through olfactory marginalia. In two footnotes, whose excessive length signals trouble, sexual difference bleeds into the body of the text as "the difference between the senses of smell and sight" (Gallop 1982: 26).

In the first fetid footnote, we learn that civilized culture's "diminution of the olfactory stimuli" was (as Jane Gallop has termed it) "a triumph of the eye over the nose" (Freud 1930: 99; Gallop 1982: 27). In the past, lowly man was sexually stimulated by the smells of menstruation—but no longer ... thanks to his evolved preference for looking, not smelling. In Freud's words:

> Visual excitations, which in contrast to the intermittent olfactory stimuli, were able to maintain a permanent effect... The diminution of the olfactory stimuli seems itself to be a consequence of man's raising himself from the ground, of his assumption of an upright gait; this made his genitals, which were previously concealed, visible. (Freud 1930: 100)

Later in the same footnote, Freud calls up all our vulgar associations of women with dogs by stipulating:

> [I]t would be incomprehensible ... that man should use the name of his most faithful friend in the animal world—the dog—as a term of abuse if that creature had not incurred his contempt through two characteristics: that it is an animal whose dominant sense is that of smell and one which has no horror of excrement, and that it is not ashamed of its sexual functions. (Freud 1930: 100)

Erect man gazes ahead and walks all over the smell of woman. But is it such a triumph? Gallop jokes: "The penis may be more visible, but female genitalia have a stronger smell" (1982: 27).

Freud summed up his perspective on women and smell best while within the second fetid footnote of *Civilization and its Discontents,* where he claimed "that neurotics, and many others besides, take exception to the fact that *"inter urinas et faeces nascimur"* (we are born between urine and feces) (1930: 106). In other words, for Freud, the child smells the mother seeing her: smell comes before seeing. Neurotics and hysterics have simply failed at repressing the mother and her smell. After all, as Freud argued, a "memory stinks just as an actual object may stink" unless it is effectively repressed (1985: 280). As a result, Freud claimed the childlike tendency to take pleasure in smell plays a significant part in the genesis of neurosis. This is why the feet and the hair, particularly odorous body parts, make such perfect fetish objects for the neurotic; they recall the body of the mother and the coprophilic pleasures of a long lost childhood. Of course, as Freud tells us, not any foot can be a treasured fetish, for it is "only dirty and evil-smelling feet [that] become sexual objects" (1905a: 155).

While not all of Freud's patients with overdetermined relationships with smell were women, many of them were, and Freud likened a "heightened sense of smell" with hysteria, a disease that predominantly affected women. Dora was supposedly disgusted by Herr K's kiss, not so much because his "member" became erect, but because it could be associated with the smell and "the function of micturition" (1905b: 31). Miss Lucy R had entirely lost her ability to smell, yet was continually haunted and pursued by one olfactory sensation after another. First, there was the smell of burnt pudding, and then (after Freud cured her of that) the smell of cigar smoke (1893–95). But the bottom line for Freud was that no matter who smelled what, it had something to do with the mother/feminine. Smell was to the feminine what the visual was to the masculine: odor, indeed, separated the girls from the boys.

Of course, all this nosy stuff appears particularly Freudian, given Freud's own relationship to Dr Fliess, the ear, nose and throat man who could attribute almost any disorder to the nose. In one letter to Fliess, Freud went so far as to suggest that the "development" of man's upright carriage was connected with the common phrase, "He turns up his nose"—meaning of course that a man with an erect nose regards himself as something particularly noble (1985: 279). The relationship between these two "noble men" is surely the subject of another text. However we can safely say that Freud's essay and letters suggest that though we may not see her, we can certainly smell her.

The relationship between "woman" and smell, so deeply rooted in Freud, is constructed as an atavistic throwback to signify not only the feminine, but also the primitive. Such a Darwinian spin on smell was also emphasized by one of Freud's contemporaries, Havelock Ellis, the great "sexologist." Ellis located an excess of "smell" in the dark races: "Odor" he said, seems "to be correlated to some extent with intensity of pigmentation, as well as hairiness" (1928: 61). As a result, Ellis repeatedly described the smell of peoples that he regarded as lower on the evolutionary scale as musky. For him, musk was an animalistic and deeply sexual smell. "Musk," said Ellis, "is the odor which not only in the animals to which it has given a name [musk-rat, musk-ox, etc.], but in many others, is a specifically sexual odor, chiefly emitted during the sexual season. The sexual odors indeed, of most animals seem to be modifications of musk" (1928: 97). Ellis specifically relates the smell of animalistic musk to black women, to lactating women, to women in general, to the Chinese, and even to the demented (1928: 60, 97–8, 107).

Following the kind of thinking that characterizes Ellis's study, musk had lost its hold as a "perfume." By the time of Ellis's post-Darwinian study, white European culture was fully invested in ridding itself of any associations, smell or otherwise, with a "primitive" animal past. Musk-like smells that had once been used with enthusiasm were now forsaken for flowery perfumes—and smell as a modern civility was invented (Corbin 1986: 74).

A Performance Guided by the *Odor di Femina*

In the history of sight and smell, photography—like flowery perfumes—disguises visual odors, the sweet stench of which seeps out of Freud's margins (pushed there by a text that otherwise constitutes a monument against smell) and into Lacan's theory of the gaze as *objet petit a*. For Lacan, the gaze as *objet petit a* operates alongside (not above) such other activities of the body as smelling, writing, touching and expelling babies and feces. And insofar as this is true, Lacan offers us a gaze configured in movement rather than fixation. The gaze's nose is no longer turned up.

The gaze as *objet petit a* describes a relation of loss between the body and its "objects" articulated in the dynamics of desire; the baby drops out of the mother's body; song comes from deep within our diaphragm and coos out of tightened lips; a tear eases itself out of a duct and seeps out through a tiny pinkened pinpricked hole, a gaze falls out of the eye. All these little things emphasize erotogenic rims of our own bodies (mouth, anus, nose, eyes, ears, genitals), off which falls some bit of one's own otherness—a little other, an *autre*, like the one falling off Lacan's own phrase "*objet petit a[utre]*," and fills up some of the lack in an other, who then expels yet another little object, creating yet another hole to be filled, and so on. As a result, we desire to have our holes filled up and we desire to fill up the holes of others. Yet every time we release an *objet* or two, we create more holes in our own bodies and then desire more *objets* from others. Lacan's story of the *objet petit a* is a never-ending story: desire only creates more desire.

For Lacan, the emphasis is on the little thing itself (the gaze, the word) *and* on the movement of the taking in of the *objet* as it becomes absorbed into the subject. The *objet petit a* is special: it initiates and takes pleasure in movement. Quite simply, one might say that the space of the *objet petit a* is not static, but rather *performative*. This emphasis on movement serves to separate Lacan's *objet petit a* from Freud's fetish.

Inevitably, the boundaries between the fetish and the *objet petit a* are blurred. They are almost synonyms. Their undecidable relationship is typically Lacanian and elusive (like a haunting aroma). Yet, even if one senses that the separation of Freud's fetish from Lacan's *objet petit a* is merely an academic exercise in splitting hairs, one cannot overlook the fact that fetishism is associated with neurosis, while the game of the *objet petit a* is not; it is desire itself.

Like Lacan, I am interested in the *odor di femina* as a fruitful *objet petit a*. Lacan's mysterious *odor di femina* exudes most memorably from his "Seminar on 'The Purloined Letter.'" According to Lacan, when in "The Purloined Letter, the Minister steals the letter from the Queen, he also takes possession of the sign of woman (Queen), and thereby becomes possessed by woman's sign, becomes castrated, becomes Queen." "He is obliged to don the role of the Queen, and even the attributes of femininity," and so to un-become a man or to become an "unbecoming man." According to Lacan, one can smell "the oddest *odor di femina*" whenever the (queer or) unbecoming Minister appears (1972: 61, 63, 66). This odor seems to exude from the text, causing the reader's eyes to water; the tears (the *objets*) that fall/follow obscure the page. Lacan compares the search for the invisible letter (that lies right before everyone's eyes) to the experience of trying to read "large letters spaced out widely across a map"; your eyes simply cannot *see* the country's name. In Lacan's wild interpretation of Poe's tale, the stolen letter is read "like an immense female body" that no one can see (but you can smell her) (1972: 66).

Lacan's use of the phrase *odor di femina* recalls Don Giovanni's own nose trap when he first smells *it* during the first act of Mozart's opera. This unseen odor of "woman" sets Giovanni off on an endless series of foreplayic seductions, as he travels on an odoriferous trail towards the mysterious *odor di femina:* a feminine *bouquet garni* lost somewhere in the soup pot. But smell plays a cruel trick on Giovanni. Following *her* scent leaves *him* chasing his own tail in an endless circle. Once the cheesecloth is torn apart, it turns out that the aroma is nothing but a common, well-known herb: the familiar smell of his own wife—the woman that he wanted to avoid at all costs.

Likewise, Catherine Clement suggests that Lacan, too, was guided by the *odor di femina* when he was searching for the meaning of Diego Velázquez's *Las Meninas*. We might thus conclude that Lacan, like Don Giovanni, was guided by something unseen. According to Clement:

> Lacan had first greeted Foucault's admirable chapter on the subject with enthusiasm [as appears in *The Order of Things*]. But he quickly changed the subject and eventually produced his own commentary on *Las Meninas,* guided as always by the *"odor di femina."* The object that occupies the geometric center of the canvas is not the king or the queen [as Foucault had argued] but rather, hidden beneath an enormous hoopskirt, the infanta's genitalia. (1983: 192)

Clement tells us that Lacan knew that even if it were possible to lift up the pounds of petticoats and the heavy armature of the infanta's hoopskirt, her secret parts, her letter(s), would always remain obscured (1983: 192–3). For the *odor di femina* that she emanates is doubly unseen. This conception of the doubly unseen is not unlike the double-sided painting (un)pictured in *Las Meninas:* we can see the back of the painting's stretched canvas and we can see the painting's painted subject (a double portrait of the king and queen) reflected in the mirror hanging on the back wall—but we cannot see the *actual* painting: it is doubly unseen. Compounding the visual confusion that takes place when a representation is nothing more than a representation of representation, *Las Meninas* describes a multitude of traditional pictorial frames that have been used throughout the history of painting. Within the rectangular pictorial surface (in addition to the back of the canvas, criss-crossed and framed by stretcher bars, and in addition to the looking-glass, which reflects the painting of the king and queen on the canvas's other side that we cannot see), the walls are covered with many other paintings (including two by Rubens) and the back wall features an open doorway flooded with light that frames a member of the queen's staff, but could be an image of *Velázquez* in masquerade. As Foucault has argued, *Las Meninas* is subjectless: it is pure representation. The painting reveals nothing. Yet, for Lacan there is a subject: our own annihilated subjectivity.

Lacan tells us that a painting annihilates us by looking back at us, without including us in the "picture." As Lacan has remarked, "The picture is in my eye. But I am not in the picture" (1978: 96). This is, of course, in reference to Lacan's famous recollection of being out at sea with some fishermen. While staring at a bit of flotsam (more trash) that had floated by—a sardine can—one of the fishermen exclaims (to Lacan): "*You see that can? Do you see it? Well it doesn't see you!*" (1978: 95). The fisherman's statement, riddled with irony, is poking fun at Lacan. The fisherman is illustrating how Lacan is "rather out of place in the picture," out on a fishing boat in the middle of the sea. For among "those fellows who were earning their livings with great difficulty," Lacan "looked like *nothing* on earth" (1978: 96)—not unlike the flotsam floating on the surface of the waves. The "joke" disturbed Lacan. For, seeing himself as the fishermen saw him, as a bit of garbage, as nothing, annihilated his perspective and so his self/subjectivity.

In Lacan's scheme of things, looking annihilates us by emphasizing our own inability to see. For, even when looking at a painting, we too are looked at from all sides, yet we are unaware of who is looking at us and from what point. And it is in this way that even an inanimate object, like the sardine can, or the infanta, or even the infanta's dress, actually does look back at us, but in such a way as to empower the object itself and not the viewer. It annihilates us. As a result, our gaze within its constructed socialization (as primary, as the only *true* sense) always falls short—like the perspective lines traveling towards the geometric center of *Las Meninas*. In Lacan's words,

"I see only from one point, but in my existence I am looked at from all sides" (1978: 72). Our eyes/"I"s are empty receptacles, like mirrors, that provide the material for misrecognition, to fulfill our mythic fantasies of being able to see, to speak. The infanta's dress becomes the clothing of a horrific idea: our own annihilation. As a result, her dress veils death's head and operates not unlike the oblique form that troubles, pulsates, dazzles and spreads out between Hans Holbein's *Ambassadors*: an anamorphic form that traps the gaze and trapped Lacan.

After walking around the room, after tilting your head in just the right way, you may apprehend Holbein's form—but what is it? A skull—empty eye sockets—glorious nothingness. In the words of Lacan, "All this shows at the very heart of the period in which the subject emerged and geometrical optics was an object of research, Holbein makes visible for us here something that is simply the subject as annihilated" or "our own nothingness in the figure of the death's head." Similarly, by approaching the canvas of *Las Meninas,* by nearly touching my nose to the canvas, a photographic detail of the cluster of roses that graces the infanta's lovely dress causes me to exclaim: "Why there is nothing there at all!" (Lacan 1978: 82, 88, 92).

But in approaching her dress as if vision were primary, I am forgetting that, for Lacan, there is a split between vision and the gaze. Vision is just one small part of the gaze as *objet petit a* and therefore must be considered in relationship to other *objets* that fall from our noses, lips and ears. For Lacan, the gaze is a polyvalent category, like thought itself. Lacan's gaze is not only a seen gaze. Recall Lacan detects that "a wild odor emanates" from the "function of *seeingness.*" Lacan's gaze is a sensate gaze that we can also smell or hear.

More than a Gaze

Page duBois writes: "If theory is a gaze, feminist theory must be more than a gaze at the same object, more than finding a new sameness" (1988: 188). For me, duBois' words are doused with a slight fragrance, an odor of difference, that fosters my decision to make such a big stink about Lacan's passing reference to the *odor di femina.* I am not the only one who has lingered over Lacan's enigmatic use of this odd Italian phrase. Clement returns to it several times in *The Lives and Legends of Jacques Lacan* and Michele Montrelay (1978) (possibly echoing Lacan) claims that femininity speaks *odor di femina:* an immediate, unmediated mode that no one can forget, a stinky language (not of flowers) that calls back to our first connections with the body of the mother. Yet, perhaps Lacan's text is smellier from his one-time mention of the *odor di femina* than one might think. It doesn't take much. The *odor di femina* may be fragile, but its essence, "tiny and almost impalpable," is enduring (Proust 1982, 1: 51).

Lacan's one drop of *odor di femina* loosens the gaze into an expanded constellation of senses. No longer overcome by the look, bodies come into play ... "a wild odor emanates." I, like Lacan (and apart from Freud), am interested in "a triumph of the gaze over the eye" (1978: 103). Turning back the pages of my text with my fingers, my eyes and my nose, the pictures elicit their own odd *odor di femina*. I smell detergent, sweat, vomit, the mother's tears, the child's sobs in the swatch of Mary Kelly's son's baby blanket. In the dermagraphic pictures from Salpêtrière, I am overcome by the smells of stale blood, sickness, fear, attacked skin, sour skin, sterilized sheets, not so recently washed hair, the armpit of a raised arm; the nervous breath of a frightened woman, skin, skin, skin. Durieu's and Delacroix's draped model smells of flowery perfume. Their photograph (which plays sensual havoc with the curve of her back, the glimpse of her left breast, and the thin, tight braid that wraps loosely around her head and falls, just right, at the nape of her neck) is painted with "the texture of perfume" (Barthes 1982: 135). In contrast, the picture's black dots (photographic accidents), which speckle the fabric backdrop and the drapery that wraps the chair and the model's lovely body as one, are signs of acrid loss. The black spots mar the vision. They mar the sweet perfume. *Le Violin d'Ingres* smells of the resin that I used to gently rub on the hair of the bow to the violin that I would never play. Its visual smell is screechingly odd, disturbing and humorous. *Las Meninas* smells of the secrets of little girls and the overwhelming scent of a big dog. Close up, *Las Meninas* smells of cadmium white, vermilion, ivory black, the hairs of a paintbrush, canvas, turpentine and linseed oil: exciting and noxious. The French ambassadors smell of knowledge, privilege, taste ... like a library or a museum or a man's beard: their smell attempts, but only attempts, to mask the *odor di femina* that emanates from the eye sockets of the skull that spins along the canvas's bottom edge.

By releasing Hope's "wild odor," my purloined images have stolen me. Though you may not see her (Hope) in Kelly's *Post-partum Document*, in the dermagraphed women from Salpêtrière, in Man Ray's *Le Violin d'Ingres*, in Durieu's and Delacroix's *Draped Model*, in Velásquez's *Las Meninas*, or in Holbein's *The French Ambassadors* ... you can certainly smell her.

Bibliography

Apter, E. (1991), *Feminizing the Fetish*, Ithaca: Cornell University Press.

Barthes, R. (1982), *Roland Barthes by Roland Barthes*, New York: Farrar, Straus & Giroux.

Clement, C. (1983), *The Lives and Legends of Jacques Lacan*, trans. A. Goldhammer, New York: Columbia University Press.

Corbin, A. (1986), *The Foul and the Fragrant*, New York: Berg.

Didi-Huberman, G. (1987), "The Figurative Incarnation of the Sentence," trans. C. Davidson, *LAICA Journal*, 5(47).

288 Scentsuality

duBois, P. (1988), *Sowing the Body*, Chicago: University of Chicago Press.
Ellis, H. ([1905] 1928), *Studies in the Psychology of Sex*, vol. IV, Philadelphia: F. A. Davis Company.
Fabian, J. (1983), *Time and the Other*, New York: Columbia University Press.
Freud, S. (1893), "Charcot," in *The Standard Edition of the Complete Psychological Works of Sigmund Freud*, trans. J. Strachey (ed.), London: Hogarth Press (1953–74), vol. 1, p. 13.
—— (1893–5), "Miss Lucy R (Case 3)" in J. Breuer and S. Freud, *Studies on Hysteria*, in *The Standard Edition*, vol. 2, pp. 106–24.
—— (1899), "Screen Memories," in *The Standard Edition*, vol. 3, pp. 301–22.
—— (1905a), *Three Essays on the Theory of Sexuality*, in *The Standard Edition*, vol. 7, pp. 136–243.
—— (1905b), *Fragment of An Analysis of a Case of Hysteria*, in *The Standard Edition*, vol. 7, pp. 3–122.
—— (1924), "A Note Upon the "Mystic Writing Pad,"" in *The Standard Edition*, vol. 19, pp. 227–34.
—— (1930), *Civilization and Its Discontents*, in *The Standard Edition*, vol. 21, pp. 59–145.
—— (1939), *Moses and Monotheism*, in *The Standard Edition*, vol. 23, pp. 1–137.
—— (1985), *The Complete Letters of Sigmund Freud to Wilhelm Fliess: 1897–1904*, trans. J.M. Masson (ed.), Cambridge: Belknap Press.
Gallop, J. (1982), *The Daughter's Seduction*, Ithaca: Cornell University Press.
Lacan, J. (1972), "Seminar on 'The Purloined Letter,'" trans. J. Mehlman, *Yale French Studies*, 48.
—— (1978), *The Four Fundamental Concepts of Psycho-analysis*, J.-A. Miller (ed.), trans. A. Sheridan, New York: Norton.
Montrelay, M. (1978), "Inquiry into Femininity," *m/f*, 1: 83–101.
Phelan, P. (1993), *Unmarked*, London & New York: Routledge.
Proust, M. (1982), *Remembrance of Things Past*, trans. C.K.S. Moncrieff and T. Kilmartin, New York: Vintage.
Rukeyser, M. (1978), "Myth," in *The Collected Poems*, New York: McGraw-Hill.
Suleiman, S.R. (1990), *Subversive Intent*, Cambridge: Harvard University Press.

25

"The Roots of the Orchis, the Iuli of Chesnuts"

The Odor of Male Solitude

Christopher Looby

There have been a few men who could smell me.

Chris Stevens (disc jockey in the television show *Northern Exposure*)

I want to read an American anti-masturbation treatise of the mid-nineteenth century and consider the ways in which this manifestly erotophobic text may be, paradoxically, erotogenic in the extreme. The text in question (and others like it) incites the very desires it condemns, and in this case it does so (at least in part) by stimulating what I will be calling the olfactory *imaginaire*, the realm of actual and fantasmatic smell sensations, immediate and vicarious responses to odors, and significations and associations attached to those sensory phenomena. Much of the pleasure of reading this anti-masturbation text or any other is owing to the way it brings the reader into imaginary proximity to the masturbating body of the sexual deviant. In its construction of this proximity—the spectacle of the masturbating body close at hand—the text demonstrates how the ostensibly anti-social practice of autoeroticism (notoriously the "solitary vice") is embedded, in the period in question, in a homosocial context that renders masturbation a phenomenon of collective male concern (the masturbator, in this literature, is almost always a boy or a man). Nineteenth-century American men didn't just masturbate; they thought concertedly about each other masturbating. In this collective thought of masturbation, the odor of semen (or its textualized, fantasmatic representation) is the embodiment as it were, of the solitary vice's inscription within a scene of male–male desire.

The Odor of Semen

In 1895, suspicious deputy chaplain W.D. Morrison thought he detected in the cell of Oscar Wilde in Wandsworth Prison a particular (and, evidently, familiar and identifiable) odor: "the odor of his cell is now so bad that the officer in charge of him has to use carbolic acid in it everyday," the chaplain wrote. "I fear from what I see and hear [and, obviously, *smell*] that perverse sexual practices are again getting the mastery over him," Morrison continued. The odor in question was that of ejaculated semen, which then, as now, was frequently likened to the smell of ammonia or chlorine. The authorities denied that Wilde had degenerated under their care into a chronic masturbator, instead attributing the smell to Jeyes's disinfectant (Ellmann 1988: 495). The chaplain was transferred to another post, and the olfactory sensation that had suggested to him a scandalous failure of (and, possibly, Wilde's unashamed resistance to) the penitentiary's disciplinary regime was, presumably, forgotten—although, if odor sensation and memory are as closely linked as they are said to be (Engen 1991; Schab 1991), Chaplain Morrison may very well, when remembering the scene of his professional mishap, have been revisited fantasmatically by Wilde's spermatic scent.

The odor of semen—one's own semen, ejaculated externally where its exposure to air allows it to volatilize, and causes its distinct pungency to register upon one's olfactory receptors—carries for men an inevitable mnemonic association with their first pubescent experiences of autoeroticism. According to Trygg Engen, "A long-term odor memory can be established with only one exposure. An episode is tagged in memory with whatever odor happens to be present. And then, like a bad habit [!], this odor connection is difficult to unlearn and forget" (Engen 1991: 6). The "domination of the first association relates to the way in which odors are committed to memory. An odor is integrated into the mental representation of an experience; it has no identifiable attribute of its own but exists as an inherent part of a unitary, holistic perceptual event" (Engen 1991: 7). Because odor sensation is so crude in itself, but becomes more acute by virtue of its intimate associations with other sensations present at the same time (especially including taste and touch), odor memory has the power to retrieve the allied sensations that were originally associated with it, reproducing imaginarily the whole multimodal sense-perceptual event. Odor memory cannot be summoned at will; it needs to be triggered by olfactory stimulation in the present, by the same odor or by a similar odor easily confused with it (although the presently sensed odor may only register unconsciously, leaving one to imagine that the odor memory was summoned voluntarily). Thus the odor of *another* man's semen, recognized as such by the man who (like Deputy Chaplain Morrison) smells it, inevitably carries with it a host of disorienting associations with the kinds of stigmatized sexual practices and erotic events that would have introduced one to that smell in the first place and taught one to recognize it: associations with one's own solitary masturbation, with external ejaculation during sex with a partner, or with experiences of mutual and/or collective masturbation, either homosexual or heterosexual.

Whatever the specific associations for particular persons, the odor of semen is, as it were, the aroma of non-procreative sex; *recognizing* that odor could be tantamount (for those who subscribe to the hegemonic nineteenth-century sexual–reproductive ideology) to a confession that one has personal experience of one or another contraceptive sexual practice. According to the dominant sexual ideology, semen is properly deposited inside a woman's vagina, where, unexposed to air, its odor would not make itself known to the nose. But when a man recognizes the odor of another man's semen, the recognition itself is a kind of homosexual event, a scented rupture in the surface homosociality of everyday life: a revelation of the strong, pervasive presence in normal daily homosocial experience of the volatile male–male erotic bonds that subtend it.

In the United States, half a century before Morrison's charged encounter with the odor of Oscar Wilde's semen, masturbation phobia had also prevailed rather widely, although at least one authority, the physician Homer Bostwick, an authority on "spermatorrhea" (the "disease" of nocturnal emission and involuntary spermatic discharge) and other "seminal diseases," including masturbation and masturbatory insanity, found the odor of semen not unpleasant at all. In his published work on the subject, *A Treatise on the Nature and Treatment of Seminal Diseases, Impotency, and Other Kindred Affections: with Practical Directions for the Management and Removal of the Causes Producing Them; Together with Hints for Young Men*, Bostwick observed that "[t]he smell of semen is specific, heavy, affecting the nostrils, yet not disagreeable. The same odor is observed in the roots of the orchis, the iuli of chestnuts, and the antherae of many plants" (1847: 23). To this rather lyrical description of the smell of the sexual secretion he liked to call "the very cream and essence of the blood" (1847: 81), Bostwick added, even more unnecessarily, and without explaining how he had come by the information, that "[t]he taste of semen is fatuous, and somewhat acrid," and that it "has a strong and peculiar odor, and a saltish taste" (1847: 23, 22). All that one can suggest to account for Bostwick seeming acquaintance with this taste, rather surprisingly suggested in this virulently hostile anti-masturbation tract, is that he does often refer, throughout the book, to "the hand of the physician" (Bostwick 1847: 10), as well as to the need of his depraved patients for "one friendly hand outstretched to save them" (1847: 14), and he testifies as to the etiolated condition of the penis of chronic masturbators that "this organ feels like a whipcord" (1847: 135).

Actually, to be perfectly just, Bostwick doesn't exactly say that *he himself* has tasted or even smelled semen; he may have gotten his knowledge secondhand. The sensory information is given impersonally: "It has a ... taste..."; "The taste ... is ..." And it is, of course, part of the standard protocol of chemistry research to give a preliminary gross description of the sensory qualities of a substance that will then be analyzed chemically. The actual fact of the matter seems less important, however, than the evocative intensity of the moment in the text, an intensity barely disguised by the embedding of the reported odor sensation in a cool prose announcing assorted facts from philology, chemistry, hunting lore and so forth:

> Semen is a word derived from the Latin word "*sero*" to *sow*. It has a strong and peculiar odor, and a saltish taste. It is composed of the following parts, according to the analysis of Professor Vauqelin:
>
> | | |
> |---|---|
> | Water | 900 |
> | Animal Mucilage | 60 |
> | Soda | 10 |
> | Sulphate of Lime | 30 |
>
> The smell of the semen of quadrupeds, when at heat, is so penetrating as to render their flesh fetid and useless, unless castrated. Thus the flesh of the stag, *tempore coitus*, is unfit to eat. The taste of semen is fatuous and somewhat acrid. In the testes, its consistence is thin and diluted; but in the vesiculae seminales, viscid, dense and rather pellucid; and by venery and debility it is rendered thinner. (Bostwick 1847: 22–3)

Eve Kosofsky Sedgwick, writing of Nietzsche's penchant for metaphorically describing, as smelling- or sniffing-out, his ability to detect the lies of civilized morality, remarks that he "put the scent back into sentimentality" (Sedgwick 1990: 149). That is, he aggressively restored to the modern emotional psychology of goodwill, pity, love and so forth (the sentimentality of which he deplored as vicarious and therefore mendacious) the corporeal dimension of bodily, sensual proximity it otherwise wished to repress. Bostwick's rhetoric is everywhere allied with a sort of sentimental Christian moralism that disguises a deep and malicious antagonism toward bodily pleasure. Nietzsche's insistence that civilized lies stink, and that their exposure is best figured as an act of olfactory detection and discrimination, should not lead us to imagine, however, that the mere restoration and acknowledgment of olfactory experience is necessarily or intrinsically liberating. The repression of olfaction may be an essential component of bourgeois hypocrisy, but repression was not the only reaction to olfaction in nineteenth-century middle-class respectable society. It was also elaborately cultivated and socially constructed, with different smells marked as pleasant or unpleasant, disgusting or exalted, pure or filthy—or some double-binding combination of such antithetical values. It perhaps shouldn't surprise us that Bostwick, whose book celebrates and enforces modern bourgeois civilized morality in its grotesque, punitive extremity, should at once appeal with undisguised delectation to taboo sensations of taste and smell *and* also condemn them. Georges Bataille has written of "the profound complicity of law and the violation of law," of the fact that—especially in the domain of the erotic— "taboos founded on terror are not only there to be obeyed," but also to be affirmed negatively by transgression. The "mainspring of eroticism" is the way that transgression "suspends a taboo without suppressing it" (Bataille 1986: 36, 48). In Bostwick's taboo-enforcing text, the forbidden action (erotic self-stimulation) must be evoked powerfully, sensuously, odoriferously, and thereby invested with an aura of excitement, precisely so that its condemnation and prohibition may then have the delicious character of violence. (The scandalous aroma here is at least given a saving, manly association with the heady odor of a rutting stag.)

Bostwick's *On Seminal Diseases* is replete with the intimate details of men's bodies, even as it preaches against most of those bodies' pleasures. Much of the essential drama of the book is economically represented in the two passages quoted above in which the explosive moment of bodily sensation—of the taste and smell of a particular bodily fluid—is discursively enclosed by the dispassionate rhetoric of etymology, the macho allusion to stag-hunting, and the scientific ritual of empirical description. Such prophylactic textual surroundings probably failed perfectly to neutralize the evoked sensations, and cannot suppress even today, when the taste of latex may be more familiar to many of us than that of semen, a strong whiff of a specific nostalgic charm.

On Seminal Diseases may be construed as, among other things, an epistolary novel of a deeply sentimental sort. Until page 47 it is a general treatise on the health of the sexual organs; from there to page 223 it consists of case histories of individual sufferers from sexual diseases, most of them presented in the form of letters from patients appealing (in the most abject and sentimental terms) to the physician for help and describing their symptoms in sometimes vivid detail. In this respect the text harks back formally to the ur-text of anti-masturbation ideology, the early-eighteenth-century *Onania*, which began as a modest pamphlet of about sixty pages but grew by the sixteenth edition (London 1737) to 194 pages along with a supplement of 142 pages, nearly the entirety of the additions consisting of letters from repentant and unrepentant masturbators (MacDonald 1967: 424–5). With a few exceptions, Bostwick's correspondents are male, and they usually complain of one or another kind of masculine depletion: they lose semen involuntarily, they lack semen altogether, their genital organs are small, they are chronically sexually unaroused. Bostwick's entire regimen of "medical discipline" addresses this epidemic of "impaired venereal power" in a variety of ways, all calculated to effect "a complete restoration of virile power" (Bostwick 1847: 57, 93, 94). On Bostwick's telling, which is essentially the same as that of the medical orthodoxy of the time, there is a general "spermatic economy": semen *is* virile power, and its loss is a positive debit to the masculine account (Barker-Benfield 1976: 175–88). It is a resource to be husbanded, not wasted.

The spermatic economy is an individual bodily economy, but not, however, only that, in important ways the spermatic economy is transindividual, collective: seminal resources are a communal property. The virile restoration effected by Bostwick is the therapeutic gift of one man to another, male physician to male patient. The chief stigmatized form of wasteful, debilitating venery—masturbation—is markedly a solitary, antisocial practice, and it is frequently attended by a pathological "aversion to going out"; restoration of masculine power is simultaneously a restoration to sexual potency and continence, *and* a return to solidarity with the "friends and acquaintances" whom the sufferer had previously "tried to shun" (Bostwick 1847: 95).

Masturbation is constructed in moral literature, as Thomas Laqueur has written, chiefly as a threat to human solidarity and not as a specifically sexual evil. In this literature, reaching back to the eighteenth century and to the anonymous *Onania* and the Swiss Dr Tissot's *L'Onanisme,* masturbation is "a fundamentally asocial or socially degenerative practice," and as such is most frequently contrasted with "the vital, socially constructive act of heterosexual intercourse" (Laqueur 1990: 229). Anti-masturbation literature, however, despite its usual posing of a stark choice between horrifying degeneration (for onanists who do not reform themselves) and marriage and procreation (for those who do)—and in this regard as well Bostwick is perfectly typical—nevertheless constitutes, given its countless juicy narratives of young persons discovering genital pleasures, a "vast corpus of incendiary porn whose erotogenic power is not diminished by the obligatory horrifying, cautionary end" (Laqueur 1990: 228).

Laqueur is right to cite this literature as corroboration for Foucault's now familiar claim that the institutions of moral and erotic discipline do not merely repress or control sexual desire, but incite it in order to shape it (Laqueur 1990: 228; Foucault 1980). The "disgust" which these texts (themselves curiously figured by Bostwick as "emanat[ions]") have "excited" in "properly constituted minds" seems to testify, ironically, to the availability of different, improper sensations that the same texts can arouse in those with "depraved tastes and prurient imaginations." The erotogenic power and the erotophobic power are not completely disjunctive; they originate in the same place. And it may be that *both* responses (pleasurably excited or disgusted) are, at least in part, aroused particularly by the olfactory powers of the text. Bostwick's exploitation of these powers strikingly resembles that of certain, other writers of mid-nineteenth-century America, in whose texts the olfactory *imaginaire* is also crucially related to issues of male sexual conduct and passional freedom. The literary practices of Walt Whitman, Francis Parkman, Herman Melville and Thomas Wentworth Higginson provide a context for understanding Bostwick's charged engagement with the odor of male solitude.

The Olfactory Text

Among Bostwick's American literary contemporaries were a number of writers whose texts aimed to be olfactory in an active sense: to produce olfactory sensations in the reader's body in seeming defiance of the nearly odorless nature of the printed book. This project of textual production of imaginary olfactory sensation is an especially striking one, contravening as it does the civilized regime of odorlessness that characterizes bourgeois modern society. It constitutes a particular instance of the "implantation of perversions" so named by Foucault (Foucault 1980: 36–49). Walt Whitman, Homer Bostwick's contemporary, wrote in the first edition of *Leaves of Grass* (1855), "The scent of these arm-pits is aroma finer than prayer" (Whitman 1982: 51). "There is something in staying close to men and women … and in the contact and odor of them that pleases the soul well" (1982: 120), he averred. Given the persistent Whitmanesque fantasy of the poet's actual bodily presence within the text or through the text ("I pass so poorly with the paper and types … I must pass with the contact of bodies and souls"; "Camerado, this is no book, / Who touches this touches a man" [1982: 89, 611]), it follows that the fantasmatic bodily contact between writer and reader that the poetry strives to effect is potentially attended by a fantasmatic smelling of, for instance, the poet's armpit odor as well.

Leaves of Grass is indeed a redolent text: the very first page mentions "perfumes," "fragrance," "smoke of my own breath," "sniff of green leaves" (1982: 27). In the revised and enlarged 1860 edition of *Leaves of Grass,* the renewed and elaborated figure of the poetic text as itself the poet's body is accompanied by the incorporation of additional olfactory moments in newly-added poems: "Scented Herbage of My Breast," for instance, one of the lyrics in "Calamus" (1982: 268–70). Whitman's explanation, in a contemporary letter, of his choice of the calamus or sweet-flag as "the token of comrades" (1982: 273) to be exchanged by youths as ritual signs of their ardent mutual devotion, emphasizes its "aromatic" quality—the "fresh, aquatic, pungent bouquet" (1982: 1356 n. 268.1)—of this variety of grass or rush that grows characteristically by the margins of ponds. What Whitman called the "recherché or ethereal sense" of this sign thus seems directly to emanate from its scent (1982: 1356 n. 268.1). The dominant conceit in "Calamus" is that the poem *Leaves of Grass* grows materially out of the ground above the poet's tomb, as if directly rooted in his buried hairy, upturned chest. (It is perhaps not irrelevant in this connection that the midline of the chest as well as the nipples and areolae are two of the major sebaceous scent-gland regions of the human body [Stoddart 1990: 58 Table 3.2].) The esoteric meaning of the poem—its celebration together of both masturbation and male-homoerotic love in defiance of "all the standards hitherto published"—is figured as a "faint odor" that may be inhaled by those who later pass by the grave (Whitman 1982: 268): according to the logic of this figure, reading equals sniffing. In "Song of Myself" the calamus is mentioned following one of Whitman's many autoerotic allusions, his enchanted declaration that "If I worship one thing more than another it shall be the spread of my own body, or any part of it, ... You my rich blood! your milky stream pale strippings of my life! ... Root of wash'd sweet-flag! ... it shall be you! ... I dote on myself, there is that lot of me and all so luscious" (1982: 211–12).

The vigorous association of Whitman's textual redolence with masturbation particularly ("The pulse pounding through palms and trembling encircling fingers, the young man all color'd, red, ashamed, angry" [1982: 262]), and with unorthodox sexual practices more generally, hardly needs elaboration. Michael Moon has shown how elaborately involved *Leaves of Grass* was in contesting the proliferating discourses of male purity and anti-masturbation that were increasingly prevalent in his day. These discourses sought to proscribe many different kinds of male bodily pleasure, but especially autoerotic and homoerotic forms of gratification. What Moon describes as "the desire to locate a central place for the body in the practices of writing and reading; the desire somehow to open in the literary text a space in which the actual physical presence of the writer might come into loving contact with readers" was intimately linked to Whitman's "desire to oppose the increasingly phobic attitude to men's taking pleasure in their own and in other men's bodies which Whitman's culture began manifesting in the 1830s and after, the years of Whitman's first youth" (Moon 1991: 14). However, Whitman's attempt to project his body into or through the text ran inevitably into the problem of "the impossibility of doing so literally." What Moon calls the "frustrating but ultimately incontrovertible conditions of writing and embodiment that actually render it impossible for him to produce in his writing more than metonymic substitutes for such contact" (1991: 5, 6) sadly give the lie, on this account, to Whitman's famous claim that he "[w]ho touches this [book] touches a man."

But are the disembodying conditions of writing so utterly "incontrovertible," finally? Sensory hallucinations are often indistinguishable from the real thing, and phantom olfactory sensations are often remarkably vivid. If a literary text—a piece of writing—induces in its reader a hallucinated sensation (say, that of the smell of Whitman's armpits), this may need to be counted as far less than the actual sensible touch of the poet's body itself but it is certainly something other (and more) than a mere metonymic substitute for that body. It is a sensation, for the reader, of physical proximity to the writer, a fantasmatic encounter (subjectively experienced as real) with a material exudation of the poet's body. The awakened sensation—the event in the reader's body—may be neurologically indistinguishable (or nearly so) from the "real" thing.

Among Bostwick's American literary contemporaries, olfactory textuality—the incitement of such phantom smell sensations—was a matter of some persistent interest. Unlike Whitman's *Leaves of Grass*, Francis Parkman's

The Oregon Trail ([1849] 1982) sets its fantasmatic productions of olfactory sensations within a context that overtly pays heed to the reigning bourgeois value of odorlessness. Along with his cousin and traveling companion, Quincy A. Shaw, Parkman is often in search of a "bath, which the heat of the weather, joined to our prejudices, had rendered very desirable" (Parkman [1849] 1982: 19). Parkman, historian and floriculturalist, betrays his attitude toward odor most clearly in his *The Book of Roses* (1866), a treatise on rose culture that presents the breeding of superior hybrid varieties as an elaborate allegory of the civilizing process, with the eradication of inferior "races" of flowers coinciding with the progressive elimination of their smell. In his career as a rose breeder—indeed, in the whole modern history of rose eugenics—strong scent has generally been sacrificed to the preferred qualities of size, color and fullness of bloom.

Parkman's demotion of scent in rose culture matches his embarrassment or self-consciousness in *The Oregon Trail* about his own body odor when he can't bathe and when he's suffering from chronic diarrhea. The rank odor of his own and his companions' bodies—the pungent odor of unbathed men in frontier camps—is one texture of scents Parkman offers for his readers' olfactory imaginations, but the most curious phantom scent in the text emanates from a scene in which Parkman is bragging to some Indians about the complete superiority of his (white) civilization to theirs. In the midst of a scene in which Parkman addresses a gathering of Indians in an attempt to overawe them with claims about the advantages of his culture, he suddenly hears himself propound what he knows to be the specious claim that "all the [white] men were brave warriors." He is then

> assailed by sharp twinges of conscience, for I fancied I could perceive a fra-grance of perfumery in the air, and a vision arose before me of white-kid gloves and silken moustaches with the mild and gentle countenances of numerous fair-haired young men. But I recovered myself and began again. (Parkman [1849] 1982: 260)

Parkman frames this momentary drama of self-distraction and self-recovery as one in which his conscience reproaches him for exaggerating the masculine bravery of his fellow Bostonians, when in fact—as he believes—many of them are foppish and weak. But I take this passage to be, first of all, a lesson on the hallucination of olfactory experience as a supplement to reading. (At the moment that this olfactory hallucination is summoned, Parkman displaces smell by sight—"a *vision* arose before me"—as if to banish the contaminating and compromising sensory mode of smell by means of the distanced and contemptuous reference to the *appearance* of the scented Bostonians. But the verb, *arose*, seems subliminally to reinvoke endophonically via its homonym—*a rose*—the odors of the scent-associated fields of floriculture and perfumery, and perhaps even the distinctive odor of attar of rose, a familiar component of colognes. Thus a sound reinvokes an odor that had been displaced by Parkman's advertence to sight.) At other places in the text Parkman reports on smells he really encountered in the material sensorium, and asks the reader to imagine them; here he reports on a smell he himself imagined or "fancied"—fancied he "perceive[d]"—a "fragrance of perfumery" of some "fair-haired young men." Parkman *fantasized* this odor as he addressed the Indians (obviously it was not materially present); and as a fantasy product, the imagined scent sensation must be counted as an effect of an unacknowledged desire, a disowned longing for the smell of what he is overtly denigrating.

Parkman's aversive desire for the odor of these young men is notably not for the natural smell of their bodies, but for a concocted fragrance that they wear to replace or mask their own odors. Prepared fragrances, ironically, are formulated to mimic the very same human body odors they are used to replace: what perfumers call the "top notes" of these aromatic compositions are usually made from the extracted sexual secretions of flowers (which often mimic animals' sex pheromones) while the "middle notes" are derived from resinous materials which resemble sex steroids' odors, and the "base notes are mammalian sex attractants with a distinctly urinous or faecal odor"—i.e. musk and civet (Stoddart 1990: 162–3). When a perfume—a complex olfactory text—is sniffed, the more volatile floral notes are intensely conspicuous, while the powerfully erotogenic lower notes are often registered only unconsciously. "In offering to the perceiver a cocktail of sex attractant odors at low concentration in the base notes, [perfumes] subconsciously reveal what consciously the strident top notes seek to hide"—i.e. they simulate and accentuate the natural sexual and excretory odors of the body (Stoddart 1990: 163). Parkman's fantasy fixes on the artificial scent the young men wore, as if to distance himself from the odors proper to their bodies, but the "perfumery" he is sniffing in his imagination replicates those bodies' odors anyway—or replicates their sex-attractant secretions. As Whitman's reader is invited to sniff the poet, Parkman takes a whiff of these scented young men, and invites us to participate vicariously in this olfactory hallucination. If what defines a sexual act as masturbation is the "absent object," the "phantom" provided by the "power of fancy" that "rouse[s] the organs form'd for nobler ends"—as a poem included in a 1767 *Short Treatise on Onanism* deliriously phrased it (qtd. in Haller and Haller 1974: 202)—then Parkman's daydreaming scent sensation, with its unmistakable overtones of illicit, stigmatized sexuality, is masturbatory certainly, but also seems effectively to elide the difference between the homoerotic and the autocratic.

The fantasmatic literary production of smell is powerfully in evidence, to take one more example contemporaneous with Bostwick, Whitman and Parkman, in Melville's *Moby-Dick* ([1851] 1972), most extravagantly in Chapter 91, "The Pequod Meets the Rose-Bud," where the reader is told "that the many noses on the Pequod's deck proved more vigilant discoverers than the three pairs of eyes aloft," thus reorienting the readers attention away from the ocular to the nasal. "A peculiar and not very pleasant smell was smelt in the sea" (Melville [1851] 1972: 512). The sweet-smelling-sounding *Rosebud*, a French ship, has chosen to attach to its sides two whales—one, a corpse of a whale that "died unmolested on the sea" and has rotted as it floated, the other, "one of those problematical whales that seem to dry up and die with a sort of prodigious dyspepsia, or indigestion," the two whales together exhaling "an unsavory odor" that announces their approaching presence to other ships some time before they are espied ([1851] 1972: 512).

The *Pequod* soon "entrapped in the smell" of "this aromatic ship"; the *Rosebud*'s captain—punningly, a former "Cologne manufacturer" ([1851] 1972: 513, 515)—doesn't know that within the blasted whale's unsavory carcass is to be found the deliciously aromatic and commercially valuable ambergris, and so the unscrupulous mate Stubb cleverly contrives to persuade the unsuspecting French captain to abandon the carcasses, under the mistaken impression that his crew will catch a fever from them, Stubb, of course, is scheming to harvest the ambergris himself, and is proud to have thus "diddled" the Frenchman, as he twice puts it (Melville [1851] 1972: 517). As the *Rosebud* pulls away from the miasmic carcasses, Stubb plunges a spade into one malodorous whale's body, in search of the precious ambergris:

> Stubb was beginning to look disappointed, especially as the horrible nosegay increased, when suddenly from out of the very heart of this plague, there stole a faint stream of perfume, which flowed through the tide of bad smells without being absorbed by it, as one river will flow into and then along with another, without at all blending with it for a time. (Melville [1851] 1972: 518)

Melville's punning association of this odorous emanation with that of semen—he's talking, naturally, of *sperm* whales, and Stubb's accession to the wonderful odor is won by his "diddl[ing]" of the Frenchman—needs scarcely more comment than did Whitman's. The *textual* nature of olfactory experience—the way different scents cross and mingle, "flow into and then along with [one] another," blending but distinguishable—seems (as with Parkman) to instruct us in reading. *Moby-Dick* is notoriously a multilayered text, one whose most accessible patterns of meaning might be received as "horrible," while it always promises an eventual accession to secret deposits of a sweeter revelation. The distinction described here—a "horrible nosegay" or "plague" versus a delectable "faint stream of perfume"—asks readers to use their noses, as it were, in realizing or activating the text's esoteric meaning. To actualize the sensory/semiotic *difference* between two contrasted odors virtually requires a willful olfactory hallucination.

Inviting the reader to enter into the text's olfactory *imaginaire*, Melville is nowhere more seductive than in "A Squeeze of the Hand," three chapters after the narrative of the *Rosebud*. Ishmael's rapturous description of the collective project of sperm-squeezing on board ship is rich in double-entendre: the seamen who are squeezing the congealed lumps of sperm to render them fluid soon find each other's softened and slippery hands in ecstatic contact, while the "gentle globules" break and "discharge all their opulence" and the squeezers "snuff up that uncontaminated aroma—literally and truly, like the smell of spring violets" or the odor of a "musky meadow" ([1851] 1972: 526–7), The direct appeal to the reader—"Come; let us squeeze hands all round; nay, let us all squeeze ourselves into each other, let us squeeze ourselves universally into the very milk and sperm of kindness" ([1851] 1972: 527)—beckons him into the enveloping redolence of the spermy scene. Melville, like Parkman, Whitman and Bostwick, strives to stimulate his readers' imaginary collective experience of a powerful odor sensation, but like Whitman (and unlike Parkman and Bostwick) he is celebrating the power of the olfactory to release the homoerotic and autoerotic desires it evokes.

"If, in the simple process of writing, one could physically impart to this page the fragrance of this spray of azalea beside me, what a wonder would it seem!" wrote Thomas Wentworth Higginson in an essay called "The Procession of the Flowers" (1862: 657). Higginson, a radical American clergyman whose abolitionist writings aimed to move his readers to take up arms against slavery and whose sentimental nature writings tried to represent the heavy, exotic scents of the flowers he rapturously loved, approaches, like Whitman, the limit of physical sensation against which his textual erotics is pressing. If, in the simple process of writing, Whitman or Parkman or Melville could have imparted to the page the "pungent bouquet" of the calamus, the "fragrance of perfumery" associated with effeminate young Bostonian men, or the "uncontaminated aroma" of the squeezed whale sperm, they no doubt would have taken advantage of such a wonder. But it may be that in inciting their readers to *imagine* such olfactory sensations they did something more wonderful; they aroused in those readers certain stigmatized desires with which those odors were inextricably associated, autoerotic and homoerotic desires secreted within the olfactory memories the text urged its readers to retrieve.

Medical Odorama

The campaign against masturbation from the eighteenth century onward needs to be seen, as Laqueur has written, less as addressed to "a problem of excess or wicked sexual desire" than as part of a "more general debate about the unleashing of desire in a commercial economy and about the possibility of human community in these circumstances" (Laqueur 1990: 229). Masturbation is construed, in this view, as "a fundamentally asocial or socially degenerative practice," "the channeling of healthy desire back into itself" rather than into socially productive heterosexual intercourse

(Laqueur 1990: 229). While it seems true to describe masturbation as in some basic way antisocial—it is a turning in upon the self, upon the self's own body, a turning away from others (leaving aside, for the moment, the possible fantasmatic presence of another/others, which would reintroduce a scenario of the social)—it is equally important to notice the ways in which even the most intimate phenomenology of masturbation relocates selfhood in the socius, as well as the ways in which masturbation and the masturbator have been discursively relocated as objects of social concern in the modern period. The masturbator may be acting antisocially, but society will not let the masturbator alone.

In Bostwick's rendering, the intimacies of the doctor's examining room are designed to reinscribe the deviant energies of autoeroticism within the social text, and they do this materially via the intensely tactile, quasi-erotic bonds between the doctor (metonymized, as we have seen, most frequently by his "hand") and the patient (present in the scenario chiefly in the form of his disordered genital–urinary and excretory systems). Bostwick published *On Seminal Diseases* at about the time that the proportion of various medical methods preferred for treating masturbation was shifting from an emphasis on non-invasive therapies (such as the water cure, dietary reform and so forth) to surgical intervention. According to Rene Spitz, "It is only in the second half of the nineteenth century that sadism becomes the foremost characteristic of the campaign against masturbation" (1952: 499). Clitoridectomy; blistering of the thighs, genitals and spinal region; cauterization of the spine and genitals; infibulation of the prepuce and labia majora; circumcision—these were among what Spitz calls the "innumerable, varied and subtle practices of a refined cruelty" (1952: 505).

Bostwick's case histories consist largely of descriptions of what he did to his patients' urethras and rectal cavities. His usual practice was to invade the patient's urethra with a "bougie" (a tapering cylindrical instrument made of a material such as rubber, metal or waxed linen, used for purposes of dilation, exploration and medication), and then cauterize the prostatic portion of the urethra. On Bostwick's unsurprising account, this is usually a very painful experience for the patient, who often faints dead away (Bostwick 1847: 70, 75, 89, 96, 192). This catheterization and cauterization is repeated at frequent intervals, and is the centerpiece of Bostwick's system of treatment: it is by virtue of this repetitive subjection of the masturbator to painful genital invasion that his autocratic habits are supposed to be eradicated.

Bostwick seems to be oblivious to the erotic dynamics of this encounter between his hands and the other men's penises and anuses. (In one of his few case histories of female patients, he describes—proudly, it seems—how "[d]uring [his] examination her excitement was so great that she could with difficulty lay upon the speculum chair" [1847: 204], but he never discusses the possibility of sexual arousal that is equally present during his contact with male patients.) The possibility that at least some of his patients were actually getting off on the experience may seem remote to us. The prevalence of doctor–patient scenarios in pornography, however, should alert us to the erotic potential of the medical encounter, and Bostwick's rhetoric of discipline, pain and suffering has an unmistakable sadomasochistic atmosphere about it.

Bostwick's patients usually masturbated alone, but more than a few of them began masturbating socially, as he acknowledges—usually in school (1847: 100, 131, 133, 234). Bostwick's effort is to convert this collaborative scenario of pleasure-in-self-stimulation into the collaborative medical scenario of pain-in-genital-manipulation. In so doing, it aims to replace an implicitly homoerotic intersubjective sexual encounter with a punitive, sex-phobic, homosocial intersubjective medical encounter. The place of odor in this transformation is important, and perhaps crucial: in the case histories that comprise the largest portion of the book we no longer read of the "not disagreeable" odor of semen introduced to us earlier, but instead of "flatulency" as a side effect of "involuntary seminal emissions" (1847: 147; cf. 191, 192). We read, in addition, that "catarrh, or chronic inflammation of the bladder ... is quite important to understand as connected with seminal diseases," that the "mucus discharged" in consequence is sometimes of an "enormous" quantity, and that "the odor of the matter discharged is very offensive" (1847: 231, 232). The odor of semen, so lyrically evoked earlier in the text, is displaced in the case histories by evocations of other bodily products—blood, intestinal gas, stools and pus most prominently—and by their associated odors.

One of the most powerfully olfactorily-evocative therapeutic regimens detailed in the book is also one of Bostwick's most common: he often applies up to forty leeches to the perineum and/or abdomen and inner thighs of a patient, and then has the patient stand over a steaming vat of boiling water until the leeches drop off, so that the steam keeps up the bleeding for a while longer. These post-leeching "warm fomentations" (1847: 110) are often rendered aromatic by quantities of poppy heads and hops, which are later formed into poultices and directly applied to the bleeding parts. Bostwick's therapeutic regimen thus appears to aim to interfere with the pleasurable associations of semen odor memory in several ways: by associating that odor memory with excruciating sensations in the doctor's office, and by substituting familiar odor sensations coded as disgusting (gas, pus, etc.). If we assume that the text still wants to work on its readers by cueing them to recall odors and their associations, to summon phantom odor sensations, then the therapy may work in some degree on the reader of the book as well as on the patient in the examination room.

If Bostwick's therapy succeeds, his patients will never smell semen again. Their ejaculations will only occur when their penises are inside vaginas. On Bostwick's self-aggrandizing account, his regimens are remarkably successful, achieving cures even in cases other physicians would call hopeless. And while

On Seminal Diseases is, among other things, a promotional device designed
to lure patients to his clinic, it also aims to affect its readers more generally,
warning young men away from the practices that might bring them under
his scary discipline, and encouraging those who are sometime masturbators
to leave off their dangerous self-indulgences before it is too late.

Pornography—there has never been any secret about this—is designed
to induce the whole range of human sexual somatic responses. Bostwick's
tract—and this may be true of many, if not most, comparable texts—
disavows such pornographic intentions, but plainly this disavowal is
somewhat disingenuous. It *needs* to arouse its readers' bodies so as to
associate that arousal effectively with punitive threats. It invites the always-
potentially masturbatory reader, who may initially identify with the sexually
anxious clients of Dr. Bostwick, instead to occupy the physician's scopic,
stigmatizing relationship to the masturbating male body. It invites this reader
to remove himself from the always-potentially-homoerotic relationship of
one masturbating man to another, and instead to occupy the safely-alibied
position of the caring physician in the properly homosocial relationship of
doctor–patient. It invites the male reader, for whom the odor of semen has
had, heretofore, aleatory associations with purposeless, perverse pleasures,
to associate that odor hereafter with scandal, and to associate autoeroticism
hereafter with the other intensely stigmatized odors of the lower bodily
stratum. By stimulating the olfactory *imaginaire*, even by fantasmatically
inducing a proscribed olfactory sensation, Bostwick's *On Seminal Diseases*
addresses itself not only to the monitoring consciences of its readers, but to
their self-pleasuring and self-punishing fleshly bodies.

Bibliography

Barker-Benfield, G.J. (1976), *The Horrors of the Half-Known Life*, New York: Harper &
    Row.
Bataille, G. (1986), *Erotism*, trans. M. Dalwood, San Francisco: City Lights Books.
Bostwick, H. (1847), *A Treatise on the Nature and Treatment of Seminal Diseases, Impotency
    and Other Kindred Affections*, New York: Burgess, Stringer & Co.
Ellmann, R. (1988), *Oscar Wilde*, New York: Knopf.
Engen, T. (1991), *Odor Sensation and Memory*, New York: Praeger.
Foucault, M. (1980), *The History of Sexuality*, vol. 1, trans. R. Hurley, New York: Vintage.
Haller, J.S., and Haller, R.M. (1974), *The Physician and Sexuality in Victorian America*,
    Urbana: University of Illinois Press.
Higginson, T.W. (1862), "The Procession of the Flowers," *The Atlantic Monthly*, 10
    (December): 649–57.
Laqueur, T. (1990), *Making Sex*, Cambridge: Harvard University Press.
MacDonald, R.H. (1967), "The Frightful Consequences of Onanism," *Journal of the
    History of Ideas*, 28: 423–31.
Melville, H. ([1851] 1972), *Moby-Dick; or, The Whale*, New York: Penguin.
Moon, M. (1991), *Disseminating Whitman*, Cambridge: Harvard University Press.

Parkman, F. ([1849] 1982), *The Oregon Trail*, New York: Penguin.

—— (1866), *The Book of Roses*, Boston: Tilton.

Schab, F.R. (1991), "Odor Memory," *Psychological Bulletin*, 109: 242–51.

Sedgwick, E.K. (1990), *Epistemology of the Closet*, Berkeley & Los Angeles: University of California Press.

Spitz, R.A. (1952), "Authority and Masturbation," *The Psychoanalytic Quarterly*, 21: 490–527.

Stoddart, D.M. (1990), *The Scented Ape*, Cambridge: Cambridge University Press.

Whitman, W. (1982), *Complete Poetry and Collected Prose*, New York: Library of America.

26
Queer Smells
Fragrances of Late Capitalism or Scents of Subversion?

Mark Graham

Sight has been described as the modernist sense par excellence (Levin 1993). It is the sense that discriminates, divides and orders the world into mutually exclusive categories. Smell, by contrast, has been dubbed the sense of the postmodern (Classen, Howes and Synnott 1994: 203–5), the sense that confuses categories and challenges boundaries. It is difficult to localize, hard to contain and has the character of flux and transitoriness. If this is acknowledged to be so, then one can immediately note some interesting affinities between the character of smells and recent theorizations of gender and sexuality often gathered under the rubric of "queer." Queer theories are suspicious of categorical neatness, and in particular the heterosexual-homosexual binary that fractures so much of Western culture (Sedgwick 1990; Warner 1994; Seidman 1997: 93). For Judith Butler (1990), gender, sex and sexuality are practical accomplishments that are brought into existence through performative creation. That is to say, gendered norms are repeatedly enacted and create over time the illusion that there are two essential genders—male and female—and that these are expressions of two fundamental sexes. Furthermore, sexual desire ought to occur *between* the two genders in the form of prescribed heterosexuality. In fact, argues Butler, these correspondences, in which gender follows sex and desire follows gender, are themselves the effects of performative acts, not the causes of them. Precisely because they are the results of social practices and not eternal essences, these effects are open to contestation, they are inherently unstable and they are always in a state of actual or potential flux and transition. In short, they are highly reminiscent of smells.

But if smell is the sense of the postmodern, perhaps it also reflects some-thing of the character of late capitalism, the historical, social and economic juncture that has produced postmodern and queer theories—in particular, the tendency of capitalism to dissolve distinctions, to fragment subjectivity, to encourage and even require flux and change (Mandel 1975; Jameson 1984). But if smells and the understanding of them seem to be in tune with the postmodern and late capitalism, as well as theories of gender performativity, it seems reasonable to ask whether they are also complicit in its logic. When, for example, the perfume industry, which has been built on pedaling essences of heterosexual man and heterosexual woman for centuries, appears, at least partly, to have abandoned its heteronormative bias in ways that appear to be queer, just how radical are queer theories themselves? There is another complicity at work here which is also of interest. I refer to the ocularcentrism that has left its mark on queer writings. For the most part, queer theories have tended to preoccupy themselves with visual contestations of heteronormative gender and sexuality. Once the bias is recognized, it may alert theorists to the queer potential of thinking about desire beyond the visual. Scents, then, can provide both a redolent example for assessing the critical impact of queer theories and also the opportunity to broaden the queer sensorium.

Queer Smells

In some advertisements for scents decidedly queer things have been hap-pening. In one advertisement, for *Lynx* (1996) for men, a young woman borrows her boyfriend's cologne. Once outside a woman who passes her on the stairs is transfixed by her scent. Later, when riding the bus, three teenage girls stare longingly at her. Back home, and none too pleased about her experiences, she angrily returns the cologne to her boyfriend who laughs with amusement.

In another television advertisement for *AXE* (1998), a handsome young man in a elevator sprays himself with the cologne while buttoning up his shirt. As he leaves the elevator, another young but far less attractive man enters it. He shares the lift with a succession of women, who, judging by his state of disarray every time the lift doors open, all ravish him between floors. His irresistibility is thanks to the lingering scent of *AXE*. On his final journey, the doors are about to close when they are suddenly forced open by a male hand wearing a fingerless leather glove. The hand belongs to a large, hirsute, leather queen who lecherously eyes the man in the lift. Aware of what he is in for the young man swallows nervously and the rest is left to the imagination. Having been reduced to a sexual toy for the female passengers by the power of the scent, his ultimate degradation is to become the sexual plaything of a gay, leather clone.

What can be said about the logic of desire operating in these advertisements? *Lynx*, the cologne for men, makes the woman that wears it desirable to those people attracted to the male gender. In the advertisement, this is restricted to heterosexual women, but homosexual men ought also to be swayed by the scent. The *AXE* advertisement depicts this with the help of a dubious stereotype of a predatory gay man. By the same logic, the scent that makes a woman irresistible to heterosexual men should also make her the object of lesbian desire. As far as I am aware, no advertisement portrays lesbian desire like this. Neither do I know of any advertisement in which a heterosexual man mistakenly uses a woman's perfume. If he were to do so, he would presumably become attractive to other heterosexual men and lesbians, but unattractive to gay men and heterosexual women. The transformation of the male heterosexual into an object of attraction for other heterosexual men is, it seems, still too daring for the industry. But whatever the combination of genders involved, desire that conforms exclusively with heterosexual demands appears to have been derailed.

Writings on the performative nature of gender, sex and sexuality challenge the nature of desire when "gender does not necessarily follow from sex, and desire or sexuality generally does not seem to follow from gender" (Butler 1990: 135–6). The logic of desire employed by the perfume industry in the preceding examples in its representations of the sense of smell and the power of scents, which is the logic that interests me here, appears to be in step with performative theories. Indeed, as I shall show, it may have gone a step further in that it seems to have dispensed with the need for sexed and gendered bodies altogether.

Smelly Genders

Many smells are gendered in that they are classed as masculine or feminine. But what if gender is not only ascribed to smells but is itself considered to be a smell? In Melanesia, for example, personhood is a relational matter involving the flow of tangible and intangible elements between persons, persons and animals, and persons and other beings such as ancestors (Strathern 1988). Gender in this cultural context is not understood as an immutable essence or difference. Rather, it is continually created and transformed along with the flow of substances—blood, semen, mother's milk, foods, gifts, odors—between persons. Among the Hua of New Guinea, the odors of menstruation are considered to be harmful to men who should avoid inhaling in the presence of menstruating women (Meigs 1984). The reason for the various taboos is that the Hua define gender more in terms of fluids and scents than in terms of external anatomy. In other words, gender determining substances are considered to be transactable. They can be passed on between persons and can alter the gender of whoever gives and receives them. However, a shift in gender among the Hua does not automatically translate into a shift in desire. The man who inhales in the presence of a menstruating woman does not thereby start to desire other men. Desire among the Hua is still expected to follow gender, even if gender is not wholly understood as determined by anatomy. Nonetheless, what the Hua example, and others like it from Melanesia, show is that models of gender need neither assume the coincidence of sex and gender nor rely as heavily on visual models of gender difference and essentialist notions of male and female gender as those found in Euro-American societies (see Howes 2003). Developments in the perfume industry point to similar ideas present within Western consumer culture.

The Heteronormative Odor

The recent queer tinkerings with how scents are normally marketed are relatively few and go against the grain of the industry as a whole. Perfumes are still more often sold with the promise that they will bolster or awaken heterosexual desire. In advertising, scents are associated with typically masculine or feminine characteristics and pursuits. *Boss for Men* has been advertised as a "commanding fragrance." Could it perhaps be fifty milliliters of patriarchal authority? *Givenchy Gentleman* suggests that the buyer think of it as "investment spending." Is it bottled business acumen? Bijan manufactures *DNA for Men*. It is sold in a bottle shaped like a DNA strand. The suggestion is that the scent contains the building blocks of masculinity. The product description is cryptic: "*DNA* fragrances do not contain deoxyribonucleic acid (DNA) except as included in the ingredient list on product packaging" (Classen, Howes and Synnott 1994: 191). In one of the advertisements for *DNA*, from 1993, the designer Bijan is shown holding his baby son in his arms while his young daughter kisses the baby's knee. The top caption in the advertisement reads: "DNA ... it's the reason you have your father's eyes, your mother's smile ... Bijan's perfume." The bottom caption reads: "Bijan with *his* DNA ... son Nicolas and daughter Alexandra." The message here is once again cryptic, and perhaps one shouldn't expect too much exactitude from a perfume advertisement as the genre is notable for its vagueness. What the caption seems to be suggesting is that the scent is somehow an essential expression of who you are in the same way as Bijan's own children are genetic expressions of who he is (although no more than fifty per cent). *DNA* is a product that derives its character from vague similarities to heterosexual reproduction.

The claim, however implicit, that scents supplement the gender of heterosexual men and women and awaken or reinforce their desirability for the "other" sex is one that raises some troubling questions for a heteronormative model of desire. Marketing strategies that sell scents as substances able to enhance and supplement a gender that is inadequate admit that the aspects of gender that are sexually desirable are at least partially constructed. Much advertising presents men and women in conventionally gendered behaviors and settings at the same time as their gendering appears to be constantly in need of supplementation in the form of consumer durables. Heteronormative gender is portrayed as a precarious accomplishment, one that can never be taken for granted, and one that is never finished: lack haunts it perpetually.

One very simple and perhaps reassuring way to explain this lack is to attribute it to chemical imbalance. *Herbal Sensations* is a preparation that is said to work by traveling throughout the body freeing testosterone (www.herbalsensations.com). Testosterone, the Internet advertisement for the substance reports, stimulates sexual activity in men and women, but with advancing age it becomes bound to various compounds in the body and sexual stimulation declines. Among its effects *Herbal Sensations* counts firmer erections for men, more multiple orgasms and climaxes, solving impotency problems, restoring women's interest in sex, lowering cholesterol and relieving premenstrual tension and prostate problems. The advertisement also comes with the assurance about the preparation: "[A very] important point for women is that it FREES UP, and does not ADD testosterone to the body. So you maintain your natural balance and [do] not have to worry about becoming masculine! (The difference is YOU may be pursuing HIM!)." *Herbal Sensations* locates sexual drive in testosterone, a substance locked inside the body but one that can alter gendered behavior—women become more sexually predatory. As the advertising hastens to assure potential buyers, the sexuality remains firmly within heteronormative bounds. But what of other preparations that are said to be capable of influencing desire in ways that dispense with gender and sexual preference altogether?

Bottled Gay: *INTENSE*, the Homonormative "Scent"

INTENSE, "The World's First Gay Pheromone Product," is advertised as "the scent of a man." *INTENSE* is supposed to contain the "gay pheromone" N10Z. It is a "pheromone splash" developed exclusively for 10% PRODUCTIONS (www.10percent.com, an Internet retailer of goods aimed at the gay and lesbian market) with the gay male consumer in mind. The advertising leaflet that accompanies the "scent" explains that some people are mysteriously more attractive than others and that this has been shown to be caused by the power of pheromones, natural attractants that send airborne signals from the body to other people. The pheromones work by stimulating the vomeronasal organ (VNO) which is found in humans a few centimeters inside the nose in the form of a small pit. Some scientists claim that it is connected to the hypothalamus, "the gland in the brain which triggers the chemicals responsible for emotions and desire." Other scientists argue that there are no neural connections between the VNO and the brain and that it may only be a vestigial organ (see Taylor 1997). As much as that may be, scientists at the Human Pheromone Science Institute, the leaflet informs us, have discovered "the proper chemical mixture of human pheromones that can result in same-sex attraction between men." *INTENSE*, readers are told, "is designed for gay men who want to spice up their social life, improve their self-confidence and make themselves mysteriously irresistible." The majority of people are odorblind for pheromones, although I have heard *INTENSE* described by someone who can smell them as reminiscent of a "rancid armpit." Its lack of odor allows men to wear it without masking the scent of their favorite cologne. To the question "Does *INTENSE* work?" the leaflet answers "Yes." "Respondents in consumer studies have reported overwhelmingly that *INTENSE* has made them feel more "romantic, alluring, more confident in social situations," and noticed that people tended to cluster around them more." There is "significant evidence," the leaflet claims, from studies carried out at the Chemical Senses Center in Philadelphia, PA, the University of Utah School of Medicine and other research centers that pheromones affect the behaviors of those exposed to them. Researchers at the University of Kentucky, it is claimed, "discovered that subjects exposed to pictures of men that were sprayed with the human pheromones found these pictures more sexually attractive than pictures of men that were not sprayed with pheromones." In England, a test was done on national television—although the program is not named—using twin brothers. One brother was sprayed with the pheromone and then both brothers were introduced to test subjects. The sprayed twin was found to be more attractive than the unsprayed. And, finally, a chair in a dentist's waiting room that had been sprayed with pheromones was the one most likely to be chosen by patients. But whatever the promises made by *INTENSE* the leaflet is careful to point out that the "splash" is *not* an aphrodisiac: "*INTENSE* simply adds more pheromones to your body which increases the chance that someone will receive and be stimulated by them."

Apparent in the advertising brochure for *INTENSE* is a notion of essentialism. The erotic desire of men for men can quite literally be bottled in the form of *INTENSE*. This goes very much against the grain of queer theoretical critiques of sexual types and the necessary coincidence of sex, genders and desires that are part of heteronormative and indeed homonormative regimes. *INTENSE* appears to be a homonormative scent. But what is also apparent from the advertising blurb is that the desires elicited by *INTENSE* and other pheromone combinations need not be confined to relations between gay men, or even humans in general; a dentist's chair has the potential to become desirable.

At first glance, it seems that *INTENSE* contains a specific "gay pheromone," N10Z, but a careful reading of the advertising leaflet makes it clear that *INTENSE* contains "the proper chemical mixture of human pheromones that can result in same-sex attraction between men." This would suggest that a skilled chemist could concoct all manner of pheromone combinations able to stimulate sexual attraction between every conceivable gender and sexual mix: heterosexual males for homosexual males, heterosexual females for homosexual females who have been doused in the pheromones of a heterosexual male, transsexual M2F for F2M, M2F for M2F, and so on. The combinatorial possibilities are many. Don't forget the dentist's chair!

Pheromone preparations for heterosexuals are also commercially available. One such product is *APC for Men*. APC stands for Androstenone Pheromone Concentrate. The email that brought this product to my attention introduced it with a promise: "Be a magnet that ONLY ATTRACTS WOMEN!!" (www. apcformen.com). The reassurance suggests some degree of nervousness about who will be magnetized by the concentrate. Who else but women does it have in mind? The advertising does not say, but it does provide some interesting examples from the animal kingdom to illustrate the potency of pheromones. "Scientists have long known that certain hormones, called pheromones, trigger strong sexual desire in animals. This is the reason that male dogs are driven crazy by a female in heat." And: "In animals and insects this "chemical compound" is irresistible. For example, when a glass rod is doused with pheromones from a female cockroach, the males go crazy and actually try to mate with the rod." APC promises to be the "quick and easy way for men like you to attract the women you've always dreamed about. *Beautiful women, that up until now, were out of reach.*" Why were they out of reach? The advertisement provides the answer: "until now, you used to need exotic [sic] cars and good looks to attract certain women, *the women we really want.*" But according to the advertisement appearances—good looks and the right car—are no longer necessary. The chemicals will do the job as women "subconsciously detect the pheromones and … suddenly find you more sexually attractive."

The nervous assurances about only attracting women, together with the implicit understanding that it will not attract other men, and the use of crude zoological comparisons between heterosexual attraction and rutting dogs and cockroaches cannot save these advertisements, and also the advertisement for *INTENSE*, from a dilemma. They have admitted one of the main arguments of queer theory, namely, that desire does *not* necessarily follow gendered persons. Desire in the form of a smell is understood to be a quality in its own right. It is a force of attraction, that can be congealed into an object—in this case a scent—and enjoy a life of its own. This receives comic expression in one of the most recent *AXE* (2002) advertisements for men's cologne. In it a young man sprays himself with the scent and immediately becomes attractive to women. He is bitten on the chest by a mosquito—it too finds him irresistible—which is eaten by a frog. The frog then immediately goes on to mate with another frog. The unfortunate amphibian is caught in a net and served as frog's legs at a French restaurant where the old man who eats them immediately attracts the attention of a beautiful young woman. They are about to consummate their passion when he dies of heart failure.

In his grave the worms eat him and one of them ends up in a tequila bottle. A young man in a Mexican bar swallows the worm along with his tequila and immediately attracts the attention of the women in the bar ...

Even if this saga of nomadic desire is a product of the advertiser's fantasy, it points nonetheless to a theory of attraction that is at variance with Western heteronormative regimes in which sex, gender and desire ought all to coincide. (There are even examples of cross-species erotic attraction present.) Although intended to effect just such a coincidence, the logic in the advertisements in fact ensures its disruption (assuming that the scents work), because desire is located in the fragrance, not in the consumer who uses it. Hence, the attraction the cologne elicits bears no necessary relationship to the sex or gender of the person wearing it. The genie of desire has been let out of the perfume bottle and is on the loose.

A World without Gender: The Unisex Scent

In 1994, Calvin Klein released *CKOne*, the company's first unisex fragrance. The scent is described as "clear, pure and contemporary with a refreshingly new point of view." Two years later Calvin Klein released another unisex fragrance, *CKBe*. This time: "Calvin Klein takes a closer look at who we are within this ageless, raceless, genderless world." It does more. "It invites us to take risks, make mistakes, be unpredictable. It invites us to close our eyes, to open our minds, and to dream" (www.scentagious.com). The advertising text for *CKBe* is particularly striking for its utopian and disembodied description of the world as one without age, race or gender.

Recent business rhetoric that extols the virtues of diversity argues that discrimination on the grounds of age, race and gender is detrimental to global capitalist production. Companies that want to survive in a competitive market require a diverse workforce to ensure their flexibility and ability to innovate. They must be able to sell their goods and services to a diverse range of consumers who want to feel recognized, not exploited or ignored, by corporate businesses. But the new production processes of global capitalism have not abolished class (Harvey 1996). On the contrary, new forms of class inequality and injustice have appeared in their wake in the lowest levels of the Western service sectors and in developing countries. It is surely significant that the advertisement for *CKBe* does not claim that the world is classless. Moreover, the dream of disembodiment, it is important to recall, has been a fantasy of the male Western philosophical tradition for millennia (Bordo 1993). The apparently positive message of the advertising rests, therefore, on some problematic silences and assumptions about class, gender and the body.

The two scents from Calvin Klein are by no means the only unisex scents on the market, other examples include *Bvlgari Black* by Bvlgari, *Chevrefeuille* from the exclusive House of Creed and *Dalimix* by Salvador Dali. *Dalimix*, which was launched in 1996, the same year as *CKBe*, is sold in a bottle shaped like a man's chin below a woman's mouth. Was this the transsexual scent of the 1990s? The desire these scents are supposed to elicit does not operate within the neatly dichotomized channels of a heteronormative gender system. Its direction is unclear and its form protean. In the case of *CKBe*, it seems that no differences are necessary at all in order to drive desire, and one is left wondering how desire ever gets started in the first place.

This short, fragrant journey started with conventional heteronormative scents, continued on past homonormative scents and finished with unisex scents. For heteronormative scents, desire is essentialized as part of a two-sexed and two-gendered world and occurs *between* two sexes and two genders, although the heteronormative scents do occasionally acknowledge, albeit nervously, that desire may be independent of gender and sex. In the case of *INTENSE*, a homonormative scent, desire is also essentialized and enhanced *within* the same sex and gender. But *INTENSE* is marketed as a chemical that can be bottled, and that has the capacity to elicit desire for objects that are not sexed or gendered in any conventional sense. Indeed, the object of desire may even be inanimate. The unisex scents elicit desire that can be both between and within sexes and genders. In fact, it is not always clear if there are sexes and genders in this "genderless" world. These latter fragrances are scents for a generalized humanity without essences. To varying degrees all three kinds of scent loosen the ties between sex, gender and desire. And in all three cases, desire can or does break free of a two-sex/two-gender order. In the case of unisex scents, sex and gender fade in an androgynous world and it is unclear if sexual desire persists at all.

Flexible Fragrances

Why is it that such apparently innocuous commodities as perfumes and colognes, which, if anything, have been used to bolster heteronormative gender, have been resignified as desire that is free-floating from any natural, that is to say anatomical, substrate? If the perfume industry has been willing to dispense with gender as part of a marketing experiment at about the same time as queer theories of gender performativity took off, then just how radical are these theories?

According to the advertising for *CKBe*, the consumers of unisex fragrances are without age, race or gender. They are blank slates on which desire can be sprayed. These unisex fragrances can be worn by anyone and, as such, are flexible fragrances capable of producing desiring effects among any combination of people independently of the qualities of the object of desire. The "flexibility" of unisex scents does clearly resonate with the characteristics of late-capitalist production in which workers are flexible, and adaptable to the shifting demands of the production process. Such flexibility is needed to guarantee the business performance of companies in a rapidly changing market.

Rosemary Hennessy (2000), while not wanting to abandon the critical take on heteronormativity afforded by queer theoretical approaches, sees them as complicit with commodification and consumer culture. Flexible gender codes, fluid sexualities and sexual identities, she argues, resonate and are compatible with the mobility and adaptability required of service workers, and the new fluid forms of the commodity (2000: 108–9). Employing a similar materialist critique, Max Kirsch (2000) sees elements of queer theory as promoting individualism and the fragmentation of working-class struggle. In short, according to these authors there is nothing in queer approaches to sexuality and gender to disrupt capitalism, even if it may challenge some aspects of the heteronormative order.

In *The Transparency of Evil* (1990), Jean Baudrillard argues that contemporary existence occurs in a trans-world. This is a world marked by a confusion of boundaries, a promiscuous intersecting of states and a loss of specificity and difference in a world of movement in which everything is always *trans*itional. Baudrillard himself uses the term "transsexual" to refer to what he sees as the breakdown of the categories of gender and sex. He also argues that this transsexual state of affairs extends to the breakdown of boundaries between economic, political and aesthetic domains. Baudrillard's vision is that of an actual and potential world in which signifiers are cut adrift from signifieds, and "race," "class" and "gender" no longer unambiguously denote any object. Subjects in this world do not express a natural substrate nor do they arise within a post-structural logic of relations of positive and negative value, the homosexual negatively opposed to heterosexual, black versus white, high culture versus low culture, labor versus capital and so forth. Rather, the identities of subjects are not straightforwardly relative to anything. In such a world, where there are no clear relations between things, value is difficult to assign and becomes *ambi*-valent (although this does not mean that inequalities grounded in them disappear). According to Baudrillard, the value that has displaced that of the natural and structural logics is that of the fractal (1990: 5). The fractal repeats itself. It generates itself from within itself and not in relation to others against which it must be defined.

Does such a world have its own distinctive odor? What fragrance would *one* choose if *one* simply wants to *be* what *one* is while escaping insertion into an invidious system of gender and sex distinctions? If the advertisers are to be believed, *CKOne* and *CKBe* would seem to be good choices. They belong to a world lacking in basic distinctions between age, race and gender. In short, they exist in a world of positives. It is no coincidence that the advertising for *CKBe* "invites us to close our eyes, to open our minds, and to dream." Once again, a parallel with Melanesia can be drawn. As Gell points out, among the Umeda of New Guinea, the word for "dream" (*yinugwi*) is close to that for "smell" (*nugwi*). For the Umeda, smells are like dreams in which things usually hidden, that is to say unavailable to vision, are revealed (Gell 1977: 32). Closing down the visual shuts out the greatest device for making clear-cut distinctions. Vision is the sense of differentiation par excellence. How unlike it is to the sense of smell and the shifting, fluctuating and imprecise qualities of its objects, odors.

Beyond the Visual: Expanding the Queer Sensorium

Appearance is held up as one of the cornerstones of desire in psychoanalysis. Freud locates one of the decisive moments in the development of infant sexuality in the dis-cover-y that the mother lacks the penis/phallus. And although this scene of reve(a)lation is not supposed to be taken too literally, its visual bias is clear enough. This ocularcentrism is even more apparent in Lacan's writings. For Lacan, the ego is precipitated through its recognition of itself in the mirror. This is the "theater" of the ego's emergence in which it is able to view (*thea*) itself (Borch-Jacobsen 1991: 43–71). The dominance of the visual in Freud's and Lacan's work is inseparable from the subsequent gendering of the subject and how it is channeled into the correct form of object choice, that is heterosexual desire. How ironic, then, that smell, the "lowest" of the senses in the West, is presented as capable of undermining this, the highest stage of sexual development, at least in a heteronormative order.

Normative heterosexuality owes its always contingent integrity and exist-ence to what it is not. It is *not* homosexuality, it is *not* the perversions, it is *not* a sin. Abjected to outside the heterosexual citadel, the sexual others of the heteronormative regime constantly threaten to storm the gates and are always a ghostly presence that haunts any definition of what heterosexuality is. This is not a comfortable state of affairs for an ideology that demands that it be crystal clear where heterosexuality begins and ends. One consequence, as queer theorists have pointed out, is that heterosexuality's integrity is dependent on what and where it is not. It constantly refers beyond itself to an elsewhere. Such a post-structuralist view of meaning is distinctly odoriferous.

Like meaning, smells refer beyond themselves to an elsewhere. A smell links the person who smells the odor or scent with its source. Odors act as a bridge between persons and the material world around them for the smell that enters your nostrils is but a diluted form of the object that emits the smells. Smells also bridge distances between people in a very tangible manner. The smell of another person cannot be ignored short of refusing to breathe. One can close one's eyes against offending sights and efforts can be made to reduce noise, but smells, and especially offensive odors, are insistent and unavoidable. In short, olfaction confuses and violates boundaries. Smells are also transient. A smell may be present one moment and absent the next. Smells shift position and it is often difficult to determine exactly where they begin and end. It has been noted that odors are very often present in rites of passage (Howes 1987) where smells are employed to symbolize transitions and shifts in status (Gell 1977: 27). The ability of smells to transcend boundaries is exploited in the use of incense in rituals. Inhaling the incense binds together the congregation and makes everyone olfactory participants in the proceedings, whether they like it or not.

It is the transient and elusive qualities of fragrances and aromas that lend them their appeal. Scents are often described in a language remarkable for its lack of precision. Adjectives like "mysterious," "evocative," "suggestive," "enigmatic" and "ineffable" abound. Just think of the language of wine connoisseurs as they struggle to find words to describe a wine's bouquet (Lehrer 1983). Some perfume advertisements dispense with words entirely. It is only a small step from this to abolishing the scent altogether to maximize its mystery and ineffability. Try to describe an odorless scent. And yet this odorless "scent" now exists in the form of *INTENSE* and other pheromone products, and, moreover, they are meant to be the most seductive of them all and the most mysterious and discreet in the way they weave their magic.

While it is certainly true that the visual and the auditory also include many instances of sights and sounds that are difficult, if not impossible, to contain within a semantic framework, the olfactory surely qualifies as the most slippery. If gender and desire can be understood as free-floating qualities that can occur in different combinations, whether it be the gendered fluids and smells of the Hua or gay pheromones, is there something about smells that makes them suitable for the task of embodying these qualities? Is the olfactory the queerest of the senses? The question is intriguing, but my main aim here is not to award the prize for the queerest sense. I do not believe that any sense is inherently more or less queer. The extent to which different senses lend themselves to a queer project is historically and culturally variable. Rather, I want to argue that the queer sensorium should be broadened to include senses other than the visual.

The ocularcentrism of Western cultures extends into models of gender, sex and desire and queer theories have not freed themselves from it. Starting with Butler's own attention to drag (Butler 1990: 136–9), the theatrical dimension of the "performative" is evident in the choice of examples (see, for example, Smith 1999). Ocularcentrism is part of Euro-American cultural common sense and it informs the theoretical sense too. If the "common sense" "senses" are examined with a mind to broadening the "theoretical sense" (cf. Herzfeld 1997: 305), then a deeper understanding of one's own ethnocentrism in the field of gender, sexuality and desire may be provided. There is no room here to speculate about what touches, pressures or caresses might count as queer. Or to ask which tastes blended into sweet or sour, smooth and mellow, or sharp and tangy combinations can send taste buds into queer spasms. This is still largely uncharted territory. A few attempts have, however, been made within musicology to identify queerness in sound.

Of Schubert's *Unfinished Symphony*, Susan McClary writes that "the opening theme becomes a pretext for deflection and exploration," and that "it invites us to forgo the security of centered, stable tonality, and, instead to experience—and even enjoy—a flexible sense of self." "Schubert's movement," she writes, "resembles uncannily some of the narrative structures that gay writers and critics are exploring today" (1994: 215, 233). The falsetto, excessive vibrato and trill in singing have all at one time or another been seen as unnatural, or even degenerate forms of vocal expression. Why the fuss? Virtuoso singers were denounced in 1755 for their "monstrous inversion of things" and because "they over do, confound and disfigure every thing" (Kostenbaum 1993: 165, 168, 184). They did not conform to a structure and were difficult to classify. They "deviated" and were too flexible. It would seem that their voices were like smells.

Conclusion

The criticism that queer theories of sexuality and gender merely reflect and are complicit with the logic of late-capitalist production and consumer culture, may not be entirely groundless, but nor is it entirely fair. As a critical enterprise, queer theories of gender and sexuality are ambiguously positioned as they must to some extent inhabit and thus run the risk of seeming to endorse the very order they seek to question. Indeed, there is an ambiguity at the very heart of capitalism, not least in its relationship to desire. In *Anti-Oedipus*, Deleuze and Guattari (1984) argue that capitalism operates along two vectors simultaneously. It subverts or "deterritorializes" the traditional constraints on an individual's desires at the same time as it attempts to "reterritorialize" desire within the state, the oedipal family and consumerism. The ways in which desire is presented as a smell display a similar ambiguity. On the one hand, they are meant to confirm heteronormative and homonormative demands in the form of commodities and yet on the other are sold as commodities that undermine them in ideas about a potentially nomadic and disruptive desire. These are the queer smells that seem to have escaped territorialization within oedipalized bodies. But have they thereby freed themselves from the culture of late capitalism?

Some of the more egregious results of a simplistic voluntarist theory of desire, when placed at the service of commodity capitalism, are evident in the utopian promise made by scents like *CKBe*: becoming an object of desire requires no more effort than choosing your eau de cologne. These scents promise the wearer identity choices that are divorced from structural inequalities of class and race, and a genderless world that echoes male fantasies of disembodiment. Such fantasies are parasitic on a visualism that supports the illusion of a distant and disengaged regard, rather than embodied, sensual involvement with others in the often messy and frequently unjust particularities of life. Yet when located more explicitly within the context of late capitalism, queer interrogations of gender and sexuality can also help to facilitate critical assessment and engagement with the forms of voluntarism implied by these scents. The voluntarism these consumer choices imply, and of which these selfsame queer theories are sometimes accused, challenges the heteronormative logic of sex, gender and desire which has been a mainstay of the perfume industry and which permeates society. They provide Western consumers with an alternative olfactory imaginary that is at least suggestive of other gender and sexual possibilities, even if one is not always convinced of the power of the scents. Smells—the "essences" of desire—flaunt gendered and sexed boundaries and scramble the categories that sustain them as everyone partakes aromatically of everyone else. Desires that are olfactory, but also aural and tactile, may be less easy to compartmentalize and less amenable to a rigid heteronormative and homonormative categorization of gender and sexuality than a distant disembodied participation through the visual. Indeed, if more attention is paid to these senses a greater range and ubiquity of queer desires may be discovered.

The gender-bending of the 1960s onwards was very much about visual culture. It is, therefore, perhaps not surprising that the initial attention of performative theories has largely been to visual phenomena. Manufacturers are now offering desires in a bottle and theories of gender performativity need to catch up with commercial developments. Once more it may be time for the Owl of Minerva to fly off into the dusk—only this time to the strains of Schubert's *Unfinished Symphony* and reeking of *CKBe*.

Bibliography

Baudrillard, J. (1990), *The Transparency of Evil*, trans. J. Benedict, London: Verso.
Bordo, S. (1993), *Unbearable Weight*, Berkeley: University of California Press.
Borsch-Jacobsen, M. (1991), *Lacan: The Absolute Master*, trans. D. Brick, Stanford: Stanford University Press.
Butler, J. (1990), *Gender Trouble*, London: Routledge.
Classen, C., Howes, D. and Synnott, A. (1994), *Aroma*, London: Routledge.
Deleuze, G. and Guattari, F. (1984), *Anti-Oedipus*, London: Athlone Press.
Gell, A. (1977), "Magic, Perfume, Dream…," in I. Lewis (ed.), *Symbols and Sentiments*, London: Academic Press.
Gregor, T. and Tuzin, D. (eds) (2001), *Gender in Amazonia and Melanesia*, Berkeley: University of California Press.
Harvey, D. (1996), *Justice, Nature and the Geography of Difference*, Oxford: Blackwell.
Hennessey, R. (2000), *Profit and Pleasure*, New York: Routledge.
Herzfeld, M. (1997), "Anthropology: A Practice of Theory," *International Social Sciences Journal*, 153: 301–18.
Howes, D. (1987), "Olfaction and Transition," *Canadian Review of Sociology and Anthropology*, 24 (3): 398–416.
—— (2003), *Sensual Relations*, Ann Arbor: The University of Michigan Press.
Jameson, F. (1984), "Postmodernism, or the Cultural Logic of Late Capitalism," *New Left Review*, 146: 53–93.
Kirsch, M.H. (2000), *Queer Theory and Social Change*, London: Routledge.

Kostenbaum, W. (1993), *The Queen's Throat*, New York: Vintage Books.

Lehrer, A. (1983), *Wine and Conversation*, Bloomington: Indiana University Press.

Levin, D. (ed.) (1993), *Modernity and the Hegemony of Vision*, Berkeley: University of California Press.

McClary, S. (1994), "Constructions of Subjectivity in Schubert's Music," in P. Brett, E. Wood and G. Thomas (eds), *Queering the Pitch*, New York: Routledge.

Mandel, E. (1975), *Late Capitalism*, London: New Left Books.

Meigs, A. (1984), *Food, Sex and Pollution*, Brunswick, NJ: Rutgers University Press.

Sedgwick, E.K. (1990), *Epistemology of the Closet*, Harmondsworth: Penguin

Seidman, S. (1997), *Difference Troubles*, Cambridge: Cambridge University Press.

Smith, P.J. (ed.) (1999), *The Queer Sixties*, New York: Routledge.

Strathern, M. (1988), *The Gender of the Gift*, Berkeley: University of California Press.

Synnott, A. (1993), *The Body Social*, London: Routledge.

Taylor, R. (1997), "The Sixth Sense," *New Scientist*, 616: 36–40.

Warner, M. (ed.) (1994), *Fear of a Queer Planet*, Minneapolis: University of Minnesota Press.

In Noritoshi Hirakawa's
Garden of Nirvana

Jennifer Fisher and Jim Drobnick

I defy any amateur of painting to love a picture as much as a fetishist loves a shoe.

Georges Bataille (Foster 1996)

An unsettling dissonance exists between the metaphysical title of Noritoshi Hirakawa's installation, *Garden of Nirvana*, and its earthy materiality. Contrary to what might be imagined by the evocative words—a sylvan retreat, a lush tropical grotto, a serene oasis—the installation is banally comprised of a number of women's underwear clamped to metallic hoops suspended above visitors' heads. Formally, it is a study in contrasts: delicate, droopy clothing held by a clinical, industrial apparatus. An attentive viewer can easily make out stains, frayed edges, and other marks of wear on the intimate apparel, although some look department store fresh. Any question of whether they are "real" or not is answered not by sight, but by the sense of smell. One may readily rise on tiptoe to get within sniffing distance, but for most visitors, the vinegary, musky odor detected upon entering the room is proof enough of their bodily provenance. A sign that reads "Dear Miss, Thank you for contributing your white(y) panties. Right now! N.H." and points in the direction of a private changing room, ostensibly reveals the method by which the articles were procured: voluntary donation. It soon becomes obvious that the aromatic "chandeliers" of panties are not the only element of this spectacle—we too are on display, by both passersby gazing through the street-level window and by the gallery attendant.

The label "provocateur" inevitably arises when artists address sexual taboos and bodily processes. With the work of Hirakawa, a photographer

320

who has also worked in audio, video, performance and installation, the label is certainly fitting, yet doesn't go far in explaining the affective power of some of his work. In a positive vein, one could argue that Hirakawa focuses on highlighting and transgressing restrictive moral codes that, for the most part, center on the body. His photographs record individuals (mostly women) breaking the confines of moral inhibitions and disciplined behavior. Photographing women in men's restrooms, for instance, or the puddle resulting from women urinating in the street, challenges societal conventions regarding the gendering of public space and inconsistent norms of acceptable bodily conduct. Hirakawa is also an impresario of the hidden and overlooked. In collecting and displaying objects that bear traces of the body, such as menstrual pads and underwear, the artist attempts to recuperate corporeal processes that society shuns and endeavors to render invisible. The homogenizing dictates of culture are candidly subverted by Hirakawa's portrayal of the diversity of personal desires and physiological needs.

Yet even as this work confronts the arbitrary controls placed upon pleasure and the body, disturbing questions emerge concerning the politics of representing, objectifying and commodifying his "collaborators" and the products of their bodies. Hirakawa likens his practice—in which strangers are encouraged to act out suppressed desires—to sociological investigations. That his subjects are mostly women, however, immediately raises suspicions of patriarchal manipulation, whether the activity is framed as art or social science. Coercion may not be directly present, but troubling aspects of voyeurism and exploitation permeate these works, implicating viewers in a realm of foggy gender politics. While some critics such as Jean-Christophe Ammann (1993) align Hirakawa's work with the iconic scandals of Manet and Courbet, raising the legacy of the avant-garde is not necessarily an effective legitimating strategy. As works such as *Olympia* and *Origins of the World*, and Hirakawa's, contest a certain type of bourgeois puritanism, they also problematically reiterate the privilege of male desire. The collaborators' disclosures, which have been harvested in the promise of a liberating friendship, are provided few safeguards against potential misuse. This is perhaps most evident in Hirakawa's series of photographs, *Dreams of Tokyo*, which features women looking into the camera and exposing their crotches. While the work includes the proviso that it can never be shown in Japan—to protect the reputations of the subjects—this doesn't prevent their images from being published in reviews and articles distributed in that country.

The history of women's underwear in the West confirms its connection between the parallel constructions of taboo and male desire. Fashion historians Anne Hollander (1978: 132–4) and Valerie Steele (1996: 115–41) have traced the trajectory of underwear from being "an absolute masculine prerogative" (i.e. worn only by men) to an erotic obsession when adopted by women. Long taboo for any respectable woman, a "dirty-minded" interest in women's underpants arose as pant-like undergarments began to be worn by middle class women in the 1850s. Before this time any separation of women's legs by cloth had been regarded as obscene or unholy. Pants were worn only by female acrobats and prostitutes, and such professions were viewed as sexually depraved. This legacy of sexual taboo intensified the eroticism associated with women's underpants. In Paris the can-can teased the audience with suggestive views of frilly underwear. Eventually even "virtuous wives" began to artfully conceal their genitals in seductive play which intensified the thrill of exposure in what Steele calls, because it is so commonplace, "normal" fetishizing (1996: 164).

The focus that *Garden of Nirvana* places on the sensorial aspects of panties—their stains, smell and textures—characterizes, in Steele's terms, that of a "true" fetishist. Whereas normal fetishism is directed toward the artifacts of a specific person, the true fetishist is aroused by the smell and feel of the panties themselves (1996: 124). Steele relates how, in Japan, vending machines have been stocked with underpants "guaranteed to have been worn by a Japanese schoolgirl" at $30 apiece. Describing a context where Japanese law prohibits the representation of female pubic hair, yet where no-panty cafes and panty auctions are longstanding popular attractions, Steele notes that "the ubiquity in Japan of panty voyeurism is so great that not only specialist fetish magazines, but also mainstream periodicals cater to it" (Steele 1996: 123).

Garden of Nirvana equates women and flowers, with odor being the experiential link. Likewise, the writer Octave Uzanne compares a woman in lingerie to a flower, "whose innumerable petals become more and more beautiful and delicate as you reach the sweet depths of the innermost petals. She is like a rare orchid, who surrenders the fragrance of her mysteries only in the intimacies of love" (Steele 1996: 117). Interest in the "fragrant mysteries" associated with women's clothing is classically known as "perversion" in the sexology and psychoanalytic literature. Freud, for instance, conceded the vital connection between sexuality and olfaction in the animal kingdom, yet relegated it to an inconsequential status in humans. In the evolutionary scheme of development, humankind had risen up onto two legs, thus diminishing the role of smell; to link sex and smell again carries with it the danger of regression, of the re-emergence of the animal, in short, the threat of psychosis or neurosis (see Brill 1932; Freud 1961: 46–7; Krafft-Ebing 1998). Neglecting to distinguish between the proper objects of disgust and desire elicits condemning nomenclatures such as infantilism and coprophilia. Yet, as Steele and others have argued, defining conclusively what constitutes "normal" and "deviant" behavior is an impossible task, one hopelessly compromised by ideological and other biases. Not the least of which is the sexist rhetoric used to situate and enforce gender relations: women who fail to live up to the fragrant mystery of Uzanne "are traitors to the ideal of femininity and objects of disgust" (Classen, Howes and Synnott 1994: 164).

Historian Alain Corbin (1986) traces the contemporary intolerance towards odor back to the Enlightenment and the development of an "olfactory vigilance" in regards to bodily emanations and civic space. The project of modernity has also involved a rationalization of the senses, in which vision was prioritized to such a degree that "olfactory silence" was a direct outcome (Classen, Howes and Synnott 1994: 1–10). The conflation of desire and disgust promulgated in *Garden of Nirvana* thus taps into two centuries of odor anxiety, both in the personal and public realms. Hirakawa violates not only the assumed predominance of the visual in the ideology of the gallery, but also one's sense of private space and identity. The enforced intimacy is confrontational—the odor is unavoidable, one cannot help but to breathe it in. In some ways the piece positions itself as a litmus test of sensitivity and sensibility: How quickly does one react? Is it prudishly or pruriently? A decision based on instinct or intellect? Regardless of the response, odor is the key element in confusing the segregated domains of the biological and the social, the somatic and the semiotic.

Besides the allusions to fetishism, one might also be inclined to reflect upon *Garden of Nirvana* in the context of Buddhist practices. Does the installation trivialize nirvana as a ribald "heaven" of "getting-into-women's-pants" or does it have more subtle implications? Nirvana describes the state of final emancipation, a state beyond attachment. Literally the term means "blown out," a combination of the Sanskrit *van* (to breathe or blow), with *nir* (the negation). It encompasses a blissful experience of knowing the absolute, which is distinct from quotidian consciousness, yet undefinable. Being "blown away" thus evokes the obliviousness of care, induced by the intoxication, joy or ecstasy of the state of nirvana.

Relevant to this installation are Buddhist spiritual practices that have deployed the outrageous to collapse dualist distinctions between the sacred and profane. A popular Zen story illustrates a method of seeking enlightenment in the most repugnant of objects: when a master was asked "What is the Buddha?," he answered "That pile of excrement in the courtyard." There is a tradition within Buddhism of meditation on what is "disgusting"—corpses, skulls or feces—in order to cultivate dispassion (see Hamilton 1995; Collins 1997). Yet at the same time, nirvana, in Tantric and Zen traditions, can be found both through the deliberate heightening of the senses as well as through the ascetic control of them. In bringing the focus to what is conventionally "disgusting," *Garden of Nirvana* can be contemplated as a clash of tasteful and distasteful objects, ugly and beautiful experiences, desirable and repulsive sensations. The Buddha, reputedly, never articulated what nirvana *was*, only what it *was not*. Both underwear (by being concealed) and odor (by its ethereality) are provocative metaphors for the state of nirvana, which exists everywhere yet is invisible.

Garden of Nirvana evidences the materiality of bodily processes that resides on the razor's edge between revelation and offense. Smell here has an anarchic potential. Despite its supposed primality, it is suffused with cultural problematics. It provides an ineluctable encounter that at once exposes and exceeds the project of civilization which measures its "success" by the degree of alienation from the body. Whether or not disgust can be defined as a natural or a learned response, or desire as the result of instinct or cultural determination, in either case, the viscerality of the body is unavoidable. Hirakawa constructs an installation where repelling and emancipatory sensations uneasily coexist, where the process of aesthetic negotiation foregrounds the embeddedness of social conditioning, as well its capacity for being overturned.

Bibliography

Ammann, J.-C. (1993), "Noritoshi Hirakawa," in *Noritoshi Hirakawa*, Frankfurt am Main: Museum für Moderne Kunst.

Brill, A.A. (1932), "The Sense of Smell in the Neuroses and Psychoses," *Psychoanalytic Quarterly*, 1: 7–42.

Classen, C., Howes, D. and Synnott, A. (1994), *Aroma*, New York & London: Routledge.

Collins, S. (1997), "The Body in Theravada Buddhist Monasticism," in S. Coakley (ed.), *Religion and the Body*, Cambridge: Cambridge University Press, pp. 185–204.

Corbin, A. (1986), *The Foul and the Fragrant*, Cambridge MA: Harvard University Press.

Foster, H. (1996), *The Return of the Real*, Cambridge MA & London: MIT Press.

Freud, S. (1961), *Civilization and Its Discontents*, trans. J. Strachey, New York: Norton.

Hamilton, S. (1995), "From the Buddha to Buddhaghosa," in J.M. Law (ed.), *Religious Reflections on the Body*, Bloomington & Indianapolis: Indiana University Press, pp. 46–63.

Hollander, A. (1978), *Seeing Through Clothes*, New York: Penguin.

Krafft-Ebing, R. (1998), *Psychopathia Sexualis*, trans. F.S. Klaf, New York: Arcade.

Steele, V. (1996), *Fetish*, Oxford: Oxford University Press.

Part VI

Volatile Art

Preface

[H]e maintained that the sense of smell could procure pleasures equal to those obtained through sight or hearing, each of the senses being capable, by virtue of a natural aptitude supplemented by an erudite education, of perceiving new impressions, magnifying these tenfold, and coordinating them to compose the whole that constitutes a work of art. After all, he argued, it was no more abnormal to have an art that consisted of picking out odorous fluids than it was to have other arts based on a selection of sound waves or the impact of variously colored rays on the retina of the eye; only, just as no one, without a special intuitive faculty developed by study, could distinguish a painting by a great master from a paltry daub, or a Beethoven theme from a tune by Clapisson, so no one, without a preliminary initiation, could help confusing at first a *bouquet* created by a true artist with a potpourri concocted by a manufacturer for sale in grocers' shops and cheap bazaars.

Joris-Karl Huysmans, *Against Nature*

Much like the non-visual senses of touch and taste, the sense of smell has been subject to exclusion and dismissal from the realm of the aesthetic despite the logical argument of Joris-Karl Huysmans, who in the above epigraph maintains the equivalence of light rays, sound waves and aromatic inhalations in prompting aesthetic perceptions. While some philosophers acknowledge an implicit, theoretical potential for fragrance as an artistic medium—Croce, for instance, remarks expansively that "all sense impressions can enter into expressions and aesthetic formulations" (1992: 20)—in most theories smell serves as the test case by which the limits of the aesthetic are set, or as the negative example which foregrounds the virtues and justifies the conventional hierarchy of the visual and musical arts. Arguments mobilized against smell as an aesthetically viable sensory mode range from the arbitrary (since some odors are repugnant, none can be aesthetic), to the biological (smell is a primal and functional sense, too immediate and sensuous for elevated pursuits), to the semantic and physical (smells lack a clearly defined language and an intrinsic structure of order and measurement). The

327

ideological bias in assessing the potential for smell in art by aestheticians is evidenced by the comparisons often utilized, e.g. that the aroma of coffee or the fragrance of a flower cannot possibly compare to an orchestral symphony or large-scale narrative painting. The absence of any mention of an existing olfactory artwork underscores the biased stakes in this debate. To admit smell to the pantheon of arts would undermine the central aesthetic tenets that have been operative for over two centuries: Kant's (1974: 35–7) notion of disinterestedness (smells are too subjective and disturbingly implicate the beholder's body) and Hegel's (1988: 622) privileging of autonomy (olfactory artworks defy stability by utilizing evaporating objects, ethereal ambiences and performative experiences). However, as the texts in this section point out, the qualities of scent which deny it aesthetic viability within traditional aesthetics—evocativeness, intimacy, variability, primality, evanescence and so on—often turn out to be the very qualities most attractive to artists seeking to redefine aesthetic experience. Artists have not waited for theoretical justification in order to incorporate the presence of smells in artworks. They have utilized perfumes, fragrant substances, atomizers and malodorous ambiances regardless of the so-called impossibility of scents and the sense of smell to participate in aesthetic experience. Fragrant artworks, in fact, have appeared in such numbers that it is now possible to conduct investigations into their unique characteristics (see e.g. Roudnitska 1977; Drobnick 1998 and [2002] 2005; Banes 2001). The chapters in this section will examine a few examples of olfactory creativity in Japanese court culture, contemporary art and digital media.

Beyond the ocularcentric definitions of art prevailing in the modern West, smell has generated sophisticated and refined aesthetic experiences in other cultures and eras. Nowhere was this more so than in Japan during the Heian period. This section's discussion of art and scent begins with Aileen Gatten's examination of the Japanese incense ceremony, *kōdō*. Using the eleventh-century novel *The Tale of Genji* and its extended portrayal of an incense contest, Gatten describes a society in which art, life and scent are intimately intertwined. The competition, based on events occurring in elite imperial circles, tests the participants' artistry in blending incense and composing poetry, and becomes a manner of meditating upon the seasons and natural phenomena. Not only is scent the means by which courtiers display artistic skill and demonstrate individualistic taste and discrimination, it is also is the medium for allusive romantic communications, the confirmation of one's social standing, an instigation for aristocratic rivalries, and ultimately the characterization of a person's innermost being. Like the related form of *sadō*, the way of tea, *kōdō* was eventually codified and although its current practice is more leisurely and gamelike, it continues to offer an example of a multisensory aesthetic (see also Morita 1992).

While aestheticians have attempted to establish inherent properties and objective criteria by which to articulate the limits of art and its separation from non-art, many artists, especially avant-garde and contemporary ones, have made it their mission to extend notions of the aesthetic into new domains. Although artistic engagement with scent extends back to the Renaissance, it is within the aesthetic pluralism unleashed in the postwar era that scents have found surprising currency. Aromatic artworks counteract the increasing virtualization of experience and the hegemony of visual media, as well as concentrating on quotidian experiences and the actuality of materials. "Eating Nothing" by Jim Drobnick surveys three kinds of olfactory artworks that pivot on the thematic of cooking aromas, but have strategically dispensed with the presence of food itself. Each of these three thematics—supplying enticing odors but denying food as an exercise in power and torture, using aromas for retail marketing and consumer behavior modification and isolating food smells to evoke nostalgic feelings in home decorating—reveal the increasing integration of olfactory technologies into everyday life. Artists working with smell are keenly aware of such cultural developments, and the works presented in this chapter draw from the contexts of war, advertising and manufactured sentimentality as much as they posit an emergent olfactory counterpolitics.

Clara Ursitti's *Self-Portrait in Scent: Sketch #1* articulates her own identity via a somewhat clinical-looking selection of odorous compounds. The list is the "recipe" of ingredients that have been isolated by state-of-the-art scientific odor analysis and the perceptive nose of her collaborator Dr George Dodd, synthetically recreated in a laboratory and uniquely blended to comprise one of her olfactory artworks. Subsuming self-definition within an invisible mist of aromachemicals, Ursitti reinvents what is traditionally a visual artistic genre. Instead of the isolated and disinterested eye of the pure aesthetic gaze, the artist demands an engaged and interested nose. Ursitti's self-portrait, called a "sketch" because it enumerates only the most evident constituents of her olfactory signature, creates fascination and awe by the sheer complexity of the composition (the number of compounds could eventually be in the hundreds) and demystifies the scapegoated phenomenon of body odor (it's just a cocktail of molecules after all) (Drobnick 2002). In a sense, the artwork continues the discussion of *flaireurs* from Part III and, in an ultimate fashion, manifests Alain Corbin's linking of scent and identity that began in the late eighteenth century but could only be accomplished with contemporary olfactory technologies.

Mark Paterson's "Digital Scratch and Virtual Sniff" assesses the utilizations of olfaction in various forms of media throughout the postwar era, from the augmented cinematic experiences of Smell-O-Vision and Odorama to computer desktop applications introduced by DigiScents and iSmell. Paterson discusses the successes and failures of these and other olfactory media attempts, noting that it is not only technological limitations that defeat effective implementation of truly multisensory multimedia, but also pejorative cultural attitudes against any kind of odoriferous intrusion into entertainment activities or users' home environments. The promises of olfactory media in the recent past have also tended to hyperbolize its capabilities, yet the desire for the inclusion of smell to humanize and de-alienate the circumscribed sensescape of audiovisual technology is a persistent one. Aldous Huxley's "scent organ," with its orchestrations of spices, herbs and musks, prophesied the coming of age for fragrant pursuits, but it may turn out that aromatized emails, videogames and online retailing will be the first olfactory mass media.

Jim Drobnick

Bibliography

Banes, S. (2001), "Olfactory Performances," *TDR*, 45(1): 68–76.
Croce, B. (1992), *The Aesthetic as the Science of Expression and of the Linguistic in General*, trans. C. Lyas, Cambridge: Cambridge University Press.
Drobnick, J. (1998), "Reveries, Assaults and Evaporating Presences," *Parachute*, 89: 10–19.
—— (2002), "Clara Ursitti: Scents of a Woman," *Tessera*, 32: 85–97.
—— ([2002] 2005), "Volatile Architectures," in D. Howes (ed.), *Empire of the Senses*, Oxford: Berg.
Kant, I. (1974), *Anthropology from a Pragmatic Point of View*, trans. M.J. Gregor, The Hague: Martinus Nijhoff.
Hegel, G.W.F. (1988), *Aesthetics*, vol. II, trans. T.M. Knox, Oxford: Clarendon Press.
Huysmans, J.-K. ([1884] 1959), *Against Nature*, Middlesex: Penguin.
Morita, K. (1992), *The Book of Incense*, Tokyo & New York: Kodansha International.
Roudnitska, E. (1977), *L'Esthétique en question*, Paris: Presses Universitaires de France.

28
A Wisp of Smoke
Scent and Character in *The Tale of Genji*

Aileen Gatten

One warm and cloudy day in late October some years ago, I attended a demonstration of *kōdō*, the incense ceremony, at Tennōji in southern Osaka. Our gathering was held in a secluded garden at the edge of the temple grounds. Nearly all the participants wore formal Japanese dress; the ceremony took place in the restrained setting of a tea room. Yet the atmosphere was relaxed, almost playful, for we had been invited to take part in a highly aesthetic amusement: the matching of several kinds of incense.

Although an incense ceremony varies in accordance with the virtuosity of its participants, the goal is the same: to discriminate between three or more varieties of aloeswood incense, and to recognize and identify those which one has sampled previously. In order to accomplish this goal, one must possess a good nose, preferably improved by lessons in the sampling of incense, and an ability to concentrate on the nature of a scent. Even in its simplest forms, the incense ceremony is a combination of intellectual discipline, rare sensations and easy sociability.

A stimulating pastime, I thought as I left the temple. Elegant, serene, exclusive—but is that all there is to it? I had come to the incense ceremony in an attempt to make more tangible my knowledge of the role of incense in the Heian period, and most particularly in the eleventh-century *The Tale of Genji*. Instead I found that the modern ceremony has lost the practicality which, together with its important aesthetic qualities, had defined the Heian view of incense. Where the incense ceremony of today is an art so refined that it makes little inroad into the daily life even of those who study it, incense in the Heian period was an indispensable part of an aristocrat's life.

Incense at that time was not limited to Buddhist ceremonies and the perfuming of clothing and rooms. Nor was it a craft left to merchants. The compounding of incense was an art requiring as much training and skill as any other polite accomplishment: and, like music, poetry or calligraphy, the incense produced by a Heian aristocrat often benefited from closely guarded techniques passed down by illustrious ancestors.

One reason why incense was held in such high esteem arose from the customs of upper-class Heian society. People rarely *saw* each other. Even members of the same sex, if not on close terms, met with a curtain between them. To make matters worse, in the case of romantic conversations, the man might not hear the voice of the woman whom he was courting until the romance reached its later stages. Until then he had to be content with the voice of a lady's maid repeating her mistress' message. Thus, one of the few means of forming an opinion of one's companion was the scent emanating from his or her quarters.

Until the fourteenth century, "incense" in Japan referred to the blending of fragrant wood and other plant and animal products, nearly all of which were obtained from the Middle East, India, Indonesia, Indochina and the Philippines, and imported through China, Korea and later the Ryūkyū Islands. The port of entry for these exotic materials was Dazaifu in northwest Kyushu. From there the incense ingredients were forwarded by the assistant viceroy to the imperial palace and the great houses of the capital. The difficulty and expense of transporting ingredients from such distances insured that they would be always scarce and extremely expensive: hence, the compounding of incense was, from the start, a pastime only of the wealthy. Its leaders were the imperial family, the Fujiwara clan, and certain priests of the great temples of Nara and Kyoto (Yamada 1942: 319–24).

The ingredients for incense fall into two major categories: plant and animal. The plant products are by far the larger, and may be subdivided into fragrant wood—including aloes (*jinkō* or *senkō*), sandalwood (*byakudan*) and camphor (*ryūnō*); fragrant resins—amber (*kunroku*), frankincense (*nyūkō*), benzoin (*ansokkō*), storax (*sogōkō*) and galbanum (*fūshikō*); and dried leaves, roots and flowers, especially those of the pine (*kanshō*) and lily (*ukkonkō*). Animal products consisted mainly of deer musk (*jakō*) and seashells (*kaikō*).

These ingredients, together with various kinds of incense already blended, made their way to Japan in the mid-sixth century, when Buddhism and the accessories necessary for its ritual were introduced from the kingdom of Paekche in southwest Korea. Although incense was originally used in Japan for Buddhist ceremonies, it was quickly secularized by the Nara court. The Shōsōin repository in Nara preserves silver censers, clothes perfumers and sachets from this period.

The art of blending incense reached its peak in the early Heian period. The first recorded incense competition—a gathering to compare the quality of several kinds of incense compounded by the contestants—took place in the early ninth century, under the auspices of Prince Kaya, the seventh son of Emperor Kammu (r. 781–806). The prince, a patron and talented blender of incense, codified the Six Scents (*rokushu*) with Fujiwara Fuyutsugu, the Minister of the Left, in the reign of Emperor Nimmyō (r. 833–50), a period generally regarded as the golden age of incense. During this time the aristocracy stopped using imported Chinese blends, and turned to the manufacture of incense which better reflected Japanese tastes.

The Six Scents, as defined by the twelfth-century *Kunshū Ruishō*, "Selections from the Incense Anthologies," by the poet-priest Jakuren, are as follows: Plum Blossom (*Baika*), Lotus Leaf (*Kayō*), Chamberlain (*Jijū*), Chrysanthemum (*Kikka*), Fallen Leaves (*Rakuyō*), and Black (*Kurobō*). Each scent corresponds to a season, suggested by the name of the scent. Thus Plum Blossom is linked with spring, Lotus Leaf with summer, Chamberlain with the autumn wind and Black with deepest winter. No season is given for the Chrysanthemum and Fallen Leaves incense, although their names indicate that they represent the transition from autumn to winter.

All Six Scents are compounded of the same six ingredients: aloes, cloves, seashells, amber, sandalwood and musk. The quantity of each and the order of combination vary with the scent. Each scent is further defined by the addition of a characteristic seventh element: if spikenard were added to the six ingredients, for example, one would have Lotus Leaf; but if frankincense were added instead, one would have created a Black incense.

The *Kunshū Ruishō* reveals the closely guarded recipes of eminent incense-blenders of the ninth century. A glance at a few famous methods of making incense may prove interesting:

Lotus Leaf. By Lord Kintada.
   Spikenard: one *bu*
   Aloes: seven *ryō*, two *bu*
   Seashells: two *ryō*, two *bu*
   Sandalwood: two *shu*
   Mature lily petals or musk: two *bu*
   Cloves: two *ryō*, two *bu*
   Benzoin: one *bu* (optional)

Plum Blossom. By Prince Kaya.
   Aloes: eight *ryō*, two *bu*
   Seashells: three *ryō*, two *bu*
   Spikenard: one *bu*
   Sandalwood: two *bu*, three *shu*
   Cloves: two *ryō*, two *bu*
   Musk: one *bu*
   Amber: one *bu*

A batch of the finished product varied from one to one-and-a-half pounds. (One *ryō* = four *bu* = twenty-four *shu*. A *ryō* was equivalent to about one-tenth of a pound.) The order in which the ingredients were combined seems to have been of some importance. Shigeno no Sadanushi, a ninth-century courtier famous for his Plum Blossom and Black blends, advises: "First combine the aloes and cloves. Then add the seashells, sandalwood and finally the musk" (Yamada 1942: 294).

The ingredients were brayed in iron mortars about the size of a modern rice bowl. The mixture was then moistened with plum pulp, honey or arrowroot sap, pounded with a pestle from five hundred to three thousand times, and rolled into balls about the size of marbles. The final steps are outlined in the T'ang treatise *Hsiang p'u*, "Taxonomy of Incense": "When all the ingredients have been blended, store the incense in an inexpensive, well-used vessel. Seal it with wax-coated paper in a quiet dwelling. Bury the vessel in three to five inches of earth and leave it there for a month and some days. Remove and open immediately" (Yamada 1942: 311).

Burying the incense, preferably near a tree or water, helped to blend and mature the scents. Once unsealed, however, the incense had to be burned as soon as possible. If left exposed to the air for any length of time, incense tended to dry out and lose much of its scent.

The rules governing the burning of incense were as stringent as those of combining and maturing ingredients. They are outlined in detail in *Go-Fushimi-in Shinkan Takimono no Hō*, "A Treatise on Incense in the Hand of the Retired Emperor Go-Fushimi":

> First burn some hardwood to make charcoal, and stir it well. Charcoal should be buried in the ashes of the censer in order to warm them. Place additional hot charcoal on top of the ashes, and leave it there for some time. When the charcoal on the ashes is quite cool, bury it in the ashes, top with another hot piece of charcoal, and let it warm the ashes for a while.
>
> When you wish to burn incense, remove the uppermost charcoal and replace it with the incense. It is best to wait until the ashes are fairly cool. Let the incense smoke until its scent becomes apparent. Burn the incense slowly and evenly, and, after an interval, extinguish it ...
>
> If extinguished after a short period, all smoke will vanish and the incense will last a long time. After the incense has been burned and extinguished, its scent will usually linger. If one burns incense properly this evening, for example..., one need not burn more until four or five days hence. (qtd. in Yamada 1942: 297–8)

Incense, however, cannot be considered apart from its accessories, which not only identified the variety of incense but also offered further opportunity for the creator to display his or her taste. Incense made its formal appearance in vitreous or ceramic jars, four to a box. The box itself was usually made of lacquer and lavishly decorated. The censers, or *hitori*, in which the incense was burned had scalloped wooden bases lined with ceramic or copper, and were topped by a decorative copper grille. Incense, then, played an important role in aristocratic society by revealing one's taste, indeed one's personality, as eloquently as did performance on the *koto* or the nuances of handwriting. In *The Tale of Genji*, that register of taste, the social utility of incense extends into the realm of literary technique: for here the author develops and defines her characters through the device of incense.

One example of how scent not only identifies but also enhances the personality of a character in the *Genji* occurs in Chapter 25, "*Hotaru*" (translated by Edward Seidensticker as "Fireflies").

Prince Hotaru, Genji's half-brother and the greatest aesthete of the novel, comes to Genji's mansion to court a lovely young woman named Tamakazura. Hotaru has never seen the lady; he has not heard her voice, or seen so much as a scrap of her handwriting. His opinion must be formed solely on the basis of Tamakazura's incense. Not long after this episode, an extremely comical lady appears, who could be the antithesis of Tamakazura. She is the lady from Ōmi, a daughter of Tō no Chūjō, Genji's great rival. The lady from Ōmi not only composes ridiculous poems and speaks in a dialect which jars the ears of the Kyoto aristocrats; she also puts too much honey in her incense, which makes it sweet and cloying and drives away suitors of taste.

Scent is also important to the male characters of *The Tale of Genji*, and reaches a peak with the appearance of Kaoru (whom the world believes Genji's son) and Niou, Genji's grandson. Even the names of the two characters prepare us for the role of scent in determining their personalities: Kaoru is short for Kaoru Chūjō, "the Fragrant Captain," and Niou for Niou Miya, "His Perfumed Highness" (Murasaki Shikibu 1976: 740). The contrast between the naturally fragrant Kaoru and the artificially perfumed Niou is most evident in Chapter 42, "Niou Miya." We are first introduced to Kaoru:

> There was nothing in his face or manner, to be sure, that brought people up short, but there was a compelling gentleness that was unique and suggested limitless depths.
> And there was the fragrance he gave off, quite unlike anything else in this world. Let him make the slightest motion and it had a mysterious power to trail off behind him like a "hundred-pace incense." ... He used no perfume, nor did he scent his robes, but somehow a fragrance that had been sealed deep inside a Chinese chest would emerge the more ravishing for his presence...
> Niou was his rival in everything and especially in the competition to be pleasantly scented. The blending of perfumes would become his work for days on end ... Perfumes were central to his pursuit of good taste. (Murasaki Shikibu 1976: 739–40)

Kaoru possesses a natural fragrance so pervasive and refined that it resembles the "hundred-pace" incense (*hyakubu*) often used for scenting clothes. His fragrance enhances other perfumes of nature—scented wood, plum blossoms and purple trousers (*fujibakama*); and yet it is a source of embarrassment. Unable to conduct love affairs in the secrecy appropriate to the times, Kaoru is forced by his inescapable fragrance to become shy with women, aloof from society, and overly interested in religion.

Kaoru's fragrance is also the cause of Niou's extreme involvement in the blending of fine incense. The two young men carry on the amiable rivalry of their forebears Genji and Tō no Chūjō; yet where the latter competed for women in their youth and political power in maturity, the young Niou attempts to best his rival in somewhat more trivial realms; for whereas Kaoru gives a new perfume to plants already fragrant, Niou must rob these same plants of their scent in order to improve his own perfume. He neglects the lovely but scentless maiden flower and *hagi* celebrated by the poets, and instead devotes his attention to the drying of fragrant flowers in order to compound new and unusual blends of incense. None, however, seems to please the flamboyant Niou so much as does Kaoru's fragrance.

Incense is most developed as a topic in the thirty-second chapter of *The Tale of Genji*, *"Umegae"*—"A Branch of Plum." Here the author shows us unquestionably that incense, like the other arts practiced by the aristocracy of the time, is a reflection of personality.

At the beginning of the chapter, Genji is thirty-nine years old. His daughter by the Lady of Akashi is now eleven, and her initiation ceremony, her official entry into womanhood, is to be held at Genji's mansion. There is naturally a great to-do over the preparation of materials for her initiation and subsequent entry into court. Genji is ambitious to make his daughter the favorite of the young crown prince, and, when the crown prince becomes emperor, to have her become empress, thus gaining the influential position of potential grandfather to the next emperor. Everything the girl brings with her must therefore be of the finest quality, and among these necessities are, of course, a full set of incense. Thus Genji turns the preparations into a contest among proven talents to see which scents will be judged worthy to accompany his daughter to court:

> The time had come to review the perfumes ... [The prince] went over them very carefully, finding this and that delicate flaw, for the finest perfumes are sometimes just a shade too insistent or too bland...
>
> [Asagao's] "dark" winter incense was judged the best, somehow gentler and yet deeper than the others. The prince decided that among the autumn scents, the "chamberlain's perfumes," as they are called, Genji's had an intimacy which however did not insist upon itself. Of Murasaki's three, the plum or spring perfume was especially bright and original, with a tartness that was rather daring...
>
> Observing the competition from her summer quarter, the lady of the orange blossoms was characteristically reticent, as inconspicuous as a wisp of smoke from a censer. She finally submitted a single perfume, a summer lotus-leaf blend with a pungency that was gentle but firm. In the winter quarter the Akashi lady ... submitted a "hundred pace" sachet ... of very great delicacy and refinement.

The prince announced that each of the perfumes was obviously the result of careful thought and that each had much to recommend it... The moon rose, there was wine, the talk was of old times ... The mixture of scents inside the hall was magical. (Murasaki Shikibu 1976: 511–14)

Here, then, is the incense competition (* indicates the winner):

Spring	Summer	Autumn	Winter	Sachet
("Plum Blossom")	("Lotus Leaf")	("Chamberlain")	("Black")	("Hundred-Pace")
*Murasaki	Lady of the	Murasaki	Murasaki	Lady of Akashi
Asagao	Orange Blossoms	*Genji	Genji	
			*Asagao	

As Genji remarks, Prince Hotaru's judgment is of "a harmless sort," designed to please everyone. No contestant wins in more than one category, and each has the honor of sending one kind of incense to court with Genji's daughter.

It is not surprising that Murasaki triumphs in the "Plum Blossom" competition. Throughout the *Genji* she is identified with the red plum blossom, and with spring itself. The four quarters of Genji's Rokujō mansion are named after the seasons, and Murasaki occupies the spring quarter. Indeed, the incense contest probably takes place in her quarter.

The text mentions that Murasaki bases her blends of incense on the "secret Hachijō tradition." This refers to the recipes of a ninth-century connoisseur of incense, Prince Motoyasu, known as the Hachijō Prince because of his residence. Motoyasu was a son of Emperor Nimmyō, another devotee of incense, and is said to have inherited many of his father's secret recipes (Tamagami 1968a: 311). The *Kunshū Ruishō* lists Prince Motoyasu as a specialist in the blending of Plum Blossom, Chamberlain and Black incense (Yamada 1942: 290)—exactly the three kinds submitted by Murasaki.

Prince Hotaru describes Murasaki's winning incense as *hanayaka*—"bright, cheerful"; *imamekashi*—"stylish, just right for the occasion"; and *sukoshi hayashi*—"a bit tart, sharp." All these modifiers could describe not only Murasaki's incense, but Murasaki herself. Her personality is decidedly tart. Of all Genji's ladies, she is probably the cleverest, the one most capable of defeating Genji in verbal duels. At one point Genji rebukes her for being too clever, and wonders why Murasaki does not model her behavior on someone like his cousin Princess Asagao.

Asagao wins the most difficult competition, that for the best Black incense This category has the largest number of entries, submitted by three of the most admirable characters in *The Tale of Genji*. Asagao's Black incense, sealed in an indigo jar and identified by the symbol of winter, a pine branch, is awarded first place because of two qualities: it is *kokoro nikushi*—"elegant, enviably so"; and *shizuka nari*—"quiet, calm, tranquil."

Not only are these modifiers appropriate to the winter season: they too are a fine description of Asagao herself. She has led a quiet and reclusive life, first as the daughter of an imperial prince, then as the high priestess of the Kamo Shrine in Kyoto. At the time of the incense contest she is living in elegant seclusion, quite aloof from society. Her quiet and refined life has given her the finest of taste.

Genji defeats Murasaki in the autumn incense category, because his Chamberlain's incense has "intimacy." In the original text the word used is *namamekashi*—a word suggesting warmth, gentleness and fullness, as well as fine breeding and a certain sexiness. Readers of *The Tale of Genji* will agree that this adjective—and scent—capture the nature of Genji himself.

The narrator of "A Branch of Plum" expresses surprise that Genji had acquired the secret formulae for two scents dating from the time of Emperor Nimmyō. Her surprise, we are told in the *Kakaishō*, a medieval *Genji* commentary, is because the formulae were not to be revealed to men. Genji's two blends were no longer secret by the time of the *Kakaishō*, however. The methods for compounding his Black and Chamberlain's incense are given in detail, together with the elegant names of the scents:

> It says in the *Gōkō Hihō* ["Secret Incense Formulae"]: "For 'Raven' [Black], mix together four *ryō* of aloes, two *ryō* of cloves, one *bu* of sandalwood, one *ryō* of oil of cloves (add an extra two *bu* if desired), one *bu* of musk, and one *bu* of amber.
>
> "For 'Gleanings' [Chamberlain], combine four *ryō* of aloes, two *ryō* of cloves, one *ryō* of seashells, one *ryō* of spikenard, one scant *ryō* of mature lily petals (one method adds musk, another yellow lily petals), and one *bu* of orange leaf extract.
>
> "Mix with honey and pound three thousand times with a pestle. Warm the seashells and add them to the mixture. Coat with honey. The mixture should be yellowish-black. It must not be too black.
>
> "These two methods are not to be transmitted to men. This is the command of the Jōwa emperor [Emperor Nimmyō]. The methods were presented by the late Shigeno no Chokushi, lady in waiting, on the third day of the Second Month in the sixth year of Engi [906]." (Tamagami 1968b: 410–11)

The ladies were asked to submit two kinds of incense each, but only Asagao does so. Murasaki submits three, and the other two ladies present one each. Let us examine the reasons for this.

The lady of the orange blossoms lives in the summer quarter of Genji's mansion, and, ever since her introduction in the eleventh chapter, "Hanachirusato" ("The Orange Blossoms"), she has been associated with summer. Hence her summer incense. Prince Hotaru describes it as *shimeyaka*, "quiet," a word used often in describing night, or gentle rain. This brings to mind the visit Genji pays the lady in Chapter 11, which takes place on a summer night, during a break in the constant, quiet rain. Prince Hotaru also calls her incense *natsukashi*, a word which gives a feeling of friendliness, familiarity and attraction.

The lady of the orange blossoms is not an outgoing woman, and will go to some trouble to avoid competing with the other ladies. Hence her one incense, in an otherwise uncontested category.

The Akashi lady is quite another case. The girl over whom all the fuss is being made is her only daughter; but because the Akashi lady was born outside the limits of the capital, of noble but somewhat eccentric parents, her daughter has been adopted by Murasaki, who comes of more proper lineage. The daughter has been living in Murasaki's quarters now for several years. The Akashi lady is a proud woman. She resents Murasaki for having taken charge of her daughter, even though it is for the girl's benefit. What is more, the Akashi lady has never forgiven Murasaki for holding the highest place in Genji's affections. This is why, although the Akashi lady is the occupant of the winter quarter of Genji's mansion, and would therefore be expected to submit a winter incense, she withdraws from the competition. Rather than be defeated by her rival, she instead submits a sachet.

The "hundred-pace" incense submitted by the Akashi lady was based, we are told in the text, on a formula by Minamoto Kintada, adapted from a blend of the "earlier Suzaku emperor."

Minamoto Kintada, who supplies us above with a recipe for Lotus Leaf incense, is listed in the *Kunshū Ruishō* as one of the few experts in blending superb incense for every season (Yamada 1942: 290). His recipe for "hundred-pace" incense, however, has not come down to us. The author's "earlier Suzaku emperor" is thought to be Emperor Uda, who reigned in the last years of the ninth century. Since Kintada served an emperor known to history as Suzaku, it seems to have been necessary to distinguish the two rulers.

The Akashi lady, a relative of the imperial family, has this famous formula in her possession. Although she does not want to risk defeat by entering the winter incense competition, her pride dictates that her entry derive from the glorious days of incense blending. Prince Hotaru rules her sachet *kokoro okite suguretari*, "of an unsurpassed nature," a judgment which cannot help but please the lady.

The text of "A Branch of Plum" mentions that Genji, Murasaki and the Akashi lady use recipes handed down from emperors, princes and courtiers of the ninth century. As the author tells us, the same traditions were subsequently taken up by a variety of people and made into something new and distinctive.

The tradition continues to this day, but has of course undergone some changes. In the fourteenth century, the informal pastime of incense competitions, like that of tea drinking, was formalized into a Way. Just as *sadō*, "the way of tea" or the tea ceremony, came into existence, so did *kōdō*, "the way of incense."

In the Heian period, as we have just seen, sizeable amounts of fragrant ingredients were combined to form balls of incense. These were placed directly on the hot ashes in a censer: the heat generated from the buried charcoal seems to have burned the incense rather quickly. And although incense competitions like that in *The Tale of Genji* seem to have been one way of exhibiting good taste, the primary reason for the manufacture of incense in the Heian period was eminently practical. Incense was used daily, in order to keep rooms and clothing attractively scented, and thereby to hint subtly at a personality which remained concealed behind shutters, blinds and curtains.

The incense ceremony which evolved in the fourteenth century contrasts sharply with its Heian predecessor. Where the Heian aesthetic stressed the colorful and the diverse in its incense, the Muromachi sought beauty in the monochrome and in simplicity. The Six Scents and their six basic ingredients were replaced by a single scent, aloes. The incense balls of the Heian period gave way to a tiny fragment of aloes burning slowly on gold or silver leaf in a ceramic brazier the size of a teacup.

The greatest difference between incense use in the eleventh and fourteenth centuries, though, was the purpose it served. The fundamental goal of the Muromachi incense competition was to discern, through the sampling of several pieces of aloes, which was the superior wood. This goal, translated into aesthetic rather than practical terms, was to "attain, through the scent, the realm of highest knowledgeable beauty" (Yamada 1942: 316). The creation of individual combinations of incense was supplanted by the appreciation and evaluation of rare kinds of aloes.

The *kōdō* of today is much like that of the fourteenth century. Certain technological improvements have taken place: the gold or silver leaf on which the aloes rested has been replaced by a silver grille which burns the incense slowly and evenly. But the small porcelain brazier passing from hand to hand at Tennōji probably does not differ much in size and shape from those used five centuries ago; nor do the warm ashes, carefully sculpted into a cone, which cushion the grille and the aloes.

The ceremony itself is not unlike the tea ceremony. One receives the brazier from the person on the left, bows and picks it up, turning it three times with the elbows held out at right angles to the body. Forming a funnel with the hand over the brazier, one samples the incense three times, contemplating the scent while doing so. The brazier is then turned three times and passed on, with a bow, to the next person.

Adepts of the incense ceremony are able to discern the several types of aloes on the basis of the Five Bouquets (*gomi*) (sweet, bitter, spicy, sour and salt) and the Six Countries (*rokkoku*) of origin (Kyara, Rakoku [Thailand], Manaban, Manaka, Sumatora [Sumatra] and Sasora). For example, an incense named Tōdaiji after the great Nara temple is recognized as aloes from Kyara (assumed to be either Java or the Malay Peninsula) with a bouquet, in diminishing order, of sweet, spicy, sour and salt.

The beginner is set a far simpler task. All that is required is that one distinguish three different scents, and remember them. *Shōchikubai* is the simplest of such games.

The three scents, *Shō* (Pine), *Chiku* (Bamboo), and *Bai* (Plum) are first presented in a *tameshi*, or trial run. Each scent is identified by the master of ceremonies before it is passed on to the participants. When everyone has had an opportunity to sample the three scents, the packets containing the incense are shuffled to mix up the order. The three scents are then passed around again, and one must identify them by their characteristic odor.

This is more difficult than it may seem. One cannot rely on the memory of familiar fragrances: the scent named Pine, for instance, does not smell especially like a pine forest, nor does the Plum resemble the fragrance of a plum blossom. The scents are entrancing but abstract; they are distinct when one samples them, and have passed from memory by the second round.

Each participant had been given paper and a small writing-box before the game began; at the end of the second round, we brushed our opinions of which incense was sampled first, second and third. Approximately twenty people took part: all but one failed to identify the scents correctly, according to the secretary. The woman who succeeded in doing so had taken lessons in *kōdō*.

Shōchikubai was succeeded by a more difficult game. The first round was again a *tameshi*: the scents passed around were named for the Three Scenic Views—Matsushima, Ama no Hashidate and Itsukushima. But the second round included an unknown scent, called *fune*, "the boat," mixed in with the previous three. When our answers had been duly recorded, the secretary announced that no one had recognized all four scents in their correct order. We were ranked according to how many scents were correctly identified. A score of three ranked one as *asagiri*, "morning mist"; two as *yūgiri*, "evening mist"; and one as *kumogiri*, "fog."

There were certain similarities to the Heian incense competition—the elegance, the leisurely quality, a feeling of well-being and relaxation. But the *kōdō* of today is much more of a game, at least in its simpler aspects; it lacks the critical spirit and practicality of the incense competition in *The Tale of Genji*. In either case, however, the way of incense makes demands on a sense rarely associated with art, except the arts of cooking and wine-tasting—the sense of smell.

Bibliography

Murasaki Shikibu (1976), *The Tale of Genji*, trans. E.G. Seidensticker, New York: Alfred A. Knopf.
Tamagami, T. (1968a), *Genji Monogatari Hyōshaku*, vol. 6, Tokyo: Kadokawa Shoten.
—— (ed.) (1968b), *Shimeishō, Kakaishō*, Tokyo: Kadokawa Shoten.
Yamada, K. (1942), *Tōa Kōryō Shi*, Tokyo: Tōyōdō.

29

Eating Nothing

Cooking Aromas in Art and Culture

Jim Drobnick

The experience of eating things is invariably a synesthetic one, yet the senses of taste and smell are privileged as the arbiters of what constitutes a delicious meal. As two of the most linked of senses, their interdependence exists on a number of levels: physiologically, they are "the chemical senses," ones that respond, "ingest" and engage on a molecular level; perceptually, the experience of flavor is a combination of circulating aromas and sensations on the tongue—in fact, many foods are not identifiable without smell, such as coffee, chocolate, apricots and garlic (Vroon 1997); philosophically, the two have been constantly denigrated as mere survival mechanisms, or so animalistic and subjective as to be unsuitable for reasoning and knowledge (Korsmeyer 1999); and aesthetically, despite the enjoyments of haute cuisine and complex perfumes, they are given little artistic potential compared to the "higher," more noble senses of vision and hearing. Historically then, taste and smell converge on biological and social grounds, being intimately bound to physicality and to the body's interior functions, as well as being embedded within analogous discourses of intellectual disenfranchisement.

Given such a "natural" pairing of taste and smell, and the bio-cultural *cul de sac* which they jointly occupy, what happens when the two are severed, their seemingly organic relationship ruptured? What issues arise when the distinctive aromas of cooking separate from the tangible experience of food? What meanings and practices are generated in that newfound chasm between these otherwise inextricable senses—for example, when the act of consumption only involves platefuls of air? In other words, eating nothing? The development of innovative sensory applications in recent years, and the technological intensification of others, make these questions timely and worthy of consideration. In both cultural and artistic contexts, scents have been disengaged from their causal sources, a move which undermines the indexical characteristic of smells and endows them with alternative capabilities. In the process, conditions are created in which political and ethical problematics become manifest. Interweaving thoughts about art, history and various social phenomena, my discussion here examines three compelling sites that dissolve the inevitability of the food/aroma dyad in the realms of the body, public space and domestic life.

Odor Pangs

Exaggerating the gap between foodstuffs and their aromas creates distance between craving and fulfilment. Because the delectable airs of cooking stimulate in both psychological and physiological manners—prompting the expectation of a tasty experience, as well as inciting the salivary glands to secrete and commence the process of digestion—the act of severing the smell of food from its gustatory enjoyment can be a cruel deprivation. To sniff, but not partake, breaks the anticipatory rhythm of desire and gratification. Detaching smells from food can therefore involve an exercise of power in which arbitrary, moralistic and sadistic impulses thrive.

The rift between aroma and food has often been used to make evident class distinctions. T. McLean's nineteenth-century illustration, *Living Made Easy* (1830), satirizes the callous indifference that emerged when the industrial revolution created an emergent class of wealthy entrepreneurs. Depicted are a series of emaciated, impoverished men, hunched over and clad in tattered clothes, with noses hovering over pipes that emit small bursts of aromas. The caption explains:

> CHARITY TUBES, to convey the Smell from the Tables of the RICH, for the benefit of the POOR OPERATIVES. Particularly recommended to the Philanthropy of those who have made large fortunes by Machinery.

McLean's humor is based on the preposterousness of the scenario and its heartless, contradictory logic: such cynical, pseudo-philanthropy serves not to alleviate hunger but instead inflames dissatisfaction, and thus heightens the disparity between the haves and have nots. The aromatic excess is a remainder, but not a leftover (which in times past went to servants, the poor and pets), and bears no nutritional value. Such a virtual feast operates chiefly on a semiotic level: the aromatic presence signifies the lack of any substantive food or solace, and any savoriness of the experience only conveys the message that a person possessing a certain social prestige can offer meaningless, scroogelike gestures of charity and still elicit gratitude.

An historical variant of McLean's illustration was recorded by Alexander Barclay, a sixteenth-century courtier. Apparently it was common practice at certain courts to circulate tantalizing dishes at banquets, with some specifically destined to be consumed only by those high in social ranking. Those who were lower could but sniff the delicacies and complain amongst themselves (Miller 1997). Here the envy caused by the ostentatious presentation of a food's fragrance was precisely the point.

Gluttony, a cousin, perhaps, of food envy, has been singled out as the primary and most notorious of sins since the fourth century when Christian clerics first enumerated the principal vices. As a "gateway" sin, its fleshly indulgence led to other, more insidious infractions, or so the theory went, and numerous diatribes were issued about the evils of excessive dining and drinking (Miller 1997; Prose 2003). The punishment for gluttony (Hell, of course!) followed an economy of justice conspicuous for its literalness: overindulgence in mortal life would be penalized by brutal denial in the hereafter. Fra Angelico, in his depiction of the Last Judgment, portrays a table of unconverted gluttons savoring plates of food and eyeing a flask of wine. Bestial demons with snakelike appendages clutch the sinners' hair and straightjacket their arms. The never-to-be diners' outstretched necks and flared nostrils greedily inhale whiffs of the meal but are forever prevented from satisfying their gustatory passions. It is a mercilessly condemning vision that increases Barclay's torment by several degrees—eternal and constant hunger, kept aroused by Satan's aroma-producing flames, enacts retribution for those who could not cleave sinner from dinner.

A version of this temptation scenario graced the world's media recently in the context of street magician David Blaine's forty-four-day retreat from food. Staged in a Plexiglas box suspended forty feet in the air by a crane, Blaine became a cynosure for activists, publicity seekers and carnivalesque interventions. A fast food proprietor, obviously familiar with at least the principle of Fra Angelico's method of subjecting woe, set up a mobile kitchen near the fasting spectacle to feed visitors and, in the process, to waft the smells of cooking hamburgers towards the hunger artist. Like so many others expressing little sympathy for Blaine's act of self-imprisoned asceticism, the manager dismissed the olfactory distress that might be caused by his business: "If he doesn't like it, that's tough. We can't move the smell" (ITV 2003).

Such "torture," however, pales in comparison to contemporary practices of punishment that often feature suffocating stenches and humiliating filthiness as means of coercion. Detainees that refuse food can find the smells of cooking or rotting food thrust into their space. Similarly, for those kept on near-starvation diets, enticing or nauseating aromas inhumanely exacerbate their ordeal. Abusive smells are in some ways an ideal means of torture—they leave no marks on the body. These and other olfactory tactics, such as incapacitating malodorants or stinging sprays, are newly in vogue, as military technicians seek to develop nonlethal forms of assault that provide soldiers with the means to stun and deter, without resorting to gunfire. Weaponized odors are the military spin-off from advances in the fragrance and flavor industry. For the survivors of such methods of torture and other traumatic circumstances, the smell of roasting meat or cooking odors can be inseparably associated with the events and trigger flashbacks and episodes of extreme panic (see Hinton et al., in this volume).

Besides functioning as a technique of torture, the divorce of aromas from the satisfaction of eating has been used by artists to elaborate an oppositional politics. On August 15, 1963, the Japanese performance collaborative Hi Red Center held a dinner in Tokyo's Citizen's Hall to commemorate the ending of the war, VJ Day—not, as was customary in postwar Japan, to mark the anniversary of the Hiroshima and Nagasaki bombings earlier in the month. Selling expensive tickets that suggested the serving of a sumptuous, full-course meal, the three members of the group permitted patrons to enter the restaurant. When the time to eat arrived, however, it was only the artists who proceeded to feast while the deceived visitors could only inhale the aromas and watch. Hi Red Center's inversion of the callous social relations illustrated in *Living Made Easy* left the well-to-do of Citizen's Hall famished, a gesture recognizing that satiety can be a sign of unreflective conformity and complacent self-satisfaction. In this context of a VJ Day commemoration, Hi Red Center's aromatic denial of food was equated with the mainstream Japanese disavowal of Japan's own militaristic, colonial acts during World War II and the role the nation itself played in being victimized by wartime adversaries. The performance's fragrant expectation and disappointing denouement inserted a critical wedge into what the artists felt was a hypocritical moral consensus. According to Nam June Paik, Hi Red Center's challenge highlighted the anti-celebratory message: "Why don't we call it as it is, that is, 'War Defeat Day'?" (Paik 1994: 80).

The persecuting practices appearing in McLean, Fra Angelico, state-sponsored torture and Hi Red Center exemplify odor taunting as an exercise of power, whether it is driven by class indifference, religious sadism, lawless intimidation or social reproach. Although the types of hunger present in these situations operate on various levels—real, symbolic, temporary, eternal, hierarchical, critical—they reveal the acute ethical problematics that can arise when the link between aroma and food is destabilized.

The Sense of S(m)ell

Online reviews of Kentucky Fried Chicken invariably mention the fast food retailer's characteristic smell. Whether people judge it to be enticing or repulsive, it is undeniably distinctive. KFC is but one example of the smell of food being vented into the air, often by specialized diffusing technology, to travel far beyond its source, following people, meeting them unawares, flaring their nostrils even when out of sight of the scent's origin. Circulating through the streets, occupying a neighborhood, lurking around corners in the mall and other indoor marketplaces, these odors are out for a stroll, trolling for potential customers to entice. Such scents intend to influence from a distance; they strategically expand the gap between food and its aroma to advance a series of corporate interests, in particular, consumer appeal, brand identity, space territorialization and, ultimately, behavioral modification.

One of the most accelerating trends of the past decade concerns promoting products in a holistic, immersive fashion—sensory marketing. Also called environmental or experiential marketing, as well as "atmospherics," this mode of consumer address seeks to engage the entire sensory field. Developed as a countermeasure to the visual overload and desensitization by conventional advertising practices, it advocates the enhancement of retail environments to target individuals on ambient, visceral levels (Weisman 2003; Kotler 1973/74). Atmospheric selling depends upon framing shoppers within a pleasurable, stimulating context, so much so that the environment of the store virtually carries more significance than the products themselves. Researchers have shown that a pleasant odor elevates the mood of patrons, improves a store's image, enriches the evaluations of products, increases the time consumers spend in a store and their intention to return and, most importantly, boosts both the price shoppers are willing to pay for a product and the amount of spending in a store overall (Botschen and Crowther 2001; Schifferstein and Blok 2002).

The sense of smell is the most striking component of sensory marketing. Considered by some in the field to be "the fourth dimension" (X3D Technologies 2004), scent is touted as a radical shift in perceptual impact that propels marketing into a universe of unlimited influence over the consumer's psyche. Part of the excitement is due to the sophisticated advances in scent analysis and synthesis, as well as new technologies of computerized odor dispersal—all of which fundamentally expand the possibilities for custom-made scents. Cooking aromas may be aerated into streets or mall corridors— such as the grilling of steaks from restaurants, buttered popcorn from movie theaters, or baking bread from ovens located in grocery stores—converting cooking's volatile excess into olfactory advertisements. A surprising number of aromas, even in restaurants, however tantalizing they may be, are ingeniously simulated. Food scents issue from vending machines, billboards, cash registers, product displays and store entrances, and are by now intrinsic to the experience of coffee shops (Starbucks), snackeries (Cinnabons), microbreweries, pizzerias and any eatery situated in a mall, subway station, airport or other enclosed, highly-trafficked building. Some locations forbid actual cooking. Fortunately for proprietors, practically any scent—from fresh-baked cookies to sizzling hamburgers—can be convincingly simulated (Spector 2003; Schlosser 2001).

The other reason for scent's predominance in current marketing strategies is that it provides a solution to a problem plaguing the contemporary food service industry: the sensory impoverishment and unpalatability of industrialized food production. Sterile packaging that obstructs firsthand sensory evaluation, plant breeding that intensifies the visual appeal or extends the shelf-life of produce but leaves it with little taste or smell, mass processing and long storage times that deplete flavor—these sources of blandness have all been ameliorated by injecting scents into the consumer experience. Bi-Lo supermarkets and Perkins, the restaurant chain, have utilized the simulated scent of apple pies to encourage sales, with reportedly dramatic results (Gillen 2004). Vending machines are now outfitted with diffusers so that their glass and steel-encased contents can be promoted at a distance, thus "catch[ing] customers by the nose" (*Newsmonthly of Vending* 2004). And scents are now being embedded into the lining of food containers to mitigate the effects of flavor "scalping." Can consumers tell whether the intense aroma comes from the food or the packaging? Scent's invisibility is the key to bolstering the illusion (fantasy?) of a product's freshness (Paul 2003).

Smell is a sense deemed immediate and believable, hence rendering it the perfect means to connote "realness." No one suspects smells, least of all the ones that mimic the aromas of cooking food. With their supposedly organic origin, they can be argued to be unavoidable as well as harmless—the smell of business. The robust aromas, for instance, percolating through specialty coffee outlets, not only from the brewing pots of coffee but also from the overt display of burlap bags and wooden barrels of coffee beans, potently convey the atmosphere of a nineteenth-century shop. Such smells transport customers to a faux bohemian realm, a supposedly more authentic past, a time before agribusiness monopolies; it is a sensorial ploy that masks the standardization of food production and its industrialized, exploitative practices (Roseberry 1996). Through the technique of "odor priming," retailers choose scents that cue thematic associations (Schifferstein and Blok 2002). Food scents, such as mulled wine and Christmas dinner aerated in Woolworths, have been utilized to rouse holiday thoughts, or like the chocolate ambiance sprayed into Superdrug stores, have summoned the gift-giving of Valentine's Day. The fragrance of ice cream was diffused at parlor entrances to "invoke feelings of satisfaction, well-being and health associated with handmade ice cream" (Losowsky 2002; *Gelato Bar & Pasticceria* 2002).

An added value for scent for marketers lies in its pivotal role in generating a "total brand experience" (Losowsky 2002). Distinctive graphics are only one aspect of marketing campaigns; also vital is a company's or retailer's "fragrance logo" and "corporate odor identity" (La Via del Profumo; Damian and Damian, in this volume). As a manager for Air France confides: "The more a brand is present on all possible points of contact with a consumer, the stronger the brand is and the more the consumer retains a brand image" (Weisman 2003).

The belief in the success of smell in cementing brand consciousness is based on three interrelated factors: *recognition, memory* and *emotionality.* Recognition, or attention, is key in a competitive marketplace. The novelty of scent can differentiate a store or service from the crowd of similar establishments, which may translate into an economic edge (Davies et al. 2003). The second factor, olfaction's special relationship to memory, reinforces brand consciousness through the process of *odor imprinting*. Once customers learn to associate a scent with a precise place or product, such an affinity can last a lifetime. Emotionality, the third factor, is the main reason why scent is touted as the supreme sales technique. Odors directly influence physical, cognitive and affective states. Smell is the only sense that instantly connects to the brain's emotional center, the amygdala and the limbic system, and thus olfactory experiences can be more intense than visual or auditory perceptions. Given that the emotions figure prominently in the act of purchasing—reputedly two-thirds of buying choices are due to subjective, extra-logical consideration—utilizing smell promises to activate a consumer's involuntary responses and bypass rational decision making (Botschen and Crowther 2001; Weisman 2003).

As much as researchers downplay their interest in olfactory determinism, commentators from the food and retail industry are completely candid about the Pavlovian effects of smell in the marketplace. Anxiety about subliminal advertising has waned since it first appeared in the 1950s, mostly because its effects proved to be unfounded, yet there is a resurgence in developing a practice of behavior modification through the use of smell—"the new hidden persuader" (Butler et al. 1999). While visual ads can be ignored and mood music tuned out, a consumer's control over their inhalations ends upon entering a retailer's atmospheric domain. More than 400,000 aromatic compounds exist, each of which bears the potential to be biochemically and emotionally active. Research indicates that the most powerful effects occur when the scent is barely noticeable, setting the stage for "olfactory muzak" and subliminal manipulation to be unleashed with little awareness of the part of the consumer (Butler et al. 1999; Damian and Damian, in this volume).

Despite the selective successes of perfume bans, second-hand smoke restrictions and laws against air pollution, the atmosphere is for the most part fair game for corporate olfactory marketing. Publicly aerated scents like those emanating from KFC generally function without monitoring or governance. More expansive than signs or billboards, able to overrun property lines and architectural boundaries, scents elude municipal codes regulating the aesthetics of the city. Enhanced by special ventilators, synthesized scents are specifically designed to be distributed as widely as possible. What medium of advertising, after all, could be freer than the wind? Market share is concomitant with atmospheric dominance, and when fast food outlets like KFC olfatively declare their presence and territorially mark a neighborhood, everyone within sniffing range ingests their product without intending, let alone consenting. The one mitigating danger that KFC and other olfactory marketers face is the triumph of their own proliferation. As more smells are pumped into the urban environment, the risk of competing odors merging into less-than-appetizing blends also increases, and so too the chances of inadvertently creating tainted clouds that confuse or repulse prospective customers.

Such swirling mixtures often occur in urban and crowded scenes. Travel literature, for example, is often peppered with descriptions of the smells of spices, fruits, open-air markets and cooking that lend an air of cultural and culinary distinctiveness to a tourist destination. In fact, inhaling the distinct smells of a locale is often equated with authentic tourist experience. But for those with more sensitive olfactory constitutions, the visceral aromas of fragrant foods can generate fear and condemnation. Food and cooking odors unfamiliar to mainstream sensibilities are often the ostensible basis for anti-immigrant bias and xenophobia (see Manalansan in this volume). Such olfactory antipathies have led to lawsuits against the smell of a neighbor's cooking (Losowsky 2002), bylaws aimed at ethnic restaurants (Mickleburgh 2004), and the segregation of minorities via zoning regulations and residential patterns. So-called offensive cooking odors not only provide markers of difference that can be perceived, and thus targeted, they also underscore the fragility (and impracticality) of a civic order based on the presumption of purity.

All of this serves as an extended introduction to a work by Michael Rakowitz that strategically utilizes the odors of cooking to interrogate urban spatial politics. Real estate speculators in New York City, despite years of activist protest and critique, continue to treat space as an abstract, purely economic entity, while endangering the viability of long-established communities. Rakowitz's installation, *Rise* (2001), intervenes into the incessant cycle of appropriation and redevelopment by channeling one of the volatile essences of a community—the smell of baking—into the center of the gentrification process.

Real estate companies often deploy art exhibitions to help advertise and provide caché to properties about to be placed on the market. When invited to participate in one such show sponsored by TriBeach Holdings, then grooming a property in Chinatown to construct generic condos for an expanding SoHo clientele, Rakowitz conceived a work that olfactively implicated the developer's community-busting practices. The exhibition site, a building on Lafayette Street, had recently evicted its tenants, which included a network of Chinese businesses and cultural institutions, along with a vital community center. The artist collaborated with the Fei Dar Bakery, located next door, to vent the aromas from its ovens into the newly emptied office spaces, thus surreptitiously reintroducing a fragrant symbol of those vacated. A ventilation duct rigged to ascend from the roof of the bakery to the ninth floor, 125 feet skyward, permeated the exhibition space with the scent of freshly baking pastries. The smell inevitably drew visitors to the bakery downstairs to make purchases, meet and talk with the owner and other local patrons, and to get the community's own viewpoint on the building's sale and its effects on the neighborhood.

For Rakowitz, the aromas served as a "disarming [and] innocuous vehicle" within which "hover[ed] an idea more dangerous and threatening: the socially excluded have breached the fortress and circumvented the structures that usually impede their presence" (Rakowitz 2003). In effect, the pervading smell of Chinese pastries subtly corrupted the commodification and deracination of space, as well as the supposed virtues of development, by recuperating what would normally be considered superfluous, redirecting it into a place conventionally protected under the logic of private property, and transforming it into a powerful symbol of a vibrant, Chinese American cultural context. As much as the aroma transgressed the shell of the edifice, proving it to be vulnerable to external factors, it also asserted a connectedness between the building and its environment—through the sharing of atmospheres. Able to breathe in the pastries, but not to taste them (except for a brief time at the opening), gallerygoers were compelled to performatively *complete* the smell (see Gell in this volume): to go to the source and cognitively connect the aroma to the bakery and, by extension, to the residents in the community at large. In the process, visitors became informed of the interlinking politics and economics of space radically changing the building and surrounding community.

The "rise" of the title, therefore, denotes not only the workings of dough rising and the ascending oven fumes, or the building itself as a high-rise, but also alludes to "rising up" and the hope that locals and sympathetic others could organize to confront the injustice of sacrificing the Chinese community's well-being for the sake of development. Like the appealing aromas in sensory marketing, people were influenced physiologically and affectively by the pleasant scent emanating from the Fei Dar Bakery, but here, as was the case with the performance by Hi Red Center, smell wielded a critical edge. Importantly, *Rise* depended on a real rather than an artificial scent. The odor's definite location in the environment offered material, living proof of the presence of the imperiled community. Making perceptible the social and economic relations that together constitute public space, Rakowitz exposed the destructive forces of "development," as well as activated a potentially empowering counter-response.

Nosealgia

If the immersive strategies of atmospheric marketing have permeated the once integral body of the bourgeois subject and reconfigured public space within an olfactory politics of molecular manipulation, they have also infiltrated the central refuge of bourgeois identity: the domestic hearth. Eating habits in the postmodern era radically reconceive notions of what J.P. Aron calls the home's "alimentary topography" (Maldonado 1991: 41). Rupturing the traditional distinctions between the places where food is prepared and where it is consumed, the contemporary predominance of snack foods, instant preparation, irregular eating times and the rarity of communal family meals have contributed to restructuring the activities that conventionally occurred in the kitchen and dining room (Bell and Valentine 1997). Food preparation now occurs in several places in the house, and consumption anywhere, anytime.

Parallel to this social trend, and in many ways responding to it, is an expanding genre of merchandise: room sprays and related products that feature "edible scents." Numerous manufacturers, from The Body Shop to independents selling homemade products online, provide a sumptuous array of smells designed to make consumers lick their lips. Claire Burke offers a room spray, Applejack & Peel, which blends the "welcoming aroma of baked apples warmed with cinnamon, spice, and a twist of citrus." Botanicus sells mouth-watering hot chocolate, creme de cafe, and pound, coffee and apple cake travel candles. The catalogue from Primal Elements is even more extensive: its candles feature the scents of cinnamon apple, almond biscotti, banana nut bread, roasted chestnuts, peanut butter, ginger bears, candy canes and many other savory treats. Explicitly working the maternal theme is a candle by Triple Swirl Sensations, entitled Grandma's Kitchen, which blends successive layers of pumpkin pie, sugar cookies and vanilla maple pecan scents. The label on its glass container, a cross between a Mason jar and a cookie jar, boasts that "Nothing will stop you quicker in your steps than the aroma of Grandma's freshly baked goodies. Pulling them hot from the oven … you've now designated yourself the 'official' family taste tester." So that no one is confused by the chemical contents of these artificial scents and their use with actual comestibles, Crabtree & Evelyn warns buyers of its Salad Greens room spray: "Not for consumption. Avoid spraying on food."

What is particularly notable about these domestic atmospherics is the eclipse of food by its synthesized aroma. Aromas no longer evidence cooking practice; they exist autonomously and extemporaneously. Edible scent room sprays disregard notions of segregated and distinct areas for preparation and consumption—cooking aromas can now suffuse any room in the home, at a moment's notice, whenever and wherever one wishes. (Compare this situation to the one noted by Margaret Visser (1991: 83) whereby up until 1950 hostesses were chided by etiquette standard-bearer Emily Post to keep food odors relegated to the kitchen, lest the smells impose themselves impolitely upon guests seated in the dining room). Contemporary food preparation, for many, has now been almost entirely eliminated, relegated to the mysteries of commercial manufacturing, which is the equivalent of "nowhere," or utopia. While the popularity of room sprays is in part due to the enjoyment of pleasurable smells without the fuss of cooking, it is precisely their detachment from an identifiable source that foregrounds other kinds of value—symbolic ones—in this case, those that are compensatory and nostalgic.

In a foodscape populated by processed, frozen, take-out and microwaveable products, the kitchen as a gastronomic arena is an estranged place. The idea of investing labor to prepare something to eat seems archaic, inefficient, tedious. Yet there remains a longing for homemade cooking, and here is where edible scents perform a *compensatory* function. Edible scents offer the relish of cooking, but without any actual exertion. Daniel Harris remarks that with the demise of real cooking, fantasies proliferate in an inverse relationship; the less cooking that is done, the more an embellished "aesthetic of deliciousness" is produced through food photography, product marketing and cooking shows (Harris 2000: 175–6). Disunited from their associated foods, and without calories, edible scents displace the gustatory to become the apotheosis of food's purest essence. Further, edible scents compensate for the numerous food scares that beset consumers' awareness. Trans-fats, toxic additives, growth hormones, irradiation, mad cow disease—these are only a few of the worries that plague the act of eating, and room sprays position themselves as the perfect way to indulge without fear. Marketers also stigmatize the smells of naturally fragrant ingredients, especially garlic and onions. Like deodorant advertisements that inspire anxiety about the body's emanations, the rhetoric accompanying room sprays implores consumers to mask or neutralize the supposedly unappetizing odors of living.

The ambiance evoked by room sprays is decidedly tilted towards nostalgia, or what I call *nosealgia*. My term refers to the calculatedness of these sprays to stimulate fragrant reminiscences and a longing for traditional family values. That so many of the edibles represented in room sprays pertain to home-baked delights, especially ones associated with holidays, intimately wraps users in a cozy olfactory blanket of childhood succor. Room sprays could be considered another aspect of what Tomas Maldonado terms "the technology of the quotidian," a series of practices that seek to assuage the effects of industrialization and urbanization, thus stabilizing daily life in capitalist society (1991: 37–8). Edible scent room sprays are special in the sense that they function therapeutically as well as nostalgically; in their sugary, syrupy, carbo-centricity they promote an idyllic version of the home that supposedly existed prior to radical modern shifts of the twentieth century, harking back to the time of one's parents, grandparents, or even the rosy quaintness of the nineteenth century and its pastoral dreams. Holiday foods spark childhood memories of being indulged by grandparents, as well as the enjoyment of temporary freedom from daily dietary regimens (Lupton 1994; see also Hirsch in this volume).

For Svetlana Boym, nostalgia (and by extrapolation, nosealgia) is the yearning for a home that never existed. It is at once a feeling of loss, displacement and aching for the past, as well as a romantic captivation with one's own fiction of an ideal home:

Modern nostalgia is a mourning for the impossibility of mythical return, for the loss of an enchanted world with clear borders and values; it could be a secular expression of a spiritual longing, a nostalgia for an absolute, a home that is both physical and spiritual, the edenic unity of time and space before entry into history. (2001: 8)

Boym theorizes that there are two forms of nostalgia: restorative and reflective. Restorative nostalgia assuages its pain by rebuilding the lost, childhood home, and attempts to reinstate a prelapsarian fullness of experience. By this definition, edible scent room sprays are highly restorative. The celebrated ability of smells to evoke moods, times and places from the past is especially suited to gestures of recapturing lost auras. The second kind of nostalgia, by contrast, foregrounds ambivalency, fragmentation, irony, criticality. Reflective nostalgia carries within it a defamiliarizing, dialectical sensibility, one that interrogates the activity of longing as much as it participates in its aspirations (Boym 2001: 49–50).

In the realm of art, as opposed to scented home decor, such a distinction between restorative and reflective nostalgia is instructive. Alex Sandover's installation, *Synesthesia (Nuclear Families)* (2000), engages with the longings of domestic nostalgia put into play by edible scent room sprays, but it simultaneously foregrounds the tenuousness of the postwar scene of familial serenity. With a wall-sized photo-mural picturing an iconic 1950s-era dining room, and prominent video inserts that offer peeks inside a black-and-white tiled floor and formica cupboard kitchen, one might assume that a restorative, compensatory logic is at work. True to its title, the visual is augmented by other sensory components, notably a soundtrack and a series of computer-diffused scents, which immerse visitors in a retro *tranche de vie*. The twenty-minute cycle of video-audio-olfactory sensations witnesses an aproned woman in the process of preparing a meal and cleaning up afterwards. Synchronized rustles, squishes, crackles, squeaks, clangs and thuds accompany her movements, and the associated smells of roast chicken, stuffing, apple pie and vanilla custard provide confirmation about what is being cooked. Like edible scent room sprays, *Synesthesia* creates an environment that capitalizes upon the capacity of smells to evoke the past and stir nostalgic sentiments.

Yet the experience of the installation calls into question the mechanisms of memory and association as much as it acts restoratively. The meal's consumption, for instance, is not shown, and the appreciative family circle never materializes, cutting short the conventional narrative arc that ends with a Norman Rockwell gathering of generations around the table. All parts of the cooking process are presented—the repetitive, unromantic labor of chopping, kneading, wiping-up—so that no individual part, especially the end product, is isolated and fetishized. Views of the action in the scenario are always partial because the cook constantly moves in and out of the frame, denying a transcendent perspective. And with regards to the aromas suffusing the exhibition space, this is where *Synesthesia* most decidedly departs from the restorative nature of room sprays and enters into what Boym calls "nostalgic dissidence" (Boym 2001: 354). Even though the aromas fill the installation's atmosphere, they do not allow the indulgence of passive immersion. Much guesswork goes into identifying the scents as they appear. While smells are cued to the visible sequence of gestures, visitors in the gallery's black box experience a tense ambiguity in terms of when the next scent will occur and what coordinated action will be its trigger. The fragrance of apple pie, for example, is easily discerned, but the hit of methane and lit match indicating the stove being fired up, the musty wood odor accompanying the opening of the cupboard, or the sharpness of bleach in the cleaning stage are unexpected and interrupt the edible nostalgic reverie. Discussions and disagreements invariably emerge among viewers with differing olfactory abilities, memories and knowledge, and so the interpretive process is kept open and engaged. Smells also progress from one to the next, thus preventing a singular type of immersion with a unitary affect. Heterogeneous and surprising mixtures inevitably arise, sometimes building into an overwhelming blur of presumably pleasant smells.

Contrary to the predominant logic of "feeling" at work with the nosealgic experience of edible scent room sprays, *Synesthesia* demonstrates that smells are not inimical to the critical process. By vexing the difference between aromas and food, it reveals telling gaps between experience and expectation, memory and imagination. Beyond revisiting the archetype of Donna Reed domestic perfection, or restoring the nurturing essence of what is felt by many as a golden era, the unpredictability of smells in Sandover's installation focuses reflection upon the processes of historicization, nostalgia and stereotyping themselves.

Once unleashed from their substantive tether to food, aromas are notoriously volatile. On the one hand, the platefuls of air described above percolate with diverse symbolic meanings; on the other, they lend themselves to being utilized in ethically compromised practices, such as torture, manipulation and fantasy. Another way to write about the apparent shift from gastronomy to perfumology would be to frame it within the contemporary strains placed upon the Enlightenment notion of the bourgeois subject by state and corporate interests, interests which sabotage notions of bodily integrity and free will, as well as commodify and normalize what is presumed to be individualistic pursuits of happiness. Odors, however, are uncontainable. They tend to frustrate attempts to be harnessed and can impel mercurial reactions. That the new scent technologies and techniques have been resourcefully recuperated by artists with an activist practice introduces scent as a means for critical thought, which can then serve as the basis for an olfactory counterpolitics—an unexpected and nascent methodology, surely, but one redolent with possibilities.

Bibliography

Bell, D. and Valentine, G. (1997), *Consuming Geographies*, New York & London: Routledge.

Botschen, G. and Crowther, D. (2001), "The Semiology of Aesthetic Atmospherics to Study Environmental Design Effects in Retail Outlets," http://www.londonmet. ac.uk/depts/bssm/research/ssm/workingpapers.cfm.

Boym, S. (2001), *The Future of Nostalgia*, New York: Basic Books.

Butler, D., Gibson, H. and Gibson, K. (1999), "Attention All Shoppers," *Time*, 2 August, 154, http://www.ecomist.com.au/Time%20Article.htm.

Davies, B.J, Kooijmanb, D. and Warda, P. (2003), "The Sweet Smell of Success," *Journal of Marketing Management*, 1 June, 19: 611–627.

Gelato Bar & Pasticceria. (2002), "Special: Ice Cream," 4(18), http://www.ilgelato. net/numero18/i-sp-gel.htm.

Gillen, S. (2004), "It's an Ol-Factory," *Denver Business Journal*, 26 April, http://denver. bizjournals.com/denver/stories/2004/04/26/smallb1.html?page=2.

Harris, D. (2000), *Cute, Quaint, Hungry and Romantic*, New York: Basic Books.

ITV (2003), "Blaine's Burger 'Torture,'" 9 September, http://www.itv.com/news/144678. html.

Korsmeyer, C. (1999), *Making Sense of Taste*, Ithaca & London: Cornell University Press.

Kotler, P. (1973/74), "Atmospherics as a Marketing Tool," *Journal of Retailing*, Winter, 49: 48–64.

La Via del Profumo (n.d.), "Olfactory Marketing," http://www.profumo.it/perfume/ olfactory_communication/olfactory_marketing.htm.

Losowsky, A. (2002), "The Nose Has It," *Hotline*, July, http://www.losowsky.com/ archives/005913.html.

Lupton, D. (1994), "Food, Memory and Meaning," *The Sociological Review*, 42(4): 664–85.

Maldonado, T. (1991), "The Idea of Comfort," *Design Issues*, Autumn, 8: 35–43.

Mickleburgh, R. (2004), "Scents and Sensibility Clash in Ritzy West Vancouver," *Globe & Mail*, 18 November: A11.

Miller, W.I. (1997), "Gluttony," *Representations*, 60: 92–112.

Newsmonthly of Vending, Foodservice, Coffee Service and Coin-Operated Recreational Services (2004), "Advertising Executive Sees New Scent Technology and Vending as Powerful Brand-Building Vehicle," January, 44, http://www.scentair.com/pdf/ newscentart.pdf.

Paik, N.J. (1994), "To Catch Up or Not to Catch Up with the West," in A. Munroe (ed.), *Japanese Art After 1945*, New York: Abrams, pp. 77–81.

Paul, N.C. (2003), "Aroma-added Packaging Aims to Allure You," *The Christian Science Monitor*, 4 August, http://www.csmonitor.com/2003/0804/p15s01–wmcn.html.

Prose, F. (2003), *Gluttony*, Oxford: Oxford University Press; New York: New York Public Library.

Rakowitz, M. (2003), *Circumventions*, Paris: Onestar Press; New York: Dena Foundation for Contemporary Art.

Roseberry, W. (1996), "The Rise of Yuppie Coffees and the Reimagination of Class in the United States," *American Anthropologist*, 98(4): 762–75.

Sandover, A. (2000), *Synesthesia*, New York: Henry Urbach Architecture.

Schifferstein, H.N.J. and Blok, S.T. (2002), "The Signal Function of Thematically (In)congruent Ambient Scents in a Retail Environment," *Chemical Senses*, 27: 539–49.

Schlosser, E. (2001), *Fast Food Nation*, New York: Houghton Mifflin.

Spector, A. (2003), "New Tech Makes Dollars by Appealing to Senses," *Nation's Restaurant News*, 19 May, http://www.nrn.com.

Visser, M. (1991), *The Rituals of Dinner*, Toronto: HarperCollins.

Vroon, P. (1997), *Smell: The Secret Seducer*, New York: Farrar, Straus & Giroux.

Weisman, K. (2003), "Brands Turn on to Senses," *International Herald Tribune*, 4 December, http://www.iht.com/articles/120122.html.

X3D Technologies (2004), "ScentAir Technologies Integrates Scent Systems with X3D Technologies," http://www.x3d.com/news/press 2004–04–30 scentair.html.

30
Self-Portrait in Scent
Sketch #1

Clara Ursitti

propionic acid
butyric acid
iso-valeric acid
acetic acid
heptatonic acid
2–methyl acetonic acid
putresine
trimethyle amine
heptane thiol
carbon disulphite
marcapto ethanol
iso-eugenol
acetones
androstene dieneone
skatole

(1994)

31

Digital Scratch and Virtual Sniff

Simulating Scents

Mark W.D. Paterson

The scent organ was playing a delightfully refreshing Herbal Capriccio—
rippling arpeggios of thyme and lavender, of rosemary, basil, myrtle, tarragon;
a series of daring modulations through the spice keys into ambergris; and a
slow return through sandalwood, camphor, cedar and newmown hay (with
occasional subtle touches of discord—a whiff of kidney pudding, the faintest
suspicion of pig's dung) back to the simple aromatics with which the piece
began.

Aldous Huxley, *Brave New World*

The sensory imaginary in works of fiction is often an interesting, if not
accurate, guide to future technological developments. Aldous Huxley's
Brave New World ([1932] 2004), for example, proposed the "feelies" as an
alternative to the "movies," where tactual effects were provided along with
the visual component in a large theater. This has not come about in the form
he envisaged, yet the technologies of touch in computer-aided design have
become rapidly accepted, and in the case of videogames nearly ubiquitous.
Similarly, in this same work of dystopian fiction, the "scent organ" fulfils a
theatrical function by pumping a range of smells into public space in a way
comparable to the production of sound, and sometimes as an accompaniment
to the feelies. Why not have smell symphonies, as articulate in the production
of odorific tones as sonic ones? And, by the same logic that sound came to
accompany the image in the age of the "talkies," why not the other sensory
modalities like touch and smell? As a gimmick this has worked through the

use of scratch 'n' sniff cards, most infamously in John Waters' "Odorama" film, *Polyester* (1981). However, in terms of more serious commercial use, just like the "feelies," Huxley's "scent organ" becomes transposed from the setting of the public theater into the realm of the computer desktop.

The human–computer interface has incorporated non-textual elements for a long time. Current computer and videogame interactions, for instance, encourage "hands on" experience, allowing tactile and aural input and providing visual, aural and tactile feedback. Of course, the noticeably missing sensory channels are taste and smell, and the apparent absurdity of producing smell through desktop computers has been met with both excitement and opprobrium by pundits and commentators. An important and illustrative example is DigiScent's iSmell device, a "personal scent synthesizer" for desktop computers, much hyped and celebrated in a *Wired* magazine cover story which featured the author's experiences of a working prototype (Platt 1999). Yet two years later an article in the same magazine bemoaned its non-appearance, describing how the company had folded: "In some ways the Digiscents experience will push back [the release of smell synthesizers] by a few years" (Manjoo 2001). The purpose of this chapter is not simply to ask "What went wrong?," since this is partly due to the business model of the company. However, some of the strong reactions evinced by journalists and the public about the use of smell in the expanded sensory space of the computer desktop are illustrative of the undervalued role of smell in Western society's sensory episteme. The DigiScents episode shows the limitations of thinking "multimedia" as not being truly "multisensory," and reveals related issues concerning simulation, commodification and the use of scent as yet another e-tailing (electronic retailing) tool.

A Brief History of Smell as Media

Perhaps the earliest example of smell as media occurred in 1906 when S. L. Rothafel, the owner of a film theater in Forest City, PA, dipped cotton in rose scent and held it in front of an electric fan, thereby suffusing the theater with floral fragrance during the newsreel screening of a Pasadena Rose Bowl game (Ijsselsteijn 2003). In the 1950s, to compete with the increasingly popular medium of television, the move towards immersive and multisensory cinema formats revived technologies that were available in the late nineteenth and early twentieth centuries, such as 3D and widescreen. To differentiate cinema from television, filmmakers sought to enhance the cinematic experience with psychological impact and physiological arousal. Some of these technologies were visual, such as Cinemascope and Cinerama, based on advances in projection and lenses. Some were tactile, such as Percepto technology used for the 1959 film *The Tingler*, which added vibration to individual cinema seats.

Around 1960, two olfactory cinematic technologies arrived, Smell-O-Vision and Aromarama. Both used a scent track on the film itself to trigger odors, analogous to a soundtrack. And both technologies faced problems common to any form of smell media. Firstly, there was the challenge of synchronizing the release of odors with specific audio-visual events in the film, in which the immediacy of the audio-visual was restrained by the slow diffusion of scent, especially in a large theater space. Secondly, the dispersal and change of one scent into another was not instantaneous, and had to be carefully managed if odorific confusion was not desired. Fast and efficient dispersal and subsequent removal was a necessity for such technologies. Aromarama distributed scents through the air conditioning system, and used Freon gas to help dispense the smells. This did not work well enough, though, and often left an unpleasant mixture of smells. The flagship production for Aromarama was an Italian travel feature about China entitled *Beyond the Great Wall* (1958), whose tagline read: "You must breathe it to believe it!" Throughout the film a range of thirty-one odors were released sequentially. The fidelity of the odors were generally felt to be lacking, however, as one critic opined:

> A beautiful old pine grove in Peking, for instance, smells rather like a subway rest room on disinfectant day. Besides, the odors are strong enough to give a bloodhound a headache. What is more, the smells are not always removed as rapidly as the scene requires: at one point, the audience distinctly smells grass in the middle of the Gobi desert. (*Time Magazine* 1959: 57)

The following year brought the Smell-O-Vision film *Scent of Mystery*, which featured the slogan: "First they moved (1895)! Then they talked (1927)! Now they smell!" Smell-O-Vision used a system of pipes to dispense scents from under each theater seat, but again the fidelity of the smells was compromised by problems of dispersal. A *New York Times* reviewer dismissed the "novel stimulation" as "bunk," beginning the review brusquely: "If there is anything of lasting value to be learned from ... *Scent of Mystery*, it is that motion pictures and synthetic smells do not mix" (Crowther 1960: 9). Smell-O-Vision was also listed in *Time Magazine*'s (2000) reader-polled "Top 100 worst ideas of all time."

After the critical and commercial failure of these scent technologies in the cinema, it would be surprising if anyone revisited the territory of enhancing the cinema audience experience through smell, but that is exactly what occurred in John Waters' 1981 film *Polyester*, which used "Odorama." Deliberately conceived as an affectionate pastiche of 1950s cinema and the kitsch experimentation of the 1960s, the audience was famously provided with scratch 'n' sniff cards imprinted with synthetic smells. At various points in the film a number appeared in the corner of the screen, suggesting that the corresponding number on the card be scratched and sniffed. According to Lefcowitz (2002), the worst smell was dirty socks. Something of this mischievous sense of humor and warm homage to an earlier generation of movies was revisited for the 2003 film *Rugrats go Wild!*, which also distributed Odorama scratch 'n' sniff cards in direct tribute to Waters' *Polyester*, with some of the smells being flowers, strawberries and an infant's feet. Bearing in mind the commercial failure of smell-enabled films, the resurfacing of these smell media through different generations of films, cable TV (accompanying four episodes of *The Wild Thornberrys* on Nickleodeon in 1999), an upcoming scratch 'n' sniff comic book (Boom! Studios' *Zombie Tales*) and even English National Opera's scratch 'n' sniff production of Prokofiev's *Love for Three Oranges* (1988) is testament to the significance of smell as media in popular memory, if not exactly as cinematic success.

These same difficulties in smell media were faced by DigiScents Corp., which in 1999 announced a smell interface for personal computers, and produced a working prototype that was demonstrated at trade shows. From an odor palette of 100 to 150 primary scents, a vast range of smells could be from synthesized, from coffee beans to wood smoke. Through the iSmell device, argued the founders of DigiScents Joel Bellenson and Dexster Smith, web browsing experiences could be enhanced by smelling the products on offer, or becoming immersed in interactive adventures by adding digitally produced smells (Platt 1999: 258; Brownstein 2000). Reminiscent of Huxley's "scent organ," it was also envisaged that there could be an additional smell track encoded onto DVD films, videogames and websites. The encoding of such media with smell data meant that, despite a working prototype being demonstrated and enthused upon by journalists, and even by digital and performance artists (see e.g. deLahunta 2003), it became rendered unto history as yet another obsolete gimmick—the latest "next big thing" that never happened.

Despite the failure of the iSmell device, an alternative artificial scent generator has been recently undergoing trials courtesy of TriSenx. Independent of the now-defunct DigiScents, TriSenx, which stands for Tri-Sensory Enhanced Net Xperience, has been publicizing "scent domes"—scent generators connected to the computer desktop. Roughly the size of a toaster, the device consists of a circular cartridge containing separate chambers of chemical scents, with a fan outputting combinations of the scents to produce approximations of complex smells. In 2004 a UK Internet provider was conducting trials to investigate the scent domes' e-marketing potential, especially for supermarkets interested in tempting customers with the smell of fresh produce and travel agencies seeking to sell trips to exotic locations. Trials were also underway for scents to be delivered by email. While the scent of roses may not be as romantic as a real bouquet, a fragranced email from a lover or suitor may have a more profound effect than text alone. Building on the commonplace observation that smells have a direct connection with people's emotions, an anthropologist straightforwardly described the effects of the scent dome: "Smells trigger very powerful and deep-seated emotional responses, and this additional element to the Internet will enhance users' online experience by adding that crucial third dimension" (Knight 2004).

The role of olfaction within ambient media, that is, media that can drift from peripheral consciousness to the focus of our attention and back again, is an area of increasing interest. Scents can be noticed almost instantaneously, but unlike the rapid refresh rates of video or audio, current olfactory technology takes time to evolve one odor into the next. For the most part, scent is additive. If two scents are present simultaneously, these often combine into a newly perceived scent unless they are clear and distinct, such as lemon and mint. A scent symphony would therefore be a slow, ambient piece that slowly resolves one scent into another, or that can simultaneously produce multiple distinct smells like chords in music.

In terms of ambient media, there are advantages in this. Since scent as a sign is not necessarily tied to any referent, artificial smells can be used as protean signaling devices. For instance, could not the smell of cinnamon, diffused in the morning air as one left the door, indicate heavy traffic on the way to work? Kaye (2002) explores this notion of smell as ambient media signaling states or events, and calls them "smicons." As an element of the human–computer interface, then, smell and other ambient media can extend the way that information is displayed to the user, and explore that area between focused attention and peripheral awareness. Ishii et al.'s (1998) ambientROOM, for example, is a complete immersive environment, a prototype combination of digital and naturalistic, analog workspace where information is displayed in indirect ways to the user:

> One area for further exploration is the fuzzy boundary between the background and foreground of awareness. When a new process or activity catches our interest, it is often integrated smoothly into our foreground awareness. (Ishii et al. 1998: 174)

In this ambientROOM, graspable items such as bottles form ways of objectifying and interacting with information, and ambient sound such as artificial traffic noise or a babbling stream can signify email activity. Most interesting, however, is the significance of smell in prompting crossovers between background and foreground awareness, a factor noted by Kaye (2002; 2004). Going beyond the commonplace associations of smell, such as the scent of roses for romance, the use of smell within ambient media can open to association with a wide variety of events. To trigger the nostalgic odor of bubblegum or crayons to create reminders or rewards within the workplace, for example, is to forge new sensory associations, what Stevenson (2001: 562; Stevenson, Boakes and Prescott 1998) terms "learned synesthesia."

The Pejorative Senses of Smell, or That Website Stinks!

The negative associations attributed to smell in cultural history are echoed in the strangely hostile reaction by technology commentators to the idea of a scent synthesizer or desktop smell device. In contrast to *Wired*'s enthusiastic greeting of the new epoch of smell-enabled desktops, websites such as techdirt. com offered scathing comments and outright hostility. The suggestion that multimedia content may soon be accompanied by smells, as was the case with the iSmell device, "invariably provokes a knee-jerk reaction of disbelief or even hostility," wrote one IT journalist (*PC Pro* 2000). The difficulty in assimilating claims made by companies like DigiScents and TriSenx about the usefulness and novelty of smell in a desktop environment is historically tainted by association with the cinematic smell media of Aromarama, Smell-O-Vision and Odorama. Read in an unironic and unsympathetic way, these cinematic smell media are seen as, at best, mere gimmickry and, at worst, a technological cul-de-sac which sets back the serious adoption of smell in the digital domain. It was with this form of tech-savvy negativity that the Internet hoax RealAroma website was set up.

When the company Real Networks first came out with the Real Player software for listening to streaming audio on computers in the mid 1990s, a site for a faux product called RealAroma arrived, boasting the ability to deliver scents over an Internet connection. On the RealAroma site, the use of CUseeMe ("see you, see me") software, an actual product which allows real-time video conferencing over the Internet, was parodied with a bogus description of "SmellU-SmellMe" software. This non-existent software and technology was informed perhaps by the incessant innovation and perceived gimmickry of an ever-expanding and increasingly commercialized Internet. Based on this parody, a story on the website techdirt.com, "The Return of iSmell—How to Sniff Out a Bad Idea," skeptically charted the rebirth of smell media through the iSmell and TriSenx devices described above, referring back to the failed experiments in cinema, and arguing that it brings "a whole new meaning to the phrase 'that website stinks'" (TechDirt.com 2004). Other contributors to the site humorously suggested the possibility of smell viruses, where stenches could be triggered in millions of homes in the same way that email viruses spread. Envisioning a scenario where smell devices become increasingly popular on desktops, one contributor wrote a fake newspaper report:

> The entire world woke up to fecal (and other) smells today, as the Smell Virus infected another 200,000,000 machines. This virus causes the DigiScents peripheral to emit odors that cannot be properly be described in a family newspaper. This virus takes advantage of a weakness in Internet Explorer (all versions 5 and 6), and so far Microsoft has not been able to find a patch. (TechDirt.com 2004)

Such cynical responses to new smell media may be partly apportioned to a healthy resistance to innovation for innovation's sake, especially in a commercial form where money is increasingly derived from Internet-based activities. Another factor is the particularity of the sense of smell and its history of being disregarded, which is compounded by the failed experiments and mixture of earnest belief and self-aware pastiche that such cinematic smell media encompassed. A further factor to consider is that of scent and control: while scratch 'n' sniff is a basic technology, one which is voluntary and does not impose on the user, ambient smell is more intrusive and persistent. Bad smells are feared as invasions into one's personal space and, even more so, their persistence reveals the lack of control one has over the environment. It is also likely that the odor extends beyond the confines of the desktop, and may leak into other spaces in the home or office. One final factor involves the often involuntary emotional reaction engendered by smell. In a carefully managed affective life, smell may evoke pleasant reveries, like a cyber-Proust, perhaps. But smells may also intrude into one's psychic life and release unwanted memories, or possibly disturb individuals in other unpleasant ways.

Smelling, Browsing, Shopping

> Can you smell a ripe peach online? Can you accidentally discover a shoe that feels so good you impulsively take three pair?
>
> Paco Underhill, *Why We Buy*

The retail environment is a relentlessly sensual place, and shopping is therefore a notably sensual experience. There is almost a child-like behavioral regression engaged by browsing shoppers: they reach out and touch, caress, hold and play with objects; they smell or taste pencils, pens, foodstuffs, soaps; they see and interact with the colors of the carpets, walls and objects; and they listen to music in the store, or the advice of friends, or even the music they wish to buy. A retail psychologist advises: "There's barely one of our senses that doesn't get assaulted the minute we walk through the door" (BBC 2002). Some of these sensory experiences register consciously, and some are used as unconscious cues. There are fairly well-known techniques in retail psychology, and smell is used frequently (see e.g. Paterson 2005). The most familiar is the wafting the smell of baking bread throughout a supermarket, which forms what Underhill calls "an olfactory trail" of "warm, homely scents" (2003: 164) that inevitably directs shoppers from every aisle toward the bakery section. Of course, with online retailing the sensual shopper is frustrated. Despite its ease and convenience, as yet the texture of clothing, the smell of a new perfume or the taste of a new chocolate bar cannot be experienced. Hence Underhill's lament: shoppers can browse for myriad goods and services and, like my mother, even conduct supermarket shopping online. Yet how can the warm smell of baking bread or the tempting juicy ripeness of a peach be conveyed?

The massive growth of online or electronic retailing (e-tail) prompts new ways to think about the materiality and sensuality of virtual objects. While some online products and retail environments exist in a shadowy netherworld between the actual and the virtual, in terms of stock supply, warehousing and delivery processes, it has been found that, even in the case of the supply of pure services as opposed to products in an online retail environment, customers need to browse and be assured of a physical existence of the company and/or product. Retail psychology literature refers to this as "service tangibility," where "tangible cues in the environment help shape consumer attitudes and behavior" (Koernig 2003: 152). In the case of services as opposed to products, it has been found that the more intangible a product is, the more these tangible cues are sought. This is the case in the physical environment of the store, where ambient and sensory factors such as smell, air quality and lighting obviously affect consumer response. Importantly this translates to an online retail environment, where the tangible cues become different, using pictures, symbols, facts and informational items within the website to accomplish the sense of a physical, and therefore reassuring and dependable, presence of the services or objects.

Desktop devices such as the iSmell and TriSenx scent synthesizers extend and supplement the visual aesthetic, introducing smell into desktop commerce. If going shopping is a multi-sensory experience, it is only fitting that online shopping allows touch, taste and smell too. Such smell devices feature a multifaceted array of olfactory symbolic means, including connotations (common cultural associations), learned synesthetic associations (the smell of crayons or freshly-mown grass signifying childhood), and purely arbitrary olfactory codes (cinnamon signaling highway traffic, and so on).[1] In the online retail environment, the power of smell media has promise, and despite the existence of two consumer-based desktop scent synthesizers, has yet to deliver. To present the sensual, experiential aspect of shopping, that is, to bring the full sensory retail environment of the physical store back home via the desktop, inexpensive scent synthesizers that have the fidelity to accompany the browsing of fruit in an online supermarket site would greatly increase the available tangible cues for ordinary consumers. But the democratization of smell synthesizers, and the apparent benefits to online retail experiences, is still some way off. Writing about this in his book on retail psychology, Paco Underhill discusses the missing sensory experiences and mentions a "box" that recreates "realistic smells," presumably a prototype of iSmell. His conclusion, and a sentiment I find fitting to summarize the promise of smell in online retail, is: "Not too believable or widespread yet, but it could bring my ripe peach online someday" (Underhill 2003: 223).

Perhaps the true test of such technologies comes when something so direct and profound as the smell of nostalgia, of ambient signaling, or the smell of juicy ripeness can be reproduced. When the simulation of such smells, through inexpensive scent synthesis, is integrated into the human–computer interface, and consumers' multisensory retail experiences become truly multimedia in online shopping, then scent will be properly accommodated as an important component of digital media. In short, it is not technology at present that is the problem—but a shift in cultural attitude.

Note

1. There are other electronic ambient smell devices, such as the ScentAir, the Aerome and the Olfacom (Kaye 2004: 56; www.osmooze.com), devices that plug into the computer and offer the controlled release of odor, at various scales from the computer desktop to large commercial spaces. While some of these scents can invoke mood-altering effects, these devices are basically electronically-controlled, precision air fresheners.

Bibliography

BBC (2002), "Who's Playing Mind Games With You?," 19 April, http://news.bbc.co.uk/1/hi/programmes/working_lunch/guides/consumer/1939231.stm.
—— (2004), "E-mail Tries Out a Sense of Smell," 19 February, http://news.bbc.co.uk/1/hi/technology/3502821.stm.
Brownstein, M. (2000), "Click & Sniff!," *Computer Technology Review*, http://www.findarticles.com/cf_dls/m0BRZ/4_20/62408983/p1/article.jhtml.
Crowther, B. (1960), "How Does it Smell?," *New York Times*, 28 February, Section 2: 9.
deLahunta, S. (2003), "Sniffable Media," *Performance Research*, 8(3): 85–6.
Huxley, A. ([1932] 2004), *Brave New World*, London: Vintage Classics.
Ijsselsteijn, W.A. (2003), "Presence in the Past," in G. Riva, F. Davide and W.A. Ijsselsteijn (eds), *Being There*, Amsterdam: IOS Press, pp. 18–39.
Ishii, H., Wisneski, C., Brave, S., Dahley, A., Gorbet, M., Ullmer, B. and Yarin, P. (1998), "ambientROOM," *CHI 98: ACM Conference on Human Factors & Computing Systems*, New York: ACM Press, pp. 173–4.
Kaye, J. (2002), "The Olfactory Display of Abstract Information," http://xenia.media.mit.edu/_jofish/writing/smell.as.media.short.paper.pdf.
—— (2004), "Making Scents," *Interactions*, 11(1): 48–61.
Knight, W. (2004), "Smelly Device Would Liven Up Web Browsing," *New Scientist*, 20 (February): 22.
Koernig, S. K. (2003), "E-Scapes," *Psychology and Marketing*, 20(2): 151–67.
Lefcowitz, E. (2002), "Retro Future," http://www.retrofuture.com/smell-o-vision.html.

Manjoo, F. (2001), "Vaporware 2001," *Wired News*, http: //www.wired.com/news/ technology/0,1282,49326,00.html.

Paterson, M.W.D. (2005), *Consumption and Everyday Life*, London: Routledge.

PC Pro (2000), "Get Ready for Fragrant Web Sites," 6 December 2000, http://www. pcpro.co.uk/news/news_story.php?id=23182.

Platt, C. (1999), "You've Got Smell!," *Wired*, 7(11): 256–63.

RealAroma, http://web.archive.org/web/1996/1231045934/http://realaroma.com.

Stevenson, R. J. (2001), "The Acquisition of Odor Qualities," *The Quarterly Journal of Experimental Psychology*, 54A(2): 561–77.

Stevenson, R.J., Boakes, R.A. and Prescott, J. (1998), "Changes in Flavour Sweetness Resulting from Implicit Learning of a Simultaneous Flavour–Sweetness Association," *Learning and Motivation*, 29: 113–32.

TechDirt.com (2004), "The Return of iSmell," 19 February, http://www.techdirt.com/ articles/20040219/0842244.shtml.

Time Magazine (1959), "A Sock in the Nose," 21 December, 57.

—— (2000), "The 100 Worst Ideas of the Century," 19 January, http://www.time. com/time100/worstideas.html.

Underhill, P. (2003), *Why We Buy*, New York: Texere.

Part VII

Sublime Essences

Preface

When consciousness rules breath, with inbreath we can smell all perfumes.

Kaushitika Upanishad (Mascaró)

It is fitting to end this anthology with mystical and sublime olfactory phenomena. Emotionally vivid, mysteriously evocative, evanescent yet powerfully present—these are some of the qualities that make smells so compelling to experience and contemplate. They are also representative, perhaps in a dramatic way, of what is not known or understood about smell and its processes of perception and cognition. The continuing use of herbs, incense and aromatic oils in spiritual practices from Neolithic times to the present day testifies to the endlessly varying esoteric significance that odors embody, giving credence to the claim by Gaston Bachelard that "Odors in and of themselves make myths possible" (qtd. in Le Guérer 1992: 128; see also Detienne [1972] 1994; Fischer-Rizzi 1996; Worwood 1999). As much as an aromatic atmosphere of worship focuses attention, sets a mood, and creates the collective "we-feeling" remarked upon by Largey and Watson in Part I, scents have been perpetually endowed with divine qualities, even, at times, the ability to prompt the incarnation of deities themselves, such as expressed in the Buddhist tradition of the *gandhakuti*, or "perfumed chamber," in which it is said that a combination of gold, sandalwood and camphor has the ability to materialize the Buddha himself (Strong 1977: 405–6). Exquisite fragrances can be the reward of disciplined asceticism and the attainment of enlightenment consciousness, as the quote from the *Upanishads* above implies (see Muktananda 1981: 14, 59), and, contrarily, abject odors can be the focus of meditative practice and serve as the path to nirvana, as found in Hirakawa's visceral version of Theravada Buddhism discussed in Part V. In the following chapters, Christian, Muslim, New Guinean, Hindu and New Age spiritualities, while emerging from different contexts, can be seen to share a number of traits as people from diverse eras and locations around the globe employ olfactory media to channel communication between earthly and transcendental worlds.

In the consciousness of premodern Christians, scent could be considered both a divine blessing and a sign of being divine. The legendary "odor of sanctity," the supernatural fragrance radiated by individuals in a state of grace, gave perceptible proof to the belief that the power of spirituality prevailed over physical limitations and the body's innate corruptibility. The scent of one such saint, Teresa of Avila, cured illnesses and worked miracles, and survived her own death undiminished in relics and objects she had touched. Beyond the odor of sanctity, other odoriferous phenomena so infused premodern Christian thinking and practices that, as Constance Classen remarks in her chapter, there is a temptation to speak of it as an "olfactory theology." As much as sublimely pleasant scents belonged the virtuous, and alluded to the sweet fragrances of heaven, unpleasant odors were believed to be emitted by the sinful, of whom the Devil was the foulest, with his lair in Hell discharging the most unbearable of stenches. As suggested by the many references to olfaction in the Bible, and in the writings of commentators like St John of the Cross, smell often served as a primary model for human–divine interaction. The ancient associations between smell and spirit aligned with the popular belief that odors revealed the inner truth of objects, thus producing a conception of the soul itself as an entity akin to, if not directly constituted by, scent.

Smell is no less complex or less integrated in the Muslim context, which has its own traditions of scented saints (Evans 2002). The chapter by Françoise Aubaile-Sallenave examines religious practices and rites of passage present throughout North African and Middle Eastern Arabic culture, where scent is found to accompany life's most eventful moments. Prayer, for instance, requires the adept to undergo a process of purification. Scented ablutions, based on precedents by Mohammed, prepare the body, breath and mental state prior to entering a mosque or engaging in religious acts. Fumigations, incense, fragrant amulets and sachets, aromatic oils and foods, and other odorous mixtures greet individuals at transitional, and therefore vulnerable, episodes in their lifetime (see Howes 1991). Birth, circumcision, marriage, sickness and death—each life situation co-exists with certain dangers, and each features the use of specialized herbs, unguents or scents to garner protection against malevolent forces, to preserve health and well-being, and to ensure one's proper progression through the ceremony.

Alfred Gell's "Magic, Perfume, Dream..." explores the importance of the olfactory in the magical spells of Umeda villagers in Papua New Guinea, and in the process contributes a number of significant observations about the sense of smell in general. Magic, he argues, is the practice that commingles matter and meaning. Smells function particularly well in magical contexts, for they possess an ambivalent status: attached as they are to the physical world in their origin, their volatility as they escape and disappear into the atmosphere accords them equal standing in the realm of abstraction. In other words, scents are substances that both operate in the real world and yet are as near to becoming a concept as material things can get. It is this dual aspect of smells that lends it efficacy as a divinatory tool in the Umedan worldview, allowing it to act as a medium of exchange between the earthly and spiritual worlds, and making it conducive to the seeking of visions and successful hunting. Lest the inference be made that such magical thinking only pertains to non-Western cultures, Gell points out a similar logic underlying the purchase of perfumes in the West. Like the Umedan magical substance *oktesap*, which imparts to the user a symbolic awareness of the ideal order, perfume offers its own form of transcendence to its wearer, only in this case it is the awareness of "the sweet life"—the promise and goal of the "religion" of consumerism.

Sanskrit literature is replete with fragrant imagery, and David Shulman's chapter on "The Scent of Memory" analyzes poetry, proverbs, mythological tales and devotional writings to ascertain the significance of olfaction in South Indian culture. "Memory" assumes multifaceted meanings in the framework of Hinduism, referring at once to the wistful remembrances of separated lovers in romantic poems, the yearning of devotees attempting to bridge the gulf between themselves and distant divinities, and to the efforts of individuals trying to address the particular challenges of their karmic past—odorous déjà vus so to speak. As Shulman argues, odors here are not just the instigations for recollection (as is understood by the "Proustian effect" mentioned in Section IV), they are the content of the memories themselves and can reconstitute forgotten contexts. Smells also carry the ability to effect major transformations of identity, and figure prominently in scenarios of redemption. Most importantly, it is the subtlety and immateriality of fragrance that imbues it with profound significance and influence. Invisible but everpresent, smells harbor essential existential truths and provide access to ultimate reality.

The final chapter in this section derives not from a specific spiritual tradition or cultural literature, but from interviews with thousands of North Americans who have encountered what William Guggenheim and Judith Guggenheim label "after-death communications" (ADCs). Featured here are ADCs of the olfactory variety, in which bereaved individuals report the spontaneous smelling of fragrances that were in some way intimately linked to the recently deceased. These supernatural experiences could be categorized as phantosmias, or olfactory hallucinations, but the pleasant and meaningful aromas recorded in these anecdotes differ sharply from the sustained and often foul sensations attributed to neurological or psychiatric dysfunctions that can have debilitating consequences (see Greenberg 1992; Hummel and Nordin 2005). Like near-death and out of body experiences, olfactory ADCs strike people regardless of their denominational background, can inspire transformational emotional affects and appear to miraculously defy understanding within current scientific paradigms. While these clairolfactive experiences exist on the edge of believability—to both readers and the witnesses themselves—the healing conferred upon those afflicted with grief, and the comfort provided about the eternality of the spirit, are unmistakable. The Guggenheim's collection of odoriferous events contemporizes the premodern phenomena of the odor of sanctity and the scent-like soul discussed at the beginning of this section, and provides raw research into what is evidently a widespread pan-religious belief in the afterlife.

Jim Drobnick

Bibliography

Detienne, M. ([1972] 1994), *The Gardens of Adonis*, trans. J. Lloyd, Princeton: Princeton University Press.

Evans, S. (2002), "The Scent of a Martyr," *Numen*, 49: 193–211.

Fischer-Rizzi, S. (1996), *The Complete Incense Book*, New York: Sterling.

Greenberg, M.S. (1992), "Olfactory Hallucinations," in M.J. Serby and K.L. Chobor (eds), *Science of Olfaction*, New York: Springer-Verlag, pp. 467–99.

Howes, D. (1991), "Olfaction and Transition," *The Varieties of Sensory Experience*, Boulder, CO: Westview, pp. 128–47.

Hummel, T. and Nordin, S. (2005), "Olfactory Disorders and their Consequences for Quality of Life," *Acta Oto-Laryngologica*, 125(2): 116–21.

Le Guérer (1992), *Scent*, New York: Random House.

Mascaró, J. (1978), *The Upanishads*, New York: Penguin.

Muktananda, S. (1981), *Where Are You Going?*, South Fallsburg, NY: SYDA Foundation.

Strong, J.S. (1977), "*Gandhakuti*," *History of Religions*, 16(4): 390–406.

Worwood, V.A. (1999), *The Fragrant Heavens*, Novato, CA: New World Library.

32

The Breath of God

Sacred Histories of Scent

Constance Classen

In modernity the sense of smell is usually associated with instincts and emotions rather than with reason or spirituality. With few exceptions, smell and smells have been discredited and removed from the arena of intellectual discourse, and, in many cases, from cultural life in general. In this deodorized ambience traditional olfactory concepts such as the "odor of sanctity" appear to be simply quaint relics of a more credulous age and not worthy of serious attention.

Prior to the modern, post-Enlightenment, era, however, smell was taken very seriously in the West. Nowhere is this more evident than in the importance assigned to things olfactory by the Church. The concept of the odor of sanctity, which we moderns tend to dismiss as a marginal (and suspect) phenomenon of an outmoded religious life, pre-modern society located at the center of a complex olfactory and spiritual network which encompassed the entire cosmos. As Piero Camporesi has written in *The Anatomy of the Senses*: "Both hell and paradise could be condensed into drops in the boiling still: celestial and infernal distillations opened the senses to an understanding of distant places" (1994: 125). To understand the historical significance of odor in Christianity, we must put aside our modern olfactory prejudices and explore the aromatic vapors produced by the fervid stills of earlier imaginations, from the stenches of hell to the sweet scents of heaven.

The Odor of Sanctity

Belief in an odor of sanctity was based on the notion that Christians who lived in a state of grace would be infused with the divine scent of the Holy

Spirit—the breath of God. This divine fragrance served as a means of making the presence of God known to others. St Paul in his second letter to the Corinthians (2: 14) wrote that God "uses us to spread abroad the fragrance of the knowledge of himself." An odor of sanctity was not the only, or even a necessary, sign of sainthood, but it was popularly regarded as one of the most notable.

Most commonly, an odor of sanctity is said to occur on or after the death of a saint. It was said of the eighth-century St Hubert of Brittany:

> When [St Hubert] breathed his last, there spread throughout Brittany an odor so sweet, that it seemed as if God had brought together all the flowers of spring to symbolize the heavenly sweetness which Hubert would enjoy in Paradise. (Geurin 1878: 312)

According to reports, when the coffin of St Francis Xavier was opened four months after his death in the sixteenth century, his body was found to be incorrupt and sweet-smelling, although no spices or balm had been used to prepare it for burial (Cobham Brewer 1966: 512).

A supernatural fragrance might also be noted during a saint's lifetime. In a story which indicates how sacred olfactory power might be translated into temporal power, the seventh-century St Valery is said to have interrupted a lecture given by St Colomban with his powerful odor of sanctity. Rather than being annoyed, however, St Colomban declared to the odoriferous Valery: "It is you, not I, who are the veritable head of this monastery" (Cobham Brewer 1966: 512). The thirteenth-century Blessed Herman of Steinfeld exhaled an odor of sanctity—"like a garden full of roses, lilies, violets, poppies and all kinds of fragrant flowers"—every time he said grace (Geurin 1878: 275). In the seventeenth century the nun Giovanna Maria della Croce left a trail of celestial fragrance wherever she went, enabling her fellow nuns to trace her movements around the convent (Thurston 1952: 229).

While there are hundreds of accounts of instances of the odor of sanctity in the annals of Christian sainthood, certain individuals were particularly renowned for their supernatural scents such as Teresa of Avila (1515–82). A description of the various olfactory phenomena which reputedly characterized her life and death will help the reader enter into the more redolent mentality of an earlier time and provide a basis for further exploring the sacred history of scent.

Teresa of Avila

Teresa of Avila, also known as Teresa of Jesus, was born in Spain in 1515. As a youth she entered the Carmelite order, which she subsequently undertook to radically reform. Teresa wrote several theological works, including *The Way of Perfection* and *The Interior Castle*, along with her autobiography. These writings and the numerous testimonies of friends and colleagues concerning Teresa's life and death provide a rich fund of information about one of Christianity's most venerated saints. Teresa is probably best known for her mystical raptures, during which she was alternately tormented by the Devil and pierced by the love of God. These raptures were occasionally accompanied by olfactory sensations. Of an unwilling visit to hell, for example, she wrote; "The entrance seemed like a long narrow lane ... and on the ground there was a filthy mud which reeked of pestilential odors" (Teresa 1972: 143). The most notable olfactory phenomena associated with the saint, however, do not concern her renowned raptures, but the odor of sanctity diffused by her body just prior to, and after, death.

During her last illness, Teresa is said to have emitted a fragrance so powerful that it scented everything she touched. This scent remained on her clothes, on the dishes she used, and even in the water with which the dishes were washed. So persistent was this fragrance that, many days after the saint's death, a nun who noticed a sweet odor in the kitchen traced it to a salt shaker that Teresa had used (Ribera 1908: 339–40).

As a treatment for her illness, the saint was prescribed a medicine with a very unpleasant odor. It happened that this medicine was spilt over her bed-clothes just as the Duchess of Alba was coming for a visit. Teresa apologized for the foul odor but the Duchess responded; "Don't worry, Mother, for you smell instead as if you had been sprinkled with perfume" (Ribera 1908: 334). On another occasion, a priest, smelling the fragrant breath of the saint, suspected she was freshening her breath with scented candies. When he asked her attendant about this, the woman replied that Teresa was barely able to eat any food because the odor made her nauseous (a chronic affliction of the saint). Much less, therefore, could she have tolerated a strongly flavored candy (Ribera 1908: 340).

After Teresa's death, in 1582, her body retained its fragrance. So overpowering was this scent, indeed, that it was necessary to keep the window of the room open during the saint's wake. The priest in attendance declared it a marvel "that a dead body ... which causes more disgust than anything else in this life because of the unbearable stench it usually gives off ... could produce such a fragrant scent" (Ribera 1908: 340).

When St Teresa was interred, odors were noted coming from the sepulcher, particularly on the feast days of those saints for whom she had had a special devotion. These odors were said to sometimes smell like lilies, and sometimes like jasmine or violet. Intrigued by the sweet scents, the nuns decided to have the saint's coffin opened to see if her body were incorrupt. When the coffin was taken out it was found to be rotten. Dirt and mold had entered through the rotted wood and covered the body of the saint. Nonetheless, while the saint's clothes were decayed and moldy-smelling, the body itself was whole and fragrant. The nuns removed the soiled clothes and washed the body, an act which filled the whole nunnery with fragrance for several days. Impressed by such signs of sanctity, the priest who had overseen the disinterment cut off the left hand from the corpse and presented it as an important relic to the Carmelite nunnery in Lisbon. The body was then reinterred (Ribera 1908: 527–8).

The fragrance of St Teresa's corpse was not only wondrous in itself, it also performed wonders. One of its reported powers was to cure people who suffered from anosmia—the lack of a sense of smell. During the saint's wake, for example, a nun who had lost her sense of smell regretted not being able to smell the fragrance emanating from the body. On kissing the saint's foot, however, she recovered her lost sense and was able to experience the same fragrance as her sisters. In the Lisbon nunnery where St Teresa's hand had been taken, there was a novice born without a sense of smell. On bringing the hand close to her nose the novice felt a warm vapor penetrating her nostrils followed by a sensation of odor. To test whether she had actually recovered her sense of smell the nuns brought different scents to the novice and she was able to distinguish those which were fragrant from those which were foul. In Alba, where the saint was buried, a man who had lost his sense of smell for almost two years due to a severe cold recovered it after putting a cloth which had touched the saint's arm on his head. After four days he was able to smell herbal scents, following which he regained his sense of smell in its entirety (Ribera 1908: 340, 546, 558).

Curiosity about the nature of the fragrance emitted by St Teresa's body led to a number of experiments being performed. One was conducted in the presence of the Lisbon Inquisitor. At that time a portion of civet was found to lose its scent after being brought in contact with St Teresa's hand. This was considered noteworthy indeed in those days when it was generally believed that "there is nothing which can take away the good odor from civet or musk" (Paracelsus 1894: 61).

As Teresa's reputation for sanctity grew, so did the demand for relics. So incorruptible was her flesh, that it was said that to have a piece of it was as good as having bones of other saints. Desirous to return the saint's body to its birthplace, a group of Carmelite priests had it secretly disinterred from the convent of Alba, in 1585, and taken to Avila. The nuns of Alba were alerted to their loss by a strong fragrance which penetrated the choir where they were reciting matins. They tracked the scent to the main door of the convent, but by that time the body had already been removed. As a consolation, the fathers had left St Teresa's left arm (less the hand which had previously been removed) for the nuns of Alba (Ribera 1908: 529–30, 536).

In Avila St Teresa's body was examined by physicians, who declared it miraculous that a corpse which had never been embalmed nor treated in any way could be so well preserved and so sweet-smelling. In Alba the arm which had been left behind was discovered to produce a fragrant oil which impregnated the cloths in which it was kept wrapped. Each time this happened the scented material would be given away as a relic and the arm wrapped in a fresh cloth (Ribera 1908: 532, 536).

The inhabitants of Alba, however, were not content to remain with only an arm of St Teresa after having possessed the whole body. After much negotiation, the Pope finally ordered that the holy corpse be returned to Alba. On its trip back, in 1586, the body reportedly exhaled such an irresistible odor that, as it was carried by a cornfield, the workers were enticed to drop their flails and follow it. From then on St Teresa's body remained in Alba (Ribera 1908: 532).

Heavenly Scents

The olfactory phenomena which pervade the history of Teresa were understood within the context of age-old beliefs concerning the natural and supernatural qualities of smell. The Christian concept of the odor of sanctity had its roots in the aromatic myths and rituals of the ancient world. The gods of Greece and Rome were believed to exhale the sweet scent of ambrosia, a mythical liquid which served both as food and perfume to the deities. In classical mythology, a supernatural fragrance is one of the characteristic signs of the presence of a deity.

The gods of antiquity not only emitted good odors, they also delighted in receiving them. Fragrant floral garlands, incense, and burnt offerings were all rendered as olfactory tributes to the deities by their followers. In return, it was believed that the gods would occasionally grant the gift of immortality, or at least of corporeal incorruptibility, to a favored mortal by anointing him or her with ambrosia. Thus humans and deities were united in an olfactory cycle, whereby sweet scents traveled up from earth to the gods and down from the gods to earth.

The early Christians made ample use of olfactory imagery drawn from ancient traditions in their writings. The actual employment of perfumes and incense, however, tended to be associated with debauchery and idolatry within Christianity. Prayers, it was held, were the "incense" of Christians, and righteousness, the "perfume." The Church father Origen wrote that Christians "regard the spirit of every good man as an altar, from which ascends incense truly and intelligibly sweet-smelling—the prayers from a pure conscience." God, it was argued, "needs neither blood nor the savor of sacrifices, nor the fragrance of flowers and incense, himself being perfect fragrance" (Atchley 1909: 84, 81).

The ancient custom of offering sweet scents to the gods was too deep-rooted, however, for the early Christians to eradicate. Although the personal use of perfume continued to be discouraged by the Church, incense soon came to be an accepted part of Christian ritual, and fragrant flowers a customary decoration for churches and shrines. Even prayer—the symbolic incense *par excellence*—would eventually be literally sweetened by persons employing rosaries of perfumed beads.

Christians, furthermore, like most peoples of the ancient world, deemed it appropriate that spiritual qualities should be made manifest by perceptible signs, such as odor. Recorded experiences of a perceptible "odor of sanctity" can be found as early as the second century. St Polycarp is said to have given off "a fragrant odor as of the fumes of frankincense" when burnt at the stake in 155 (an ordeal he managed to survive). Later that century a group of persecuted Christians are reported to have met their martyrdom "perfumed with the glad odor of Christ, so that some thought that they had been anointed with worldly ointment" (Eusebius 1953: 241, 281).

In Christian tradition fragrance was closely associated with spiritual integrity and malodor with moral corruption. Baptism, it was believed, made it possible to start one's spiritual life free of the stench of sin. The sweet odor assigned to the baptized soul was considered to be due to the soul being infused with the fragrant Holy Spirit. St John of the Cross writes in his *Spiritual Canticle*:

> So profuse are these odors at times that the soul seems to be enveloped in delight and bathed in inestimable glory. Not only is it conscious itself of them, but they even overflow it, so that those who know how to discern these things can perceive them. The soul in this state seems to them as a delectable garden. (1864: 98)

There was a further notion that the soul was scented by the perfumed ointment—chrism—used in the baptismal rite. Medieval legend held that chrism came directly from the scented exudations of the Tree of Life in the Garden of Eden and therefore partook of its vivifying power (Albert 1990: 83–4). This power was referred to in the Book of Enoch (25: 9–10) where it was said of persons chosen by God that "the sweet odor [of the Tree of Life] shall enter into their bones; and they shall live a long life." The chrism employed in baptism, with its legendary association with the Tree of Life, was thought to confer on those who received it spiritual immortality by imbuing them with the essence of life.

By overcoming sin, saints were believed to overcome, to a certain extent, the physical corruption thought to have entered the world with the original sin of Adam and Eve. This was the explanation for why, when saints were ill, they sometimes smelled sweet rather than foul, and why their bodies on occasion remained fragrant and incorrupt after death. Scriptural support for this phenomenon came from Psalm 16: 10 which says of God: "Thou wilt not suffer thy Holy one to see corruption."

The customary appearance of an odor of sanctity on the death of a saint had to do with the belief that the saint's sweet-scented soul left the body at that time, thus making its odor manifest. In fact, it would seem to have been a commonplace that the departure of the soul at death created a perceptible odor. Jacob Boehme wrote in the seventeenth century that "when [the common man] sees a blue vapor go forth out of the mouth of a dying man (which makes a strong smell all over the chamber) then he supposes that is the soul" (1910: 479).

As the odor of sanctity indicated the triumph of spiritual virtue over physical corruption, it was often considered able to heal physical ills. Numerous stories in saint lore refer to the healing power of the fragrance associated with a saint. In many cases the healing scents are said to arise from the saint's corpse. The fact that corpses at this time were usually held to spread disease by their odor, made the curative power of the scents produced by the saint's corpse another example of how the natural order of bodily decay was reversed in the case of the saint through supernatural grace.

Aside from healing, a variety of wonders are associated with odors of sanctity. The seventeenth-century Dutch nun Mary Margaret of the Angels, deliciously fragrant during life, is said to have prayed that after her death her body might provide oil for the sanctuary lamp. When Mary Margaret died her corpse was left on its bier in the convent chapel. After a few months the body began to produce an aromatic oil, which reportedly provided ample fragrant fuel for a sanctuary lamp (along with curing many invalids) (Imbert-Gourbeyre 1996: 303–4). St Martin of Tours, in turn, reportedly once calmed a storm with his scent (a legend in keeping with the common notion that evil spirits and odors caused storms). The tempest was threatening to sink a ship at sea when the saint was invoked by the sailors on board. A fragrant odor immediately filled the ship, and the sea was promptly stilled by this pouring of scent on troubled waters (Atchley 1909: 108–9).

Along with their physical powers, odors of sanctity have the reputed ability to induce repentance and offer spiritual consolation. Teresa's odor was said to soften peoples' hearts and fill them with praises for God (Ribera 1908: 546). In pre-modern Europe scents were commonly thought to have a potent effect on the spirit, in part because of a perceived similarity in nature between the airiness of odors and the airiness of spirits, and in part because odors were believed to rise through the nose to the brain, the imagined seat of the soul. Odors of sanctity could hence provide the soul with a direct infusion of divine joy and grace.

The divinely sweet scent of the odor of sanctity was deemed to constitute a foretaste of heaven. According to popular belief heaven, and everything associated with it, was pervaded by fragrance. A seventh-century English account of a "near-death" experience brings out this celestial redolence. In this account, the soul of a man presumed dead journeys through the divine realms. He first visits hell with its malodors. He then journeys to "a very broad and pleasant plain, full of such a fragrance of growing flowers that the marvelous sweetness of the scent quickly dispelled the foul stench of the gloomy furnace which had hung around me" (Colgrave and Mynors 1969: 493). This, he is told by his spirit guide, is the "waiting room" for heaven. The presence of heaven itself is communicated to the soul by a fragrance so wonderful "that the scent which I had thought superlative before, when I savored it, now seemed to me a very ordinary fragrance." Not being ready yet to enter the celestial kingdom, however, the man must content himself with a whiff of divine delights and return to earth and life (Colgrave and Mynors 1969: 495–6).

Not all accounts of the odor of sanctity were taken seriously by the Church or the public. Skeptics suspected that the aromatics with which bodies were sometimes buried could give rise to false reports of odors of sanctity. In order to dispel such suspicions, accounts of the odor of sanctity frequently emphasize that the saint's body was buried without the use of any spices or herbs and that the incorruption of the body was verified by physicians.

In fact, reports of encounters with divine beings, ecstasies, and other supernatural phenomena, were disbelieved more often than not by Church officials, particularly after the wonder-working Middle Ages. There were political, as well as religious, reasons for such official disbelief, as the Church wished to retain control over the power of popular devotion.

Hellish Scents

The converse of the sweet scents of heaven was the stench of hell. In the twelfth-century St Hildegard of Bingen (who herself exhaled the odor of sanctity) described hell as "a long and wide marsh filled with filth and vermin of many types and emitting the worst stink," or as a "ditch ... filled with a fierce fire that gave forth a tremendous stink" (1994: 157, 165). Later writers produced more detailed commentaries on the olfactory and other torments of hell. Thus one seventeenth-century Jesuit warned of "the stench of sulfur, the stink of gangrene, the breath of ... foul-smelling bodies in a completely enclosed sewer" that awaited sinners in hell. According to another account the malodor of hell was so powerful that "the smells of this world ... would not altogether be as strong smelling as a mere drop of [hell's] burning stench" (Camporesi 1991: 60, 52–3, 109).

As the ruler of hell and the ultimate sinner, the Devil was likewise portrayed as foul-smelling; reeking of sulfur or excrement. Many holy persons faced olfactory assaults from the Devil as part of their struggle for sanctity. In the fifteenth century St Francesca Romana was tormented by diabolic ill odors until she thought "the whole house [would] perish of suffocation from such a stench" (Camporesi 1988: 55). The malodor of the Devil was deemed to have the didactic purpose of communicating the repulsive nature of sin. St Hildegard stated: "The stink surrounding the uncleanness of the devil is so that the people who had been seduced by him will smell the stink and turn away from their own mistakes" (Hildegard of Bingen 1986: 362). (Hildegard also believed that the Devil induced Eve to sin by injecting her with his poisonous breath.)

As in the case of the Devil, a corrupt odor was thought to arise from sinful humans. Saint Philip Neri is related to have had the following experience of this unholy stench:

> One morning when [Philip] laid his hand on the head of a possessed person, such a pestilential smell was left upon his hand, that though he washed it with soap and different sweet-scented things, the stench lasted for three days, during which he gave his hand to several persons to smell, in order that they might take occasion from it to avoid sin more carefully. (Bacci 1902: 354)

The ability to smell human sin is found in a number of hagiographies. The early Christian saint Hilarion was said to have been able "to know from the odor of the body, the clothing, and the things that anyone had touched, what devil or what vice had predominance over him" (Jerome 1952: 266). In the Middle Ages Saint Bernardino stated that "When I enter a city … all the good and evil that is done in it comes into my head … everything that smells sweet or that stinks" (Origo 1962: 37).

In their sleuthing of sin, these saints were following the model of the Messiah given in the Book of Isaiah (11: 3) which suggests that the Messiah, when he comes, will judge people by his sense of smell, rather than by sight or hearing. Smell could thus be presented as the paradigmatic sense for the divination of sin or sanctity.

Certain holy persons with hypersensitive noses found not only sin, but many worldly substances associated with sin, unbearably malodorous. This was particularly the case with food, which seemed to some ascetics to reek of corruption. As noted above, Teresa of Avila had great difficulties overcoming the nausea she felt at the taste and smell of food. The thirteenth-century Mary of Oignes likewise had periods in which "she could not in any way endure even the smell of meat, or of anything cooked, nor of wine" (Thurston 1952: 342).

Worldly perfumes might also seem foul in comparison to the scents of heaven. In the seventeenth century the nun Giovanna Maria della Croce of Roveredo would faint at the smell of perfumes such as musk and amber. Novices who came to the Order wearing scented necklaces (as were common in those redolent times) were obliged to leave them at the convent gate to save Giovanna Maria from an olfactory indisposition. The only perfume the holy nun could tolerate was her own sweet scent of sanctity (Thurston 1952: 229–30).

Some saints courted foul earthly odors in order to mortify their sense of smell and be better able to carry out works of charity among the poor and ill. St Catherine of Genoa, for example, cured herself of the repugnance she felt at the stench emanating from the sores of the ill by rubbing her nose with pus. The Jesuit priest Peter Claver, working among African slaves living and dying in crowded, unsanitary conditions, had to cope with odors so foul they "completely numbed the senses." "Yet such sordid, smelly, fetid and intolerable dwellings were a garden of delights for this evangelical worker," his biographer writes. When Peter Claver himself died, his body exuded a sweet odor "so exuberant that it could be smelt from far away" (Camporesi 1994: 183, 151).

While the association of holiness with fragrance and sinfulness with stench is the general rule in Christian hagiography, there are exceptions. Aspiring saints were sometimes warned against sweet scents of diabolic origins:

> [At times] the deceiver maketh a sweet smell to come, as if it were from heaven ... in order that ye may think that God, on account of your holy life, sends you his grace and his comfort, and so think well of yourselves, and become proud. (Morton 1968: 105–7)

Furthermore, there are instances of saints being notoriously bad-smelling. In the fifth century the saintly ascetic Simeon Stylites (who gained renown for making his home on top of a pillar) repelled his fellow monks by the stench emanating from his self-inflicted wounds. In the twelfth century the young Alpais of Cudot stank so horribly from illness that her mother refused to feed her. (The Heavenly Mother, however, cured Alpais of her illness, her stench, and also of the need to ever eat again.)

Various rationales were offered for the presence of foul odors in a holy person. In the case of stench arising from illness or wounds, the reason given might be that the person's faith was being tried by God or by Satan. Stench arising from a lack of hygiene was usually interpreted as an instance of the meritorious rejection of sensual luxuries—such as baths and perfumes—on the part of the holy person. In such cases of "holy stench," foul odor served as a potent reminder of the importance of transcending worldly values and prejudices in the pursuit of the divine. Nonetheless, if the saint's body sometimes stunk, the saint's *soul* was invariably characterized as fragrant. Indeed, when Simeon Stylites was found dead on top of his pillar, his "true" odor manifested itself; "a scented perfume which, from its sweet smell, made one's heart merry" (Harvey 1999).

Holy Virgins and Aromatic Pain

While in modernity fragrance is often considered a superficial, rather frivolous aspect of existence, in earlier eras it was frequently associated with the most intense of life's experiences. The phenomenon of the odor of sanctity, for example, was coupled both with glorious visions of the Divine and with racking experiences of physical and spiritual pain. St Teresa, for instance, wrote that she had endured "unbearable pains" which, "according to the physicians, were the worst one can have [in this life]" (Teresa 1972: 143).

The suffering of the saints began with an ascetic way of life. Two of the basic practices of asceticism, celibacy and fasting, had important olfactory associations. Sexual activity, for example, was considered by many physicians to be a source of malodor. St Philip Neri, hence, had the support of contemporary medical science when he covered his nose on passing a "woman of bad character," declaring that moral impurity gave off the worst smell in the world (Bacci 1902: 249). Virginity, by contrast, uncontaminated by the corrupt fluids of coitus, was held to be sweet-scented. Thus, after having experienced the remarkable fragrance of Philip Neri, a penitent did not hesitate to assign its cause to the father's virginal purity. Likewise, it was said of St Teresa that her virginity helped keep her body from decaying after death: "As Our Lord preserved her from all unchastity during her life, in a perfect state of virginity, so he kept her from all corruption after death" (Ribera 1908: 528).

In a similar way, fasting supposedly decreased bodily corruption and odor by reducing the amount of organic material "decaying" within the body. Saints often found they were compensated for their fasting by receiving divine savors which left them satiated and filled with fragrance. For example, Catherine of Siena, one of the most stringent of fasters, was able to savor the fragrant body and blood of Christ for several days after communion" (Catherine of Siena 1980: 239). Of Philip Neri, it was said that:

> In receiving the Lord's Body he had an extraordinary sensible sweetness, making all the gestures which people do who taste something very sweet; for this reason he used to select the largest hosts he could find, that the holy specks might remain in him a longer time, and that he might taste the longer that delicious food. (Bacci 1902: 147)

As a special sign of holy suffering, saints sometimes manifested stigmata, marks on the body resembling the wounds of the crucified Christ. These stigmata were often notable for their fragrance. For example the wounds which St Veronica of Giuliani (d. 1727) intermittently displayed on her hands, feet, and side "emitted so delicious a fragrance throughout the whole of the convent that this alone was sufficient to inform the nuns whenever the stigmata had been renewed" (Thurston 1952: 228).

While odors of sanctity are recorded of both men and women, they seem to be more frequent and more prominent in the lives, or Lives, of women. This is also the case with penitential practices such as severe fasting, saintly illnesses, and stigmata. Why this gender difference in expressions of sanctity? Men, it has been argued, who could serve as preachers, missionaries or Church officials, had the whole world as a field in which to manifest or acquire holiness. Although holy women might engage with the world through such deeds as acts of charity or the foundation and direction of nunneries, they were considerably more limited in their opportunities for religious expression. The body and soul, rather than the world, were a woman's primary field of action. Odors of sanctity (along with other supernatural signs such as stigmata) drew attention to the sacred importance of the work undertaken by women within their restricted sphere (Weinstein and Bell 1982: 236).

Popular ideology, furthermore, deemed women to be especially marked for suffering, first of all through childbirth, and second through their supposed closer association with the body and the emotions. Female saints, it was believed, could play a special role in the redemption of the world through undertaking the "womanly" role of suffering and serving as sacrificial victims. For the holy woman herself, however, undergoing this torment was not simply a matter of suffering silently but of being an actor in a vital cosmic drama in which she could identify with the crucified Christ and assist in the expiation of sin and the saving of souls. The odor of sanctity arising from the tortured body of the saint marked such cosmic suffering as no ordinary pain, but a sweet sacrifice to God.

Olfactory Theology

Odors of sanctity were the subject of considerable theological elaboration in pre-modernity, as well as being the stuff of legend. The Bible, with its numerous references to olfaction, provided the primary basis for such elaboration. Indeed, even minor biblical references to odor could inspire an extended commentary on the theology of smell. John Wycliffe, for example, made use of the possible etymology of the biblical Jericho as "place of fragrance" to produce the following statement:

> Jericho is the ... smelling that men should have, for each man in this life should smell Christ and follow him ... For this smell is Christ ... and his way is [the] smelling of a full field that God has blessed [Gen 27: 27], and this smell had Jacob and other fathers who believed in Christ. (Arnold 1869: 107–8)

The Song of Songs, with its dialogue between an aromatic bride and a scented bridegroom, provided a particularly rich source of olfactory imagery for theological expositions. Using *The Song of Songs* as his inspiration, John of the Cross, for instance, wrote an extensive commentary on the olfactory dialogue between the soul and Christ. The virtues of the soul, said St John, "are like the budding flowers of a garden ... opening under the inspirations of the Holy Ghost—and [diffusing] most marvelous perfumes in great variety." Christ, in turn, is a flower exhaling "divine odors, fragrance, grace, and beauty" (John of the Cross 1864: 129, 126). The soul and Christ attract each other until they unite, on a symbolic bed of flowers, in a spiritual marriage.

By making smell a primary model for the interaction between the soul and God, St John conveyed the notion of an attraction based on intangible and invisible virtues, and a pursuit of the divine grounded in faith rather than knowledge. In saint lore, as we have seen, this olfactory pursuit of the divine was sometimes presented, as quite literal. Farmworkers, attracted by the odor of sanctity, drop their tools to follow Teresa of Avila's corpse on its journey back to Alba.

Popular theology linked many of the olfactory references in Scripture and in Christian legend to create an aromatic history of Christianity. This history begins in the fragrant Garden of Eden with its two trees: the Tree of Life and the Tree of the Knowledge of Good and Evil. The Tree of Life was held to be "ineffable for the goodness of its sweet scent" (Apocalypse 8: 3). The Tree of the Knowledge of Good and Evil, by contrast, contained within itself the seeds of corruption, for it was by eating its fruit that Adam and Eve lost their immortality and made themselves prey to the stench and decay of death.

Drawing on ancient imagery, Jacob Boehme wrote a detailed account of the olfactory fall of man. Adam and Eve, said Boehme, lived in a world of perfect fragrance. The Devil, however, tempted the pair with the corrupt forbidden fruit, referred to ironically by Boehme as "sugar." The first humans' consumption of this worldly product brought dung into being, and introduced stench to the Garden of Eden. This unacceptable antithesis of human stench and divine fragrance made it necessary for Adam and Eve to be expelled from Paradise. The Devil's punishment for his misdeed was to eternally dwell in the excremental filth of the world he has corrupted:

> God has prepared such a dwelling-house for him, as Adam lets forth (from the earthly sugar) at the nethermost exit; and that shall be left for him at the corruption of the earth ... and then that pleasant smell of the stink of sin and abominations ... shall remain for him, and that sugar he shall eat eternally. (Boehme 1910: 410)

With the birth of Christ a new aromatic history begins. The gifts of myrrh and frankincense offered to Jesus on his birth by the Magi forecast the Son of God's future—the bitterness of myrrh represents death, and the fragrance of frankincense, divine life. The perfume poured over Jesus by Mary Magdalene signifies the homage of humanity to Christ's divinity. Jesus's resurrection of Lazarus from the stench of death indicates that humanity is to be saved from physical and moral corruption. At Jesus's death aromatics once again come to the fore in scripture: his body is buried with spices—aromatic omens of divine immortality (Albert 1990: 208–30).

Popular tradition similarly went beyond Scripture in its olfactory interpretations of the birth, death, and resurrection of Christ. One sixth-century manuscript, the *Transitus Mariae*, for example, indicated that Jesus was conceived through smell. In the account presented there the Holy Spirit penetrates Mary as a sweet odor. Her response to this olfactory grace is to offer up incense to God, thus replying to fragrance with fragrance (Harvey 1998).

If smell has lost much of its traditional meaning for us in the modern West, why was it so important for our forebears? The evident answer to this comes from the ancient association of smell with the spirit. When in the Jewish–Hellenic Book of the Secrets of Enoch (30: 8–9) the various senses are linked with different body parts, smell is assigned to the soul. This association was based on the identification of the sense of smell with the breath, and hence with the life force.

The verse in Isaiah in which the Messiah is said to judge by smell rather than sight or hearing was interpreted by both Christians and Jewish theologians as indicating the high spiritual value of the sense of smell. In the twelfth century Ibn Ezra commented on this passage:

> The ear is sometimes deceived in hearing sounds, which are only imaginary; the eye, too, sees things in motion, which in reality are at rest; the sense of smell alone is not deceived. (Friedlander 1873: 60)

Centuries later John Calvin made a similar interpretation:

> We ought to attend, first of all, to the metaphor in the verb *smell*, which means that Christ will be so shrewd that he will not need to learn from what he hears, or from what he sees; for by *smelling* alone he will perceive what would otherwise be unknown. (Calvin 1981: 376)

Therefore, while smell was customarily ranked third in importance of the senses, after sight and hearing, when it came to religion olfaction was sometimes given a certain priority over the other senses.

Smell also had a traditional association with the mind. Odors were thought, to have a direct connection with thought by virtue of their traveling up the nose to the brain. The Latin word *sagax* (sagacious), meant both a keen sense of smell and a shrewd mind. The seventh-century theologian, Isidore of Seville, wrote that to smell is to know (Schrader 1975: 352). According to the twelfth-century Hildegard of Bingen:

> By our *nose* God displays the wisdom that lies like a fragrant sense of order in all works of art, just as we ought to know through our ability to smell whatever wisdom has to arrange. (1987: 130)

In the sixteenth century, Girolamo Cardano wrote that a good sense of smell was a sign of a good mind, because both the brain and the sense of smell function according to similar principles (Schrader 1975: 353, 355). His contemporary Francis of Sales compared the acts of meditation and contemplation to the act of smelling:

> Meditation is like smelling first a carnation, then a rose, then rosemary, thyme, jasmine, orange flower, each one separately; contemplation is equivalent to

smelling the scented liquid distilled from all those flowers put together. (1962: 231)

In the seventeenth century the "mystical odorist" Lorenzo Magalotti wrote of the importance of immersing the imagination in a continual bath of perfumes:

> from which the imagination, impregnated and satiated, will rise … imbuing the soul with vapors purified of every vestige of matter, which when they reach the mind act as a pure spiritual suffumigation, inundating it with so unique a harmony that all plurality is banished. (Camporesi 1988: 184)

These examples are sufficient to show that in pre-modern Europe there existed an understanding of olfaction that was fundamentally different from that which reigns today. Yet it is not difficult to see why smell was accorded the status that it had, for the nature of odor renders smell an apt vehicle for expressing concepts about knowledge and divinity. Odor, emanating from the interior of objects, can readily be understood as conveying inner truth and intrinsic worth. The common association of odor with the breath and with the life-force makes smell a source of elemental power, and therefore an appropriate symbol and medium for divine life and power. Odors can strongly attract or repel, rendering them forceful metaphors for moral good and evil. Odors are also ethereal, they cannot be grasped or retained; in their elusiveness they convey a sense of both the mysterious presence and the mysterious absence of God. Finally, odors are ineffable, they transcend our ability to define them through language, as religious experience itself is said to do.

Placed in this context, the traditional belief in the odor of sanctity becomes intelligible as more than mere superstition. The concept of the odor of sanctity is, in fact, the essence of a whole way of life and thought; a rich and rare fragrance, scented with holy pain and mystical rapture, impossible to distill from the secularized values of modernity.

Bibliography

Albert, J.-P. (1990), *Odeurs de sainteté*, Paris: Editions de l'Ecole des Hautes Etudes en Sciences Sociales.

Arnold, T. (ed.) (1869), *Select English Works of John Wyclif*, 3 vols., Oxford: Clarendon.

Atchley, E. (1909), *A History of the Use of Incense in Divine Worship*, London: Longmans, Green & Co.

Bacci, P. (1902), *The Life of St. Philip Neri*, 2 vols., trans. F. Antrobus, London: Kegan Paul, Trench, Trubner & Co.

Boehme, J. (1910), *The Three Principles of the Divine Essence*, trans. J. Sparrow, London: John M. Watkins.

Bynum, C. (1987), *Holy Feast and Holy Fast*, Berkeley: University of California Press.

Calvin, J. (1981), *Commentary on the Book of the Prophet Isaiah*, vol. 1, trans. J. Pringle, Grand Rapids MI: Baker Book House.

Camporesi, P. (1988), *Incorruptible Flesh*, trans. T. Croft-Murray and H. Elsom, Cambridge: Cambridge University Press.

—— (1991), *Fear of Hell*, trans. L. Byatt, Cambridge: Polity Press.

—— (1994), *The Anatomy of the Senses*, trans. A. Cameron, Cambridge: Polity Press.

Catherine of Siena (1980), *The Dialogue*, trans. S. Noeffke, New York: Paulist Press.

Cobham Brewer, E. (1966), *A Dictionary of Miracles*, Detroit: Gale Research Company.

Colgrave, B. and Mynors, R. (eds) (1969), *Bede's Ecclesiastical History of the English People*, Oxford: Clarendon.

Eusebius (1953), *Ecclesiastical History*, trans. R.J. Deferrari, New York: Fathers of the Church.

Francis de Sales (1962), *The Love of God*, trans. V. Kerns, Westminster: Newman Press.

Friedlander, M. (ed.) (1873), *The Commentary of Ibn Ezra on Isaiah*, vol. 1, New York: Philip Feldheim.

Geurin, P. (ed.) (1878), *Les Petites Bollandistes*, 17 vols., Paris: Bloud et Barral.

Harvey, S.A. (1998), "Incense Offerings in the Syriac *Transitus Mariae*," in A. Malherbe, F. Norris and J. Thompson (eds), *The Early Church in its Context*, Leiden: E.J. Brill.

—— (1999), "Olfactory Knowing," in G.J. Reinink and A.C. Klugkist (eds), *Change and Continuity in Syriac Christianity*, Louvain: Peeters Press.

Hildegard of Bingen (1986), *Scivias*, trans. B. Hozeski, Santa Fe NM: Bear & Co.

—— (1987), *Book of Divine Works with Letters and Songs*, ed. M. Fox, Santa Fe: Bear Company.

—— (1994), *The Book of the Rewards of Life*, trans. B. Hozeski, New York: Garland.

Imbert-Gourbeyre, A. (1996), *La Stigmatisation*, J. Bouflet (ed.), Grenoble: Editions Jérome Millon.

Jerome (1952), "Life of St. Hilarion," in R.J. Defarrari (ed.), *Early Christian Biographies*, Washington: Catholic University of America Press.

John of the Cross (1864), "Spiritual Canticle," in *The Complete Works of Saint John of the Cross*, vol. 2, trans. D. Lewis, London: Longmans, Green & Co.

Malory, T. (1889), *Le Morte d'Arthur*, M.O. Sommer (ed.), London: D. Nutt.

Morton, J. (1968), *The Ancren Riwle*, New York: Johnson Reprint Corporation.

Origo, I. (1962), *The World of San Bernardino*, New York: Harcourt, Brace & World.

Paracelsus (1894), *The Hermetic and Alchemical Writings*, A.E. Waite (ed.), London: James Elliot.

Ribera, F. de (1908), *Vida de Santa Teresa de Jesús*, Barcelona: Gustavo Gili.

Schrader, L. (1975), *Sensación y sinestesia*, Madrid: Editorial Gredos.

Teresa de Jesús (1972), *Libro de la vida*, in *Obras completas*, E. de la Madre de Dios and O. Steggink (eds), Madrid: Biblioteca de Autores Cristianos.

Thurston, H. (1952), *The Physical Phenomena of Mysticism*, J.H. Crehan (ed.), London: Burns & Oates.

Weinstein, D. and Bell, R.M. (1982), *Saints and Society*, Chicago: University of Chicago Press.

33
Bodies, Odors and Perfumes in Arab-Muslim Societies

Françoise Aubaile-Sallenave

In Arab-Muslim societies, odors and perfumes occupy a specific place. The importance of fragrance is attested by the pleasure and the attention individuals bring to scenting themselves, their clothes, household furniture and even certain objects. The odors that are considered to be "good" convey well-being—they are a way of fostering contentment with oneself and with others. Because of the great interest attached to odor, there are noteworthy circumstances during which the body must emit "good odors" and thus provide the necessary quietude for the accomplishment of certain actions, such as when conducting religious practices or at the crucial moments in a person's life, for instance birth, circumcision, marriage and death; thus, an entire series of products and practices are brought into play to make the body smell better. The primary practice consists of the use of plain (or pure) water; after that there are complex practices that utilize fumigations, soaking oils, distilled waters, scented pastries, beverages, spices and aromatic leaves, in a range of forms. The body integrates these odors into itself, which then confer to the person's personality new powers and protections, but also the sense of well-being and self-confidence, thus playing an important role in relationships.

After reviewing some of my studies that evidence the importance of odors and scented plants in the language and practices of Arab-Muslim societies, I will analyze some of the diverse aromatic means that represent the eventful moments of life, notably in the exercise of religion and in rites of passage.

Religious Practices

To enter the sacred confines of the mosque, to pray and to present oneself to God, requires a perfect purity which expresses itself by a total "cleanliness" and a good scent. Everything that leaves the body—breath, sweat, sexual secretions—is considered impure and "foul," which is conveyed by the Arabic term *muntîn*. This is why so much effort is invested in purifying the zones of the body and making them pleasantly scented; it is felt to be an abandonment of one's responsibilities to "neglect to make oneself nicely scented, and because of this, to smell bad" (Kazimirski 1980). The breath, *nak'ha*, is perhaps the exhalation of which individuals are most concerned. In the religious context, where purity expresses itself by the metaphor of perfume but also by the perfume itself, it is said that those who fast have the purest breath in the eyes of Allah, even more than musk perfume (an-Nawawî 1975: 212) and, according to Ghazali, the prophet said: "Your mouths are a way of passage for the Koran, scent them thus and put *suwak* in them" (Bouhdiba 1975: 171). In these societies, where the cuisine features a great number of spicy condiments, Mohammed forbade going to the mosque when one has eaten garlic or onion "because the angels also suffer that which men suffer" (an-Nawawî 1975: 286).

Before performing any religious act, one must practice ablutions. The minor ablution *al-wûdû*, which cleanses impurities before undertaking *salat*, ritual prayer, consists of carefully washing the face (nose, mouth, ears), the hands (and arms until the elbow), the feet (and the ankles). This ablution is repeated before each of the five daily prayers. *Al-ghusl* is the ablution of the entire body that is mandatory after a major pollution (sexual act, menstruation, childbirth, contact with an impure thing or animal etc.), which can be repeated multiple times a week. The term *ightasala*, which bears a large semantic range, signifies "to wash oneself, to purify oneself by ablutions" as well as "to rub up with perfumes" (Belot 1955), which also imparts to this action an inherent religious character. A number of *hadith* [supplements to the Koran recounting the sayings and actions of Mohammed] recall "Aisha scenting the Prophet and his beard" before prayer while reciting: "I scented the messenger of God with the most aromatic perfumes that I could find until I saw the shine of perfume on his head and on his beard" (al-Bokhâri 1977, III: 126–7). It is these oils, infused with the scent of flowers, fragrant wood or leaves, which make the Prophet's hair and beard so shiny. All of these obligations explain the existence of such a large number of bathing establishments, *hammâm* (pl. *hammâmât*), that each town has sheltered for centuries and which most often originate from religious institutions.

Rites of Passage

Transitional periods are the moments in which a person is particularly weakened and vulnerable to all sorts of bad influences—*jnûn* evils, jealousy or the unhappiness of a parent, neighbor, etc.—of which a single contact can generate the evil eye and so forth. This is why one must have recourse to multiple protections of a magical character; these are fumigations, made in the *kânûn*, comprised of certain scented plants, harmel seeds (*Peganum harmala*), gum resin of *fasûkh* (*Ferula communis*) with an acrid odor, benzoin resin (*jâwî*) of various kinds (white, black, red, green), aloe wood (*'ûd*) and also certain animal parts (stinging sea-urchins, animal hair etc.). One also can construct a garland of protective seeds, teeth, small mirrors and, for brides, a necklace made of cloves, sometimes with Saharan nutgrass (*Cyperus rotundus*)—these are all amulets, as well as are the sacred texts inserted in a leather or silver case, a case which can also contain seeds, vegetable powders or animal parts (hair, teeth, stingers etc.). These are the instruments with which one creates an "armor" to protect oneself from the very beginning of life and all throughout it.

The Newborn

From birth, a strongly scented universe surrounds the infant: these include massages, fumigations, aromatic seeds put under its pillow and in sachets put near its head (Aubaile-Sallenave 1997). This happens practically universally in the Arab-Muslim world. Despite the nuances pertaining to various cultural traditions, everywhere the goal is to maximize the protection of this frail being.

In Dhufar, the room where the woman gives birth is smoke-filled with aromas and crushed incense to neutralize the emanations of the body in labor and to maintain the purity of the place (Bonnet-Chelhi 2002: 100).

When the infant is born, its body is covered with a sticky viscous layer, the *vernix caseosa*, the odor of which resembles fatty cheese. If this product, which is rich in antibiotic substances, protects the fragile epidermis of the newborn, its odor, by contrast, is one of the reasons why the newborn is wiped off. Even in ancient times, Greek doctors of the first century had difficulty convincing people not to "scrape" newborns (Soranos d'Ephèse 1988, II: 89). Besides, newborns are often subjected to a ritual that consists, after wiping it off, of washing it in water more or less salted, or even scrubbing it in salted oil or pure salt. This ritual is practiced in the Middle East, Syria, Palestine, North Arabia, West Iran (Morgenstern 1966: 13), Qatar, Turkey and the regions of the ancient Turkish empire, the Balkans, Greece, as well as in some parts of North Africa, notably Kasbah in Algeria. The practice has a physiological goal, to strengthen the skin, but most of all it is magical, to resist exterior forces, and to endow the newborn with salt's multiple symbolic values: purification, incorruptibility, union (Aubaile-Sallenave 1988). The salt also grants the newborn the power to give off good odor. In the countryside of Anatolia, one directly salts the body of the newborn and leaves it to remain for ten minutes; it is a practice for the benefit of the infant, in particular, so that its mouth and its breath do not smell bad. The salting is followed immediately by a washing in water perfumed with cloves or myrtle (Nicolas 1972: 101–3). In Anatolia, the Balkans, south Macedonia and Bulgaria, one bathes the baby in salted water "so that its feet or other parts of the body do not smell bad" (Garnett and Stuart-Glennie 1890: 69, 315; Paunovska 1964: 261), which attests to popular Turkish folk saying *tûzlasounlar-da qoqma* ("Be salted and you will not smell bad"), an insult addressed to a person of no value (Barbier de Meynard 1881).

Ointments and massages aim to protect the baby, strengthen its skin, and generally accompany it to prevent manipulations that might influence its eventual psychology and physique, according to the reasoning of benevolent magic. In the Maghreb region of North Africa, after the midwife wipes the newborn, it is coated with olive oil or butter for multiple days, both substances of which have protective values. In Fez, the oil is sometimes scented with cloves, the aroma of which is considered a good omen, or a blend of henna, a plant from paradise rich in *baraka* (blessed energy) (Mas 1960: 29, 30).

The newborn's first food is scented. After wiping the infant, the midwife passes her index finger along its mouth to clean the mucous. In Tlemcen, one washes the mouth of the baby with a cumin pacifier, *kemoussa*. A fine, clean cloth is dipped into the powdered cumin and soaked in orange flower water before being inserted into the baby's mouth (Zerdoumi 1970: 92). In Mettidja, the midwife, after removing the newborn's mucous, makes it suck on a drop of *ftour el-mezioud*, "the newborn's first meal," which is a mixture of lemon juice, cochineal, cumin and asafetida. In the neighborhood of Blida, the composition is a semi-liquid pasta made of white marrube, garlic, wild blackberry sprouts, round mint and thyme leaves, all crushed in a mortar (Desparmet 1918: 123–4).

Maternal breastfeeding is a general rule. Mothers are very attentive to the taste and odor of their milk. Forbidden foods are numerous but vary according to group: in Tunisia, one generally avoids spicy foods, which can make the milk spicy; lemon and acidic foods, which sour milk; cabbage, turnips and cauliflower, which give the newborn a bad taste and odor. Likewise, eggs can make the infant mute, and garlic and mint dry up the mother's milk (Hubert 1984: 122).

Circumcision

Circumcision is an act associated with the Arabic term *tahar*, meaning to clean or purify; it is a ritual that children undergo at ages that vary according to the population. In the Maghreb, it is often a collective ceremony where children are between four and ten years old. On the day before, one puts a little henna in their palms and they carry protective amulets. During the ceremony, incense smoke, benzoin and also at times cascarilla (*Croton eluteria*), all pleasant odors, fill the atmosphere so that the blood spilled does not attract *jnûn*. The few drops of blood fall on a dish full of specially chosen earth, which will then be thrown out. The foreskin is taken and buried.

This act gives off a good odor to those who undergo it. In a culture that popularly employs physiognomic theories, a person's physique is a moral image and foulness is associated with ugly morals: "adulterers are the most foul people" according to Ibn al-Jawzi (Bell 1979: 30), the non-circumcised *lakhnun* and *al-khanun* emit, semantically speaking, a bad odor (Kazimirski 1980, II: 981). In 1935, Charles Le Cœur told how Sara infantrymen got circumcised because the Teda women of Tibesti refused to go out with them since they smelled bad. Without a doubt, he adds, the women were sincere (Le Cœur 1935: 49).

In societies that are rich in perfume and where individuals scents themselves freely, like in South Arabia, the body of the circumcised is coated with oil scented with amber and saffron, and tinted yellow by the addition of turmeric. For adults planning to marry, circumcision is a necessary passage and can be painful when done as an adult (Thesiger [1959] 1978: 392).

Spouses

Marriage is an important passage that is subject to precise, complex and codified rituals in each society. Spouses must be in a pure state so that all the steps of marriage and the union unwind perfectly. Plants rich in *baraka*, like henna, decorate the hands, wrists and feet of the spouses. The would-be bride especially takes care to renew the purifications each day during this time, which can last up to a week before the union. To be pure equally signifies to smell good and to be scented.

In the complex marriage rituals of North Africa, hair is one of the principal symbolic agents of the passage of a young girl to a married woman. During the festivities leading up to the meeting with her husband, she will keep her hair free and unattached, being "unraveled" is a sign of total acceptance of the role of motherhood. This open situation makes her vulnerable because hair is, in Islamic societies, one of the elements of the body with the most symbolic value, for it has the ability to be a zone of passage between the interior body and the exterior world, and notably to capture external impurities (from sickness, death, those generated by *jnûn*, etc.). This property makes her nearly always considered as being impure and bad smelling. Thus, during the three to seven days preceding the union, the young woman goes each afternoon to *hammâm* with her friends to wash and to scent her hair and her body. The care that one links with her has its object in the happy consummation of marriage. This is consistent with washing her hair every day, after spreading a mix of henna and saffron powder—both loaded with *baraka*—rose petals, clove, oak moss, coriander, nutgrass (*Cyperus*), lavender, yellow sweet clover and all the most powerfully scented plants (see Aubaile-Sallenave 1987: 352–4).

To have pleasant smelling breath, the bride chews mastic (*Pistacia lentiscus* L.), from the island of Chio, which today still is reputed to have the best tree bark harvest. One also uses teeth cleaners fabricated out of aromatic wood (see Portères 1974). Called *swak*, in North Africa they are made from the bark of a walnut tree that scents and blushes the mouth, gums and lips all at the same time. Dried fennel sticks, or *Ammi visnaga* (toothpick plant), also serve this function and, in the Middle East and in East Africa, wooden sticks are made of *Salvadora persica* Garcin (toothbrush tree). The use of *swak* is one of the major recommendations of Mohammed, abundantly revived by the *hadith* and everpresent. In the thirteenth century, when the use of exotic aromas was much embraced, it was "advised to each spouse, during coitus, to keep some nutmeg or clove in the mouth in order to have scented breath" (Ibn Khalsûn 1996: 61, 87).

The strong aroma of saffron and its use as an efficient dye are dual properties which confer upon it a great cultural value. Its yellow color has been considered erotic since antiquity (in India and Persia), and it has been associated with marriage ceremonies and sexual relations since the pre-Islamic period in Arabia and in subsequent Muslim societies. Its use in scenting the body and clothes of spouses has longstanding textual support (Aubaile-Sallenave 1992: 51). Saffron face decorations practiced in the Berber populations of the Maghreb, as well as in the oases of the North Sahara, carry both cosmetic and disease prevention properties. They protect against the evil eye and *jnûn*, especially when the fiancée occupies that fragile state with unattached hair and unraveled girdle (Aubaile-Sallenave 1987: 353; Champault 1969: 141, 191).

Along with saffron, the strong animal scents of musk, amber and civet were also much used in ancient times in amorous relationships. These three scents have powerful sexual connotations.

If the married woman wore make-up and was pleasingly scented, her body must be equally attractive, which, nearly everywhere, signified a certain stoutness; this state was, with men as with women, a sign of beauty, force, health, wealth and prosperity. Moreover, the plump body, judged to be the canon of beauty, generated good odors that were reinforced by aromatic ointments: *damakha,* that is, to abundantly anoint the body with perfumes, leads to *dimkhah,* "a stout woman or she-camel," and also "a fresh and mature date." Recall the image of the rounded body in the numerous stories of *1,001 Nights;* they are principally from seventeenth- and eighteenth-century Egypt. The standard of beauty was thus to have large hips and a trim waistline. And for a long time, women looked for and still look for all of the possible means to gain weight and become attractive to their husband. Scholarly and popular Arab literature is quite prolix on the foods needed to gain weight—these are principally aromatic plants: fenugreek seeds (Arab *holba*), sesame, caraway seeds, gladioli and iris bulbs, salep (from the Arab *sahlab,* which is a starch made from the bulbs of various orchids according to the regions and the ingredient of a popular nutritious beverage in Turkey and Egypt), and round and long nutgrasses (*Cyperus esculentus, C. longus*) etc.

Health always has a "good" odor. However, the dry and thin body is associated with bad odor. The sick generate unpleasant odors that indicate illness. The mutilated body as well and, in particular, those castrated emit a bad odor. This perfection of the body is equally required for the sacrificed ram of *aîd el-kebîr*; it must be whole, an adult and without imperfection (Kazimirski 1980, I: 1370; Aubaile-Sallenave 1999: 103–4).

The Dead

Along with the funeral prayer, the shroud and the sepulchre, the funeral unguent is a religious obligation for every Muslim. It is common knowledge that "all the faithfully deceased must be properly scented three times: at the moment of death, after the funeral bathing, and when one wraps the shroud" (D'Ohsson 1788: 306). To say scented is to say fumigated, as was done in the seventeenth century. This is still true. For the funeral bathing, *ghassl djenaze* ("washing the cadaver"), one uses scented waters. After the viscera are removed, which is not always practiced, the body is washed in lukewarm water, often with a brew of leaves from *sidr* (*Zizyphus lotus*, jujube tree), Accacia (*Acacia arabica*) or *hurd* (*Curcuma longa*, turmeric). The head and beard must be washed with a brew of flowers or leaves from mallow, *khitmi* (*Althea*), *salamah*, a sage plant; in Mohammed's Arabia, one washed the head with camphor water. Next one puts a cotton swab soaked in camphor in the natural openings—in Egypt they add cloves. After wiping the body, one often scrubs it with a ritual scented mix called *hanût*, which consists of flower-infused water (from an orange tree or a rose), or even with musk or sandalwood. The body is then covered with a white shroud sprayed with sacred well water from Zem Zem and sometimes fumigated with *jawî*, or benzoin. Certainly, these scents serve to repel insects, but in preserving the body from decomposition, they forecast the afterlife in Paradise. They confer the necessary purity to those who are about to be led away by the archangel of death, Azra'il. It is the reason why one scrubs camphor onto the eight parts of the body that participate in prayer during the time of prostration—forehead, nose, hands, feet and knees—as well as to preserve from worms and postpone the body's putrefaction (see D'Ohsson 1788, II: 301–2).

In Arabic-Muslim societies, many bodily odors qualified as "good" play an important role as purifier and protector, but scents also act as a form of pleasure. Indeed, they can be at once fragrant and malodorous, as in the case of fumigations by the resins of *Ferula*, *fasûkh*, of black benzoin, *jawî khal*, of stinging sea-urchins or of various animal hairs and so on. To smell "good" odors generates a number of positive values: good thoughts, good dispositions and an atmosphere free from maleficent aggression. A good odor foreshadows a beautiful future: this is the reasoning attached to the tradition of making a Maghrebin infant smell good odors when it is forty days old. While bad odors cause a wasting away, "good" odors contribute to healing, they signal a state of health and help to maintain good humor. Thus, these aromatic practices confer a new personality to one's body and play a major role in magico-religious knowledge and social relations.

Note

Translated from French by Kathryn Hunter

Bibliography

al-Bokhâri (10th C.), ([1903] 1977), *al-sahih (Les Traditions Islamiques)*, trans. O. Houdas and W. Marcais, 4 vol., Paris: Adrien Maisonnneuve.

an-Nawawî (13th C.), (1975), *Riyadh al-salihin*, "Gardens of the Righteous," trans. M.Z. Khan, London: Curzon Press.

Aubaile-Sallenave, F. (1987), "Les soins de la chevelure chez les Musulmans au Moyen Age," in D. Menjot (ed.), *Les Soins de Beauté*, Nice: Centre d'Études Mediévales, pp. 347–65.

—— (1988), "Le sel de l'alliance," *Journal d'Agriculture Traditionnelle et de Botanique Appliquée*, 35: 303–23.

—— (1992), "Safran de joie, safran interdit," in M.J. Cano and L. Ferre (eds), *La Ciencia en la España medieval*, Granada: Universidad, pp. 124–47.

—— (1997), "Le monde traditionnel des odeurs et des saveurs chez le petit enfant maghrebin," in B. Schaal (ed.), *L'odorat chez l'enfant*, Paris: Presses Universitaires de France, pp. 186–208.

—— (1999), "Le souffle des parfums," in D. Musset and C. Fabre-Vassas (eds), *Odeurs et Parfums*, Paris: CTHS, pp. 93–115.

—— (2002), *Histoire Naturelle et Culturelle des Plantes à Parfum*, Paris: Ibis Press.

Barbier de Meynard, A.C. (1881), *Dictionnaire turc-français*, Paris: Leroux.

Belot, J.-B. (1955), (17th ed.), *al-Farâid al-durrayah*, Beirut: n.p.

Bell, N. (1979) *Love Theory in Later Hanbalite Islam*, Albany: SUNY Press.

Bonnet-Chelhi, N. (2002), *Cueilleurs de lait, brûleurs de sang*, Doctoral thesis, Paris V.

Bouhdiba A., (1975), *La sexualité en Islam*, Paris: PUF.

Champault, D. (1969), *Une oasis du Sahara nord-occidental, Tabelbala*, Paris: CNRS.

Desparmet, J. (1918–1921), "Ethnographie traditionnelle de la Mettidja," *Revue Africaine*, 1918: 117–50.

D'Ohsson, M. (1788), *Tableau général de I"Empire Ottoman*, Paris: Didot.

Dozy, R. ([1881] 1967), *Supplement aux dictionnaires arabes*, 2 vol., Leyden/Paris: Brill/ Maisonneuve & Larose.

Garnett, L.M.J. and Stuart-Glennie, J.S. (1890), *The Women of Turkey and Their Folklore*, 2 vol., London: n.p.

Hubert, A. (1984), *Le Pain et l'Olive*, Paris: CNRS.

Ibn Khalsûn (13th C.) (1996), *Kitâb al-aghdhîya*, trans. S. Gigandet (ed.), Damas: l'Institut Français d'Études Arabes de Damas.

Kazimirski, A. ([1860] 1980), *Dictionnaire Arabe-Français*, 2 vol., Beirut: Librairie du Liban.

Lane, E.W. (1863), *An Arabic–English Lexicon*, 8 vol., Beirut: n.p.

Le Cœur Ch. (1935), "Le Tibesti et les Tédas," *Journal de la Société des Africanistes*, V: 41–60.

Mas, M. (1960), "La petite enfance à Fès et à Rabat," *Annales de l'Institu d'Etudes Orientales*, XVII: 1–144.

Morgenstern, J. (1966), *Rites of Birth, Marriage, Death and Kindred Occasions Among the Semites*, Cincinnati & Chicago: Hebrew Union College Press & Quadrangle Books.

Nicolas, M. (1972), *Croyances et pratiques populaires turques concernant les naissances*, Paris: POF.

Paunovska, B. (1964), "L'accouchement en Macédoine du point de vue de l'ethnologue comme éducateur sanitaire," *VI Congrès Internationale des Sciences Anthropologiques et Ethnographiques*, Paris: Musée de l'Homme, pp. 259–63.

Portères, R. (1974), "Un curieux élément culturel arabico-islamique el néo-africain," *JATBA*, Paris: Muséum.

Soranos d'Ephèse, S. (1st C.), (1988), *Ginaïsia*, trans. P. Burguière, D. Gourevitch and Y. Malines (eds), Paris: Belles Lettres.

Thesiger, W. ([1959] 1978), *Le désert des déserts*, Paris: Plon.

Zerdoumi, N. (1970), *Enfants d'hier*, Paris: Maspero.

34
Magic, Perfume, Dream…

Alfred Gell

I

The Umeda[1] term which corresponds most closely to our word "magic" is *sap* (ginger). Besides referring to the varieties of *zingiber*, both wild and cultivated, that Umedas use in their magic, *sap*, as a suffixed element, means "the magic of such-and-such" thus: *oktesap*—the magic of pig-killing, *kwisap*—the cassowary-hunters magic, and so forth. It's on the first of these, *oktesap*, the magic of killing pigs, that I want to focus attention here. The ethnography involved is very simple, no spell, no cult, no ritual of any kind being involved. Yet the manner of operation of this *oktesap*, is, in its extreme simplicity, revealing in a way which many more complicated magical procedures are not. The problem of "magical efficacy"—the underlying problem with which this essay is concerned—is not, I think, which will be ultimately clarified by more field research. The factual material available is plentiful and of high quality. Unfortunately, it is also paradoxical, and the difficulties of interpretation only seem to multiply the richer the material is. Hence the usefulness of restricting oneself to the simplest possible examples.

But there is also another, more immediate reason why I want to look particularly at the *oktesap* example. In a famous paper, Evans-Pritchard (1929) commented on the ephemeral nature of the Zande spell, as contrasted with the highly standardized incantations characteristic of Trobriand magic. The Trobriand word for magic is *megwa* "spell" and the material element "is of minor importance," whereas, in Zande, the word for magic is *ngwa* which really means "wood" but which Evans-Pritchard says refers to the "strange woods and rare roots" used in magic. Now I would like to make two suggestions in this connection: (i) that there is a complementarity between (standardized, formulaic) spells and *magical substances*; and (ii) where the "bias" of the system is away from spells (Trobriand-type) and toward substances (Zande-type) we will find a corresponding increase in the importance of the *olfactory* element in magic. Evans-Pritchard, it is true, does not single out scentedness as one of the characteristic features of the "strange woods and rare roots" used in Zande magic, thereby preventing us from pursuing this idea further in relation to the Zande material. Fortunately, I can be fairly explicit on this score where my own New Guinean material is concerned. In Umeda, at least, odoriferousness and magical significance were closely correlated, though not, to be sure, exclusively so. In numerous contexts, informants explicitly stated that it was the *smell* of a magical preparation which endowed it with its efficacy (*zingiber*-based medicines are prime examples of this). *Oketesap*, a common medicine consisting of a variety of *zingiber*, plus turmeric and perhaps some other ingredients which were not revealed to me, kept in a tightly bound sachet of bark (the porous underbark of *Gnetum gnemon*) is entirely typical of Umeda magic as a whole. *Oktesap* works by smell, that is, the sachet containing the medicine is kept in the net-bag of the owner, gently infusing both the bag itself and the surrounding atmosphere with the special *sap* aroma. *Oktesap* is, in short, a magical perfume, attractive to the wild pigs which are the most highly sought-after local game animals. There would seem to be very little to explain here at all. Perfumes are attractive, and this is simply a perfume supposedly attractive to pigs. In fact, there is rather more to it than this, since as I will describe later, the *oktesap* has a more subtle effect via the influence it has on the dream-experiences of the hunter who possesses it.

But for the present let me restrict myself to the straightforward problem of perfume as an attractant, here a means of attracting wild pigs, or, in a more general sense, attracting *good hunting*. There seems to be no problem here only so long as we do not speculate on the specific character of olfactory experience in general, including our own. Once we begin to do so, I think it will become immediately apparent that the olfactory domain is one of the least explored aspects of human symbolic experience, but not, for that reason, one of the least significant. Just how, and in what sense does perfume "attract"? The semiological status of smells is indeed highly ambiguous, for it would seem that we are dealing neither with a system of "chemical communication" which could be handled within a purely ethological perspective, nor yet with a "sign-system"—since the smell-aspect of the world is so intimately bound up with its purely physical and physiological constitution that it can in no sense be considered conventional. Somewhere in between the stimulus and the sign a place must be found for the restricted language of smells, traces which unlike words only partially detach themselves from the world of objects to which they refer. However fragmentary, a phenomenological analysis of the olfactory domain would, I think, be a great help in coming to understand the cognitive basis of magic, because it is here that our own experience is most congruent with that of practitioners of magic—at least, the "magic of substances" to which I have alluded. Nor is this the only reason: for it would seem that this semiological ambiguity of the smell-sign, which does not properly detach itself from the world, points directly to an analogous ambiguity in the status of the magical sign, which refers to, and also *alters* the world. The phenomenon of magic confronts us with a situation in which matter and meaning become miscible fluids, a scandal, of course, from the standpoint of scientific method. Looking at all this from the angle just indicated—the olfactory dimension which is both part of, and a reference to, the world—assists us not only in coming to grips with magical techniques which make direct use of odoriferous substances, but also in understanding, in a more general way, how this paradoxical "mixing" takes place.

II

A color always remains the prisoner of an enclosing form; by contrast, the smell of an object always *escapes*—it is an active principle. But if a further contrast is drawn between smell and sound—another quality which shares the ability to escape from the object—smell is distinguished by formlessness, indefinability and lack of clear articulation. Smells are characteristically incomplete. They are completed, in the first place, by their source, which is where they become so highly concentrated that they cease to be smells and become substances. Apart from this a smell is completed, not only by the actual source, but also by the context. Because smells are so intimately bound up with the world, the context of a smell is not other smells (in the sense that the context of a linguistic sign is the rest of language, only in relation to which it outlines its distinctive meaning)—but simply the world. We do not discover the meaning of a certain smell by distinguishing it from other smells (we have no independent means of codifying these distinctions) but by distinguishing contexts within which particular smells have a typical value.

This incompleteness, this extreme determination of olfactory meanings by non-olfactory contexts, means that for us, olfactory sensations are in the main only tangential to the business of living. For each and every kind of experience, there is a characteristic olfactory accompaniment, yet it is rare for an experience to be dominated or thematized by this particular sensory mode. Eating and drinking, parties and country walks all involve a dimension of olfactory pleasure, yet it is true of none of them that they are worthwhile on that basis alone (to be able only to *smell* food, without any prospect of eating it is torture, not pleasure). The pleasures of this sense only adumbrate those of richer sensory content. This is to say that just as the smell only acquires definiteness in relation to a context, so the pleasures that this sense confers rarely appertain to the olfactory dimension per se rather to the context with which a particular smell is typically associated. In this respect, though, the very impalpability of olfactory pleasure is also its special advantage, because a smell may give access to a pleasure more intense than could ever be realized in practice, albeit the access given is only vicarious. Many more wines promise to be reasonably drinkable, than actually are. Because all wines of a certain type smell broadly similar (to my inexpert nose at least) the smell of a wine is, for me, the smell of *absolute wine*—a wine I have not tasted once. As soon as I have begun to drink I can tell good from bad readily enough. Perhaps this observation can be generalized; our response to smell is typical rather than specific, general rather than particular. And this is not without importance when one comes to consider the olfactory aspect of magic.

Another thing one can readily see is that the pleasures of the sense of smell tend to be anticipatory, or retrospective, rather than being climactic. The sense of smell comes into play most when the other senses are in suspense, at moments, one could say, of *materialization* and *dematerialization*, the coming into being and passing away of things, situations, circumstances which hold our attention vividly while they are present (suppressing olfactory awareness, whose role is restricted to announcing them prior to their arrival, and commemorating them when they are gone). For example, a merely prospective meal is heralded, and its specific nature is somewhat suggested, by wafts of cooking smells coming from the direction of the kitchen, gradually assuming an ampler and more concrete character ... Or alternatively, where other standards are in operation and diners are sedulously isolated from the kitchen area with its suggestive aromas, the same function (of olfactory anticipation) is performed by the distribution of scented aperitifs, whose minor alcoholic importance is secondary, surely, to their role as aromatic stimulants to hunger (hunger becoming frankly desirable only because the aperitif provides an olfactory context which promises its speedy satisfaction). The smell of something cooking or the tang of an aperitif mark a transition from concept, expectation, to fact—a notional meal to the actual one—and conversely the standard and familiar postprandial aromatics, nuts, cheeses, coffee and cigars set a seal of finality on the dematerialization of a meal, now only an insubstantial trace. A mere aroma, in its very lack of substance is more *like* a concept than it is like a "thing" in the usual sense, and it is really quite appropriate that the olfactory sense should play its greatest role at junctures when it is precisely this attribute of a meal (meal-concept or meal-fact) which is in the balance.

III

To manifest itself as a smell is the nearest an objective reality can go towards becoming a concept without leaving the realm of the sensible altogether: as such, the dematerialization of the concrete thing as the evaporated essence of itself serves as the model for exchange between this world and

another, disembodied one. In a poem entitled *All Souls' Night*, Yeats writes
that it is:

> ... a ghost's right,
> His element is so fine
> Being sharpened by his deaths
> To drink from the wine-breath
> While our gross palates drink from the whole wine.

These lines suggest, not only the familiar idea that it is the smell of an offering
which is the portion of its unworldly recipient, but also that the recipient (*His
element is so fine / Being sharpened by his death* ...) is different in nature to the
part of the offering he receives, only in being if anything still more tenuous.
There is a profound connection between the olfactory dimension and the
dimension of other-worldliness, which is only inadequately expressed in
the phrase "odor of sanctity." The very words "spirit" and "essence" reveal
the fact that the vehicle for an ideal or absolute truth which would be, at
the same time, concretely within reach, would have to be something like a
vapor, a distillate of more mundane reality. Platonism, idealism, spiritualism
seem to haunt any discourse which concerns itself with the sense of smell
and the kind of experience it gives us access to, and I will show that this is
no less the case when we come to consider the concept of smelling among
the Umeda villagers of New Guinea, for whom smelling is intimately connected with dreaming, and for whom dreaming means having access to a
higher truth. But all this must be related back, I would argue, to the incompleteness, the disembodiedness of smells as such, which makes them the
model for the ideal which hovers on the edge of actualization, something
not quite in being but which announces itself as an odor which corresponds
to a context within which the ideal is. The olfactory exchange between the
gross and spirit worlds can be understood not only in the sense of the subtle
sacrificial portion ascending skywards, but also in the other direction, as the
presentation, in the vehicle of an impalpable but distinctly perceptible odor,
of an ideal order which could be real.

This idea may not carry much conviction. But consider the facts which
surround the apparently simple institution of perfume-wearing, as familiar to
us as it is the New Guineans of whom I shall speak later. It does not seem to
me that the wearing of perfume is to be accounted for either as the attempt
to trigger an innate ethological mechanism—if the mechanism existed so
would the means of triggering it without recourse to artifice—nor yet as a
purely customary signal, since there is no consistent meaning encoded in
perfume, as there is, say, in wearing black (for mourning) or white (for the
bride). Perfume does not have a discrete communication function (though I
do not say that it does not communicate). It does not say "I love you," "I am
available"—these are messages which imply a recipient, and the message of

perfume is not specific as to its recipient. Some perfumes say "I am rich," but only by implication, for the message really is "I am wearing a perfume that rich people also wear," i.e. the meaning of perfume is a function of context, and it is characteristic of smells, as I said earlier, that the context dominates the sign. Perfume-wearing is resorted to routinely, like tooth-brushing (also not devoid of magical overtones), with the result that its "message" is weakened by the absence of diacritical weighting: "wearing perfume" is not much more "marked" than "not wearing perfume." The language of code, message, sender and recipient is inappropriate to perfume—the real meaning of the custom of wearing perfume lies less in the communicative ends it may contingently serve, than in the *act* of putting it on. It is not sufficient to say, simply, that this is auto-communicative; since, just as perfume does not have a diacritical meaning for others, it may lack one also where the wearer himself or herself is concerned. Perfume is not a language or a substitute for language. Nor yet is it a technique, efficacious in a straightforwardly instrumental way. It is a symbolic presentation.

What the characteristic atmosphere of expensive perfume enveloping a woman can do is give us access to an ideal which is perhaps only lamely expressed except by that precise olfactory sensation. Perfume is symbolic, not linguistic, because it does what language could *not* do—express an ideal, an archetypal wholeness, which surpasses language while language remains subservient to the more or less worldly business of communicating (I agree that language can be used symbolically as well as communicatively: poets and magicians do this). Perfume has to do with the transcendent, the transcendence which, while always inaccessible, can thematize the experienced world. I said earlier that a smell is always incomplete by itself, that it acquires a meaning not by contrast with other smells, but by association with a context within which it is *typical*. Where perfume is concerned this completion is contextual also: the perfume is not completed by the idea "roses, patchouli, musk, alcohol..."—or whatever the actual constituents of the perfume may be (they are probably quite unfamiliar) but by the idea of the perfume *situation*. The constituents of perfume as substance are not the constituents of perfume as experience: just as an odor permeates a place, an occasion, a situation, so the context comes to permeate the odor-sign and becomes inseparably part of it. But if we try to define what that context of perfume, the perfume situation, really is, it is apparent that this is an instance of an odor-sign giving vicarious access to a kind of experience not really matched by anything in real life.

At any rate, perfume advertisements of the kind which commonly occur in the glossies, notwithstanding the combined efforts of the most expert copywriters and photographers, sometimes achieve a quite egregious degree of bathos, even for advertisements. Trade-names like *Nuits d'amour* or *Stolen Kisses* linearize the essentially indirect relationship between perfume and sexual happiness in a way which, seeming to lay bare the motives of perfume wearers, exposes them to ridicule. A perfume does not seduce: it sets up a context of seduction. This context is not the mundane one, the actual tangible elements of the scene, only a kind of aura which, enveloping everything, assures us that the scene is typical, that it is the realization, in the here-and-now, of a pre-ordained scheme. Perfume evokes a transcendence (of the world but not in it)—it could be called *the transcendence of the sweet life*. But because it is perfume (spirit, halfway between thing and idea) it almost partakes of the nature of the transcendence (otherwise dimly adumbrated in images, musical sounds, vague feelings and desires) while still remaining part of the world.

In real terms, the transcendence of the sweet life is inaccessible, but while we are content to remain under the spell cast by perfume, so redolent of everything that is typical of that life, it seems that the otherwise separate spheres of the actual and the transcendent merge together partially, the communication between the two having been established in the olfactory domain. This is really having access to a charmed universe in which good fortune is the law of life. This possibility or actuality of the charmed universe in which the good happens, not contingently, but typically and as a consequence of something pre-established is what perfume communicates, or better, appresents. This is what I wished to indicate when I said earlier that the significance of the custom of wearing perfume lay less in the socially communicative ends it served than in the act of putting it on. For to open up a channel of communication between these domains (the real world and the transcendence of the sweet life) is extremely propitious. A shift of boundaries, of contexts, has occurred, and the ideal intersects with the real, or rather, it should be impossible to tell which is which.

It is surely correct to say that wearing perfume is a *magical* act.

IV

An Umeda man will sleep with his net-bag beside him on the bed, or may, for want of anything better, use it as his pillow. In waking life the bag hardly leaves his shoulder, and its contents (tools, ornaments, magical substances and food) summarize his life and its activities. This is the bag which contains the sachet of the magical perfume *oktesap*. It is believed that the sleeping man, imbibing the magical aroma of *oktesap*, will thereupon dream a dream which betokens good hunting according to the system of dream-augury followed by the Umedas. *Oktesap* has, therefore, two distinct modes of operation: it is, first of all a perfume used by hunters, used in the same vaguely propitiatory way as perfumes are in the west (*oktesap* creates a context of good hunting)—and secondly a means of so influencing a hunter's dreams that hunting success follows necessarily.

It may be of interest to say something at this point about Umeda dream-augury. The Umeda word for "dream" (*yinugwi*) is, in fact, very close to the

Umeda word for a smell (*nugwi*). Umedas were very sensitive to both. They were brilliant at detecting the faintest hint of the smoke from a campfire in the depths of the forest, or at distinguishing (by the freshness or otherwise of the scent), whether pig-tracks were new or old, or where a cuscus might be concealed aloft. They were always on the alert for olfactory clues which might lead them to discover things otherwise kept hidden. Their attitude towards dreams was only a more complex instance of the same thing: a dream was always a clue giving access to something hidden—the world of spirits, ghosts, or the future fate of the dreamer and/or his immediate associates. Some dreams simply reflected accurately a state of affairs which would duly come to pass (unless avoided by counter-action). Others were interpretable by means of a standard set of symbol-identifications. The dream which foretold the killing of a pig was one such dream; for it did not take the form of a direct representation of the event (to dream of killing a pig was an evil omen, an indication of illness and death in the local community)—the dream indicative of hunting success was dreaming of making love to a woman.

The substitution of "making love" for "killing a pig" is not arbitrary. Eating, violence (hunting), and sexuality, are alternative "modes" of a single basic activity which the Umeda language expresses by means of only one verb (*tadv*). In dreams, the modes are switched round—"hunting" becomes "lovemaking," and "lovemaking" becomes "eating" (the dream which prefigures the successful consummation of a love affair is "your sister comes and give you some food"). It is as if the displacement of the action from the plane of real life to the plane of the dream brought about a systematic shift in *tadv*-modalities, for it is by no means the case that hunting and lovemaking are substitutable as activities in normal existence. In fact, they are regarded as being mutually inimical to the highest degree: the actual practice of lovemaking robs the hunter of his luck—pigs can smell a man who has been in contact with women, particularly those who are menstruating. The ideal hunter is a chaste bachelor, who, shunning contact with women, makes an ascetic vocation of the chase. Such a young man will, however, dream of the women from whom he has absented himself: and having been aroused by his dream he will take his bow and arrow and slip away into the forest, speaking to nobody, emboldened in the belief that a pig must come his way. It is not hard to surmise the psychological value of the incentive to hunting the dream must provide, nor the continuous stimulus of the wafts of *oktesap* perfume issuing from the hunter's net-bag. The "focusing" power of magic has been discussed elsewhere (Tambiah 1968; Douglas 1966, ch. 4). What interests me particularly, though, is the relation between the perfume and the dream-augury, and the light they conjointly shed on the question of the efficacy of symbolic action.

It would appear, both from the fact that the *oktesap* perfume is believed to be conducive to the pig-killing dream, and from the very marked similarity of the words for smelling and dreaming in Umeda (both being based on the element *nug*, "smell") that the connection between smell-experiences and dream-experiences in Umeda is very close. They could, I think, be seen as two aspects of a single faculty or activity—the faculty of having cognizance of things at a remove—just as the various modes of eating, sexuality, violence, etc. referred to previously are "aspects" of a single basic activity. Seen in this light the *oktesap* perfume no longer need be seen as having two separate ways of working (as an attractant and as a dream-stimulant)—but only one, in that the kind of access to the ideal order possible in the dream state is only an intensification of that already present in the "perfume state."

Perfumes, in their disembodiedness and typicality serve as the vehicles for symbolic awareness of an ideal order: the "perfume state" is a state in which perfume becomes for the wearer (and for others under its spell) much less a sign of good fortune or happiness or the sweet life, than a condition for that life. That is to say that the context has permeated the sign, and has become so inseparable from it, that what might be—from the standpoint of one outside the system—an "association" endowed with only contingent significance, has acquired in the light of "perfumed consciousness" the force of something inscribed in the fabric of the world. Perfumed consciousness grasps the world as something emanating from the sign, ordered according to necessities imposed by the sign, because the sign and the idealities which are the context of the sign are inseparable. The dream-state is more complex than this, but is also, analytically, more familiar. The similarity between the two is possibly most apparent in the way in which a dream colors subsequent waking perception of events, so that the day following a memorable or fateful dream gains a characteristic feeling-tone corresponding to the tenor of the previous night's dream. This "atmospheric" modulation of waking experience by dreams is not unlike the effects achieved by perfumes. But dream consciousness is autonomous in a way in which perfume-experiences are not. Except where special techniques are employed, as they sometimes are, to direct the course dream experiences will take—the *oktesap* magic I have mentioned is one such technique—the worldly interests of the dreamer are not in play on the plane of the dream. The splendors or abasements of the dreaming soul do not "count" in the sense that the erotic or hunting feats achieved under the propitious influence of perfumes, magical or otherwise, obviously do. Their value in terms of real life is only indirect, monitory, prognosticatory, or inspirational as the case may be. At the same time the relative fullness of the dream experience contrasts with the tenuousness of perfume, however vividly suggestive. The dream seems to hold out the possibility of direct access to the transcendent, mitigated only by forgetfulness, and the barriers to understanding posed by elliptical symbolism (such as the "shift" from "hunting" to "love-making" and "lovemaking" to "eating" described above). In the dream transcendence is revealed as fully constituted, leaving little enough room, usually, for the subject's manipulations. Perfume, on the other hand, while it can only dimly prefigure what the dream vividly shows, admits readily of intervention by the subject in pursuit of certain ends. It is not a surprise to find the value of the dream, in the Umeda system, is that of infallible augury, while the value of perfume is as a means of manipulating transcendence actively.

Perhaps, one might go on to say, a fully developed magical technique is always founded (like the *oktesap* technique I have described) on a conjunction of two such elements, an element of constituted transcendence (the world as it ideally, typically, is, "in the light of eternity") and on the other hand a symbolic technique for making this eternal order part of an integral situational reality, by so using signs (magical perfumes, incantations, gestures) that the transcendence invoked comes into being naturally as the implicit context of the signs used. Divination and augury, for instance, presuppose the existence of a pre-given, authentic, "truth of the world" by seeking access to it: where the historian *reconstructs* the past, the diviner tries to re-establish contact with it directly as an eternal present, and augury, similarly, reposes on the idea of prediction not from "observed regularities" but from messages emanating from a future already enacting itself but out of our sight. Divination and augury respect the pre-givenness of the world "as it really is" and only try to achieve as direct as possible intuition of the totality of which the current situation affords us partial glimpses only. Magic differs from these, "passive," forms of ritual action only in actively seeking to condition the occurrence of events in the immediate situation by specifying their symbolic context in the light of the pre-established totality or the "truth of the world."

Magic—or purposive ritual generally—can be viewed as *manipulated augury*. Spells (e.g. the familiar example from *Coral Gardens* "The belly of my garden leavens, the belly of my garden rises ... reclines ... grows to the size of a bush hen's nest ... etc.") depict a favorable outcome as a means of bringing it about. But the depiction—the description—is not of this or that actual garden, canoe, etc. but of the lineaments of an essential one (just as the smell of roses is not the smell of this or that particular rose, but *the*, typical, absolute rose-smell ...). The factor of *standardization* in the morphology of the spell corresponds to the factor of typicality in smells, which makes them magically efficacious. There is no room for idiosyncrasy, for anything merely personal or improvisatory, in magical language, which must evoke not a contingent, situational reality, but that reality "as it really is" stripped of everything inessential: the spell is standardized because the reality it evokes is no less so.

The lesson of the example I have considered seems to be that magic seeks its effect neither in miracles, nor yet in technical manipulations of a would-be rational kind, but by means of a rhetoric which annuls the distinction between the contingent situation and the regularities of the overall pattern of meanings which the rhetoric evokes. While the magician speaks, he is every magician: the garden he addresses is the epitome of all gardens. He normalizes the situation. In the same way, I have tried to suggest, perfume could be said to normalize the situation of seduction, by placing it in the context of the transcendence of the sweet life, a generalized pattern of pre-established harmonies latent in every contingent encounter; the real intersects with the ideal and a happy outcome is assured.

Note

1. Umeda village (pop. ca. 200) is one of a group of four known as the Waina-Sowanda villages situated in the West Sepik district of New Guinea. A monograph on the Umeda (*Metamorphosis of the Cassowaries*) is in press (1975). Further information on the culture is contained in an article published in *Man* (Gell 1971) devoted to Umeda penis-sheathing practices. The Umeda are a small, relatively isolated group, maintaining themselves by small-scale shifting agriculture, sago palm culture, collecting and hunting. Fieldwork in Waina-Sowanda was carried out in 1969–70, supported by a grant from the Social Science Research Council and the Horniman Scholarship Fund.

Bibliography

Douglas, M. (1966), *Purity and Danger*, London: Routledge, Kegan & Paul.
Evans-Prichard, E.E. (1929), "The Morphology and Function of Magic," *American Anthropologist*.
Gell, A. (1971), "Penis Sheathing and Ritual Status in a West Sepik Village," *Man* (N.S.), 6: 165–81.
—— (1975), *Metamorphosis of the Cassowaries*, London: Athlone Press.
Tambiah, S.J. (1968), "The Magical Power of Words," *Man* (N.S.), 3: 175–208.

35

The Scent of Memory in Hindu South India

David Shulman

In one of the most famous, and most poignant, verses in classical Sanskrit literature, Kālidāsa's amnesiac hero, Dusyanta, gives voice to the strange disquiet that arises in him as he overhears a beautiful song:

> Seeing rare beauty,
> hearing lovely sounds,
> even a happy man
> becomes strangely uneasy ...
> perhaps he remembers,
> without knowing why,
> loves of another life
> buried deep in his being.

> (*Abhijnanasakuntala* 5.2 in Miller 1984: 134)

The verse sets the scene for a dramatic and evocative enactment of the themes of human memory and forgetting; the royal hero is about to repudiate his recent bride, Śakuntalā, whom he fails to recognize when she reappears in his court—for his memory of their recent nuptials and passionate love has been completely erased by an irascible sage's curse. But the verse just cited, which adumbrates this unhappy encounter, focuses rather on the sudden *recovery*, through aesthetic experience, of earlier memories that have been "lost" to consciousness. The unease and sense of longing that a person feels upon encountering beauty are here attributed to the sudden reemergence of buried, karmic memories from earlier births. The verse presents us with two examples, visual and auditory, of the aesthetic trigger capable of producing this type of response; sight and sound are, perhaps, the most obvious vehicles for conventional aesthetic perception (etymologies aside). But the Hindu tradition in fact refers to the phenomenon of karmic memory generally by another term, drawn from the realm of smell. Such a buried, unconscious memory carried over from a person's former lives is known as *vāsanā*—literally, an odor. Each one of us bears a nearly endless number of such odors within his mind without being aware of their presence; but these scent-memories are activated by the conjunction of formerly familiar circumstances, by experiencing again a specific context, and, as we have seen, by coming into contact with beauty (see O'Flaherty 1984: 220–30). The notion of *vāsanā* is the conventional Hindu explanation for the universal sense of déjà vu: the reawakened "odor" presents us with a real, although intangible, memory from our distant past, from beyond the boundary of this particular present experience of birth and growth; if we think that we have been in this place before, seen this sight, heard this music, it is because we indeed *have*—perhaps more than once, perhaps a great many times—even though we cannot recall the precise circumstances of those former occasions. The subtle, revivified "scent" is the bearer of this powerful but ambiguous knowledge, whose content is rarely explicit and defined. Note that the emotion that habitually accompanies this process is one of wonder and amazement, and at the same time of disquiet and uneasy longing. *Vāsanā* makes the past present again, but at the same time, as with any memory, it establishes a gap, a distance, a sense of loss.

Sanskrit love-poetry offers many examples of this connection among odor, memory and a painful distance. Let us look at another verse, this time one that is content to remain within the confines of a single lifetime:

> Before I met him,
> I was a virgin:
> now he is my husband.
> But these spring nights
> are just the same,
>> still soaked in the fragrance of jasmine
>> and of the ripening *kadamba* blossoms
>> carried by the wind,
> and I'm still me –
> the same woman –
> yet how I long now
> with all my heart
> for the way we played at making love
> there, on the river bank
> under a canopy of reeds.

(Jha 1967: 1.4)

This somewhat unusual nostalgic statement is a study in continuity and inner dissonance, delicately expressed in the timeless, crystal tones of the *kāvya* style. *Kāvya* seeks to delineate a moment in its very essence and then to freeze it in perfect form; but this "freezing" effect is itself part of the poem's theme, a problematic subject for its reflection. The speaker cries from her heart; "I am who I am" (*sa caivāsmi*)—uncannily echoing the words of the Vedic sacrificer who, having gone through all the upheavals of the sacrifice (an ascent to heaven and a return; a ritual death and rebirth through the rite), must similarly proclaim that he remains just the person he was before (*idam aham ya evāsmi so 'ham*) (see Heesterman 1978: 92). *Kāvya* and Vedic sacrifice both deliberately remove themselves from time and change. But the stated continuity is, nonetheless, utterly misleading: although the nights are the same intoxicating wonder, and the two actors are unchanged, the inner reality has been painfully transformed; the woman looks back with longing at the early unfolding of her love, a moment lost now beyond recovery. The striking element, for our purposes, is, however, the place of the jasmine and *kadamba* fragrance in the speaker's awareness (and in the poem's overall effect). These powerful smells serve both as the chief indicators of a presumed continuity and as the essential vehicles for memory; they identify the spring nights for what they are and thereby create the conditions for the speaker's flooding sensation of simultaneous familiarity and loss. Reading the poem, one feels that the perception it describes is, in fact, actually initiated and largely determined by the impact of this fragrance, by far the poem's most prominent sensory feature. One whiff of jasmine, and the woman's existential reality is at once made clear.

Thus, in India, one smells his way back into his past, which recedes even as it becomes present in this way. We shall explore more carefully below the reasons for this connection and the underlying conceptions it represents. First we must fill in the outlines of the picture that is emerging. To take another example, a more conventional one, in this case from the collection of Sanskrit love-poems known as the *Caurapañcāsikā* (attributed to the medieval poet Bilhana):

Even now I can see her,
her lovely eyes tremulous
with fright,
as she was waving a lotus that was our toy
to drive away a bee drawn in hunger
to her lips
by her unbearably
sweet scent.

(qtd. in Miller 1971: 59)

Tradition identifies the speaker as a "thief of love" who has had an affair with the king's daughter and, having been captured by the irate father, whiles away the hours before his execution by composing these verses suffused by memory. But even if we choose to ignore this story that traditionally frames the poems, we are left with a series of recollected vignettes: each verse begins with the nostalgic *adyāpi*, "even now ...," and proceeds to concretize a moment drawn out of the speaker's past; the mood is one of wistful recollection from a position of present loneliness or loss. Most of the verses are quite devoid of odors (they are replete with visual and verbal themes), but the above example nicely illustrates the linkage we are exploring. The girl's "unbearable" fragrance is *durdhara*, an ambiguous adjective that can mean both "irresistible" and "difficult to be remembered." There is, perhaps, a hint here of the notorious difficulty we have in remembering smells in their absence, although once again it is the smell itself that permeates the quality of the speaker's memory and that serves as the crucial pivot of the verse—for the lover, by implication, is undoubtedly identified here with the bee, helplessly drawn to the heroine's lips, overpowered by her sensuous scent. It is this image, metaphorically extended to the speaker, that forms the substance of his memory. The specific fragrance may have disappeared, but the sense of its former power informs the *general* process of remembering, which is itself seen as a kind of smelling—an experience at once enticing and somewhat painful, in that it generates the emotions of yearning and desire.

To smell is to remember, and thus to become aware of separation: thus in the Tamil version of the *Rāmāyana* by Kampaṉ (to switch to the more specific, regional context that will occupy us below), Rāma, searching for his beloved Sītā, who has been kidnapped by the demon Rāvaṇa, is given a collection of her ornaments and jewels, gathered and preserved by the monkeys near the place where these jewels had fallen; Rāma sniffs at them—and they become flowers in his arms (Kampaṉ, *Irāmāvatāram* 4.210). The moment is deeply ambiguous: he has, on the one hand, recovered something of Sītā's presence, which intoxicates him by its immediacy and precious reality; on the other hand, he is even more aware than before of the extent of his loss, of his beloved's absence, of the tormenting state of separation that he must continue to endure. The smell, by its very presence, embodies this sense of separation. Even without the factor of memory, this equation still stands—indeed, it functions as something of a convention. The sweet fragrances of springtime, the season of love, are literary markers of painful yearning: the southern quarter (home of the Malaya Hill, which fills the air with the scent of its sandal trees) is said to emit, at the onset of spring, a fragrant breeze (*gandhavaha*) that is like a sigh of pain (*vyalīkaniśvāsa*) (Kālidāsa, *Kumārasambhava* 3.25). Another royal hero of Kālidāsa's can exclaim:

The wind from the southern mountain,
fragrant with amaranth pollen,
fresh with scents of budding flowers,
often incites an aimless longing.

(*Mālavikāgnimitra* 3.9 in Gerow 1984: 278)

And, elsewhere in the same play:

The youthful season comes of age –
the mango tree is covered with fruit;
amaranth blossoms everywhere,
and longing fills the heart.

(*Mālavikāgnimitra* 5.2 in Gerow 1984: 303)

Longing of this sort exists in its own right, even without an object; and, as in the case of the scent-memories mentioned earlier, with the disquiet they induce, there is an outstanding olfactory aspect to this sensation. The medieval devotional poets, such as Jayadeva (thirteenth century), take over this convention and apply it to the state of the devotee yearning for his god:

The south wind fans love to flame
and blossoming flowers crack open the hearts
of separated lovers,
while your companion, o Krsna,
dwells alone.

(*Gitagovinda* 5.2)

We are left, then, with the following observation: in Indian poetry, the notions of smell and memory are deeply bound up with one another as well as with the closely related notion of traumatic separation, the concomitant emotions of unsatisfied longing and desire, and the consciousness of distance and loss. How are we to understand this relation? Why is memory identified as an odor? And why the emphasis on the painful side of memory, especially the memory of love? It would appear that the role of smells in the latter case—the poetry of love—goes beyond that of being a simple function of the poets' interest in states of separation. Something in the very nature of smells fits them admirably to this symbolic slot, allows them to suggest a generalized atmosphere of separation and yearning. We may begin by observing a congruence between odors and the Hindu concept of an ultimate but hidden reality, often described as *sūkṣma*—subtle, delicate, invisible, seemingly immaterial, but actually constituting an essential level of being that is far more pervasive and more significant than everyday, perceived phenomena. Many texts make smells their major metaphor for unchanging, natural essence: "Even if you grind sandalwood, it will never lose its fragrance. Burn aloe-wood, but it will never smell bad. You can infuse an onion with many fragrances, but it will never lose its stench" (Ativīrarāmapāṇṭivar 1970: 18–19). These statements, taken from a medieval Tamil collection of gnomic utterances appropriately named "The Fragrant Collection" (Naṟuṅtŏkai), are meant to support other hallowed pronouncements of both descriptive and prescriptive character (e.g. "A woman's beauty lies in never talking back to her husband," "Greatness or smallness result only from one's own actions"). Smells function here as markers of a stable order of truthful being. On a somewhat more rarefied level, we find the fragrance of a flower serving as a metaphor for the subtle presence of the ultimate reality—that of God:

> In fire, you are the heat.
>   In flowers, you are the scent.
> Among stones, you are the diamond...
> Everything, you are everything,
> the sense, the substance, of everything.

> (Paripāṭal 3.63–4, 68 in Ramanujan 1985: 218; cf. Cuntaramūrtti 1964: 690)

The medieval devotional poets develop this theme to considerable lengths; the Tamil Tevāram poems, for example (seventh through ninth centuries), are redolent of powerful odors associated with Śiva's shrines and, more specifically, with Śiva himself. For, as Nietzsche knew, God can be detected by his smell:

> Hawks haunt the reeking
> begging-bowl he carries;
> his adornment
> is ashes;
> his matted hair is piled
> high upon his head.

> (Ramanujan 1985: 736)

Śiva, smeared with ashes taken from the burning ground, uses as his begging-bowl the stinking skull of the god Brahmā, whom Śiva decapitated in punishment for arrogance; demons swarm around this repulsive bowl as the god wanders the world in search of alms (Ramanujan 1985: 13). The presence of this deity is thus marked by the stench (nāṟṟam) of death and decay:

> He cut off the head
> of the hostile Brahmin (= Brahmā)
> and filled it with Viṣṇu's blood
> as he carried the corpse on his shoulder
> for all to see...

> (Ramanujan 1985: 686)

In addition, we must recall the terrible odor of the elephant skin, still covered with coagulated blood, which Śiva flayed from its demon-owner and in which he habitually drapes himself. But these harsh smells are also mitigated by that of the garland of "sharp-scented *kŏṉṟai*" (Ramanujan 1985: 279) that the god wears and, of course, by the sweet fragrances that perfume the shrines that are his homes:

> I saw him in Kāṉāṭṭumuḷḷūr
> where the crooked *talai*
>   enveloped by its leaves and prickly thorns,
> puts forth its buds in the groves
>   thick with fragrance and fresh honey
> while the dark *kuvaḷai* flowers, savoring the honey in their mouths,
>   close their eyes in slumber
> in the paddy-fields.

(Ramanujan 1985: 404)

The aromatic atmosphere of worship in the South Indian temple is here consistently transposed to the natural landscape in which the god, himself a radiating center of strong odors, is situated. Specific smells indicate his presence, even as the more general *notion* of smell figuratively expresses his nature as hidden, delicate, divine essence.

We arrive thus at an ontology of odor: like the repressed *karmic* memory, all the more real and more overpowering by virtue of being unconscious (in Hindu, not Freudian, metaphysics!), an odor constitutes a specific, undeniable, but still invisible presence. Intangibility is here an argument for reality, for a force representing a more essential form of existence. In this context it is important to note that the *vāsanā*-odor does not merely trigger a lost memory (that is accomplished by various contingent factors, e.g. the aesthetic experiences mentioned earlier), but rather actually comprises the content of the memory. *Vāsanā* is the *karmic* trace itself, the subtle stuff of remembering, an intangible, evocative, ambiguous, yet highly specific presence latent in the mind. We are dealing not with an indeterminate fantasy but with an unknown or only partly known reality. At the same time, as we have seen, *vāsanā* embodies the dynamism of distance—like the elusive, time-bound, transient scent. The hidden essence of being tantalizes by its fragile manifestations. We normally approach it through fragmentary symbols (Shulman 1986)—and here we observe that odors partake of the quintessential symbolic faculty of simultaneously "making present" (representing) and determining an absence. The symbolized whole eludes its symbolic container; the subtle reality of an odor induces the awareness of loss. Yet, in effect, the basic relationships in this analogy are reversed: whereas the symbol (especially the linguistic symbol) is a gross and partial representation of the partly absent signified, the scent is itself the elusive essence given to manifestation in other, cruder forms. It is not merely an iconic or indexical sign, in the Peircean sense, but rather embodies an identity that belongs to a superior reality; moreover, as a sign, it merges utterly with a context, or a content, whose essence the scent does not merely represent but rather effectively comprises. The conjunction of intangibility and obvious immediacy marks smells off from other signs; in sharp contrast with linguistic symbols, for example, which, at best, tend toward the suprasymbolic, pointing mutely beyond themselves, an odor tends happily toward the infrasymbolic. If it suggests separation, it also constitutes an immediate reality of true, essential being.

All this might suggest that the apprehension of smells may well incorporate an even more powerful sense of a tantalizing and poignant presence than does an ordinary symbol, which in any case conditions us to partiality. For the scent is really there, imbued with unmistakable power, clearly capable of generating and sustaining an entire context—however elusive the scent-substance of this context may be. At the same time, for all the association of smells with essential levels of reality, we are not necessarily dealing with static entities. Quite the contrary: within the fluid world of Hindu identity-boundaries, odors often function as major indicators of transition and transformation. The hideous, foul-smelling demoness Pūtanā tries to kill the infant Kṛṣṇa by nursing him from her breasts, which have been smeared with virulent poison; Kṛṣṇa, impervious to the poison, sucks Pūtanā's life away; but when the villagers come to burn her body, it gives off a marvelous sweet odor of aloe-wood—the sign that her evil past has been completely destroyed by Krsna nursing at her breast (*Bhāgavatapurāṇa* 10.6.34). Even more striking are the cases in which odors symbolize the outstanding moment of identity-transformation in the Hindu life-cycle—that of marriage and sexual union. A famous case from the Epic is that of the Fish-Maiden Satyavatī, born from a fish and brought up among the fishermen; as a result of making love with the great sage Parāśara (in a boat in the middle of the river), this woman's congenital fishy odor was replaced by a sweet fragrance that could be detected miles away—hence her names, Gandhavati ("the fragrant") and Yojanāgandhā ("fragrant for miles"). Later in her career, she is wooed by and married to Śantanu, who is overpowered by her "indescribably wonderful odor" while walking one day in the forest; her combination of beauty, sweetness and fragrance (*rūpamādhuryagandha*) convinces this king at once that she is the bride he wants, and thus Satyavati is catapulted into a new life at the royal court (*Mahābhārata* 1931). Note that here it is the woman whose basic odor is transformed, even as it is the context of *her* life that is radically changed by marriage; the sage Parāśara's initial blessing, which produces her magical perfume, is simply the first step in her elevation to queenship and to a decisive role in the development of the Epic's tale. In this North Indian story, the woman naturally adapts herself to a new identity in her husband's world, and the natural sign of the transition is the prophetic change of smell.

In the Tamil South, the picture is somewhat different, although here, too, marriage is an event characteristically described by its odor. The heroine of an ancient Tamil love-poem, having described to her companion a meeting with her lover, ends by praying:

> May the sweet smells
> of my marriage in our house
> cling to no man
> but him,
> and that will be good.
> It will guarantee a lasting place for us
> in this world that doesn't last.

(Kalittŏkai 54 in Ramanujan 1985: 200)

The sweet smells (*aruñ kaṭi*) mentioned here are actually synonymous with weddings and marriages (cf. Cīttalaiccāttaṉar, *Maṇimekalai* 16.98); in a later period, we find a similar notion in the apparent conflation in popular awareness of two homonymous roots *mana*—"to be united, to wed, embrace" and "to emit fragrance" (Burrow and Emeneau 1961). A wedding is thus *tirumaṇam*, which resonates strongly with *maṇam*, "smell"; poetic usage sometimes plays with these overtones. But whereas the *Mahābhārata's* Satyavatī assimilates a new identity, and therefore emits a different odor, by being deflowered (and later married), the South Indian fragrances of marriage point to a continuity of identity on the part of the bride, an identity intensified, perhaps, by the fulfillment of her womanhood in marriage and still symbolically focused on her fragrance. This, perhaps, is what we might expect in any case, given the South Indian preference for cross-cousin marriages, which effectively ensure that the woman remains securely entrenched within her own native subcaste (*kulam*)—in marked contrast with the North Indian pattern, in which the bride exchanges her native patrilineage for a wholly alien other (see Hudson 1978: 116–7). Note that in the verse just quoted, the "sweet smells of marriage" are immediately linked to the speaker's fantasy of stability and continuity, her hopes for a "lasting place ... in this world that doesn't last." In the context of Tamil marriages, fragrance is the external marker of a deeply rooted identity that can flower and unfold, without losing its essential character, in sexual union, in the life of the home, in love.

For love itself (*aṉpu, aruḷ*) is a fragrance, whether it be the love of man and woman or of man and God: in both cases, a hidden or latent feeling emerges, like a subtle odor, from the recesses of inner being that are the proper dwelling-place for a deeper truth. In the implicit metaphysics of the Tamil universe, the unmanifest "inner" properly contains its apparent container, the gross outer form; life is a process of manifestation of this delicate but pervasive and powerful inner being, although this process is also deeply interwoven with a contrary movement of demanifestation, of reabsorption within the invisible innerness of things. In whichever direction one moves (we are, in fact, normally moving in both ways simultaneously), the basic vehicle of experience and perception is feeling (*uṇarcci*), which, like memory, is a subtle smell at once embodying and indicating the dynamic yet hidden essence. Marriage is, perhaps, the outstanding expression of this movement within reality—an unfolding from within, but also a merging of outer with inner being, at once emergence outward and return—hence its identification as a fragrance with connotations of continuity and quintessential identity.

And married love is a powerful perfume that carries an existential truth. In the remainder of this chapter, we shall examine two stories that touch upon this theme, structured in both cases around the same motif of the woman's naturally fragrant hair.

The first text suggests the complexities that can overtake the sweet fragrances of marriage when a rival relationship—that of the devotee and his god—enters into the equation:

> The Pāṇṭiya king imprisoned his enemy, the Chola, who had come to attack him at the town of Kāḷipuram. After some time the Chola sent a message to his captor to say that he had come not to fight, but to see the beauty of Kāḷipuram; moreover, he would happily bestow all his wealth and his daughter on the Pāṇṭiyaṉ. The latter freed him from prison and asked him to send for his daughter; when he saw her beauty, he agreed to wed her.
>
> After the ceremony, in the bridal chamber, the king looked carefully at his bride and said, "You are as beautiful as Pārvatī; you seem to be no mortal woman but a goddess. Because of the natural fragrance of your hair, you are named Sugandhakeśī [*sugandha*, "fragrance"; *keśa*, "hair"]. Therefore not I but Śiva is your husband: live happily with him." The bride said, "Surely you are jesting in order to test me. Is it right to speak like this to a bride? You are my husband, and I can think of no one else." Said the king: "Transfer the desire you feel for me to Śiva." "No," said the girl, "be he king of kings or god of gods, I will pay no attention to him. *You* are my lord."
>
> The king then took his bride to the temple. The priests had already performed the night service and locked the five doors of the shrine. By his powers of devotion and truthful speech, the Pāṇṭiya king made the doors open one by one and took Sugandhakeśī into the inner shrine. Pointing to the god, he said to her, "Behold your husband; unite with him in bliss." She refused, insisting, "*You* are my husband," At this the king grew angry and took his sword in his hand. The god appeared, smiling, and asked, "Why have you brought me this woman you have wed?" "I married her thinking of you" answered the king. "You took her hand in love; now take her home," said Śiva. "You must take her," demanded the king, "otherwise I shall take my life." He laid his sword on his neck. Śiva quickly stretched forth his hands and embraced Sugandhakeśī, taking her into the *liṅga* [Śiva's sign]. Her bracelets and anklets remained on the left side of the *liṅga,* and the natural fragrance of her hair still fills the nearby wood. (Ayar 1899: 16.2–39, 17.2–42; see also Shulman 1980: 162–5)

This story fits into an important series of South Indian myths about thwarted marriages of one kind or another; the unusual feature here is the mirror-relation of king and god, each equally reluctant to marry (or to stay married to) this particular bride. Siva achieves his local consort at this shrine, Kāḷaiyārkoyil (Kāṇapper) in the far south of the Tamil country, by virtue of his devotee's violent threats, which effectively coerce the deity to accept the unwanted gift. But this shotgun marriage is, in fact, a success after all, as one can surmise from the perfume that still lingers over the god's symbol and in the neighboring forest—the ultimate indication that Sugandhakeśī has finally transferred her allegiance from the human husband who rejects her, despite her wholly proper arguments and pleas, to the divine consort that he has picked for her in his stead. We cannot be sure that this act of rejection is not planned as a further humiliation of the Pāṇṭiya king's Chola rival, the father of the bride; if this is the case, then the bridegroom's pious preaching to his new wife—to direct her love toward Śiva—would ring rather hollow, even if in the end the girl is forced into an apotheosis that improves upon her initial status. Or does it? The husband himself seems convinced that his wife is divine right from the start, both because of her obvious beauty and because of her most salient feature, the natural fragrance of her hair. This is the real sign of her identity, persisting beyond the transformation described in the myth; and while the text vividly portrays the winsome, entirely human reaction of this woman to her husband's perplexing behavior, the motif of the stable identity-perfume does suggest a relation to the deeper level of reality that is lived out, in this case, by Sugandhakeśī's merger with the god. Indeed, the more likely explanation of the Pāṇṭiya bridegroom's actions is that he has made a choice implicitly guided by this same hierarchy of levels: there is a tension at work here between sexual love in the context of marriage and the home and the love of man and god; the king prefers, so to speak, the latter "fragrance" to the former, an exclusive, rather violent, and self-abnegating service to the deity over union with his wedded wife, despite her divinely scented hair. The interesting point is that the two contexts, the bridal chamber and the temple, are in the end both equally redolent of the same intoxicating scent; the fragrances of marriage and worship are really one, even if the logic of the king's choice requires him to limit his contact with this aroma to one specific, indubitably legitimate context. If, as we have seen, smells can conjure up, indeed essentially constitute, given contexts, here we should note that, as with the *vāsanā* memory-trace, differing contexts can claim their own regulating influence upon the functioning of a single odor-sign.

Sugandhakeśī's fragrant tresses mark her off as potentially divine, but she is not the only Tamil heroine to enjoy this shocking faculty: there is an even more famous story, from the great shrine of Maturai (not very distant from Kāḷaiyārkoyil), which turns upon this very motif. The story, known best from the medieval (seventeenth-century?) retelling of Parañcotimuṇivar (1965) in the *Tiruviḷaiyāṭarpurāṇam* (see also Perumparrappuliyurnampi 1972), was embroidered around a much more ancient Tamil poem from the Caṅkam-period anthology *Kuṟuntŏkai* (2):

> You live by seeking fragrant honey,
> bee with lovely wings –
> don't tell me what I want to hear
> but what you really know:
> is there any flower
> that smells as sweet
> as the long hair of this woman
>   with her rows of perfect teeth
>   and the peacock's grace
> who loves me well?

The poem is attributed to an Iṟaiyaṉār; the name means "lord" or "god." That, and the fact that the poem fits the Caṅkam-period aesthetic ambience with its suggestive techniques and conventions, is all we know about it. But the medieval tradition offers a rich narrative setting to the poem and, at the same time, elaborates upon its central rhetorical image:

> The Pāṇṭiya king was walking in his garden, one day, in the company of his wife, when he became aware of a powerful fragrance—not, he realized, that of the sweet south-wind, infused with the scent of blossoming flowers, but rather of his wife's long hair. Idly he wondered: do bees also recognize this fragrance? Is it natural or artificially produced? He decided that he would give a bag of a thousand gold-pieces to any poet who could divine this still unuttered thought of his and express it in verse.
>
> All the poets of Maturai searched diligently through their minds, filled with endless knowledge, but they were unable to discover the king's hidden thought. Meanwhile, a temple-pest named Tarumi, who wished to get married but had no parents to help him with the expenses of the wedding, prayed to Lord Śiva for help: "Lord, you know everything; you must also know what is in the king's mind. Please compose a verse and give it to me." Śiva at once composed a verse [*Kuṟuntŏkai* 2, quoted above] and offered it to Tarumi, who rushed with it into the poets' assembly [*kaḷakam*] like someone who has found an ancient treasure.
>
> The poets studied the poem with interest, marveling at its richness of expression and meaning; they took it to the king and expounded its import, and the king at once recognized that the poem expressed his thought perfectly. He ordered the bag of gold to be given to Tarumi. But just as the latter was about to cut down the bag, Nakkīrar, the President of the Caṅkam Academy, cried out, "Stop! There is a flaw [*kuṟṟam*] in this verse." Tarumi sadly took the poem back to Siva in the temple. "I am not complaining about losing all that money," he said to the god, "but if those foolish poets find fault with your poem, who will think well of you in the future? And why did you give me an imperfect poem? This reproach affects you, not me."

Śiva was goaded into action. Dressed as a poet [*pulavaṉ*], with a bag for his betel-nut and yak-tail fails waving on either side, he strode into the poets' hall and demanded, "Who has found fault with my poem?" Nakkīrar answered proudly, "I have." "And what is the fault?" Nakkīrar superciliously explained, "It is not a fault of language [*cŏl*] but of meaning [*pŏruḷ*]; hair can have no fragrance unless one puts flowers in it."

Śiva: "Is that true even for lovely *padminī* women, paragons of beauty?"
Nakkīrar: "Precisely."
Śiva: "And what about the divine women who belong to Ālavāyuṭaiyāṉ [Śiva at Maturai]?"
Nakkīrar: "They, too, put *mandāra* flowers in their hair."
Śiva: "And Ñāṉappūṉkotai, the goddess whose tresses are graced with wisdom, and who dwells in half the body of the god you worship, the lord [Śiva] of Kāḷatti?"
Nakkīrar: "Her case, too, is the same."

At this point Śiva opened slightly the third eye in his forehead, which burns whatever it sees; but the obstinate academician, though feeling the heat upon his body, remained unperturbed: "Even if you were all eyes, like Indra, the flaw in your verse would still be a flaw!" By now, however, the fire was unbearable, and Nakkīrar was forced to jump into the water of the Golden Lotus Tank, while the god disappeared.

The Caṅkam poets were desolated at this loss: "It will be a miracle," they said, "if this sin of arguing with the god of Ālavāy will ever be healed." They begged Śiva to forgive Nakkīrar for arguing with him out of the arrogance of learning. Śiva and the goddess joined the group of poets at the edge of the tank. Nakkirar, looking up from within the water, could see only the god; Śiva pervaded all his senses, and he, the crusty old scholar, was overpowered by love. Still floating in the tank, he composed a poem in praise of Śiva's shrine at Kāḷatti; Śiva extended his hand and pulled him out of the water. Tarumi could now be given his gold. But Nakkīrar, apparently traumatized by his experience, had forgotten all his previous knowledge of grammar [*ilakkaṇam*] and had to learn everything again, from the beginning, from the sage Agastya. When he then reexamined all his old compositions, he discovered, to his horror, many mistakes. "The proverb is right" he concluded; "those with only a little knowledge are the most arrogant."

This complex and beautiful tale, which is susceptible to analysis on many levels (see Heifetz and Rao 1987; Dhurjati 1986; and Shulman 2001), presents us, among other features, with an interesting opposition: on the one hand, the learned but rule-bound poets and scholars, committed to their traditional notions of right and wrong, propriety and mistake; on the other, the unpredictable, spontaneous, playful deity, who is capable of improvising a poem along more or less conventional lines but who does so only to help his devotee, and, perhaps, for the sheer, purposeless joy of the exercise. The former group also represents the weighty tradition of the cultural past, a tradition both sustained and partly undermined by the deity in his transcendent position in the temple (outside of and definitely separate from the Caṅkam Academy). But this opposition, which extends to further levels not directly related to our concerns (e.g. court-poet [*kavi*] versus *bhakti*-poet; author versus "non-author"), is also perfectly suited to the essential thrust of the ancient poem's basic image, that of the beloved's naturally fragrant hair. The wider opposition, it seems, is thus one of nature versus culture; other women put flowers in their hair, according to custom (as Nakkīrar, the stubborn pedant, notes), but the Pāṇṭiya queen has no need for such tricks. If there is any doubt about this gift, it is dispelled by Śiva's interrogation of Nakkīrar and the queen's adoption of the wider series of Śiva's dancing-girls at Maturai and his divine consort at Kāḷatti; Nakkīrar's refusal to accept the fact of their natural perfume leads to his near-incineration. The god's intervention and easy triumph establish the obvious superiority, in the view of this text, of nature—free, unbounded, ultimately real—over culture (even if to us this perspective is, or course, itself a cultural artifact par excellence). The natural fragrance is correlated to the natural powers of the god, who clearly transcends and, indeed, *overrules* all hallowed rules and forms; cultural norms are relegated to a lower rung in the hierarchy of being, whose upper rungs are accessible through the spontaneous, irrational impulse of devotional love. This relative ontology is accompanied by an epistemology, which is also keyed to the notion of fragrance: the queen's fragrant tresses, which initiate the entire development of the story through the king's idle speculations, suggest a kind of knowledge—knowledge of a reality, beyond conventional cultural forms, which the king senses (without really penetrating), which Nakkīrar foolishly denies (in the face of an overwhelming demonstration of its truth), and which the god momentarily makes immediately present before the other poets and king. Nakkīrar, obsessed with knowledge of a different, clearly inferior sort, is unable to recognize this more pressing truth; the king, as befits the South Indian royal image, is characteristically on its margins, still vaguely in doubt as to the real origin of the fragrance he detects; Śiva playfully, and for once unambiguously, proclaims a hidden identity. The natural fragrance that is the subject of his poem hints at being at its most irreducible, and most real, the level of being most closely related to the god's own limitless, aimless, indeterminate, "inner" existence. We should note that this lesson emerges, again, from a context of marriage—both the Pāṇṭiya king's marriage to his sweet-smelling queen and the dream of the impoverished Tarumi, eager to marry, who begs a poem from "Iṟaiyaṉār," the god.

Let us sum up the major features of smell in the South Indian sources we have been studying. Smells function in the poems and stories as characteristic markers of identity, capable of transformation, but generally linked to the sense of profound, essential layers of experience and being. Emerging from the inner, hidden world, retaining its features of subtlety, delicacy, and pervasiveness, they are the stuff of immediate, irreducible reality in its manifestations (or, potentially, in its contrary movement of re-absorption). Their very intangibility allows them to maintain the essential force of continuity, to reconstitute lost or forgotten contexts, to re-present unconscious memories and hidden, unrecognized truths. In the Sanskrit materials, this latter function is also predominantly connected to experiences of separation, distance, and longing. And a final feature is stressed in the last story we have quoted—that of spontaneity, the natural freedom of the divine being at work in odors or in relation to them. Let us conclude with a well-known Tamil proverb: *kaḻutaikkut těriyumā karppūravācanai*—"Does the ass know the scent of the camphor he carries?" Note that the scent indicates, as we by now expect, a higher reality; the only question is that of its presentation to consciousness. Devotional poets use this same image to express their hope and their despair:

> Like the donkey
> laden with a burden of fragrant saffron,
> harried through a wasteland,
> half-dead, I stumble,
> father—trapped
> in a whirling vortex.
> And you, my heart –
> who go on weeping?
> I am too much a fool
> to cry out to Hara
>   of the lovely eyes.
> Show me in your mercy
> some way to be saved,
> father, lord
> dwelling in Itaimarutu.

(Cuntaramūrtti Tevāram)

The poet, burdened by forgetfulness, unable to keep Siva constantly in his mind, sees *himself* as the proverbial donkey unable to break through the tragic and pathetic limitations of consciousness. Yet, if we follow his image to its further limit, it is clear that the god is truly there after all, amazingly close, if he could but sense him—a subtle, precious, essential, utterly real, potentially redemptive fragrance.

Bibliography

Atiṿīrarāmapāṇṭivar (1970), *Naṟuntŏkai*, in *Nītinūṟ kŏtto*, Madras: n.p.

Ayar, C. (1899), *Tirukkāṉapper ĕṉṉum kāḷaiyārkoyiṟpurāṇam*, Madras: n.p.

Burrow, T. and Emeneau, M.B. (1961), *Dravidian Etymological Dictionary*, Oxford: Clarendon Press.

Cīttalaiccāttāṉar (c. 500), *Maṇimekalai*, n.p.: n.p.

Cuntaramūrtti (1964), *Tevāram*, Tarumapuram: n.p.

Dhūrjaṭi (1986), *Kāḷahastīsvaraśatakamu*, in H. Heifetz and V.N. Rao (eds), *For the Lord of the Animals*, Berkeley: University of California Press.

Gerow, E. (trans.) (1984), "Mālavikā and Agnimitra," in E.S. Miller (ed.), *Theater of Memory*, New York: Columbia University Press.

Heesterman, J.C. (1978), "Veda and Dharma," in W.D. O'Flaherty and J.D.M. Derrett (eds), *The Concept of Duty in South Asia*, New Delhi: Vikas.

Heifetz, H. and Rao, V.N. (1987), *For the Lord of the Animals*, Berkeley: University of California Press.

Hudson, D. (1978), "Śiva, Mīnākṣī, Viṣṇu," in B. Stein (ed.), *South Indian Temples*, New Delhi: Vikas.

Jha, G. (ed.) (1967), *Mammaṭa: Kāvyaprakāśa*, Varanasi: Bharatiya Vidya Prakasan.

Kampaṉ (n.d.), *Iramavataram*, n.p.: n.p.

Mahābhārata (1931), Southern Recension, Madras: n.p.

Miller, B.S. (ed.) (1971), *Phantasies of a Love-Thief*, New York: Columbia University Press.

—— (ed.) (1984), *Theater of Memory*, New York: Columbia University Press.

O'Flaherty, W.D. (1984), *Dreams, Illusion and Other Realities*, Chicago: University of Chicago Press.

Parañcotimuṉivar (1965), *Tiruviḷaiyāṭarpurāṇam*, Madras: n.p.

Pĕrumpaṟṟappuliyūrnampi (1972), *Tiruvālavāyuṭaiyār*, 3rd ed., Tiruvaṉmiyūr: n.p.

Ramanujan, A.K. (ed. and trans.) (1985), *Poems of Love and War*, New York: Columbia University Press.

Shulman, D. (1980), *Tamil Temple Myths*, Princeton: Princeton University Press.

—— (1986), "Terror of Symbols and Symbols of Terror," *History of Religions*, 26(2): 101–24.

—— (2001), "From Author to Non-Author in Tamil Literary Legend," in *The Wisdom of Poets*, Oxford: Oxford University Press.

36
Olfactory After-Death Communications

William Guggenheim and Judith Guggenheim

The accounts in this chapter involve smelling a fragrance that is associated with a specific deceased family member or friend. They are a relatively common type of after-death communication (ADC), and we call these olfactory ADCs. Typical scents include the fragrance of a perfume, cologne or aftershave lotion; the essence of roses or other flowers; and the aroma of a food, beverage, tobacco or commercial product. The variety of odors that can be identified is virtually unlimited. During an olfactory ADC experience people reported smelling a fragrance that was clearly out of context with their surroundings. The room or area they were in was suddenly filled with a particular aroma, but it had no physical source. Occasionally, two or more people who are together in the same place at the same time can smell this scent. In fact, an olfactory ADC is the one type of ADC that is most often shared by a group of people.

Kathryn, a homemaker in Virginia, received a demonstration of caring from her mother, who died of cancer at age seventy-five:

> One afternoon, just a couple of weeks after my mother died, I was lying on my bed sobbing. Suddenly, my room was flooded with the scent of green apples. I stopped crying in a flash and sat up in bed, sniffing the air like a bird dog.
>
> It was no little maybe, maybe-not kind of thing. My whole bedroom was permeated with this wonderful aroma! The green apple smell just filled up the room and it didn't go away. It lasted for a full minute or possibly longer.
>
> My mother had a wonderful air freshener she used at home that was the fragrance of green apples. I never smelled it anywhere else. I loved it and always made a big to-do over how marvelous it was.

It is the only scent that I identify with my mother—and absolutely no one else. I knew this was a signal from her to help me get my act together. I was so grateful for the contact, as it helped me enormously.

Aromas have a strong effect on our emotions and can produce a marked change in our mood. Kathryn's mother chose the one scent her daughter associated exclusively with her, and it quickly achieved the desired result.

Elizabeth is a private investor in the Southeast. She had this engaging encounter eight years after her grandmother died at age ninety-eight of natural causes:

I was sitting in a chair nursing my baby. All of a sudden, I felt a cool breeze brush by me. My grandmother always wore this perfume called *Blue Waltz*—a really old brand.

The room filled up with that fragrance, and I knew she was there. I had an overwhelming sense of feeling her love.

My little boy stopped nursing and opened his eyes. He turned to look where I felt my grandmother was standing and made little cooing sounds.

She was there for probably fifteen minutes. I told her that I was happy and healthy and how much I appreciated her coming. I knew she was really excited because this was her first great-grand baby.

Many women wear a favorite perfume or cologne for years, which might be called their "signature scent." This makes it very easy to recognize them when they return, just as Elizabeth was able to do when her deceased grandmother stopped by for a short visit.

Sharon, age thirty-four, works in community relations in Florida. She had this charming visit from her grandmother, who died of old age:

My grandmother had a very particular scent about her—it was her very own. Sometimes elderly people just have their own scent.

Hers was lovely—it was not offensive at all. It was a nice, comforting, grandmotherly smell, and there was some lavender associated with it too. She always used lavender soap for bathing and kept bars of it in drawers with her clothes. I hadn't smelled that scent since I had last seen her.

The following spring, about a year after my grandmother's death, I was walking up the stairs in my town house. Her scent was just everywhere! It was very clear and very real to me.

I sat down on the stairs and started to giggle. I said, "What are you doing here, Grandma?" There was a humor in the air and a kind of "Hello!"

Most people have a pleasant personal scent that can be enhanced by the fragrance of soaps, bath powders, shampoos, lotions and assorted toiletries and cosmetics. Their clothing may also retain the odor of cedar chests, mothballs or sachets.

Vera is a hairdresser in Arizona. She was given a dramatic new appreciation for life from her father about fifteen years after he died of cancer at age forty:

> I was in the hospital to have our first child. We were thrilled because we had wanted a baby and had waited so long to finally have one.
>
> Suddenly, I was in a lot of trouble! My contractions were strong, yet I stopped dilating, and nothing was happening. The doctor said they had to do an emergency cesarean.
>
> On the way to the operating room, we stopped at the blood lab. I was alone in the corridor when suddenly I could smell the aroma of my father!
>
> He had been a furrier by occupation. His aroma was the combination of animal skin and tannic acid he had used to tan hides. It's a very distinct odor—there's no other smell like it. It's a very clean fragrance and was very much a part of my father.
>
> I could feel my daddy was there with me, and I relaxed. A peaceful feeling came over me, and I knew everything was going to be fine.

Many industrial and occupational odors are absorbed by those who work with foods and chemicals over a long period of time. Vera's father acquired an unusual yet pleasant personal scent that was related to his profession. Even fifteen years later, Vera was able to easily recognize this familiar, unmistakable fragrance.

Peter is a salesman in Florida. He and his wife, Vivian, had a series of olfactory ADCs shortly after their twenty-year-old daughter, April, died of a brain hemorrhage following an automobile accident:

> Vivian told me she had been in April's bedroom and smelled an overwhelming fragrance of roses. As she told me that, I thought, "Well, honey, whatever is going to help you get through this—great." But I knew neither we, nor our neighbors, nor anybody else around us had roses.
>
> The following day we were in April's bedroom together. Vivian was standing on one side of the bed, and I was on the other side. We were talking and grieving and crying and asking, "Why? Why did this happen? How are we ever going to get through this?"
>
> Then I had the most overwhelming fragrance of roses you can imagine! You cannot stick your nose in a rosebud and smell the intensity of that fragrance. I took this as a sign from April, "Hey, I am in a better place!"
>
> For the next six to eight weeks, though the fragrance wasn't there constantly, sometimes when we went into April's bedroom we would smell a powerful scent of roses.
>
> At those times we would say to our daughter, "Hi, April. We understand. We both smell the roses. Thank you for letting us know that you're in a better place."

Some people in our culture tend to be a "doubting Thomas" about another person's experience until they have a similar one of their own.

SUBLIME ESSENCES

Emory, age thirty-six, is a legal secretary in New York. He had this impressive group experience after his foster father died of cancer:

> There is a tradition in the Jewish faith of saying the Kaddish on the anniversary of a person's death. It is a prayer recited by mourners after the death of a close relative.
>
> Since my foster father didn't leave any children behind of his own flesh and blood, I had taken it upon myself to say the Kaddish for him every year.
>
> Not being Jewish, I am not part of a synagogue. However, I can go on the anniversary of Dad's death and say the prayer. This particular time, my wife and a friend went with me.
>
> On the way down from the sanctuary, we all smelled pipe tobacco in the elevator. It smelled like an apple pie out cooling on a window sill.
>
> Later, I asked my foster mom about it. I knew that Dad had given up smoking cigarettes, but I didn't know he had become a pipe smoker before he died. When she told me that his tobacco smelled like apple pie, I was about ready to pick my jaw up off the floor!

Since Emory had two witnesses who also smelled the aroma of pipe tobacco in the elevator, he could be certain his experience was real. This is also an evidential account because Emory learned his father had been a pipe smoker, which was something he hadn't known before.

Spontaneously smelling a fragrance that you associate with a deceased loved one may trigger a flood of warm, loving memories of that person. And having an olfactory ADC at a special time or place can provide much comfort and support when you realize you are still in the thoughts and in the heart of the one who has died.

Copyright Acknowledgments

Chapter 18 by Marcel Proust, "Another Memory," in *The Complete Short Stories of Marcel Proust*, translated by Joachim Neugroschel, New York: Cooper Square Press, 2001, pp. 186–8. Reprinted by permission of Cooper Square Press.

Chapter 19 by Mandy Aftel is from "Perfumed Obsession," *Tin House*, April 2005, 23: 106–11. Reprinted by permission.

Chapter 21 by John J. Steele was originally published as "The Anthropology of Smell and Scent in Ancient Egypt and South American Shamanism," in S. Van Toller and G.H. Dodd (eds), *Fragrance: The Psychology and Biology of Perfume*, London and New York: Elsevier Applied Science, 1992, pp. 287–302. Reprinted by permission of Springer Science and Business Media. Abridged.

Chapter 22 by Richard T. Gray is from "The Dialectic of 'Enscentment': Patrick Süskind's *Das Parfum* as Critical History of Enlightenment Culture," *PMLA*, 1993, 108: 489–505. Reprinted by permission of the Modern Language Association of America. Quotations from Patrick Süskind's *Perfume: The Story of a Murder*, trans. J.E. Woods. Copyright © 1986 by Alfred A. Knopf, Inc. Used by permission of Alfred A. Knopf, a division of Random House, Inc. Abridged.

Chapter 23 by Richard H. Stamelman is from "The Eros—and Thanatos—of Scents," *SITES*, January 2002, 6(1): 79–102. Reprinted by permission of Taylor & Francis Ltd., http://www.tandf.co.uk/journals. Abridged.

Chapter 24 by Carol Mavor is from "*Odor di Femina*: Though You May Not See Her, You Can Certainly Smell Her," *Cultural Studies*, 1998, 12(1): 51–81. Reprinted by permission of Taylor & Francis Ltd., http://www.tandf.co.uk/journals. Abridged.

Chapter 25 by Christopher Looby is from "'The Roots of the Orchis, the Iuli of Chesnuts': The Odor of Male Solitude," in Paula Bennett and Vernon A. Rosario II (eds), *Solitary Pleasures*, New York and London: Routledge, 1995, pp. 163–87. Reprinted by permission of Routledge/Taylor & Francis Books, Inc. © 1995. Abridged.

Chapter 27 by Jennifer Fisher and Jim Drobnick was originally published as "In the *Garden of Nirvana*: An Interview with Noritoshi Hirakawa," *Parachute*, 1997, October/November/December, 88: 31–5. Reprinted with permission. Abridged.

Chapter 28 by Aileen Gatten is from "A Wisp of Smoke: Scent and Character in *The Tale of Genji*," *Monumenta Nipponica*, 1977, XXXII: 1: 35–48. Reprinted with permission of *Monumenta Nipponica*. Abridged.

Chapter 29 by Jim Drobnick was originally published as "Platefuls of Air," *Public*, 2004, 30: 175–93. Reprinted with permission by the Public Access Collective. Abridged.

Chapter 32 by Constance Classen is from "The Breath of God: Sacred Histories of Scent," in *The Color of Angels: Cosmology, Gender and the Aesthetic Imagination*, New York and London: Routledge, 1998, pp. 36–60. Reprinted by permission of Taylor & Francis Ltd. Abridged.

Chapter 33 by Françoise Aubaile-Sallenave was originally published as "Corps, Odeurs, Parfums dans les Sociétés Arabo-Musulmanes," in Jane Cobbi and Robert Dulau (eds), *Sentir: Pour une Anthropologie des Odeurs*, *Eurasie* 13, Paris: L'Harmattan, 2004, pp. 181–92. Reprinted with permission by L'Harmattan. Translated by Kathryn Hunter.

Chapter 34 by Alfred Gell is from "Magic, Perfume, Dream..." in Ioan Lewis (ed.), *Symbols and Sentiments: Cross-Cultural Studies in Symbolism*, London, New York and San Francisco: Academic Press, 1977, pp. 25–37. Reprinted by permission of Elsevier. Abridged.

Chapter 35 by David Shulman is from "The Scent of Memory in Hindu South India," *Res* 13, Spring 1987, pp. 123–33. © 1987 by the President and Fellows of Harvard College. Reprinted by permission of the Peabody Museum Press, Harvard University. Quotations from B.S. Miller's (ed.), *Phantasies of a Love-Thief* and *Theater of Memory*, and from A.K. Ramanujan's (ed. and trans.), *Poems of Love and War* are copyright 1971, 1984 and 1985 Columbia University Press, and are reprinted by permission of the publisher. Abridged.

Chapter 36 by William Guggenheim and Judith A. Guggenheim is from "Smelling a Fragrance: Olfactory After-Death Communications," in *Hello From Heaven!*, New York: Bantam, 1995, pp. 62–75. Reprinted by permission of Bantam Books, a division of Random House. © 1995 by William Guggenheim III and Judith A. Guggenheim. Abridged.

Notes on Contributors

Mandy Aftel (www.aftelier.com) is a natural perfumer and author of *Essence and Alchemy* (2001).

Françoise Aubaile-Sallenave is a Research Fellow in Anthropology and Ethnobiology at CNRS—Muséum National d'Histoire Naturelle, Paris.

Dara Chhean is in the Health Services Administration program at the University of Massachusetts, Lowell.

Constance Classen is the author of *Worlds of Sense* (1993) and *The Color of Angels* (1998), co-author of *Aroma* (1994), and editor of *The Book of Touch* (2005).

Erik Cohen is Professor Emeritus at The Hebrew University of Jerusalem. His books include *The Chinese Vegetarian Festival in Phuket* (2001) and *Contemporary Tourism* (2004).

Alain Corbin is Professor of Contemporary History at the Sorbonne and author of *The Foul and the Fragrant* (1986), *Women for Hire* (1990), *Time, Desire and Horror* (1995) and *Village Bells* (1998).

Peter Damian and **Kate Damian** are the authors of *Aromatherapy: Scent and Psyche* (1995). They founded Windrose Aromatics and offer training in practical and theoretical applications of essential oils.

Jim Drobnick is a Postdoctoral Fellow at the University of Manchester. He is the editor of *Aural Cultures* (2004), co-author of *Museopathy* (2002), and is working on a book on smell in contemporary art.

Rodolphe el-Khoury is Chair of the School of Architecture Studies at California College of the Arts, co-author of *Monolithic Architecture* (1996), and co-editor of *Architecture: In Fashion* (1994).

435

Jennifer Fisher is Assistant Professor in Visual Arts at York University and co-author of *CounterPoses* (2002). She has essays in *Naming a Practice* (1996), *Foodculture* (2000) and *Caught in the Act* (2005), and is working on an anthology about the sixth sense.

Aileen Gatten is adjunct researcher in the Center for Japanese Studies, University of Michigan. She is co-editor of *New Leaves* (1993) and translator of Jin'ichi Konishi's *A History of Japanese Literature*, vols. 1–3 (1986, 1986, 1991).

Alfred Gell (1945–1997) was the author of *The Metamorphosis of the Cassowaries* (1975), *The Anthropology of Time* (1992), *Wrapping in Images* (1993) and *Art and Agency* (1998).

Mark Graham is Associate Professor of Social Anthropology at Stockholm University and the Editor-in-Chief of *Ethnos*. His book, *Receiving Strangers*, is forthcoming.

Richard T. Gray is Byron W. and Alice L. Lockwood Professor of the Humanities in Germanics at the University of Washington. He is the author of *Constructive Destruction* (1987), *Stations of the Divided Subject* (1995) and *About Face* (2004).

William Guggenheim III and **Judith Guggenheim**'s extensive research into after-death communication experiences is collected in *Hello From Heaven!* (1995) (www.after-death.com).

Rachel S. Herz is a Visiting Professor at Brown University. She has published numerous articles on olfactory perception and cognition and is currently writing a book on the psychology of smell.

Devon E. Hinton is Assistant Professor of Psychiatry at Massachusetts General Hospital, Harvard Medical School, and is the co-editor of the upcoming *Culture and Panic Disorder*.

Alan R. Hirsch is the Neurological Director of the Smell and Taste Treatment and Research Foundation in Chicago (www.smellandtaste.org) and the author of numerous articles on the psychological power of scent.

Alan Hyde is Professor at the Rutgers University School of Law at Newark, and the author of *Bodies of Law* (1997) and *Working in Silicon Valley* (2003).

Helen Keller (1880–1968) was an activist on the behalf of socialism, women's rights, and the blind and deaf. Her books include *My Life* (1902), *The World I Live In* (1908) and *Out of the Dark* (1913).

Gale Largey is Professor of Sociology at Mansfield University. He is the author of socio-historical monographs on Pennsylvanian communities and the producer of six documentaries.

Christopher Looby is Professor of English and Vice Chair for Graduate Studies at the University of California, Los Angeles. He is the author of *Voicing America* (1997) and *The Complete Civil War Journal and Selected Letters of T.W. Higginson* (2000).

Martin F. Manalansan IV is Associate Professor of Anthropology and Asian American Studies at the University of Illinois, Urbana-Champaign. He is the author of *Global Divas* (2003) and the upcoming *Altered Tastes*.

Eleanor Margolies is a writer, theater-maker, and editor of *Puppet Notebook*.

Carol Mavor is Professor of Art at the University of North Carolina at Chapel Hill and the author of *Pleasures Taken* (1995), *Becoming* (1999) and the forthcoming *Reading Boyishly*.

Mark W.D. Paterson is a Lecturer in Philosophy and Cultural Studies at the University of the West of England, Bristol, and author of *Consumption and Everyday Life* (2005).

Vuth Pich is a social worker at the Arbour Counseling Center and the Massachusetts Department of Mental Health.

Mark H. Pollack is the Directory of Anxiety Disorders at Massachusetts General Hospital and an Associate Professor of Psychiatry.

J. Douglas Porteous is Professor of Geography at the University of Victoria, British Columbia. He the author of *Landscapes of the Mind* (1990) and *Environmental Aesthetics* (1996), and co-author of *Domicide* (2001).

Marcel Proust (1871–1922) was the author of the multi-volume work *In Search of Lost Time*.

Hans J. Rindisbacher is Professor in German and Russian at Pomona College. He is the author of *The Smell of Books* (1992) and editor/translator of *STILLSTAND switches* (1992).

Lucienne A. Roubin (d. 1999) was the author of *Le Monde des Odeurs* (1990).

Oliver Sacks is a practicing neurologist whose books include *Awakenings* (1973), *The Man Who Mistook His Wife for a Hat* (1985), *An Anthropologist on Mars* (1995), *Uncle Tungsten* (2001) and *Oaxaca Journal* (2002).

David Shulman is Professor of Indian Studies at Hebrew University, Jerusalem and the author of *The Hungry God* (1993), *The Wisdom of Poets* (2001) and *Behind the Mask* (2005).

Richard H. Stamelman is Professor in Comparative Literature at Williams College. His books include *Lost Beyond Telling* (1990) and translations of Edmond Jabès and Yves Bonnefoy.

John J. Steele is an archeologist, author and fragrance designer employing rare botanical essential oils. He is a co-author of *Earthmind* (1989).

Luca Turin is a biophysicist, CTO of the odorant design firm Flexitral and the author of numerous scientific articles.

Donald Tuzin is Professor of Anthropology at the University of California, San Diego, and the author of *The Cassowary's Revenge* (1997) and *Social Complexity in the Making* (2001).

Clara Ursitti is a Glasgow-based artist who recently exhibited at the Centre for Contemporary Art, Glasgow, the Centre for Contemporary Photography, Melbourne, and is completing a scent work for the British Library, London.

Rod Watson teaches Sociology at the University of Manchester. He has published a range of praxiological studies of embodied action.

Index

439

Lightning Source UK Ltd.
Milton Keynes UK
UKOW051506191112

202433UK00003B/1/P